On Being Normal and Other Disorders

On Being Normal and Other Disorders

A Manual for Clinical Psychodiagnostics

Paul Verhaeghe

Translated by
Sigi Jottkandt

LONDON AND NEW YORK

First published 2004 by Other Press

This edition published in 2008 by
Karnac Books Ltd.

Published 2018 by Routledge
2 Park Square, Milton Park, Abingdon, Oxon OX14 4RN
711 Third Avenue, New York, NY 10017, USA

Routledge is an imprint of the Taylor & Francis Group, an informa business

Copyright © 2008 by Paul Verhaeghe

The rights of Paul Verhaeghe to be identified as the author of this work have been asserted in accordance with §§ 77 and 78 of the Copyright Design and Patents Act 1988.

All rights reserved. No part of this book may be reprinted or reproduced or utilised in any form or by any electronic, mechanical, or other means, now known or hereafter invented, including photocopying and recording, or in any information storage or retrieval system, without permission in writing from the publishers.

Notice:
Product or corporate names may be trademarks or registered trademarks, and are used only for identification and explanation without intent to infringe.

British Library Cataloguing in Publication Data
A C.I.P. for this book is available from the British Library

ISBN-13: 9781855756885 (pbk)

For Sarah and Sander

Contents

Preface ix

Acknowledgments xiii

I: DIAGNOSTICS AND DISCOURSE   1

1. Introduction: Clinical Psychodiagnostics versus Medical Diagnostics   3

2. Categorical Diagnostics versus Clinical Praxis: A Matter of Impossibility   19

3. The Impotence of Epistemology   37

4. Know-how in Clinical Practice: Doxa as the Result of Impotence and Impossibility   71

5. Conclusion: The Need for a Metapsychology   127

II: METAPSYCHOLOGY   149

6. Identity as a Relational Structure   153

7. Defense in Double Time: A Linear Model   181

8. From a Linear to a Circular Model: On Becoming a Subject   207

9. Etiology and Evolution: Nature, Nurture, and the Theory of the Drive   235

10. Conclusion: The Subject's Position in Relation to Anxiety, Guilt, and Depression   259

III: POSITIONS AND STRUCTURES OF THE SUBJECT — 283

11. The Actualpathological Position: Panic Disorder and Somatization — 289

12. Between Actualpathology and Psychopathology: Post-Traumatic Stress Disorder and Borderline — 313

13. The Psychopathological Position of the Subject: Hysteria and Obsessional Neurosis — 351

14. Perverse Structure versus Perverse Traits — 397

15. The Psychotic Structure of the Subject — 429

CONCLUSION: DIAGNOSIS AND TREATMENT — 459

References — 465

Index — 497

Preface

When I was a student, my professors taught me that man was something "made." Gender was nothing but a sociocultural construction and psychopathology the effect of an adverse environment. The emphasis in both the human sciences and in the wider cultural and artistic milieu was on the interpretation of the underlying layers. Looking back, we should have anticipated how a couple of decades later the pendulum would swing back in the other direction. Now we're in the heyday of genetics, where everything is supposed to be genetically determined. Interpretation is no longer necessary, everything substantial can be found on the surface—"what you see is what you get"—and psychology has been reduced to a behavioral science.

Happily, there are signs of a movement away from this polarization. I'm seeing evidence of an increasing interest in the original imbrication of both heredity and environment. The sheer complexity of human behavior demands that we reconsider the nonvisible mental, constructions directing it. And for this, of course, interpretation is indispensable.

This book emerges out of the same context, focusing on clinical *psycho-diagnostics*. Nevertheless, a reader looking for a discussion of methods and specific testing procedures will be disappointed. This is not to say that I consider such techniques unimportant. It's just that, for me, such methods are productive only when they are applied from within the framework of a determining metapsychological theory, and this is where the book's emphasis will be placed. The real need for such a theoretical foundation is demonstrated in Part I, where I show how a categorizing diagnostic based upon atheoretical observations is doomed to fail. Such a diagnostic, furthermore, leads to a paradigmatic approach in clinical practice that loses the vital connection between diagnosis and therapy.

It is this connection that becomes pivotal in Part II, which serves to develop the theoretical ground mentioned earlier. In this section, I argue that the connection between diagnosis and treatment can only be made through a conceptual understanding that holds the vicissitudes of identity as utterly central. In this case, the emphasis will be on the relation between the subject and the Other. This is not by coincidence: the main contention of this book will be that identity is acquired only in relation to the Other. Consequently, any potential pathology must also be diagnosed on the basis of this relationship. Finally, it is only through this relationship that the treatment can be effective. This latter idea is confirmed by numerous studies that reveal the therapeutic relationship itself as the decisive instrument.

This argument is based on my reading of Freudian and Lacanian psychoanalysis, simply because this is the theory I know best. The expression "my reading" is deliberate. Even Freud and Lacan need to be submitted to empirical scientific evidence, and I have tried to do this as much as possible. In the process, a number of their theses have been contradicted, a number of them confirmed. But all current clinical theories have significant data that have no way of being empirically tested. The question of whether one will ever be able to completely test everything is moot.

With this theoretical background in hand, the chapters in Part III analyze the various possible differential-diagnostic relationships occurring between subjects and the Other. The reader will encounter a number of the classic concepts of psychoanalysis—neurosis, psychosis, perversion—as well as the less well-known opposition between an actualpsychology and a psychopathology. Wherever possible, I refer to the DSM categories and, especially, to recent findings in empirical research. In keeping with the general intent of this book, I discuss the implications of a certain differential diagnosis for the treatment at every turn. More specifically, I indicate what kind of therapeutic relationship we can expect, depending on a given diagnosis, and how this relationship will determine the treatment, in whatever form it takes.

Combining analytic theory with contemporary empirical research in this way carries a double risk: analysts may reject this diagnostic theory on the grounds that it is not analytical enough. Clinicians coming out of other traditions, on the other hand, may consider the book unserviceable because of its foundation in what they consider an outdated theory. I can only hope that I reach the critical reader who is prepared to test his or her own experiences against what is put forward here.

Acknowledgments

Knowledge is a collective enterprise and I am very happy to acknowledge here the help of a number of friends and colleagues. V. De Gucht (Leiden, Holland), S. Bogaerts (Tilburg, Holland), S. Soenen (Leuven, Belgium) have helped me a lot by giving me the results of their research before they were actually published. R. Vermote (University Center, Kortenberg, Belgium) helped me to find my way in the borderline maze. Repeated talks with J. Feher-Gurewich (Harvard, U.S.A.) and E. Welldon (Tavistock, U.K.) enlightened me in the study of the ever-intangible perversion. J. Mertens and J. Braeckman (Ghent University, Belgium) convinced me of the importance of the evolutionary point of view.

My doctoral students, D. Blomme, F. Declercq, A. De Rick, I. De Groote, A. Lievrouw, E. Van Compernolle and S. Vanheule read the first versions of the manuscript repeatedly. Initially hesitant but with increasing enthusiasm, they have reversed the roles and obliged me time and again to rewrite "everything." Without the practical help of my secretary, E. Vandenbussche, the manuscript would never have left my hard drive.

Sigi Jottkandt took care of the English version and went even further than that: her questions during the translation obliged me to reword a number of ideas in a much better way. The copy editor at Other Press, Sigrid Asmus, did a very thorough job, polishing the book into its current form.

Finally, the English edition would not have been produced without the enthusiasm of Judith Feher-Gurewich (Other Press, New York). Our discussions and conversations on Lacan and Freud started a number of years ago and are far from finished. The book is in large part a direct outcome of this interaction.

I
DIAGNOSTICS AND DISCOURSE

"Go and name the things"

I
Introduction: Clinical Psychodiagnostics versus Medical Diagnostics

A 4-year-old child wakes up one morning with a rash. She is sweating, apathetic. The young, and therefore worried, parents call the doctor who does a quick examination, concludes it is chicken pox, reassures the parents, and prescribes an anti-itching powder.

This short sequence is a perfect illustration of medical diagnostics; incidentally, it is a perfect illustration of an implicit social relationship as well, something that we will return to later. The young patient displays a number of symptoms that are collated by the doctor so as to identify—diagnose—a distinct syndrome. This is done in accordance with an established knowledge that maintains both a notion of etiology and a clear diagnostic distinction between health and illness. In this way, the doctor makes a diagnosis, usually with the help of various instruments (thermometer, stethoscope, etc.), forms a prognosis, and suggests a treatment on the basis of her observations. The intent is to return to the status quo ante, the earlier state. The model is in fact essentially circular and can be put schematically in this way:

- Symptoms are gathered together into an objectively generalized syndrome,

4   ON BEING NORMAL AND OTHER DISORDERS

- In accordance with an established knowledge, which includes an etiology and a clear distinction between health and illness,
- The result is a diagnosis and prognosis reached by way of an instrumentally assisted diagnostic,
- The aim: treatment and a return to the previous state.

A 15-year-old and his concerned parents come to a psychologist for a consultation. He has been caught joyriding by the police. The parents not only want the psychologist to diagnose him, they want rapid treatment as well. The juvenile court is threatening to take drastic measures since this was not the boy's first time. How can the psychodiagnostic process here be compared with the medical process described above?

FROM SYMPTOMS TO SYNDROME

The first interview adds more information. The boy does not simply steal cars per se. They have to be Mercedes. Once in the driver's seat, he drives around apparently aimlessly on his own. Each time, he leaves the car unharmed in another part of the country and hitchhikes home. The boy himself cannot give any explanation for his behavior except for the fact that he has an expressed preference for this kind of car. While the diagnosis "joyriding" remains the same—at most it could be substituted with "maladjusted behavior"—where are the symptoms that could be gathered into an objective, universalized syndrome?

In the second interview, the psychologist focuses on the family situation. The boy is an only child whose parents are undergoing a marital crisis. The mother is from a privileged background, the father is working class but has raised himself to a higher socioeconomic status. At the time, each fell in love with the other's otherness, now they reproach one another for it—a fairly typical scenario. The mother has taken a lover, the father works himself to death and retreats from confrontation. He works himself to death for . . . Mercedes. And entirely coincidentally, the region where the boy leaves his cars is where his mother was born and where her last name still holds a certain prestige.

The as-yet undiagnosed symptoms now appear in a completely different light. Whose symptoms are we talking about anyway? The son is caught between his parents, his behavior clearly cannot be understood outside of its context. From a psychoanalytic perspective one would say that his behavior provides an answer to the desire of the Other, that is, his parents, with the proviso, however, that the boy himself is not, or is only barely aware of it. "The unconscious is the discourse of the Other" (Lacan). Systemic theory would say that the boy shoulders the symptoms of his family. A cognitive behavioral approach would see his behavior as learned, which leads us to the following question: From whom does one learn what, and why?

Whatever approach one takes, a common factor emerges: the diagnosis cannot be limited just to the boy. The impact of the Other is fundamental. This is the first major difference between medical diagnostics and psychodiagnostics: clinical psychodiagnostics cannot be restricted to the individual. Psychic identity, with its potential psychopathology and aberrant behaviors, must be conceived in such a way that it grants the other a place equally important as the individual's.

A second difference has meanwhile emerged. Unlike what takes place in medical diagnostics, here one cannot similarly bind a number of isolated symptoms into an objective, universalizable syndrome that holds for just about every case. To the contrary, the more information the diagnostician acquires, the more specific the situation becomes, to the effect that generalization becomes all the more difficult. In medical diagnostics the symptoms are interpreted as *signs* pointing to an underlying disturbance that can be both isolated and generalized. In clinical psychodiagnostics we are confronted with *signifiers* that carry endlessly shifting meanings in any given interaction between the patient and the Other.[1] The signifier "Mercedes" will never carry the same meaning in any other clinical situation as it does here. The universal element is missing; the clinical psychodiagnostic process results in a category in which N = 1. The clinical psychodiagnostic questions are thus not so much "What disease does this patient have?" but "To whom

---

1. A sign always points to a fixed meaning: a red traffic light means stop. A signifier refers to an underlying, ever-changing signified, with the result that it is impossible to talk about a fixed meaning. Meanings are determined by the larger linguistic and sociocultural context in which this particular signifier is used. (Compare the difference of the signifier "sheaf" in these two quotations: "His sheaf was neither miserly nor spiteful" and "Alas! How many would sooner steal their brother's whole shock than add to it a single sheaf!"). See the structural linguistics of de Saussure (1976).

or what do the symptoms refer? What are their meanings and functions, and who do they relate to?" There must be an underlying and, as yet, invisible structure determining the whole that intersects in the patient.

Thus we can say that medical diagnostics and clinical psychodiagnostics are exact opposites in this respect. Medical diagnostics begins with the particular (the symptom) and moves toward the general (the syndrome), based on a semiotic system that is entirely focused on the individual's complaints. Clinical psychodiagnostics begins from the general (the incipient complaint) and proceeds toward the particular (where $N = 1$), based on a system of signifiers that is part of a wider relationship between the subject and the Other.

BASED ON AN UNDERLYING KNOWLEDGE

Despite its complexity, medical knowledge exhibits a relatively uniform character whose conceptions of etiology and of what constitutes health and illness can be readily identified. Clinical psychodiagnostics is completely different. Not only does it have no uniform character—there are many different theoretical perspectives, each with their own competing conceptions of how the mind functions—but it addresses quite a different question. With the exception of a restricted number of cases, we are not so much confronted with the question of whether someone is healthy, but whether she or he is normal or abnormal. In contrast to the absolutes of the medical norm (fever starts at 37 or 98.6 degrees), in psychodiagnostics we are confronted with the problems of a perpetually relative norm: What constitutes abnormal behavior within what kind of abnormal psychical identity? This will be our central question, which can be approached from three main angles.

Normality and Abnormality

One approach attempts to describe the difference between normality and abnormality through the lens of contemporary science, namely, through computation and quantification. Psychic normality is understood in terms of average scores, standard deviation, and modal personalities. This implies that psychic characteristics can be mathematically calculated and then presented in the famous bell-curve of normal distribution: the normal group in the middle of the graph is the largest while the left and right sides are occupied by the smaller abnormal populations.

In the clinical field, however, less emphasis is placed on quantification. Indeed, there the question is whether quantification is even possible.[2] To measure something, one needs an objective unit of measurement: cm, kilos, grades, and so on. Yet in clinical praxis such an objective unit of measurement is missing. What would depression's unit of measurement be, what would an average "depressive quotient" look like? While it is true that contemporary psychodiagnostics has a number of scales through which we try to measure anxiety, depression, and other states, in the final analysis such measurements come down to the counting of words or expressions against which patients can measure the extent of applicability to themselves.

The end result may well be of a quantitative nature. Nevertheless, such numbers invariably have a different status than those of the hard sciences because they always demand interpretation owing to the lack of an objective unit of measurement. The numerous attempts to establish such objective norms inevitably terminated with biological parameters. Aggressivity, for example, can be calculated by the objectively measurable quantity of testosterone in the blood. Nevertheless, experience shows that subjective behavior is never directly linked to these objective markers.

The saga of the so-called lie detector test is a good illustration of this. Despite objective measurements of sweat, heartbeats, and blood pressure, there is scarcely a direct correlation between the test results and the degree of truth emitted by the test subject. More broadly one can say that, in psychopathology, there is no firm link between objective, assessable parameters for a specific psychological problem and the way it is subjectively experienced and expressed (Koster van Groos 1989, p. 353; Silvestre 1981, p. 27).

---

2. Even the measurement of intelligence has long been contested. It is also not clear whether there are objective external parameters. Hence today's cautious definition: intelligence is that which intelligence testing tests.

The ultimate impossibility of achieving an objective quantification doesn't prevent approaches like this from occurring in clinical practice: "A stronger than normal separation anxiety" . . . "a severe personality disorder" . . . "an excessive midlife crisis." Such quantitative evaluations rely, at best, simply on the observer's own clinical intuition and experience. At worst, they are based on the observer's mirror image. The danger of such an intuitive diagnostics will be discussed in the following chapter.

Normality as an Ideal

Almost imperceptibly, we have come to the second approach, one that considers normality as an ideal, a utopia, which means, equally, that it doesn't exist per se. As Freud puts it: "a normal ego of this sort is, like normality in general, an ideal fiction" (1978 [1937c], p. 235). Here we encounter ideal and, hence, ideological prescriptions of how mankind ought to be. The title of the first Western psychological manuscript (from 1590) is paradigmatic in this respect: *Psychologia, hoc est de hominis perfectione* ("Psychology is the study of man's perfection") by Goclenius of Marburg.

In this approach, diagnosis takes a peculiar form: in affirming an ideal image of mankind, the clinician's work is accordingly reduced to calculating the distance between the patient and this ideal. In other words, in the majority of cases, diagnosticians appear less interested in etiology than in an immediate diagnosis, one enabling them to concentrate on the desired goal. Such reasoning is clearly visible in the way psychodiagnostic tests often contain an ideal result, the difference between which and the patient's score serves only to represent how far he or she still has to go. Also surely not coincidental is the way the diagnostician often talks about the need to "grade" certain tests. Suddenly, we have become teachers and treatment becomes a question of learning or of (re-)education through which the pupil must be brought as closely into line as possible with this ideal result. Moreover, such an approach presupposes that one can define this ideal of normality. Seeing as how we are not dealing with an objective external norm (fever starts at 37 or 98.6 degrees), but with an always relative—because socially determined—norm, such a task is far from simple and leaves the result open to further discussion.[3]

How one handles the treatment within such an approach is reminiscent of what we earlier described as intuitive diagnostics: it seems practical, a matter of sound judgment, of personal ethics, and so on . . . When, in his *Ethics Seminar*, Lacan (1992 [1959–1960], pp. 8–10) summed up the therapeutic ideals as human love, authenticity, and independence, many therapists nodded enthusiastically. But this assent only served to make Lacan's subsequent rejection of these ideals all the more disconcerting. Beyond the attractiveness of their—incidentally, continually changing—contents (i.e., the ideals), the underlying formal system tends to be overlooked. This latter is nothing other than a coercive ideology, yet one more alienation imposed on contemporary *homo psychologicus* through which the therapist determines the client's "good." Meanwhile a confusion reigns between psychotherapy and (re-)education. The latter is unrealizable without ideals, while the former belongs to a different order. People frequently get into difficulties when their ideals have been shattered.[4] But to spoon-feed them new ideals at such a time, albeit with therapeutic intent, resembles a detoxification treatment that replaces opium with morphine. Instead, psychotherapy must give them the chance to interrogate the *how*s and *wherefore*s of these ideals, that is, their subjective history, so that certain choices can be (re-)made.[5]

---

3. A simple example. Ernest Jones (1931) identified three ideals as the goal of analysis: "happiness," understood as a state free from anxiety; "efficiency," that is, "the full utilization of the person's potential," and "adaptation to reality" especially in "relation to one's fellows." With Bettelheim (1979), we can say that someone who is completely free of anxiety will never realize anything at all, because anxiety is the human driving force par excellence. This idea was given a genetic and species-specific basis by Monod (1970). The second criterion, "the full utilization of a person's potential," is in complete contradiction with the first, as well as appearing somewhat exhausting. The third criterion became Hartmann's (1939) cardinal question, for which we can immediately offer an example, from only a slightly later date, of a man by the name of Eichmann as someone who was perfectly adapted to his social reality.

4. A contemporary example of this, occurring among counsellors, is burnout syndrome (Vanheule, 2001a–c).

5. This is impossible with certain patients due to a combination of biological, psychological and social factors. At such moments, one leaves the field of psychotherapy proper to work from a much more forceful angle.

The dangers of such a treatment, however, go beyond alienation—indeed, alienation is probably inevitable in any form of psychotherapy. Thomas Szasz glimpsed the snake in the grass most keenly (1972, p. 26): "Every rule or norm of psychological health generates a new category of mental illness." The role of segregation in the psychopathological industry now comes into sharp relief: a certain group designates itself Normal by categorizing others as Abnormal ("I'm okay, you're not okay, therefore everything is okay"). That people subsequently wanted such normality for others, too, lends the whole thing an altruistic shine, the same as that by which colonialization, for example, is also justified. The examples of such misuse are most clearly visible in totalitarian regimes, where psychiatry and psychodiagnostics quickly become abused for such ends.[6] Because of our lack of distance, it is much harder to acknowledge the applicability of this charge closer to home. Nevertheless, we can at least give two contemporary examples. First, one of the most significant personality disorders today is that of the *antisocial* personality. Second, yesterday's pervert has been rechristened the so-called paraphile, in distinction from his normal (healthy?) counterpart, the normophile.[7] No further comment is necessary.

The results of regarding normality in terms of the ideal can be summarized thus: first, psychopathology and criminality become so interwoven that the knife begins to cut both ways. Criminal behavior becomes acceptable because it is explicable; psychopathological behavior becomes

---

6. This has been easy to recognize in the history of the "free west." One need only look at this segregation in the example of Benjamin Rush, father of American psychiatry. Following the American civil war (itself fought over the issue of segregation), this scientist discovered two new forms of mental illness, *Anarchia* and *Revolutiona*, both all but incurable disorders, demanding radical "medical" treatment. This keen observer later laid claim to another great discovery regarding the "breakdown in the belief principle or the power to believe." This intellectual power is subject to disturbance or illness, leading to an inability to believe in things that are manifestly obvious to belief itself. The most significant subcategory of this dangerous disorder concerns "people who refuse to believe in the benefit of medicine." Anyone at all familiar with the structuration of the hysterical clinic and the relationship between the Hysteric's and Master's discourses might readily recognize a number of things here.

7. "Normophilia: a condition of being erotosexually in conformity with the standards as dictated by customary, religious, or legal authority" (Money 1988, p. 214). Paraphilia, hence, is being not "in conformity."

punishable because it is deviant. It is no coincidence, therefore, that an ever-increasing number of psychiatric patients are beginning to populate Dutch prisons (Beyaert 1987; De Ridder 1987). Second, psychiatry and clinical psychology become the judges of the social order, with the prosecutors of the pathological society at one extreme and the guardians of the public good at the other. With the latter, the practice of psychology becomes transformed into a form of social coercion and obligatory adaptation. Cautionary warnings against this are found more often in a number of the gems of world literature (see, for example, Huxley's *Brave New World* and Orwell's *1984*) than in our own field. This ought to be more than enough to address the ethical aspects of clinical psychological practice. To think naively in terms of adapted or unadapted behavior, or even desired or undesired behavior, is to enter into dangerous waters. Who desires what, and in whose name?

Normality as a Developmental Process

The third perspective approaches normality in terms of a developmental process. Here, normality is regarded as something that requires long-term study, something that cannot be grasped in a single take. This seems to me, for a number of reasons, the most legitimate approach. Diagnosis, and even therapy, often entail merely a single, momentary take whose transitory nature gets forgotten. The earliest historical example is Bertha Pappenheim, better known by her pseudonym Anna O. As one of the most pathological cases in *Studies on Hysteria* (Freud and Breuer 1978 [1895d]) she was later rediagnosed as a schizophrenic psychotic (Bram 1965). Great was the surprise, therefore, when it was discovered that—counter to all expectations connected with such a diagnosis—she led a miraculously full and creative life in the forty years following her treatment (Freeman 1977).

This developmental notion is found in a number of writers, most often in connection with the idea that human life undergoes a number of phases, wherein each period announces a distinct problem and its accompanying potential disorders. The model for this idea is to be found in the organic somatic development of mankind, which does indeed possess quantitative criteria, deviations from which yield indications of pathological disturbance. But to transplant this idea wholesale into clinical psychology is considerably more problematic. A fair amount of developmental psychological results are as much (or more) determined by environmental factors than by nature, and hence will have different characteristics from culture to culture. What I simply wish to underline here is the way all psychological development takes place in interaction with an Other, and that the impact of such an Other must not be neglected in clinical psychodiagnostics.[8]

In addition, one must note how this way of thinking emphasizes a linear, chronological time-scheme. In the case of psychopathology, an alternative temporal structure can just as easily be put forward, one based on retroactivity, or *Nachträglichkeit*, in which elements from the past are interpreted by way of the present (Freud 1978 [1918b]). A depressive patient, for example, will stress the negative elements of his life's story because of his depression. But to consider this negative past the cause of his depression would be to jump to a conclusion too quickly.

Beyond these remarks, it is nonetheless clear that in certain cultures an experienced clinician can quite properly make out a number of more or less typical life stages. The problem is that this observation inevitably relies on the concept of normality as an average. How long does the toddler's negativism phase last? What is an average puberty crisis? What is a typical midlife crisis? Even if we find statistics for such things, these will also be relative, and need reinterpretation in the light of the specificity of each particular patient. The judgment ultimately depends on the clinical intuition of the individual caseworker.[9]

---

8. The Lacanian term "Other" indicates the totality of the typically human elements present in the concept of nurture (education, culture, teaching, media, etc.). These elements exert themselves in every individual through language and, hence, through the Other, particularly during development. We will return to this in detail later on.

9. The drama usually begins with the second generation, with the pupils' application of the theory. The phases that originally were deduced from a large number of nuanced and hence valuable clinical experiences, and which, as a result, present only a standardized picture, are frequently adopted by the second generation as a straitjacket. The classic example is found in the idea of libidinal organization as developed by Abraham and Freud, in which a specific function is considered every time in relation to the castration complex. Fifty years later, this nuanced and difficult theory served as a chapter in practically every training course for pediatric nurses, who learned that a child must first go through the oral phase, following which he or she enters the anal phase, only to arrive finally in the genital paradise. Woe to the 3-month-old playing with his

The greatest danger in such an approach is the same one facing the entire clinical psychological field. To maintain that everything must be situated in chronological terms implies that the present can be explained on the basis of the past, and that both of these determine the future. Put differently, it implies that what is actual can be entirely explained by the past, not just disorders, but normality as well. The risk, then, is that the following message is implicitly sent: anything that can be traced back to a life history is explainable, comprehensible and, hence, *acceptable*. The hyperbolic but logical extension of the so-called "mitigating circumstances" serves as an illustration. "He beats his wife, but what do you expect? He had an unhappy childhood." Nevertheless, even insanity has ethical limits. Throughout this book, I will emphasize over and over again that these two fields—the field of clinical psychology and the field of jurisdiction and normativity—must be clearly separated.

By way of concluding this second point of comparison between medical and clinical psychological diagnostics, we can say that our field has far less univocal theoretical grounds. The main reason for this has to do with each field's different objects: illness/health versus normality/abnormality. The criteria for the latter can never be of the same order as the former since the quantitative factors can never be more than a general appraisal, while the diagnostic data must be interpreted in a specific way each time. To do this, one needs a governing metapsychological theory of psychical identity and its development.

DIAGNOSIS AND PROGNOSIS— THE DIAGNOSTIC TOOLSET

Along with measuring, the entire focus in medical diagnostics is on *looking*. Medical instruments can be understood more or less in terms

---

willy, he is too early (must be precocious)! A less familiar and more poignant example concerns support for the dying. From the Kübler-Ross studies, we know that the process of dying can pass through a number of phases that appear in a certain sequence. I myself have witnessed a case in a university hospital where a dying patient was obliged to follow the "right" sequence of these phases by the well-meaning psychologist in order to die in the "right" manner (i.e., "shock and denial, anger, bargaining, depression, acceptance"—Kübler-Ross 1969).

of an ever-increasing perfection of looking at and in the body, by which certain parameters are measured and weighed according to objective criteria. In clinical psychodiagnostics, however, the focus is on *listening*. Indeed, psychodiagnostic tools can be regarded as an attempt to develop standardized methods of listening. The results of this process, therefore, can never have the same objective status as in medical science, and the focus is not so much on the measurements themselves, but on the interpretation of the results.

Any diagnosis that uses psychological testing, even with today's computerized renditions, always yields relative results. This relativity has as much to do with the fact that the results need to be evaluated against a representative group to which the tested person belongs, as with the fact that the parameters for measurement themselves can never be exact. As I said before, there is no precise unity of measurement for anxiety, for neurosis, and other states. This is the classic problem of reliability and validity (as discussed below). Consequently, the results still require interpretation, and it is at this point that the experimental field proper is left behind. Interpretation—assuming we are dealing with valid and reliable instruments—must be performed by the diagnostician according to the principles of the theory she or he has chosen. Without interpretation, the results remain largely useless for their specific clinical psychological application, and can be employed, at best, only from sociological and epidemiological perspectives. Again, this is an argument for focusing not simply on methodology but, first and foremost, on an overarching metapsychological theory of clinical psychological diagnostics.

It is striking to observe how, in test-based diagnostics, such a metapsychology is virtually absent from most handbooks. The history of test-based diagnostics shows a clear shift in emphasis toward the theory of test *construction*, itself both important and necessary but insufficient for actual interpretation and clinical application. To the extent that tests do make use of a grounding theory of psychology in the construction process, they rely on an elementary functional psychology. The basic idea is as follows: psychological functioning can be divided into separate component functions—memory, intelligence, attention, emotion . . . —for which individual instruments of measurement can be developed. Again, the classic example is the intelligence test.

The history of the intelligence test shows the limitations of such an approach. While intelligence was originally studied as a completely isolated function, it rapidly became clear that this view was far too restricted.[10] The final outcome contradicts the basic assumptions of functional psychology: intelligence cannot be isolated, but forms part of the global psychological functioning. For example, in a Rorschach session we can easily observe how someone's intelligence functions, just as, similarly, in a typical intelligence test we might be faced with how the test subject copes with anxiety and authority.

The practical effects of this are twofold. First of all, a psychodiagnostic examination always needs to call on a variety of instruments to get ahold of the complexity of psychic functioning in its totality. The concept of independently measurable psychic functions is simply not applicable from a clinical psychological perspective. Secondly, the exam's utility will be ascertained by the interpretation of the results. To put it differently, the quantitative factors gain their function and signification only by way of qualitative factors.

REFERRAL AND TREATMENT

A decision regarding next steps will be made on the basis of the foregoing diagnostic elements. From a medical perspective, treatment typically comes next. The ideal goal is to cure, that is, to return to the state prior to the illness, with as complete a removal as possible of the symptoms. It is striking how in this context the two processes—diagnosis and treatment—can be neatly separated. As a result, they need not be performed by the same person. Indeed, with the increasing specialization of medical practice, this is becoming less and less the case.

---

10. Binet's initially relative definition rapidly became, despite his protestations, an absolute law for Terman and his colleagues to the extent that IQ became the indication of a presupposed, tangible, measurable entity "somewhere in the cortex" (Konner 1982, pp. 441–444). It is nonetheless striking how the impasse of such a line of reasoning has given rise to an ever-growing expansion of the concept. Beginning from a theory involving dual factors to one of multiple factors, and toward even further partitioning (including, with the latter, the monstrosity of "emotional intelligence"). Ultimately, it seems that "intelligence" has become a synonym for practically the entire psyche (Jansz 1986, pp. 60–61, 80–81).

In our profession, however, things are a little different. First and foremost, diagnosis and treatment are less visibly separated. It is by no means exceptional if, during the treatment, a diagnosis is changed due to emergent additional information. Indeed, research shows that additional information may change the diagnosis considerably (Dingemans, cited in Van Lieshout et al. 1987). Moreover, the diagnostic process itself inevitably entails some element of treatment. The great majority of recent studies of psychotherapeutic efficacy indicate that the most important operative factor is the therapeutic relationship, and this is established right from the first interview, even if that has a merely diagnostic aim. As a result, it is far from self-evident that the diagnostician and the therapist need be two different people. When this does occur, a predictable enough scenario ensues. Often, the therapist regards the first interview as a rapid recapitulation of what already occurred in the diagnostic examination, while the patient complains that she or he "has to say it all over again."

The second difference is potentially even more significant. The goal of medical diagnostics is to indicate the correct treatment for eliminating the illness. Earlier, we noted how psychic symptoms carry meanings and have a function that transcends the individual. Now we can go a step further and say that psychic symptoms invariably come down to a patient's economic attempt at a solution for an underlying, structurally determined problem. "Economic" here signifies an accounting paradigm of loss and gain. By "structural" I mean to indicate that the problem is not limited to the individual, but must be understood from within the terms of a relation with significant others. The teenager's joyriding, for example, was his solution to the problematic position he adopted toward his parents and their own relationship. To put it briefly, let us simply recall that classic argument of psychoanalysis: psychic symptoms are the patient's attempts at recovery.

The consequences of this view are far reaching. For instance, it implies that certain symptoms can yield more gains than losses and that, as a consequence, there can be something like a "successful" symptom. More often than not, in the course of the first clinical interview the diagnostician concludes that the client has suffered under the complaint for several months, perhaps even years. Why had there been no previous call for help? Something must have changed in the balance sheet wherein the loss has finally become too big, leading to the consultation. An important psychodiagnostic question therefore is: Why has he or she come now, what caused the change in the balance of gains and losses? Moreover, it is likely that certain symptoms, within their own defining structure, will always produce more gains than losses and, for that reason, rarely offer themselves up for analysis. Exemplary in this respect is what is involved in the fear of failure. This fear must always be understood from a structural perspective: one fails (or doesn't fail) in relation to someone else, as determined by the underlying context. The complement of this is the compulsion to succeed: one succeeds (or doesn't succeed) in relation to someone else, again within a structurally determined context. The latter symptom is rarely presented for consultation, except in contemporary cases of burnout.

The implications for treatment are radical. The patient's implicit demand almost invariably boils down to a demand for the restoration of the previous economic balance, rather than for the removal of the symptom itself. We will encounter this later on under the appellation of the "flight into health." Nevertheless, a psychotherapeutic approach ought rather to be directed toward the underlying structure. Should the therapist forget this, she unwittingly collaborates in restoring the symptom's economic gain. It is in such a way that "revolving-door" patients are made who, with each subsequent swing in the balance, knock once more at our door. Ideally, psychotherapy should not focus on the elimination of symptomatic behavior. The most important aim of the treatment is rather to effect change within the underlying, structurally determined relation with the Other through which the symptoms originally materialized. The implication, then, is that it is expressly upon this relationship that the psychodiagnostic process needs to focus.

CONCLUSION

A comparison of medical and clinical psychological diagnostic procedures reveals a number of significant differences.[11] Central to medical diagnostics is the gaze, whose focus is on detecting signs that point

---

11. In this account I have reduced medical diagnostics to a purely mechanical-biological matter. Contemporary medical practice is, fortunately, taking more and more psychological factors into account.

toward objective, measurable parameters. In contrast, in clinical psychological diagnostics the focus is laid primarily on listening to signifiers that remain open to interpretation. Medical signs pertain to an illness scenario; signifiers, on the other hand, derive their meaning and function from a specific relation with an Other. The distinction between illness and health can be measured and generalized, but psychic normality and abnormality are always relative and, hence, particular. Moreover, certain psychic symptoms can best be understood as attempts at a solution for a particular structural relation with the Other.

Consequently, any data resulting from a psychodiagnostic examination must invariably be interpreted. The basis for such interpretation must be a governing grounding theory, combining quantitative, experimental-diagnostic results on the one hand, with a clinical psychological theory of the development of psychic identity on the other. In clinical practice, we frequently encounter an intuitive diagnostic that fails to take the previously discussed limitations into account. Such a diagnostic practice is best described as an exercise in naming, evoking the Biblical injunction to "go and name the things." It is this practice that is the subject of the first part of this book. The second part offers an elaboration of a metapsychology that forms the basis for clinical psychodiagnostics proper. The third part discusses the differential diagnostics itself based on this model.

2
Categorical Diagnostics versus Clinical Praxis: A Matter of Impossibility

THE BANKRUPTCY OF CLASSICAL PSYCHODIAGNOSTICS: QUESTIONING THE INDISPUTABLE MASTER

Clinical psychodiagnostics has its origin in medical practice, and emerged historically out of psychiatry. The implications are thus that clinical psychodiagnostics not only developed out of a particular type of knowledge, but also that it possesses a very specific relationship with the object of this knowledge, namely, the patient. The contribution of this relationship to the doctor's success or failure with his patients, beyond the mere question of his or her knowledge, is considerable, because it is precisely in and through this relationship—and never apart from it—that such knowledge operates.

Nevertheless, this relationship is implicit, and the participants—both doctor and patient—are barely aware of it. Even in medical school, this critical factor remains simultaneously both tacit and axiomatic. The medical student not only acquires knowledge and technique but, through constant contact with instructors, also learns how to behave in relation to patients. This only becomes explicit in situations of crisis, when the relationship as such takes center stage and the respective positions of both participants are called into question.

Such a crisis occurred in the second half of the last century. Psychotherapy and insanity were suddenly "in," but the character of the medical therapist, complete with needle and electroshock apparatus, became extremely suspect. Thus anti-psychiatry was born. Not only did partisans of this view attack the (lack of) treatment and the institution, but the authoritarian relationship between doctor and patient also became the special target of critique. Notable figures such as Cooper, Laing, and Szasz saw this primarily as a power relationship, one clinched by the psychiatric labels themselves (Cooper 1967; Laing 1960; Szasz 1972). Psychodiagnostic categorizations themselves subsequently came under heavy fire, with schizophrenia as the favorite target.

This social movement can best be understood (in Lacan's terms) as a clash between an hysterical and a master discourse, one whose most significant effect was to strengthen the master's position.[1] The most important consequence for us is that a number of scientific studies occurred in its wake, enabling the entire psychodiagnostic enterprise to be evaluated for the first time. The results were even worse than expected. Here are some of them.

What Is Abnormal?

One of the earliest studies begins with the commonsensical idea that the distinction between psychic normality and abnormality is not so hard to make. So claimed Lorenz (1984, pp. 101, 186), the famous ethologist who asserted that everyone has the intuitive ability to see quickly what is abnormal, based on a kind of Gestalt perception. This harks back to the widespread superstition about the dog that immediately startles whenever a psychiatric patient (the alienated, *alien*—in other words, the other) enters, the dog's bark testifying to the patient's abnormality. A diagnostician clearly has to have a fine nose! Phillips's experiment (1963) delivered some surprising results in this respect. This sociologist made a table of two columns comprising five categories. The first column comprised descriptions of:

---

1. These terms will be explained later (see Verhaeghe 1987, 2000a).

1. A paranoid schizophrenic
2. A schizophrenic
3. A person with anxiety depression
4. A phobic person with obsessive traits
5. A normal person

The second column ran as follows:

1. (Nothing was added to the description of the behavior.)
2. "Who regularly went to his pastor to talk about his situation"
3. "Who regularly went to his doctor to discuss his situation"
4. "Who regularly went to his psychiatrist to discuss his situation"
5. "Who was in a mental hospital on account of his situation"

Phillips (1963) presented the twenty-five categories he obtained in this way to 300 lay people (married white women), in order to assess the relation between psychiatric problems and social rejection. The results are hallucinatory: it was not the behavioral description that was decisive, but the extent and type of help sought. The normal person in the mental hospital is mad and socially rejected; the paranoid schizophrenic who does not seek help is normal and socially accepted. In other words, the idea of a ubiquitous differential-diagnostic intuition is an illusion.

One might dismiss these results by pointing out that it involved lay people, not professionals. But Temerlin's study (1968) offers a devastating retort. He asked an actor to play a normal person, interviewed him about his case history, and presented the audiotape to experts from our profession: twenty-five psychiatrists, twenty-five psychologists, and forty-five psychology students. Before listening to the tape they heard a very respected colleague tell how "this patient's subtlety makes him seem neurotic but in fact he is completely psychotic." The result: fifteen psychiatrists diagnose psychosis and ten neurosis; seven psychologists find him psychotic, fifteen neurotic, and three healthy; among the students, five diagnose him psychotic, thirty-five neurotic, and five found the man sane. Conclusion: the clinical intuition of professionals is evidently just as unreliable as that of lay people—and three cheers for the students. In more or less comparable experiments, Langer and Abelson (1974) and Lange and Van der Valk (1983) obtained analogous results: suggestion determines what one sees. Nearly two centuries ago Gall's student, the phrenologist Spurzheim, discovered the same thing. Presented with the skull of the genial astronomer Laplace, he measured and demonstrated with great enthusiasm the "cranial knobs" which were supposed to explain the specific intellectual capacities of the presumed genius. His enthusiasm rapidly dissipated once he was informed he was working with the skull of an imbecile (Deelman 1986, p. 141).

The Suggestibility Effect

Once again, one can dismiss these unwelcome results by claiming that the bias of the suggestibility effect would not appear in normal diagnostic circumstances. Indeed, in a later phase of Temerlin's (1968) experiment, the tape was replayed without suggestion. Out of the twenty-one test subjects, nine subsequently found the man neurotic and twelve pronounced him normal. Obviously, the presence or absence of suggestion is decisive.

It can, moreover, be virtually invisible. There is an impersonal kind of suggestion that is much more difficult to measure and that can be situated both on a microcosmic and on a macrocosmic level. On the macrocosmic level we find the fashion for diagnostic models that changes over time. All that is needed is for an authority to discover a new syndrome, or to breathe new life into an old one, for a massive increase in this diagnosis to occur. An example in this respect is the sudden revival of the old Tourette's syndrome following the publication of Oliver Sacks's (1986) best-seller, *The Man Who Mistook His Wife for a Hat* (1986 [1985]; see Minderaa et al. 1988). In the meantime, this has been replaced by the more recent rage for ADHD. Throughout the history of psychiatry and clinical psychodiagnostics, various such fads can be identified. Clearly there are epidemics in psychological disorders as well, but the question is, Who falls prey to them, the patient or the clinician?

On a smaller scale, something similar occurs with the observation that some diagnoses are made with greater frequency in certain institutions than in others, largely as a result of the particular hobbyhorses of the individuals in charge (one clinician, for example, detecting epilepsy everywhere, while another finds hysteria). Such was Abraham's comment to Eitingon—that, since leaving the Burghölzi clinic, he "found" far less dementia praecox and a lot more hysteria. An institution's intellectual climate of the time doubtless has a lot to do with it.[2]

The least obvious yet nevertheless most important form of suggestion is found in the ubiquitous idea of the expectation of illness. This was tellingly put into words by one of my MD friends: "The moment someone enters my consultation room, they are a suspect."[3] Rosenhan's findings (1973, 1975) are seminal in this respect. He sent a number of test subjects to American mental hospitals, asking them to present symptoms resembling hallucinations. The supposed patients were told to behave completely normally from the moment they were admitted to the hospital, and to answer all case history and diagnostic exams in an ordinary way. The result: every single one of them was labeled psychotic, albeit with the epithet "in remission." The beauty of it was that the clinicians in the institutions were able to explain the disorder on the basis of the true case histories of these pseudo-patients. The power of secondary elaboration is evidently not limited to dreaming.[4]

Some may try to contradict these results by invoking a deontological argument; that is, given such initial indications no institution would refuse them admittance. Besides, the disappearance of symptoms shortly after admittance is, after all, not so rare . . . In the second part of his experiment, Rosenhan (1975) gave the institutions a "second chance." He published his results, shook his admonishing finger, and let it be known that in the following months further "normal" test subjects would be sent for admittance, in the hope that this time the right diagnosis would be made. And, in fact, this time the normal patients were exposed. Unfortunately for the institutions, however, Rosenhan hadn't actually sent anyone.

---

2. The Burghölzi clinic (Zürich) was run by Eugen Bleuler from 1898, where he developed and taught his theory of dementia praecox (schizophrenia) to Abraham and Jung, among others. See Karl Abraham, Letter to Eitington of March 8, 1908, cited in Maleval (1981, p. 281).

3. Or in the words of "Dr. Knock," the archetypal medical doctor created by Jules Romains (1923): "A healthy man is a patient who ignores the fact that he is ill."

4. "Secondary elaboration" is a Freudian concept that explains how the ego subsequently revises the dream's content in order to make it into a logical and coherent narrative. We will encounter this function again later on.

Recounting these research results invariably produces a reaction of disbelief and defense: such things are impossible. We can cover ourselves by pointing to the lay character of the experiment (Phillips), to the suggestibility effect (Temerlin), or to the deontological errors. The hope is that with extensive enough diagnostic interviews, performed with adequate care, something useful will nevertheless come out of it. But at this point we encounter research by Sandifer et al. (1970). This time it is an open project, without a hidden agenda. Case history interviews with real psychiatric patients were videotaped and shown to experienced psychiatrists. The aim of the research was clearly explained to the participants beforehand: "to observe when and how a diagnosis is made and to what extent agreement is reached between different diagnosticians." The results are breathtaking: regardless of the length of the interviews, the majority of diagnoses are made within the first three minutes, less than half of the clinical data is used, and the agreement among the different diagnosticians is depressingly low.

What further became evident from this project was the diagnosticians' own immunity from additional information: once a specific diagnosis had been made, new information contradicting this diagnosis was neither heard nor seen. Rooymans (1986) cites the research results by Gauron and Dickinson (1970), Elstein et al. (1978), and Blois (1980), whose combined results led him to the following conclusion: "Provisional judgement, vital as a guideline in the diagnostic process, can mutate into prejudice" (p. 22).

The results of such findings brought the societal ideological upheaval indoors as well. The former psychodiagnostic categories and accompanying methods had lost so much of their credibility that a worldwide search began for an accessible and, above all, reliable system for psychodiagnostics. It was as if a new Enlightenment was taking shape, whose final form we know today as the DSM.

THE DSM-DIAGNOSTICS:
THE ANONYMOUS NEW MASTER

These fairly well-known critiques of the psychiatric diagnostic system resulted in the agreement that the creation of a clear, objective, and preferably international categorization should be given priority.

This in turn gave rise to the establishment of codified nosological systems in the hope that this would increase the reliability of diagnostic pronouncements. An important first step was made by the World Health Organization, which included in their International Classification of Diseases (ICD) a separate section for psychopathology and psychiatric disorders. Faithful to their own political tendencies, the Americans quickly replaced this system with their own model, which was subsequently exported through the usual (i.e., pharmacological) promotional channels to the rest of the world. This is the *Diagnostic and Statistical Manual of Mental Disorders*, usually known as the "DSM," first published in 1952, and most recently reedited as the *DSM-IV-TR* (2000).[5]

At first sight this doesn't seem like such a bad choice, given that the initial results surrounding the *ICD-9* were not particularly rosy. For example, Van Lieshout et al. (1987) examined the extent to which different diagnosticians come to the same ICD diagnosis in clinical practice. They made a comparison between: (1) the admission and discharge diagnoses, (2) the discharge diagnosis and the diagnosis on readmittance in the same institution, and (3) the discharge diagnosis of institution X and the diagnosis on readmittance to institution Y.

The data were drawn from the *Patient Register of Intramural Mental Health Care*, whose abbreviation in Dutch renders an excellent illustration of the power of the signifier: "PIGG." Their conclusion requires no further explanation: "The conformity among diagnosticians concerning PIGG-diagnoses [sic] at differing points in time is minimal, particularly in cases of diagnosticians arriving at diagnoses independently of each other. Technical factors alone cannot explain why there is a higher chance of a patient's receiving a different admission's diagnosis on readmittance to another institution within a year, from the one given at the previous discharge" (Van Lieshout et al. 1987, p. 243). Those cases

---

5. The first version of the ICD containing a classification of psychiatric disorders is the *ICD-6* (1948). The *ICD-9* (1975) was considered problematic by the APA (American Psychiatric Association) for application in the United States, so they installed a "task force" [sic], which led to the development of the *DSM-III* (1983). Its many shortcomings gave rise to a revised version, the *DSM-III-R* (1987). Since then the *DSM-IV* (2000) and the *DSM-IV-TR* (2000) have appeared, developed more or less in dialogue with the *ICD-10*. Throughout the different editions, increasing importance was attached to empirical verification.

showing close correspondence frequently involved categories such as dementia and addiction; in other words, the kinds of categories in which conformity would have been present anyway, without the application of the *ICD 9*.

Now, one might argue that the information available to the diagnosticians might have been too limited for them to make a correct ICD classification. But the researchers themselves reject this idea: they cite research by Dingemans demonstrating that the addition of further clinical information results in an even more unreliable classification. Anyone with clinical experience can confirm this. Having a limited amount of data leads to a rapid diagnosis. Once therapy begins and more clinical material becomes available, clinical judgment becomes increasingly nuanced, making a univocal diagnosis less likely and ultimately even impossible.

Understanding the DSM's Success

The question now is, how much weight does the DSM carry? For the inexperienced student, who is frequently ignorant of the history of our profession, the DSM (and particularly its descriptions of the personality disorders), seems to be the mother of all things. But in the process one tends to forget about the rest of the family.

The success of the DSM can be historically understood as emerging from the anti-psychiatry movement, more specifically from dissatisfaction with confusing psychodiagnostic terminology and the accompanying multiplicity of disparate theories and opinions. From the beginning, the aim of the APA's so-called task force was to construct a diagnostic system grounded in sound observation. Before long, however, this task force discovered what every philosopher and epistemologist could have predicted beforehand: simply that their atheoretical, purely observational approach did not yield the desired results. To put it more concretely, the DSM's descriptions of Axis one are insufficient. At this point, we have to take note of the growing importance and success of Axis two, because this axis of the personality disorders is precisely an attempt to leave the purely descriptive aspect behind, and to order the observational data back into categories again.

As such, the introduction of the personality disorders testifies to sound thinking. This is the good news. The bad news is that, because the intent was to maintain a purely descriptive approach to categorization, the transition to a truly structural approach was not made, because that would have presupposed a theoretical basis. Incidentally, it is worth asking oneself exactly what a personality disorder is and, by implication, what constitutes a "personality."

The APA's definition of a personality disorder runs as follows: "an enduring pattern of inner experience and behavior that deviates markedly from the expectations of the individual's culture, is pervasive and inflexible, has an onset in adolescence or early adulthood, is stable over time, and leads to distress or impairment" (American Psychiatric Association 2000, p. 685). Even with the most cursory examination of this definition one cannot help but conclude that personality is a synonym for the psyche itself and hence that personality disorders are psychological disorders. In other words, a new term has been invented for an old problem, but the problem itself is not solved. We could find excellent uses for Occam's razor here.

Research and Personality

Nevertheless, such remarks are insignificant in light of the ultimate goal, namely, the creation of a routinely useful and reliable diagnostic system, assuming that this goal can in fact be reached. In the meantime, there has been no shortage of research discoveries, all running parallel with one another. It is scarcely necessary to enumerate each of them, so we will restrict ourselves simply to the two most important conclusions, which turn up in just about every study.

First of all, none of the studies succeeded in demonstrating the categorical character of the personality disorders. In concrete terms, this means that there is no clear-cut demarcation between normality and pathology and that there is a considerable overlap between the different categories. And there you have it—or rather, have them, since all of a sudden clusters begin to appear, enabling groups to form.

Among the multiplicity of the personality types, three main groups can be identified, which we can name, innocently enough, A,

B, and C. A contains paranoid, schizoid, and schizotypical personality types; B is made up of theatrical, antisocial, narcissistic, and borderline personality disorders; C includes obsessive-compulsive, dependent, evasive, and passive-aggressive types. These clusters acquire separate headings in the *DSM-III-R*: A is the odd-eccentric, B the dramatic-emotional-erratic, C the anxious-fearful. It doesn't take much to realize that this is indeed an ABC of psychiatry, where A stands for psychosis, B for psychopathy, and C for the neuroses. But it is only insofar as these designations are meaningful within the metapsychological theory of the one who uses them that we can obtain useful results because, at the end of the day, diagnoses and treatments are possible only when generated in the context of such a conceptual environment.

Shouldn't we now cheer, having been persuaded that this clustering gives us hard evidence of the factual reality of these three primary pathologies, and that classical psychiatry was right after all? Alas, depending on the choice of material and the way the clustering is done, different overlappings are produced (Schopp and Trull 1993). Firm data fail to offer any certainty, and leave us only with the illusion of certainty.[6] Hellinga (1992) lists these overlaps; it suffices here to mention only the most striking ones, in the sense that they precisely traverse the three primary pathologies. There is, for example, an overlap between the borderline and the schizotypical, between the schizoid and the evasive, between the passive-aggressive and the whole of Cluster B, as well as between the schizotypical and the obsessive-compulsive.[7]

---

6. Often all it takes to persuade the public is to produce numbers and formulas. What one forgets is that how the factor analysis is done—the choice of variables and the choice of procedure—is decisive for the results of the research. The rabbit indeed comes out of the hat, but that is because it was presupposed to be there beforehand. This is why research into IQ based on factor analysis hit a dead-end and was given up (cf Gould 1984). The same goes, probably even more so, for research into the "personality." The problem is not so much the mathematical methods in themselves but the variables that are used, because they always contain an arbitrary choice. In the symposium of *The Symptom* (June 11, 1994), the eminent Dutch scientist Van Praag remarked that, in spite of intensive worldwide research we still do not have useful biological "markers," and that the psychic entities—among which he counts the DSM personality disorders—are not usable, scientifically speaking, because they are too fuzzy as variables.

7. On the overlap between schizoid and evasive, borderline and schizotypical, see Kalus et al. (1993). On the overlap between passive-aggressive and the B-cluster, see Millon (1993).

Going further, it doesn't take long to see that what we encounter here are nothing but the old, yet still smoldering, differential diagnostic issues, such as, for instance, that between obsessional neurosis and schizophrenia in the last-mentioned overlap, and between hysterical psychosis and psychosis in the first. In order to address these issues, a theoretically driven approach is required; observation in itself is not enough.

Modalities of Treatment

The first group of critical remarks already puts the very idea of personality disorder into serious question. The second group concerns the modalities of their application. It became rapidly clear that the very same patients received a different diagnosis depending on the instrument used (questionnaires, semistructured interviews), and that even with the same instrument many people fit the criteria for several personality disorders. In fact the studies (Hellinga 1992) discuss an average of 3.75 to 4.60 personality disorders per patient![8] The most frequent diagnosis, then, is of course the latest DSM blanket term, namely Personality Disorder Not Otherwise Specified.

Personality Types

As well as critiquing existing conditions, we can also anticipate subsequent problems. This has to do with the as yet limited character of the represented personality types. The *DSM-III* contained eleven such types, the *DSM-III-R* was extended with the appearance of the "self-defeating and sadistic personality disorder," albeit only in the appendix; the *DSM-IV* tentatively introduces the "depressive personality disorder" and pushes the passive-aggressive personality disorder

---

8. A recent study shows that 69 percent of all cases could have resulted in multiple diagnoses; semistructured interviews yield an average of four personality disorders per patient (Livesley et al. 1994). A still more recent review study speaks carefully of "patterns of co-morbidity"; what is remarkable in all the reviewed studies is the way such patterns are the rule, not the exception (Millon and Davis 1996).

into the appendix. In the meantime, voices defending the depressive personality disorder have been raised, as well as the dysthymic and the hyperthymic personality disorders, while all indications point to distinguishing a hypochondriac personality disorder as well. In other words, the gate is wide open, and soon all the antiquated psychiatric entities will have found their contemporary equivalents, albeit with the suffix "personality disorder." And immediately, all the old problems will return as well, all the more so because of the DSM's sole emphasis on empirical observation, without any conceptual guide to act as a compass.[9]

DSM Pros and Cons

We can conclude, therefore, that the chief difference between the DSM diagnostics and their antecedents comes down to the fact that the DSM diagnostics have greater international currency than any preceding nosological system, and this is unquestionably a significant gain. So concurs a review of all recent studies of the DSM diagnostic (Jongedijk 2001). But beyond this immediate benefit, Jongedijk also lists a number of clear disadvantages: the impoverishment of the differential diagnostics, a very weak connection with the treatment, an unclear differentiation of the categories, and the problem of whether to assign a patient to one specific category or another based on threshold values. Moreover, he demonstrates that the DSM's highly praised empirical basis is an illusion. The various categories "didn't come into being through scientific research, but are the product of historical traditions, social developments or conflicts of interests" (p. 315). These same errors and shortcomings are found in every categorical psychodiagnostic approach (cf infra). However, in this case these mistakes can be rectified only with difficulty, precisely because the corrections of a guiding metapsychological theory were repudiated a priori.

---

9. Just how old they are can be illustrated by a letter from Jung, who wrote to Freud on September 11, 1907: "Once again I discovered to my satisfaction that without your ideas psychiatry will inevitably go to the dogs, as has already happened with Kraepelin. Anatomy and attempts at classification are still the rule—sidelines that lead nowhere" (cited in McGuire 1994, p. 86).

Meanwhile, we have lost sight of one of the most important motivations of the anti-psychiatric movement, namely, to address the typically authoritarian relation between the expert and the patient. So the final question is: Has the DSM diagnostic changed anything in the relationship between diagnosticians and patients? The answer is an unqualified no. From such a perspective, the expert remains an objective observer who inspects an object of study in an outside world—psychopathology belongs to the "kernel" of a personality—upon which the requisite conclusions are subsequently based. In the case of the DSM, this observer is reduced to nothing but that—a pure and simple gaze that nevertheless maps the outside world from an ascendant position. Its method? "Go and name the things."

CONCLUSION: THE IMPOSSIBILITY OF $S_1 \to S_2$

Closer analysis of the foregoing shows how the psychodiagnostic process has two components, namely form and content. The latter amounts to the question of naming: the diagnostician attempts to identify and correctly label a certain psychic situation, deviation, behavior . . . At the same time, a certain form is at work, invariably involving a specific relationship between the one who names (the diagnostician) and the one who is named (the patient). This relationship frequently remains hidden from view and has received far too little attention in the psychodiagnostic literature. When it has been highlighted, it has been through the agency of a critical social movement rather than through internal concern with the diagnostic process itself.

These two aspects converge at the point of "deviance"—and we know rejection is never far off here. [Translator's note: the author is making a wordplay here between the Dutch word for deviant (*afwijking*) and for rejection (*afwijzing*), words that are identical except for the sound of the single consonant that separates them.] The use of terms such as "normal," "deviant," "undesirable," and so on inevitably implies a norm that implicitly carries a power relation. This means that right from the start there is a danger of a crossover between the juridical-normative and the clinical-psychodiagnostic fields. We must be expressly aware of and attentive to this.

A Failure of Categories

One of the primary contentions of this book will be that content (naming) and form (relation) are two sides of the same diagnostic coin and that each performs a role in every psychodiagnostic process. Going deeper into the available data, it seems fairly clear that the categorizing psychodiagnostic process implies a certain failure at the level of labeling. Firstly, in contemporary psychodiagnostics just as in the earlier varieties, there are no general, mutually exclusive categories that can be isolated per se. Such categories can only be regarded as ideally conceived types, from which reality will always diverge. Secondly, the internal reliability of the proposed categories is depressingly low.

Both failures are usually seen as merely cosmetic flaws that, with further research, will vanish with time. However, it is my contention that these mistakes are structural in nature and will therefore endure (cf infra). In Part 3 of this book we will develop psychodiagnostics based on the structural relationship between the individual and the Other. The persistent failure of categorization with regard to content makes this relational aspect all the more important. Unfortunately, the relational aspect often becomes almost exclusively a power relationship, which is put to work in order to combat failure at the level of content. A diagnostic pronouncement is accepted not so much because it is correct (it can never be entirely correct), but because a confirmed authority presents it. Coming from a weak authority figure, it will not be accepted, regardless of its (in-)accuracy.

Such material easily lends itself to a Foucauldian reading, whose discourse theory asserts that a power relation is inaugurated in a dominant discourse through language. Foucault's own application and combining of the judicial and the clinical fields constitute a direct illustration of this.[10] However, there are a number of reasons why I have chosen Lacanian discourse theory as the basis for interpretation. Lacan's theory brings us much closer to the clinical field as such, while Foucault remains within the sociohistorical field. Moreover, Lacan's theory is elaborated in a more formally structural way, enabling us to make

---

10. See Michel Foucault, *The Order of Discourse* (1975); its applications in *Discipline and Punish* (1977), *Madness and Civilization* (1972), *The Birth of the Clinic* (1997).

anticipatory explanations and predictions. From a scientific point of view, this makes it a lot more attractive.[11]

The Agent and the Other

Discussion of discourse theory is reserved for our next chapter. But, in anticipation, let me already observe how the psychodiagnostic process, as described above, perfectly encapsulates what Lacan calls the "discourse of the Master." The speaker or the agent of this discourse occupies the master's position (indicated by S_1), which is the position from which he speaks and acts. His speech acts are directed toward the other (indicated by S_2), who is subjected to the master's knowledge. The relationship between agent → other, present in every discourse between the two, thus takes the following form in the discourse of the master: $S_1 \rightarrow S_2$. Occupying the position of agent, the master-diagnostician reduces the other-patient to his knowledge. In psychodiagnostics, the diagnostician is the agent who, in the form of the master signifier, S_1, must produce knowledge about the other contained in the signifiers, S_2. This is the upper level of the discourse: the agent → other, in this case $S_1 \rightarrow S_2$.

In his theory of the four discourses, Lacan states that an unbridgeable gap separates every agent and other, which he calls the disjunction of impossibility. This disjunction can be understood conceptually and belongs to what everyone intuitively knows: no message ever reaches the other the way the speaker intends it; every communication at least partially contains an internal failure.

$$\text{impossibility}$$
$$S_1 \rightarrow S_2$$

Applied to psychodiagnostics, the implication is that the master, S_1, is unable to definitively name the other through the S_2; to "go and name the things" is apparently not such an easy task. Practically everyone has had the experience of this impossibility, both in research and in day-to-day practice, and it gives rise not only to the previously

---

11. For the discourse theory, see Lacan (1991 [1969–70]). For an applied explication, see Verhaeghe (2001b).

mentioned clamor for more research, but also to flight—either to higher up in the hierarchy, or into the safety of the group (cf infra). It is no coincidence that the three professions Freud dubbed "impossible" are each implicated in the master position: governing, educating, and analyzing (Freud 1978 [1937c]).

Nevertheless, this disjunction of impossibility at first appears to be of a practical, and hence solvable nature. Just a bit more research, preferably strictly objective and scientific, and the ultimate system will be found. In Lacan's discourse theory, this is not the case. The relationship between the agent and the other has to do with merely the *upper* level of each discourse; what it veils is a fundamental relationship containing a second underlying disjunction. Extending this first disjunction to its underlying second one, the disjunction of impotence, shows that there is a lot more going on.[12] The impossibility of reaching

---

12. The deeper I go into Lacan's discourse theory, the more apparent its profoundly new character in comparison with other theories of communication becomes to me, largely because of these disjunctions and the structural relation that inheres between them. The far-reaching character of this discovery is of the same order as Freud's pronouncements concerning the impossibility of governing, educating, curing, but—because of its structural nature—it is much more useful here. The repercussions of this, as is well-known, reach as far as the famous Lacanian expressions, "There is no Other of the Other," "The Woman does not exist," and "The Sexual Relation does not exist," which can only be understood from within their structural conceptualization, beyond their misuse as slogans. Their inherently difficult character is typically ascribed to Lacan's abstract style. This is only partly correct. The real cause for misunderstanding lies rather in a persistent, defensive not-wanting-to-know, because the theory makes a number of certainties teeter, not only in our working domain, but also in our very way of life, and this causes a kind of conceptual loneliness. Hence my delight when I discovered an analogous idea in a completely different field, that is, in the work of a sociobiologist, who compares human science to the acts of a tinkerer. I will leave to the reader's imagination its relevance to Freud's joke about the "logic of the kettle" (Freud 1978 [1900a], pp. 119–120):

> According to the tinkerer theory, human behavior and experience are basically good and decent and healthy and warm and cooperative and intelligent, but something has gone a bit wrong somewhere. A fuse has blown in the child-rearing process or a tube has overheated in the psyche or an evil madman has taken over the controls [. . .] All we need to do is some tinkering: change the teaching apparatus or administer the right kind of psychotherapy or kick out the king and queen or institute socialism or at least print less money, and then everything will be just fine. If you can do more

a final diagnostic pronouncement has to do with this underlying impotence. In Lacan, this impotence is structurally determined and hence insoluble. I would like to suggest that, rather than losing our way among the diagnostic trees, we must uncover the structure of the diagnostic forest, namely, what this impotence involves.

Consequently, this leads to the question of an underlying epistemology, which will be addressed in Chapter 3: the *impossibility* of the diagnostic naming is founded on an epistemological *impotence*.

INSTALLING A CERTAIN RELATIONSHIP

It would be naive to think that the above-mentioned impossibility shuts clinical practice down per se. In spite of all the difficulties, diagnoses continue to be made and exchanged, and categorizing systems of classification continue to be applied. At this point the second aspect, the power relation, comes more fully into the picture.

How this happens is fairly easy to explain, despite the many forms in which it appears. The impossibility of maintaining the position of the master makes one retreat into the anonymous safety of the group. The formula dates back to Socrates, albeit more as admonition than advice: if *episteme* (loosely translated: knowledge) is unable to ground *arètè* (loosely translated: truth), one settles for *doxa* (group conviction, dogmatism). In other words, one rationalizes in accordance with the recognized and approved paradigm of a collective authority that anonymizes the master figure because it is hidden behind an apparently unanimous, conventional system. The conscious argument concerns what is considered the accuracy of the theory; the subtext shows how this accuracy is actually the product of shared conventions. Kuhn's

---

than one of these things and, preferably, get rid of your present wife at the same time, you will not only be just fine, you will stumble upon paradise on earth. [. . .] Everything will not be just fine. After we make the change, even if it improves us, we will still be full of the flaws of the human condition. [. . .] the behavioral or social tinkerer are merely reluctant to face these things, just as the average person is. That is why they are not good poets. Good poets not only face them, they dwell upon them in order to show us how to live in spite of them. [Konner 1982, pp. 414–415]

(1970) history of scientific thought offers many perfect illustrations of this.

From the perspective of discourse theory, the language of clinical practice inevitably retreats into the discourse of the university, which is a safer option for the individual in the face of impossibility. The apparent agent of this discourse is collective knowledge, the convention of communal knowledge that directs itself toward the other as an object. However, the structure of this discourse enables us to predict its effects completely independently of the specific contents of the discourse—the specific nature of the implied knowledge is all but irrelevant. This relation will be the subject of our fourth chapter.

3
The Impotence of Epistemology

In the previous chapter I argued that at the level of content—the identification and the naming of a psychic disorder—clinical psychodiagnostics always implies at least a partial failure. In this chapter we will see how this failure has everything to do with the problem of naming itself. What does one call a certain phenomenon? What influenced that choice of name? What are its effects? This is not just a philosophical but also an epistemological problem: What do the nosological designations refer to? In other words, What is the relationship between the nosological designations and clinical reality? The specificity of this question shouldn't blind us to its more general, epistemological nature.

In the first section, we will review the historical background in an attempt to discover the object of clinical psychodiagnostics and to see how it came into being. The second section examines the relation between psychodiagnostic designations and clinical reality from a wider perspective, namely, how science conceives of the relationship between words and things. The third section concludes that one cannot avoid making ethical choices, and that the object of psychodiagnostics is first and foremost a *relation* rather than an object per se.

THE OBJECT OF PSYCHODIAGNOSTICS

The question of the object of clinical psychodiagnostics is only one instance of a much larger problem: How does science relate to the reality that it studies? One often hears how science is defined through its objectives and methods. Its history begins with the western interpretation of Plato in the subject–object division, which redoubles as the opposition between psyche and soma. The Platonic psyche is an active, organizing entity perpetually searching for eternal and unchangeable Ideas, today's "invariants," which are known to mankind only through their shadows.[1] With the Western rediscovery of Aristotle, this entity became coupled with the empirical object and, by implication, its observation. The pre-Socratic argument of Heraclitus ("Everything changes, nothing remains") was forgotten.

In the meantime, these ideas have become quite literally self-explanatory and we can scarcely imagine any other way of thinking. The subject–object divide, renamed as the body–soul dualism, completely determines how we think. A holistic structural approach, wherein each part is indeed only a part of a larger whole, conflicts with the inherent dualism in our way of thinking. This is reflected, moreover, in our training: soma for the medical world, psyche for the human sciences. Attempts to join these two a priori separated structures together—*psycho-soma*-tics— are indeed nothing but attempts to glue a preconceived break together.

As a consequence, Western science was for many years reduced to a search for the invariants of various intuited phenomena, and delivered all sorts of observational classifications of presumed ontological essences as the foundation for every breed of science. In addition, from Descartes more or less onward, the scientific method has been characterized by the imperative principle of objectivity, confirming this fundamental dualism (*res cogitans* versus *res extensa*).[2] The scientific manual is immediately legible: an objective, "Cartesian" reconnaissance of the

---

1. This is the well-known Platonic metaphor of the cave, where captive individuals see only the shadows of the "true objects" while believing them to be real. Our contemporary variation of it involves the captive individual once more, fettered this time to his television set, zapping through "reality."

2. The effects of this dualism on our thought processes, particularly in scientific thought, cannot be overrated, and go a lot further than binary thinking in terms of either body (nature, sex, woman, etc.) or soul (nurture, gender, man, etc.). It implies,

"Aristotelian" object so as to find the underlying "Platonic" invariant. The quotation marks here are mandatory and help to indicate the superfluity of their predicates, which have little to do with their origins. The patent is German, but they are assembled in Taiwan.

This approach overlooks at least two subtle distinctions. First, that in Plato the psyche is the actively organizing principle, meaning that objects are ultimately only the means by which the subjective psyche "recalls" the Ideas. As a result, these Ideas (the invariants of today) only exist in thought, not in reality.[3] Secondly, that Descartes wrote his *Discourse on Method* (1968) with the explicit and profoundly subjective intent to gain clarity and certainty for his own actions and non-actions. These two remarks ultimately send us back to the most important axiom of philosophy's founder, Socrates: "Know thyself." Everything else follows from this. The idea that science is ultimately nothing but the anthropomorphization of the world will also be found later in Hegel.

Nor do things stop with Descartes. Under Kant, the very concept of what science is will be shaken to its foundations. To put it schematically, Kant concludes that science can never study the thing-in-itself, the Real, but only the thing as it appears to us. Consequently, science can only construct a representation of reality, nothing more. The next major tremor in scientific thought will be caused by Darwin, in whose aftershocks all science comes to acquire an evolutionary stamp. With Darwin, every actual object acquires a relative character, as representing only one phase within a larger evolutionary process. Noticeably, it is in the positive sciences that Kant and Darwin have had the most

---

for instance, the need for an ultimate or final ground, such as the Cause, which is nevertheless nothing more than the self-mirroring of the terms. We already see the same thing in Aristotle, who had to accept a final, unmovable prime mover along with his postulated movable spheres. That the latter are precisely an artifact of the thought process itself presupposes that one can distance oneself from such dualistic modes of thought—and that is precisely the ultimate difficulty, because of the apparently "self-evident" nature of such thought processes. Lacan sharply criticizes this dualistic thinking throughout his entire work, particularly in Seminar XX (1998 [1972-73]). For further discussion, see Verhaeghe (2001b).

3. A question posed by my then 6-year-old son: "Dad, how come there are so many different birds? Wouldn't it be better if they had only made one that we could just call 'bird'? Wouldn't that have been much easier?" We are Platonic in heart and soul, and especially in our thought processes.

impact; so far, at least, they have made little impression on the human sciences. Evolutionary psychology has barely got off the ground. In the hopes of being similarly scientific, the majority of the human sciences continue to reflect the naive empirical-Aristotelian model that the hardier brothers of the hard sciences have already left behind.

In psychodiagnostics, the effects of this model are clearly visible. Science is the objective study of the object—of the immutable object, no less. As a result, phenomenological diversity must be reduced to its universalizable essence. This is why the history of psychopathology can chiefly be understood as the history of a changing and ever-increasing nomenclature that tries to embrace the essence of clinical reality. Its concrete realization is found in every manual and, indeed, in the very idea of a manual itself. It is no coincidence that Griesinger's *The Pathology and Therapy of Mental Illness*, and particularly the second edition of 1867—see Bercherie (1980)—is known as the first modern psychiatric manual. After all, it is the first book that contains a systematic nosological classification.

This process becomes most obvious the moment the clinic comes into being. In the psychodiagnostic field, we find Pinel (Bercherie 1980), who emphasizes observation and classification: the object is the mental illness, the method is, in the first instance, looking and listening, through which an inductive system of classification is developed. Objectively knowing the distinct clinical pictures or syndromes ought to make an exchange possible among different researchers. Pinel had an aversion to theory because it would take us too far from clinical practice and, moreover, would prevent us from seeing things as they are. For him observation and classification were the name of the game that took a comment by Condillac as its motto: "A perfect science would be a perfect language." As far as treatment was concerned, Pinel favored a pragmatic approach, the effects of which still reverberate in contemporary practice today, albeit in a somewhat surreptitious manner, as the so-called "moral treatment."

Pure, Unprejudiced Observation

Today's confrontation with the impossibilities in our field has meant that a number of researchers see something fortuitous in this historical starting point: independent of every theoretical prejudice, these would-be pioneers could freely and without prejudice approach the clinic as a tabula rasa. This is the myth of the absolute zero-point, of the true Discoverer who steadily opens up a new, previously undiscovered field and gives it a name. The inventory of this field will then be adapted and enlarged to such an extent that finally the theory is experienced as a burden that can no longer be carried nor manipulated. Hence, the lamenting of a return to this state of pure, unprejudiced observation whose aim is to objectively describe the object and whose scientific classification of mental illness could serve as a basis for the theory and treatment.

Halfway through the previous century, this categorization was suspended. The relatively sudden impact of pharmacology on the clinic, from 1960 onward, further enforced this moratorium, which reduced a previously rich diversity to a number of templates, and in turn engendering the historically predictable reaction against what came to be known as "labeling." Classification has now taken the place of diagnostics, and the distinction between classification and diagnostic systems has been lost (Van Hoorde 1986a,b). As a result, we are left empty-handed. Clinical knowledge is disappearing and thus so is the clinic itself. The former all-too-rich diversity has been lost, and is replaced by a tendency toward a globalist psychiatry characterized by fluent transitions between neurosis and psychosis, while perversion seems to have been reserved for forensic psychiatry and potential literary uses. Griesinger's idea of a "unary psychosis" is not too far off here.[4] Furthermore, a number of peculiar neurobiological diagnostic kinds of logic are emerging: if someone responds favorably to antidepressants, she or he must suffer from a depressive disorder; if someone responds favorably to antianxiety medication, he or she must suffer from an anxiety disorder. The diagnosis imposes itself, even when there is a lot of additional clinical data besides depression and anxiety in the case history.[5]

In the turbid wake of all this, the DSM came into being as the material result of the nostalgia for the tabula rasa. This diagnostic clas-

---

4. "Unary psychosis" describes the idea that there is only one psychopathology whose different forms of appearance are determined according to when the illness erupts in the patient's lifetime.

5. For more examples, see Zarifian (1988).

sification system is presumed to be atheoretical, and to be based solely on observation and empirical verification, by which one arrives at categorization and labeling. What I called the globalist tendency collapses into its opposite here, which Vandereycken (1988), not without some justification, calls the Diagnostic and Statistical *Mania*: hundreds of categories have been distinguished while a number of classic syndromes have disappeared. These categories are assumed to be directly perceptible "in the field"—presupposing a certain transparency of the object—and the implication is that the only points left worth discussing revolve either around the question of the name (in cases of a monothetic ordination) or the way the characteristics should be grouped, along with the accompanying code number (in case of a polythetic ordination).

The fact that this transparency is not so self-evident is shown by the transition from the so-called "archetypal" to a "prototypical" classification.[6] Here, one is prepared to sacrifice one's original aim (of finding invariants) and to replace it with multidirectional, fragmented, and quantitatively determined cross-sections of the clinical reality, all for the lack of the rigorous analysis that a theoretically driven approach can provide. In this way, a number of diagnoses can only be reached when at least x number of symptoms, distributed over at least y of the

---

6. For the sake of clarity, these concepts should be explained. "Classical" psychiatric classification is *monothetic* and *archetypal*, indicating that a patient belongs to a single diagnostic class, based on ideal archetypes or principle classes. These two characteristics (indeed, requirements) are the main reason why classical diagnostic systems are always incomplete, because these requirements are impossible to meet in clinical practice. Opposed to this is the contemporary alternative, called *polythetic* and *prototypical*. Polythetic implies that the "criteria for in- or exclusion are clearly defined and of which one must meet a specified number in order to be attributed to a certain class" (de Jong and van de Brink 1986, p. 430). Not all of the characteristics therefore need to be present. Prototypical indicates that certain characteristics are more important than others, so that each category is organized around the best, or prototypical example of that category which functions as a cognitive point of reference; for instance, the nightingale belongs more fully to the prototypical category of birds than a chicken, having not only wings and feathers, but song and flight as well (de Jong and van de Brink, ibid.). The reader with literary inclinations will immediately recall Borges's classification of animals from *The Book of Imaginary Beings* (1984). The moral of Borges's fable is of course the arbitrary nature of every classification whose final criterion rests on the classifying subject itself, and not the classified object.

z itemized categories, appear for a sufficiently long period, frequently within certain age limits.[7] Here is an example:

Diagnostic criteria for 301.83 Borderline Personality Disorder

A pervasive pattern of instability of interpersonal relationships, self-image, and affects, and marked impulsivity beginning by early adulthood and present in a variety of contexts, as indicated by five (or more) of the following:

1. *frantic efforts to avoid real or imagined abandonment.* **Note**: *Do not include suicidal or self-mutilating behavior covered in Criterion 5.*
2. *a pattern of unstable and intense interpersonal relationships characterized by alternating between extremes of idealization and devaluation*
3. *identity disturbance: markedly and persistently unstable self-image or sense of self*
4. *impulsivity in at least two areas that are potentially self-damaging (e.g., spending, sex, substance abuse, reckless driving, binge eating).* **Note**: *Do not include suicidal or self-mutilating behavior covered in Criterion 5.*
5. *recurrent suicidal behavior, gestures, or threats, or self-mutilating behavior*
6. *affective instability due to a marked reactivity of mood (e.g., intense episodic dysphoria, irritability, or anxiety usually lasting a few hours and only rarely more than a few days)*
7. *chronic feelings of emptiness*
8. *inappropriate, intense anger or difficulty controlling anger (e.g., frequent displays of temper, constant anger, recurrent physical fights)*
9. *transient, stress-related paranoid ideation or severe dissociative symptoms.* [APA 2000, p. 710]

It is immediately striking how the diagnosis itself already demands arbitrary thresholds: a diagnosis of borderline has to meet at least five

---

7. This idea is anything but new. The distinction between a real illness and its accompanying variations, for example, can already be found in Charcot's distinction between "real" hysteria and *"les formes frustes,"* the reduced versions. This same idea forms the basis for the difference between the so-called primary and secondary symptoms, a division that appears in almost every diagnostic system. This is invariably the result of the attempt to hold to the notion of observable invariants.

of the nine characteristics. Why five? Why not four or six? No one can give a meaningful answer to this question; the "border" has to be located somewhere. Moreover, for a characteristic to be present, a certain quantity has to be transgressed each time: *intense, marked, frequent, recurrent, markedly and persistently, frantic*. The diagnostician must weigh things up, asking him or herself: is this intense enough, is this sufficiently inadequate or marked?

Such calibration is not founded on any conceptual basis. Rather, that is precisely what is avoided. In other words, we have made the complete transition to arbitrary-normative categories. With this, the second problem arises, because an arbitrary-normative categorization does not exist, in the sense that nothing simply falls out of the sky. If there can be no categorization founded upon a theoretical basis, the diagnostician unavoidably falls back on social-cultural criteria, in other words, on the collective norms. This is what is happening right now. Biological psychiatry's ascendance finds its mirror image in the emergence of social psychiatry.[8] No wonder that in many publications we now read how socially deviant behavior is more representative than the so-called psychiatric symptomatology (is there still a difference?). There is even less reason to wonder why the majority of diagnosed cases stem from Cluster B, that is the anti-social, theatrical, narcissistic, and borderline personality disorders. Like the Queen's letter in the famous Poe story "The Purloined Letter," it is so obvious that nobody even sees it anymore.

We can regard this quantitative aspect as an artifact of a purely observational method that founds itself on the image, on the Imaginary. If one is prohibited from making theoretical distinctions, only comparative logic remains.[9] The arbitrary nature of such quantitative arguments

---

8. E. M. Coles makes the same observation: "The best examples of artificial or equivalence taxa are probably the DSM personality disorders. [. . .] By not distinguishing between natural/identity taxa and artificial/equivalence taxa, the later editions of the DSM have *encouraged the nonmedical role of psychiatry as social constraint*" (Coles 1996, my italics).

9. By theory I mean the Symbolic order, whose triangular structure enables the difference between two terms to be made clear through a third. The Imaginary order, in contrast, is always dual and hence comparative, precluding definitive conclusions. An example of an Imaginary form of diagnosis would say, for example, that a paranoid-type person becomes fully paranoid when he starts behaving too paranoiacally:

resides in the arbitrariness of the chosen criteria. Berden (1986), for one, demonstrates how, when applied to the same group of children, two different systems (*DSM-III* and the Weinberg criteria) for diagnosing major depressive disorders deliver two different groups as results; as if that weren't enough, the administering psychiatrist suggests yet another classification.[10]

What can we conclude from these developments? Chiefly that, historically, scientific development has progressively increased the distance in the relation between the subject and the Other, and purports to find complete certainty in an apparently immutable object. The DSM is the most recent attempt at this in our profession, aiming to establish once and for all the invariants of the clinical psychodiagnostic field.

In the meantime it has become clear that this attempt has failed, a failure that can be located on the following two levels, among others. On the one hand, the ideal of perfect communication fails because of the deficiency of what were hoped to be unanimous results. On the other, the classification system is forced to call on arbitrary quantitative criteria in order to delimit the borders between different categories.

Beyond these failings, we find a still more fundamental shortcoming. The problem with the DSM is not simply a result of the DSM's own failure. As explained above, this manual is the final culmination of a certain scientific tradition that upholds the centrality of the object's transparency and immutability, albeit as a problem often enough. For the DSM, this operated not so much as a problem but as an assumption: the object *is* transparent. Hence one of the most overriding problems of epistemology was not taken into consideration, namely, what is the relationship between the scientific description and the object of study, in this case, between the nosological designation and its clinical reality? Or, more broadly: What is the relationship between the word and the thing?

"[. . .] a paranoiac was a nasty person, an intolerant one, a bad-humored type, proud, mistrustful, irritable, and who overestimated himself. This feature formed the foundation of paranoia—when the paranoiac was far too paranoid, he would end up deluding" (Lacan 1993 [1955–56], p. 4).

10. The third classification, that of the administering psychiatrist, was the most useful because here depression was considered a component, a symptom within a larger diagnosis (depression within a hysterical pathology among others), giving rise thereby to therapeutic considerations (Berden 1986).

Such questions dominate the history of philosophy and, later, of epistemology, so that rather than reinventing the wheel we need only to examine their history. What quickly becomes clear, above and beyond all their various nuances and refinements, is how two fundamentally different approaches stand opposed to one another, in short, those called idealism (Plato, Hegel) and materialism (Aristotle, Marx). This opposition is, moreover, associated with certain linguistic considerations that are best understood by the opposition between nominalism and realism. We will discuss this opposition in more detail in an attempt to make things clearer.

EPISTEMOLOGICAL IMPOTENCE: A CONSTRUCTIVE MISUNDERSTANDING

The Naive Point of Departure: $S_2 = a$

The first approach is not only the simplest and most naive but probably also the most prevalent, if only implicitly. It assumes a natural, stable, regulated order that is independent of the observer. The scientist's task is primarily to observe, to discover. The ultimate goal is to name. Condillac expressed it best in his previously cited motto, "a perfect science would be a perfect language," one that science adapts from the biblical injunction "go and name the things."

Essentially, there's little difference here between the botanist and the diagnostician: each has his given bank of assorted flowers possessing their own internally regulated systems, founded on rigorous laws. The researcher's task is to discover and chart this system and to insert each individual sort or species into its rightful place.

> The supreme Being is not subjected to less certain laws in producing diseases or in maturing morbific humours, than in growing plants or animals. . . . He who observes attentively the order, the time, the hour at which the attack of quart fever begins, the phenomena of shivering, of heat, in a word all the symptoms proper to it, will have as many reasons to believe that this disease is a species as he has to believe that a plant is a species because it grows, flowers, and dies always in the same way. [Sydenham 1772, quoted in Foucault 1997, p. 7]

Such research results in an objectively recognizable and generalizable nosological system conceived as a scientific mirror-image of reality. Mistakes can happen, but the assumption is of a progressive, cumulative development.

A number of the consequences of such an approach are immediately apparent. In this view, there is only one correct way of ordering, independent of and prior to any research. The scientist's task is to discover and understand this order in a progressive, cumulative way. Such an ordering seems to have been accomplished in botany with the Linnaean system, but psychodiagnostics still has a long way to go. Secondly, this approach situates all certainty in the object, being persuaded that a precise order, a fixed lawfulness, exists independently of the researcher who merely gives it a name: "What's in a name? That which we call a rose, by any other name, would smell as sweet" (Shakespeare, *Romeo and Juliet*, Act II, Scene 2). This harks back to medieval realism, as a Catholic-inspired rewriting of Plato and Aristotle, which holds that in reality there is a preexisting order and lawfulness determined by God. This brings us to the third consequence: the ground, the foundation of this system, has to be looked for in a specific belief. This is most obvious with the guaranteeing God of Descartes, for instance, but it doesn't hide the fact that such a final ground can just as well be the belief in the unchangeable laws of nature. Its most beautiful illustration is found in Spinoza, whose analogy between God and Nature (*Deus sive Natura*) ended up in a guaranteeing pantheism. It is not by chance that a figure like Einstein, his a-religious position notwithstanding, repeatedly gestured toward that *Deus sive Natura*, a compound that appears in an exemplary way in his statement that "God does not play dice with the universe," a response to what was for him the unacceptable indeterminacy of quantum mechanics.

That such a perspective has far-reaching consequences at the ethical level is less immediately clear but not therefore without its own dangers. In medieval times it was connected with the idea of predestination, through which everything is preordained and against which all resistance and innovation were forbidden because they went against the divine, that is to say, natural order of things. Such logic returns today whenever something is disputed with the argument that it is "against nature." This is in fact—regardless of its apparent scientificity—a legacy of medieval religious convictions whose emphasis is on creationism.[11] Darwin is execrated as a heretic, Kant is too difficult, all certainty lies in faith.

Approaches to Language

Further consideration shows how this perspective depends on a naive approach to language. The thing dwells in the external world, waiting until the right word is found for it. In terms of discourse theory, this implies that in scientific activity, knowledge (S_2) is equivalent to the object of study (a), which, by these means, becomes transparent. But this is not even true of children's language, except perhaps in onomatopoeia. Medieval realism is untenable, even for the frequently cited example of botany. Lévi-Strauss (1976) demonstrates in *The Savage Mind* how the classification systems of certain South American tribes are more efficient than that of Linnaeus insofar as the system has a different functionality (the quest for food). Apparently, a rose is not always just a rose. The empirical speaks because somebody made it speak. Who is it that's speaking anyway?

$$\text{Negative answer:} \quad \begin{array}{c} S_2 \\ \downarrow \\ a \end{array}$$

This brings us to a second approach, radically opposed to the first. Its starting point is the idea that we gain access to reality only through our individual representations based on perception. While we provide the links, build categorizations, and construct abstractions that appear empirically recognizable, these nevertheless exist only in the mind and are imposed upon reality afterwards, in a second moment. "It is the theory that determines what observation tells us."[12] From this perspec-

---

11. A grievous example from today: homosexuality is "against nature," that is, against a supposedly divine or natural law. Hence, AIDS is said to be the just punishment of this natural God. Such "natural" arguments are always ethically suspect.

12. Thomä and Kächele, cited in Den Boer (1987, p. 40). For those who wish to hear it from a real scientific angle, we refer them to Einstein's famous comment, "It is the theory which decides what we can observe" (cited in Cosmides and Tooby 2001, p. 4).

tive, there is no preexisting order, it is we who create and impose it. In the final analysis, this imposition always happens in the same way: by naming, through the giving of names. Hence the name of this approach, nominalism, which dates back to William of Occam.

From this second perspective, scientific activity becomes a little less rosy. The secure hold of the first perspective, whereby only a single correct order was conceivable, is replaced here by an evidently unavoidable subjectivity. Certainty is no longer on the side of the object; it is the subject who now takes this place. The ultimate stumbling block is always the same, though: language as the giving of names. It was for this reason that Occam sought a remedy in his razor. As we saw before, such a breaking point can easily be found in psychodiagnostics.

The extension of this approach leads to the extremes of solipsism, even to nihilism, where nothing is assured and any word can mean anything. This ultimately leads to the denial of the existence of the world itself—had there been no one to name the world, the world would not exist.[13] A more moderate version runs: science can only make constructions and models of reality and test them on their predictive merit. Scientific progress is the replacing of one model by another that is presumed to be a better approximation of reality at the time. Nevertheless, a model remains first and last a model, nothing more.

Linguistics and deSaussure

Here as well, we can make a connection with linguistics, more specifically with that of Ferdinand de Saussure (1976). Rather than an equivalence between the word and the thing, we now find a division between the acoustic image, called the signifier, and the signified, beyond both of which lies the thing itself. Saussure holds that the relationship between the signifier and the signified is arbitrary. For instance, there is nothing in the signified "dog" that requires us to use the signifier "dog" for it

---

13. Strangely enough, the clinician will recognize two possible positions for the subject here. The first is the obsessional, whereby the subject, throughout all his doubts, keeps looking for the final referent; the second involves the psychotic's denial. This correspondence is no coincidence, having everything to do with the relationship between the subject and the Real by way of the Symbolic, of which science is only one example.

(proof of which is found in the way different languages use different signifiers: dog, *chien*, *Hund*, *hond* . . .). The speaker can thus "choose," as it were, what signifier he or she wants to use. Nevertheless, the choice has already been made. Saussure calls this the forced choice of language (*"la carte forcée"*): choices are possible, but have been made long before us. The arbitrary relationship and the forced choice leads him to the importance of convention: language rests on an agreement between its speakers and, hence, not on an internal relationship between signifier and signified, let alone between word and thing. Moreover, signifiers in themselves are meaningless. The production of meaning comes from the difference between the mutual signifiers, indicating that it is always the context that produces signification. A single signifier signifies nothing; it is only in the combination of several signifiers that meaning is produced, drawn from the surrounding signifiers.[14]

Combining the nominalist approach with Saussure's linguistics leads to a surprising inference. While in the realist approach, things come to us out of the Real, as it were, needing simply a name, now it is from words, from the Symbolic, that an effect is made on the Real. From this perspective, so-called reality is at least partially a product of the Symbolic, reality becomes *materialized, realized*. Reality is indeed what has been actualized, made operational for us. [Translator's note: The Dutch word for reality, *werkelijkheid*, has connotations not only of actuality and reality, but also connotes the word work (*werk*). The author is making a pun here that cannot easily be rendered into equivalent English. A literal translation would go something like, reality is indeed what becomes real/works for us.] With the expression "to realize something," we return to the relationship between the Real and the Symbolic. One "realizes something for oneself" and hence it exists, that is, for the name-giver. The Real always ex-sists, independently of the Symbolic. So-called reification, the fact that things are called into life by words, is less the exception than the rule in human reality.[15]

---

14. A simple example can clarify this: "Public hysteria became so encompassing that intervention was necessary"; "Hysteria still presents medical science with a number of questions"; "Hysteria à la Charcot has become a rare phenomenon today." The signifier hysteria has three different signifieds, determined by the context.

15. Note that in realism just as in nominalism, a thing without a name also has no existence in human consciousness.

Approaches to the DSM Diagnostics

Applying these two approaches to science in general, and to psychodiagnostics in particular, it quickly becomes clear how the aforementioned nostalgia for the absolute zero point of observation boils down to a contemporary redaction of medieval realism. Moreover, to think in this way amounts to an absolute determinism: the invariants are fixed, together with the laws governing the underlying relations.

Postmodern science, in contrast, is both neo-Kantian and neo-Darwinian. Since "the thing-in-itself" can never be known, science concentrates on "the thing-for-itself," which must be conceived in terms of evolutionary adaptation. Following on the heels of this, the development of quantum mechanics and evolutionary theory has made determinism questionable, shifting the emphasis onto contingency.[16] Contemporary science leans toward a new version of nominalism: *we* make constructions, models of reality whose impact and range we try to empirically verify. Nevertheless each signifier remains a signifier, even those at a higher level of abstraction.[17] Working with subjectively determined systems, science consequently demands that we pay particular attention to intersubjectivity. It is this that dictates a scientific system's generalizability. To put it in Saussurian terms: convention determines everything, and belongs not to the *object* but to the *subject*.

---

16. Lacan developed such a view of causality and determinism in his paper, "The Purloined Letter" (In his *Ecrits: A selection*, 1977) and in Seminar 11 (1994 [1964]). Briefly, he considers causality as belonging to the order of contingency, whereas its ensuing elaboration belongs to determinism. Both cause and determinism, moreover, stand in a clear underlying relation understood by way of the difference between repetition compulsion (cause) and repetition (determinism). The clinical application is found in the study of traumatic neurosis (cf below, Chapter 12). For a more extensive discussion of Lacan's theory of causality and determinism, see Verhaeghe (2002b, pp. 119–145).

17. The difference between so-called higher levels of abstraction in language hides a more fundamental characteristic of human language, that is, the radical gap between words and things—there is never a correspondence, every signifier is "abstract." Lacan expresses this laconically: for as long as a child says woof-woof to the dog, and meow-meow to the cat, she doesn't speak. It is only when she is able to say woof-woof to the cat, and meow-meow to the dog, that we can then say she does indeed speak.

This latter idea has not yet penetrated the task force of the DSM. Their philosophical approach is more akin to medieval realism. Here we encounter two classic terms of psychodiagnostics, namely, reliability and validity. Usually, reliability is put forward first—and with good reason, because it is the only term that can be more or less measured. Indeed, on closer inspection, this reliability or arbitration-consensus, is nothing other than the previously mentioned convention and the extent to which it is followed. Validity, on the other hand, concerns the "correspondence between intellect and thing" of Thomas Aquinas (*adequatio intellectus et rei*), or the extent to which the name of the object corresponds to the object, the degree to which one measures or diagnoses what one intended to measure or diagnose. It must be said that in this respect the available quantitative material makes for some very sorry considerations, immediately raising the question of how this validity can be measured in the first place in the light of the epistemological problems discussed above.[18]

All of the emphasis seems to lie on this shared convention. It is amusing to see that Freud already reached this conclusion, albeit only anecdotally. In his study on Schreber (1978 [1911c]), which represents his attempt to conceptualize psychosis psychoanalytically on the basis of a patient's own report of a delusional system, Freud makes the observation that, crazy as it seems, this delusional system displays all the characteristics of a theory. He then asks himself what the difference might be between psychoanalysis, deemed insane by his opponents, and the insane theory of the paranoid Schreber? The sole guarantee for Freud lies in the conclusion that only one person believed in Schreber's theory (namely, the patient himself), whereas Freud's had more "believers," in other words, the community of analysts. This anecdotal evocation of convention as the final ground of science acquires epistemological airs when someone like Stengers, half a century later (and independently of Freud, because she doesn't appear familiar with this part of his study on Schreber) elevates this same argument to the final criterion of how to determine what science is: science is what concerns the *inter*-est of scientists; it is that

---

18. See the study by H. Rooymans (1986, pp. 18–21). For a more conceptual approach, see Mooij (1988, pp. 72–78).

around which scientists commonly assemble (Stengers 1989, pp. 165–167).

In short, from an epistemological perspective, certainty is not found on the side of the object, but on that of the subject, and then chiefly among the scientific community of the subjects, namely, convention.[19] At this point, we must leave the specific field of psychodiagnostics so as to give this epistemological problem further consideration. The value of this for the field of psychodiagnostics will quickly become apparent.

Science as a Symbolic System: A Constructive Misunderstanding

The impasse of nominalism and realism can be given in linguistic terms, but linguistics in itself is not enough. Indeed, linguistics pays very little attention to the speaker as subject, and it is precisely this subject that is the object of psychodiagnostics. Here, however, a bridge appears in the form of psychoanalysis: both Freud and Lacan study the human being first and foremost as a being that manipulates symbols and undergoes their effects. This will be our own starting point as well.

Science, in any of its forms, is first and foremost a *symbolic* system through which we can study so-called reality. To put it concretely: it is a system that cannot but operate through signifiers.[20] The difference between humans and animals can serve as an illustration. Animals have

---

19. Anyone who imagines scientific certainty has to do with the extent of its serviceability is referred to all the concrete and successful experiments based on scientific theories that were later discovered to be wrong and, vice versa, to all procedures that occur without the aid of scientific theories.

20. The best illustration is algebra, where the signified of the signifiers X, Y, or Z can shift constantly within the system itself. Algebra is a perfect illustration of what lies at the base of modernity and modern science: the mathematization of reality, and the accompanying break with Aristotelian thinking, which remains stuck in the conviction that things can be studied in their empirical essence. Newton was the first to resolutely distance himself from this. Kant will confirm it later with the idea that we can have knowledge only of "the thing-for-itself." Incidentally Lacan sees such a mathematical approach to reality as the perfect proof of the primacy of the signifier on top of the Real. Mankind is the bearer not of a real essence, but of a symbolic system separated from the Real and through which this Real is interrogated. In our time, science is the primary form of this questioning (see De Kesel 2002, pp. 61–65).

no need of science because they have direct knowledge of their surroundings, that is to say, an unmediated knowledge that operates through sign-systems originating in their phylogenetic and ontogenetic development by way of imprinting and prewired connections. Despite the frequent complexity of animal communication systems, it is precisely as a result of their unmediated nature that they lack one central characteristic of mankind's, namely, the ability to reflect. This brings us to the two next characteristics.

Because science is a symbolic system, this implies a number of things. First of all, its mode of operation is *displacement*. This was one of Freud's first discoveries regarding the functioning of the psychic apparatus, and it was precisely on its operation that he would found his treatment, namely, free association. This is simultaneously one of Saussure's main contentions as well: signifiers, like signifieds, must be understood as part of a series, that is, in a flow. The relation between the two is *arbitrary*; it is the context that generates signification, founded upon difference. In order to have a symbolic system, there must be at least two signifiers, which Lacan represents as S_1 and S_2.

Secondly, *lack* is the primary condition that makes displacement possible. Without lack, displacement cannot occur in the symbolic system. The combination of lack and displacement makes *reflection* possible: to think about thinking and to make choices founded upon such a mediated meta-standpoint. As regards lack, we can point to Freud's assumption of the loss of an original, undivided relationship with a primal object (the mother), resulting in an endless search for the restoration of this original relationship. Even the logical need for lack in the functioning of a symbolic system can be shown, see Gödel's argument on this score. A simple children's toy gives a practical illustration. Think of those sliding tile puzzles that only work if there is one tile missing to provide a preliminary opening space.

The strongest argument for the need for such a lack is found in clinical practice, particularly in the psychotic's use of language. In the naive complaint about the possibilities of human communication, the dream is of a univocal and unambiguous language, that is, a language without displacement and lack, containing an ever-unchanging meaning. Psychotic patients who haven't passed through symbolic castration and, hence, have no lack at their disposal, at times exhibit such a "language."[21] This reminds me of the "as-if" personality and the "computer memory" that are sometimes found in psychotics. Both come down to the same thing: the so-called high-functioning psychotic or autistic person stores every social situation they have experienced in memory. From this data bank, the person retrieves what is needed for an appropriate reaction in a subsequent situation, in which she or he ultimately does nothing but replay the original situation. The human being's quintessential creativity, in the sense of displacement among signifiers—and thus within the entire symbolic system—is absent, because its precondition has not been met.

This precondition is a little peculiar because it involves something that might be considered a failure. By this I am referring to the way that ordinary human language is unable to get ahold of the thing-in-itself, so that there is always a gap between every form of symbolization and the Real.[22] In Lacanian psychoanalysis, this is known as the lack in the Symbolic order, signaled paradoxically by the object (*a*). But this paradox disappears once we understand its accompanying logic: this *Real* object (*a*) is lacking in the *Symbolic*,[23] and refers to Freud's originally lost object, that which never can be refound and for which every one of us continues to search. It is precisely this object that is lost by and through the acquisition of language, the object that we have left behind, the "answer" to desire *beyond* words.

The effect of this fundamental condition and its mode of functioning is double: not only the object, but also the speaker is continuously displaced by the signifiers, to become a divided subject. "A signifier represents a subject for another signifier," says Lacan, following the

---

21. A clinical illustration can be found in a fascinating case study by Sterba. It concerns a 5-year-old patient who had to forge a new linguistic expression for every new situation, and whose literal memories always referred to a singular situation (Sterba 1990 [1933]).

22. Summarized powerfully by the painter Magritte: "This is not a pipe." The same goes for scientific representations as well, regardless of their empirical character.

23. Again, we can make a comparison with Kant's "thing-in-itself" and "thing-for-itself" wherein the first thing is the Real, while the second can be Imaginary as well as Symbolic. The difference between Kant and Freud or Lacan is that with the latter two this object has everything to do with the drive, which indeed drives us toward something without our being able to name it.

Freudian "the ego is not master in its own house" (Freud 1978 [1917a], p. 143). One recognizes, in the first place, a psychological doubling in this divided being: I am the son/daughter of, but also husband/wife of, father/mother of, brother/sister of . . . From an analytic point of view, the division goes considerably further: the subject does not speak, it is spoken. As a result, the subject floats on top of the spoken words. Indeed, when "I" speak, I do not know what "I" am about to say, unless I am reading it or have learned it by heart. In all other cases, "I" is spoken by a desire outside my consciousness that drives me, sometimes with my approval, sometimes without. And what I do say always comes, in the final analysis, from the Other (see the section on alienation in Chapter 8).

Terms of Lacan's Discourse Theory

In the meantime, we have assembled enough information to discuss Lacan's discourse theory more explicitly. Each discourse is made up of four terms: the two signifiers S_1 and S_2, necessary for displacement; the divided subject $\bar{S}$ as an effect; and lack, expressed through the lost object (a) as a condition of possibility. There are four different discourses, because the four terms (in a fixed sequence) can change across the four different positions: the agent or the speaker, the other or the one spoken to, and the product. What Lacan calls the truth lies beneath the agent, as the starting position of each discourse. Within these four fixed positions are two disjunctions, one above, the other underneath. Moreover, and even more importantly, each discourse epitomizes a certain social interrelation, depending on how the disjunctions are handled.

Positions in each discourse:

$$\begin{array}{ccc} \text{apparent agent} & \rightarrow & \text{other} \\ \uparrow & & \downarrow \\ \text{truth} & // & \text{product} \end{array}$$

Normal discourse (that is to say, the *Hysteric's discourse*) is as follows: the divided subject $\bar{S}$ is driven by the truth of the lost and hence desired object (a), whereupon this subject turns the other into a master, S_1, who must produce the relevant knowledge, S_2:

$$\begin{array}{ccc} \$ & \rightarrow & S_1 \\ \uparrow & & \downarrow \\ a & // & S_2 \end{array}$$

A simple and at the same time fundamental example of this discourse is the Oedipus complex. Confronted with the question presented by its drive (a), the child (S) is split and turns toward the father (S_1) in an attempt to find an answer (S_2). But the reply will never suffice for answering the question about the departure point in this particular drive and that particular desire.

The discourse of science, for Lacan, is a *discourse of the Master*.[24]

$$\begin{array}{ccc} S_1 & \rightarrow & S_2 \\ \uparrow & & \downarrow \\ \$ & // & a \end{array}$$

Lack and Possibility

Rather than elaborating these formulas in all their complexity (see instead Verhaeghe 2000a, pp. 95–118), I simply wish to highlight here what is essential for our subject. The essence of discourse theory is as follows: *the lack of object, that is, the object* (a), *is both the cause and the condition of possibility of every symbolic system, and therefore also of science*. It is the cause because it is precisely the loss of the Real effected through language that drives our endless attempts to recover this Real. It is the condition of possibility because it maintains the necessary opening of the Symbolic system that enables displacement to take place.[25]

---

24. In Chapter 8, in the section on alienation and separation in the formation of the subject, I will conclude that the Master discourse, with its alienation and separation, can be understood as the Freudian primal repression by which man definitively leaves the Real for the Symbolic at the oedipal crossroads. Only from that moment on do knowledge and, hence, science become possible. The consequences both for the individual and for science are identical on at least one point, namely, the longing for the One, the Universal, the third point; in short, the longing for the Master signifier that would be able to plug the gap between words and things. We'll encounter this longing again when we discuss the *savoir-faire* of diagnostic practice—in other words, the diagnostic paradigms (see Chapter 4).

25. With this, Lacan has formulated his own answer to the epistemological question of causality: Who or what is the unmovable mover, the last ground of science?

As a result, every symbolic system—and thus science too—will never be able to reach the "thing." Indeed, as a symbolic system, science increasingly *produces* this lack of object, which is why the object (*a*) appears in the righthand space below. It is this that I call the constructive misunderstanding that lies at the foundation of every science.[26] The more scientific—that is to say, symbolic—we become, the further from the Real we are, from the very thing we wanted to get ahold of in the first place. But what we gain in the meantime is a perpetually changing model of reality. That this is not merely a hypothesis is shown by the ever more impossible objects of theoretical physics, which the scientists themselves confess to not knowing whether or not they really exist.[27]

Consequences

The consequences are beyond far-reaching. The relationship between man and thing is one of a fundamental impotence. This allows us to interrogate the epistemological problem expressed in the deadlock of nominalism-realism in a different way: namely, what is the relationship between the subject and the thing, and what roles do the Other, language, and lack play? Science is only one of the forms this relationship takes on; there are also ethics, religion, and art. On this note, let us turn back to our main concern, namely, diagnostics, taking with us the question of the effects of this impotence on this field.

FROM OBJECT TO RELATIONSHIP

The Impotence of a Nominalist Diagnostics

To the extent that psychodiagnostic practice boils down to an application of the Master's discourse, we can, on the basis of the dis-

---

His answer: the undetermined or lost part, that which drives us to find the correct determination (Lacan 1994 [1964], p. 22 ff; see also Verhaeghe 2002a).

26. More broadly, in Lacanian terms this can be understood in terms of the relationship between the *automaton* and the *tuchè* (see below).

27. The more impossible they become, the more florid their names; from quarks to charm.

course theory, make a number of predictions concerning the consequences of this application in practice.

First, we can answer the following question: On what grounds does the diagnostician-master reach his diagnosis? The formula of the Master's discourse demonstrates that its starting point is the denial of its own self-division. In each discourse, the agent is only seemingly the driving force; its real source lies hidden underneath. In the Master's discourse, the master signifier is only the apparent agent; its underlying truth is that even the master is a divided subject who has equally had to make a number of choices. In the context of the DSM, we can say here that the so-called pure observation of the DSM task force comes down, in the first instance, to the clinical judgment of the task force, that is to say, to their intuition and experience, and hence ultimately to their own psychic identities. The absence of clear-cut external criteria makes such a fallback inevitable, and one that in itself is not necessarily wrong. The chief point is that one recognizes it, and that such diagnostic criteria (one's own self) be handled within a framework of structural relations.

Secondly, the lack and failure, which the master signifier tries to counter in the movement from S_1 to S_2, constitute precisely the *product* of this movement, called the object (a). Every diagnostician-master attempts to make the right pronouncement, legitimately shored up by a theory that is assumed to be a perfect mirror image of empirical reality. In practice this only rarely succeeds; patients never fully answer to the diagnostician's pronouncement. The pronunciation itself consequently *produces* the failure of diagnostics as a system. Lacan rightly observes that to permanently take on the position of the master would amount to a permanent silence. From the moment one speaks, one chases after an ever-receding Real—that is, the object (a)—without ever being able to reach it completely.

Thirdly, the disjunction of impossibility that separately joins the upper terms is based on the underlying disjunction of impotence. The latter grounds the impossibility, and this in its turn masks the impotence. For as long as one concentrates on refining, improving, and adapting diagnostic denominations within the Master's discourse (the upper level of the discourse), one can pass over its structurally determined failure (the lower level of the discourse). These disjunctions are the most difficult part of the discourse theory because they involve a perpetual failure in the relationship between two positions. The basic gap concerns the relationship between the subject and the Real.

$$\uparrow \begin{array}{c} \text{apparent agent} \\ \text{truth} \end{array} \begin{array}{c} \rightarrow \\ // \end{array} \begin{array}{c} \text{other} \\ \text{product} \end{array} \downarrow$$

$$\uparrow \frac{S_1}{\$} \begin{array}{c} \rightarrow \\ // \end{array} \frac{S_2}{a} \downarrow$$

Lacan's discourse theory shows, therefore, how the disjunction of impossibility between agent and other (in this case, with the diagnostician-agent as the master signifier, and the patient as the as yet unsignified object of theory and diagnostics) is secretly propped up by an underlying impotence between the truth and the product (here, the diagnostician's truth as a divided subject, and the place of the lack—object (a)—as the waste product of the Master's discourse). With this we can see how the lack is, moreover, the product of the attempt to answer it, to which the agent is driven by its own self-division.

Diagnosis as a Cover-up of the Division: Knowledge versus Truth

The production of "masterly" nosological names fails to correspond to something in reality. Rather, they *cover over* something of the Real in that reality. What is classically regarded as the function of diagnostics, that a more accurate diagnosis would result in better treatment, is frequently an illusion.[28] In this case, an improved diagnosis does not

---

28. This is the reason, for that matter, why Koster Van Groos (1989, p. 352) does not consider the *DSM-III* craze as all that dangerous: "Many young psychiatrists are almost incapable of using concepts other than those of the *DSM-III*. Nevertheless it is questionable whether this is so serious from a practical point of view. It would only be serious in cases when a diagnosis really has some implication for the treatment. And it is precisely that which can be doubted." The idea that a better diagnosis in a master discourse would allow for better treatment is an illusion. Independently of the diagnosis, the treatment will always hystericize the patient, that is, oblige him or her to take a hysterical position. This is a structural necessity: it is only the hysterical position of the subject that enables it to subvert the alienating identifications in the signifier (Soler 1986, pp. 52, 57).

necessarily imply better treatment, for the simple reason that within the Master discourse, the diagnosis, and especially the diagnostic statement, *is* the treatment.[29] Giving a name always carries with it the implication of the illusion of control and mastery. Nothing is worse than not being able to name something; once a name has been found, it seems manageable. In this discourse, giving an explanatory label to madness has the same function as calling lightning the "sparks of Thor's hammer," namely, the reduction of anxiety.[30]

The role of diagnostics has to be sought elsewhere. The positing of a master diagnosis instates a certain *relationship* and this is not so much an effect as an aim in itself, albeit one that is rarely conscious.[31] It is here that we make the transition to the idea of discourse as a structure, as something determining a social relation. Nominalism can thus be understood as the installation of the discourse of the master, an installation that is *demanded* by the subject out of his discontent. Hence Vandermeersch, in critiquing both ego-analysis and cognitive psychology, rightly observes that people acquire their identity through "authority figures," and that the omnipresent feelings of dependence and problems have to do with "the fundamental anxiety that without the authorities, one would not know who one is" (Vandermeersch 1978, p. 73). Mankind's discontent is the discontent of the split subject whose

---

29. Classical psychiatry emphasized the elaborate formulations of the *status praesens* and the patient's case history, after which one arrived, as it were, at a standstill, with the expressed hope that sooner or later "the" remedy would be found. It was not uncommon for the patient's condition to improve during the many case-history interviews. Ever since pharmacology took over, things seem to be the other way around: now we imagine we have "the" remedy, but we no longer know what it is for. It reminds me of a book by D. Adams, *The Hitchhiker's Guide to the Galaxy*. People worked for millennia improving their computers in order to answer the final question. Finally, they succeeded and received the answer: it was "42." The only problem was that, in the meantime, they had forgotten what the question was.

30. This is one of the most important and frequently undervalued of the effective factors in any form of psychotherapy: so-called verbalization, or, in contemporary jargon, "mentalization."

31. Nowhere is this better expressed than in Lewis Carroll's *Alice in Wonderland*. As Humpty Dumpty said: "When I use a word, it means just what I choose it to mean—neither more nor less," and when Alice questioned whether you can make words mean so many different things, he replied: "The question is, which is to be Master, that's all."

division lies firstly between being and signifiers, and secondly between the signifiers themselves (see Chapter 8). The relationship between the oppressor and the oppressed that a figure like Szasz talks so much about, and which he sees so abundantly in our field, is found in the first instance, *internally*. This is Freud's famous "splitting of the Ego" or Lacan's divided subject, with the defense mechanisms acting as a divider.

This relationship is only brought out into the open in a second instance as a question: at certain moments, the subject *asks for* the installation of a master discourse in an attempt to escape from the unpleasure of its self-division. Anyone with clinical experience knows that at a certain moment the patient will demand, even insist upon, receiving a master signifier ("You must tell me what I have/am suffering from"), with which he or she can ultimately coincide. Lacan expresses this in a play of words that cannot be translated: "*Le significant-maître surgit de m'être/maître à moi-même*"; ("The master signifier rises to be myself / to belong to myself / to be master of myself" (Lacan 1991 [1969–1970], p. 178). Here, diagnosis becomes synonymous with band-aid therapy, despite the invariable failure of such treatment.

Such failure is included in the sequel, where what was originally an internal fight becomes externally projected toward an opponent who is called on to assume the impossible position of the guaranteeing master. This is nothing other than the typical relationship between the hysterical discourse and the discourse of the master.

$$\uparrow \frac{\$}{a} \quad \xrightarrow{} \quad \frac{S_1}{S_2} \downarrow$$

The divided subject $\$$ addresses itself to the undivided other, S_1, in an attempt to receive an answer that will cancel out its self-division. But all this master figure can produce is knowledge, S_2, which will never suffice as an answer to the division. On the contrary, it has little or nothing to do with it (this is the meaning of the double slash //). Returning to our initial example of the adolescent and his joyriding: the master can communicate to the parents his knowledge of puberty, of how the joyriding represents a typical reaction to authority at this age, of the attractiveness of what is prohibited, and so on. In response to the hysterical demand, he thus produces a master discourse:

$$\uparrow \frac{S_1}{\$} \quad \xrightarrow{\;\;//\;\;} \quad \frac{S_2}{a} \downarrow$$

Knowledge, S_2, is draped like a veil over the other. This will have both an alleviating and a soothing effect, albeit not for long. Such knowledge says nothing about the underlying truth of the symptom that is implied in the subject-division of this particular father, this particular mother, and this particular son. Furthermore, because the application of knowledge fails for this specific situation, it becomes all the more enigmatic, and knowledge produces its own failure and lack in the form of the object (a) as product.

Here we come across a prototypical conflict that holds for the entire symbolic field but that carries special weight in the field of psychotherapy and its accompanying psychodiagnostics. I mean the conflict between ethics and science, or more specifically, between truth and knowledge. Supposed to be value-free, science presents an objective model of reality that contains as many nuances as possible. Nevertheless, at times, certain decisions must be made, along with certain choices, revealing thereby the deficiency of the concept of scientific objectivity. Indeed, the more nuanced science becomes, the more difficult it is to make a clear-cut decision. At this point, we have left the field of science and entered ethics and, thus, the realm of choice.

Knoweldge and Truth

As discourse theory expresses it, knowledge is a term, while truth is a position, and each has a completely different range. To the extent that we deal with the register of knowledge, it implies the existence of a correct and an incorrect knowledge; in our case a correct or incorrect diagnosis and treatment. In the register of truth, on the other hand, we encounter the opposition between a true and a false speech.

Correct versus incorrect: this belongs a priori to the field of knowledge, and hence to the learning process. Immediately, this implies a pedagogical figure, the learned master who transmits his knowledge. From this we acquire a number of typical characteristics. Firstly, that knowledge is cumulative; we know more now than we did fifty years ago. Secondly, that knowledge can be generalized: John's bronchitis is the same as Vladimir's. Thirdly, that knowledge can be transmitted through instruction; in roughly thirty years, we cover the distance that once took humanity two millennia. And fourthly, that knowledge aspires to completion: one day we will know everything; today's hiatus is merely temporary.

On the other side, we find the second opposition in the register of truth: true versus false. The difference between this register and the first cannot be emphasized strongly enough, as a comparison of its characteristics with the previous opposition reveals. First, the cumulative character is entirely missing. The whole history of psychology, education, and philosophy shows how mankind wrestles over and over again with the same questions, and how the answers successively relieve one another over the ages and are taken up again under different names without ever reaching a definitive conclusion. Hence the second characteristic of knowledge, generalization, is completely absent. Under collectivizing names, problems within the human condition may resemble one another, but the moment we are faced with these in clinical practice the differences become so glaring that we can only conclude that there is an extreme particularity: every "case" is always unique. The third characteristic, the ability to transmit knowledge through instruction, consequently shifts to another order. Where knowledge is noncumulative and particularity rules, truth can only ever be skirted around, nothing more. The fourth characteristic reverts to an opposite: in the register of truth, the incompleteness becomes structurally determined. Words, and hence knowledge always fall short of catching the ultimate truth. Lacan talks about "the half-saying of truth." The unsayable part can only be evoked, it can never be fully expressed. Precisely at this point, people create art and religion in an attempt to call forth the unspeakable.

Learning and knowledge belong to science, truth lurks in the field of ethics. The difficulty begins the moment one confuses the two.[32]

---

32. To make the esoteric character of the difference between science and truth a bit less esoteric, I present an everyday example: the sexual enlightenment of young children. Formerly taboo, it has now become obligatory, so much so that it has inaugurated a whole torrent of publications of handy books for unhandy parents, amply supplied with the requisite pictures (reality teaching!), in which everything is explained from start to finish and from flower to bee if needed. The aim of such enlightenment was to eliminate infantile sexual theories (anal, oral, cloacal theories of birth), which, as has been known since Freud, can be the forerunners of later neurotic symp-

Confronted with a question from the second register, truth, someone from the positive sciences will try to answer it by appealing to the first register, knowledge. What is sexual identity, what does a normal sexual relationship look like, what is the right education, what is a normal relation towards authority? Ethical questions such as these, ubiquitous in psychotherapy, will never receive definitive answers in knowledge; at best all we can get are some hints.[33]

Nominalist Diagnostics in Action: Referral, Flight, and Burnout

Sooner or later, everyone working in the psychodiagnostic field experiences this structural impossibility and impotence. Its consequences can be predicted and are easily recognizable.

---

toms (the idea of the need for enlightenment in fact goes back to Freud (1978 [1907c]). In the meantime, we have learned that this goal will not be achieved: despite all the enlightenment campaigns, children continue to create their own theories. What is the cause of this failure? It is because this enlightenment usually produces the correct answer to the wrong question: it provides a technical-scientific explanation for conception and sexuality, in the conviction that this does the job. The child's question—and indeed, it is very much a question—is not solely directed toward this knowledge, but aims at the underlying truth as well: Where do I come from, what links my father to my mother and vice versa, what is my place in all this? The old-fashioned explanation—"Babies arrive when Mommies and Daddies love each other very dearly"—lies a bit closer to the register of truth and demonstrates at the same time the possibility of a lie—in a not inconsiderable number of cases, a baby is underway precisely at the point when Mommy and Daddy don't love each other all that dearly anymore . . . It is in this register that the child's interrogations occur that, given the nature of the questioning, will never receive a final answer. Hence the child continues to explore it, both in fantasy (the infantile-sexual theories) and in practice (through the most well-known play of children: to play daddy and mummy, coupled with playing doctors and nurses). "Total" enlightenment has to account for both registers, both the technical-scientific and the ethical.

33. Examples from daily clinical practice include post-traumatic stress disorders, the relation toward authority, sexual and relational problems, every possible difficulty with regard to procreation, and so on. Despite the vast body of scientific knowledge in all of these concerns, clinical praxis always invokes a confrontation with ethical choices for which knowledge in itself can give no answer. This becomes all the more evident whenever we deal with psychopathology.

Having reached this point, I can now advance a perhaps somewhat absolute statement concerning the triptych of the classical Master's discourse, diagnosis-theory-treatment. Psychodiagnostics represents classical psychiatry; psychoanalysis and everything that follows it, whether supportive or antagonistic, represents theory, while treatment stands for referral. Such a statement is at first sight strange, even a little shocking. A moment of reflection, however, quickly reveals its applicability. Classical psychiatry is synonymous with psychodiagnostics because clinicians have for decades gathered and labeled careful observations in a manner that seems almost impossible today. The theory has retroactively become psychoanalysis because this was the first coherent conceptualization of human psychological functioning.[34] Referral has become the usual practice, precisely because of the failure of the Master's discourse; the impossibility of maintaining this position makes a referral to another master necessary in the hope that the next one will be able to finish the job.[35]

With the perpetual failure of the Master's discourse, the drama of the individual clinician as the always impossible incarnation of the master figure begins. Here we encounter a paradox: it is the *patient* who demands the establishment of the master signifier and of the master. Once this has been established, the destruction of the Master's discourse becomes possible. An internal division is externalized, enabling the subject to replay events in a safer context. The person who has been forced into the master's role becomes the dupe, particularly if she or he makes the error of believing in it. The need to make this role explicit or, even better, of explicitly discussing its implications, seems

---

34. Psychoanalytic interpretations of psychiatric entities are ubiquitous. In response to those who would point to other theories, I simply wish to stress how I am often struck by the multiple and frequent use of psychoanalytic concepts when reading otherwise inspired clinical descriptions and—irony of ironies—even at times in critiques of psychoanalytic theory. Psychoanalysis has doubtless instated a knowledge, albeit one that is unable to be used within the clinic to the extent that the latter operates under the Master's discourse. "For to use the technique that he [Freud] established, outside the experience to which it was applied, is as stupid as to toil at the oars when the ship is on sand" (Lacan 1977 [1959], p. 221).

35. Referral is often enough an initiative of the patient, who—once the master has demonstrated his failure—begins to look for another master.

imperative to me because when this does not occur taking on the character of the dupe becomes inevitable.

This is easily recognizable at the level of the individual: our institutions—both residential and outpatient—can be characterized by what I would call flight. One flees from the client; that is to say, from the impossible position of the master that the client demands. The flight may occur in one of two directions: either up into the hierarchy, whereby one becomes unreachable and hence inviolable; or into the illusory safety of the group, with its endless team meetings and the like through which one attempts to maintain an impossible position by sharing it with others. In cases where flight is impossible, we come across the relatively widespread "burnout syndrome," especially among those who attempted their utmost best (Vanheule 2001a–c).

This brings us to the level of conceptualization. It's weird how one always refers to dead masters when founding the master's position, carefully forgetting the way, while alive, and usually at the end of their careers, they themselves frequently reached an impasse in their own theorizations. Three classic examples: at the end of his successful mapping of hysteria, Charcot rejects his own theory, throwing it overboard and putting all his hopes in the new approach by Janet. Similarly, at the end of his career, Bleuler writes a little book called *Autistic Undisciplined Thinking in Medicine and How to Overcome It*, in which he not only distances himself from his own conceptualization of schizophrenia, but at the same time labels clinical practice impossible. (Schotte, one of my own psychiatric fathers, referred to "the illusion of psychiatry" from time to time in his courses.) Last but not least is Freud who, toward the end of his career, similarly calls governing and educating the two impossible professions, to which he then adds analyzing.[36] We can include an even more recent example: as chair of the IPA (International Psychoanalytical Association)—a master position as paradoxical as they come—Otto Kernberg published a powerful argument against the normalization tendencies in psychoanalytic training (Kernberg 1996b).

Pinel understood this intuitively. As one of the founding fathers of the clinic, he would do only two things: give disorders a name and provide moral treatment. He did not want to know about theory; theory was

---

36. For Charcot, see Pichot (1968); for Bleuler, see Szasz (1983); for Freud (1978 [1937c]), p. 248.

a superfluous luxury. One might thus talk of a gap between his naming and his system of treatment, seeing as how the vital link between the two—that is, a theory—is missing. But nothing could be less true: in this case theory is not only superfluous, but even the source of the failure. In the master discourse, naming itself suffices, and Pinel's moral treatment is the ideal answer because it strengthens the previously installed social bond. Let us not forget that he is the inventor not only of the psychiatric institution, but of the *chef de clinique*, the clinical director, as well.

Anyone who imagines they can and must permanently occupy this impossible master position will go astray sooner or later. "The non-dupes err," writes Lacan—he who thinks he is not duped by this position either becomes a victim of it himself or victimizes others.[37] At this point, another register opens, that of the social bond and of ethics.

Ethics and Social Bond

In our previous chapter, we concluded that psychodiagnostic categorization is far from easy. This chapter has shown the underlying reason for this: its epistemology contains a structurally determined impotence that makes it impossible to arrive at a definitive solution in this field. Scientists try to gain knowledge about reality, but this knowledge can never be fully conclusive. As a symbolic system, science nevertheless has an intersubjective criterion; we can talk only about a hypothetical realism.[38] Confronted with the same difficulty,

---

37. A Lacanian wordplay on the foundation of the master's discourse: the No/Name of the father, *"le nom-du-père"* / *"le non du père"* / *"les non-dupes errent."* This is his expression for the basis of authoritarian patriarchy that can only function because it is accepted by its individual members who submit themselves to it. Beyond the naive idea of liberation through an insurrection against it, Lacan demonstrates that such an insurrection can only lead to an endorsement of the system that one fights, hence his "the non-dupes err," "those who think that they are not duped err" (Lacan 1991 [1969–1970]).

38. This idea comes from Campbell and Lorenz and can be expressed as follows: every being lives in an environment, an "Umwelt," in which the "Um" is determined by the being, not by the "Welt" as such; accordingly, each being constructs its own world picture, and this construction is based on the being's specific cognitive organs that are evolutionarily based, just like the world itself. The extensive testing and corrections in this reciprocal development form the constructive basis for what science is (Lorenz 1975).

the psychodiagnostician and/or psychotherapist has, moreover, to gain knowledge of how their patients have gathered and ordered their own knowledge of reality, albeit in a pathological way.[39] The object of the "psy" sciences is, consequently, not so much an object but *a relationship between the subject and the outside world.*

The first conclusion that impresses itself upon us is that the difference between the normal and the abnormal is often made in an arbitrarily normative way. These norms are historically developed within a sociocultural context and are even recorded, albeit from a jurisdictional frame of reference. Here, abnormality is synonymous with social deviation, whose possible sanctioning is an essentially judicial process that has the protection of a third party as its principal function. Doubtless there is a need for psy-specialists in this field of work as well. This broaches the question of responsibility within the impossible mixture of truth and knowledge. From a Freudian perspective, everyone is responsible for what they do (Mooij 1988, pp. 150–163). There are ethical limits to madness too. This takes nothing away from the court-appointed psy-specialist's ability to explain the so-called deviant behavior by referring to the patient's history. This explanation is not to be confused with explaining away, and must be considered in relation to potential remedies. In *Discipline and Punish* (1977), Foucault already demonstrated how repression is the least appropriate path. At this point, the demand for psychotherapy begins, which in the judicial field is all too often confused with enforced reeducation.

This brings us to our second conclusion. As opposed to the social-juridical realm, in the field of psychotherapy the subject's demand is

---

39. "The psychotherapist studies the study of reality. One could say that he is the epistemologist or scientist of more or less private epistemologies. [. . .] This parallel is too limited. Firstly, during psychotherapy this recursiveness seems to 'quadrate'. The psychotherapist thinks about what the client thinks about his thinking, about what the client thinks about the therapist's philosophy" (Cambien 1981, 1987, pp. 530–531). We can add that this boils down to the empirical study of the client's private language, emerging from the Other as a reaction to the object (*a*), a private language upon which this particular client has based his construction of reality. Of course, the therapist also has his or her own language emerging out of the scientific Other, grounding yet another construction. On top of all this, the study of the language and hence of the reality of the client must pass through yet a third system, which is the conventionally shared common language.

central, and the only criterion for normality or abnormality rests with the subject itself. Where there is no demand for change, there can be no place for psychotherapy. In fact, it is on this point that the most telling difference between psychotherapy and the social-normative comes into view: for the latter, the question always comes from a third party. The fact that in the field of psychotherapy the demand for change comes from the subject itself, incidentally, is no guarantee against the ambiguous character of the question, but I will return to this later.

The third and final conclusion is that the clinician *consciously* has to make ethical choices. Insofar as the clinician is inscribed into the social field, she or he is a (re-)educator, grounding both the diagnosis and the specific intervention in the social norms to which she or he subscribes. Here, diagnosis amounts to measuring the extent of the patient's distance from these intended norms, although discovering the reason for this distance is not strictly necessary. In the process, one invariably comes up against the impossibility in the master discourse: therapy à la "Emperor Jozef" that Freud often refers to is given up only with the greatest reluctance.[40] To the extent that clinicians inscribe themselves in the field of psychotherapy, they must leave the master discourse, allowing another subject to take the central position and to direct its demand toward them.

Unfortunately, such a conscious choice is not often made in today's practice. While naive empiricism is increasingly being left behind in the positive sciences, in the human sciences, oddly enough, it is increasingly being introduced, without taking its fundamental epistemological problems into account. The difference between knowledge and truth, and the field of tension between the general-categorical and the particular-subjective, is not given enough emphasis, despite its ubiquity in the clinic. In its place we find a predictable strategy—predictable from the perspective of discourse theory, that is. The untenability of the master discourse results in a shift into another discourse, that of the university, the consequences of which are discussed in the next chapter.

---

40. Freud frequently uses this analogy, which refers to the Austrian Emperor Jozef II who, from his almighty and benevolent position as an enlightened dictator, wished to impose upon his people what he considered to be their "good," only to be perpetually confronted by the fact that his people did not want it (see Freud 1978 [1913c], *Standard Edition* (*SE*) 12, p. 133; 1978 [1916–1917], *SE* 16, p. 432; 1978 [1919a], *SE* 17, p. 167).

4
Know-how in Clinical Practice: Doxa as the Result of Impotence and Impossibility

INTRODUCTION

A completely comprehensive theory, supported by an effective epistemology, would seem to be an illusion. Nevertheless, Candide must continue to cultivate his garden (translator's note: as in the final pages of Voltaire's *Candide*). Clearly, for the field worker, job satisfaction in itself is not enough: her work must also be conceptually grounded, which is why she scours the markets seeking the definitive scientific justification for her job.

Such "definitiveness" quickly becomes relative, and yesterday's certainties have become today's cast-offs. For a growing number of people the ensuing doubt is barely tolerable. Consequently, we see the emergence of a highly characteristic solution, which was anticipated and critiqued as long ago as Socrates: if *epistèmè* (knowledge) is unable to found *arètè* (truth), people fall back on *doxa* (opinion), or in today's terms "paradigm." We have already seen this in Kuhn (1970), who reintroduced these ideas into contemporary terminology.

The contextualizing paradigm's real function, apparently, is to guide. Depending on which psychological theory is chosen, one intervenes in x or y manner. Still, as the years go on, it is becoming increasingly clear to me that the most divergent paradigms do not necessarily lead to particularly divergent practices. Indeed, in a number of cases, such practices proved profoundly monotonous, compared to the raucous ways the various doxa competed with one another. Presently we will see how even what seem to be diametrically opposite paradigms ultimately amount to the same thing, particularly when it comes to their mutual disdain for the subject.

In other words, the paradigm's function is not, after all, to guide a practice, whatever people might say. It has recently become increasingly clear that the effective factors in therapeutic practice are very much the same, beyond and above the various different paradigms. Every theoretically based clinical practice (psychoanalytic, cognitive behavioral, systemic, experiential . . .) has its good and bad therapists, and this evidently has less to do with the particular theory than with the way these therapists are (un-)able to handle these common factors. No, the paradigm's real function is to create nest warmth, that is to say, to offer an articulated and hence security-providing framework for its followers, collected around a central credo that supplies a comforting answer to the ever-threatening Real of the clinic. We will subsequently see how this framework only incidentally influences clinical practice, and that these influences are not as diverse as one might imagine.

What we might call the "props" of these doxa can be very large or quite limited. Because of their small size, the smaller ones immediately reveal what is involved. A quick, if ironic recital gives us the Exemplary Case, the Latest One-Hit Wonder and the Guilt-tripping Drama Queen. In practice these three are frequently found in combination with each other such as, for example, every Latest One-Hit Wonder also contains a Guilt-tripping aspect as well, and an Exemplary Case is always useful to have on hand.

Exemplary Case Paradigms

Exemplary case paradigms are all those famous, if not infamous, case studies that are perpetually being rehearsed within certain circles. A quick glance back shows how every clinical master had one or even several star patients: for Charcot, it was Blanche Wittman; for Janet, Madeleine and Nadia took center stage; Flournoy chose Hélène Smith;

Jung had Helene Preiswerk, and for Binswanger it was Ellen West; Mary Barnes performed the role for the Kingsley Hall Therapeutic community . . . The list is endless, and as a final example, we offer Freud's own five case studies (see Ellenberger 1970, pp. 891–893, and Maleval 1984, p. 112).

Beyond this, it is an open secret that the principal patient of each of these great figures was himself. The exemplary, or any rate first case of this is to be found in Robert Burton, with his *Anatomy of Melancholy* (1621). Even Pavlov only came to the study of psychiatry after a so-called heart neurosis (Ellenberger 1970, p. 850). Freud himself begins from the same point as any student of the humanities: everyone always looks first for him- or herself in the array of theories, but this more or less always fails. Despite whatever his masters told him, and everything that was written in the textbooks, Freud, with his problematic train phobias and hypochondriac complaints, was unable to recognize himself. All that was left was to start looking for his own subject, Sigmund. That his patients aided him in his search is known by everyone in clinical practice. Hence, from *Studies on Hysteria* to *The Interpretation of Dreams* and *The Psychopathology of Everyday Life*, we get the story of a journey of discovery through the continent called Sigmund Freud. That he, and a number of other major figures, was able to go beyond this starting point and to elevate it into a theory is precisely why they are major figures. Ellenberger talks about "creative illness" and makes the inescapable comparison with the shaman (pp. 888–891 and passim).

The heroic historical narratives prefer to pass over this aspect in silence, instead presenting an image of an isolated toiler, neglecting wife and children and inventing earth-shattering theories for starvation wages while producing a number of unforgettable standard case-studies along the way.[1] Their paradigmatic effect can be seen in the way the

---

1. In the light of the heroic historical narratives, it is no coincidence that the English *Standard Edition* of Freud's works excels in its de-subjectivation. I refer to the way Freud's originally informal language has been turned into a technical and impersonal jargon (*Besetzung* becomes cathexis, *Anlehnung* is turned into anaclitic, and so on; "The biggest shortcoming of the translations is that, through their use of abstractions, they make it easy for the reader to distance himself from what Freud sought to teach about the inner life of man and of the reader himself. Psychoanalysis becomes in English translation something that refers and applies to others as a system of intellectual constructs" (Bettelheim 1983, p. 6 and passim).

second generation, that of the master's students, is unable to produce its own case studies perpetually returning to those of the master's, which are then deemed classics. To give an example, it is very difficult to find a psychoanalytic study or clinical demonstration of a psychotic patient who is not constantly being compared with Schreber. It almost seems as if every modern-day psychotic has to model himself according to the near perfect Schreber-profile, whose case thus comes to function as a kind of clinical bed of Procrustes.[2] Originally these case studies introduced innovative conceptual and pragmatic insights; now they have become standard weights obstructing every change.

What I call the Latest One-Hit Wonders start out from the idea that simplicity is the primary attribute of truth, and that anything can be explained on the basis of a limited etiology. Treffers (1988) likens this to a traveling circus: "Decades-long group discussions, symposia and workshops were organized during those years, [. . .] There are a number of other traveling circuses, and the names of the most important acrobats and other attractions are easily filled in: the now bankrupted traveling MBD Circus (Minimal Brain Damage), a traveling circus for The Whole Family, a traveling circus for Body Language (extended thanks to popular demand) and the traveling circus for Autism. Recently I was confronted with the traveling Incest circus."

These limited exploratory frameworks follow one another in rapid succession (fear of failure, borderline, ADHD . . .) and have apparently only one thing in common beside their short-lived nature: the initial enthusiasm of their followers, which frequently appears in the form of a proselytizing zeal. Thus I was once asked by an alarmed doctor whether it was "really true that *everything* could be explained by and treated as hyperventilation?" Yet there is another, more important mutual factor: the cause or etiology is always situated in an accusatory way outside the subject, in some so-called third party. Either the parents didn't do their job or the social machinery failed, launching one onto the somatic roller coaster. This is even more true of those I refer to as the guilt-tripping drama queens, as this is their leading trait.

---

2. Procrustes was one of Theseus' challengers whose bed could fit anyone, albeit rather uncomfortably. If it was too short, Procrustes would chop off the offending lengths of limb; too long, and the victim's limbs would be stretched to fit the bed. See Plutarch's *Life of Theseus*.

The chief difference between the Latest One-Hit Wonders and the *Guilt-Tripping Drama Queens* is the much wider range of the latter, a quality that always appeals to the sense of guilt ever-present in everyone ("Use every man after his desert, and who shall 'scape whipping?"—Shakespeare, *Hamlet,* Act II, Scene 2), cleverly channeling it into larger, nameless entities. The example that first comes to mind is youth addiction. Over three decades, we have had four different exploratory models, each creating its own individual furor at the time. In the '60s, drug addiction was explained as an expression of youth protest against an authoritarian society. Yet, in the wake of the bankruptcy of May '68, the same addiction was explained as the alleged general feeling of defeat and alienation among the youth of the very same society. From the '70s on, in contrast, drug use was interpreted primarily as one of the effects of a society of excessive consumption, overloaded with well-being and opportunities. But this failed to account for similar drug problems in underprivileged and poor segments of society. The explanation was then sought in the weakening of family ties: the torrent of divorces and open marriages operated as a destabilizing factor for youth. At the same time, it was discovered that young people coming from stable economic and strict family structures had their own drug problems, collapsing this exploratory framework as well. In the '80s the one-size-fits-all response was economic insecurity combined with unemployment, until the discovery that drug abuse was the order of the day in certain highly specialized, professional circles (Di Gennaro 1987). All this calls to mind the image of a weary social worker who, casting anxious eyes to heaven after his latest ongoing training session ("Remotivation of Unemployed Addicted Youth"), shuffles into the nearest bar and orders a double whiskey.

The next example belongs to the same, albeit larger field: youth deviance. Summing up the commonsensical attitude that has characterized the prevailing approach for a number of years, Walgrave (1979) observes,

> Our society is heavily directed toward economic progress and hence, has become too competitive and too materialistic. A number of people cannot cope with the daily struggle any more [. . .]. Therefore a group of people exists on the borders of normal society. [. . .] These families live an irregular life, the kids are neglected. In such situations, it is normal for young people to be unable to adapt to society's demands.

They remain psychologically immature, have a lack of psychic inhibitions; they do poorly at school, remain unemployed. [. . .] The prevailing image of youth care programs immediately follows on from these ideas. While society must defend itself against such behavior, the teenagers themselves ought not to be regarded as responsible for it. They are in fact the victims of the circumstances in which they are forced to live. [pp. 2–3]

Immediately after presenting this oh-so-understandable explanation, Walgrave proceeds to throw cold water on it. Within scarcely a page, this comprehensive construction falls to pieces. In accordance with the Porterfield study and ensuing research into the "dark number," it is revealed that this framework does not so much present us with the etiology of deviant behavior, but rather with the jurisdictional criteria[3] for selection, scarcely covering 15 percent of the estimated total . . .[4]

It should be evident that these are examples of a form of social critique. The accusatory and exculpatory aspects seem self-evident because it is a matter of youth, drugs, and deviant behavior. But these aspects, as we will see, go much further than that. *The question of guilt lies at the heart of the more global paradigms as well.*

A Word about Paradigms

The larger paradigms are found alongside and through these more limited and limiting conceptual frameworks. Their size does not pre-

---

3. Incidentally, I am convinced that the same form of reasoning can be applied to patients in residential psychiatric care. While Morel's concept of degeneration may have become politically incorrect, it has not disappeared; it has just gone undercover. A study by Giel, Wiersma, and De Jong (1987) concerning the relationship between social class and psychic disorders demonstrates that in the diagnosis of schizophrenia, too, it is more a question of social *selection* than of social *causation*.

4. The etiological question that has to be asked here reverses the classical one. Walgrave (1979) appropriately asks now: "Why did x % of youth get stuck in delinquency while the rest did not?" The same reversal can be applied to the study of perversion. Moll was the first to discard both the degeneration and traumatic incidents hypotheses (Sulloway 1979, pp. 303–305). Every childhood suffers these last in all of their far-reaching banality, which is the reason one must ask why a particular individual *remains* a pervert while another normalizes (see Chapter 14 below).

vent them from formally displaying the characteristics of a doxa, which can be briefly summed up as follows: blinding you to what lies outside the frame, they force you to see what lies within it—even with the trigger-effect: "Can't you see it?"—while simultaneously reifying it.[5] In the preliminary interviews, the therapist imagines herself to be discovering things, while in most cases she will do nothing but confirm—confirm what was presented in the training. Real discovery means one has to leave the well-trodden paths of the doxa and blaze one's own trail. Hence the therapist and the patient both need the same thing: the ability to reflect that makes both distance and choice possible.

Today, we can identify three such paradigms, each one initially seeming quite different from the others: the medical-biological one, the psychological one, and the psychoanalytic one. The last is considered corny and outdated, while the medical paradigm has increasingly become the Real Thing, as the psychological paradigm is doing its utmost best to lose its soft image and look as hard as possible by importing elements from the medical corner. My argument is this: in spite of their differences, these three paradigms are identical to the extent that their application makes them function as a University discourse (as discussed below). This doesn't necessarily have to be the case, but clinical practice testifies to it being less often the exception than the rule.

These paradigms can indeed be studied as realizations of the University discourse, the latter being a regression from the Master's discourse. Here the power of discourse theory lies in its predictive value: whatever the differences between the paradigms in terms of content, on a formal level they will institute the very same social bond, including the identical relations of impotence and impossibility. This is the

---

5. An unforgettable illustration of this for me is that of the onion skin and the blackbird's testicles. When I was a student, everyone who went through practical training in biology sat through a session in the first hour in which it was patiently explained, with the aid of enormous panels (Power Point did not exist), what slivers of onion skin and blackbird testicles would look like under the microscope. Then came the magic moment when 120 young, would-be scientists simultaneously bowed their heads over the enchanted instrument and, with half-closed eyes, discovered a hitherto unsuspected world. It was our luck to have a malicious training assistant who convinced everyone that we actually saw "it" (mitochondrion, nucleus, etc.) . . . despite the light not being switched on under the slide. I have never needed another warning against suggestion.

most important thing: beyond the ever-present seduction of different concepts, theories, and explanations, we must concentrate our full attention on the almost incidentally created *social relations*.

THE MEDICAL-BIOLOGICAL PARADIGM, OR THE WET DREAM OF HARD SCIENCE

Because this approach sounds simple, it is therefore easy to sell: the cause of all human affliction is located in one way or another in the body. Therefore, diagnosis and treatment ultimately have to be grounded there as well, at least once science knows everything that there is to know. The old fashioned anatomical (or *anato*)-pathological model has today been replaced by a neurobiological-genetic one, but this is nothing but a turning of the tables. History, however, has shown that things are a little more complex.

From Dualism . . .

The starting point of what we call "reductive materialism" can be found in the fifth century B.C., with Democritus. Its basic argument is that both the ontological and the actual can be reduced to their fundamental composite particles. With Descartes and Newton, the emphasis is on mechanics, whose laws would explain "everything." In Descartes' *Discourse on Method*, the laws of mechanics are the same as the ones governing nature. With Newton, this becomes "the billiard ball universe." Its explicit application to mankind is found in De La Mettrie's *Man as a Machine* (1758), with Changeux's *Neuronal Man* (1983) as a modern variation.

Meanwhile, Plato inaugurated a division between soul and body one that became hierarchized in medieval times: the soul is the highest good, the flesh is weak and perishable, subordinated to the eternal soul. With Descartes, this philosophical background will cause a division in thought and hence in education: the body belongs to the medical department, the soul is reserved for the shepherds of the soul—or the psyche as psychologists call it. Since the Enlightenment, the shift in emphasis from the religious-spiritual to the profane-material has brought the vilified body back into the center of the scientific enterprise, always within this materialistic-mechanical way of thinking, and along with the already mentioned division between body and soul.

Applied to our subject, psychopathology and psychodiagnostics, the same dualistic ideas quickly reappear.[6] At this point, we can turn to Condillac and eighteenth-century materialism, of which positivism is a later offshoot. Prototypical for Condillac is his concept of "the statue." He begins with a fictional human statue that initially has only one sense-organ, resulting in a single perception. After the statue acquires a second sense-organ, and hence a second perception, other functions get installed: a memory of the first perception; a comparison between the first and the second; a judgment containing a reflection and, finally, a desiring imagination that is able to present the no longer visible object. These are the so-called human faculties, which, for Condillac, always come down to transformed perceptions focused on the body as a material medium. We will encounter these faculties again in the psychology of the functions, dressed this time in somewhat more contemporary garb.

The scientific method that is based on these premises can be described as follows: science is a mental activity that always begins with the observation of phenomena, that is, sensation, whose aim is the application of a systematic ordering of that observation through the comparison, differentiation, and classification of the elements according to their resemblances and differences. In other words, decomposition and recomposition based on observation. The entirety is orchestrated by language, hence Condillac's famous remark that a perfect science would be a perfect language. With regard to psychodiagnostics, this would lead us to the ideal of a perfectly closed nosological system of categorizations and denominations.

It must be emphasized that this approach was primarily dualistic, meaning that the psyche and the soma occupied equal places. For instance, half a century later, we will encounter this again in Leuret, who

---

6. Much of the ensuing historical account was derived from the following sources: Beauchesne (1986), Bercherie (1980), De Kroon (1999), Ellenberger (1970). The classic works of Michel Foucault also continue to provide a source of inspiration.

in his *Fragments psychologiques sur la folie* (1834) places hallucination into two categories:

1. Psychic hallucinations, missing the sensory element, but with a xenopathic or "alien-subject" character. Its normal variations can be found in "inspiration," which seems to come from outside the subject and does not necessarily have to be sensory or sensual, as with the Muses, for example.
2. Psycho-sensory hallucinations resembling the first, but with a sensory quality. This quality is explained by referring to a perceptual-neurological factor that is thought to play a role here.

The two types sit beside one another in the dualistic line of reasoning of Pinel and Esquirol, where certain psychopathological deviations are the consequence of clearly visible, somatic disorders, such as idiocy. In contrast, madness in its pure form, has no lesional basis and can be described as an unknown functional change in the psychic apparatus.

. . . to the Opposition between Anatomists and Functionalists . . .

This dualism was gradually left behind, firstly with Gall's phrenology at the end of the eighteenth century. As a neuroanatomist, Gall discovered the difference between the grey and white matter in the brain. From this, he developed a speculative theory about where the mental faculties in the cortex were located, convinced as he was of a quantitatively proportional correlation: the larger a certain region in the brain, the more important the faculty that it contained. This is the theory of the so-called cranial knobs, which postulates that each psychic function belongs to a part of the brain that can be topographically identified and isolated. In this manner, Gall and his pupils isolated some thirty-five faculties in as many corresponding knobs, including ones for poetry, for mathematics, and even one for conflict.

The immense success of this theory is still evident in certain colloquial expressions in German and Dutch where to "have a knob" for something means to have a particular talent for it. Nevertheless, this success was unable to prevent Gall's phrenology from being officially condemned by the Austrian government in 1802 (because of its allegedly antireligious content), forcing him to leave the country. One of the reasons for its success was that it seemed as if he had found a material substrate for monomania, a nosological category of Esquirol's that was causing a great furor at that time. As partial afflictions involving a single faculty, the various monomanias were thought to correspond with the yet-to-be discovered responsible knobs. In complementing each other perfectly, the success of these theories was more or less inevitable.

From Gall onward, two different approaches to psychopathology went into action: it was the anatomists versus the functionalists. The anatomists toed the phrenological line, advocating a certain monism: every mental alienation presupposes a specific cause in the brain that must be hunted down. Pinel's moral etiology and treatment was tossed out as old-fashioned. More skeptical, and remaining within the dualistic reasoning of a Pinel and Esquirol, were the functionalists. For them, cerebral lesions are in most cases either undetectable or their relationship to psychopathology cannot be demonstrated. They do not deny that the body plays a role, but refuse to recognize it as the exclusive causal factor. For the functionalists, the cause of psychopathology lies outside the body but has effects on this body's functions. Hence their name: functionalism, functional disturbances.

After Gall, the opposition between the anatomists and the functionalists gets consolidated by Georget. He will introduce a division that will continue to govern the clinic until today. In *On Madness* (1820), he distinguishes between:

1. Mental deviations that are merely symptoms of a known organic disorder. The causal factor lies in the body. From a nosological perspective, he locates the "acute delusions" here, which are nothing but a symptom of an already discovered organic disorder. In this category, for instance, we find delirium caused by fever, brain damage, and the intoxication psychoses.
2. "Madness" proper, as an idiopathic affliction whose cause is unknown, and which is expressed by purely functional disturbances. While the symptoms are of a psychological nature, this does not mean that they have no impact on the body. The cause must be sought in the moral realm.

Furthermore—and this is what is new—Georget introduces the idea of evolution within these afflictions, an idea that forms the basis for what will later be called the "dynamic" point of view.[7]

This division is the precursor to the subsequent partition of neurology and psychiatry, recently given new form in the split between neuro-psychology and clinical psychology. Here, too, we find another of today's oppositions: the first group focuses primarily on the illness, the second on the patient.

As a result, the two conceptions that originally sat alongside one other, or even merged with one another, are now replaced by an opposition between the anatomists and the functionalists. But the scales will soon tip heavily toward the anatomical side because of a certain discovery. From that moment onward, anato-pathology becomes the new Enlightenment in nosological thought. I refer here to Bayle's discovery of paralytic dementia.

... to the Anato-pathological Paradigm

Appearing in 1822, Bayle's discovery emerges almost simultaneously with Georget's theory. Nevertheless, its effect will only appear some twenty years later and, under Kraepelin's influence, will color contemporary nosological and diagnostic thought in a lasting way.

The effect of this discovery has to be seen against its historical background. The phenomenon of general paralysis (*paralysie générale*) was known long before Bayle, and was considered to be a symptom or complication of the terminal stages of several diseases. It is precisely this thesis that he will reverse: general paralysis is caused by a single organic factor; it is a single disease that evolves through different stages. At a stroke, nosology seemed a whole lot simpler. At least three different illnesses could be reduced to a larger whole, of which each is an evolutionary stage; the previously random symptom of general paralysis is now unified into a single syndrome whose organic causality has been proved. Bayle's discoveries can be briefly summarized as follows:

---

7. This evolutionary aspect, with its concentration on etiology and case histories, has meanwhile more or less been wiped out by the DSM approach. Hence, as in the game, it's back to the beginning: "Do not pass Go. Do not collect $200."

1. General paralysis is caused by a chronic inflammation of the brain (meningitis of the arachnoid membrane).
2. This inflammation leads to a psychopathology that normally undergoes three stages, spread over several years:
   - delusion with exaltation (or occasionally depression);
   - delusion with mania, megalomania, furor, agitation, logorrhea;
   - delusion with deterioration, amnesia and dementia.

We will come back to the question of the value of this description. Bayle propagates his discovery as the prototype for the entire field of psychopathology: every psychopathological disturbance is merely a symptom of an underlying anato-pathological process. From 1850 on, this idea becomes ubiquitous. Research into psychosis, chronic alcoholism, epilepsy, and even hysteria becomes the search for their underlying somatic bases. "General paralysis," better known to us as "paralytic dementia," becomes the Medusa-head around which a whole generation of researchers became paralyzed, with Kraepelin as her principal victim. With this discovery, the balance is also tipped and etiological research becomes exclusively directed at the body: every psychopathology has an organic base and is therefore organically treatable. Anato-pathology is a fact. Virchow's *Cellularpathology* (1858) becomes the leading paradigm that extends into the entire field of medicine, culminating in enormous progress in this field.

As for the value of this discovery for psychopathology, we have to consider it carefully—one must first distinguish between the value of the discovery itself and the idealizing generalization that followed afterward. Bayle's discovery became the subject of subsequent research, enabling Fournier in 1879 to demonstrate a connection with a syphilitic etiology, while in 1905 Schaudinn discovered *Treponema pallidum* in the infected sexual organs.[8] In 1913, Noguchi demonstrated the presence of *Treponema* in the brains of paralytic dementia patients. These therapeutic attempts were topped off with Mahoney's 1943 discovery

---

8. This discovery is itself a beautiful example of a paradigm's effect: the anato-pathologists were unable to make the cause of paralytic dementia perceptible because their methods, founded on their paradigm, had the exact opposite effect. Schaudinn, a zoologist, used different techniques emerging from his own paradigm (without the coloring of the slides) and obtained immediate results.

that penicillin could be used, making paralytic dementia today a rare phenomenon. Such, at least, were the discoveries, still revolutionary today.

But once we examine the accompanying idealizations, the Medusa-head aspect becomes more equivocal. Paralytic dementia becomes the paradigm par excellence of the *syndrome*, as developed later by Kraepelin; according to Kraepelin, psychopathology ought to distinguish among syndromes that possess the same cause, exhibit the same somatic and psychological clinical picture, and follow the same evolution.

Unfortunately, even in the case of paralytic dementia, this idea of a uniform syndrome is more dream than reality, something that is usually forgotten thanks to the subsequent idealizations. Despite its clear organicism, the unequivocal factor is missing, meaning that the diagnosis isn't unequivocal either. Only a limited number of syphilitic patients develop paralytic dementia, for example, forcing one to rethink its organic causality. The long cherished idea that there could be two viruses at play, only one of which caused paralytic dementia, was never proved and finally had to be given up (see Ey and colleagues 1974, pp. 835–836). The clinical evolutionary picture for psychopathology, for instance, can take many different forms; every textbook presents different classifications, most of which, moreover, contain "rare" or "atypical" forms. For example, the most frequent form before the turn of the century, megalomania, appears to have been replaced after the First World War by a simple form of dementia, a shift that a famous clinician like Rümke recognizes as being the effect of the dominant discourse, and which certainly doesn't tally with the idea of an unequivocal somatic cause (Rümke 1971, p. 78).

These difficulties argue against an exclusively organic approach. We may conclude with Bayle then, that the somatic part of a certain disorder was indeed discovered, but that the mind–body division and—in the case of general paralysis—the exclusion of the psyche, inevitably lead to the classic deadlocks of the artificial dichotomy psyche–soma; all we can do is make an entreaty to try to think beyond this dichotomy.[9] The

---

9. This is a long-standing appeal that has delivered little in the way of results. The reason for this has to do with our shortage of concepts for so-called holistic thought: our vocabulary continually forces us to think in terms of division, which literally "speaks for itself."

unequivocal and one-to-one correspondence between somatic etiology and psychopathology that Kraepelin so desired is an illusion, leading Nijs, in 1987, to invert Kraepelin's statement in the following way: "Organically caused psychiatric disturbances are typical to the extent that they are atypical."

The Paradigm: Kraepelin and the Uniform Syndrome

Despite the difficulties of applying the idea of the "uniform syndrome," paralytic dementia became the leading paradigm. The idea of the uniform syndrome is nothing but another name for the Platonic invariant. As a result, in the second half of the nineteenth century, research concentrated on the search for the anatomical substrates of every psychopathology, and for epilepsy, chronic alcoholism, and hysteria in particular. Autopsy became the primary research method, through which one hoped to find "it," despite not really knowing what "it" was.

Nevertheless, the results failed to materialize. Consequently, that conviction weakened and, instead, the idea of degeneration took center stage as a reversed illustration of Darwin's theory of evolution. With Freud, however, a new path was blazed: psychopathology concerns not simply the body but also and even primarily the psyche. The failure of anato-pathology in hysteria—see Charcot—inaugurated *psycho*therapy and *psycho*diagnostics. From this period onward, the anato-pathological conviction wanes and there is renewed attention to more wide-ranging approaches that take the interaction between the individual and his surroundings as a central theme.

This does not exclude the idea of an organic determination continuing to play in the background. The power of this ideal increased once clinical experience with paralytic dementia disappeared. Indeed, thanks to successful treatment, it has become quite rare, meaning that many clinicians in training do not experience the restrictions of the purely organic causal factor described above. The Kraepelinian ideal will receive fresh blood from the 1950s onward, due to the purely accidental pharmacological discovery of the precursors of neuroleptics. If chemical substances can exercise a more or less normalizing influence on psychotic behavior, then its cause and etiology must be on the biochemical level as well (Bouhuys and Van Den Hoofdakker 1986).

Meanwhile, this anato-pathological model has more or less become history, having been replaced by a new show pony, namely genetics and, more specifically for our field, behavioral genetics. Dressed up in a different outfit, it is the very same belief. A torrent of quantitative research has been published in the past decade, all demonstrating that certain behavioral characteristics are significantly determined by genetics, with only a limited environmental influence (for a review and a critique, see Fonagy et al. 2002, pp. 97–145). Nevertheless, it is enough just to examine recent changes in elementary bodily characteristics (such as bodily length, onset of menses) to see that the environment has a massive and, above all, barely understood influence on features that are undeniably genetically determined. It becomes all the more complex once we study non-elementary characteristics such as schizophrenia and delinquent behavior.[10] Nevertheless, this conviction is rapidly gaining ever more ground as the new doxa. Rather than "anatomy is destiny," the bell now tolls: "genes are destiny." The difficulty of thinking about the interaction between nature and nurture is avoided. Behavioral genetics are the Latest One-Act Wonder.

The Hidden Moral in the Story: The University Discourse

So far we have recounted the history of this paradigm, emphasizing its factual content. But beyond this, we need to call attention to another aspect, namely, its formal mode of operation. My argument is that such

---

10. The following are two classic studies. With regard to schizophrenia, it was shown that adopted children with one schizophrenic parent do indeed run a higher risk of psychiatric disorders, on condition that they have been adopted into a dysfunctional family (Tienari et al. 1994). Bohman (1996) showed the same thing for children of convicts, who—after adoption—run a higher risk of offending, with the same condition that the adoptive family was dysfunctional. The most persuasive research comes from Suomi (1997, 2000) concerning an impressive experimental-empirical research with . . . rhesus monkeys. Genetically highly reactive individuals display highly reactive behavior as adults (including alcoholism), if they were peer-reared and maternally deprived, whereas if reared by the mother, the genetic effect was canceled. His conclusion is very clear: genetic vulnerability is reversible.

a paradigm operates chiefly according to the University discourse, through which certain relationships and positions are imperceptibly imposed on the participants. Furthermore, this occurs independently of both the content and the scientific quality of the paradigm.

The reason why we encounter the University discourse here has to do with the radical impossibility of maintaining the Master's discourse (Lacan 1991 [1969–1970]). The University discourse is easier and, moreover, fits in with today's scientific climate. The positions and disjunctions remain the same, but the terms have undergone a quarter-turn shift from those of the master discourse.

$$\uparrow \frac{S_2}{S_1} \quad \overset{\rightarrow}{{/\!/}} \quad \frac{a}{S} \downarrow$$

To put it schematically: this time the agent is the knowledge base from which the diagnostician and therapist approach the other as an object to whom this knowledge can be applied. Behind the agent lies the unquestioned and unquestionable master signifier. The product of this approach is that the other, placed in the position of an object, becomes more of a divided subject than ever. The relation between this subject and the master theory comes down to an unbridgeable gap, meaning that the upper relationship becomes impossible as well. The whole is moreover supported by a certain conception of science that ultimately excludes the subject as such. In spite of its apparent objectivity, this approach is fundamentally morally-ethically colored through and through. Let us look at it more closely.

Compelling Explanations

Knowledge, S_2, occupies the place of the agent. This knowledge is not merely knowledge per se, but first and foremost a certain conviction: it *has to* be so, reality *has to* correspond to this knowledge. To the extent that reality doesn't yet correspond to it, it is only a matter of time. The basis of this conviction is found in a now incontrovertible master signifier S_1, which serves as a shining example. We already found one such compelling expectation—a doxa—back in 1917 with the reference to Kraepelin and paralytic dementia:

> The nature of most mental disorders is still unknown. *But there can be no doubt that* future research shall enlighten the question and un-

cover new facts in a science which is for the moment only in its infancy. In this domain, the disorders caused by syphilis provide us with a vast field of investigation. It is logical to assume that we will succeed in discovering the causes of other forms of madness, and hence to prevent them, maybe cure them, *although for the moment we don't have any indication whatsoever*. [Quoted in Szasz 1983, p. 45]

In response to this, we can cite another celebrity: "In an attempt to go further into the psychological, people cling to newly discovered somatic phenomena, or pin all hope on experiments through which something measurable, visible, a curve that can be mapped onto a graph, must finally come to light."[11]

The scientific outlook is the positivist, even scientistic paradigm.[12] Its specific conviction with respect to our field can be put this way:

---

11. My italics. The first is from Kraepelin (1917), *One Hundred Years of Psychiatry*, pp. 151–152, quoted in Szasz (1983, p. 45). The second is from Karl Jaspers, *Allgemeine Psychopathologie*, p. 5 (quoted in Vandereycken 1988, p. 79). One encounters the same logic in a publication by Van Praag (2000). He reexamines an earlier publication of his, dating from 1974, in which he expressed the hope that biological research into depression would provide us with more precise referrals and more selective antidepressants. Twenty-five years later, he is obliged to conclude that this has not happened, but seeing as how his expectations have also not been contradicted, he holds to his hope. While there is life there is hope, that much is clear.

12. On this point, Lacan made a provocative statement that—unsurprisingly— created the usual uproar: modern science can be regarded as an expression of paranoia (Lacan 1992 [1959–1960], pp. 129–132). Such a statement has to be understood within its larger context to avoid its becoming simply a catchphrase. Lacan starts out from the idea that, through acceding to language, we lose the "Thing" for all time, even the very Thing we are-in-ourselves. This is how he reads what is found both in Kant and in neo-Kantianism, and that meanwhile has become common knowledge in contemporary epistemology: science can only approach reality by way of models or constructs, period. The re-finding of the object can only occur through the auspices of an unsublatable lack, hence every approach must ultimately fail, resulting in a continual metonymy. Lacan applies this idea to what he calls the three great sublimations, that is, art, religion, and science, which he links respectively with hysteria, obsessional neurosis, and paranoia. Art and hysteria are always organized around this lack; creativity is based on the recognition that the Other can never definitively fill in this void, and that the Other, moreover, is held responsible for this impossibility. Religion and obsessional neurosis try to avoid the lack by installing an Almighty Other in the center, who is supposed to supply the Answer; the lack and the accompanying guilt are then assumed by the subject itself. Today's empirical science and paranoia start out from a disbelief in the definitive loss of the Thing and thereby ground them-

every psychological disorder has, that is to say, *must* have an organic cause. While this cause has already been found for a number of disorders, the others need further, intensive research, which will eventually lead to their discovery as well. In the meantime, for lack of anything better, we must content ourselves with psychotherapy, but the day will soon come when a pill, or a surgical intervention will suffice. The implication of such a scientific approach is immediately clear: if schizophrenia, for instance, is caused by a disturbance in neurotransmitters, then psychotherapy doesn't make much sense. Rather, one must consider pharmacological, even neurosurgical interventions, if necessary. From this perspective, research into the schizophrenogenic family is an outdated anachronism that ought not to be funded.

We have already seen how the unprovability of this paradigm can be conceived in terms of an epistemological impossibility; this means that what we are dealing with here is a doxa. Its success, despite its lack of scientific persuasiveness, has to do with its hidden moral component, which we shall come to shortly. Put in terms of discourse theory, what we see here is the relation between knowledge (S_2), as the apparent agent, and a belief in the master signifier (S_1) occupying the position of truth and in fact governing the whole thing.

Illness as an Essence

If we pursue the structure of the University discourse further, we find that the other is reduced to an object, producing a heightened awareness of division and subjectivity on the patient's side. Illness is defined as a nosological *essence*, for which the patient supplies only the fertile soil, a temporary dwelling. To put it more strongly, as a substrate, the patient muddies the disease's pure expression, just as soil that is too barren or too rich has effects on the form of the plant that happens to grow on it. "Anyone who describes an illness, has to make a careful differentia-

---

selves in a correlative omnipotence of thought, through which the complete mastery of reality can be imagined. From a Lacanian perspective, it is more effective to recognize the lack as such and to shape science from this recognition accordingly. In neo-Darwinian terms, the aim is not so much to find the "missing link" as it is to take the "missing" bit seriously. By this I mean the bar indicating both the division in every subject and the bit that remains perpetually unreachable because of this division.

tion between the symptoms that necessarily go with it and are specific to it, and the symptoms that are only accidental and coincidental, such as the symptoms depending on the temperament and the age of the patient," writes Sydenhan in 1772 (cited in Foucault 1997, p. 27).

The very same subdivision between the *essential*, which belongs to the illness's essence, and the *secondary*, which is caused by the specificity of the patient, can be found throughout the history of nosology, in Charcot (real hysteria versus "formes frustes," or weaker versions), just as in Bleuler and Schneider (primary versus secondary symptoms), to name only the principal figures. The emphasis of medical science is not on the patient but on the illness, an idea we have already seen in the DSM with its stress on the various "disorders." The patient must be abstracted away if a clear picture is to emerge: "The Creator has established the course of most diseases by means of invariable laws that can be discovered quickly enough, *if the patient does not interrupt or disturb the course of the illness.*"[13] When the body is considered a mere substrate, the subject is at most the passive victim of an organic agent. The etiological agent lies, like a "foreign body," a *Fremdkörper*, outside the subject itself, who has little to do with it aside from being "overtaken" by it.

To put this in terms of discourse theory, in the University discourse, one finds an object rather than a subject in the place of the other. Objectification and desubjectivation are well-known in medical practice. This is, in fact, the classic critique of the medical model: being reduced to a "case" (the ulcer in room 2B) generates indignation in the patient—that is, a demand for recognition as an individual human being. But there is one tiny detail: in this discourse the subject is, quite precisely, *produced* by this approach; without it, there would not have been any subject whatsoever. With this approach, it appears in the position of the *product*. Such a protest, incidentally, conceals an underlying benefit for the subject itself, and therefore needs to be taken, at least partially, with a grain of salt. This becomes clearer once we take the ethical-moral aspect into account. The argument is quite simple: if a certain psychopathology has an organic explanation, then there is no such thing as a guilty party. There are only victims of accidental gene combinations, of exter-

---

13. My italics. Zimmerman (1800), *Traité de l'expérience en médecine*, quoted in Foucault (1997, p. 35).

nal, nonhuman toxins, and so on. The parties themselves are not to blame, that's the ultimate message.[14] However, should the same disorder have a psychological etiology, then we would have to look for a cause in the psyche itself, and hence for a causal agent, either in the environment or, more frighteningly, in the mirror. This opens up a quasi-juridical process in which it is not just the patient, but the parents and the partner as well, who must all take their places in front of a prosecuting jury of psy's (Fischer and van Vliet 1986, pp. 137–139, 148).

This is the advantage of the anato-pathological paradigm for the patient: he or she is acquitted and, moreover, can protest that his or her subjectivity wasn't taken into account. The consequences of such an approach go much further than one would imagine. In fact, they color the entire mentality of our health-care system,[15] which can be summed up in the following slogan: "Health is everyone's free right." The result, predictably enough, is that everyone avoids their own responsibility and choices. Lung cancer? No problem, just sue the tobacco industry, it's all their fault! Alcoholism? That is simply an illness that one "has" (I *have* the flu; I *suffer* from alcoholism), what an awful tragedy!

Put in terms of discourse theory, what we encounter here are the disjunctions, which go considerably further than the purely anato-pathological or medical aspect of this approach. On the upper level, it becomes apparent that knowledge is never fully able to grasp the object; there is always a gap and a remainder. On the lower level, it is clear that the subject, in the position of the product, neither has nor wants anything to do with the master signifier S_1 in the position of cause and of truth. The double bar // will never be overcome.

We are now in a position to examine the other paradigm in which the moral element is explicitly foregrounded.

---

14. In an informal study in a British outpatient center for children, parents were asked what they considered the cause of their child's problems. "It surprised no one [of the researchers] that they all put brain chemistry at the top of the list. It was more surprising that "bad genes" came second, peers third, and early life experiences a poor fifth, just ahead of food additives." (Fonagy et al. 2002, pp. 98–99). This clearly shows how the neurological-genetic paradigm has penetrated the contemporary popular discourse. The advantage of this for the subject is discussed above.

15. Translator's Note: The Belgian national health care system is a single-payer, government-funded system comparable to those in Scandinavia.

THE MORAL TREATMENT PARADIGM: TO TEACH SOMEBODY MORES

We could, fairly arbitrarily, begin with Pinel (1754–1826), one of the founding fathers of what would later become psychiatry and psychopathology. Like every founding father, he is described in mythical terms: heir to the French Revolution, severer of the chains that fettered the mentally ill, and so on. His essential significance lies neither in the field of nosology nor in that of theory. Pinel is important because of his method: he was the founder of the *clinic*, that is to say, of the determined and systematic approach through which mental illness acquired its distinctive status, institutions, and treatment.

With regard to theory, he took a rather peculiar stance: he remained skeptical of any form of theory that, as far as he was concerned, moved too rapidly away from observation. Hence one cannot talk about Pinelian theory. Rather, he proposed a pragmatic approach, a form of know-how (*savoir-faire*) that enters history under the name of the "moral treatment" (*traitement moral*). This approach accords with his views on etiology. He distinguishes between three groups of pathogenic factors:

- Physical causes (trauma, organic diseases);
- Hereditary causes (debility);
- Moral causes.

Deeming the first two practically incurable, he concentrates on the third group. His ensuing treatment model recalls the Hippocratic idea of illness, in which illness is the body's healthy defensive reaction to an imbalance, and whose normal result is health. It is clear that such a conception of illness has important repercussions for the way the person who was then called the "alienist" responds. Pinel sums this up in three basic rules:

- He has to wait;
- He has to avoid any intervention that disturbs the natural course of the illness (because its ultimate goal is health);
- He must help the illness progress.

It is precisely this last that constitutes the "moral treatment."

The underlying theory originates in sensationalism: the contents of the sick mind stem largely from deleterious perceptions and sensations, that is, Pinel's third etiological factor. Consequently, curing boils down to the presentation of health-inducing perceptions and sensations, combined with the patient's removal from the harmful environment so that his or her psychic "faculties" can recover their balance. The practical effects of this project meant that special institutions had to be created for the recovery process—psychiatric hospitals—where the healthy perceptions could be effective. This gave rise to the application of a variety of cures (mud, water, sun and other baths) intended to create healing perceptions. Each one of these cures forms only part of a total approach because these institutions will eventually give birth to the clinic, the characteristic, all-encompassing *regime* that is to effect moral healing in the form of a kind of strict paternal order that is incarnated by the clinical director himself.

With this we have already sketched a brief outline of the core of the moral treatment model: people become mentally ill because of deleterious perceptions, ideas, norms; psychotherapy occurs by grace of a master figure whose correcting interventions take place within the context of a larger environment, or—more precisely—inside a totalitarian discourse that has no room for the subject's division. Note here that morals are considered health inducing. After Freud, this gets reversed, and morals seem to become the most significant deleterious factor (Vandermeersch 1978, p. 45). Later on, this core will be mitigated somewhat, but in essence it remains unchanged. For instance, for Pinel, the mental faculties were autonomous and nonhierarchized. Psychic functioning was a process of interaction in which upsets of balance could take place, resulting in psychopathology. From Esquirol (1772–1840) onward, a hierarchical order gets introduced: at the top of the faculties lies a function that controls, selects, and synthesizes, namely, the ego as the center of attention. Consequently, psychological disturbances are conceived as an effect of an imbalance between the lower faculties and the higher attention function of the ego.

This shift is significant because it continues to determine contemporary thinking; even today, psychology is frequently simply an "egology," with the emphasis today on what are termed cognitions. While in Pinel's time people were permitted to be both passionate and rational, now rationality dominates. Throughout history, the pendulum has swung back and forth: in pragmatic eras, man is thought to be rational (*cool*), while in more expressive periods passion is allowed. Anyone unlucky enough to respond to period X with image Y deviates from the ideal norm.

Guislain and Phrénopathie

Somewhat closer to us in time is Guislain (1797–1860). He replaced what was then termed madness (*folie*) with *phrénopathie*, understood as "a psychological reaction to a state of phrenalgia." We can extract two things from this description: a psychological reaction and phrenalgia. Guislain looks for the model of the psychological reaction in normality. For him, there are always both normal and pathological variations, and he remarks dryly that the success of the treatment depends on the degree of distance between the pathological and the normal. He conceives of "phrenalgia" as a moral affliction (*une douleur morale*), and it is precisely this aspect that will subsequently become a bone of contention. As a general practitioner in Ghent, he was able to keep abreast of the same families for many decades, which taught him, firstly, that the cause of psychopathology was always to be found in what he called the moral sphere and, secondly, that this cause was almost invariably kept from outsiders. As a result, his position was that "one must look behind the scenes." This idea finally became commonly accepted, and influenced, for example, Griesinger's theory of conflict, and consequently Freud as well (see, for example, his notions of conflict and defense).

With regard to specifically nosological classifications, Guislain remains adamant that the pure forms are very rare and that one mostly encounters hybrid forms in the clinic. This is unquestionably true. What is weird is how the vast majority of us continue to think and rationalize in terms of strictly separated species, turning clinical experience into a kind of aberration of the pure, rational, nosological system.

The beauty of it—which is precisely why Guislain was picked here—is the superb confusion that appears in his terminology, which is by no means accidental: in it, "moral" states are rechristened as medical-organic afflictions (*phrenalgia, phrenopathie*), blurring the differences in content between the two paradigms.

Protagoras to Pinel

We took Pinel as an arbitrary starting point. We could just as easily add a number of other writers from around the same time to the discussion, but this won't be necessary for our purposes. The moral conception of illness actually goes directly back to Protagoras and from the beginning exhibits the very same paradox. This sophist from the fifth century B.C. became well known for his argument that "man is the measure of all things" (*homo mensura*), thus reducing all perceptions to the subjectivity of the perceiving subject, and hence to a merely individual truth. What person X perceives is not necessarily the same as person Y; but the two different perceptions of the same reality are nevertheless each "true," albeit only for a single person. Even Protagoras, however, allowed that certain perceptions are better than others, namely, those belonging to healthy rather than sick persons. He conceives of a pedagogical role for the therapist, who must teach the patient-pupil the proper perceptions. What is better is what has better actual effects. As a result, we are faced with a paradox: the actual is only subjectively perceptible, while different "better actual effects" result from different perceptions. The master position becomes inevitable here, and that is precisely what we find with Pinel's *chef de clinique*. Historically speaking, it is here that the enlightened appeal to reason always shows up as the decisive argument, from Kant ("The only feature common to all mental disorders is the loss of common sense (sensus communis) and the compensatory development of a unique, private sense (sensus privatus) of reasoning") to Monod.[16]

In this way a line can be drawn from the Greek sophists to Pinel. We can pass over this quietly—it is old-fashioned, goes back to pre-scientific times, and the like. However, when we make the step to contemporary psychological approaches we are in for a double surprise.

---

16. Protagoras of Abdera, in P. Edwards, ed., 1972. *The Encylopaedia of Philosophy*, vol. 5, pp. 505–507; Kant, "*Anthropologie in pragmatischer Hinsicht*," in E. Cassirer, ed., 1922. *I. Kant's Werke*, Berlin: Bruno Cassirer, VIII. After a scientific rejection of all "natural" or "religious" laws of human behaviour, Monod makes a plea for scientific-rational objectivity as the basis for all human endeavors. He is smart enough to name this objectivity as an ethical, and therefore arbitrary stance (Monod 1970, p. 188 ff).

Firstly, we find almost exactly the same problems in today's psy-clinical practice. You don't need much clinical experience to discover that most psychological problems are concerned with psychosexual identity ("What does it mean to be a man? What does it mean to be a woman?"), with the psychosexual relationship ("Where do I stand in relation to the other, my partner?") and with the relationship toward authority (classically the father, nowadays less clear). It is also well known that these problems always imply a conflict between pleasure and unpleasure in every conceivable form (from anxiety to jouissance). The contemporary clinic, in other words, is still very much a *moral* clinic, although the signifier "moral" has been unilaterally replaced by the "psychological."[17] The reason for this substitution is not only historical, but also epistemological. The term "moral" doesn't fit very well into a positive-scientific way of thinking, and "ethical" only barely, but "psychological" does the job nicely.

The second surprise concerns the difference between the contemporary clinic and the medical-biological approach described above, which one would expect to be substantial. Isn't the subject, after all, the main focus of clinical psychology, not the body? Closer examination, however, reveals a surprising result. The difference between clinical psychological and medical biological approaches is minor, provided that in both situations they take place within the University discourse. The most important difference seems to come down to the fact that, compared with the organic-medical approach, today's "moral treatment" is unable to convincingly refer to a master signifier in the same way, so that it is more a question of *aspiring* toward a guaranteeing

---

17. Over the last decade there has been a change in the demand for psychotherapy in that it has been extended toward what is clearly a "moral" direction. The reason is probably connected with the loss of the grand narratives on the one hand, and the omnipresent psychologizing of everything and everyone, on the other. As a result, patients infrequently come for consultation because of clearly defined symptoms. Rather, they come into the consultation room bearing their soul on a platter—"*la condition humaine*" (Malraux)—expecting the therapist to be the new provider of meaning. This reminds me of Freud's final sentences in *Studies on Hysteria* (Freud and Breuer 1978 [1895d]), where he says that his treatment can transform his patients' hysterical misery into common unhappiness, but that the normal human problems inherent to life he is unable to help with. I get the impression that a number of today's consultations begin at the point where Freud drew the finish line.

master signifier S_1. This is, incidentally, more or less the sole difference, for we encounter the same ideas again, with the very same deadlocks. Consequently, the implications of today's moral treatment, that is, psychotherapy within the terms of the University discourse, are identical to those of the organic-medical treatment, with the exception of the aforementioned aspiration. We have already mapped them out through the University discourse, and can take them up again here virtually unchanged. To avoid repeating myself, I shall pay special attention to the subject, because one would expect it to have a central place within this approach.

The Exoneration and Infantilization of the Subject

The upper level of the University discourse shows how an object appears in the position of the other to which knowledge is then applied. In the organic-medical approach, the subject is regarded as a victim of external biological agents. In what we might call the hidden moral paradigm, the subject is a victim of its environment (parents, family, job), which must be objectively studied and mapped out—the enmeshed family, the disengaged family, the schizophrenic mother, the hysterogenic father. This means that the medical-biological line of reasoning can also be applied, but with psychological concepts for content. The psychological becomes pseudo-medical. This equivalence doesn't mean that psychology acquires medical contents (in the sense of MBD, ADHD,[18] or lack of oxygen at birth, for example), but points to a formal similarity: the etiological agent is located *outside* the subject, who remains more or less unimplicated in it but is, rather, assailed by it. The medical and the psychological are both alienating discourses precisely because of this exclusion of the subject.

Hence, in the University discourse (whether clinical-psychological or anato-pathological), we encounter a diagnostic logic that excludes the subject: the subject is merely a product that an agent, such as a foreign body, psychic virus, or bacteria, has acted on. Such an etiology

---

18. Anyone who might find these abbreviations irritating should consult Orwell's *1984*, more specifically, his reflections in the appendix on the power of abbreviations in Newspeak.

can seem quite psychological. Every time anxiety, for example, is explained and diagnosed through reference to a birth trauma, or hysteria by a traumatic experience before the patient was four, or learning difficulties by the parents' divorce, it sounds quite psychological.[19] Nevertheless, this logic is fundamentally alien to the subject, referring to something that comes from the outside and that can be objectively retraced.

The metaphor that we used with the organic biological paradigm, where illness was a plant and the subject its soil, applies here as well. This time the poorly developed plant represents the subject that has languished because of a bad soil. Both diagnosis and treatment start with the definition of an ideal plant and an ideal terrain. The subject—the plant—comes into the picture only as a goal, a final product of the process that is primarily concentrated on the improvement of the potting mix. Diagnosis here does not so much measure the subject's difficulties as the distance between the subject and the presented ideal. We obtain, as it were, a picture of a gradually elaborated path that starts out far from the norm and ends up in perfect accord with it. The subject will be situated in its corresponding place on this continuum through which one can then estimate the distance he or she still has to cover.[20]

What is striking in this approach is how difficult it is to found the treatment: what is one to do with the irrevocable "facts"? An external etiology implies an external treatment. In bronchitis, the subject becomes the victim of an attack by a bunch of little critters; one is given antibiotics to kill the bacteria. But what should one do if the subject is the victim of a birth trauma, the parents' divorce, or . . . ? In such cases, the only real antibiotic, in the etymological sense of the word (translator's note: *Anti-biotics*: literally anti-life), would seem to be that most radical one, evoking the *mè funai* of the chorus in *Oedipus Rex*: "It would have been better never to have been born." In this context, one reaches for a double arsenal, with reparative techniques (the original learn-

---

19. This has meanwhile become common parlance. A colleague working in prisons told me that inmates themselves nowadays explain their criminal behavior by referring to their unhappy youth—James Joyce's "He had a great future behind him" in reverse. The opposite can also be found as analysands discover in analysis that, in spite of their present symptoms, they have had a happy childhood.

20. See earlier, where normality was discussed as an ideal.

ing process must be redone) and various abreaction predicaments (rebirthing, primal scream) on the one hand, and recovery techniques for changing the originally faulty substrate into an ideal form on the other. In both cases, therapy runs the risk of deteriorating into a patronizing helping hand. The subject, in all of this, is exonerated of guilt; it is purely the environment that is to blame. The price is infantilization. As a flawed product, the subject is nothing but the raw material upon which other, better designers will do their job; nothing but the starting point for a new improved edition.

Enforcing the Ideal

This turns the vast majority of contemporary therapeutic approaches into covertly moral projects, not so much because they conduct everything under the banner of the ideal (in whatever version) but because they coercively enforce it. Hence, psychopathology is considered a failure to correspond with a certain ideal and treatment boils down to an educative process, a kind of relearning of this ideal. The moral dimension is expressly present, although now disguised under a pseudoscientific veil: psychological health becomes a coercive yoke, an obligatory conformity to a prescribed norm as the incarnation of the health ideal. The difference between psychotherapy, education, and re-education becomes completely blurred.[21]

No wonder that educational psychology, cognitive psychology, and psychotherapy have become confused today, and that one frequently talks about psychological training, preferably in groups where the effects of transference and identification are much greater. When Foudraine wanted to demedicalize his ward in Chestnut Lodge, the most

---

21. For utter clarity: Every form of psychotherapy implies an educative process. My critique concerns how this process is applied. A good way to express this is in terms of Lacanian discourse theory. In the University discourse and the discourse of the Master, the pupil has no impact whatsoever. In the yet-to-be discussed Analytic discourse, the stress is on the subject's own input. This may seem trivial at first sight, but it is not. One of the factors that has meanwhile been discovered regarding the efficacy of any treatment concerns precisely the amount of input the patient him- or herself has in the therapeutic process. It is precisely this input that is rendered impossible by the discourses of the university and the master.

fitting new name he found for it was "School for Living."[22] What makes this still weirder is that, after Freud, we do have some concept of the subjective implication: ideas such as the "benefit of illness" and "choice of neurosis" can serve us as beacons for avoiding this subject-infantilizing approach. We might add that Freud himself originally used these ideas of external factors, because that was how his hysterical patients presented it: something attacked them from outside—see his first theory of trauma. But long before he officially gave up on this theory, he wrote that the so-called "foreign bodies" formed part of the subject's ego, meaning that from the early Freud onward we must look for the etiology in the subject itself (Freud and Breuer 1978 [1895d], pp. 6–16).

The results of such an external approach can easily be foreseen: maintaining this objectifying and patriarchal mode will lead patients to denounce the entire psy-enterprise, just as they did with the older medical model.[23] Nevertheless, complaining about it doesn't prevent them also from benefiting from it, through the patient's self-exoneration, which is why the system endures. But it also creates fertile ground for all kinds of alternative healers, some of whom may be more willing to listen than regular therapists.

---

22. "I forbade the 'patients' to use this language and told them to use the term 'students' instead. The word 'patient' became taboo. I renamed Upper Cottage a 'School for Living' and Julia had the job of making a large sign stating 'THIS IS A SCHOOL FOR LIVING' to hang on the wall. The sign 'Nursing Office' became the 'Educational Office', and when the staff asked to be included I renamed them 'assistant educators'" (Foudraine 1973, p. 337). My critique notwithstanding, this book continues to be a must-read.

23. The repetition of history is a tragicomedy. The first psychoanalytic approach argued that psychopathology originated in unconscious determinations. The treatment was directed toward bringing these into consciousness, which in Freud's initial phase came down to imposing interpretations that would lead the patient to "insight" and, consequently, to choose the correct path. Within a very short time the treatment became a conflict—many patients didn't want the master's "correct" knowledge. The result became known as resistance. The same thing is about to happen now with cognitive behavior therapy. They too have discovered that psychopathology is the result of the patient's faulty cognitions that must be corrected. They will soon discover their own version of resistance. In Lacan's follow-up of Freud's later theory, he argues that one of the central problems of psychopathology and subject-division is this *not wanting to know*, and this requires a different approach than pure insight-therapy.

Rejecting the Subject

The idea that, as a result of the moral approach, the subject itself can be blamed and therefore rejected is at first sight perhaps even more surprising than simply the chill exclusion of the subject. Unexpectedly enough, we find an illustration of this in Thomas Szasz. This well-known freedom fighter from the anti-psychiatry movement has always presented himself as a defender of the rights of the mentally ill; he was a relentless critic of everything and everyone who threatened these rights. It is less well known that he ultimately rejected the patient, and that this is a necessary consequence of his approach.

His basic thesis is as simple as it is seductive: psychopathology is an effect of oppression, comparable to the medieval Inquisition. Moreover, he makes a black-and-white distinction between illness on the one hand and psychic difficulties on the other. Illness is biological and belongs to the field of the positive medical sciences, the world of laboratories and scanners. Natural science for him is the only genuine form of science. In contrast, psychiatry and psychology, to which psychic troubles belong as general problems in human life, inevitably have to enter the fields of morals and ethics, and therefore are unscientific by definition (Pols 1984, p. 58 and passim). As a result, he argues against enforced institutional psychiatry and in favor of what is known as "contractual" treatment, whereby patients come for consultation of their own free will with the aim of regaining their lost freedom or autonomy.

These arguments seem beautiful, human, modern, and so on. Nevertheless, they become somewhat less attractive once we follow his reasoning through to its final consequences, which inevitably lead to a deadlock and a paradox.

Let us deal with the deadlock first. Everything to do with institutional psychiatry Szasz interprets in terms of the relationship between oppressor and oppressed. In itself this is not new. As an idea it can be put into the context of much wider theories than anti-psychiatry, where mental illness is reduced to a question of power and oppression. Let us sum them up. In philosophy, we encounter this idea in Hegel, Schopenhauer, and Nietzsche. In our own field, it already takes center stage from the moral treatment model onward. In Freud, the important but often neglected opposition between passive and active is apparent throughout his work. In Adler, we find the theory of masculine protest and organ inferiority. Behavioral therapy is an open-and-shut case of power at work, while in systemic therapy the ideas of one-up and one-down speak for themselves. In ego analysis, the concepts of resistance and adaptation are fundamental. Lesser gods are Bakker with his theory on the territorium and Laborit with his similarly ethologically inspired ideas of hierarchy and dominance. With Foucault, we find an explicit relation between discourse and power. Finally, Lacan equates the discourse of the unconscious with the discourse of the Master and considers the latter the necessary precondition for every possible discourse and hence for every possible social relationship. Consequently, he does not naively reject this master discourse but links it structurally to the three other discourses.

In other words, if Szasz centralizes the idea of power and oppression, he inserts himself into a long tradition. But with this he makes a substantial error of interpretation: the relationship between oppressor and oppressed is primarily *internal* to the subject that is divided between its desire and its truth, and this relationship only becomes externalized afterward, resulting in the creation of oppressive instances, institutions, and so forth. For both Lacan and Freud, family and society are the effects of a certain subject-formation, not causes, albeit in a perpetually circular relationship (Freud 1978 [1930]; Lacan 1990 [1974], pp. 28, 30).

Szasz concentrates on these effects and calls them causes. His error becomes visible in the deadlock we can observe in his treatment: when one removes all external oppressive factors, the individual psychopathology remains. Precisely at that moment, Szasz's attitude shifts into the rejection mentioned above: the patients cannot cope with their liberty, with their autonomy.

This brings us to the paradox. Despite all of his pleas for freedom and autonomy, his theory finally amounts to a direct rejection of the patient. Why? Because his (in many respects justified) critique of institutional psychiatry, and his black-and-white distinction between science and ethics lead him back to the moral treatment model of the alienist, upon which his thought acquires a remarkable moral stance. He advocates the freedom, responsibility, and autonomy of the subject, values that he assumes institutional psychiatry shuns. Yet this implies that, for Szasz, the patient appears in a totally different light. In place of the medical psychiatric criterion that in a certain sense declared the patient both innocent and helpless, Szasz now gives us a moral value judgment that very rapidly becomes a prejudice. The striking thing about his line of reasoning is that it enables us ultimately to align Szasz with someone like Slater (1961, 1965), who argued that hysteria does not exist and that hysterical symptoms, lacking biological foundation, are proof that the patient is healthy.

For Szasz, mental illness does not exist, but the associated behavior does. So-called psychiatric patients are people who avoid their responsibility, who make unjustified use of their sick role. Thus we find the following notable saying from this liberator of the mentally ill: "The facts are, that, in the main, so-called mad-men [. . .] are not so much disturbed as they are disturbing; it is not so much that they themselves suffer (although they may), but that they make others suffer (Szasz 1976, p. 36). With this, Szasz not only distances himself from the vindicating effect of certain psychotherapeutic theories (the subject is himself responsible for his behavior and has to assume this responsibility), but goes a considerable step further (if they don't assume their responsibility, they are "disturbing mad-men"). Finally, we encounter here an accusatory prejudice that returns us to the idea of simulations, infantile adults, even criminals. Psychopathological labels are turned into pseudo-scientific excuses to "punish" "deviants," a process that is not all that rare in the psy-enterprise. Already in 1939, Hartmann noted that his colleagues had no difficulty claiming "that those who do not share our political or general outlook on life are neurotic or psychotic." That this still happens today is well known.

Aspiring toward the S_1: The Appeal to the Primal Father

In the Discourse of the University, the other is turned into an object of knowledge, forcing the subject to feel its subjectivity more than ever as the product of such a de-subjectivizing approach. This discourse is supported by an underlying master signifier that serves to guarantee the discourse's accuracy.[24] In the anato-pathological approach, we

---

24. Elsewhere I have called this "automaton"-science and have outlined the consequences of such an epistemological choice. One of them is that automaton-science must always appeal to an ultimate, final cause, a point of certainty outside itself that

could locate the paradigmatic discovery of dementia paralytica in this place, which has been replaced by behavioral genetics today. In the clinical-psychological-moral approach we see this function become personalized: the guarantee becomes embodied in a specific master-figure. Just as "made in Germany" guarantees quality, "Mr. X has said that . . ." certifies its truth.

In itself, this is a very interesting arrangement and a direct confirmation of Lacan's interpretation of the Freudian Oedipus complex. The father as a guarantee can only function by grace of a super-father, a primal father. While Freud believed this to be historical reality, for Lacan it is a neurotic illusion: there is no "big Other" founding "the Other" although in itself this hasn't prevented both Freud and Lacan from being installed or even installing themselves in the position of the master signifier S_1.

Such a personification of the university discourse's underlying guarantee has far-reaching consequences: the guarantee is not so much given by the master's theory as by his or her associated *ideology*. This is easier to see in the field of clinical psychology because the problems it treats are indeed moral problems.[25] It will become more visible still once we go from diagnosis to treatment—which is, after all, the aim of psychodiagnostics.

With regard to treatment, we encounter an ostensible opposition: either one strives for a completely objective approach—which is impossible—or one goes in the opposite direction and the therapist becomes the new Messiah, or meaning provider. Both approaches presuppose a master-figure in the form of the therapist who both knows and is able to instruct his patients in how psychologically normal people behave. A

---

guarantees the truth of the system, the *deus sive natura*. With Freud, we can identify this as the oedipal father. From a Lacanian perspective this is "the Other of the Other," or the all-guaranteeing master-figure, while in terms of discourse theory, it is the S_1 (Verhaeghe 2002b).

25. This is becoming much less the case in the natural sciences. Nevertheless, hard scientists are recently coming to the conclusion that their methods are inevitably colored by subjectivity, with the result that such subjectivity is increasingly becoming their object of study (see Norretransders 2001).

third possibility—that of abstinence (cf infra)—is entirely overlooked.[26] Abstinence means that, in an attempt to handle this division differently, the therapist avoids imposing her desire onto the other and creates a situation in which the subject's own subjectivity and accompanying division can be taken into account.

---

26. During the fiftieth anniversary of the Dutch Society for Psychotherapy, Bergin (1980; for a discussion, see de Haan 1980) openly said that religion and morality co-determine the degree of the cure's therapeutic efficacy, and that the role of the therapist boils down to giving a moral judgment about the client's lifestyle. His comments received a violent reaction. Seven years later, a conference was organized in Holland around the theme of mental health and philosophies of life. Dijkhuis (Dijkhuis and Mooren 1988) stated unequivocally that therapists pay too much attention to the constituent problems and don't focus enough on the problems in the underlying philosophy of life. This is paradoxical, because "The core of the psychological view of human behavior is ultimately located in the normative determination of this behavior, determined by what people consider good or bad in their social behavior with others. Emotional, cognitive and psychosomatic reactions take place in the light of qualitative and normative dimensions of human life: that is, the way one gives form to one's own norms and values in the social relations with others and oneself" (p. 15). He drew out the obvious therapeutic implications: "Psychotherapy is more than creating a condition in which specific symptoms can be changed; it is also the creation of a condition in which the clients' normative attitudes can change" (p. 29). In the same discussion, Mooren pointed out that many therapists are convinced of "the impossibility of combining directions and roles when questions about the philosophy of life enter the discussion" (p. 43). The danger lies in the therapeutic modeling, the hidden preaching, driven by the unspoken feeling of superiority of someone possessing a certain religion or ideology (e.g., the believers vis-à-vis the poor heathens, but also the enlightened freethinkers against the naive believers).

Freud had already foreseen the danger long before the term "modeling" became fashionable: "otherwise the outcome of one's [therapeutic] efforts is by no means certain. It depends principally on the intensity of the sense of guilt; [. . .] Perhaps it may depend, too, on whether the personality of the analyst allows of the patient's putting him in the place of his ego ideal, and this involves a temptation for the analyst to play the part of prophet, savior, and redeemer to the patient. Since the rules of analysis are diametrically opposed to the physician's making use of his personality in any such manner, it must be honestly confessed that here we have another limitation to the effectiveness of analysis; after all, analysis does not set out to make pathological reactions impossible, but to give the patient's ego *freedom* to decide one way or the other" (1978 [1923b], *SE* 19, p. 50).

Where this does not happen, diagnosis and the cure become an authoritative form of help in which the therapist wants "the best" for his client. This best, however, implies a value judgment and, hence, can only ever be arbitrary: thus *homo mensura* must call upon a "superhomo supermensura." Here we find the same deadlock as in the biological approach, where the underlying dualism between psyche and soma inevitably gives rise to an internal dualism, namely, the homunculus theory: someone has a headache because a smaller person in his brain has a headache, which is caused by an even smaller person in his even smaller brain, and so on.

The foundational master signifier S_1, the Other of the Other, continues to recede ever further toward the horizon. Some idea of the danger of benevolent therapeutic help can be given by a Lacanian saying. He scans it in three bars that each time delineate the enclosed problem more sharply: "It is a fact of experience that what I want is the good of others in the image of my own. That doesn't cost so much. What I want is the good of others provided that it remains in the image of my own. I would even say that the whole thing deteriorates so rapidly that it becomes: provided that it depends on my efforts." (Lacan 1992 [1959–1960], p. 187). Here we can turn to Freud who, not coincidentally in a paper on transference, categorically dismissed such an attitude, precisely because "psycho-analytic treatment is founded on truthfulness" (1978 [1915a], p. 164) by which he simultaneously recognizes its greatest ethical value.

Nostalgia for the Father

This issue has become all the more problematic as a result of the social evolution of attitudes toward authority. Roughly speaking, for half a century the overly severe father has been regarded as the cause of every psychopathology in his children: the patriarch, the leader of the primal horde who raised his children into neurotically contorted milksops. The sexual revolution, antiauthoritarian models of upbringing, learning-in-freedom and Sommerville schools were all corrections to this, based on its opposite. Quantitative criteria were used as well: an overly severe father causes frustration and neurosis in his children; an excessively severe monster-father goes a step further, causing psychosis in his offspring. Strangely enough, we hear pleadings, almost supplications today for the return of this father patriarch: "More structure!" . . . "the Name of the Father has to be installed!" A severe father might not be all that much fun, but an absent father is even worse. People talk more generally about the loss of the grand narratives, the myths: human beings need a meaning-bestowing belief in something, whether it is religion, politics, or . . . science. A final, desperate attempt to sit on the fence is found in the eternally returning quantitative logic: the father must be authoritarian, but not too much so.

Here, the moral treatment model turns into nostalgia for the primal horde: "Long before he was in the world . . . there was the father who knew that a Little Hans would come who . . ."[27] The anato-pathological model has less need of this nostalgia because there the installation of the S_1 seems more secure. From a psychoanalytic perspective, two comments can be made. First, this pleading for a return fails to make an essential distinction between the real father, the imaginary father image, and the symbolic function of the father. Second, with Lacan we can go beyond the Freudian call for the primal father-master ("You are looking for a master, you will find one")[28] as a typically neurotic and perpetually failed solution to one's own self-division; the failure is inherent in the structure of the Master discourse itself. This is not to say that this type of solution is not exercised just as much in science (*deus sive natura*), in politics (Papa Stalin and Co.), and in religion (from the Pope to Khomeini) as on the individual-clinical level.

The application of the two paradigms, the savoir-faire (know-how) of both medical and psychological practice, is nothing but a phenomenalization of the University discourse. To found a practice upon this demands the politics of the ostrich. Without awareness of that one is confronted with impossibility and impotence. In our field, this can be seen in Freud's concept of the "impossible professions": educating, governing, analyzing. Nor did this stop his own theory from being turned into a paradigm in a very short time as well.

---

27. The allusion is to Freud's intervention with a 5-year-old phobic child; see Freud 1978 [1909b], *SE* 10.

28. This is the prophetic answer that Lacan gave to the May '68 students who interrupted his seminar (Lacan 1977 [1969]).

THE ANALYTIC PARADIGM: PROMISE AND DECAY

Freud's originality lies in his daring originality. This tautology can be found at the origin of every scientific innovation: every time someone risks leaving the beaten path, the chance of something new appears. The associated paradox is that, following this fruitful side track, a group of disciples emerges to defend the master's orthodoxy. Anything is allowed, so long as it is written by the master. In the name of an original thinker, originality itself becomes forbidden.

Before examining the psychoanalytic paradigm, I will first explain Freud's original vision of psychopathology, for which a well-known expression can serve as a guide: the flight into health. Next we will look at Freud's own evolution, which, starting out from a positive scientific model and colliding with its deadlocks, inevitably culminated in certain ethical implications. Moreover, it will become clear that this ethic was implicitly present from the beginning despite its being hidden under the various different names of objectivity. Finally, we will be able to pinpoint the moment when, after Freud, this decay into an "analytic paradigm" occurred.

Freud: The Flight into Health

One reproach often leveled at psychoanalysis is that it makes *any* behavior suspect, constantly shifting the border between what is normal and abnormal. This reproach has to do with Freud's expansion of the concept of the symptom; from an analytic perspective, anything that can be traced back to the history of a subject's formation is a symptom. Such a statement says nothing about the pathological or normal character of this symptom, only about its place, signification, and function within the economy of a particular subject. Israel (1984) expressed this position in terms of a wish: that one day a diagnostics independent of all pathological connotation would emerge.

The reproach, therefore, doesn't go far enough. Freud didn't so much shift the frontiers between normality and abnormality as explode them. The "flight into health" of our title can serve as a paradoxical leitmotif here. We encounter it, for instance, in a case study of obsessional neurosis (1978 [1909d]), where it refers to what is no doubt quite a remarkable process: the patient recovers in order to escape from the truth that is on the brink of emerging through the analytic process. In his paper "On Beginning the Treatment" (1978 [1913c], Freud uses the metaphor of the set of scales: on the one side is the loss, namely, the subjective pain caused by the symptoms; on the other, the gain, the primary and secondary advantage of the illness. This balance as fully determines the moment when someone appeals for treatment as when they stop it.

This is, incidentally, common knowledge for every clinician: the moment that someone asks for help is almost never contemporaneous with when the symptom started. Typically, the pathological structure is much older, while the demand for help almost always seems to come too late. This is the most important starting point for the intake sessions: Why has the patient come now, at this specific moment? To put it differently, what has changed in the symptom's balance sheet of gains and losses that makes a demand for help needed now? At the same time, the equivocal quality of many demands for help becomes transparent: most patients want nothing more than a restoration of the original balance, not the dissolution of the structure—this is evident from another Freudian case study, this time concerning a hysteric (1978 [1905e]). Hence the consultations will be stopped once the balance is restored, while nothing has fundamentally changed—this, then, is the flight into health. Its opposite is still more paradoxical: the therapeutic negative reaction, in which the analysis runs beautifully, but the patient suffers even more profoundly. The revelation of too much truth is not always easy to take, and it is not by chance that Lacan puts an ethical imperative at the foundation of the analytic process and of the unconscious: "*Whatever it is, I must go there*" (Lacan 1994 [1964], p. 33).

The subversion of health into illness suggests a fundamentally different vision of psychopathology in general, and of the symptom in particular. After psychoanalysis, it is well known that a psychopathological symptom is an attempt at cure, more specifically, an attempt to reach a solution within a given psychic structure. This still revolutionary idea is in fact age-old as it perfectly reflects the Hippocratic view of illness (as discussed above): illness is an organism's healthy reaction to an imbalance, a reaction that normally ends in health. Its accompanying symptoms are attempts to adapt to it. In the first half of the twentieth century this mechanism was even reversed. A psychosis? No problem. Transform it into malaria and the psychosis will vanish (known as the "Von Sackel" treatment). It is almost like the implicit rule of folk psychology: solve a problem by creating a bigger one.

Back to Freud then. His explosion of the border between the normal and the abnormal can be seen at any number of points. It is enough simply to consult the index of the German *Gesammelte Werke* under "Normal" and "Normale Menschen." It extends over ten columns, and we encounter just about every pathological phenomenon.[29] His foundational texts present the same combination every time, from *The Interpretation of Dreams* to *The Psychopathology of Everyday Life* and *Jokes and Their Relationship to the Unconscious*: there is practically no difference between the "healthy" and the "sick" mind. It is not by chance, moreover, that this intermingling occurs; it takes on an increasingly structural importance throughout the development of Freud's theory, as can be illustrated through three main themes.

First, sexuality. The so-called normal sexual relationship is a normative illusion; there is only a "norm-mal(e)," a male norm, whose short-term variations are provided by the periodical statistics supplied, à la Hite and Masters and Johnson, and which any interested person can consult freely to see how many orgasms she or he is entitled to within the various age categories. For Freud, the human being starts out from a polymorphous perverse sexuality whose original instincts get perverted into the typical human drive. There is no natural norm for human psychosexuality. The central diagnostic problem concerns the difference between the perverse traits that are found in everyone, and the perverse structure of the subject (see Chapter 14 of this book).

Second, repression. From his earliest writings, Freud uses the terms normal and pathological to describe this process. The difference between the two kinds will never be elaborated except in quantitative terms: pathology implies an excessive repression. The moment he formulates the concept of primal repression as a necessary preceding state for "secondary" repression, it becomes evident that this primal repression is structurally necessary for every subject, thus blurring the distinction even more.[30]

---

29. Freud, "Gesamtregister," *Gesammelte Werke*, vol. XVIII, pp. 295–399.

30. This has been extensively discussed elsewhere. See Verhaeghe (2000a, pp. 25–55, 141–195).

Immediately following this, we encounter the idea of the splitting of the subject, the *Spaltung*. Originally, Freud limited this to extreme cases of hysteria, but eventually he will universalize this process: every subject becomes divided during its development, and this division is focused on the acquisition of language and the accompanying loss of immediacy (Freud 1978 [1940e], pp. 275–276). Freudianly speaking, this enables one to specify a person's pathology on the basis of their relation to the lack that language has installed: repression, disavowal, foreclosure. With Lacan, this will become the subject's relation towards the lack in the Other, opening up the idea of a structural clinic. As someone once quipped, there are three ways of being normal: neurotically, psychotically, and perversely.

The World of Make-believe

Therefore, the reproach we began with is at least partly on target: psychoanalysis has undeniably exploded the difference between normality and abnormality. The question now is whether this is justified? Is it possible to neglect this difference? Is it not rather that analysis has created an unfortunate artifact? The story of the Emperor's new clothes can serve to illustrate this. Freud takes the place of the child who dares to reveal the truth in the face of reigning appearances: everyone knows that the Emperor is walking around naked, but no one has the guts to say it.[31] This is precisely one of the fundamental characteristics of what Lacan calls "*le monde du semblant,*" the world of make-believe, and the reproach directed at Freud belongs to it. An example of this is found in the remarkable screening list designed to detect psychic anomalies in schoolchildren.

1. School problems such as low scoring, top scoring, and irregular scoring;
2. Social problems with peers and brothers and sisters, such as the aggressive child, the submissive child and the braggart;

---

31. Hence the confusion the moment the institutions got rid of the uniforms: Who was the patient? Hence, too, the way TV documentaries about "psychiatric patients" almost inevitably put mentally handicapped or geriatric patients on display; at least with these groups "it" is visually clear.

3. Relations with parents and other authority figures, such as annoying behavior, docile behavior, obsequiousness;
4. Clearly perceptible behavior, such as tics, nail-biting, thumb-sucking and interests that are more appropriate to the opposite sex, such as the boyish girl and the girlish boy. [Radin 1962, p. 392]

No further comment is needed here.

Freud's Evolution: From Scientism to Ethics

Right from the start, Freud wrestles with what he calls the choice of the neuroses (the *Neurosenwahl*): how is it that someone chooses this particular psychopathology, and not a different one? The term itself is a little misleading: it does not concern just the neuroses, but also what Freud later called the narcissistic neuroses, that is, psychosis. As an illustration, it is enough to recall the peculiar term, neuropsychoses of defense (*Abwehr-Neuropsychosen*), among which Freud includes hysteria as well as paranoia. What is striking is his introduction of the idea of choice: the subject itself has always been a part of its pathology; it is not just the victim but the actor as well.

In this light, it seems as if Freud has been concerned with differential diagnostics from the outset. This is only partially true, because this distinction is developed through and together with the treatment. To the extent that Freud discovers hysteria and obsessional neurosis, he is developing the psychoanalytic method. The classical pre- and, more especially, post-Freudian gap between diagnosis and treatment thus entirely disappears. The way a patient goes through his or her analysis—more accurately, the specific form that the transference takes—enables a diagnosis to be made, with the result that the final diagnosis can only be made during the treatment.

The choice of neurosis, the "*Neurosenwahl*," therefore does not exist as a kind of separate diagnostic field: nosology, analytical theory, and practice together form a single indivisible whole. Freud's developments can be divided into two major strands. The first concerns the discovery and theory of defense. The second deals with the transference as the relationship between the divided subject and the Other. One can formulate this differently: the first concerns the primacy of the pleasure principle and the signifier, the second puts forward the dimension of the Real, where the Lacanian idea of jouissance is found. We will see that there is a special relationship between these two developments, making it possible, for example, to locate psychosis more precisely. This will subsequently form the touchstone for the decay of the psychoanalytic paradigm.

Defense

First of all defense, the pleasure principle and resistance. The subtitle of Freud's well-known paper of 1894, "The Neuro-Psychoses of Defence," already indicates the reach this concept is supposed to have: "An attempt at a psychological theory of acquired hysteria, of many phobias and obsessions and of certain hallucinatory psychoses" (1978 [1894a]. Freud believed he had found the key to practically the entire field of psychopathology: the ego finds itself in a conflictual situation and manages it through a form of defense. The development of this thesis will form the heart of Freud's theory and practice, at least for as long as the pleasure principle serves as a fundamental axiom. This theory is relatively simple: every subject strives for pleasure, which means as low and as constant a level of tension (in today's terms: arousal) as possible. A conflictual situation creates an unpleasurable rise in tension, which is precisely what the defense, whether pathological or not, aims to avoid (because there is also such a thing as a normal defense for Freud). It is precisely the changing of this fundamental axiom that will generate the second major strand, through which psychosis, perversion, and neurosis can be radically distinguished, which is not yet the case with the first. See Freud's main title: "Neuro-Psychoses of Defence," and the enumeration in the juxtaposed subtitle.

Freud will develop this first strand from three different angles that each provide an answer to a question about the choice of neurosis. The questions can be put as follows: Defend against what? When? How? In the first place, the question of what is being defended against will produce a medically inspired differential diagnostics. This is the theory of trauma. Freud distinguishes between an external, etiological agent, which he calls the foreign bodies (*Fremdkörper*), who attack the subject from the outside, as it were. Once his trauma theory has been completed with the theory of fantasy, however, this will change: the subject plays its own part in this etiology, hence the term "choice of neurosis."

This first distinction soon proves insufficient. Consequently, Freud poses another question, namely, When did the defense become necessary? In his famous correspondence with Fliess, he describes a number of life stages, each determinative for a specific pathology.[32] A couple of years later, Karl Abraham would take this up again with his theory of libidinal development. We see a sort of psychoanalytic genesis here, whose implicit presupposition is that the earlier a pathology establishes itself, the more severe it will be. The limited value of this idea can be shown through a specific application of it: from such a perspective, the earlier determined hysteria should be a more severe pathology than the later determined paranoia (Lacan 1977 [1949], p. 5).

This approach is also insufficient for grasping the diversity of the clinic, and Freud continues to search. The next question he poses concerns the "how" of the defense. In answer to this, he elaborates the following idea. Every form of psychopathology has a mechanism of defense of its own. Thus hysteria can be characterized by repression, obsessional neurosis by isolation and reaction-formation, psychosis by projection.

It is important to underscore how this threefold conceptualization in Freud's first theory only becomes clear in the post-Freudian retake of it. In Freud himself, these three approaches are parts of a larger whole. After Freud, each approach will be individually seized upon as a unique explanatory model. In my discussion of the decay, this will be well illustrated for psychosis.

The Real and the Transference

That's it for the first major strand we find in Freud. We can understand it in terms of the upper level of a discourse: the agent tries to grasp the other but comes up against an impossibility each time.

The second major strand in his theory will undermine this first one in its very fundamentals, and can be understood as the lower level of a discourse, wherein the product can never come into relation with the truth that drives it. This second line of development concerns the Real and the transference, that is, the discovery of the importance of the

---

32. See the letters of May 30, 1896, and December 6, 1896, in Masson (1995, pp. 187–190, 207–215).

Other in subject-formation. It is precisely here that Lacan will transform his "return to Freud" into a continuation of Freud, with his concept of jouissance and the double disjunction that inheres in discourse.

Let us look at this in more detail. Until 1920, Freud thinks almost exclusively in terms of the pleasure principle, that is, a human being always aims at abreacting the tension caused by a desire until it reaches zero. Psychopathology boils down every time to a failure of this pleasure principle—whose result is unpleasure, that is, tension—whether because of an external trauma, or because at a certain point in the development something went wrong, or because of the wrong defense. Both the defense and the treatment run according to the laws of the signifier, that is, according to this pleasure principle, as one can read it in its entirety in "Beyond the Pleasure Principle" (1978 [1920g]). Desire is expressed in words, in "representations." Defense works on these representations by shifting them, repressing them, reversing them into their opposites, occasionally even rejecting them, with the result that the original words and their accompanying desire are no longer available to consciousness. Therapy tries to counter this by neutralizing the defense and making the original representation available to consciousness once more. In this way, a conscious abreaction can take place following the laws of the normal pleasure principle. Treatment can thus be pragmatically understood as a means for realizing full speech, whose consequence is that normal satisfaction becomes possible. The entire enterprise is grounded by the strong conviction that "everything" can be said, that "the" perfect sexual relationship does exist and that "the" father therefore forms the guaranteeing keystone.

Incidentally, this way of thinking closely corresponds with certain behavioral and later educational-psychological principles: the anxiety-provoking stimulus becomes linked (as Freud puts it, *verknüpft*) or associated with another stimulus that itself will provoke anxiety later on; therapy needs to undo this bad linking or association and bring the original coupling to light, and must subsequently extinguish it. The whole thing is governed by the conviction that the human being wants to avoid pain. Right from the outset, there are enormous differences as well. For example, Freud will be much more interested in the how, the what, and the why of the defense mechanisms causing these associations. The chief difference concerns something of a more conceptual order; early behaviorism presupposes a correspondence between objects and signifiers (hence the eternally returning demand in early behavioral therapy for the complaint to be concretized), while Freud's later evolution is based entirely on the lack of correspondence between them, as described already in his "Project" (1978 [1950a (1895)]). The starting point is also different. Freud will always be attentive to the internal drive, that is to the actual source of the anxiety that only becomes associatively hooked onto an external hanger in a second moment.

In this first period, Freud believes his treatment can offer a definitive solution through verbalization. Meanwhile, the problems with which his patients are wrestling can be brought into clearer focus: they are all sexual problems, in the widest sense of the word. His patients are wrestling with questions about their psychosexual identity and the accompanying sexual relationships. These questions, moreover, are always combined with (the narrative of) the parents and hence with authority. Freud will recap this in his theory of the Oedipus complex. Therapy must put patients into a position of being able to verbalize the defective mode by which they feel pleasure, and replace it with the correct one.

Along the way, he gets confronted with the impossibility of bringing the treatment to an end. In the course of this evolution, his first theory—that of the pleasure principle—collapses with the discovery that there is something beyond the pleasure principle, something that always causes the pleasure principle to fail; the discovery, in other words, that full speech, the ability to say everything, is impossible. Here Freud rediscovers the dimension of the Real and this time he will take it wholly into account.[33] Beyond representation, that is, beyond the signifier, lies something that cannot be libidinally bound and therefore cannot be abreacted, something for which even the repetition compulsion fails, so that the pleasure principle can never achieve a total

---

33. I say "rediscovery" because he had already been confronted with it at the time of his first theory of trauma. Nevertheless there is an important difference. In this first theory, the causal trauma is largely external (the traumatizing other). In his second theory, such an external trauma adheres to a structurally determined inner trauma, more specifically the subject's own drive that can never be finally abreacted. Lacan will later reiterate this with his laconic term "object *a*" and, more broadly, as the register of the Real (see Chapter 12).

discharge of tension.[34] He finds the basis for this in the first narcissistic injury in the relationship between child and Other, and will ground a new theory of the transference precisely at this point: the idea of a transference *neurosis* (Freud 1978 [1920g], pp. 18–23).

We can best chart this by using the disjunctions of Lacanian discourse theory. In neurosis, the disjunction of impossibility is central: the pleasure principle is ultimately doomed to fail, and every life's story is a depiction of the various attempts to cope with this failure. This first disjunction (impossibility) masks the underlying grounding and guaranteeing disjunction of the impotence, that is, the incapacity of the subject to get hold of the Real through the product of discourse. In clinical terms, there is no final signifier, no final story that will grasp psychosexual identity, and, hence, also no symbolically preset relationship between the two genders. No single authority—no oedipal father—is able ultimately to define this signifier or this relationship. Instead, the four discourses sketch four different routes through which the subject can elaborate four different forms of social bonds around this impotence to obtain total satisfaction. This is as much as saying that there are four ways of circling around the Real at those points where the Symbolic fails: the function of the father, sexual difference, and the sexual relationship. Neurosis, or even more broadly, culture, is always an attempt at an answer. In this, one consults a guaranteeing, self-establishing authority who installed a normative and conventional attitude toward pleasure and desire, and who makes it possible to adopt an attitude both toward one's own body and toward the body of the other.

At this point, the psychotic fault line comes into view. The psychotic stands outside discourse, outside the auto-constituted oedipal father and, hence, outside the securing effects of the discourse framework. The impotence is missing, meaning that the impossibility is no

---

34. Repetition compulsion is a mechanism aimed at decanting certain elements of the Real into words but also one that, because it is unable to do so, continues to function compulsively (see Chapter 12 on the traumatic neurosis, where the trauma is continually repeated in nightmares, without the dream ever succeeding in imaging "it"). The aim of this verbalization is to enable the traumatic Real to be psychically elaborated and dischargeable in the manner of the pleasure principle (see Freud 1978 [1920g]).

longer guaranteed. The Real remains unprocessed, with the result that the transference, as an imaginary processing, is missing and appears in another form that is experienced as "monolithic." The narcissistic injury Freud talks about as the foundation of neurosis in "Beyond the Pleasure Principle" is of a totally different order here; it may even be absent. Hence the expression, "narcissistic neurosis."

Ethics and the Guaranteeing Figure

Regarded thus, Freud's theory is characterized by two main strands: on the one side, the signifier, and on the other, the Real. The dimension of the signifier implies both the Symbolic and the Imaginary, two orders that circle the Real and characterize a particular neurosis. Psychoanalysis as a treatment is based on a neurotic disposition, which is to say that it is based on the disposition of the signifier. It became clear to Freud, even at this stage, that this was not enough, and that such a treatment, at least, contains a structural impossibility. This later becomes the problem of the so-called interminable analysis, for which one must look for a method of treatment that can offer something beyond words.

One can thus read Freud as a scientistic, positivist thinker, a *Freud, Biologist of the Mind* (Sulloway 1979). From such a perspective, one invariably ends up in the same deadlocks as positive science itself, as becomes more apparent from its paradigmatic applications where something of the order of the Real keeps escaping. Nevertheless another reading is possible, one that shows how, starting indeed from the angle of the hard sciences, Freud finally confronted its deadlocks. Looking back over these deadlocks shows, moreover, that the ethical dimension was implicitly there from the beginning. The reason for this is simple. Ethics, both in the larger social sense as in the narrower, subjectively determined meaning of the word, is an essential part of every clinical practice because each patient's demand for (and in) the treatment carries an ethical problem.

Ethics as the core of every treatment. But if this is the case, how come Freud paid so little attention to it in the course of his psychoanalytic conceptualization? Beginning in a time of the hard sciences, a laboratory atmosphere even, Freud will be the first to chart the problems of the desiring subject. The scrupulously careful schemas of "The Psychopathology of Everyday Life," the unraveling of the dream mechanisms, the dynamic relationship between repression and symptoms, these "Selected Topics" testify to a research mentality. The frequently mechanical-seeming descriptions in the hydraulic model didn't leave much room for ethical questions, as has become even more apparent in post-Freudianism.

But this applies only for what we've called Freud's point of departure. The reason that Freud remains one of the determining figures for contemporary thought, alongside Marx and Darwin, is precisely because he was able to overcome the problems of his starting point. This overcoming can be summed up in a nutshell. Firstly, Freud heard the ethical implications of his patients' demands: neurosis is always the effect of a conflict between a desire and a prohibition in which the desire seems to belong to the subject and the prohibition appears to come from the outside (recall "Studies on Hysteria"). Following this, Freud tried throughout a certain period to answer the neurotic demand by taking on the role of the father himself, albeit in a corrected re-edition (the highlight of this moment was "Totem and Taboo"). Finally, he discovered and questioned the internal impossibility of this response and of taking this position, so that psychoanalysis comes to join the list of the impossible occupations (Freud 1978 [1937c] and 1978 [1939 (1937–1939)]).

The conflicts at the base of neurosis can have as many contents as there are subjects. In terms of a formal structure, however, there is a recurrent phenomenon: the divided subject always seeks an external figure who can provide a form of certainty, that is, a figure that can serve as a guarantee against one's own self-division, firstly with respect to the drive and secondly with regard to the Other. Freud came to understand this fairly early on and discovered, moreover, that this sought-after figure is colored by infantile memories of the parents, primarily of the father. The therapeutic instrument thus becomes the transference through which the therapist comes to carry the weight of the original authority.

With such reasoning, no distinction can be made between the classical moral treatment and this first Freudian conceptualization. In both cases, the original, failed authority is replaced by a new, improved re-edition. The difference begins only from the moment Freud discovers the ever-recurring failure of the guaranteeing oedipal function, and the subject's implication in both the construction and destruction of this figure. The laborious process of construction and working through thus becomes the core of the cure, and simultaneously founds the difference between therapies that operate on the basis of suggestion, and analysis whose task is to analyze the conditions of the possibility of suggestion.

This is what Freud described as transference: the weight assigned to the therapist comes from elsewhere. Furthermore, experience shows how this weight always has an ethical character, in that the patient expects yet fears judgment, wants advice, approval, and to be loved, and all this invariably in relation to what yields either pleasure or unpleasure. In brief, she or he searches for a master (S_1) who preaches knowledge (S_2) in an attempt to make the drive manageable. The therapist is put into position of the oedipal guarantor, or let's simply say, the primal father who, according to little Hans, has an intimate relationship with God because he appears to know everything (Freud 1978 [1909b], pp. 26–27). I say, appears, because this is where the next set of troubles begins: sooner or later, the guaranteeing figure fails, and this failure is then also transferred onto the figure of the analyst in the course of the treatment. It becomes increasingly clear that it is this relationship that is central, both in pathogenesis and in the course of the treatment, and that all previous conceptualizations must be reconsidered in this light.

Lacan takes this up and reconceives it in terms of the subject's formation, which takes place in relation to the Other. The symbolic system developed meanwhile displays an essential lack—there is no Other of the Other—whose consequence is that the discourse of the Master contains both an impossibility and an impotence. The confrontation with this lack in the "all-knowing" symbolic system and hence in the Other, provokes an anxiety about the unprocessed Real, resulting in a never-ending search for an imaginary master figure who should nonetheless be able to provide an answer.

The radical difference between this and the previously discussed paradigmatic ideas can now, with the Lacanian conceptualization of the last Freudian shift, be made out: it is senseless to identify the therapeutic figure with the master figure. The Freud who assumed he could teach Dora how to desire falls off his pedestal. The core of Freud's treatment model is that the master figure is a creation, a neurotic construction built in an attempt to rid oneself of division. To the extent that the therapist permits the patient to turn him into this master figure through the transference, and insofar as the therapeutic process stops at this point, he merely repeats the original process. Psychoanalysis, rather, is ultimately the analysis of this construction process, of its necessity and subjective modalities. Its aim can be defined in these paradoxical terms: the aim of analysis is to analyze that which originally made analysis possible, namely the transference.[35]

Deterioration: Dr. Ernesto Morales and the Last Freudian[36]

At this point the reasoning pertinent to the anato-pathological paradigm can be repeated. It is not because psychoanalytic concepts are used that we have escaped paradigmatic deterioration. Each discourse can be filled in with any kind of signifier. It is its formal structure that determines how it is manifested. Whenever psychoanalytic jargon is used within a university discourse, the implications are the same as in the two other paradigms.

To repeat the argument behind this would only be to repeat myself—I thus leave its application to the cognitive abilities of the reader. What must be underscored is that the psychoanalytic model is unfortunately very apt for what I want to call the oedipalization of clinical

---

35. An important question is whether analysis then automatically leads to individual choices, to a personal ethic in the analysand. The medieval Catholic rereading of Socrates reappears here: know thyself and you will become virtuous. In this context, it is worth mentioning the Lacanian aim of analysis: to install a new social bond through the analytic discourse, "one that would not be a semblance." This implies that a social bond should be possible beyond the collage-effect of the assembling master figure. This seems like a beautiful but almost impossible dream, because it goes precisely against the essential division of the subject. Either this division is not essential, and hence can be modified, whereby another discourse becomes possible, or it is indeed essential and then this other discourse remains only an ideal to try to emulate.

I have no answer to this. Instead, I shall present a specific clinical experience that was also familiar to Freud: it is surely no coincidence that neurotics always belong to the category of people who try to be too moral, who—as Freud put it—want to be better than they ever can be. The end of the treatment becomes therefore not so much the creation of a new morality, but more the creative assumption, the taking upon oneself of a previously existing, arbitrary ethic, that until then had only been followed or fought against. And this, too, is a choice.

36. See the novel *The Treatment*, by Daniel Menaker, Knopf, 1998.

theory and practice. Both Lacan and Freud became preeminent master figures, so that it is enough simply to cite them to turn an argument into a truth, a sin my own work occasionally falls into as well although I try to avoid this as much as I can.

Psychosis and the University Discourse

Applying the psychoanalytic model according to the terms of the university discourse like this will inevitably mean choosing certain contents from this model. It is not by chance that in the subsequent paradigmatic decay, the focus is on the first Freud, that of the scientist, thereby avoiding the deadlocks of the second. This is what post-Freudianism illustrates: certain ideas are picked out from the first theory and become subsequently generalized. The first angle, that of the trauma and its defense, for instance, appears in those approaches to psychosis that in one way or another foreground a particular parental intervention as the causal factor for psychosis. This is, amongst others, typical of a certain Anglo-American approach to Freud and psychosis (Freud 1978 [1911c]). His standard model, Schreber, had a father who is described as a Prussian fanatic of indoor gymnastics, with a taste for a variety of sadistic instruments. He then forms the cause, the external traumatic cause, of his son's psychotic pathology, an idea upon which two successful plays were actually based. It is clear that this approach is not only insufficient, but even wrong (Schreber 2000).

The same idea—psychosis based on defense against an external etiological agent—can be found in another, if less immediately recognizable manner from an area that analysts usually reject as foreign to their discipline, namely, the field of organically caused psychoses. The logic remains the same: an organically caused psychosis implies a biological agent that the subject has fallen victim to—analysis is superfluous here and analysts leave the field free for the medical doctors. But this is also wrong, because even the so-called somatic psychosis cannot unilaterally be explained merely by appealing to an external etiological agent. For an example, we can look to the previously discussed icon of such an approach, that is, paralytic dementia. Its relative rarity today means one forgets that only a small percentage of syphilitic patients developed paralytic dementia (Ey et al. 1974, pp. 835–836). The somatic etiology seems inadequate for explaining this psychosis. This goes for every psychopathology that invariably must be considered a result of a complex interaction between dispositional and environmental factors, in addition to which, moreover, we must also take the subject's choice into account.

The second approach—when to defend—will be also be developed in the post-Freudian period as an explanation for psychosis. Here we see the theory of object relations and the libidinal developmental stages. With this, Abraham's original vision has been forgotten and suddenly everyone is convinced that psychosis must be the earliest established pathology, going even as far back as the prenatal stage. Therapy becomes a question of a monitored regression to this stage when things went wrong, followed by a monitored progression to genital normality. This approach is also inadequate, albeit only because it cannot explain the emergence of psychosis at a later date. This way of thinking, moreover, inevitably leads to the idea, along the lines of Melanie Klein, that everyone possesses a "psychotic nucleus" which, under the right conditions, will come to light; thus there is no structural difference between the neurotic and the psychotic positions.[37]

The third perspective—how to defend—was developed primarily by Anna Freud, with her famous *The Ego and the Mechanisms of Defence* (1979). Ego psychology will be founded on it, culminating in the analysis of defense. For psychosis, projection was initially put forward as the characteristic mechanism, but the vagueness of this concept, combined with its generalized nature, meant that this was abandoned fairly quickly. In its place, we commonly get nothing more than the pronouncement, "psychotic defenses," which are then usually specified by saying they concern processes that were established "very early on" and have every chance of opening pathways to "regression." In other words, despite the lack of an individual mechanism, the idea that a specific mechanism of defense lies and must lie at the root of psychosis is maintained.

The same idea can be found in certain Lacanian approaches to psychosis. It has, in the meantime, become fairly well known that Lacan offered the mechanism of foreclosure as a working hypothesis and guiding concept for research. Today it seems as if this hypothesis has already deteriorated into an established and hence confirmable knowledge.

---

37. Along these lines, we get, not all that rarely unfortunately, the following conclusion to a diagnostic inquiry: "The patient shows a neurotic upper structure with an underlying psychotic layer." All that is missing now is perversion.

Psychosis is the expression of a special kind of neurosis, meaning within the reign of the signifier. In addition, the clinical aspects become immensely narrowed down: it is a matter of *the* foreclosure and *the* psychosis, exemplified by the binding model of Schreber. The incontrovertible heterogeneity of the clinic is not reflected in the theory, so that the plea one hears everywhere for a structural approach ultimately comes down to the already-mentioned historically datable idea of the unitary psychosis. Lacan himself was much more nuanced: "It can be argued—albeit not without some hesitation—that clinical types arise from structures. Only in the case of the hysterical discourse is this certain and transferable" (Lacan 2001, p. 557).

The Place of the Subject

The diversity of these types of theories carries with it the risk that a certain vital question gets overlooked: What is the place and role of the subject itself in the development of its psychopathology? As we saw earlier, the University discourse inevitably results in an objectifying approach, resulting in both the exoneration and infantilization of the patient. Freud offered a more nuanced perspective from the start: both dispositional factors and the environment are influential, but the patient him- or herself also has some element of choice in the pathogenesis. Hence the idea that the patient is supposed to take an active role in the treatment. What happens to this view after Freud?

To my knowledge, Janet, a contemporary of Freud's, was the first to take aim at this idea when he described psychoanalysis as "a criminal inquiry which must find a culprit, a past event responsible for the manifested troubles."[38] Here we find two possibilities for the deterioration. Either the patient is once again exonerated, and something or someone else lies at the root of the pathology; or the patient him or herself is blamed as the sole cause of his or her pathology. In both cases the complexity of Freud's theory is lost.[39] The exoneration is well-

---

38. Janet (1921), *Les méditations psychologiques*, p. 224, quoted in Roudinesco (1986, p. 252).
39. In Part II, on the formation of identity, I will show how this complexity has to do with another conception of the relationship between I and Other or the inside and outside.

known, it is the famous unhappy childhood that is taken into account as mitigating circumstances. Blaming the patient (see above with Szasz) is rarer, but it is there whenever depression is said to come down to a moral mistake and cowardice on the patient's part. We even find this in Freud, specifically in the *Studies on Hysteria*, where he talks about a relation between moral courage and cowardice in the emergence of hysteria, an idea that Lacan takes up again with regard to depression in *Television* (1990 [1974]).[40]

It thus becomes clear how every paradigmatic application of the University discourse—regardless of its theoretical and actual content—has a central impact on the position of the patient. This impact has far-reaching repercussions, both for the diagnostics as for the treatment, both of which—no matter how scientific and objective they may appear—always imply the adoption of an ethical position.

---

40. "Thus the mechanism which produces hysteria represents on the one hand an act of moral cowardice [. . .]; more frequently, of course, we shall conclude that a greater amount of moral courage would have been of advantage to the person concerned" (Freud and Breuer, 1978 [1895d], *SE* 2, p. 123). "For example, we qualify sadness as depression, [. . .] But it isn't a state of the soul, it is simply a moral failing, as Dante, and even Spinoza, said: a sin, which means a moral weakness, which is, ultimately, located only in relation to thought" (Lacan 1990 [1974], p. 22).

5
Conclusion: The Need for a Metapsychology

On the basis of Part I of this book, I can put forward the following conclusion: *every paradigm offers its own specific way of handling the question of guilt*. The question of etiology is a scientific and hence unblemished renaming of the quest for a culprit whose two extremities are the exoneration of the subject by way of an external causality, and the blaming of the subject through an internal causality.

We can deplore this, complain about it, reject it, and so on. In so doing, we run the risk of bypassing a ubiquitous clinical reality, namely, that every psychopathology, indeed every psyche, centers around this question of guilt. To sum up, the central theme in Sophocles' *Oedipus Rex* is not so much the well-known murder and incest story; that is already history when the tragedy begins. The central question is the quest for the culprit, and its irony is that he who searches is himself the guilty party. Immediately following on from this comes the well-known rule of thumb: the patient with a sense of illness is neurotic; the psychotic is the one in whom this is missing; the pervert is the one who denies it. Retranslated this means: the one who displays *a sense of guilt* is neurotic—as with Oedipus; the one who doesn't is psychotic; the one who denies guilt is perverse.

Consequently, it is the neurotic subject who deserves our help. The perverse subject, with its rejection of guilt, is quickly shunted off to the criminal side. The psychotic, in his or her radical difference, becomes stigmatized as uncanny, as not being one of us. Moreover, the question of whether manic-depressive disorders can be considered part of psychosis is representative of this: the manic-depressive patient does indeed have a sense of guilt, but is it so exaggerated that it is no longer credible.

The classic explanation for this ubiquity is that this sense of guilt is a culturally determined and hence contingent inheritance of Judeo-Christian culture (from original sin to the Flood, mea culpa, mea maxima culpa), and that this would have been different under another, better cultural background. This argument is too limited: the sense of guilt remains just as central in Eastern cultures, with the concept of karma for example, or in the Japanese concept of *On*.[1] Duyckaerts (1988) reminds us of Lerner's ingenious experiments that demonstrated over and over again that, as far as the observer is concerned, the victim is always the guilty party and gets what he or she deserves, and this—within the setup of the experiments—in the face of all reality. The conviction that everyone gets what they deserve is deeply rooted.[2]

Hence these paradigms' mistake is not that they inevitably revolve around the question of guilt. Their mistake is that each paradigm itself is nothing but a defensive, disguised *answer* to this question of guilt, just like the answers of the patients themselves. In this sense, our science is nothing but a culturally shared fiction that provides an answer to a private fiction. Nevertheless, we expect more from a scientific approach. If we wish to construct a clinical and differential diagnostics, then we have to take the following as a basic starting point: *How does a particular subject handle the question of guilt?*

In order to answer this question, we need two things. First, we need to elaborate a metapsychology that gives the relationship between subject and other a central place, most particularly in relation to the

---

1. An unforgettable description of *On*, an untranslatable term expressing the Japanese concept of guilt, can be found in Ruth Benedict's *The Chrysanthemum and the Sword* (1988).

2. M. J. Lerner (1980), *The Belief in a Just World: A Fundamental Delusion*, pp. xv, 209, cited and discussed in Duyckaerts (1988).

question of guilt. We will redefine this as the subject's relation to the structural lack in the Symbolic (the Other) with respect to the Real of the drive. Such a theory, constructed preferably in accordance with the demands of contemporary science, belongs of necessity to the University discourse. Here we encounter a second necessity: in its clinical application, we must make the radical choice for the discourse of the Analyst, during the diagnostic phase as well. Its formula demonstrates its difference both from the Master and the University discourses:

$$\uparrow \frac{a}{S_2} \quad \genfrac{}{}{0pt}{}{\rightarrow}{//} \quad \frac{S}{S_1} \downarrow$$

Its fundamental difference from the two other discourses is that the emphasis is put on the subject's division that is caused by its inner drive, creating S_1 as the product. To the extent that the therapist is attributed this position, she or he can only assume it as a subject that is *supposed* to know (*le sujet-supposé-savoir*). It is precisely this attribution that gets the patient to speak, enabling the knowledge S_2—located expressly in the patient—to come to the surface.

To apply this discourse is less of a technical matter than an explicit ethical choice in favor of a certain social bond that is radically different from that of the University or the Master discourse. In this sense it cannot easily be taught, having everything to do with the way the clinician as a subject has assumed a certain relationship toward authority and knowledge. To put it differently: it has to do with the extent to which the clinician can handle his or her own pleasure and anxiety. Consequently, in what follows I will focus on what can indeed be taught, namely the metapsychology that is indispensable for it.

WHAT IS THE AIM OF CLINICAL PSYCHODIAGNOSTICS?

This question is so obvious that it is hardly ever asked. A facetious answer might be that the aim of psychodiagnostic investigation is to fill the archives. That this is still all too often the case has to do precisely with the fact that this question is hardly ever posed. This is why it is our first point. One doesn't need much experience to conclude that, independently of the stated goal, at least two different kinds of psychodiagnostics exist: a juridical-social one and a clinical psychodiagnostics. Mixing the two together ends in insurmountable difficulties, which is why the difference between them must be explained.

Juridical-social Diagnostics

As far as juridical-social diagnostics and its associated aims are concerned, we must first note how, until a couple of decades ago, clinical psychiatry in Belgium (and in most West European countries) belonged to the Department of Justice, and was only fairly recently shifted to the Department of Public Health. Hence it was only recently that patients officially became patients; previously, they belonged to the group of marginals and deviants who fell under the custody of legal jurisdiction. You can read about it in Foucault's *Madness and Civilization*.

Against such a background, psychological abnormality is synonymous with the idea of social deviance, in which someone harms himself or a third party and therefore needs psychiatric treatment. The aim is clearly the protection of the social order; the care of the patient itself only comes in afterward. The proceedings run from probation, to obligatory psychotherapy, to collocation. The nosological categories here are well-known: perversions, addictions, and everything that is summed up under the heading of psychopathy. The common denominator is the fact that the patient fails to live up to the juridically established norm. In more contemporary language—psychopathy has a bit of an obsolete ring these days—we find the so-called personality disorders, particularly the antisocial, narcissistic, and borderline personality disorders that are, incidentally, found in combination more often than not in clinical practice. To explain this in terms of co-morbidity is not so much to solve it (although it is presented in that way), but rather evidence of the failure of this approach.

The expression we just used—"the juridically established norm"—evinces the arbitrariness of this approach.[3] The norm here is nothing other than the law, in the sense of the penal code that hereby acquires

---

3. Arbitrariness, that is, from the clinical perspective. In the field of jurisdiction, such norms are established preferably according to the rules of democratic proceedings.

an apparently nosological character. It entails a double arbitrariness: on the one hand this law differs from state to state and is variable over time; on the other hand, this law only becomes operative in the event of harm, either of the third party or of the person himself. Where there is no harm, there is no cause for a juridical intervention, despite the existence of a clear psychopathology.

The difficulties with this kind of diagnostics and its accompanying aim are well known. Here we are confronted with the problem of accountability on the one hand and the practice of enforced psychotherapy on the other. Today it's not the least bit unusual for a judge to call in the assistance of a psy-expert to establish the guilt or otherwise of the accused. I get the impression that on occasion this boils down to something like a game of ping-pong where the judge, as the representative of the social order, passes his or her responsibility onto a supposedly "expert other" who then, rather than the judge, is responsible for the decision. Moreover, this entails a common misunderstanding: explaining a behavior is not synonymous with accepting it. For Freud, the subject always remains responsible, even for its unconscious productions, meaning that madness has its own ethical limit too. However, the judging and the psychoanalytic/psychotherapeutic positions are impossible to reconcile with one another.

In clinical praxis, enforced psychotherapy is unfortunately all too well known. The judge sends the exhibitionist, the addict, and so on to the expert, whose mission is to "do something about it!" But if the demand doesn't come from the patient him or herself, the clinician is butting up against a brick wall, making both diagnosis and treatment impossible. Indeed, she or he will typically be regarded as an arm of the authorities. The result is that the patient either reacts passive-aggressively or with a falsely cooperative attitude. Both situations make a genuine diagnosis impossible. The only solution is to turn this inoperative relation into one of trust between the therapist and patient who, in the best-case scenario, then generates the demand him- or herself. But success is far from guaranteed.

Such a juridical diagnostics is ultimately nothing other than the legal manifestation of something that can be found, if only obliquely, in every society. Every socius possesses its own intuitive diagnostics that it applies to the other according to the norms of the larger social group that he or she belongs to. The same instrument is always used to measure the other, that is, the ideal image one has of oneself. If the other matches it, he or she is accepted as normal; if not, rejection will follow.

At the bottom of such a practice lies an anxiety about the other's otherness and, especially, anxiety about the other in oneself. Such a separation consequently aims rather at avoiding questions about one's own psychic division and its accompanying problems. To put it briefly, one looks for reassurance in conformity, and forgets the parable about the fly who, seeing a large assembly of its confrères, rushes to join them only to find itself dangling from the flypaper a few minutes later.

This conformity reveals its hidden intent, namely, the protection of one's own security; here, by calling the otherness in the other bad or ill or abnormal, one identifies oneself as good or well or normal. It is not hard to see how this might lead to racism. One only hopes that its juridical and hence symbolic manifestations are attentive to such things.

Clinical Psychodiagnostics

Contrasted with this juridical diagnostics is clinical psychodiagnostics. The norm here is the subject itself who comes with a demand for help; diagnosis and treatment are one inseparable totality. It is only in this form that genuine clinical therapeutic work becomes possible.

Note that someone might be deviant on the juridical-social level, but that this does not necessarily produce a demand for help. Conversely, someone can seem perfectly normal at that level but nevertheless make a clear demand for help. Examples are rife. Just think of those people who appear to have everything, who seem completely adapted, but who then suddenly commit suicide. In contrast are those who develop symptoms but never ask help for them. A friend—a radiologist—once told me that he saw patients suffering claustrophobic attacks in his office on a weekly basis (it must be admitted that his office lent itself rather well to this). In response to his by now standard question of why they didn't seek help for it, he always got the same answer from them "I don't think I need it." The idea that for the subject a symptom can represent a form of solution failed to add up in this medically educated expert's mind.

The chief difficulty in the clinical field proper thus has to do with the absence of a demand for help from those people who nevertheless display obvious problems. Classic in this respect are psychotic patients, addicts, and among young people almost every psychological-educational problem.[4] The clinician's job is additionally more complex here: he or she must first of all succeed in gaining the patient's confidence and then find out whether a demand exists in the patient him- or herself.

Reducing the diagnosis to clinical diagnostics is doubtless just that, a reduction that possesses a certain form of treatment or counseling as its aim. The clinical field is wider than just the psycho-therapeutic field. The residential clinic in particular also carries a medical and social aspect. Nevertheless it seems clear that counselors who try to handle of all these aspects at the same time ultimately succeed in doing nothing. Indeed, reduction has pure practicality in mind here. No one can be a psychotherapist, a social worker, a judge, and a medical doctor at the same time.

In our approach, it is the patient and his or her demand that are made central. It is only by doing this that the clinical combination of diagnosis and treatment becomes possible. The question now becomes one that concerns our metapsychology. What should one avoid, what ought one to aim for?

PITFALLS TO AVOID

Three things must be avoided at all costs if we want to arrive at a useful metapsychology for clinical psychodiagnostics. To put it facetiously: botanics, Lady Justice, and the archive.

First, *avoid drowning in a phenomenology of externally observable phenomena*. The call for a back-to-basics in observation, for starting out from a tabula rasa, has always been an illusion; one sees only what one was taught to see. Theory, even etymologically speaking, is what conducts the voyage, telling us what to look at, from Herodotus to Baedeker to Michelin—hence the importance of a good travel guide (Van Hoorde

---

4. This confronts us with the question of the patient's autonomy and his or her own right to decide. Psychotherapy, as we understand it, presupposes such an autonomy. When the patient does not have a demand of his or her own, we enter another discourse where the ever-problematic conjunction between the clinical and the juridical field is explicitly brought into central focus.

1987). The seemingly objective classification of externally observable phenomena is arbitrary and ultimately leads to the clearest form of the Master discourse: "go and name the things." The saga of the DSM also serves us as a warning here: the predictable side-effects are an exhausting fragmentation of the complaint, desubjectivation and "statistiatry" rather than psychiatry. This can only result in a psychodiagnostic botanics that is of little use in clinical practice.

Second, *avoid value judgments*. To make a diagnosis on the basis of desirable or undesirable behavior, adapted or unadapted behavior, is merely social conformity and belongs more properly to the social-juridical order. The first part of this book was a structural presentation of the consequences inherent in the paradigmatic applications, that is, the accusatory or exculpatory effect in combination with the infantilization of the subject. Making a value judgment for a diagnosis, moreover, loses sight of an essential point—namely, that the symptom can be comprehended as a subject's attempt at stabilizing something within its preexisting structure. This blind spot has a clear connection with the first point of caution: any phenomenological screening that takes place independently of a theory can only measure symptoms in terms of adaptation and desirability. Consequently, the ensuing treatment will be solely focused on the elimination of the unadapted behavior, without regard for or, even worse, counter to the psychic structure of subject.

Third: *ensure that there are therapeutic effects*. Here, too, a clear connection can be made between the two previous pitfalls. From (1), the simple enumeration of symptoms, one arrives at (2), a negative value judgment disguised as a diagnosis, resulting in (3), the fact that therapy can only be an exercise in the suppression or removal of symptoms. As far as I'm concerned, these are not therapeutic consequences, but an enterprise in enforcing social conformity. Nor, in most cases, will any attention be paid to the etiology. The sorry result of such a psychodiagnostics is that its primary purpose is to fill the archives.

This last pitfall is doubtless the most dangerous and, unfortunately, also the most frequent. Recent research constantly stresses how vitally important it is that the diagnostics be meaningful for the ensuing treatment (Schotte and De Doncker 2000; Vertommen 1996). Nevertheless in scientific practice the entire focus is on the empirical validation of test-diagnostic instruments. This is in itself not a bad thing, but scarcely any attention is paid to the need for a metapsychology for understanding the subject of the diagnosis. In clinical practice, it still happens far too often that a patient must first undergo a careful and lengthy diagnostic procedure, based on the specific diagnostic traditions of a particular institution or center. An extensive diagnostic report follows, written and discussed during the team meeting. Then comes the treatment, which runs according to the long-standing traditions of that particular institution or center, that is to say, *almost completely independently of the diagnostic process*. In fact, without that diagnostic procedure, the patient would have been subjected to the very same treatment anyway. And it is not at all uncommon for the therapist then to repeat, at least partially, the diagnostic phase, albeit this time from his or her own angle and therapeutic approach.

Treatment—A Clinical Example

To clarify the connection between the aims of the diagnostic procedure and the treatment, here is a clinical example. Since 1995, "Education projects for violent sexual offenders" have been installed in Belgium, aimed at offering alternative measures instead of punishments to sexual perpetrators. The referrals, primarily for cases of exhibitionism, rape, and incest, usually come from the Department of Justice. Experience shows that the referrals are made because of transgressive behavior and, particularly, that the severity of the proceedings is linked to the seriousness of the transgression. From this perspective, for example, rape is regarded as worse than exhibitionism. The latter is usually referred for an average of three months, while rapists get a period of three years. The experience of clinical workers in this area nevertheless is the exact opposite. Rapists frequently display a relatively normal personality profile, while exhibitionists nearly always possess very complex personality disorders. Translating a juridical diagnosis (based on the observation of unadapted behavior and focused on relapse prevention) into a clinical psycho-diagnosis (aimed at the underlying problem of the subject in order to change this) absolutely doesn't work. Needed alongside and following the juridical diagnosis is a clinical psycho-diagnosis, whose additional difficulty is that the client must, in the first instance, be motivated to cooperate. In such a psycho-diagnosis, a distinction between paraphiliac traits and perverse structures (see Chapter 14 below) is of decisive importance for predicting the possibility of change. This is precisely why we need a metapsychology.

POSITIVE CHARACTERIZATIONS FOR TREATMENT

The essential requirements can be given as follows. One, clinical psychodiagnostics has to be based *on a developmental perspective*. Two, such diagnostics must be founded *on the relationship between subject and Other*.[5] This must, as a consequence, produce three, *a formal-logical structure founded on an etiological analysis*.

These three requirements form a single whole consistent with clinical practice. Indeed, the subject's identity develops in relation to the Other and this has immediate effects on the way he or she relates to all others.[6] The source of a symptom, indeed of a psychopathology, has to be sought in the modalities of these relationships. Through the transference, the treatment becomes a repetition of this relation between subject and other, aimed precisely at changing it.

This way of thinking is primarily characterized by its difference from diagnoses that are restricted to the "personality," and by the fact that it takes the Other fully into account. It suffices to recall our earlier example of the joyriding son. Even with such a seemingly restricted phenomenon, it soon became clear that the diagnosis could not be limited to the individual, but had to take the wider situation into account, preferably in structural terms. Today, such an approach is more or less present in practically every clinical psychological theory, although often only implicitly. It is found most explicitly in Lacanian psychoanalysis ("The Unconscious is the discourse of the Other") and in systemic therapy (the scapegoat, the carrier of the symptom). But even in

---

5. The concept of the Other comes from Lacan's theory of subject-formation. It denotes firstly the most important others—the parental figures—and subsequently everyone else who follows in their footsteps as a significant other. But it also refers to language, because of the way these others' influence manifests itself through words. In this way, the highly abstract concept of "the Other" is at the same time quite empirical.

6. Lacan expresses this as follows: "the realization of the subject in his signifying dependence in the locus of the Other" (Lacan 1994 [1964], p. 206).

the cognitive approach, the other is normally taken into account too, although largely only because the emphasis of this approach on the learning processes means it cannot do without the figure of the other—one learns from, for, or in opposition to someone.[7]

Dependence on the Other

The developmental perspective is clear. The intent of clinical psychodiagnostics is to make conclusions about a person's psychological identity. Such an identity is not there from day one, but acquires form and content through a never-ending relationship with others. The very first layer of identity has its origin in the mirror stage, where the child identifies with the complete image presented by the other: "Thou art that" (Lacan 1977 [1949], p. 7). As we will see later, the ensuing development runs along similar lines, alternating continuously between alienation (coinciding with the other) and separation (keeping one's distance from the other).

This means that the foundation of development boils down to the subject's relation of dependence on the Other. The subject must identify with the image presented by the other, that is to say, it must identify itself with the desire of the Other. The mirror stage shows us the ground layer and, hence, the very first alienation, but the constitution of identity goes much further than this purely specular aspect. Identity formation also means that the subject must identify with the image that is presented through the *words* of the other. Speech takes on here the primary weight, not so much as a way of communicating, but as a source of identity. Consequently, the Other is not just the flesh-and-blood

---

7. A fortiori, this also applies for clinical training. In our field, a scientific background is a necessary but not in itself complete prerequisite. During the reform of psychiatric training in Holland, the so-called master–pupil relationship was raised as one of the most important mainstays of the training. This can be entirely understood by way of the theory of identity formation, in the sense that the trainee acquires a new relationship toward others (the patients) through an Other (his medical psychiatric master, Pinel's *chef de clinique*). This also shows that there is always something that escapes any knowledge that is expressible in words, and that this something is evidently essential for clinical practice.

other but, more specifically, the speaking other. Above all, this Other is not unidimensional, far from it. Every child is faced with opposing desires, emanating from the father, the mother, and others. Choosing one means *not* choosing the other, with the result that such a choice is burdened with conflict and finally comes down to the question "Who do you love best?" One can always find the traces of such conflict in future pathologies.

All this demands further discussion. In the meantime, on the basis of the foregoing, we can simply stress the following: psychic identity is not something static and unchangeable. Quite the opposite in fact. It is a continuous, dynamic, developmental conglomerate of symbolic processes centered around an identification mechanism, known today as "social learning." The idea of an auto-constitutive, quasi-permanent personality gets completely shaken up. Immediately we find the grounds here for the possibility of psychic change. And indeed this, too, will occur within the context of a relation, more particularly in the "therapeutic alliance"—meaning the transference.

Such a view of development is not, however, without its own difficulties. A first such difficulty concerns the temporal aspect. In genetic psychology, one studies the development of a number of psychic functions in the various stages of childhood. The concepts of maturation, retarded and advanced development, regression, progression, and fixation are all central notions here. Such expressions already show how a purely linear model of development doesn't ring true in practice. The idea of a succession of stages, each following the next in a fully baked sequence, simply doesn't add up with clinical experience. Freud initially tried to construct a chronological-causal logic too, a type of *post hoc ergo propter hoc* (after and because of X comes Y). He had to give up this idea, precisely because of his clinical experience. In the end, he was to discover that the unconscious has no concept of time.[8]

---

8. Freud elaborated this in a well-known archaeological metaphor in which he posits that all previous elements are maintained in the psychic function, next to and by way of newer ones (Freud 1978 [1930], pp. 69–71). It is only with the post-Freudians that this becomes formalized into stages. Here is Lacan's comment on this: "Ferenczi is the one who started to put the famous stages into everyone's heads. Freud refers to it. [. . .] Ferenczi brought him something, and he made use of it. [. . .] In taking up this structural point of view, we are directly following Freud, because that is where he ended up. [. . .] Actually, what Freud always insisted upon was exactly

Here we come up against the need for an alternative temporal sequence, where what occurred before only acquires meaning from what follows, and where the meaning of the past is only "virtual" and can therefore be rewritten. The naive argument, that a traumatic event at 3 years old inevitably has an effect twenty years on, is certainly naive and, in principle, undemonstrable. The case is rather the opposite: at a specific stage of one's life, an earlier event can acquire a traumatic meaning in the light of subsequent information whose influence is always exercised through signifiers. This is the effect of an already mentioned Freudian concept, *Nachträglichkeit*, or retroactivity.[9]

This immediately reveals the linguistic slant of our view of development: a signifier acquires (always provisional) meaning from the context of other signifiers, such that the addition of new signifiers immediately brings with it a change in meaning. In Saussure's structural linguistics, meaning comes into being retroactively from the "quilting point" (*le point de capiton*), and every signifier gains meaning only from its context. As far as the subject's identity is concerned, one effect of this ever-expanding chain of meaning is that identity changes in accordance with each adjustment of the chain.

A straightforward developmental logic is therefore difficult to maintain. In clinical psychodiagnostics we always have to deal with a previously constructed development. This was, for example, also Stern's finding (1985) regarding Mahler's (1968) idea of symbiosis: it is practically invisible in small children but in adults can be reconstructed and has enormous relevance for the clinic. In Lacan, the expression "development" is absent; he always speaks in terms of the future, the subject's realization.

The second difficulty with regard to development is that with this idea one inevitably falls back into the impasse of the question of guilt. To the extent that psychic identity and psychopathology have to do with development, there must also be something like a pathological

---

the opposite, namely the preservation, at every level, of what may be considered as different stages" (1991 [1953–1954], p. 127–128). This discussion is continued in Seminar XI in dialogue with F. Dolto (1994 [1964]).

9. Lacan elaborates this in his "mathemes." The relevant text, "Subversion of the Subject and the dialectic of desire," is anything but simple; for an excellent commentary, see Van Haute (2002).

development. The next step to guilt becomes more or less unavoidable, resulting in the previously discussed opposition between an approach that exonerates and, accordingly, desubjectivizes the subject, and an approach that subjectivizes and therefore blames the subject. As we have already seen, a paradigmatic deteriorization can manifest itself in one of two ways. Either the Other is exonerated, and the patient him or herself is blamed for the symptoms, or the patient is completely freed of all blame and the guilt lies in the other, whether the other may be the environment or the body.

In both cases, one goes beyond the clinic as such: Who would deny that parents and family have an influence on children, a pathological influence if need be? In reverse, who would deny that children are always putting their own stamp on their surroundings, and thereby helping to create their own environment? We find both these experiential possibilities in the Freudian term the "*choice* of neurosis." The word choice cannot be taken literally here because that would imply the idea of a conscious choice with which this has nothing to do at all. Lacan will revisit this in his discussion of the logical "*vel*": an either/or choice that is no choice at all, as in "your money or your life" (Lacan 1994 [1964], pp. 209–213).

Such an impasse mainly has to do with the dual nature of the two alternatives: one of them must have done "it." From a psychoanalytic perspective, this deadlock can be escaped through centralizing the cause of the question of guilt, that is, the underlying lack in relation to which a position must be chosen. Later we will see how, in the course of this positioning, both the subject and the other acquire content and identity.

The Basis of Relation

The second positive characteristic of our project concerns the necessity of basing clinical psychodiagnostics on the *relation* between the subject and the Other. The perspective described above could still be interpreted as a process that forms the basis of the development of a core personality that can subsequently be described in categorical terms. This is far from our intent. Even from the perspective of a developmental model it is clear that it is more a question of the core relation between the subject and the Other.

Conclusion: The Need for a Metapsychology 141

Such a description immediately calls to mind the idea of an interactive "two-bodies psychology" that attempts to chart the different interpersonal relationships. Such an approach is bound to fail, simply because the relationship we are talking about cannot be located between two "personalities." On the contrary, from a clinical point of view, we are always dealing with the divided subject, and therefore with a relation between two divisions. Furthermore, the first relation is internal to the subject (the relation to the other in oneself, that is, to the drive). In addition, there is also an external relation (that between the divided subject and the also divided Other). In view of the fact that the external dialogue experiences the effects of the internal relation and vice versa, a completely different perception of inside and outside, both of self and Other, needs to be developed.

The relation with the foregoing is easy to see: the relational aspect emerges in the dialectic between the subject and the Other, where it is constantly being elaborated and extended. This fact was the basis for one of the most important of Freud's discoveries, namely, the transference.

The transference is classically understood in terms of love–hate relationships, to which Lacan added a third, the passion of not-wanting-to-know. Such a partitioning has the disadvantage of sliding too rapidly into a push-me–pull-you effect, thereby reducing transference to a mere repetition of a supposedly original love or hate relationship toward the parents. It is far more instructive to understand love in terms of "having the need for" and hate in terms of "keeping one's distance from." Considered thus, love can be interpreted in terms of being directed toward symbiosis (Eros), and hate toward separation (Thanatos). The third trend (not-wanting-to-know) has to do with the division of the subject and the way this division appears in the relation with the Other concerning knowledge. This latter might seem a little strange at first sight. It becomes slightly less so once we realize that every treatment, regardless of what form it takes, always implies a learning process that takes place precisely in the relation between the subject and the Other. In this sense, a certain relation toward knowledge is of particular importance to the success of a treatment. This relation has little or nothing to do with the patient's intelligence and everything to do with his or her relation toward the Other whose knowledge is either accepted or rejected.

This is why the structural aspect in the transference acquires a special emphasis, as this is what will gain shape through what is known as the *fundamental fantasy*, the cognitive-affective script through which we approach the world. Without question, this contains a repetitive aspect, but it also simultaneously opens up the possibility for creating something new. Again, I am referring to the importance of the way the divided subject acquires its identity by way of the speaking Other. It is on this basis that the subject takes certain positions both in relation to itself and toward the other, from whence the treatment can entail both a repetition and the possibility for change. Always lying in the background of such a relationship is the most important clinical phenomenon: anxiety. This aspect requires constant attention. A positive transference in this respect shouldn't be understood so much in terms of love, but rather in terms of an orientation toward symbiosis and identification. Conversely, a negative transference is not so much hate, but an orientation toward separation and expulsion. Both forms of transferential relationship closely adhere to a specific manifestation of the underlying anxiety, whether it is separation anxiety, or an anxiety about being reduced to the passive position.

The final question concerning transference is, then, What attitude does the divided subject take toward the divided other: alienation or separation? As we will see later on, this position concerns two important elements, namely gender and authority.

Three Relational Structures

In conclusion, we can formulate the aim of clinical psychodiagnostics as follows: to derive on the basis of an etiological reasoning the formal-logical structure of the subject's relation toward its drive and toward the Other. The intention is thus not to categorize personalities but to study structural relationships. What position does a subject take in relation to the Other with respect to lack? What is the connection between this positioning and the subject's symptoms? What can be changed in this relationship in order to change the symptoms?

The advantage to such an approach is its coherence with the etiology, diagnostics, and treatment. A potential psychopathology emerges from and concerns the relation between the subject and the Other, is diagnosed on this basis, and must be changed through the dialectic of the transference. The entire process, moreover, occurs through the same medium, language, which is both the source of identity and the working instrument par excellence for diagnosis and treatment.

In anticipation of our later discussion, we can already identify three such relational structures: that of the neurotic, the pervert, and the psychotic. Each implies a different relation toward the Other, that is to say, toward the lack in the Other. The symptoms must be understood in terms of this relationship, and—despite some apparent resemblances—may be very different, depending on the structure through which they appear. Since this relation is founded on language, which forms the basis for subject-formation, each of these structures will imply a different way of being-in-language. This too, along with the relation toward the Other, will be of decisive importance for both the diagnosis and the treatment.

CONCLUSION: THE CATEGORICAL VERSUS THE PARTICULAR

A clinical psychodiagnostic theory that ultimately produces only three structures is at first sight a little disappointing. Where is the diversity of the clinic? How can one, with only three keys, do justice to the particularity of each individual patient? Where should we locate depression, where do clients suffering from addiction find a place, what about borderline cases? The fact that we will subsequently understand these omnipresent clinical phenomena from the starting point of the three structures of the subject (and not as separate structures in themselves) doesn't really answer this criticism very satisfactorily. A structural diagnosis is useful only if it can be situated between two other approaches: the categorical, on the one hand, and the particular, on the other.

The categorical diagnostics is more or less synonymous with the traditional psychiatric nomenclature, albeit dressed up in today's clothes. Nowadays one will, for the most part, have to call upon the DSM headings for this category. Experience shows that the processes by which this DSM categorization is reached are usually more interesting than the final result. Most clinicians today agree that a DSM diagnosis in itself only narrowly relates to the subsequent treatment.

Accordingly, the result of this categorical diagnostics is never enough. We need a proper clinical psychodiagnostics that enables us to clearly state the structural relation that the subject takes toward the Other. Moreover, this statement should simultaneously enable us to make conclusions about the potential possibilities or impossibilities for treatment.

This does not mean that the psychodiagnostic inquiry is over at this point. The subsequent and even imperative next step concerns particularity: a particular subject possessing a certain structure (whether neurotic, psychotic, or perverse) will produce a completely unique implementation of this structural relationship. The diagnostic process, which in most cases will already form part of the treatment at this point, will have to explore the particularity of this specific subject in his or her relation to the Other; therefore the diagnostic process will have to go back to the particular history of this relationship. To the extent that this third part of the psychodiagnostic inquiry contains a form of categorization, it will always be a categorization in which $N = 1$.

Myths and Unique Content

This reciprocity between the universal and the particular is our reply to the persistent temptation offered by the paradigmatic position, which reduces the patient to an invariant that can exist only on paper. The diagnosis has to be threefold: categorial, structural, and particularizing in terms of content.

Confronted with the same problem, Freud already found a solution: he gestures to foundational myths of a phylogenetic nature (he even invents one himself), which always acquire a particular form in the ontogenesis.[10] In this way, every one of us is an Oedipus, a Narcissus, a primal father, a primal son, a Cordelia, an Isolde. . . . With Jung, this

---

10. It is not by chance that this part of the index in the *Standard Edition* encompasses eight pages; including the list of analogies, it adds up to fourteen (*SE* 14, pp. 177–194). When I call Jung's handling of this "imaginary," I mean that these collective myths or archetypes can serve as a new mythical identificatory image for the patient. This can only result in a further alienation, whose therapeutic results can incidentally be quite positive, belonging to the same order as the catharsis effect in the audience of Greek tragedy in the fifth century before Christ.

imaginary aspect takes on all its weight with the idea of the collective unconscious and, particularly, with the archetypes.

Such a solution contains one big disadvantage: these grounding myths highlight content more than structure, showing a certain frequently moralizing strain. They are, so to speak, too "full" and thus work determinatively in terms of content. As such, they are the very fare of a paradigmatic approach. Thus a therapist speaking enthusiastically about having a "veritable Hamlet" in analysis will probably pay less attention to those aspects for which Hamlet doesn't fit. All we can do is call for a change in emphasis: from the general content to the underlying formal structure that enables one to describe particular, unique contents. Here Lacan's peculiar signs and formulas come in handy, from the algorithm for the fantasy, to the discourse formulas, whose empty structures permit one to fill them in differently for every new clinical encounter.

By way of concluding the first part of this book, we can sum up the basic propositions while indicating at the same time what the reader can expect to encounter in Part II. My approach starts out from the idea that the relation between the subject and the Other is a lasting construction, emerging in the course of the history of the subject and to a certain extent open to change. This relationship comprises the aim of both the clinical psychodiagnostic process and the ensuing treatment. It is striking how one almost always finds the idea of defense here, whether in the form of the classic defense mechanisms, or in today's flashier "coping mechanisms."

This relationship is the framework within which all symptoms, or more broadly all behavior develops, forming the basis through which symptoms and behavior can be understood. A change in this relationship must then also bring about a change at the level of the symptoms. Throughout the different psychological approaches there is still a common element: the subject is largely unconscious of the relation and scarcely knows what it is that drives it.[11] On this basis, becoming conscious of this relational structure can be presented as a first therapeutic

---

11. The idea of unconscious processes and of a so-called "cognitive unconscious" has meanwhile largely been accepted, particularly following its endorsement by neuropsychology.

aim, with the proviso that merely becoming conscious of it is usually not enough to change it.

A psychodiagnostic metapsychological theory offers an image of how such a relationship comes into being. In this we must pay special attention to three very common clinical phenomena: anxiety, repression, and guilt. Part I of this book showed how the question of guilt is surreptitiously implicit in the classical question of etiology; making this explicit can only be a gain. Anxiety and depression are universally present in the clinic and therefore deserve a central place. We will see that we can make important psychodiagnostic distinctions with regard to both that have important repercussions for the treatment.

Once again, these phenomena must be understood in terms of the relation between the subject and the Other. Anxiety, for instance, may involve two completely different aspects of this relationship: separation anxiety on the one hand and anxiety about symbiosis on the other. As we will see, anxiety about losing the other is the most primary of the two and also the most well known. Anxiety about symbiosis, understood as an anxiety about dependence, or anxiety about losing control, is at least as important. Moreover, both forms of anxiety can straightaway be coupled with the question of guilt: Who is responsible for what? Finally, we will understand depression as the effect of a certain failure in the relation between the subject and the Other, through which the subject suffers a loss of identity.

Such a relation comes into being in the course of development during which certain periods are more important than others. This does not imply a linearly determined developmental model, with neatly delineated phases or periods. Instead the two central notions are those of the subject's position and retroactivity. The idea of "positions" comes from Melanie Klein, becoming further elaborated in Lacan. The underlying idea is that everyone acquires a certain position and function in relation to the first others (usually the parents) in the course of development, and that the resulting position can later on be repeated in a structurally formal way with other others. We will distinguish between an actualpathological and a psychopathological position, both of which can be present in the three different structures (neurosis, psychosis, perversion). The concept of retroactivity is originally Freudian, and was taken up again by Lacan. It has, meanwhile, largely been confirmed by studies on declarative memory. It implies that the past is not linearly determined, but is itself determined, and even rewritten, by the present. History must therefore always be read from two directions, where the direction from the present to the past is at least as important as the reverse.

The value of the still-to-be-developed metapsychology and the resulting differential diagnostics (to be addressed in Part III of this book) must be evaluated around our central aim: a clinical psychodiagnostics that must be explicitly relevant to and, hence, conceptually linked to the ensuing treatment. Otherwise it is a gauge for nothing.

II
METAPSYCHOLOGY

Overview

In Part II of this book I will develop the idea that subject-formation has to do with more than just the individual. Identity concerns the way psychological reality comes into being. Psychological reality bends the real into so-called facts, in the sense of "what is made"—the past participle of the Latin verb *facere*—and more specifically, facts that are made for and by a subject in its relation to the Other. For Freud, this has to do with how the subject handles guilt, and hence—from our angle—how it manages its own and the Other's lack. "What lie behind the sense of guilt of neurotics are always psychical realities and never factual ones. What characterizes neurotics is that they prefer psychical to factual reality and react just as seriously to thoughts as normal people do to realities" (Freud 1978 [1912–1913], p. 159).

Described in this way, psychic identity is a largely unconscious representative construction that represents both the subject's and the Other's identities, along with the relation between the two. We will call this the *fundamental fantasy*, an idea that reappears in today's theory of the mind (Gergeley and Watson 1996). The question is, how does the fundamental fantasy, or more broadly, psychic reality—normal or not—come into being?

We will approach this question through a reading of Freud and Lacan. What is striking is how closely contemporary psychoanalytic attachment theory adheres to their theories. This should not be surprising, given their common starting point (the relationship between the subject and the Other), and their shared clinical experience. We will have several occasions to refer to attachment theory here, all the more so because it has meanwhile been empirically validated.

Part II is both literally and figuratively the heart of this book. Given its contents, it is not an easy section. Identity development, or subject-formation, takes place through the mechanism of retroactivity, and its conceptualization is perhaps best approached in the same way. The reader will encounter my frequent advice to refer to earlier and later parts of the book (as cf infra and cf supra). At the end of each chapter I provide a concise summary to help further clarify the key concepts and relations. Here is an overview of what follows.

Chapter 6 sketches out how the subject comes into being in relation to the Other in the primary mother and child relation. From this, it will become clear how identity is always relative, in the sense that it cannot be understood as a substantial and separate entity but rather in terms of a relation where the distinction between the self and the other is not so easy to make.

Chapter 7 devotes special attention to the mechanisms of defense and retroactivity. We will distinguish between a first and a second period, which form the ground for the specific structure of the relation between the subject and the Other. More specifically, this will enable us to make a distinction between an actualpathology and a psychopathology.

Chapter 8 bids goodbye to the linear-chronological form of reasoning to instead present a circular model of subject-formation. Its mechanisms—alienation and separation—bring about two contradictory tendencies, each favoring a different direction in the subject–Other relation, and hence also in diagnostics and treatment.

Chapter 9 discusses something that is usually missing from contemporary psychology: the underlying causality as situated within neo-Darwinian discourse. Here I will show the affinities of this discourse with Freud's theory of the drive, and we will ultimately discover that there is a homologous structure between the drive, the unconscious, and the subject.

Finally, Chapter 10, the conclusion, will reconsider our initial questions regarding anxiety, guilt, and depression in the light of a structural psychodiagnostic theory and in the treatment associated with it.

6
Identity as a Relational Structure

SEPARATION ANXIETY AS STARTING-POINT

One of the classic criticisms of Freud is that he sexualizes everything. What this tends to overlook is the fact that, even as early as the "Project" (1978 [1950a (1895)]), Freud had already come up with a theory of the development of psychological functioning, long before there was any discussion of gender differentiation. For his theory of development, he employs a principle borrowed from psychophysics that will later become known as the pleasure principle, but which was originally called the unpleasure principle.[1] This designation is not

---

1. This unpleasure principle functions alongside the principle of constancy, the latter appearing for the first time in 1893 (see Freud and Breuer 1978 [1893a]). Freud's chief elaboration of this is found in the "Project" (1978 [1950a (1895)]), under the heading of the inertia principle. Originally neurons aim at a complete abreaction of tension until the zero level; this proves impossible because a certain tension is necessary to perform the requisite "specific actions" for survival, hence the change of this aim (= zero) in the attempt to reach a level of tension that is both constant and as low as possible. Here, Freud is clearly referring to Fechner's "universal principle of stability" (Fechner 1873). It achieves its final shape—albeit with difficulty—in 1920 (Freud 1978 [1920g], p. 9 ff).

coincidental, to the contrary in fact. Life is seen as being directed toward the experience of as little unpleasure, that is to say, tension, as possible—hence the idea of the unpleasure principle. A couple of decades later, the same idea will be used as the basis for behavioral psychology and, still later, as the foundation for learning psychology.

Freud's argument in the "Project" is as follows. The starting point for human development is an original experience of unpleasure, called pain (*Schmerz*), which is the consequence of an internal need whose prototypes are hunger and thirst.[2] Freud understands this pain as an accumulation of tension, resulting in a breakthrough of the stimuli through the so-called protective shields (*Reizschutz*), just as in cases of physical injury (Freud 1978 [1950a (1895)], pp. 298–307).[3] Because the stimuli are internal, defense is virtually impossible; running away won't help.[4] The child's reaction to this unpleasurable situation is prototypi-

---

2. This idea originally appears in the "Project." It returns later in "The Ego and the Id" (Freud 1978 [1923b], p. 22): "In the same way that tensions arising from physical needs can remain unconscious, so also can pain—a thing intermediate between external and internal perception, which behaves like an internal perception even when its source is in the external world."

3. This means that from a psychoanalytic point of view the original experience of pain can be compared to trauma. Freud (1978 [1926d], p. 170) will later compare it to the trauma caused by the drive: "The only fact we are certain of is that pain occurs in the first instance and as a regular thing whenever a stimulus which impinges on the periphery breaks through the devices of the protective shield against stimuli and proceeds to act like a continuous instinctual stimulus, against which muscular action, which is as a rule effective because it withdraws the place that is being stimulated from the stimulus, is powerless."

We can reverse the argument as well, namely, the link between pain and an underlying traumatic disorder. A case study of this link by De Witte and Van Houdenhove (2001) is very convincing. Four years after the treatment, a chronic pain syndrome persists in an adult patient suffering from acute PTSD (which can happen frequently as their review of the literature indicates). Their follow-up shows that the patient's most important complaint is about *the Other's lack of response* (whether a medical or family Other), through which both the original trauma and the current pain persist as actualpathological phenomena (cf Chapter 7 below).

4. Running away is of course impossible for the baby. The adult encounters the same impossibility whenever the danger comes from the inside—and this explains the ever-present tendency toward "externalization" (Freud 1978 [1915d], p. 146) or even projective identification, that is, the tendency to put it all onto the other.

cal and provides the foundation for all subsequent intersubjective relationships. The helpless baby turns to the other by crying. The other is supposed to take care of the "specific actions" that will relieve the inner tension (Freud 1978 [1950a (1895)], pp. 317–321; Freud 1978 [1926d], pp. 169–172). Such an intervention will always consist of a combination of acts and words, indicating to the child that the Other has understood the demand and tried to respond to it. Note that this prototypical foundation thus indissolubly links an originally somatic pain and tension with the Other. In other words, the somatic drive has an intersubjective dimension right from the very beginning.

The importance of this shift cannot be overestimated because it forms the foundation for all subsequent relations. First and primarily, the child quite literally receives the images and words for its internal experience from the other. Under normal circumstances, the mother's reaction will be a mirroring that reflects both the child's pain and its first regulation ("Does it hurt? Come here, Mommy will kiss it all better"). Moreover, from this primary interaction, the originally purely somatic tension takes on a psychological dimension. To put it more strongly, the somatic pain is transformed into psychological pain the moment that the Other doesn't respond. It is at this point we encounter the primary traumatic situation, *separation*, understood as the experience where the inner tension remains unresolved by the Other, that is, by the Other's specific action that would relieve the tension. The tension and the other are linked together by the cry. Even more, the cry is the expression or representation of the tension. And this then becomes the central problem: How can the subject express its tension, in psychological terms, in representations (*Vorstellungen*) or words? We will return to this presently.

Clinically speaking, two consequences emerge (cf infra, Chapter 10). The original experience of pain acquires an affective coloring, namely, anxiety. Separation gives rise to a primary depressive reaction displaying the main characteristic of later adult depression, namely, the loss of identity.

Let's begin with anxiety as the first and most important manifestation of unpleasure. In addition to its well-known psychological aspects, anxiety also exhibits an obvious somatic component, such as heart palpitations, respiratory difficulties, trembling (Freud 1978 [1916–

1917], p. 395; 1978 [1926d], pp. 132–133).[5] The somatic component can be directly linked to the unpleasurable rise in tension; the psychological component is how this is represented in the subject through the Other's mirroring activity. The question is, which primary situation lies at the origin of anxiety?

From a classically Freudian perspective, we would expect to find castration anxiety here. However in clinical practice this form is rarely or even never encountered. Clearly, the idea of castration anxiety needs to be reinterpreted (Verhaeghe 2001b, pp. 9–16); it is primarily a Freudian metapsychological construct (cf infra). In the light of developments by Otto Rank, one could expect to find "birth anxiety" in its place. This, too, is primarily a theoretical construct, whose most important clinical manifestation is indeed found at birth, albeit on the father's side. In former times, he was expected to remain outside the birthing room and get drunk; these days he is supposed to be passively present throughout the birth where his most noteworthy coping mechanism is a certain fumbling about with the video camera.

Empirically speaking, the first appearance of anxiety in children is easy to see: it is separation anxiety, commonly known as "8-month anxiety" because of the typical age at which it occurs. In her extensive studies of this, Ainsworth (1978) showed how, in the vast majority of 1-year-olds, the mother's disappearance and the presence of a strange figure provoke anxiety. Relief only comes once the mother returns. The evolutionary ground for this is likely to be the child's dependence upon a familiar other for its own survival.[6]

This anxiety can take two forms: automatic or expectation. Automatic or traumatic anxiety is the immediate reaction to unpleasure, that

---

5. It is strange to see that these somatic anxiety phenomena are identical to the phenomena evident in pleasurable processes, especially in sexual excitement. In itself this is already enough to suggest that human pleasure is ambiguous at best. Pleasure and unpleasure have to do with the rise and fall of tension, meaning that they belong to the same process. Lacan brings this together in his concept of jouissance, not to be confused with phallic pleasure. The latter concerns merely the loss of tension by abreaction, and works in accordance with the Freudian pleasure principle.

6. For Freud, the basis of this separation anxiety is the child's helplessness (1978 [1950a (1895)], Part I), which then returns in the fear of the dark (1978 [1905d], p. 224).

is, to the internal rise in tension. Expectation anxiety anticipates the return of the first form, and especially the other's absence, with the result that the specific action that would remove the tension does not occur. In expectation anxiety, the gaze is central: until the child acquires "object permanence," the other's absence from the child's visual field (combined with the tension) is enough to install a feeling of helplessness.[7] The result is well known: crying, which Freud sees as an attempt to abreact the tension of the drive.[8] Expectation anxiety is a reaction to the repetition of the experience of separation and thus amounts to an expectation that the other won't respond to the call. The repetition of the separation is thus the cause of the inner experience of pain becoming associated with the external loss of the object, giving rise to anxiety (Freud 1978 [1926d], p. 169).

The Depressive Reaction

Along with anxiety, we come across a second clinical consequence, the depressive reaction. This is more difficult to understand, although it is quite literally visible. The child reacts not just with anxiety to the loss of the object. Practically every language has an expression that clinically describes this reaction with great precision: crying about the separation leads to a disfigured, "*décomposé*" (French), "*vertrokken*" (Dutch) face, making the original identity hard to recognize (Assoun 1997a, 1997b, p. 27). This can only be understood in light of the yet to be discussed theory of subject-formation: psychological identity comes from the other, originally through the Other's mirroring of what the child internally experiences. Identity—the face—comes from the other, and if this other disappears then the mirror-ego, the face, disintegrates.

---

7. We find the same phenomenon in adult loss of the object, for example when a love relationship ends. Typically in such situations the bereft partner demands, even begs, the other to see him or her for one last time ("I need to see you!"). This is at least partially a regression to the original situation of separation and loss of the object, where the visual presence of the other was needed to remove the inner tension.

8. Freud (1978 [1905c]) applies this to laughter as well, which boils down to a motor form of drive abreaction. It is not by chance that laughing and crying often occur at the same time.

Lack and Alienation

Considered in this way, the process of separation brings about a major shift that can scarcely be overrated: an internal unpleasurable rise in tension is associated with the external other. The infant quite probably experiences the original internal drive as something peripheral; in any case, it can only disappear through the presence of the Other. The Other's absence will be regarded as the cause of the continuation of the inner tension. But even when this Other is present and responds with words and actions, this response will never be enough either. For the Other must continually interpret the child's crying, and there is never a perfect fit between the interpretation and the tension. At this point, we come up against a central element of identity formation: *lack*, the impossibility of ever answering the tension of the drive in full. Freud observed what every parent knows: our children seem permanently unsatisfied. "It is as though our children had remained for ever unsated" (1978 [1931b], p. 234). The demand through which the child expresses its needs leaves a remainder in the sense that the Other's interpretation of the demand will never coincide with the original need. It seems that the Other's inadequacy will always be the first thing to be blamed for what goes wrong internally.

A developmental perspective puts the most weight on separation. But this overlooks how another process also starts up at the same time, namely, identity formation, which Lacan calls *alienation* (see Chapter 8). Almost immediately, the initial experiences of (un)pleasure are introduced into the relation between the subject and the Other. In this relation, the first awareness of identity comes into being. Freud argues that this situation, in which the internal unpleasure becomes combined with the demand to the Other, leaves memory traces because of its constant repetition. He talks about "facilitations" (*Bahnungen*), whose nature promotes a later return to them (Freud 1978 [1950a (1895)] 1978 [1920g], p. 26). In terms of contemporary developmental psychology and attachment theory, this means that the child constructs a representational system in which both the image of the self and of the other come into being, with a special emphasis on the arousal (the rise in tension) that the child has experienced (Fonagy et al. 2002, pp. 36–37). The way this occurs means that a distinction between the subject's own identity and that of the other cannot easily be made. This leads to our next point, identity and the mirror stage: "It is once more a question of external and internal" (Freud 1978 [1925h], p. 237).

Identity and Mirroring

The foregoing shows how, from the very first exchange between the child and the Other, the Other is held responsible for the success of this relationship, and that this occurs prior to any form of gender differentiation. The question now is, what mechanisms play a role in this development and how do we acquire our own identity?

In both Freud and Lacan, we come across ideas concerning the developing relationship between the human being and the external world. Freud (1978 [1920g], pp. 26–28) talks about the "primal ego," the "real Ego," and even about the cell facing the external world. Lacan (1994 [1964]) discusses the "being" or the "organism." The developmental process starts with the primal ego's differentiation of three different aspects in the external world: that which produces pleasure, that which produces unpleasure, and that which produces indifference. Freud more or less describes this process in biological or even ethological terms: the primitive organism-in-process, the cell, literally takes in parts of the external world. Whatever it finds pleasurable stays inside; whatever produces an unpleasurable feeling is sent back out.

The psychoanalytic version of the biblical "In the beginning was the Word . . ." is quite prosaic: "In the beginning was incorporation and expulsion."[9] The primitive ego-in-process confronts the external world and literally incorporates parts of it. The experience of pleasure or unpleasure results in a primary differentiation. The unpleasurable part is spat out as fast as possible again, so that initially the external world and the not-I are synonymous: they are "the badlands." Conversely, the pleasurable part remains inside, meaning that the ego and pleasure are synonymous, which Freud calls the primitive pleasure-ego. These processes of incorporation and expulsion are precursors of the later intellectual function of judgment, in which confirmation (*Bejahung*) is ersatz

---

9. Freud (1978 [1925h], p. 237). This part can best be understood by reading it together with the "Project."

for incorporation—"Yes, this is mine"—and negation is the successor to the expulsion—"No, this is not mine." Note that for Freud, confirmation is on the side of Eros and fusion, while negation is the effect of the death drive's tendency toward separation and disintegration (Freud, 1978 [1925h], p. 239).

These primitive processes are well known in biology and ethology, and occur in the child in vivo, as it were. Incorporation: babies discover the world through their mouths, they quite literally "taste" it. The earliest external part—the mother's milk—is taken in and quite a lot of other things can disappear into those rapacious little mouths along the way as well. Expulsion: what is bad is spat out or shat out, and even parental advice comes to the child in this form ("This is bad, it is shit!"), even for things that are quite remote ("Don't touch the fire honey, it will bite!"). Parents rediscover the primordial anal/oral language with surprising ease when talking to their children, which then easily crosses over into adult speech. Just think of expressions like "I'm going to eat you up!" or "devouring love" or "You make me puke." It continues to live on in adult love-life in the form of kissing or, even more, in oral sex, while in psychopathology the link with bulimia and anorexia is also clear.

It is at the point where images are linked to words that what is quintessentially human about this interaction begins. This major step in development means that from that point onward, we no longer are dealing with an exchange between the organism and the external world, but with an exchange between the child and the Other. At this point we have reached the transition from the mother's breast to the mother tongue. This is why, in "Lacanese," the Other with a capital O indicates both the concrete other and the totality of what the other says to the child. As such it is an operational concept (operational because it signals its effect through the signifier) that gathers together a number of previously described processes: "specific action" (Freud), "containment" (Bion), "attachment" (Bowlby 1969, 1973). This Other has the function of the S_1, the one who guarantees both the first processing of the drive and the first layer of identity.

The use of signifiers introduces other mechanisms while the process of identity formation as such remains the same. Instead of the literal incorporation of the pleasurable "outside," we now have identification with certain signifiers of the Other (a Dutch proverb expresses this beautifully: "Whose bread we eat, his words we speak"). Rather than the literal expulsion of the unpleasurable outside, we now have the repression of what yields unpleasure, that is to say, the ejection of the signifier, resulting in its becoming unconscious again.

Sketched out in this way, this description of the relation between the organism and the outside world seems fairly simple, almost banal. Going more deeply into it, an unexpected complexity arises. First, we have to conclude that the original primal ego or being is nothing but an empty box, a container (although one directed toward a certain aim, see Chapter 9) that acquires content only from the moment it brings things in from the outside. A second consideration reveals that the outside world only exists (that is to say, exists for the developing ego) from the moment that it has been taken in and weighed up in terms of pleasure or unpleasure.[10] In other words, the seemingly simple opposition between the inside and the outside, between the subject and the object, is far more complex.

The first conclusion carries an important assumption regarding ontology, the being of mankind, namely, that there is no preexisting identity from the moment of birth. The starting points are somatic experiences of pleasure and unpleasure, combined with certain hereditarily determined, cognitive functional possibilities, and that's all. Fonagy and his colleagues confirm this in their extensive review of the relevant research (Fonagy et al. 2002, p. 207), and they conclude that the infant has no direct, introspective access to "the differential basic emotion states," let alone an innate identity. Both are formed through interactions with the external world and, especially, through what these researchers call "the social biofeedback of parental affective mirroring" (Fonagy et al. 2002, pp. 145–202; cf infra, Note 13).

The second conclusion implies that reality is not an external object but is idiosyncratically constructed in and through that primary relationship—facts, as we saw earlier, are made. This is what Freud calls psychic reality, and it will initially have ascendancy over objective

---

10. Note that the judgment of pleasure or unpleasure precedes the judgment of existence! More simply: what leaves us indifferent doesn't exist. This Freudian logic fits perfectly with Chapter 3, the philosophical-epistemological chapter from Part I. Here, Freud (1978 [1925h]) elaborates a Kantian argument that avoids the deadlock of nominalism and realism.

reality. The only thing that is really outside and that remains outside doesn't exist for the developing organism or ego, precisely because it belongs to the indifferent part. The "inside" is that part of the outside that was judged pleasurable. The recognized outside is something that once was inside but was sent back to the outside (because it was unpleasurable); hence it is a rejected inside. Moreover, the internal and external worlds are developed at the same time, in the very same process of reciprocal mirroring. It is precisely this aspect that Lacan treats in his theory of the mirror stage—the basis of his later topology—wherein the inside and the outside are reversible.[11]

At the level of the unicellular organism, incorporation and expulsion are performed literally. Higher up on the evolutionary scale we can assume that this literal operation is overtaken by perceptual functioning. In place of the real thing, the images of the outside world are taken in and organized on the basis of pleasure (food, sex) and unpleasure (danger). This must also occur in human beings. It is not by chance that in his discussion of the mirror stage—the starting point of subject-formation—Lacan refers to ethological data (Lacan 1977 [1949]).

Long before attachment theory, Lacan had already indicated the importance of the mirroring process for the development of identity.[12] Briefly summarized, his theory runs as follows. In the beginning, the child experiences the arousal coming from the pregenital drives—indicated by (a)—as external. These drives are not only pregenital, they

---

11. The simplest illustration of this is the Möbius strip. Begin with a piece of paper of approximately 50 cm long and 5 cm wide; take an end in each hand, turn both hands 180 degrees in opposite directions and glue the two extremes together. Now try to identify the upper and the lower side of the strip by drawing a line on what you consider the upper side. It is no accident that the mathematical symbol for infinity is a Möbius strip: ∞. The Klein bottle is the same thing, although now in three dimensions where "inside" and "outside" can no longer be distinguished.

12. His first paper in this respect goes back to 1936, was taken up again in 1949, and reworked in 1960 (Lacan 1966 [1958], 1977 [1949]). Many others subsequently confirmed the importance of the mother's mirroring for the child's identity formation (Bion 1962b; Jacobson 1964; Kernberg 1984; Kohut 1971, 1977; Mahler 1975; Mahler and Mcdevitt 1982; Winnicott 1967). The link with the idea of "containing," as developed by Bion (1962a) is clear. In contemporary attachment theory, mirroring is the central process: "at the core of our selves is the representation of how we were seen" (Fonagy et al. 2002, p. 348).

are also partial, meaning that the child is not able to regulate them, nor to experience them as belonging to its own body as a whole. It is only through the mother's reactions that the child gains access to its own experience, because it is the mother who presents the child with an image of what it "is." Lacan illustrated this didactically with what is known as the single-mirror construction from the optica (see Fig. 6–1). By means of an ingenious construction with a convex mirror, a bouquet of flowers and a reversed vase underneath, the image of the vase is projected around the flowers (Lacan, 1966 [1958], p. 673).

Here the flowers stand for the partial drives, the vase for the container—that is, the child's body as a totality—in which they function. Through the reflection process, the mirror causes the partial drives to appear to be clothed by the containing surface of the body, to be literally in-corporated (Latin, *corpus*, body) in the body as an experience of totality (in contrast to the partial character of the drives). It is the mother who presents this mirror with which the child identifies. Such an image is never neutral, bringing with it at the same time the earliest regulation of the drive tensions by the specific way the mother performs this mirroring. The foundational layer of identity boils down to the image presented by the other that the child takes in and which forms the base for the ego.[13]

---

13. For Freud (1978 [1923b]), too, the ego is, in the first instance, the body's surface to which psychological contents are added later. As with so many other psychological truths, this idea can already be found in common language: someone can get "under your skin." The theory described above has meanwhile largely been confirmed by empirical research, both in biofeedback studies with adults and in infant research. The first demonstrate that internal somatic changes, of which someone has no conscious awareness (e.g., blood pressure), can be made conscious and even subjected to control, on condition that these changes become associated with external visible stimuli that are in covariance with the internal changes and can be observed by the subject. The second, the infant research, demonstrates that babies are directed toward "contingency detection," that is, to the covariance of their own behavior with that of others, and that this occurs during the first months after birth, with a special emphasis on maximal resemblance. In this process, facial and vocal mirroring of affective behavior between child and caretaker takes a central position. These two empirical findings are combined in the social biofeedback theory of parental affect-mirroring. The other's mirroring of what she imagines is going on internally in the child is taken over by the child, thus making a representation possible (the basis of a child's "theory of the mind") and providing the first opportunity for regulating the

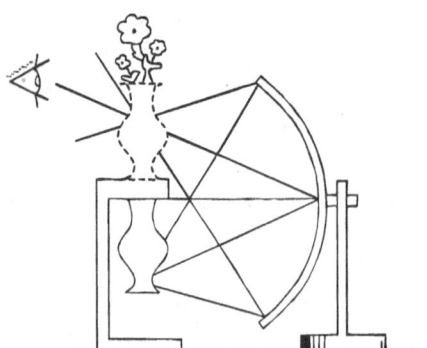

Figure 6–1. The single-mirror construction.

However, Lacan goes a lot further than the single-mirror construction. In such a model, the relation is merely dualistic. This is preeminently the order of the Imaginary and of the image, which makes no distinction between the ego and the Other. The next step is the double-mirror construction and the introduction of language (Lacan 1966 [1958]).[14] Speech presents both a lack and the accompanying Ego-Ideal—I(A)—that the subject is supposed to attain. Hence, the signifiers presented by the Other not only allow for an extension of the subject's representative construction of its own identity and that of the other, but at the same time they also enable the subject simultaneously to distance itself and be different. Therefore, the introduction of a third point is necessary, beyond the dual relation.

This introduction doesn't automatically take place. Speech can also remain in a merely dual, Imaginary perspective. In the dualistic order there are only two possibilities: complete immersion into the other, or

---

tension. As regards this latter, these authors use the concept of "affect" in a very broad sense, meaning that it can be understood as a rise in internal tension. In this way, it is quite close to the Lacanian (*a*). Needless to say, these theories permit an empirical confirmation and elaboration of Lacan's mirror stage (for all references, see Fonagy et al. 2002).

14. This theory is central to Lacan and is far more complex than what I have outlined here. For two excellent discussions, see Gallagher and Darby (1994) and Nobus (1998, pp. 101–138).

radical refusal. This becomes clear at the moment of the first awareness of an individual identity.

Such an identity is not present from the start; the first layers of identity come from outside. This is shown in the way the developing ego initially describes itself in the third person ("Lisa mad—Lisa want candy!" just as the other does ("Lisa has to be a good girl now!"). It is only later that the "I" form is used, which is also when the use of negation begins. The way this happens shows the tendency toward autonomy: it is always a negation directed toward the Other, from whom one no longer wants to just take things in, that is, to incorporate: "I don't want to!" In developmental psychology, this period is appropriately called negativism. It occurs in that period when the toddler tries to feed itself, refusing all help from the other. This same refusal can be understood in more general terms: the Other's offerings are no longer accepted just like that. This position can only be reached after and because sufficient feelings of security have been installed.[15] This means that the original separation anxiety has to be overcome in order to make its opposite appear—the desire for separation and autonomy, that is.

This brings us to the question of the subject's own identity. What the child internally experiences is mirrored and put into words by the other. It will be through these mirrorings—emanating from the outside—that identity is constructed as an answer to (*a*) (Declercq 1995). The question now is, do we merely become what the other mirrors? In such cases, development gets stuck in a dualistic relation that is unable to make a distinction between an I and an other. Separation anxiety produces ongoing dependence and a perpetual attempt to merge with the image the Other presents. Making the step to the triangular,

---

15. This becomes especially obvious in cases where security feelings haven't been installed. Children who haven't had the luxury of the original security constantly try to establish this later on with other people, usually with the opposite result. On this basis, the goal of education can be paradoxically defined thus: our children must be educated so that they are able to leave us. In oedipal terms, this comes down to the exogamy rule. Where this fails, the original incestuous situation—understood as a symbiotic relation between the subject and the first other—remains in place. The fact that this original relation was genderless means that the repetition of such a situation in adult relations is eminently possible, and that gender plays a secondary role. The most typical form is the bond between a master and his male and female groupies. Hence the cynical psychoanalytic in-joke: "Incest is fine, so long as you keep it in the family."

however, opens up the possibility of difference. This is what Freud demonstrates in his theory of the Oedipus complex.

THE OEDIPAL STRUCTURE: THE NAME-OF-THE-FATHER, DIFFERENCE, DESIRE, AND INTENTIONALITY

Between the ages of 2 and 5, a number of changes take place that have enormous implications for a child's psychological functioning and identity formation. These changes can be approached from a developmental-psychological or from a psychoanalytic point of view. From a developmental-psychological perspective, this period sees the beginnings of intentional reasoning and of a stable awareness of identity. For psychoanalysis, language and the symbolic function of the father introduce the difference between the two sexes and the two generations. The result is the subject's ability to distance itself and reflect on its own identity and the identity of the other.

By the age of one, the child has acquired the "teleological position": it can interpret certain events as the effect of something that happened before, both with human and nonhuman objects (Csibra and Gergely 1998; Tomasello 1999). It cannot build a causal explanation because it doesn't yet have an established consciousness that something ought to follow (Fonagy et al. 2002, p. 223 ff). The next step in development is the "intentional position," where the child becomes able to attribute past intentions both to itself and to others. This implies that it is able to think in terms of mental causation and that it must have an inner representation concerning "intentional mental states," both in itself and in the other (Fonagy et al. 2002, p. 237).[16] In short, desire is installed.

At 14 months, the child assumes that the other's desire is the same as its own; at 2 years it can differentiate between them and is aware

---

16. The difference between the teleological and intentional position is important from a clinical perspective. Autistic children acquire the teleological but not the intentional position (Leslie and Thaiss 1992). They fail to attribute "intentional mind states" to the other (Abell et al. 2000). This failure is caused by the lack of an inner "theory of the mind" (Gergely and Watson 1996).

that its own desire is not necessarily the same as the other's. Even more, it will give precedence to this other's desire.[17]

This implies that from age 2 onward, the child has representations about the intentions and desires of the other, enabling it to have expectations about the other's behavior. At the same time, a representation of the child's own goal-orientedness in relation to the other's comes into being through the mirroring, particularly with regard to the extent to which it answers or fails to answer this other's desire (Fonagy et al. 2002, p. 239 ff). This is the first form of a complete sense of identity, in the sense that it is a representation of the child's own identity in terms of causality and intentionality, and it takes place in relation to the other's identity.

This first identity is fairly elementary. Two-year-olds recognize themselves in the mirror through a relation of equivalence, but they are unable to distinguish between present and earlier images. This is connected with the dualistic functioning of that period, which developmental psychology calls the "psychic equivalence mode": the subject's thoughts and reality are the same, there's no awareness of a difference between representation and external reality (Fonagy et al. 2002, p. 258 ff). At the same age, we find the complete reverse as well, the "pretend mode": the child's make-believe play is completely divorced from reality, and it will make this quite clear. Should the play become too real—usually because of an intervention by an adult who wants to play along—the result is anxiety (Fonagy et al. 2002, pp. 261–263). In short, in the equivalence mode reality and thought completely coincide; in the pretend mode, they are completely separated.

From age 4 onward, the child is able to distinguish between present and earlier mirror images, and the integration of equivalence and pretend modes begins. A number of experiments demonstrate how 4-year-olds can compare their actual mirror image with previous images of themselves because they can make temporal and causal links between the present image and what they remember. Hence the beginning of

---

17. This was shown by the following experiment: toddlers are first placed in a situation where they can watch other children's food preferences and dislikes. Later, they are asked what food they would offer these others. While 2-year-old children will follow the preference previously shown, against their own individual preferences, children of 14 months present their own preference (Repacholi and Gopnik 1997).

the autobiographic and stable sense of identity is found between the ages of 4 and 5. The same thing happens on a larger scale as well: equivalence and pretend modes are integrated into a detached, reflective mode, making it possible to distinguish between inner and outer reality. The dualistic functioning is overtaken by triangulation, the "truly representational mode" (Fonagy et al. 2002, p. 263).[18]

The Two Others

It is not by chance that these latter developments coincide with the oedipal period. In what we saw above, the focus was more or less exclusively on the mother and child.[19] The oedipal structure rewrites the original separation anxiety such that this primary interaction expands into relations with a first Other and a second Other, and this occurs, moreover, inside a gender differentiation. It is precisely this rewriting that will make separation possible, beyond the original separation anxiety.

In its attempts to respond to the tension of the drive (a), the child appeals to the first Other. As a result, it identifies itself with the image presented by this Other, that is to say, it identifies with the Other's desire. In this way, a primal dual mirror-identity comes into being, along with the first regulation of the drive. To put it in terms of Lacan's first mirror construction: the vase (the surface of the body) is projected around the flowers (the partial drives). In the course of normal development, this answer is insufficient and the second Other enters the scene, resulting in a triangular interaction. In terms of Lacan's double-mirror construction, language functions as a third point through which

---

18. For a quick and clear overview of this theory, see Fonagy and Target (1996a) and Target and Fonagy (1996).

19. This is doubtless one of the most important critiques of contemporary attachment theory. There the focus is exclusively on the mother–child relationship; the father is barely mentioned and gender differentiation comes suddenly out of the blue. In other words, this theory makes the opposite mistake of Freud's: for Freud, the exclusive focus was on the father, and development seemed to start only at the age of 4. It took until 1930 before he recognized the importance of the mother, largely as a result of influences from other analysts.

the difference between the already constituted identity and the anticipated ideal identity can be measured. Lacan summed this up very neatly in his idea of the father's symbolic function, indicating that it doesn't so much concern the real figure of the father, but rather a combination of language and the Symbolic structure, as opposed to the image and the Imaginary relationship.

The child wants the mother all to itself, to be sure of getting a complete answer to (*a*). Nevertheless it finds that the mother's desire goes out not only to it, but also toward a third figure. On the basis of the cognitive developments described above, the options for identification are not only substantially expanded, but also structurally changed. The child can see itself through the gaze and words of the first Other *and* of the second Other. Moreover, it is able to see the first Other through the gaze and words of the second Other, and vice versa. The whole thing is directed by the desire to see its own desire answered. Thus, every time, the images presented offer identification possibilities with which the child will never perfectly coincide. To the contrary even. This introduces the dimension of difference between the child, the first Other and the second Other, opening up the possibility of choice. Who am I, in relation to the desire of the first Other, and in relation to the desire of the second Other, and which position do I take between those two? For Lacan, the distinguishing element in all of this is the symbolic phallus.

The first Other turns to the second Other for something the child itself is unable to give. Hence a third, mediatory point is set up between the mother and the child. The assumption will be that this Other has "it," the answer to the inner rise in tension. For the child, just what this "it" constitutes is far from clear. And the same lack of clarity lingers on in the adults. Think of expressions like "That woman really has something!" . . . "That guy's got it"; but the moment this something or "it" must be defined, we brush up against an impossibility. The sole thing to emerge from this is that "it" has something to do with gender, and is supposed to answer to our desire for an answer from the Other. The content that Freud gives this is as radical as it is naive: "it" is the real penis. Lacan abstracts it and coins it the *phallus*. The real penis can leave us with the illusion that desire, even the drive, can be satisfied. The phallus, in contrast, is a signifier and in that sense only an indicator of the dreamt-of, unreachable end-point of desire, the signifier for what would finally resolve the lack. The father is only supposed to possess this phallus, nothing more.[20]

The Phallus as Signifier

To the extent that this phallus is reduced to the Imaginary, the illusion that there can be a conclusive answer to desire through Imaginary identification remains in place. But as a Symbolic signifier, the emphasis is on the lack as such, and the subject is called on to fill it in on his or her own terms. This is the meaning of the incest prohibition and of obligatory exogamy: the child is separated from the dualistic relation, meaning that later and somewhere else it must choose to create something, namely, an identity of its own in relation to the Other.

The fact that something involving gender difference is used as an indicator for what would fulfill desire has very specific consequences. The child's turning to the father by way of the mother means that the originally genderless mother–child dialectic is characterized from this moment on by gender difference and the difference between the two generations.[21] This means, too, that gender identity is a secondary construction, based on another, previously nongenital relationship.

The establishment of the oedipal structure has far-reaching consequences for the emergence of anxiety. Initially, the child was confronted with a primary experience of unpleasure that was transformed through

---

20. The implication is that lack and desire can never be ultimately satisfied. This is a crucial difference between psychoanalysis, with its accompanying ethics, and today's mentality (in the mental health field as well). In our postmodern, voluntarist climate, the illusion reigns that the ultimate object of satisfaction not only exists, but can moreover simply be bought. Psychoanalysis starts out from the idea that every object appears within the framework of a structurally determined and hence irreversible lack. This is not just a philosophical difference because it has quite clear consequences in considering the goals of all kinds of mental health care.

21. This doesn't void the earlier pregenitality. The oedipal retake on it means that the original pathways or "facilitations" remain but acquire another meaning. More precisely, the partial drives gain a phallic interpretation, becoming "phallicized:" the child interprets the pregenital in phallo-sexual terms. This is clinically illustrated in fecal and urethral jokes, in infantile sexual theories of birth and, of course, in our own adult sexual life.

its first interactions with the Other into separation anxiety. In the dualistic relation, this amounted to the child's anxiety over its inability to fit the ideal image presented by the Other. The oedipal structure transforms this into a secondary and partial signal anxiety.

This latter aspect (the partialness) has to do with the way the subject no longer needs to satisfy the total image presented by the Other, but only the Other's (phallically interpreted) desire. In Freudian terms, this reworking means that the original separation anxiety is changed into castration anxiety for the boy, and anxiety over the loss of the Other's love in the girl (Freud 1978 [1924d]). Given Freud's concern with the real penis, he understands castration anxiety literally. With Lacan, the idea of castration acquires a completely different meaning, one beyond the anatomic Freudian reading. Imaginary castration involves an anxiety about being unable to satisfy the phallic desire of the other, either because one doesn't sufficiently have the (imaginary) phallus, or because one insufficiently is the (imaginary) phallus (remember that the phallus always functions as a signifier) (Lacan 1994 [1956–1957]).

Such "castration"-anxiety functions as a secondary or signal anxiety because it is, in itself, already a defensive processing of the underlying primary anxiety (Verhaeghe 2001b, pp. 9–17). Through this processing, the original anxiety retroactively acquires another meaning. It no longer concerns separation anxiety as such, but rather an anxiety about being in the passive position, of falling back into the earlier situation of total dependence on the Other in an undifferentiated gender identity, as in the period before the oedipal structuring.[22] It is precisely because of this structuring that one has the possibility of acquiring an identity of one's own: by separating from the Other. From this moment on, the desire for autonomy comes into being, along with an anxiety about remaining incorporated by the Other.

---

22. In his final and most powerful conceptualization of castration, Freud explicitly describes anxiety about being in the passive position as the foundation of castration anxiety (Freud 1978 [1937c], pp. 250–253). This forces us to question the concepts of gender and of sexual positioning again, independently of the oedipal and hence constructivist aspect of gender identity. The most important opposition in this discussion is not so much that between men and women as that between activity and passivity in relation to the Other.

Lacan expresses this in his formula for the oedipal structure: the metaphor of the Name-of-the-Father (Lacan 1977 [1959], p. 200):[23]

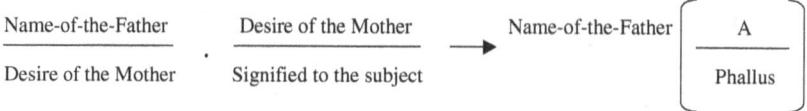

Figure 6–2. The metaphor of the Name-of–the-Father.

The original dualistic relation (the mother's desire as signified to the subject) is superseded by the Name-of-the-Father, as the signifier for the mother's desire. As a result, the child enters into the Symbolic, triangular order, where the phallus signifies the difference that enables the subject to build its own constantly shifting identity through the Other.

Conclusion

To conclude, we can say that difference and lack are introduced through the phallic signifier, which enables the transition to be made from the preoedipal, dualistic relation to the triangular oedipal structure. Where, previously, the subject was completely dependent on the first Other for an answer to the drive and, in its wake, for its own identity, now it is referred to a third figure. This not only implies that both the answer and the subject's identity have expanded, it also means the

---

23. This must be read through Lacan's theory of metaphor. The formula is:

$$\frac{S}{S'} \cdot \frac{S'}{x} \rightarrow S\left(\frac{1}{s}\right)$$

Here, S and S' are signifiers, where S comes to take the place of S', introducing the new signification x. S' vanishes into the background, S comes to the foreground, resulting in a new layer of signification s (Lacan 1977 [1959], p. 200). The same logic can be applied to repression and the return of the repressed, where S stands for the return of the repressed and S' is the repressed (cf. infra). In the paternal metaphor, the mother's desire functions as S' and is replaced by the Name-of-the-Father that introduces phallic signification. As a result, the subject is introduced into the Symbolic order that is always phallically signified, hence O/Phallus.

subject can now assume a position of distance. Language is what founds these possibilities.

LANGUAGE AND IDENTITY

In our first part, we described the typical characteristics of the Symbolic order, namely, lack, difference, and displacement. We can now discuss the functions of language. One usually tends to reduce these to communication, but the foregoing discussion enables us to present a number of the other functions of language that are more important still.[24]

The first function of language is unreservedly that of mastery. As Freud noted in his "Project," the child is born into a situation of total helplessness, having a complete passive dependence on the other. It acquires an active hold on the external world by appraising it in terms of pleasure and unpleasure, and this process takes place through representation, beginning with crying and continuing in speech. For the child, the first external world is of an internal nature, namely the child's own drive, although this will immediately be connected with the Other.[25] Language, and even more representation, opens up the possibility of regulating affect. Representational mastery such as this can be illusory—when lightning is called "sparks from Thor's hammer" or "Zeus's spears" for example. These are typical characteristics of the Imaginary: the giving of meaning, albeit in the sense of a meaning fixation. At the psychological level, these are symptoms, imaginary constructions through which the subject tries to get a grip on the thing that drives it. Even science can fall under this category, as

---

24. With this, we not only reencounter the problems discussed in Part I of this book concerning the relationship between words and things, but the very same problems are now also extended to the relation between identity and the drive.

25. A stunning illustration of this function of mastery is found in Freud's description of the fort–da game, where an 18-month-old toddler tries to master his mother's coming and going in a representative ("symbolic"—but in Lacanian terms, Imaginary) way by throwing a spool out of the cot ("Fort!") and then reeling it back in ("Da!"). The shift from passive to active position is very clear (Freud 1978 [1920g], pp. 14–16).

a meaning-providing system through which man tries to lay hands on the Real.[26] To the extent that science is a Symbolic system though, it distances itself from meaning fixation to underscore the perpetual displacement of meaning. Mathematics is an exemplary case of this.

The second function of language concerns identity. The developing ego begins as an empty container that gains content from the external world, from the Other, and above all from the Other's speech. Our identity is verbal; each human being is a story and lives in a narrative reality.[27] This is what is at the bottom of certain of Lacan's (1977 [1960]) statements, such as "The unconscious is the discourse of the Other" (*"L'inconscient, c'est le discours de l'Autre"*, p. 312). This discourse is only taken in if it's pleasurable, and, hence "Desire is the desire of the Other" (*"Le désir de l'homme, c'est le désir de l'autre"*, p. 312). This eventually ushers in the definition of the subject, albeit with a clear shift in emphasis toward the signifier: "The signifier is what represents the subject for another signifier" (*"Le signifiant, c'est ce qui représente le sujet pour un autre significant"*, p. 316). This association between language and identity introduces a very important human

---

26. Richard Feynman (Nobel physics prize 1965) constantly emphasized that to give something a name is not the same thing as understanding it. It was his father, incidentally, who taught him this at a very young age (Feynman 1999, p. 4—highly recommended for DSM devotees).

27. The clinical validity of this model is found in the conclusion that it enables an apparently paradoxical fact to be explained, namely, that identification *precedes* object choice, and that object loss frequently results in a *regression* to identification (Freud 1978 [1921c], pp. 106–107). This becomes comprehensible once we see that, as described above, a subject doesn't begin from an external object but from an identification with a pleasurable experience, and that through this process both the subject and the object come into being. Freud's mythical starting point is the "primordial satisfaction" of his "Project," where the subject and object are not yet differentiated. Only afterward is the subject able, in a second moment, to seek the object in the outside world, precisely because of the existence of the first identification. The loss of the object means that the subject is left with just the identification, known as regression. This argument is not just academic, because it allows us to understand the process underlying depression. As far as love is concerned, it gives rise to the prosaic and well-known conclusion that we always seek "ourselves" in love—identification occurs before object choice.

characteristic we will return to later: the ability to reflect, to regard something from a distance.[28]

The third function of language is communication. The important element in this function is not so much the message but rather the relation between the sender and receiver. This relation will determine how the message is—or is not—received, and more specifically whether or not it is "taken in" and kept, or returned back outside to the sender.[29] In positive relations, the message is taken in; negative relations result in rejection. Freud developed this idea with regard to the therapeutic context (positive versus negative transference). Still later, it returned in the wider concept of the therapeutic alliance that forms the basis for any therapeutic efficacy. The same focus on the relation is found in Lacanian discourse theory, especially in the idea of the social bond that characterizes each discourse.

Last but not least is the fourth function. The link between language, the outside world, and identity opens up the potential for consciousness. As we know from Freud's "Project," our quintessentially human consciousness, with its accompanying reflective ability, can only be explained through a coupling of an original, unmediated perceptual thought process with the mediation of words. He calls verbal association the condition for both conscious thought and memory, especially for what we call "declarative memory" today (Freud 1978 [1950a (1895)], pp. 364–366). At the same time, another quintessentially human phe-

---

28. Thus our identity always comes from the (words of the) Other and is therefore always alienated. This reminds me of an anecdote about Picasso, who was asked to paint a portrait of a rich businessman. Not averse to the money, he agreed but naturally painted it in his own style. After a number of sessions the businessman was finally allowed to see the end product. Picasso turned the painting toward him—it was a typical Picasso—saying: "The only thing now is that you have to try to look like it." This is how our identity is established: by trying to look like what is presented to us as ideal. Our originality lies in the choice we make between the myriad identities that are presented to us by many others.

29. Teaching is a perfect example of this: one "learns"—that is to say, one takes in signifiers—in a positive transferential relation. This latter is of far more decisive importance than any possible accuracy or inaccuracy of what is actually taught. As a result, all education runs the risk of turning into an opportunity for indoctrination.

nomenon arises, namely, the fact that a certain specific content can become unconscious again, even content that had already been verbalized and, therefore, was previously conscious but that loses this quality of consciousness. The difference between the two—conscious versus unconscious—is intimately bound up with verbalization. The "taking in" and "retaining" of the positive signifiers of the Other implies consciousness, the "sending out" of the Other's negative signifiers implies that they become unconscious (again).

One cannot overestimate the importance of this fourth function. In all probability, it is very likely one of the most important differences between mankind and animals. Defining what it is, precisely, is one of the hottest tasks of contemporary science. Animals clearly have a kind of awareness whose feedback system explains goal-directed behavior. The difference between this form of animal awareness and human consciousness has to do with the difference between the human language system and the sign system we know to exist in certain animal species. Human language gives one the ability to reflect, that is, the ability to think about oneself, the other, and the world from a certain distance, thus making choices possible. The prerequisites for this are twofold: the displacement of meaning through signifiers, and the fact that the subject fails to fully coincide with these signifiers; to put it differently, there is a lack in the Other.

Incidentally, we can make an important correlation between language, consciousness, and knowledge here. Everyone has the experience of knowing something but not being able to say it ("it's just on the tip of my tongue"). And, conversely, what we know explicitly is always expressible in words and is, hence, conscious. The first, nonconscious knowledge explains so-called "intuition": we act according to a knowledge that drives us, but that cannot or can only barely be verbalized. Conscious knowledge, on the other hand, seems a lot less effective—how many conscious decisions do we found on conscious knowledge? Freud will even ask in his "Project" why consciousness is necessary. Animals seem to function perfectly well without it, and a lot of human existential misery is precisely bound up with this characteristic. There can only be one conclusion: there is an unconscious knowledge in nondeclarative memory that has workings of its own. The importance of unconscious processes has recently been gaining increasing attention in cognitive- and neuropsychology, reducing the importance of consciousness and declarative memory (Damasio 2000; Edelman 1990; Kaplan-Solms and Solms 2000; Rogers 2001).

The linking together of signifiers not only makes consciousness possible, but simultaneously makes it possible for something to become unconscious once again: take away its signifier and the "consciousness of" something disappears. This forms the basis for a quintessentially human defense mechanism: not wanting to know. Freud coined the word for this: *repression*, the relief of expulsion.[30] In this way we encounter a division between ego–pleasurable–signifier–identification–conscious versus non-ego–unpleasurable–no signifier–repression–unconscious. To secure the pleasurable identification between the ego and the outside world, a number of barriers are installed against the unpleasurable part of the outside world. Freud calls them "stimulus barriers" or "protective shields" (*Reizschutz*) whose function he recognizes in our sense organs, for example. He was one of the first to confirm that our sense organs are no open gate to the outside world but in fact selective and, therefore, defensive organs (Freud 1978 [1920g], pp. 26–28). An ostrich mentality doesn't require one to put one's head in the sand: it is enough simply to look, listen, and smell, and the selection is already fully at work. "What is said remains forgotten behind what is said in what is heard" ("*Qu'on dise reste oublié derrière ce qui se dit dans ce qui s'entend*" Lacan 1975, p. 5).

Defense

This idea of defense is tremendously important and follows immediately from the previously described attempts at mastery. It suggests that right from the beginning of identity formation, so-called mechanisms of defense are installed and at work in the developing relation

---

30. Freud explains it as follows: "Now, too, we are in a position to state precisely what it is that repression denies to the rejected presentation in the transference neuroses: what it denies to the presentation is translation into words which shall remain attached to the object. A presentation which is not put into words, or a psychical act which is not hypercathected, remains thereafter in the *Ucs.* in a state of repression" (1978 [1915e], p. 202). Hence Freud can describe negation as an intellectual sublation of the repression, where the analysand has the signifiers at his or her conscious disposal but refuses to accept them (Freud 1978 [1925h], pp. 235–236). In the old, oral form of language, it's "I'm not eating this."

between the subject and the Other. In this way, the primitive ego defends itself against arousal. Effectively, this implies that the subject defends itself against perceptions or signifiers that would bring unpleasure. Because of the nature of the inside–outside dialectics, it is far from clear what these unpleasurable representations refer to. The primitive ego will displace them to the outside, to the Other, but the starting point remains the originally internal arousal or tension.

This displacement will color Freud's first theory. Indeed, he originally assumed that the cause of psychopathology lay exclusively in the other; this is the so-called trauma and seduction theory, which lays all the blame on the Other. Almost immediately he had to introduce an important correction. The original unpleasurable impulses have scarcely anything to do with the Other, but originate from inside. Ascribing them to the Other is already a first form of defense. Moreover, they will continue to operate from the inside, despite the subject attributing them to the Other, and are therefore experienced by the ego as incompatible. Hence Freud's name for them, deriving from the medical tradition: "foreign bodies" (*Fremdkörper*) (Freud 1978 [1926d], pp. 98–99; Freud and Breuer 1978 [1893a]; 1978 [1895d], pp. 290–291). Consequently, in his later work he is obliged to talk about a double defense: a first defense, linking the internal arousal with an external Other, and a second form that must be located entirely in the relation between the subject and the Other. This will be the topic of the next chapter.

SUMMARY

- The relation between the subject and the Other is at the heart of identity-formation from the outset, making the Other responsible for answering to the inner drive.
- The earliest identity is constructed through a dualistic mirroring of the Other's answer. The motive is furnished by separation anxiety, whose mechanisms are incorporation (identification) and expulsion (repression).
- Through the oedipal structure and language acquisition, a triangular relation is installed that enables a distinction to be made between the subject, and the first and second Other.

- The initial separation anxiety is in this way transformed into a desire for autonomy, occurring inside generational and gender differentiations.
- Language acquisition enables one to master the drive from a distance, accompanied by the development of reflective identity in the relation to the Other.
- A number of mechanisms of defense are established in the course of identity development that will determine the relation between the subject and the Other.

7
Defense in Double Time: A Linear Model

PRIMARY AND SECONDARY DEFENSES

Both psychotherapy and psychodiagnostics typically focus on the subject's speech and behavior. But far too often this overlooks the way both speech and behavior take place inside a double dialectic: between the subject and the body *and* between the subject and the Other. In the developmental model described in the previous chapter, we saw how the subject constructs a defense against the experience of unpleasurable tension right from the outset. This defense is always an attempt to master the drive by means of the Other, principally through the Other's representation of it. At the same time, this defense against and attempted mastery of what Lacan calls (*a*) is transformed into a defense against and attempted mastery of the Other. In what follows, I will develop this idea of the double defense.

The primary defense lies on the border between the verbal and what is preverbal, and determines the structure of the subject. Such a defense is, in the first instance, directed against something in the subject's own body, that is to say, against an internal arousal that breaks through the homeostasis. This defense makes an appeal to the other. The secondary defense takes place entirely verbally and lays the groundwork for symptom development. This defense implies an important shift: from that moment on, the internal problem is warded off in and through the Other, and its internal aspect becomes almost unrecognizable.

This enables us to distinguish between two different temporalities. In clinical practice, the second temporality (the linguistic one) is the most visible because it contains the mechanisms of defense as we encounter them in the patient's speech in the course of the diagnostic and therapeutic process: repression, isolation, projective identification, idealization, disavowal, and negation, each occurring in relation to the Other. Any potential psychopathology will therefore clearly be recognizable as a psychopathology. Such a second temporality of necessity falls back on a primary moment that lays the foundation for all later defense strategies.

This groundwork is unique because it contains the transition between the originally internal tension, belonging to the somatic part of the drive, and the place and function of the Other, understood as the concrete other and the source of language and symbolization in general.[1]

The nature of this primary defense determines that of the secondary defense. For instance, the secondary repression of neurosis is always built on a primary repression. Considering that this latter is located in the transition from the nonverbal to the verbal, such a primordial defense simultaneously determines how the subject enters language and, therefore, determines the specific structure of the subject as well. The acquisition of identity through the Other, as discussed in the previous chapter, is not just a question of filling in the content; it also concerns the subject's positioning in relation to the (desire of the) Other. I will come to this in Part 3 of this book, in my discussion of the differential diagnostic structures. The same logic applies to psychosis, whose primary mechanism is foreclosure, as well as to disavowal in perversion.

As we will see, the subject can remain stuck in the first temporal moment, without any significant processing of the initial problem into a second moment. Consequently, the pathology is largely limited to the

---

1. The implication is that we are confronted here with nothing less than the mythical transition between mind and body. Note that such a transition takes place through the Other; it is the Other who names what is experienced bodily.

primary processing of the originally internal somatic drive, and even if there is some resulting pathology, this will be considerably more difficult to recognize as psychopathology. We will soon come to understand these disorders in terms of actualpathology. A material consequence of remaining stuck in the primary processing is that this actualpathology will barely be audible in the verbal exchanges between the subject and the Other, meaning that we won't often encounter such actualpathology in psy-consultations.

The significance of this distinction is fully bound up with the aim of clinical psychodiagnostics, namely, the treatment. Psychotherapy, in the usual sense of the word, minimally implies that the subject's disorder is processed through the secondary defense. Being stuck at the primary level means that such a processing is missing. This does not mean that psychological treatment is impossible, just that it needs to be thought about differently.

It must be admitted that it is very difficult to make an empirical study of the primary defense mechanism. We can only deduce its existence from the way it appears in the secondary forms. It has primarily been studied with regard to primal repression in neurosis, which is why it appears here as the standard example. From a classical Freudian point of view there are three temporal moments: the return of the repressed, repression proper (or secondary repression), and primary repression.[2] In my reading, the first two are the same thing, that is, the secondary defense; primary repression is the primordial defense.

It is almost always the secondary defenses that psy-consultations confront, along with their accompanying psychopathology. The object of secondary repression concerns psychological material that has already been put into signifiers (and hence is conscious-pleasurable), but which, for one reason or another, has become unpleasurable. The underlying motive of secondary repression is thus a signal anxiety that forms the basis of the patient's not-wanting-to-know. In this way, certain thoughts are warded off, that is to say, sent back to the outside. Effectively, this means that these signifiers are kept outside consciousness, with the result that they seem to be forgotten. When the

---

2. See Freud 1978 [1911c], pp. 66–67; 1978 [1915d], p. 148; 1978 [1915e], p. 181.

affective load of these signifiers becomes displaced onto neutral words, it enables the return of the repressed to take place.

This return is the signal of a fairly typical phenomenon: the failure of every neurotic process of defense. In one way or another, the warded-off ideas always manage to break through to consciousness. The slip of the tongue is a good example of this: the repressed content always glimmers through in what is said (e.g., "I would like to thank all those who are absent here"), opening an associative pathway to the underlying material.

The return of the repressed and secondary repression are two sides of the same coin within secondary defense. The underlying ground is primary repression, that is, the primordial defense. This can be located at the transition from incorporation–expulsion to identification–repression, that is to say, at the transition from nonverbal to verbal functioning. In the course of this transition, the cognitive-affective contents must be put into a new form of expression, that is, into words. Freud hypothesizes that during this transition, certain material is not translated and remains behind on a previous level (Freud 1978 [1911c], p. 67).[3] What does make the transition is confirmed with a new status, namely, that of the Symbolic order; its mechanism is the so-called "assent" or affirmation (*Bejahung*).[4] The Symbolic order itself then becomes the defensive counter to what is left behind.

Consequently, material that fails to make the transition remains fixed at the earlier, extra-linguistic level of expression. For Freud, this material will continue to exert an attraction on the conscious verbal material and will constitute the kernel of the unconscious (Freud 1978 [1915d], p. 148). The nature of this kernel is unclear, precisely because of its lack of words. It has to do with the pressure of the drive against which the

---

3. It is no accident that one's earliest memories are almost always of a perceptual nature, having no need of language whatsoever. Dreaming is probably a remnant of this mode of functioning. The dualistic, imaginary character of it is clear: it is almost impossible to take a reflective distance while dreaming; one *is* the dream.

4. See Freud 1978 [1925h], p. 239. Freud considers affirmation an effect of Eros, in the sense of the Ego's incorporation, that is, fusion. Negation, on the other hand, is on the side of the death drive and of separation.

psyche must defend itself. Should the inhibition of these impulses fail, the subject typically experiences anxiety.[5] This anxiety appears automatically, without mediation. This is its difference from signal anxiety, where certain objects or signifiers function as mediating instances between the subject and the drive. In other words, in secondary repression signal anxiety can always be linked to the Other. This is not the case with primary repression. The automatic anxiety thus set free is intimately bound up with the originally internal process.

From a Lacanian perspective, the classic triptych—primary repression, secondary repression, and the return of the repressed—can be reduced to a twofold process that takes place simultaneously. The return of the repressed and secondary repression are two sides of the same procedure, which can best be understood through the trope of metaphor. A certain (group of) signifier(s) is placed above and in opposition to another, making the latter disappear from the conscious perceptual field but leaving behind an associative link to the vanished part. In this sense, both repression and the return of the repressed take place at the same time.[6] The same can be said for primary repression: the installation of language itself acts as a countercathexis to and on top of the Real of the drive, making the Real as such disappear while retaining a link to it.

---

5. "At any rate, the earliest outbreaks of anxiety, which are of a very intense kind, occur before the super-ego has become differentiated. It is highly probable that the immediate precipitating causes of primal repressions are quantitative factors such as an excessive degree of excitation and the breaking through of the protective shield against stimuli" (Freud 1978 [1926d], p. 94). A clear comparison to trauma can be made here because in trauma the psychic processing is also missing, resulting in a similarly unmediated and raw anxiety. Hence our argument that every instance of subject-formation begins with a structurally determined trauma that is the confrontation with the Real of the drive.

6. As we saw in the previous chapter, this can be understood in terms of Lacan's theory of metaphor, where a new signifier is placed on top of another. Although it makes the first signifier disappear, the new signifier at the same time retains an associative link to it (see Chapter 6, Note 23). The metaphor of the Name-of-the-Father is part of the basic defense against (*a*), with the proviso that the drive must already have undergone a primary processing through the (identification with the) mother's desire.

The clinical distinction between primary and secondary defense is illustrated through the different kinds of anxiety. Primary repression involves an automatic, even traumatic anxiety based on the fact that something cannot be symbolically processed. There is no meaning or signification involved. Secondary repression involves a signal anxiety, on the grounds that something should not be verbalized anymore. Here the signifiers are indeed processed, albeit defensively.

A CLINICAL ILLUSTRATION

A clinical fragment makes this clearer. A young woman comes in for consultation because of difficulties with relationships and a vague mixture of anxiety and depression—a typical illustration of "The Sexual Relationship does not exist." In the first interview, she quite prominently emphasizes the recent nature of her problems. She mentions that both of her parents are dead (her father died when she was 11, her mother during her adolescence), but that this is "unimportant" and I shouldn't worry too much about it. The here and now is all that matters. Moreover, she has no memory whatsoever about her father, merely a vague image.

From what we saw in the theoretical exposition, we can assume a secondary repression or negation at work here but one that cannot be worked on.[7] Note that her defense concerns certain ideas or memories, but that this defense simultaneously implies a very clear relational message: "You think this is important. It's not, so back off!" In the course of the second interview, the wider family is briefly discussed; an aunt with progressive ideas gets the most attention. This aunt is the only one who listens to her, the only one she can open her heart up to, "and I don't talk to her, for example, about my attic or my dentist."

This is a strange thing to say. When I ask for associations for attic and dentist, it becomes immediately clear that they function as defen-

---

7. A certain technical error frequently occurs in clinical practice here, where the therapist comes up with an opposing answer: "Your father must have been really important for you!" The need to convince the patient of this idea then makes an "analysis of the resistance" unavoidable. Lacan offers another solution, that is, the analysis of the verbal material itself (Lacan 1966 [1955], p. 323 ff; 1991 [1953–1954]).

sive metaphors and refer to anxiety-laden material. Her attic, she says, needs to be cleared out. After the sudden death of her mother, she moved everything from her mother's house, from the furniture to the family pictures, to her attic. This evokes repeated anxiety dreams in which she is chased by her mother, something that did in reality happen a couple of times . . . And the dentist? Her childhood memories of this are full of anxiety and pain, and this was the sole event when the ever-absent father (as she describes him) was with her, not her mother, "But, wait, he also stayed with me in the hospital, when I had my tonsils out . . ."

Both the diagnosis and the treatment really take off after this. Need I add that her recent problems with her partner(s) have everything to do with the apparently forgotten memories about her parents, their marital relation, and the position she took between the two of them?

This clinical fragment shows how psychic material can be missing in the first place because translating it would evoke an anxiety that is explicitly located in the relation between the subject and the Other. This can be considered the patient's not-wanting-to-know. Technically, it involves secondary repression and the signal anxiety where unpleasurable verbal material has been covered up by other verbal material. This latter makes a return of the repressed possible through the associative pathways. Both the specific defense mechanism (repression) and the transferential relationship (attributing to the therapist knowledge that is then immediately contested) raise suspicions that we are dealing with a hysterical structure (see Chapter 13).

The question now is, what lies behind the repression, assuming that the patient articulates "all" of her associations? Freudian theory enables us to presume that primary repression lies at its base. Clinically, this means that beyond the exhaustive associations, we will come up against a much more radical linguistic failure, caused by a far more radical process. In secondary repression, the repressed material can be recovered through associations; with primary repression this is impossible. This is not purely a theoretical construct. We find its empirical expression in Joseph Breuer's treatment of Anna O., the first verbal psychotherapy. Breuer discovered he could dissolve Anna O.'s mysterious symptoms on the condition that the patient herself put their history of origin into words, albeit under hypnosis. Being a classically schooled scientist, Breuer carefully took down every symptomatic appearance, thus reconstructing the whole series. His quest produces nothing less than an extremely meticulous reconstruction of the chain of signifiers. And what does he conclude? That in every case it ultimately leads to a missing word, an inability-to-say, one explicitly associated with her father, moreover.[8] The father, as the Other, was unable to provide an answer.

This should not be surprising, given that it is a study of hysteria. The lack with which the primal repression is concerned here is far more radical, and its link with trauma is clear. Trauma, too, involves a gap in the ordinary, that is to say, verbal memory, and involves a different kind of anxiety.

PATHOGENESIS: FROM (*a*) TO OTHER

The previous section dealt with normal development; the focus of this section will be on pathogenesis. Freud studied pathogenesis in reverse order, beginning with symptoms in the here and now, and seeking out their prehistory. From the very beginning he focused on defense (Freud 1978 [1894a], 1978 [1896b]). In keeping with his medical training, his aim was to discover an analogous etiological core, the *nec plus ultra* of the symptom series. Like Breuer, he tracked the substitutive signifiers back down along a receding line in an attempt to discover "the" cause. The result is described in the final chapter of the "Studies on Hysteria."[9] There he postulates a traumatic real core (see Fig. 7-1) around which the verbal associations triply circulate, with increasing resistance and, hence, anxiety as they approach the kernel: (1) chronological-centrifugal, (2) concentric-centripetal and (3) logical-associative.

---

8. Hence Breuer's early ideas concerning what he called *"retention* hysteria": originally the patient was unable to do something of a motor and/or verbal nature. The treatment nevertheless forces the patient to perform it, producing the requisite therapeutic abreaction (Freud and Breuer 1978 [1895d], p. 36).

9. Freud and Breuer 1978 (1895d), pp. 288–290, with my diagram. The way Freud presents these three layers corresponds with the evolution in his clinical approach. The reverse chronological line is characteristic of the hypno-cathartic method, as developed by Breuer. The second line represents the period of Freud's focus on symptoms and analysis of the resistance. The third and last line is the result of the free-association method.

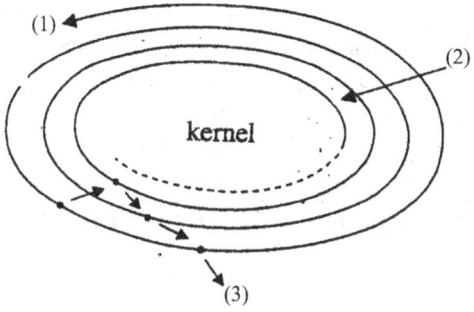

Figure 7-1. Threefold ordering of the psychic material.

This explains why, in the period of the "Studies on Hysteria," he regards an external trauma caused by the Other's drive as the moment of the etiological core, namely, seduction, incest, and sexual abuse. The trauma's specific characteristic is its nonlinguistic nature, which the treatment must try to counter. A couple of years later, with *The Interpretation of Dreams*, he concludes that a certain kernel, found also in the dream, is inherently nonverbalizable.[10] It is during the same period that Freud gives up the question of whether the trauma was real or imagined, regarding this as unanswerable.

Primary repression, as the primary mode of defense, always implies a failure: something cannot be put into words. This something remains stuck at another level of functioning as the core of the unconscious, from which it continues to exert an influence.[11] In fact, the term "pri-

---

10. Freud calls this the "navel" or mycelium of the dream, which is also simultaneously "the kernel of our being" (Freud 1978 [1900a], p. 525). Its ultimately nonverbalizable character has important consequences for the treatment: the final word can never be said; every verbal psychotherapy encounters its limit at this point (see Freud 1978 [1937c]). Freud puts it in terms of a single core and a single lack, that is, castration. In Lacan's reading it becomes doubled between an original lack—the Other's failure to produce an answer to (*a*) (in different terminology, a preoedipal lack)—and its retroactive processing in terms of gender and phallic sexuality through the oedipal structuration. (cf infra, Chapter 9).

11. This perfectly corresponds with Lacan's theory of the unconscious as a perpetually failing process, something that never completely succeeds (i.e., in producing a perfect, final representation), and, precisely because of this failure, keeps insisting and exerting an influence on conscious functioning (Lacan 1994 [1964], first chapter). This is fairly close to Freud's theory of the unconscious as a system.

mary repression" conveys the wrong impression; it is not that something is repressed. Rather it is more accurate to say that something remains at a previous level of expression. Primary repression is consequently more a primary fixation where certain material does not take part in the conversion to normal verbal representations. For Freud, the first verbalizations function as a defensive "counter-cathexis" or "border signifier" to this primal material (Freud 1978 [1911c], pp. 66–67).

Pathogenesis

This understood, we can now make a comparison between the developmental history described in the previous chapter and pathogenesis. The starting point of both is a rise in tension and the accompanying experience of unpleasure. Its cause is internal; it is in the subject's own drive, which seeks an answer in the Other. From this angle, it is not by chance that the patient's first important memories in the clinical fragment described above have to do with pain (the dentist, the tonsils operation) and the Other's presence (the father). An abnormal development implies that the internal tension of the subject gets mixed with (the external drive of) the Other. This mixture may have to do with sexual abuse, but usually comes down to the way this Other will mirror the tension of the subject and/or the way the subject interprets this mirroring. The distinction between internal and external is, moreover, far less dichotomous than one might imagine, precisely because of the way identity is formed, as we saw before. Ultimately, every internal drive will come into interaction with the Other's answer, which itself will always be based on how this Other handles his or her own drive. Consequently, the difference between the Other's drive, as the external trauma, and the subject's own drive, as the internal trauma, becomes much more indistinct. This is confirmed by clinical practice.[12] The result is that the question of "guilt" immediately becomes more problematic.

We can now link these findings to Freud's views on etiology, more specifically to his theory of the origin of the "neuropsychoses of

---

12. Anyone who has worked extensively with victims of long-term sexual abuse has been confronted with the impossibility of making a black-and-white distinction between victim and perpetrator (cf infra, Chapter 14, on perversion).

defense," taking hysteria as the main example. "*Schreck hysteria*," or "panic hysteria" is his name for the first phase, the departure point, that is, a panic attack that occurs whenever the psychological apparatus fails in its processing task: the psyche produces a blank response, a lacuna, resulting in panic (Freud 1978 [1892–1899], pp. 228–229). In the same text, Freud adds that we should not assume that a certain representation is repressed during hysterical attacks: "its primary symptom is the manifestation of fright accompanied by a gap in the psyche." This implies that in hysteria it is not so much that something is repressed, but rather that something has been left behind and remains fixated at an earlier prelinguistic level.

This remainder only becomes apparent in what Freud calls the "second stage," in the construction of a countercathexis or counter-signifier, as a failed representation of what was originally unrepresentable. This, says Freud in the same draft, is the first symbol, albeit through a "false connection."[13] This "border representation," representing the nonverbal nucleus, thus forms the first line of defense that will be developed into greater associative complexes and even fantasies. These themselves will become the target of the resistance, considered as "incompatible" with the ego—that is, with the conscious representational complex. In a conscious rejection this would be denied or negated, but in hysteria, the defense takes the form of secondary repression, through which the material is sent back outside. This second stage becomes particularly evident in clinical practice.

In today's terms, we find here the typical evolution from a panic disorder to a phobia. An originally free-floating anxiety, seemingly without an object, is secondarily linked to something that functions from that moment onward as a phobic object. In itself, this phobia is not the main problem. On the contrary, it is already a solution for an underlying problem, because it enables the patient to manage the origi-

---

13. In anticipation of what follows, we can note that this testifies to a fundamental psychoanalytic thesis, which is that this first symbol, at the same time the first symptom, is an attempt at recovery. We can be more specific about the nature of this attempt: recovery implies an attempt at psychic mastery through representation. The English language expressed this quite beautifully: *recovery* implies the idea of covering up something important, in this case by representations. The difficulty in the case of the drive is that there can be no definitive representation.

nal anxiety, albeit at a price—that is, its invalidation through the phobia. This enables us to see how and why the phobic object is a partially successful–partially failed representation of the originally anxiety-laden and impossible-to-name stimulus. Moreover, such a phobic development invariably implies an other, who receives a certain position and function within the phobic construction. It is, for example, very common for an agoraphobic mother to have to be accompanied by her daughter, without whom she cannot function in certain situations.[14]

Building on this, we can now advance a general thesis: the specific way the primary defense is established determines the structure of the subject, both in its relation to the Other and to the drive. The secondary defense is its subsequent elaboration within the Symbolic-Imaginary (that is, in a theory of the mind) and in the ensuing interactions with others. In the clinical situation (see Fig. 7–2), this elaboration will give rise to a transferential relation between the patient and the clinician, which in itself is the aim of both the diagnosis and the treatment.

Fig. 7–2 summarizes this in more abstract terms. The original experience of internal unpleasure is depicted by (a). Freud initially described this in terms of a quantitative rise in tension resulting from trauma (Freud 1978 [1894a], p. 60). This reappears later on in his theory as the "pressure" arising from the source of the drive.[15] In

$$a \rightarrow S_1$$
$$\downarrow \rightarrow \cancel{S}$$
$$S_2$$

Figure 7–2. Linear depiction of the primary and secondary defenses.

---

14. Clinically, the positions are perfectly interchangeable; it can just as well be the phobic daughter/father, (and so on), who places the mother/son in the contraphobic function. The example above must be read structurally; the content can take many different forms.

15. The concept of the drive was introduced in the "Three Essays on the Theory of Sexuality" (Freud 1978 [1905d]), but the idea is much older, particularly regarding the aspect of tension (cf infra, Chapter 9). Freud identifies two parts to the drive: a somatic part with the source and the pressure, and a psychic part with the aim and the object. The two sides are divided by a gap that cannot be bridged, the same gap as between soma and psyche.

Lacanian terms, this has to do with the Real of the drive, which is traumatic for the subject and which provokes anxiety as a first reaction (Declercq 1998). Later, Lacan will also call this the "jouissance of the body."[16]

What follows is $(a) \rightarrow S_1$, that is, the primary processing of the drive through an association with the Other. As we saw above, this association will always be an incomplete representation, through which the subject's own identity is developed. The S_1 will never fully be able to represent (a); one part of the drive remains fixated at a nonverbal level. For Freud, the S_1, as the earliest symbol, is a "false connection" in the hysterical syllogism of the *"proton pseudos."*[17] Clinically this equates to the way declarative memory of a trauma comes into being. Such memory is never exact and always contains a processing of the original trauma, and therefore functions as a defense itself.

The S_1 indicates an attempt at representation and regulation of the drive, as it is presented (mirrored) by the Other. As a result, the internal problem is shifted outward, onto a verbal dialectic between the subject and the Other that is installed at precisely this point. The way this S_1 is installed will determine the psychic structure of the subject in its relation to the Other as authority. At the same time, the primary defense determines how the subject relates to language. Here we come upon a pivotal process concerning the subject's position toward the Other as an authority on (or having knowledge of) the drive.

No wonder the implications for the differential diagnostics and treatment are so far reaching. The motive for this primary coping mecha-

---

16. This is doubtless one of the most difficult aspects of Lacanian theory, all the more so because it carries an importance change in Lacan's thinking. Where the original emphasis was first put on the "jouissance of the Other," this shifts after Seminar XX to the "jouissance of the body." There the body is understood as the really real Other (see Declercq 2000a, pp. 266–267 and Verhaeghe 2001b, pp. 99–133).

17. Freud uses the expression *"proton pseudos"* in his discussion of hysterical symptom construction. The expression itself comes from Aristotle, stating that a false thesis always goes back to a preceding false premise. In psychological terms, Freud calls this a "false connection" because the patient connects anxiety to an erroneous situation. This mechanism can be understood perfectly in terms of conditioning and the associated learning processes. See Freud 1978 [1950a (1895)], pp. 352–359; for "false connection," see Freud and Breuer 1978 [1895d], pp. 67–70.

nism is the attempt to manage an automatic, traumatic anxiety. The relation is preoedipal and dualistic, presenting only two terms that are impossible to tell apart. Either the ego merges with the answer presented by the Other, or this answer is radically refused.[18] The continuation of this process appears in the relation $S_1 \rightarrow S_2$, resulting in the divided subject $\mathcal{S}$. The way the first symbol gets installed (hysteria: primal repression) determines how the subsequent defense will function (hysteria: secondary repression). The difference between this and the primary level is that this secondary level takes place within normal linguistic functioning, represented by S_2, that is, the entire associative chain of signifiers. This is the post-oedipal, triangular level within language, through which the ego and the Other can be distinguished but never completely separated. The accompanying anxiety is of a secondary nature here, because it has already been processed through the chain of signifiers. Such anxiety functions as signal anxiety or expectancy anxiety, implying that it is a defense against the original primal anxiety. Moreover, at this stage the drive will undergo a gender differentiation, becoming a sexual-phallic impulse, all the while remaining attached to the component drives.[19]

Such a secondary defense, determined by the nature and form of the primary defense, installs a lasting relational structure between the subject, the Other and the drive, setting up a mechanism of repetition. This repetition is entirely bound up with the relation and can be given different names depending on the theory one is using: fundamental fantasy, cognitive schemes, attachment style, or reciprocal patterns. From a Lacanian perspective, this repetition occurs within the chain of

---

18. The Imaginary contains only two terms, making them, precisely for this reason, impossible to tell apart. Try, for example, to say which is the left and right side of the room you are in. One can only do this by using a third point (yourself in this case). Moreover, this example shows how there are no fixed meanings in the Symbolic order (unlike, as it is assumed, in the Imaginary), and that the meaning can always shift depending on the third point (as is typical for the Symbolic).

19. The primary drive can be understood in evolutionary terms as being directed toward survival and reproduction. (cf infra, Chapter 9). The partial or component drives must be conceived in terms of this goal-directedness, where the primary drive is harnessed to certain somatic zones (oral, anal, genital), lending the primary drive a number of specific appearances.

signifiers and is of the order of the automaton. Beyond it lies the considerably more dangerous repetition compulsion (*tuchè*) that belongs to the first level, and hence repeats the confrontation with (*a*). The best clinical illustration of it is the traumatic neurosis with its so-called reliving of the trauma.[20] An important difference between the unprocessed repetition compulsion of the tuchè and the processed repetition of the automaton is that the latter no longer implies a confrontation with the drive itself, but with an already processed version of it within the relation to the Other.

Its subsequent elaboration through the wider chain of signifiers is nothing but the filling in of the subject's identity in its structurally determined relation toward the Other. I will develop this in the following chapter in terms of the fundamental fantasy, that is, the cognitive affective script through which the subject takes up an imaginary position towards the Other. Structurally speaking, such a script always belongs to the secondary processing and can never be considered final.[21] Secondary processing points to the *proton pseudos* aspect: it is indeed an elaboration that always lies at least partially alongside the real thing, giving a rational explanation for something that can never be completely symbolized. This explains why the script is never finished: there is always a remainder, leading to the continual need for further elaboration.

---

20. *Tuchè* and *automaton* are concepts Lacan takes from Aristotle in his discussion of causality and determinism (Lacan 1994 [1964]). Briefly, the *automaton* indicates the process that both determines the associative chain (which signifier appears when?) and installs repetition in the Symbolico-Imaginary order. Free association is anything but free. The *tuchè* indicates a much more radical process where contingent real factors function as the motivating cause for putting the associative chain into action, with the precise aim of representing and mastering this Real cause. This will only partially succeed, with the result that sooner or later the associative chain re-encounters the Real. This is the repetition compulsion.

21. Secondary elaboration is a concept Freud uses in relation to dreaming (Freud 1978 [1900a], p. 499). It indicates the defensive process that transforms the dream's content into a logical and coherent narrative after awakening, over and against the dream's original unconscious source. This term can be expanded by applying it to the entire process of identity formation, where the division is similarly healed through narrativization. Fonagy employs the same basic idea involving division and identity in his term, "narrative smoothing," although without linking it to secondary elaboration (Fonagy et al. 2002, pp. 12–13).

Finally, this clarifies why the subject established in this way is always a divided subject, and divided not merely once but twice. Firstly, it is divided between the Real of the organism and the primary attempt at symbolization: $(a) \rightarrow \$ \rightarrow S_1$. Secondly, it is divided between the different signifiers, each one carrying its own further attempt at a symbolization that will never be complete: $S_1 \rightarrow \$ \rightarrow S_2$. Moreover, this division is explicitly situated in relation to the Other who is supposed to furnish the final answer, S_1. Being unable to do so, the Other consequently also shows its lack.

This latter idea, lack, demands some explanation because of its ambiguity. As we saw earlier, the starting point of human development is an internally experienced situation of drive tension and its accompanying unpleasure. This starting point becomes a lack after the first attempts at symbolization and representation have taken place. We talk about a *lack* because the representation of the original drive impulse always fails—meaning that something is missing in the Symbolic.[22] Experience shows the inevitability of this representational failure, which has to do with the division between the psyche and the soma. The impulse itself has more to do with an excessive aspect of being "too much," because the Real is something that remains insistent and demands processing. This element of being too much will become clinically visible in the study of psychosis and actualpathology.

We are now in a better position to understand the distinction Freud makes between the system unconscious or the primary repressed, and the dynamic or repressed unconscious (Freud 1978 [1915e], pp. 186–189). The system unconscious is the inscription of the drive's kernel on the body, demanding processing in the form of the insistent drive impulses. From a Lacanian perspective this is primarily an indication of a failure of processing, that is, the failure of a final symbolization. The dynamic unconscious, on the other hand, contains all of the "false connections," that is to say, all of the secondary attempts at represent-

---

22. A simple illustration makes this clearer. You look for a book in the library catalog and you find the call number: 15E337. Next you go to that section, convinced that you'll find it in that particular place, indicated by 15E337. But the book is missing. The librarian can't find a borrowing record for it either. The question now is, where exactly is it missing? The answer is, in the Symbolic, more specifically, in the position indicated by 15E337. In the Real, the book isn't missing; it must be "somewhere."

ing the original drive impulse and its accompanying defensive elaboration (Freud 1978 [1915d], pp. 148–150). Symptoms, in other words. Freud also called them "*Abkömmling des Unbewussten*," descendants of the Unconscious, where *Unbewussten* stands for system unconscious. They are the drive kernel's further attempts to reach consciousness. This is why, for Lacan, the dynamic or repressed unconscious is synonymous with the formations of the unconscious (Lacan 1998 [1957–1958]). The dynamic aspect has to do with how part of the symptom is always conscious—indeed, a slip of the tongue is spoken aloud—but contains at the same time an unconscious layer.

THE SYMPTOM AS A HINGE: A DOUBLE LAYERING

In the first clinical consultation, a patient typically presents a number of vague complaints, often focusing on depression and anxiety, which are more often than not connected with relational problems. The first goal of the consultation—in addition to discovering the underlying structure—is to extract whatever symptoms are present. This might seem strange: are not anxiety and depression themselves symptoms? To clarify this, we must first go into how psychoanalysis conceives of symptoms.

In this respect, proto-professionalization has long since taken over, both among professionals and patients unfortunately.[23] In the heyday of psychotherapy it seemed as though pretty much anything could be symptomatic, from nose-picking to the brand of one's new car. The symptom's interpretation was largely determined by the inverse ratio between the symptom's length and breadth—everything represented the genitals . . . Contrasted with this is a very specific Freudian conception, later picked up by Lacan. From *The Interpretation of Dreams* (1978 [1900a]) onward, the symptom, in the psychoanalytic meaning of the word, is an unconscious production that creates a compromise between conflicting impulses, in this way bypassing the defensive censoring line between

---

23. Proto-professionalization is a concept of de Swaan's (1984), indicating the contemporary phenomenon wherein lay people come to describe their problems in professional psychiatric and clinical psychological terms. Feeling bad becomes depression, the ordinary human curve of ups and downs means one is manic-depressive (bipolar), and so on.

the conscious and the unconscious. Or to put it more concretely, bypassing anxiety and unpleasure. This production obeys a number of laws which, precisely for this reason, makes it possible to analyze them using associative material. Lacan devoted his early seminars to this and discovered in his return to Freud that these laws can be formulated in linguistic terms.[24] In his opinion, the symptom always possesses a linguistic structure in relation to the Other, with the emphasis on metonymy (displacement) and metaphor (condensation). Precisely because of this linguistic structure, the gate is opened to potential reformulation during the course of the treatment. Free association is anything but free; it operates according to the automaton.

Let me give a classic example: Freud's forgetting of the name "Signorelli." In its place, the substitute names "Boltraffio" and "Botticelli" crop up (see Fig. 7–3). The ensuing associations demonstrate that association is not free but lawfully determined in the chain of signifiers, where certain syllables refer repeatedly to the repressed name.

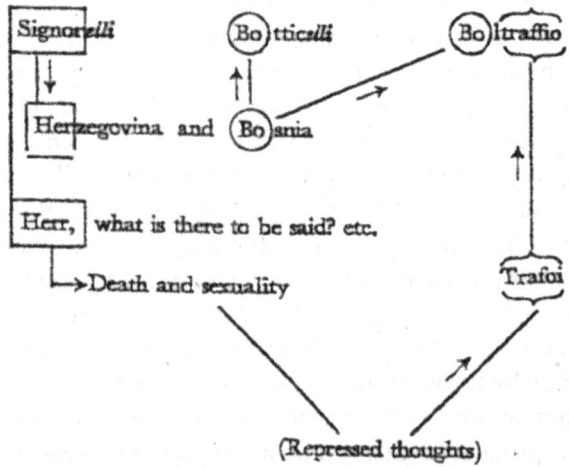

Figure 7–3. Forgetting and remembering as symptoms.

---

24. It is no accident that Lacan placed *The Purloined Letter* first in his *Écrits*, in reverse of all the other papers' chronology. In this paper he scientifically demonstrates (through a probability calculus) the determinism and automaton of the chain of signifiers.

The whole scheme is nothing but the secondary elaboration inside the secondary defensive process (Freud 1978 [1901b], pp. 1–7). The underlying primary defense process is merely referred to, but not elaborated, "Death and sexuality" and "Repressed thoughts" being incompletely represented in the secondarily processed associations. The forgetting of the name "Signorelli" is an attempt to avoid unpleasurable thoughts of impotence and death. Moreover—and this is not mentioned in the commentaries I am familiar with—this forgetting explicitly takes place within a certain relation. Freud was in discussion with someone about the extent of a Turkish patient's trust in their doctor and their resignation to Fate, although with one important exception—their sexual functioning. It was precisely this last point Freud wanted to keep out of the discussion. In other words, the topic under discussion concerns the potential impotence of the master figure (the doctor) in relation to the patient's impotence. This motive becomes all the more significant when we consider how Freud had recently lost such a patient through suicide. The failing is consequently his failing, and it is this that he cannot or will not admit to the Other. The symptom covers it up—recovery, indeed.

This illustration can serve as a model for every form of symptom construction: slips of the tongue, conversion, phobia, and obsessional thoughts. What I wish to emphasize is how every one of them is constructed in relation to an Other. This is frequently forgotten, resulting in an isolated view of the symptom. For both diagnostic and therapeutic reasons, it is vitally important that one understand the symptom as a product constructed in the light of an underlying fantasmatic relation toward the Other, a relation through which their respective identities are defined.

Such a view of the symptom has practical implications, unlike the confusion we see in the current psychoanalytic paradigm's decline. So far we have discussed the "what" of the symptom; the following question has to do with the "why." For both Freud and Lacan, insofar as every symptom is a compromise, it is always an attempt at a solution, that is, an imaginary way of responding to the lack in the Symbolic with regard to the anxiety-provoking Real. In this way we rediscover the development sketched out above, where the symptom takes its place in the subsequent elaboration of the original border signifier.

This does not mean that the symptom is purely an imaginary construction. Reduce it to this and one forgets about its substratum, which is integral to the construction itself. Freud's well-known metaphor for this is that of the oyster that creates a pearl around a grain of sand (Freud 1978 [1905e], p. 83). The grain of sand is of the order of the Real and of the tuchè, to be defended against; the pearl is the automaton-reaction to it, producing the envelope or container, that is to say, the visible external side of the symptom. On the inside, the original real starting point remains effective as a "foreign body." In the case of hysteria, Freud talks about "somatic compliance," the fact that something of the body is present in the kernel of every symptom.[25] In the more general terms of his theory, this is the so-called "root" of the drive or the point of fixation (Declercq 2000, pp. 291–312; 2002). Following Lacan, we can place the object (a) in this position. A schematic diagram of symptom formation (see Fig. 7–4) appears as follows:

(a)
traumatic real
"too much"

border representation S_1
first symbol, first symptom
= failing symbolization

↓

further elaboration:
symptoms as a compromise
in the relationship $\barS \lozenge (a) \lozenge A$
= within the fundamental fantasy.

Figure 7–4. The linear development of symptoms.

---

25. The German expression: "*Somatisches Entgegenkommen*" is stronger and more active than the English "somatic compliance." With this concept, Freud indicates how every symptom boils down to a normal or pathological process in an organ or part of the body that determines the "*Neurosenwahl*," or the subject's "choice" of a certain pathology (see Freud 1978 [1905e], pp. 40–41).

In this schema, the symptom's processing function can be seen: every symptom is an attempt to express and master the original drive impulse through signifiers, and hence through the Other. At the same time, as the symptom is constructed a certain identity is also formed for both the subject and the Other. The failure of this process is a structural necessity, resulting in the asymptotic construction of symptoms: no single symptom succeeds in finally covering up the original Real. Hence Lacan's thesis: "It doesn't stop not being written" (Lacan 1998 [1972–1973], pp. 94, 144).

Furthermore, the schema carries a very important implication: in themselves symptoms are neither normal nor abnormal. Their potentially normal or abnormal character depends on two things: one, on the degree to which a symptom does or doesn't fit within a given sociocultural context, that is, on an arbitrary-normative criterion. Two, on a subjective criterion, that is to say, the degree of the symptom's success in providing a livable compromise for the subject. These two aspects don't necessarily have to coincide; recall the difference between a juridical and a clinical diagnosis.

We can clarify this through an example we've already discussed, the fear of failure. This fear can be examined in its own right, leading to explanations that quickly fall into neurobiological considerations. Or, from a Lacanian perspective, fear of failure can be considered not as a symptom but rather the expression of a certain relation to the Other. An important clinical question is then: for whom or against whom is one failing? And which symptoms were constructed inside this relationship? Rather than simply reducing it to an individual phenomenon, such an approach can have far more fruitful diagnostic and therapeutic effects. Moreover, it simultaneously enables one to discover its counterpart: the compulsion to succeed. Just as certain people have to fail for or in opposition to someone else, others have to succeed. The latter can demand just as heavy a toll as the former, but in our current sociocultural discourse it will be considered less of a problem as it accords perfectly with the values of today's competitive society.

On this basis, we can distinguish between two groups of pathology. The first is determined by the nature of the primary defense. Depending on how the originally internal drive is taken up in relation to the Other, the subject will exhibit either a neurotic, a perverse, or a psychotic structure. These will be discussed in the following section. The second group is an extension of the first and is determined by the degree to which the secondary defense and elaboration are carried through. Some neurotic, psychotic, or perverse structures may remain stuck at the primary level, without the development of symptoms as such. We will now examine this in more detail.

ACTUALPATHOLOGY VERSUS PSYCHOPATHOLOGY: TWO FORMS OF ANXIETY

Additional analysis of the symptom's two layers enables us to distinguish between two types of symptoms. On the one hand, we find naked anxiety as such, where the subject feels overtaken by passivity and which seems to have little to say to us at first sight. This anxiety is thus also meaningless, explaining its traumatic character. As we will see later on, this reappears in the contemporary idea of the panic attack. On the other hand, we have the endless series of symptoms that are actively constructed by the subject in an attempt to master the original anxiety; in the course of this construction, the subject acquires layers of additional identity. This explains why every subject, even long before the development of psychoanalysis, is intimately convinced that his or her symptom "means" something (Ellenberger 1970; Veith 1965). Freud sees this symptomal series as an attempt at recovery, in the sense of an attempt at stabilization; as a series, it belongs to the order of the signifier, with phobia, conversion, obsessive phenomena, slips of the tongue, and hallucinations. In brief, every symptom in the classical psychoanalytic meaning of the word.

In this symptomal series, anxiety is made manageable through associating it with the signifier. Often the anxiety itself slips almost entirely away from view. The role of the symptomal series is to signal the underlying danger associatively, and thereby protect against it. Contrasted with this is traumatic anxiety, also called automatic anxiety, which surfaces in direct confrontations with the Real. In such anxiety there is no substitution by signifiers and no symbolization. The closest it comes to symbolization is to the so-called somatic anxiety equivalents, which are very carefully described by Freud and have mainly to do with respiratory problems, heart complaints, sweating and shivering, and so on.[26]

---

26. It is striking how the very same description can be found in recent studies of the so-called hyperventilation complaints and panic disorder (cf infra, Chapter 11).

From now on we will call this first type of symptom a *phenomenon*, in order to distinguish it from the symptom as such, which is a defensive construction within the signifier against the Real of the drive. In light of what we saw in the previous chapter, we can say that this automatic or traumatic anxiety merges with separation anxiety. What we call it depends on the direction we look at it from: either from the perspective of the drive impulse (automatic, traumatic anxiety) or view it as originating from the Other who fails in its meaning-providing and mirroring function (separation anxiety).

Here again we encounter the double layer of the defensive process that enabled Freud to make a significant differential diagnostic classification. What Freud, in his correspondence with Fliess, was still calling "panic hysteria" becomes rechristened "actualneurosis" in his official publications and is clearly differentiated from what he called the neuropsychoses of defense (Freud 1978 [1895b], [1896a], [1896b], [1898a]). Actualneurosis goes no further than the primary defense and the accompanying automatic anxiety; psychoneurosis, on the other hand, does nothing but try to remain as far removed as possible from the initial moment of panic by putting as many signifiers as it can on top of it. This is precisely why it constitutes an attempt at recovery.

In Part III this distinction will be applied more generally to the entire field of pathology, that is, beyond the strictly neurotic field. For this reason we will be using the expression "actualpathology" in place of "actualneurosis." We can bring this into the terms of a linear schema (See Fig. 7–5).

Actualpathology
automatic anxiety
primary defense

$a \rightarrow S_1$

$\downarrow \rightarrow \$$ **Psychopathology**
signal anxiety
secondary defense

S_2

Figure 7–5. Actualpathology versus psychopathology.

The distinction between actualpathology and psychopathology traverses the different structures of the subject: psychosis, neurosis, and perversion may remain stuck at the actualpathological position, or may continue in a further psychopathological elaboration within the chain of signifiers. As we will see in the next part, the concept of actualpathology can be extended to a number of typical disorders lying between the somatic and the psychic (panic disorder, somatization, MUS). The difference between the two types of pathology has to do with the way the anxiety is experienced. Such a distinction is not merely academic but can be found without too much difficulty in clinical practice. It is not at all unusual for patients to express anxiety about the anxiety. Here, the signal function of a specific anxiety appears quite clearly in relation to the underlying anxiety that is experienced as much more threatening.

This difference has to do with what I described above in terms of the active or passive positions. One copes with being passively surrendered to the other part (a) in oneself by taking an active position, thus shifting this other part (a) to the Other, understood as both the other as such and as language. Here, active implies a tendency toward separation, passive a tendency toward identification and fusion.

Development and the Discourse Formulas

The linear schema loses its linear character the moment we recognize that it contains two of the discourse formulas, namely, those of the master and of the hysteric. Rather than a chronological-linear time scheme, a logical temporality becomes necessary, meaning that the processes can occur at any point in "development," that is, at each point where a confrontation with (a) takes place.

$$\begin{array}{ccc} \$ & \rightarrow & S_1 \\ \uparrow & & \downarrow \\ (a) & // & S_2 \end{array} \quad \text{leads to:} \quad \begin{array}{ccc} S_1 & \rightarrow & S_2 \\ \uparrow & & \downarrow \\ \$ & // & (a) \end{array}$$

This analogy between development and the discourse formulas is no coincidence. It provides a structural illustration of how the starting point of subject-formation boils down to the relationship between the

Hysterical and the Master discourse, that is, Lacan's formulation of Freud's Oedipus complex. An original drive impulse (a) puts pressure on the subject $\slashed{S}$, becomes processed through the Other as S_1, and is thereby introduced into the sexualized interaction S_2. The result is that the original internal division between the subject and (a) is displaced onto an "external" relation, dividing the subject now between the various signifiers being emitted by the Other. Nevertheless, the gap between (a) and the divided subject keeps on insisting itself, both literally and figuratively, "under the skin."

So far we have discussed development in chronologically linear terms. In clinical practice and human reality, however, we are condemned to an eternal *hic et nunc*, where past and future are continuously determined in circular ways. For instance, it has been empirically shown that memory of traumatic events is clearly influenced by the actual circumstances of those involved (Southwick et al. 1997; Wyshak 1994). Epistemologically, this is considerably more difficult to conceive. It obliges us to attend fully to the circular nature of both defense and identity acquisition, and to the effects of the *Nachträglichkeit*, the retroactive revision. This is the subject of our next chapter.

SUMMARY

- The subject defends itself against something Real in the body by means of the Other, understood as both other and language.
- This defense takes off in a primary form that determines the subject's psychic structure (neurosis, psychosis, perversion)—that is, how the subject functions in language.
- The secondary defense is a subsequent self-protective elaboration in the Imaginary, where the material that is warded off is attributed to the Other.
- On this basis, a lasting and repetitive relation between the subject and the Other regarding lack is installed: the fundamental fantasy.
- The anxiety belonging to the primary defense is caused by the impossibility of completely mastering the drive through the Other and is of a traumatic and automatic nature. It is missing the link with the signifier.

- The anxiety belonging to the secondary defense is the result of further associative processing of the underlying drive impulse and functions as a signal anxiety. The processing through the signifier is used as a defense.
- The construction of the symptom follows the same double layering. Each symptom contains a real kernel around which a defensive superstructure is built in the Imaginary. Each symptom is therefore an attempt at "re-covery."
- Should the defensive process remain stuck at the primary level without further processing, actualpathology results. Where it does acquire further processing, one talks about psychopathology.
- Both actualpathology and psychopathology can appear in every subjective structure, that is, in neurosis, psychosis, and perversion.

8
From a Linear to a Circular Model: On Becoming a Subject

The post-Freudian reading of Freud interprets his theory as a description of linearly occurring, intrasubjective processes that feature just a single central anxiety. One speaks of an initial primary defense, followed by a second, both defensive processes taking place within a single psyche. The impact of the other is negligible and the classic psychoanalytic framework is considered to belong to an "individual" model.

Subsequent analysis nevertheless shows that these three characteristics can and must be given further development in Freud's theory. The aspect of linearity is overcome by his focus on the retroactive nature of meaning and by the discovery that there is no time in the unconscious. The emphasis on the intrapsychic disappears once we realize that his theory of the oedipal structure, with its identifications and repressions, entails a dialectic between a subject and an Other that will later be repeated through the transference. The most difficult point remains his theory of anxiety, where he obstinately maintains his emphasis on castration anxiety. Nevertheless, this doesn't take anything away from the fact that he distinguishes between two different forms of anxiety, each possessing a different foundation.[1]

---

1. These are the automatic and signal anxieties (Freud 1978 [1926d]). It is no coincidence that Freud continues to have difficulties with his theory on anxiety.

Lacan's return to Freud will make a number of implicit things explicit. The linearity is completely abandoned, to be replaced by a circular model. The intrapsychic aspect disappears and in its place the emphasis shifts toward the relation between the divided subject and the Other, understood as both language and others. The differential diagnostics is focused on the position the subject takes in relation to the Other's lack. Finally, the theory of anxiety and castration gets completely rethought. The original lack in the Symbolic in relation to the Real is replaced during subject-formation by a lack in the Symbolic in relation to the Imaginary. With this replacement, the lack becomes sexualized, setting the dialectics of gender in motion.

This is best explained by Lacan's theory of identity acquisition, that is, of subject-formation. But before we go into this, let us first discuss a number of general characteristics of his theory. Briefly, Lacan's is a conflict model; identity takes narrative form, with an emphasis on alienation, and must be understood from inside its structural context.

The Lacanian subject is a divided subject whose different parts are not only different but also often incompatible. Here we come back across Guislain's idea of conflict as the basis for pathology (see Chapter 4). For psychodiagnostics, this has a number of immediate implications. First, it implies that there is no kernel of identity or personality, only a division. Moreover, in the event of conflict there will always be a dominating and a dominated part of the identity. During the diagnostic process, the dominant part will speak the loudest, drowning out the other. The resulting danger is for the diagnostician to consider the other, dominated part as the real identity, the "true self." This is a mistake: one must instead concentrate on the division, its background history and its effects on the subject's present-day psychological functioning.

The subject obtains its divided identity through the Other by way of language, with the result that this identity is both alienated and of narrative form. Seeing as how this Other is put together out of different others who each contribute their own little part of the story, the implication is that the subject is divided between different desires

---

Without going more deeply into it, I can say here that these difficulties have mainly to do with the fact that he keeps unilaterally insisting on castration anxiety. On this point, he is corrected by Lacan (1962–1963 and 1991 [1969–1970]) and Laplanche (1980).

emanating from different others. The term alienation is part of the philosophical heritage of the 1960s, but it gains another meaning in Lacan. Identity comes into being through identification with the signifiers of the Other—hence the alienation effect—but there is no original or authentic personality beneath these alienating layers. Lacan's now-classic metaphor for this is the onion: one can peel away all of the alienating layers of identity, with tears if need be, but after the last layer there is nothing left (Lacan 1991 [1953–1954]).[2] To the extent that one can talk about a kernel, it has to do with the body and its insistence upon the psyche.

The structural aspect of this has to do with what we have already discussed and highlights the relation between the different elements in such a way that the ego and the other are no longer strictly separated entities. Both acquire their identity in relation to each other, with the accent on two central themes: authority and gender. It will be in all those relations that touch upon these two things (i.e., sex and authority) that the division and its potential accompanying conflict will become especially visible.[3]

Finally we must underscore another characteristic of Lacanian theory. Were the subject's division restricted solely to the linguistic

---

2. After the movie *Shrek*, the onion metaphor has acquired a new layer:

Shrek: "Ogres are like onions."
Donkey: "What, 'cause they stink?"
Shrek: "No . . ."
Donkey: "'Cause they make people cry?"
Shrek: "NO! They have LAYERS. There's more to us underneath. So ogres are like onions."
Donkey: "Yeah, but nobody likes onions!"

3. There is a clear resemblance here to contemporary attachment theory (Fonagy et al. 2002). There, too, identity formation begins with a somatic arousal for which an appeal is made to the other that installs a lasting relation, along with the representation of one's own and the other's identities. This "style of attachment," which can take different forms in children, has been empirically shown to be correlated with the parents' own attachment styles (Van Ijzendoorn 1992, 1995; Van Ijzendoorn and Bakermans-Kranenburg 1996). Moreover, the basis of the inner working model for the image of self and other has everything to do with the child's reaction to the desire of the mother: "The key feature of this [inner model] is how acceptable or unacceptable the child feels in the eye of the attachment figure" (Fonagy 2001, p. 12).

dimension, this would imply that human identity was located purely in the Symbolic and, hence, was entirely "constructed." Simply put, identity would merely be a game of words, through which ultimately anything would be possible. Such a view, however, overlooks our starting point, which Lacan situates explicitly in the primary relation toward the body. The manner in which he accomplishes this overcomes the classic psyche–soma dichotomy (Verhaeghe 2001b, pp. 99–126). The Real of the body is not something that operates from the outside. Just as the internal–external and ego–other are continually interwoven, so the subject and the drive remain one uncanny and always incomplete totality. The uncanny aspect of this lies in the fact that the drive continues to work in an ex-sisting way as an irreducible *nec plus ultra*. The incompleteness has to do with it's being impossible for the Symbolic to completely represent the Real of the drive. Hence Lacan's negative name for this divided totality: the "not-whole" or "not-all" (*le pas-tout*, Lacan 1998 [1972–1973]). This in itself gives rise to what he calls a circular, but nonreciprocal, structure that is continuously taken up again on another level, but which never succeeds in closing itself (cf infra, Chapter 9).

CIRCULAR AND RETROACTIVE: SUBJECT-FORMATION

In clinical practice, one commonly comes across what is known as selective listening: a patient, upon being given advice, interpretations, or therapeutic directions, hears something other than what was intended. This puts the whole idea of all forms of insight therapy—whether psychoanalytic or cognitive—seriously into question: it is not enough just to present the right solution for the treatment to be successful.[4]

Selective listening has to do with subject-formation[5] and needs to be applied not just to the patient but to the therapist as well. In the

---

4. This explains the failure of most enlightenment campaigns, from driving under the influence to health food. These appeal in particular, if not exclusively, to an already receptive part of the public. Their target group, on the contrary, begins with a negative attitude toward the message and—especially—toward the messenger, making it impossible for the content to be taken in.

5. Also see B. Fink (1995), pp. 34–79.

Freudian-based linear model above, identity is formed in relation to the outside world on the basis of pleasure and unpleasure. The initial mechanisms of incorporation and expulsion become replaced by identification and repression. From a Lacanian perspective, this outside world amounts to the speaking other and to the body as organism; the inside world is the subject. The relation between these two is similarly based on pleasure and unpleasure, but the exchange material is linguistic in nature. Identity is a chain of signifiers through which both the subject and the other gain content, along with the specific character of their relation.

Lacan's approach to identity acquisition introduces a number of new ideas to the Freudian model. The foundation of identity is still sought in infancy, but identity acquisition continues to evolve; one's identity as such is never completed. Moreover, the acquisition occurs both pro- and retroactively. Recently added content acquired through identification with new signifiers changes the meaning of the whole; conversely, previously incorporated signifiers determine the meaning of the newly added signifiers. This is what Freud calls *Nachträglichkeit* (retroactivity), whose logic, albeit unbeknownst to Freud, recalls that of structural linguistics (De Saussure 1976; Freud 1978 [1918b]). The meaning of a story is always determined by the combination of the newly added elements with what went on before. The result is a circular—not linear—identity formation; chronological time is replaced by logical time.

Consequently, we need to leave every linear form of etiological reasoning behind. Declarative memory declares above all how one situates oneself in the present. Its potential resemblance to what happened in the past is only narrowly recovered and even that, in itself, is not the purpose of the clinical interview in the first place.[6] Moreover, we can

---

6. Cf. Lacan (1977 [1953], p. 48): "I might as well be categorical: in psychoanalytic anamnesis, it is not a question of reality, but of truth, because the effect of full speech is to reorder past contingencies by conferring on them the sense of necessities to come, such as they are constituted by the little freedom through which the subject makes them present." This has very important repercussions for the aim of the treatment. The aim of psychoanalysis is not to arrive at an accurate reconstruction of the past, nor to explain (let alone justify) the present based on the history of the subject. The aim is to create possibilities for change.

reasonably assume that the way the past is brought into the story is always a falsified version, precisely because of its present-day construction.[7]

The basic mechanisms in this subject-formation are alienation and separation (Lacan 1994 [1964]; Verhaeghe 1998b). Alienation encompasses both identification and repression (more generally, defense). Separation, on the other hand, is scarcely discussed in the Freudian model. Each mechanism presents a starting point for a potential pathology that, precisely depending on its starting point, will be completely different. In cases of insufficient alienation, the subject-to-be will continue to try to fuse with the Other and will display separation anxiety. In cases of too much alienation, the subject-to-be will fly from the Other and display an obvious desire for separation.[8] Note that in both cases, the subject fails to achieve a position independent of the Other. In the first, it must continue to connect with the Other; in the second, it must

---

7. A simple clinical illustration. Summer 1980. A young academic fulfills what was then (in Belgium) the still obligatory military service. It is a period of intense boredom, characterized by meaningless watches and shoe-polishing and coped with through the consumption of considerable amounts of alcohol in the mess; a life in waiting before "real" life can start. Autumn 2000. The same man comes for consultation, complaining about panic attacks and a midlife crisis. His marriage has lost all passion, his children do nothing but present problems, his job is one confrontation after another with his superiors. During the second interview, he describes his military service as a period of joy and challenges, a time when he was still "fully alive."

Where is the "reality" in this story? And what is the "truth"? Human memory clearly has a different function than that of recording the past objectively, so much is clear. It is striking that Freud, a hundred years before the debate over "false memory," explicitly expressed his doubts about the authenticity of memories and pointed to the importance of fantasmatic distortions. His is a very nuanced discussion whose conclusion reads: "It may indeed be questioned whether we have any memories at all *from* our childhood: memories *relating* to our childhood may be all that we possess. Our childhood memories show us our earliest years not as they were but as they appeared at the later periods when the memories were aroused. In these periods of arousal, the childhood memories did not, as people are accustomed to say, *emerge*; they were *formed* at that time. And a number of motives, with no concern for historical accuracy, had a part in forming them, as well as in the selection of the memories themselves" (Freud 1978 [1899a], p. 322).

8. It is fascinating to read Lacan's theory of alienation and separation alongside the different attachment styles. In the adult, the styles are: secure/autonomous; insecure/dismissive; insecure/preoccupied; unresolved (Fonagy et al. 2002, p. 39). To be able to combine the distinctive Anglo-American focus on empiricism with the French emphasis on structure would doubtless be quite fruitful here.

constantly run away. Separation proper, in the sense of autonomy and an effective reflective function (cf infra), fails to develop, and a dependence on the Other in either direction persists. It is thus no accident that, for Lacan, the aim of the treatment boils down to separation, that is to say, to the installation of maximum difference between the subject and the other (Lacan 1994 [1964], p. 276). In what follows, we will go more deeply into these two mechanisms.

ALIENATION

Analogously with the Freudian model and in line with Lacan's reasoning, I consider a first, primary alienation as the basis for all further alienations. This process starts with a confrontation with the real part of the drive that is to be processed through the first signifier from the Other. Thus is the foundation of identity laid, immediately indicating its alienated nature. Indeed, identity's attribution comes from the Other; the subject must identify with it.[9] This occurs in a relation in which the Other assumes responsibility for removing the original unpleasure or arousal (Lacan 1994 [1964], pp. 203–216). The latter nevertheless continues to insist, resulting in the circular and never-ending character of this earliest process (see Fig. 8–1).

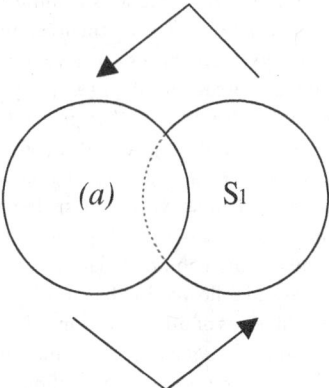

Figure 8–1. Primary alienation (primal repression).

---

9. Let us not forget that identity comes from the Latin *identitas*, meaning indeed identity, uniformity. Here Lacan assumes a radical stance: every identity is alienated

In the figure, the bottom arrow indicates the subject's appeal to the Other, from whom the subject receives the first signifier. Hence the top arrow, indicating the subject's identification with the S_1 that becomes incorporated into the subject in this way. As a result, (a) is displaced to the "external side" of the subject, and more specifically to the intersection between the two circles (see Fig. 8-2). This process will never be finished: the tension will never be completely answered for, resulting in the need for another signifier and turning subject-formation into an endless process.

The parallel between this first alienation and primary repression is unmistakable.[10] Here the subject acquires a lasting position, with respect to both language and the Other. In the early Lacan, this position was considered irreversible: one is either psychotic, perverse, or neurotic. His later conceptualizations, based on topology, put less emphasis on its irreversible nature (Maleval 2000). Clearly, Lacan's theory of alienation and separation, like the Freudian theory of (primary) repression, is by and large a theory of neurosis. Psychosis (foreclosure) and perversion (disavowal) can similarly be considered according to the same structural logic albeit, above all, to demonstrate their difference from neurosis (cf infra, Part III).

---

because it comes from the Other. It is striking how in the contemporary attachment theories mentioned above, the same argument is presented (there is no original identity, there are only representative constructions coming from the other), although without arriving at the same conclusion. Such theories describe an "alien self" but one that is restricted to pathology; nevertheless, in several places throughout the book it is admitted that everyone possesses this alien self (Fonagy et al. 2002). An earlier publication says the same thing: "This alien other probably exists in seed form in all our self-representations" (Fonagy and Target 2000, p. 865).

10. The differentiation between a primary and a secondary alienation is my interpretation of Lacan's theory in Seminar XI. This first alienation is nothing other than Freud's primary repression. As we saw earlier, primary repression comes down to fixation, that is to say, to the leaving behind of material on an earlier nonverbal level. In a letter dated May 30, 1896 and followed by the one of Dec. 6, 1896, Freud describes early infantile development in terms of different forms of expression—writing forms, *Niederschrifte* (in neurological terms, *Bahnungen*, facilitations or pathways)—of which language is the last to appear. During the transition of one writing form to another—during the development of the psychological apparatus that is—certain material is left behind in the previous form for defensive purposes. It is not so difficult to recognize here the evolution from incorporation–expulsion to identification–repression and alienation–separation (Freud 1978 [1892–1899], pp. 229–239).

The subject acquires its first identity through this process, along with an initial mastery of (*a*), coming from the Other each time. As we saw above, the representation of the drive remains structurally incomplete, whereupon a new appeal to the Other is made. The continuation of the subject-formation takes place within language and amounts to a continuous extension of the chain of signifiers through which the subject continues to acquire more identity in relation to the Other.

This acquisition process is not neutral but is constructed within a dialectic of desire. As described earlier (cf supra, Chapter 6) a reversal occurs. The Other is made responsible for answering to (*a*), but in order to receive this answer, the subject must identify with the Other's desire. Consequently, positive signifiers coming from that Other will be accepted, negative ones will be refused. The relation between the subject and the Other will come to take on specific content and form, depending on the reactions of the significant others and the choices of the subject-to-be. (see Fig. 8–2).

The earliest identity (of the mirror stage)—here indicated by S_1—receives further signifiers, S_2, from the Other in an attempt to obtain a final answer to the drive. But it is precisely the impossibility of ever receiving such a final answer that makes this process endless. From this extension over succeeding signifiers, moreover, the subject becomes divided over a number of signifiers, and will never again be able to coincide with "itself," with the S_1 of the first mirror identity.

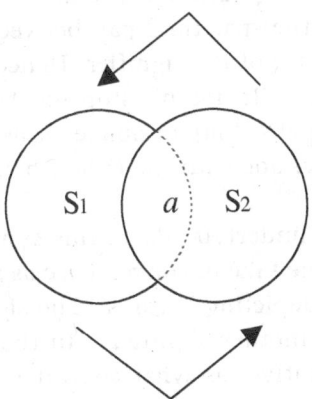

Figure 8–2. Secondary alienation (secondary repression).

This same figure illustrates the expulsion, when certain signifiers of the Other are experienced as negative and are therefore sent back outside, to the Other. In Lacan's schema (not reproduced here; see Lacan 1994 [1964], p. 240), these unpleasurable signifiers are displaced to the intersection, the common part between the two circles, where they remain operative as Freud's "foreign bodies." As a result of the primary alienation, (a) has already been displaced to this intersection, and, from the Freudian point of view, this is the nucleus of the system unconscious that continues to attract the material of the secondary repression (Freud 1978 [1911c], pp. 67–68; [1915d], p. 148). It is not by chance that Lacan indicates this intersection as the region of "non-sense," that is, the absence of sense. The expulsion comes down to the secondary repression, implying that the unpleasurable material is dissociated from the signifier, thereby becoming dynamically unconscious (Lacan, 1994 [1964], p. 211). As a result, we find in this intersection both (a), that is the result of the first alienation and primal repression, and the refused, repressed signifiers coming from the Other. We will return to this later in the discussion of separation.

Thus considered, the acquisition of identity comes down to the symbolic realization of the subject. In view of its starting point, this realization is contingent, necessary, and impossible. The contingency has to do with the chance nature of the interaction—initially centered on the body—between the subject and Other. The necessity is the result of the compelling nature of the drive tension. The impossibility is caused by the structural gap between the Real of (a) and the Symbolic character of the signifier. Hence the double negation in Lacan's statement: "It doesn't stop not being written" (Lacan 1998 [1972–1973], pp. 94, 144). In simple terms: we will never be finished with our body, nor with the Other, hence the need for more (Encore).

Along with the underlying lack, this symbolic realization can be represented for the sake of convenience as a chain (see Fig. 8–3), thus schematically depicting Lacan's "The signifier is what represents a subject for another signifier." In the background, (a) remains causally operative, as what continues to push the process (= tuchè).

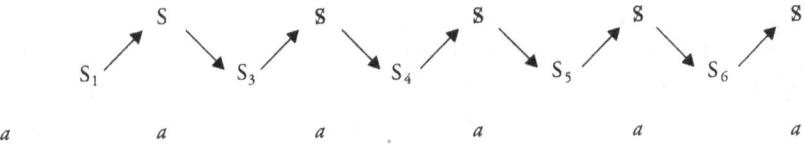

Figure 8–3. Retroactive subject-formation.

Nevertheless, a representation such as this is didactic and therefore incorrect (cf. infra, Fig. 8–5). A better rendering would be a three-dimensional network where the associative connections run in different directions. Moreover, the retroactive character has to be taken into account; as argued above, the chronological temporal perspective doesn't work. The ever-provisional end product of identity acquisition is located on the right, in the alienation of the last signifier. Each new signifier that is added causes an extension that retroactively changes the whole of the preceding chain. Conversely, the existing chain has an automaton-influence on the choice of the next signifier(s) with which the subject will identify (Lacan 1966, pp. 54–61). Determination thus works in two directions, from the present to the past and the other way around. The central question therefore concerns the position of the subject in relation to the Other and to (*a*).

In clinical praxis we are nearly always confronted with the linguistic end product of identity acquisition, and in our previous descriptions we stressed identification with the signifiers of the Other. Such an emphasis needs to be corrected in two ways.

First of all, the point of onset of a specific pathology is almost always caused by a (renewed) confrontation between the subject and its own drive (Freud 1978 [1916–1917], p. 391; [1937c], pp. 220–223). Here, we can refer more broadly to the typical life periods during which a pathology breaks through: the Oedipal period, puberty, adolescence, midlife, menopause, and—even more specifically—the first ejaculation, the onset of menses, pregnancy, and birth. These are all periods when the drive-driven body puts its demands into the foreground loud and clear. In this way, the body functions as an accidental cause, tuchè, beyond the Symbolic that consequently is called upon to do something about it.[11] What will subsequently be done with it will take place inside further subject-formation and, hence, in dependence on the Other (Assoun 1997b, p. 93 ff). It is important to pay sufficient attention to this, both in the diagnosis and in the treatment.

Secondly, and immediately following on from it, identity acquisition starts from the first exchanges between the subject-to-be and the Other (as represented in Fig. 8–1), which are contingent and almost entirely focused on the body.[12] It might sound strange, but it is there that each of us acquires our body, over and frequently counter to the original organism.[13] It is the Other, usually the mother, who invests her own desire in certain body parts and functions, either at the child's demand or not. This investment sets in motion a process that runs more or less in tandem with the body's physical maturation, but one that can never simply be reduced to the latter. More usually the opposite occurs: her demand determines how this maturation progresses; this is illustrated by the fact, for example, that children become toilet-trained at different ages in different cultures.[14] Analogous with this, the child gains its first sense of totality, prototypically in the mirror stage (Lacan

---

11. Here again, I am following the distinction Lacan makes (1994 [1964]) between causality (tuchè) and determination (automaton) (cf supra, Chapter 7). For Lacan, this causality is always accidental and real. The subsequent processing takes place through the signifier and is therefore precisely determined in and by the dependent relationship with the Other. Freud talked about "the pathogenic appeal of the drive on the ego" and about the "taming of the drive" in this respect, thus clearly indicating that such an appeal can never be fully answered but only "tamed" through the binding to signifiers during the secondary process (Freud 1978 [1937c], pp. 224–225; see also Note 18 in Chapter 9).

12. The contingency has to do with the particularity of the subject's individual body it begins with, and with the specific ways that a particular mother reacts to it.

13. Fonagy et al. (2002, p. 207 ff) also regard identity development as beginning in bodily arousal. Based on a review of developmental psychological research, they demonstrate that babies under 6 months do indeed have a sense of their body as a separate entity with causal effects on their surroundings, but that they do not have a psychic representation of it—this has to come from the Other. They call this starting point the "bodily self," with the result that they contradict their own thesis: there is, as yet, no identity, only a kind of "awareness."

14. Bodily development will thus be determining for both the upper and the lower age limit, but no more than that. See Lacan for the transition from the oral to the anal (Lacan 1991 [1960–1961], p. 164).

1977 [1949]). The view of the child's own complete image in the mirror, pointed out to it by the Other, leads to the first full experience of totality: that is "me." It is no accident that for Freud, too, the first layer of the ego boils down to a bodily surface (Freud 1978 [1923b], p. 26).

This has far-reaching consequences: the most intimate part of ourselves, "our" own body, is handed to us by the Other. According to Lacan, the unconscious is structured like a language, and in this way the body functions as the first sheet of paper upon which the Other writes its message.[15] The first Other invests in the subject's body through demand and desire—the desire of the Other, that is to say—and in the meantime the subject acquires a consciousness of having a body of its "own," along with its own desire (Lacan 1991 [1960–1961], p. 255). Consequently, the subject comes into possession of a hysterical body image, that is to say, one that is signified by the signifiers of the Other.

As peculiar as it may seem, this aspect of the theory is fairly easy to recognize in experience, both on a macro and a micro social level. At the societal level, it is always the Other (in the form of fashion, medicine, gender roles, art, health care, and more) who not only determines the look and form of the body, but in particular how it enjoys itself (its movements, food, drink, eroticism). On a micro level, the first and second Other explicitly call for the form of the subject's body, both in terms of looks and enjoyment. As such, body image forms the basic layer of identity, the first alienation in the mirror stage on top of which all further alienations through the signifier of the Other will be stacked (Lacan 1977 [1949]). It is also the way the subject acquires a first,

---

15. This is a very brief summary of a very difficult part of the theory. The unconscious is structured like a language because it consists of associations that are both synchronic and diachronic; the material consists of signifiers, in the widest sense of the word, and thus always comes from the Other, hence: "The unconscious is the discourse of the other" (Lacan 1997 [1955–1956]). These signifiers first of all represent the body and the drive in the relation between the subject and Other, hence the connection between the unconscious, the body, and eroticism. The core of the system unconscious—the real part of the drive—nevertheless remains unrepresentable and is indicated by Lacan as the "object (a)." It is precisely because of its ultimate unrepresentability and the subject's unceasing attempts to try to represent it nevertheless, that Lacan regards the (dynamic) unconscious as a border process that will always fail in its endeavours. This is one of the main theses of Seminar XI (Lacan 1994 [1964]).

albeit imaginary, mastery over its body.[16] Once this total image and total consciousness have been acquired, it retroactively becomes possible to have it disintegrate, that is to say, to have the experience of the total image falling apart. This experience of *membra disjecta*, of dismemberment (*"corps morcelé"*) can appear in the context of both psychosis (schizophrenia) and neurosis (hysteria, conversion symptoms). In both cases, the dismemberment will take place according to the stipulations, the "dotted lines" the Other has inscribed on the body.[17]

In any event, it always concerns the imaginary body, the body that we "have," inside of which the ex-sisting Real of the organism operates in a causal way.

SEPARATION—AUTONOMY AND A DESIRE OF ONE'S OWN

If alienation were all-encompassing, everyone would perfectly coincide with the story dictated to them by the Other. That this doesn't happen is because of several reasons. First, and above all, it is because the causal starting point, the drive tension (*a*), can never be fully answered; its demand continues to insist. Moreover, within the different answers of the different others, there will inevitably be contradictions. Consequently, the subject must continually make choices, confronted

---

16. Lacan expresses this in a play of words that cannot be translated: *"M'être/maître à moi-même"* (to be myself, to belong to myself, to be master of myself): the first layer of the ego originates in an appropriation, an assumption of the body through the mirror image, thus installing the illusion of mastery over this body (Lacan 1991 [1969–1970], p. 178). This is the basis for negation as well, as the basic characteristic of the ego, the *"méconnaissance*/me-connaissance" (wordplay: to deny myself/to know myself): the subject thinks it knows itself but its self-knowledge comes from the Other from the start (Lacan 1966 [1958], p. 668).

17. This is clearest in hysteria, where the conversion symptoms never follow the anato-neurological organization of the body, but rather the dotted lines on the body image that result from the Other's speech. Compare the hysterical paralyses and their classic names, which invoke this imaginary dotted line very clearly—"glove paralysis" for example. Following Janet, Freud already in 1893 (1978 [1893c]) observed how hysterical somatic symptoms run according to contemporary conceptions of the body, frequently against the laws of neurology.

with a usually unspoken question: "Who do you love best?" Independently of these internal contradictions and the ensuing division, the chain of signifiers and hence each story contains a lack, meaning that "it" can never be said. "This is what they're saying to me, but what does he or she want?" (Lacan 1994 [1964], p. 214).[18]

As a result, subject-formation contains a double lack. The original drive tension can neither be fully represented nor mastered by the Symbolic, and, precisely for this reason, this latter continues to maintain a structural opening. The excess of the Real is in the Symbolic's shortfall, its inability to "say it all," and it is this that makes up the core of the unconscious, Freud's "kernel of our being" (Freud 1978 [1900a], p. 525). Through the subject's interactions with the Other, this primordial lack is resumed within the chain of signifiers as that part of the Other's desire that cannot be fully represented and that continues to insist through the signifiers. In this, the original lack will be retroactively reworked in phallic terms (see Chapters 7 and 9). It is precisely at this point that separation comes into action.

This lack puts a limit to alienation and opens up the possibility for separation and a desire "of one's own," albeit in a continuing dependence on the Other's desire (Lacan 1994 [1964], p. 211 ff).[19] A desire "of one's own" comes down to an interpretation of the Other's desire, with the subject's own drive in the background. Such an interpretation always contains an aspect of choice for the subject itself, through which it influences its own identity formation and acquires a certain autonomy. This is how Lacan reads Freud's choice of neurosis, as the choice of a certain position in relation to (a) and the Other.

Where alienation was based on the set composed by the two circles, separation has to be sought in their intersection (see Fig. 8–4). As mentioned above, it is there that Lacan situates both the object (a) and the

---

18. In "Lacanese," this usually takes the form of the question "*Che Vuoi?*" as Lacan (1977 [1960]) expresses it in his paper "Subversion of the Subject and the Dialectic of Desire in the Freudian Unconscious."

19. This lack is also the reason why alienation and identification are usually incomplete. In the psychotic structure this partial nature (see Lacan's idea of not-whole, *le pas tout*, in Seminar XX) is absent, making the alienation and separation more monolithic and the reflective function, with its symbolic distancing ability, impossible. I will come back to this in Part III of this book.

subject's rejected (repressed) signifiers concerning the desire of the Other. Both have to be considered together, because these repressed signifiers always contain a retroactive interpretation of (*a*). We can write it as $\frac{a}{-\varphi}$

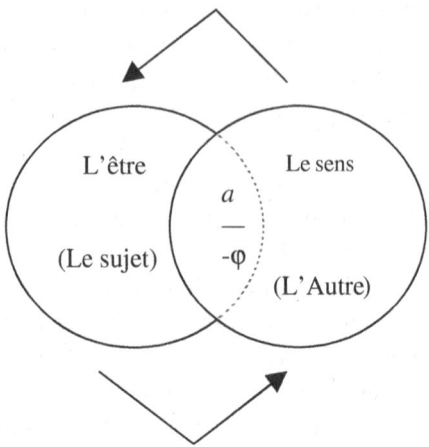

Figure 8–4. Separation.

Separation can be read both etymologically and homonymically, as in "*se parare*," to give birth to oneself, "*se parer*," to defend oneself, or to clothe oneself (Lacan 1994 [1964], pp. 214–215). The subject defends itself against its drive by obtaining a representation and, hence, mastery of it, through the Other. This explains why the original defense shifts to a defense against the Other's drive. In the course of this, the subject must interpret the desire of the Other, and such an interpretation always takes place in phallic-pregenital terms.

This latter sounds strange at first. How can separation and one's first identity occur through an interpretation—of a phallic-pregenital nature, moreover? A beautiful illustration of this can be found by watching young children. Every child, from a certain moment onward, searches for answers to the quintessential questions of origin: Where do babies come from (Where do I come from?), what is the difference between boys and girls (What is the difference between me and that other?), and what does this have to do with daddy and mummy (What are they doing?). Such questions of origin are at the same time always questions about identity, and the child must construct its own answers to them, using phallic-pregenital elements every time. Theories of birth (babies are born through the anus, the breast, etc.) are the most well-known, but not the only example. The child creates similar constructions for sexual difference and the sexual relationship. Freud calls these the infantile sexual theories (Freud 1978 [1905d], pp. 194, 226; 1978 [1908c]). Note that these infantile interpretations of the Other's lack always imply an interpretation of the relationship as well, where the subject ascribes a specific position both to itself and to the Other. This is precisely the second aspect of separation: to clothe oneself with—to give birth to oneself.

Separation presupposes the ability to detach oneself from the original dual relation with the Other, where previously the only possibilities were either to fuse entirely with, or to completely distance oneself from the other. This explains why separation can only be understood in the light of the oedipal structuring, with its redoubling of the Other, and the phallic rewriting of the drive (see Chapter 7). The most powerful proof for the necessity for this triangulation and its accompanying separation potential is found when it is missing.

Should the oedipal structure not be installed, the mother's desire and lack fail to shift to the father, that is, to the second Other. The position the subject subsequently assumes has no escape possibilities, with serious consequences both for speech and for the relation toward the Other. Lacan coined this the "holophrase" (cf below, Part III). This means that there is no break in the speech of the first Other, thus making the reflective functioning of language impossible. To "give me a break!" is out of the question. Because of this, the subject is forced to coincide with the words and hence with the total desire of the first Other, which always leads to something resembling psychosis (Lacan 1994 [1964], p. 237). In such cases, the Other has no desire outside of the subject. The subject fills in the Other's lack completely, leaving no possibility for separation, and the process of subject-formation ends at alienation. This may result in what is known as psychologically determined debility.[20] A less pronounced neurotic version can be found in

---

20. A convincing clinical illustration of this is found in Foudraine (1973). The case study "Jaap" describes a patient who never escaped from the all-encompassing alienation coming from the first Other. Traditional diagnostics, as criticized by Foudraine,

people who have sacrificed themselves for the Other, usually a mother or father, and whose whole lives are devoted to satisfying the Other's desire, maintaining only a minimal space for themselves.[21] In each case, whether in neurosis or psychosis, Imaginary dualism is paramount: either entirely without the possibility of separation (in the case of psychosis) or with only a minimal possibility (neurosis) through Symbolic triangulation.

Again I wish to emphasize that the lack found in the chain of signifiers—indicating the desire of the Other—has nothing to do with the original lack. Beneath the lack in the chain of signifiers, the original drive impulse of the subject persists. In the dialectical exchanges with the Other, the subject expects this Other to provide the answer to its own original drive impulse. Furthermore, this impulse will be attributed to the Other, albeit translated in terms of desire: What does this Other want from me?

In the confrontation with this desire that can never be fully formulated, the normal-hysterical subject produces a characteristic reaction: Does this Other really desire me, can I satisfy his or her desire? At this point, the never-ending dialectic between a subject and its objects is set in motion. A bridge is built between the subject's desire and the desire of the Other. Lacan's saying, "Desire is the desire of the Other" can thus be understood in the following way: the subject desires that the Other desires it; it desires to be desired. The clearest expression of this is found in the field of eroticism: Who takes the ini-

---

overlooks this entirely and thereby misses a number of important starting points for the treatment. The patient's central motive is anxiety about and the desire to escape from the symbiosis and the crushing alienation; the great risk of the treatment is that it is nothing but a repetition of such an alienation, despite all the best intentions . . .

21. Such a choice explains a hitherto little-understood characteristic of hysteria, namely, the social commitment of hysterical subjects, who—in their desire to answer the Other's lack—often translate this into fruitful projects. Anna O. (Bertha Pappenheim) is the classic historical example (see Freeman 1977). Nor is this subjective structure all that rare in clinicians; it largely determines the nature and intensity of the countertransference, eventually leading to *furor sanandi* (Vanheule 2001 a–c).

tiative in bed, who desires whom? The ultimate testing of the other's desire takes shape in those fantasies where the subject visualizes its own death with the intent of measuring the other's reactions: "Can she or he lose me?" (Lacan 1994 [1964], p. 214). The majority of suicidal fantasies and even suicide attempts can be understood in this context, amounting to a final test of the possibility for separation.[22]

CONCLUSION: THE FUNDAMENTAL FANTASY AS A LASTING RELATIONSHIP BETWEEN THE SUBJECT AND THE OTHER

Psychic identity is constructed in relation to the subject's own drive and to the Other through a double process—alienation and separation. Having no end, it continues to form through dialectical exchanges, thereby opening up the possibility for change. The starting point is the shift from (a) to A, being the first, primal alienation that determines the structure of the subject. The way this becomes installed determines all subsequent relations between the subject and the Other. The sequence takes place within the chain of signifiers and gives rise to the possibility of separation. The result is that identity will always be divided, the division between the different representational identity layers covering up the original division between subject and drive—see Freud's closing ideas in his "Splitting of the Ego in the Process of Defense" (1978 [1940e]). The originality of one's identity resides in the particularity of the chosen parts the subject takes over from the Other. Every subject is a unique amalgamation of the signifiers emanating from the Other; the element of choice is what guarantees its particularity (see Fig. 8–5).

---

22. According to Lacan, the relation between the subject and the Other displays an essential asymmetry at this point. The desire that speech is supposed to respond to will never be fully answered, precisely because of this dependence on language. Beyond language the Real continues to insist. The result is that the process of subject-formation in relation to the Other must continue, and there will never be a complete reciprocity between the subject and the Other. Hence Lacan's famous saying: "There is no sexual relationship."

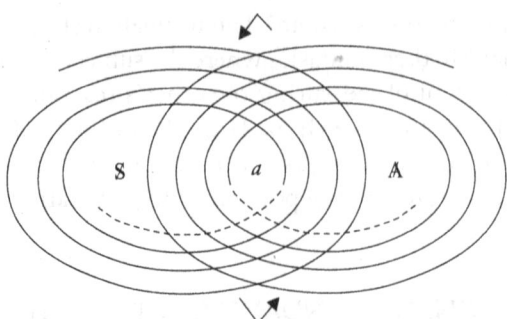

Figure 8–5. Subject-formation and the fundamental fantasy.

This structure is universally applicable and can take different forms depending on the specific reactions of the significant others to the subject's demand and choices, specifically, in the way the subject interprets the Other's lack, (the Other's desire). Freud gathers the early infantile manifestations together under the concept of infantile sexual theories, which he will rename the primal fantasies (Freud 1978 [1915f], p. 269). He considers these the basis upon which symptoms are constructed.[23] This explains why therapeutic interpretations of the symptoms always lead toward a laying bare of the underlying fantasy on which they are based (Miller 1982, 1984). Nevertheless, analysis of the symptoms is not enough; it must lead to an analysis of the transference.

---

23. The importance of this part of Freud's theory cannot be overstated. It implies a clear rupture with his original idea of trauma as an accidental cause emanating from the outside. Here he presents a structural reading of the relation between the Real and the Symbolic. Every child is confronted with the traumatic Real of its own drive and processes this defensively through the construction of Imaginary answers to a number of questions regarding origin. The material for these answers is taken from the Other, resulting in the infantile sexual fantasies. Its connection with the "family romance" is also quite clear (Freud 1978 [1909c]). See Verhaeghe 1999b, p. 190 ff). Among other things, the importance of this conceptualization has to do with its effects on the aim of the treatment. From this point onward, the re-construction of the past no longer becomes a central issue, being replaced by a focus on how the subject constructs its history.

The latter is nothing but the implementation of this underlying fantasy in the patient–therapist relation.[24]

In Lacanian terminology, this is the fundamental fantasy. It indicates the lasting relation that was originally constructed between the subject and the Other on the basis of repeated exchanges at the level of desire and lack. These original processes determine the identity of both the subject and the Other as far as it can be expressed in language, together with the specific, structural appearance of the relation between those two.[25] The fundamental fantasy is based on alienation and separation, as its formula makes clear:

$$\$ \diamond (a) \diamond A$$

The actual content of identity is the result of an identification with the images and speech coming from the Other. The Other's identity is the result of projective identification, how the subject clothes the Other with its own expectations of it. As such, the fundamental fantasy functions as a self-fulfilling prophecy.[26]

---

24. This explains a well-known clinical truth: during the treatment, the neurosis shifts to a "transference neurosis" and the symptoms acquire a transferential signification as well. This implies that both the treatment and the therapist are taken in by the relationship as designed by the fundamental fantasy.

25. Because of where it comes from, the fundamental fantasy is largely unconscious. Conscious daydreams are just the tip of the iceberg, requiring interpretation every time.

26. The joke about the car jack is a perfect illustration of this. A driver gets a flat tire on a deserted road. It's midnight, rain is pouring down, there is mud everywhere. To finish things off, he realizes he left his jack at home. Luckily, he sees a light in the distance and starts to make his way toward it. Along the way, he wonders whether these people will have a jack, but he reassures himself—in such remote areas people have to be independent. They are sure to have plenty of tools. But then he has another thought—they are peasants, probably conservative and a bit jumpy and almost certainly ill-disposed toward strangers. They will have a jack, but will refuse to give it to him! Thinking of this, he becomes more and more angry, finally ringing the bell in a total rage and when the unsuspecting resident opens the door, yells at him: "You can keep your fucking jack and you know where to put it!" Relieved, he disappears into the night.

The specificity of the fantasy's structural appearance has everything to do with the (im-)balance between alienation and separation (cf infra). In cases of insufficient alienation, the fundamental fantasy will trace out a relation in which the subject continues to try to get a guarantee from the Other. When the alienation is too severe, bringing the Other too far under the subject's skin, the fundamental fantasy will delineate a relation where the subject tries to take as much distance as it can from this Other.

At the end of the day, the fundamental fantasy can be regarded as the cognitive-affective script through which the subject approaches both itself and the Other, or more broadly, the world in general (see the contemporary concept, the "theory of the mind"). The cognitive aspect lies in the fact that the fantasy offers meanings and explanations—recall Freud's term for it: "infantile sexual *theories*." The affective aspect concerns the fact that the fantasy opens up the possibility for coping with the anxiety. This relation will determine the potential psychopathology and will reappear in the diagnostic and therapeutic situation.[27]

Effects of the Fundamental Fantasy

The opening hypothesis of our metapsychology is that every psychopathological structure (psychosis, perversion, or neurosis) can be understood as a specific manifestation of the fundamental fantasy.[28] The

---

27. Here a further connection with contemporary attachment theory can be made, showing that a partly conscious but largely unconscious representational construction is built, in the course of the attachment process, that contains both the subject's identity and that of the other, taking the form of the relation between the two. Here, too, a distinction is made between a construction that calls for a merging with the image presented by the other, and one where separation is permitted. For attachment theory, this depends on the extent to which "mentalization" and, particularly, "reflective functioning" is possible. To my mind, this differentiation is not all that clear. Making a distinction between dual imaginary and symbolic triangular functioning could be more useful here.

28. There are no specifically Lacanian research instruments, but it is my conviction that the fundamental fantasy can be researched through a number of already validated instruments. At the same time, they enable one to measure the evolution during and at the end of the treatment. One possibility is the CCRT (Core Conflictual

way the psychotic subject relates to desire and jouissance will be structurally different from that of the pervert or the neurotic. This, consequently, forms the basis for a structural differential diagnostics. Each particular subject, moreover, will fill in the structure to which he or she belongs with particular content from his or her life story that is forged in relation to particular others. This is the basis of the second feature of differential diagnostics, which focuses on the aspect of particularity. In the diagnostic situation, the clinician will then be placed in the position of the Other in relation to whom the same structural relation, based on the fundamental fantasy, will be repeated. As a result, it is precisely this relationship that becomes the aim of the diagnosis and, later, of the treatment as well.

IMPLICATIONS FOR DIFFERENTIAL DIAGNOSTICS

Ideally, alienation and separation appear in mutual balance. A sufficiently secure basis provided by the alienation—a secure attachment style—enables one to separate from the Other. This balance is missing

---

Relationship Theme Method). This is a method that was developed by Luborsky and Crits-Christoph (1998), intended to chart transferential patterns that emerge during a psychotherapy. Fragments of sessions are therefore taped and printed out. Through a coding of different narrative fragments, the extent of the repetition of certain themes and conflicts is recorded. This method is mostly used to assess which relational patterns appear in certain pathologies (in depression for instance) and to assess the changes in these patterns during the course of a psychoanalytic psychotherapy. Based on the CCRT, the same researchers developed a second method: the RAP (Relationship Anecdotes Paradigm) interview. Its main difference from the CCRT is that this second method does not use fragments from psychotherapeutic sessions but anecdotes told by respondents during an interview. A third possible instrument is offered by Bucci (1997), who correlated psychoanalytic metapsychological concepts and free association with processes occurring at the level of mental schemas. A fourth method is the Adult Attachment Interview, accessing the adult's attachment style (George et al. 1996). This focuses not on the contents of the story but on how the story is told, using a specific method (Main and Goldwyn 1995). The coherence of the discourse is then used as a gauge for the security of the attachment style. Subsequent to this, the RFS (Reflective Functioning Scale) was developed (Fonagy et al. 1991; Fonagy and Target 1997) that can be used both for the diagnosis of the attachment style and for measuring change in the course of the treatment.

in pathology. Based purely on the temporal sequence—alienation occurs first—we can make out two situations: one where there was insufficient alienation, and one where there was too much. In both cases, separation will not take place.

A deficiency in alienation implies that the subject will be unable to find enough ground in the Other upon which to construct its own identity. In some cases, the Other answers the subject's question concerning its drive inadequately, reacting in a rejecting manner. This is an "insecure/dismissive attachment" (Fonagy et al. 2002, p. 43). The primary processing of the arousal is thus missing and the secondary elaboration will also be unable to occur. The process will stop at the actualpathological level. In cases where the Other rejects the subject's drive, but manages to offer signifiers all the same, a psychopathological development will take place. In such cases, the subject tries to answer to the signifiers of the Other's desire, but the latter's reaction remains rejecting. The message the subject hears will be: try again. The result is a further alienation/identification that will also be rejected, and so on.

The end product will be insecurity and an enduring dependence on the Other. The anxiety remains close to the original separation anxiety. Indeed, if the basis for identity is insufficiently secure, the subject cannot allow itself to lose the Other. In actualpathology, the subject will experience the Other as unsatisfactory, resulting eventually in an ambivalent demand for an answer—ambivalent, because the subject does not really expect an answer. In psychopathology, separation anxiety will usually express itself in the form of an anxiety about not being good enough for the Other, about being unable to fill the latter's expectations. In the clinical context, these patients experience the therapist-diagnostician as an examiner whose role is to make value judgments, to decide whether or not they are adequate. The clinical situation will thus be transformed into a classic repetition of that relation between the subject and the Other.

At the other extreme, there is too much alienation, without the possibility of separation. This is an "insecure/preoccupied attachment" (Fonagy et al. 2002, p. 43). Here the preoccupied Other buries the subject under signifiers in such a way that there is no room for the subject or its drive. This is the exact opposite of the situation described above, because in this case it is the subject who will be the rejecting partner. The subject has been reduced to the Other's desire, resulting in anxiety toward this Other and a desire for separation. This will be replicated in the clinic in the form of a rejecting attitude on the patient's part. Anything coming from the clinician will be regarded as too threatening, too close to the skin, and therefore the subject's autonomy will have to be defended at all costs. This form of rejection will be constantly repeated, making the subject dependent on everyone and everything that it rejects.

One encounters this differential diagnostic distinction in the three different structures. Anxiety about separation is most evident in hysterical neurosis and in depression. Alienation anxiety and the need for separation are especially clear in the psychotic subject (with the stress on paranoia), but also in obsessional neurosis. In perversion, as we will see later, the emphasis is on alienation without a manifest desire for separation. This is because of the specific mechanism of defense that is at work in the perverse structure.

Examples: Anorexia and Bulimia

Alienation and separation are two processes within the linguistically structured subject–Other relation that hark back to a more primordial dialectic of incorporation and expulsion. In case this sounds too theoretical, let us conclude by discussing two striking clinical manifestations of these processes, anorexia and bulimia.

The vast majority of anorexia today can be accounted for by the sociocultural Other (the discourse), that obliges the contemporary woman—and recently also increasingly the man—to match up to certain norms in terms of bodily proportions (Orbach 2001). Such an alienation also explains the success of plastic surgery, being the most radical way of answering to the socioculturally obliged mirror image. Understood in this way, anorexia gives us a perfect illustration of the hysterical structure in the normal subject, dependent as it is on (the gaze of) the Other. Whereas in the time of Rubens one was expected to be voluptuous, nowadays it's the opposite. Nevertheless, the underlying process is identical and belongs entirely to alienation, that is, identification with the image, as the Other desires it.

Alongside and beyond this is anorexia per se, semi-independent of the sociocultural discourse. The complexity of the phenomenon requires some prudence here. Nevertheless, it is a now classic assumption that the patient's unique attitude toward his or her own body has to do with the interaction between the mother and child. Refusal is central here, specifically, the refusal to take anything in from the Other. It can be no coincidence that anorexia patients frequently exhibit very strong needs for control, combined with a fiercely competitive drive. Both phenomena can be read as attempts to acquire a position of one's own, independent of the other.[29] Its chief difference from the sociocultural form is that in anorexia proper the desire for separation is central, together with the refusal of incorporation/alienation. Its mirror image is then bulimia, where there can never be enough of the Other taken in. In both, there is a lasting dependence on the Other, whether negative or positive.

The frequently observed alternation between the two comes down to a continuous vacillation between incorporation (alienation) and expulsion (separation). Such a vacillation in itself is not so unique; however its special character resides in its real level, in combination with the age at which this vacillation occurs. The crucial question here, then, is, Why did the relation between the subject and the Other get stuck at such a primal level? The implications of this for every form of treatment are clear. The anorexic refusal to take anything in that comes from the Other represents an enormous obstacle to the therapeutic alliance, and every treatment runs the risk of repeating the original relation, along with its accompanying refusal.[30] Here, too, its mirror image can be found in the "therapeutic bulimic" patient who takes in everything from the therapist and ends the treatment with profound indigestion.

---

29. Empirical research on female patients with chronic eating disorders shows that emotional disturbances during childhood are common (70–93%), with problems with the mother foremost, along with the impossibility of talking about feelings (Noordenbos et al. 2000). This indicates the actualpathological character of this pathology. The fact that the same research shows that these patients have no "self"-confidence and are directed toward perfectionism is yet another indication—"self"-confidence develops in relation to the confidence expressed by the Other, and if this is unsuccessful there will be no "self"-confidence. The fact that this pathology is expressed at the level of the body indicates that its structure harks back to the primary exchanges of incorporation and expulsion.

30. Hence the (relative) success of group treatments where the patients treat "themselves" through mutual identification, seemingly independent of the Other as the S_1.

SUMMARY

- Identity is acquired in a circular relation toward (*a*) and the Other through the joint processes of alienation and separation.
- Alienation results in the filling in of identity's content; the lack integral to separation opens up the possibility for distance and choice.
- Because of this double process, identity is always divided, always incomplete, and above all of a narrative nature.
- The result is the construction of the fundamental fantasy that fills in the identities of the subject and the Other, along with the characteristic relation that inheres between the two.
- Pathology has to do with an internal conflict and the failure of its external processing. Symptoms are always constructed in light of the fundamental fantasy.
- In the three different subjective structures, the accent can lie either on the anxiety about, or desire for, separation.
- During the diagnostic process, the fundamental fantasy is repeated in the relation with the clinician through the transference. This fundamental fantasy is the aim of both the structural diagnosis and the treatment.

9
Etiology and Evolution: Nature, Nurture, and the Theory of the Drive

The central argument of this book so far has been that identity and pathology are developed in the relation between the subject and the Other in the confrontation with (*a*); consequently they must be diagnosed and treated within this relation as well. The leading processes are alienation and separation, each expressing an opposite tendency. The first process is directed toward merging with the other, while the second aims to realize autonomy. The accompanying anxieties are thus diametrically opposite. In the first, we encounter separation anxiety; in the second, anxiety about being reduced to a passive object of the other. The unavoidable question now has to do with the underlying motives.

Contemporary science is steeped in evolutionary and neo-Darwinist thought and empirical evidence confirming its veracity continues to mount. With the exception of evolutionary psychology, psychology has yet to take any of this on board. The former has been the object of severe criticism, and the academy, particularly in the United States, has tended to have cold feet about it, largely because of the looming specter of political correctness. But beyond this typically obsessional superego symptom, we can discern the following problems: How can one identify an evolutionarily grounded purposiveness in human behavior? How can the answer be read in the light of our overarching metapsychology, particularly with regard to the nature–nurture debate?

PURPOSIVENESS IN HUMAN BEHAVIOR

The principal question is straightforward, but carries very important implications: are humans driven by a number of underlying motives that are evolutionarily established? Both Freud and behavioral psychology emphasize pleasure and unpleasure, but each was forced to acknowledge that such a view of human motivation is too simplistic.

Darwinian theory was involved with questions of purposiveness from the outset. According to Darwin's grandfather, the three driving forces are hunger, the search for security, and lust. The translation into reproduction only comes later.[1] Contemporary evolutionary psychology takes things further. Popular conceptions understand this theory as though everything were organized in the light of reproduction, as was the case with the earlier sociobiology.[2] Every ontogenetically and phylogenetically acquired characteristic is measured on the same scale: To what extent do they help this particular organism transmit its genes to the next generation? In this way, evolutionary psychology is the

---

1. The emphasis on sexual enjoyment has to do with Erasmus Darwin's libertine lifestyle; he expressed his views on natural history in the form of erotic poetry (*The Botanic Garden*, 1794). His grandson Charles was somewhat more prudish and his theoretical emphasis shifted toward reproduction.

2. Evolutionary thinking in itself has already seen an evolution. The first revolution came with Darwin as one of the three narcissistic humiliations of humanity (Freud 1978 [1917a]). The second, neo-Darwinistic revolution (1930–40) brought us a synthesis between Mendel and Darwin. The most recent conceptualization (post-neoDarwinian) begins with sociobiology (Wilson 1975), and has now been followed by evolutionary psychology. The most important difference from the previous theories is that here the emphasis is no longer so much on group selection but on the individual and even the gene. A rapprochement with cognitive psychology and psychoanalysis has also been made in the meantime. From the cognitive angle, the emphasis is on cognitive modules that are genetically/evolutionarily based. In the psychoanalytic framework, the stress is on the interaction between the patients and the analyst in the light of a process of adaptation that possibly went wrong (Palombo 1999). For a more conceptual discussion, see Zenoni (1991).

successor to post-Freudianism, particularly when each is portrayed in caricature form. If so, then in post-Freudianism everything revolves around sex, while in evolutionary psychology it revolves around reproduction. Both perform miracles in constructing post-factum explanations, presenting an interpretation for certain behavior in the light of an a priori determined goal.

Reducing these theories to caricatures is all too easy, but their scientific credentials are of considerably more interest and nuance. The question concerning their similarities and differences is more complex and relevant, particularly when combined with the question of its significance for clinical practice. Doubtless their common ground has to do with conceptions of the body (genes, the drive, etc.). But before we go into this, a certain misunderstanding must be corrected: evolutionary psychology does not begin from the idea that the human, or more generally, every living organism is purposefully directed toward reproduction. Their opening hypothesis is that accidental genetic characteristics have, through natural selection, a greater chance of persisting if they contribute to the possibility of survival and procreation.[3] Reproductive success is hence a result rather than a goal in itself. In this way, evolutionary psychology avoids the problem of teleology.

Such a form of reasoning can be consummately applied to phylogenesis. With regard to ontogenesis and individual life, we nevertheless cannot do without the idea of purposiveness, based on the function of specifically directed behavior. The question is then, What is this function? The first person to put this problem onto the psy-agenda was Freud. By this I am referring to his theory of the drive, which I will come back to at the end of this chapter. But by way of an introduction, let us look at the difference between the answers he and others of his time came up with and those of contemporary medical thought.

Medical discourse today is all-pervasive. Medical science reduces the body to the organism, that is to say, to a combination of organic

---

3. The difference between reproduction and survival comes down to the difference between sexual and natural selection. The jury on whether these two have to be separated or considered as a single whole is still out (Braeckman 1997). As we will see later, the same question can be found in Freud, and he will finally consider the two as a peculiar whole through the so-called fusion of the drive.

systems that are placed alongside one another: blood circulation, respiratory system, reproductive system, and so on, each with its own specific function. These relatively mechanical or instrumental systems can be either healthy or sick, requiring treatment by a specialist for that specific system.

Another reading, however, is possible. The classical Greek tradition enables us to distinguish between two different systems: the *organikos* and the *phusis*. The first concerns the practical instrumental functioning of different organs. The second system not only contains the idea of growth, but also the principle of generation and, hence, of reproduction as such. The principal difference between this and contemporary medical thought is that in the classical viewpoint phusis has a different status than the organikos, the other organ systems. Even more, phusis imbues all of the other systems of the organikos. Where contemporary medical thought invokes juxtaposition, here we encounter a relation of opposition, whereby one principle runs through the other and is explicitly capable of influencing it.

Based as it is on the juxtaposition of the different organ systems, contemporary medical thought inevitably runs up against a number of inexplicable items. These are principally inexplicable because of the medical discourse's reduction of the body to mere juxtaposition. The explanation, emerging suspiciously like a deus ex machina, is that the problem must be "psychosomatic," which—in itself—does little more than confirm a self-created problem. One of the fields where contemporary medicine is most frequently confronted with this problem is with pain, which, as we have already seen, can very well be understood in terms of the primary interaction between the child and the first Other (see Chapter 6). With this, we have come across one of the earliest Freudian discoveries. The functional body or organikos can be disrupted by the phusis. This is why, in his first theory of the drive, he describes two totally different aims. On the one hand, the organism's aim is to continue to live as an organism, which Freud calls the drive for self-preservation. On the other hand, its aim is to reproduce itself, at the price of the organism itself if need be. "The individual does actually carry on a twofold existence: one to serve his own purposes and the other as a link in a chain, which he serves against his will, or at least involuntarily. [. . .] The separation of the sexual instincts from the ego-instincts would simply reflect this twofold function of the individual" (Freud 1978 [1914c], p. 78).[4] This originally somatic conflict forms the basis for the later psychological conflict where the organikos must occasionally be defeated by the phusis. It is far from accidental that Freud's drive theory is dualistic from the very beginning and will remain so.

Here we reencounter one of the central ideas of our metapsychology: pathology is inextricably bound up with an underlying conflict. On the one hand, we have incorporation–identification–alienation, being the tendency to unite and fuse with the Other. This is the requisite condition both for survival and reproduction, yielding a certain form of pleasure as a bonus. Alongside and against this we find separation as the opposing tendency, aiming toward the individual's own survival, independently of the Other. The two constantly alternate and create a tensional field within which individual life is built. This is the basis of Freud's dualistic drive theory that takes its final form in the opposition between Eros (understood as fusion) and Thanatos (understood as separation).

A comparison with evolutionary psychology quickly reveals that it is closer to these Freudian ideas than to contemporary medical discourse. Reproductive success, the basis for the inheritance of the characteristics, can only be achieved if an individual life lasts long enough to make reproduction possible. Both—a sufficiently long life as an individual and being directed toward reproduction—have to be built-in in the evolutionarily acquired characteristics and hence will find expression on the level of individual life that we cannot but interpret in terms of purposiveness. The conflict between the two (Eros as fusion, versus Thanatos, separation) can be regarded as the basis for psychopathology, albeit within the psychological processing with its accompanying complexity.

Incidentally, there is another important correspondence. Both for Freud and for evolutionary psychology, consciousness is a peripheral phenomenon, and the majority of the governing processes will occur

---

4. For Freud, too, this opposition is primarily biological (see Freud 1978 [1910i], p. 214). To offer an illuminating quote in this respect: "It has been discovered as a general fact that the ego-function of an organ is impaired if its erotogenicity—its sexual significance—is increased" (Freud 1978 [1926d], p. 89).

outside of consciousness.[5] Contemporary cognitive psychology and neuropsychology have meanwhile demonstrated this quite convincingly. Here we run across more cold feet. The fear of being associated with psychoanalytic thinking—considered outdated—has resulted in both evolutionary and neuropsychology rarely using the term "unconscious." Clinical knowledge of unconscious functioning compiled over the past century thus remains largely inaccessible to them, despite its having to do with the same thing.

The difference between the two somatic systems can explain the idea of conflict that lies at the heart of every psychopathology. But this in itself does not satisfactorily answer an important psychodiagnostic issue, namely the question of etiology.

ORGANOGENESIS VERSUS PSYCHOGENESIS: THE FALSE "NATURE VERSUS NURTURE" DEBATE

A superficial reading of our metapsychology might leave the reader with the impression that it is based on social constructivism, and that my choice is radically in favor of nurture, understood as the influence of the Other. Thus etiology ought largely to be situated on the psy-side. Such a reading fails to see two things: the real point of departure (*a*) and the ensuing interaction between (*a*) and the Other.

The nature–nurture debate is as prevalent as it is black-and-white, and testifies to a certain tendency to dichotomize, which, for one reason or another, is built into our cognitive functioning—something must either be this or that: to have them together at the same time is unthinkable. We already came across this in Part 1, in the opposition between

---

5. In their recent study, Cosmides and Tooby (2001) put this forward as the third principle of evolutionary psychology: "Consciousness is just the tip of the iceberg. As a result, your conscious experience can mislead you. [. . .]" Their metaphor is that of a president who must make decisions based on selective and frequently contradictory information that can never be fully understood. The resemblance with Freud's idea of the ego ("The ego is not the master of its own house") is readily seen, while Lacanian theory (it is not the subject, but the signifiers through which the subject is installed, that decide) even gives this idea a functional-empirical basis (pp. 15–16).

the anato-pathological and moral models. It is unquestionably one of the merits of evolutionary psychology that it has eliminated such a dichotomy with convincing empirical evidence (Cosmides and Tooby 2001, pp. 30–39). Moreover, it enables us to put forward other and better questions. Because of this debate's significance for our field, we must go into it in more detail.

The so-called standard social-science model starts out with the idea of the tabula rasa, and belongs in this sense to social constructivism. In this line of reasoning, the human mind is imagined to be empty at birth, acquiring content and modes of functioning only through interaction with the surrounding environment. Consequently, the human mind can be changed by changing that environment (reeducation, psychotherapy, rehabilitation, etc.). In sharp contrast to this is essentialism, the position that locates everything in the body, largely in terms of genetics in today's world. There the human being is considered literally to "de-velop," to un-fold what is a priori already there through the phylogenetically acquired program; everything is, hence, strictly predetermined. Change, that is to say, treatment, takes effect only through an intervention in this organic–genetic scheme (genetic engineering, psychopharmacology, neurosurgery, etc.) and psychotherapy is a load of bunkum.

Such caricatures are still around today, usually combined with a certain lip service to the so-called bio-psycho-social model. The opposition between nature versus nurture, innate versus acquired, biological versus cultural, sex versus gender, and so on, is still very much present. This is all the more peculiar because even classical ethological studies are enough to make this strict opposition disappear. A goose, for example, will find mates of its own species because of the imprinting it gets from its mother upon hatching. Should the researcher assume that maternal role, the animal will indeed subsequently try to mate later on—with people (Lorenz 1966). One can only conclude that a genetically determined, prewired learning process interacts with the environment and that behavior is shaped by this interaction. Right from the outset, the interaction between genetically determined factors and elements from the environment will determine the behavior—or, more generally, the psychological functioning—making it very difficult, if not impossible to distinguish between nature and nurture.

In other words, there is no opposition between innate and acquired; the proper object of study is the result of an indivisible whole.[6] This example already shows that environmental influences can have radical effects on the final product, and that this product always starts out with something that cannot be approached as if it were a tabula rasa—organisms learn something because, through adaptation and selection, they have acquired the possibility and specific form of this learning process, which has been genetically recorded. Two leading figures from contemporary evolutionary psychology consider instincts "complex information-processing programs," causing the organism to interpret its surroundings in particular ways (Cosmides and Tooby 2001, pp. 5, 31–38). Even within this approach, then, meaning is central.

On the basis of these empirically supported propositions we can pose another question, and that is whether these phylogenetically acquired dispositions are of a general or a specialized nature. In the first case, mankind has one general-purpose cognitive program genetically at his disposal, on the basis of which anything can be learned in interaction with the environment. In the second, it is assumed that there are—besides such a general program—a number of genetically fixed specific learning programs, adjacent and even in opposition to each other. The best-known discussion in this respect concerns language acquisition, where the general option is represented by Skinner and the specialized by Chomsky (Cosmides and Tooby 2001, p. 34). Meanwhile, it has become increasingly accepted that the second option is the correct one: clearly there are a number of prewired programs or "crib sheets," each interacting with specific elements in the environment.[7] Future evolutionary

---

6. The nature–nurture dichotomy is analogous to that of the soma–psyche, and just as false. There is no allowance made for interaction between the two separate entities, which means that we are confronted right from the beginning with a result that in itself will determine the subsequent results. Every use of the term "interaction" in the text should be read in this way. As far as this is concerned, we need to bid farewell to Plato.

7. Such crib sheets are domain-specific (applicable only to a limited domain), content-dependent (activated by certain influences in this surroundings), and functionally specialized (in opposition to a general capacity for learning). From the moment the interaction with the environment begins, a complex interaction comes into being based upon which the difference between learned versus innate disappears (Cosmides and Tooby 2001, p. 33).

psychological research will be directed toward the discovery of these specific programs, the relevant elements in the environment, and the resulting capabilities that enable humans to function in that environment.

Despite this being little more than an aspiration at present, we can already draw an important conclusion for clinical psychodiagnostics with regard to etiology and pathogenesis. To make it short and sweet: there is neither organogenesis, nor psychogenesis.[8] Both positions are wrong; etiology always returns to a complex interaction in whose result the different elements can only barely be seen. Human surroundings are so complex and diverse, moreover, that—despite the supposed presence of the same crib sheets in each individual, even in different cultures—the result will also be profoundly diverse, precisely because of the complexity and diversity of the surrounding elements. Here the paths between evolutionary psychology and clinical psychodiagnostics diverge, since evolutionary psychology is directed toward the general results of the interaction, while clinical psychodiagnostics focuses on the individual results of a single subject growing up in a particular environment.

In spite of this separation, an important correspondence remains that can also be demonstrated from another angle. We have already seen how our model of identity acquisition shares close resemblances with contemporary psychoanalytic attachment theory. In both models, the stress is on the primary interaction between the subject and the Other that forms the basis for all later relationships. While Lacanian theory tends to focus more on its subsequent elaboration, in attachment theory the emphasis is placed on the starting point, and in this respect it is closely related to the idea of crib sheets. Already with Bowlby, the starting point is the idea that a child begins with systems that are already there: an "attachment system," an "exploratory behavioral system," and a "fear system," all of which will, moreover, interact with one another (Fonagy 2001, p. 9).[9] This aspect of nature

---

8. Lacan already came to the same conclusion in 1946, in his discussion with Henri Ey, making reference to the ethology of that time (Lacan 1966 [1946], pp. 151–193).

9. In a more recent book (Fonagy et al. 2002, p. 207 ff), the traditional assumption that the baby functions in a solipsistic, almost autistic way is abandoned. From his review of the relevant research literature, Fonagy shows how, from birth onward, the baby displays an active inclination to explore. During the first three months, the focus is on self-exploration, especially through "contingency detection." Later comes

will interact with nurture from the moment of birth onward, thus making even the first results a complex whole. Future research into evolutionary psychology and contemporary neuropsychology will probably allow for further refinement of these systems.[10] Its application to clinical psychodiagnostics will represent quite a challenge.

COMPARED TO OUR METAPSYCHOLOGY

In putting this together with our metapsychology, a number of similarities immediately strike one. With regard to the question of universality, the early tendency toward incorporation and identification with the other must indeed form part of a genetically determined disposition. The same goes for the subsequent tendency toward separation and autonomy. Moreover, the establishment of such a primal relationship between the subject and the other is the basis for an ever-increasing exploration of the outside world whose origin lies in anxiety and its possibility for being managed. The most important difference is that in our approach the emphasis is on language, and more broadly on the representational constructions through which the subject defines both its own identity and that of the outside world, along with the assumption of an ensuing and irreversible self-division.

Immediately following this, the emphasis of clinical psychodiagnostics shifts to the conflict between the different representational constructions that can form the basis for psychopathology. What we consider symptoms are always attempts at a solution, attempts to make such conflicts livable. In this way, symptoms are also adaptations, and may indeed be understood as the subject's attempts at recovery.

---

the tendency for exploration and representation of the social surroundings through "non-contingency detection." Both inclinations are universal and, hence, assumed to belong to an innate learning disposition.

10. It is notable how in his latest major work a figure like Panksepp—a neurobiologist/neuropsychologist working with animals—discusses five such systems based on neurological data: lust circuits, care systems, fear and rage systems, a separation-distress or panic system, and a rough-and-tumble play system (Panksepp 1998). Clearly there is a link between these neurologically identifiable systems (albeit in animals), evolutionary psychology, and identity acquisition.

This idea of conflict has to do with the complexity of the interaction between us and our environment, between the subject and the Other. We can reasonably assume that in most animals the interaction between the individual and the outside world is more or less fixed, but in humans this is not the case. Quite the opposite in fact, since humans live in a self-created world that calls forth myriad interactive possibilities. This is at the same time the difference between an instinct and a drive. Unlike the drive, instinct functions within a stable and hence predictable interaction between a species and an outside world. The hereditarily determined learning processes that make a certain representational system possible will be surpassed in the case of the human subject. I am referring to what is generally called "culture," which will be passed through to the next generation as well, although not through genes.

With his concept of memes, Dawkins (1976) already came to this conclusion. Memes are representational constructions that lead a life of their own, as it were, and are transmitted from individual to individual, as well as between generations. Such memes are ultimately nothing other than signifiers, formulating collective ideas and aims, even a discourse. Individual manifestations of them will always be particular and, within a particular relationship between the subject and the Other, will determine the identity of both parties.

The impact of language cannot be overestimated. In both evolutionary psychology and psychoanalytic attachment theory, less emphasis is currently being put on purely behavioral studies in order to focus on the representational constructs by which the individual creates its own world (Bucci 1997; Cosmides and Tooby 2001; Fonagy et al. 2002). We have already enumerated the functions of human language: mastery, identity acquisition, communication (see Chapter 6). Its most important characteristic, and probably its chief difference from animal communication systems, is its reflective quality. The human being is able to think about thinking and therefore also about its own and the Other's identity. For precisely this reason, choices become possible and, hence, so does the ability to create something new. At the same time, the possibilities for conflict and self-division become manifest, along with the possibility of psychopathology. Psychology needs to study these representational constructs, at least if it wants to be psychology, and not merely ethology or behavioral science.

Here we come across yet another empirically supported piece of evidence: such representational constructions are largely unconscious. The unconscious is indubitably an information processing system of which we see only the tip of the iceberg. As a system, it must follow certain laws and regulations, such as those Freud concentrated on and that were subsequently taken up by Lacan. The method is free association, in combination with in-depth interviews and narrative analysis, with the precise aim of discovering what these rules are. This, together with the reflective function, then forms the basis from which psychotherapeutic changes may begin.

All this means we must now address Freud's theory of purposiveness—the drive—particularly in relation to these representational systems and the underlying conflict.

THE DRIVE AND THE REPRESENTATIONAL CONSTRUCTIONS

The problem of the drive is to be found in Freud from the outset, years before the concept itself is introduced. By this I am referring to all of his attempts to comprehend the "quantitative energetic factor" and the accompanying stimuli. One of the clinical and conceptual problems that bothers him from the start concerns the inner rise in tension, the famous "Q"-factor: the energetic flux that arises from within the body, and therefore cannot be escaped; it requires an answer.[11] This Q-factor is the central characteristic of the drive, namely the pressure (*Drang*) or excitation (*Erregung*) (Freud 1978 [1915c], p. 122). This is clear from the original name: the German *Trieb* (drive) is related to *Treiben* (to push). As an unpleasurable accumulation of excitation, it must be abreacted and lots of things can go wrong during this process, produc-

---

11. "I refer to the concept that in mental functions something is to be distinguished—a quota of affect or sum of excitation—which possesses all the characteristics of a quantity (though we have no means of measuring it), which is capable of increase, diminution, displacement and discharge, and which is spread over the memory-traces of ideas somewhat as an electric charge is spread over the surface of a body" (Freud 1978 [1894a], p. 60).

ing anything from actualneurosis to neuropsychoses of defense. The drive's aim is abreaction through mediation—bringing us back to the question of the nature of this mediation, and more specifically of its representational aspect.

Freud begins from the idea that the primal, preverbal experiences of unpleasure are retained in memory traces. He calls these traces the "pathways" or "facilitations" (*Bahnungen*, from *Bahn* meaning road) that are inscribed on the body in one way or another. Because this takes place in the preverbal period, these memory pathways must be different from ordinary, verbal memory. According to Freud, they already contain a type of organization through which a kind of automaton comes into being on a primitive level (Freud 1978 [1900a], pp. 538–539).

These pathways undergo a first evolution when they are linked with what Freud calls thing-presentations (Freud 1978 [1915e], p. 201). They constitute the ground layer of the psyche and function as goal-representations. The aim of the primitive psychic apparatus is to find the same perceptual identity in the outside world as that represented by the inner thing-presentation. The motive for this search is to relieve the inner pressure through an external intervention that comes from the other. A typical example of this is the mother's breast, as a unity of olfactory, visual, and auditory stimuli that the baby searches for in the outside world in response to the trauma of separation.

The final step in the development implies the linking of these thing-presentations to what are known as word-presentations. This step is crucial for several reasons. First, it opens up the possibility for consciousness and reflectivity, because it is only through the association with language that human (as opposed to animal, nonverbal) consciousness becomes possible. From this connection onward, the psyche functions in a different way: the aim is no longer to recover the same perceptual thing in the outside world, but to recover the same identity qua thought (Freud 1978 [1900a], pp. 319 ff, 565, 602). This introduces the idea of psychic reality. Freud regards the ego as an amalgamation of such word-presentations. He assumes that the ego functions purposively according to the pleasure principle, that is to say, it aims at reducing tension. The second reason why this step is crucial is because a number of earlier pathways or memory traces are left behind in the previous psychic system, that is, in the non-conscious, nonverbal (primary repression/

fixation) system. In other words: the kernel of the unconscious contains the first inscriptions of the drive.[12]

Such a transition from thing- to word-presentations is not self-evident, as it quite literally does not speak for itself.[13] The words have to come from the Other, through how the Other interprets the cry, and the baby itself takes those words over from the Other. Hence, the verbalization of our drive comes always from the Other—nature and nurture are intertwined from the very beginning. In the drive's transition into crying and speaking, something gets lost; the original drive does not find full expression in language, nor in the words of the Other, nor in the subject's own words later on. Something remains definitively in the system unconscious and can never become conscious, that is to say, linguistically conscious. Consequently, the drive continues to drive and there is no definitive finishing line. This is why Freud conceived of the drive as a border concept between the psychic and the somatic.

This is at least partly why the Other is always inadequate. But it has an even greater impact. The failure of such a complete translation into word-presentations is the functional definition of trauma for Freud. The energetic flux that cannot be fully expressed in words, and therefore cannot be mastered by the ego, that is, be abreacted, is traumatic (Freud 1978 [1939a (1937–1939)], p. 72 ff). Each abreaction is structurally incomplete; there is no definitive, satisfying endpoint. The result is the repetition compulsion, understood as the never-ending attempt to master this flux.

This definition applies to accidental trauma in what are known as the post-traumatic stress disorders, whose characteristic effect on the patient is dissociation: it is the gap between the traces inscribed by the accident on the body that remembers these traces, and the ego as

---

12. Freud's analysis can be inserted into contemporary notions of cognitive conditioning without too much difficulty. The original stimulus is produced by the internal drive, and gives rise to the cry, followed by the Other's response. Its repetition gives rise to a conditioned ("tracked") total schema: stimulus—crying—reaction, inscribed in a thing-presentation, that is, a preverbal cognitive schema that is repeated whenever the stimulus is reencountered. The developmental psychological advantage is that object permanence is already acquired. At a higher developmental level, the thing-presentation is changed into a word presentation.

13. Translator's Note: The author is punning here on the Dutch *"vanzelfsprekend"* (self-evident), which literally means "to speak for itself."

the conscious assimilation of word-presentations whose declarative memory is unable to recover those other traces (see Chapter 11).[14] The same goes for the drive as such; the drive is both pleasurable and traumatic in the sense that a certain part of it cannot be verbalized, and therefore cannot be mastered, but nevertheless is still fully present through a different inscription in another (nonverbal) memory. The accompanying dissociation is then the general structural split between the conscious and the unconscious resulting from what I call the structural trauma.[15]

Translation and What is Left Behind

Central to this line of reasoning is the axiomatic idea that the translation or representation of the original drive into thing-presentations and subsequently word-presentations never fully succeeds, that there is always something left behind on the previous level, causing a number of difficulties.[16] Consequently, the subject is obliged to keep trying to get this drive represented or verbalized, but continuous failure turns it into a Sisyphean task. In turn, this leads to the so-called infantile sexual theories or, more broadly, to the fundamental fantasy as an idiosyncratic representational construction that answers a structurally unanswerable problem. In the fundamental fantasy, both the drive, the Other's reaction, and the subject's own position become represented and articulated. Even more broadly, I can say that it is this impossibility that is at the basis of human creativity itself, being the endless displacing process of getting "it" done, whether in linguistic or visual form, beginning with the endless babble over religion to art, science, and—let's not forget—love.

---

14. The ego's repetition compulsion is nothing but an attempt to install this connection all the same, enabling the ego to take an active position instead of being passively submitted to this flux (Freud 1978 [1920g], p. 35).

15. Elsewhere I have described the trauma of the drive as a structural trauma for the reason that it is inevitable for every subject. Moreover, every chance or accidental trauma will always fall back on the structural trauma as already expressed, through Freud's idea that in one way or another all trauma always goes back to an "earlier" trauma. In my reading, this means that each accidental trauma gets the full weight of the structural trauma (see Verhaeghe 1997, 2001b, pp. 49–65).

16. In psychology, this is known as the problem of proprioception.

With regard to this problem of presentation, we can conclude that the starting point of the drive is somatic for Freud, and real for Lacan, but there is from the outset a connection with the Other and hence with the psychological. The leap to the psychological or the Symbolic always remains a leap, in the course of which something gets lost. Neither the baby's original cry, nor the subsequent words of the adult, let alone the Other's interpretation are able to fully translate the drive.

Here we must acknowledge the unbridgeable gap between the drive and the Other's verbal representation. It is, moreover, clearly a question of mastery where one tries to get the upper hand on the other—representation (or symbolization) is thus a means of mastery. This leads us to the most beautiful description of the drive in Freud. He tells us that the drive is not only a border concept between the psyche and the soma, it is more specifically a measure of the amount of work to be put on the psyche ("The simplest and likeliest assumption as to the nature of drives would seem to be that in itself a drive is without quality, and, so far as mental life is concerned, is only to be regarded as a measure of the demand made upon the mind for work" (Freud 1978 [1905d], p. 168; see also 1978 [1915c], p. 122; I have replaced the *Standard Edition*'s "instinct" by drive).

This gap between drive and representation can be understood as the same split between the word and the thing we discussed in Part I of this book. This gap is doubled by another antinomy residing internally in the drive itself. We saw this already in the introduction to this chapter, and we will now look at it in more detail. As will become clear, this idea of a split can be found throughout the entire psychological functioning.

DRIVE AND FINALITY

The second central problem concerns the drive's finality, or final aim, and here we encounter another internal contradiction. But before going into this, I want to first examine the aspect of mastery that evidently also belongs to the drive's finality.

The drive, in the sense of pressure, is first and foremost traumatic for the organism or the primitive ego that is passively subjected to it. The ego's attempt to master the pressure can always be understood as an attempt to take the active position. The active-passive opposition is central here, and can be detected throughout Freud's entire oeuvre (Verhaeghe 2000b).

Hence the use Freud occasionally makes of the idea of a "drive for mastery" although this, in my reading, does not so much concern a separate drive but rather a certain characteristic of the drive as such.[17] In addition, in a more specific context, he uses a second, analogous term, namely overwhelming (*Bewältigung*). What the subject must actively master is the drive's arousal, the inner pressure.[18] When Freud discusses repetition compulsion in "Beyond the Pleasure Principle," he will ascribe it precisely to this drive for mastery, that is, the ego's never-ending attempt to get a grip on the underlying trauma and, above all, on the

---

17. In his "Three Essays on Sexuality," Freud describes a drive for mastery operating independently of sexuality, and becoming linked to sex later on, thus giving rise to sexual sadism. It aims not so much to harm as to have control over someone, as opposed to being passively subjected to them (Freud 1978 [1905d], pp. 192–193).

18. For Freud, such a mastery boils down to a "binding" of the original free energy or tension by way of association with representations. This term "binding" comes from the "Project," where Freud says that the energy or pressure resulting from unpleasurable experiences has to be "bound" through the pathways (*Bahnungen*, "facilitations" in the official translation) and through their linking up with the ego in order to make them controllable. The next step to the incorporation/alienation in subject-formation is not hard to make. In contemporary terminology, this means that these impulses must be inhibited, thereby becoming subject to control (Freud 1978 [1950a (1895)], pp. 376–383). Later, Freud will link this differentiation between bounded and unbound energy to two different forms of psychological functioning, the secondary and primary processes respectively. In the primary process, the connection with word-presentations is missing, thus causing an endless displacement and a continued search by the subject for a perceptual equivalence between an inner representation and an object in the outside world (in accordance with the pleasure principle). In the secondary process, the drive impulse is associated with a word-presentation, which makes both inhibition and control possible. This is accompanied by the subject's search for a correspondence between an external world and thought (following the reality principle) (Freud 1978 [1911b]). A further application can be found in Freud's final trauma theory (Freud 1978 [1920g]), where he regards the retroactive and intrusive effect of the trauma on the patient's psychological functioning as an effect of the unbound character, that is to say, unrepresentable, and hence making it impossible to inhibit the character of the traumatic experience. The link between Eros and binding, between Thanatos and unbinding, is clear and is found later on (Freud 1978 [1940a], p. 148).

ensuing rise in tension (Freud 1978 [1920g]). In this way, the drive for mastery is the expression of the dualism where one part actively tries to take hold of the other, and vice versa. As we saw in our previous chapter, this attempt to master the drive takes place through the Other, meaning that it ultimately comes down to an attempt to master the Other.

For Freud, the repetition compulsion is not merely an attempt at mastery, but also has to do with what he considers to be the basic aim of the drive: the desire to return to an original state. The question is, What could this original state be? In accordance with the pleasure principle, it must involve minimizing the tension to as low a state as possible. Consequently, for Freud the final aim is to get rid of every form of tension and to recover the original tensionless state. The surprising, pleasurable aim of the drive is, then, nothing but death, hence its new name, the death drive.[19] We have to conclude that, opposed to this there is another drive tendency at work at the same time, one that operates in such a way that the level of tension rises. The question then becomes, Which original state is restored? To answer this, Freud consults the Aristophanes fable of the original undivided androgynous being described in Plato's *Symposium*. The aim of this drive is fusion, the restoration of the undivided being, and hence its name, Eros.

With this, we can bring the final dualism of the Freudian drive into the picture as it bears on our metapsychology—to which it is in fact quite close.[20] The first aim of the drive is to (re-)join the other, and to fuse the different parts back into a greater whole, albeit with an ever-increasing rise in tension. This is the goal of Eros, as the source of the

---

19. He links this to the "principle of neuronic inertia" as discussed in his "Project" (Freud 1978 [1920g], *SE* 18, p. 63).

20. It is striking how, in his elaborations in "*Beyond the Pleasure Principle*" and elsewhere, Freud tries to hold on to his dualism, and thereby runs into even more trouble. He can equate the life drive to the sexual drive, but that obliges him to equate the death drive to the ego drives, which is in contradiction with the aim of self-preservation. His attempts to link the respective drives to a single instance—the ego versus the id—fail as well. As a result, he has to abandon his strict dualism, and to think in terms of a combination of drives. On the phenomenological level, that is to say, at the level of the symptoms, the two drives always appear together; it is nothing but the old story of the pearl and the grain of sand. Freud's difficulties concerning the drive's duality are an artifact of his previously discussed binary dualism.

drive toward incorporation/identification. The other aim is the relief of all tension through the unbinding of the composite parts. This is the goal of Thanatos, the source of the drive toward separation and autonomy. Its ultimate effect is the most thoroughgoing form of separation, that is, death. The drive as such can therefore be characterized as a continuous back-and-forth movement between these two opposite aims (Freud 1978 [1940a], p. 148).[21]

This inner conflict in the drive, along with the impossibility of obtaining a final representation, explains why the drive can never be fully satisfied: should one of the aims be reached, the other cannot be achieved. Satisfaction, in the sense of fully attaining the end goal, is never complete.

CONCLUSION: A CIRCULAR BUT NONRECIPROCAL STRUCTURE

Freud's theory of the drive can be summed up as follows. Right from the outset, the drive is both pleasurable and traumatic for the subject. The subject's reaction to this is to try to master it, understood as an attempt to relieve the tension. This attempt is double: it takes place both through action and through language, but in both cases an appeal is made to the Other. This causes a displacement to occur. Both the drive itself and the failed representation are attributed to the other, and for neither will the other's answer or specific action ever be sufficient. The resultant problematic Freud discusses in terms of activity and passivity. Being passively subjected to the drive causes pleasure and unpleasure; even the baby goes for the active direction: from being suckled to active sucking. The same inversion can be seen throughout the entire pregenital spectrum, as well as in later adult relations.

This active–passive dialectic that occurs first and foremost in the relation between the subject and its own drive will be brought into

---

21. It is notable that in Freud's theory Eros operates through representation, and the death drive "in silence" (1978 [1930a], SE 21, p. 120). Moreover, both basic drives always operate in combination. Cases of diffusion are rare; Freud refers to melancholy as "a culture of the death drive" (1978 [1923b], SE 19, p. 58), and to the ambivalence in obsessional neurosis (*ibid.*, p 42).

the relation between the subject and the Other from the start. It is from the Other, after all, that an answer will be expected. This is why Freud himself was seduced by his seduction and trauma theory, which is ultimately nothing but the expression of this shift that takes place in every one of us. Where, initially, this occurred through the ungendered mother–child relation, it will later become sexualized through the oedipal structure, in the sense of being divided across the two different genders. For Freud, the libido is always active-masculine, although he repeatedly voices doubts about the analogy active–passive and male–female. At any rate, the subject's original attempts to master its own drive are displaced from the outset into an attempt to master the Other. This is why, at the end of his oeuvre, Freud can state that the most dreaded position is the passive one. By this we must understand a passive position in relation to the drive and its displacement into the relation to the other. The problem that keeps on insisting has to do with the evidently essential dissatisfaction of the drive, which acquires its shape in the opposition between Eros and Thanatos. In his final notes, Freud (1978 [1941f], p. 300) writes: "There is always something lacking for complete discharge and satisfaction."[22]

Between Freud and Lacan

The entire problematic can be studied in much greater detail in Lacan. I present only the broadest outline of it here.

One of the most important differences between Freud and Lacan is that Lacan refers the double and contradictory aim of the drive to a double loss and double lack (Lacan 1994 [1964], pp. 204–205). Based on this, he interprets Freud's dualism as a self-sustaining pendulum motion where one side inevitably sends the subject over to the other side and vice versa.

For Lacan, the Real of the organism functions as the accidental causality because life itself implies a primordial loss. This is the loss of

---

22. This problem is literally present throughout Freud's work. In a letter to Fliess (Freud 1878 [1892–1899], p. 222) he already writes that shame, morality, and disgust are not enough to explain sexual aversion. There must be an internal factor at work in sexuality itself that causes the dissatisfaction. The quote in the text above dates from shortly before his death.

eternal life that occurs, paradoxically enough, at the moment one is born as a sexually differentiated living being through the specific cell division that is meiosis. He explains this with his metaphor of the *"lamella,"* mythically indicating by this something that flies away at birth, the lamella as pure life instinct (Lacan 1994 [1964], p. 205). As strange as this idea may seem, it derives from a biological fact: nonsexual reproduction (parthogenesis) primarily implies the possibility of eternal life (as with the unicellullar organisms); sexual reproduction implies the death of the individual. Every organism wants to undo this loss; every organism wants to return to the previous state of being. This is the axiomatic single-mindedness one can see in the drive. In other words, every organism wants to go back to the previous state of eternal life, a situation that precedes sexual differentiation.

In the human being, this attempt at return, which forms the reaction to the primal loss, occurs through the mediation of the Symbolic and the Imaginary, which is at the same time the level where psychosexual identity takes shape. This has an important consequence: it means that the primal loss or lack, belonging to the order of the Real, is answered on the second level, that of representation, that is to say, in the orders of the Imaginary and the Symbolic. The original loss is thereby sexualized; more specifically, it is expressed in phallo-representational terms, and the attempt to return to the original loss takes place within the phallic-representational order. Nevertheless, this answer will never be enough to reach the original goal, that is, eternal life for the individual. This is where Lacan encounters the second loss, this time in the Symbolic. No signifier is able to answer and cancel out the primal lack, that is to say, to fully articulate desire.

This installs a certain deterministic dialectic. The real loss of the organism—the loss of eternal life—is rewritten as a phallic lack in the relation between the subject and the Other. This is the transition Freud described from the relation between the baby and its internal drive, to the relation between the baby and the first Other, and then to the sexually differentiated, oedipal relation between mother, child, father, and phallus (Lacan 1994 [1964], p. 181).[23] From that moment on, the drive

---

23. Discussions are missing in the English translation: see also the French version [Lacan 1973 [1964]. *Le Séminaire XI: Les Quatres concepts fondamentaux de la psychoanalyse*. Paris: Seuil, pp. 62, 95–96.

operates as a partial drive, with the ever-present combination of the life and death drives.

The result is *The Human Condition* (Malraux). We end up with a circular but nonreciprocal relation: "It doesn't stop not being written" (Lacan 1998 [1972–1973], pp. 94, 144). The loss at the level of the asexual Real causes the individual, sexually differentiated life to be one long determined attempt to return to the earlier eternal life. This search acquires form at another dialectical level, starting with the mother and child and traditionally ending with a man and woman. The attempt to return takes place within the dialectics of the Symbolic and the Imaginary, determined in a systematic way (automaton), but this return inevitably confronts the irreversibility of the cause (tuchè). The resulting structural incompatibility keeps the pendulum going.

We can easily recognize this account in Lacan's theory of causality and determinism, and of the unconscious as a perpetually failing border process. Ultimately, his theory deals with an homologous structure that returns on different levels, and is both circular and nonreciprocal (Lacan 1994 [1964], p. 207). The introduction of a new element causes a previous element to disappear, but the new one makes every effort to restore the loss. The result is the exact opposite: the loss is confirmed again, yet on another, advanced level. And there the same process is repeated, with identical results. Inside this homologous structure, one can discern a number of steps (Lacan 1994 [1964], pp. 203–215).

First, the acquisition of life. The introduction of sexually differentiated life forms implies the loss of eternal life. This latter, the *Zoë* of the classical Greeks, functions as a pole of attraction for the individual life, *Bios*, that wants to return to it. The way this return occurs is once more through sexual reproduction, meaning that, ironically enough, the original loss is confirmed again. From that moment onward the life and death drives are inextricably combined.

Secondly, the formation of the ego. This is the primary alienation of the mirror stage. The living being acquires an initial mastery and identity through the externally imposed body image, which in the following stage is translated into the master signifier "I," understood as "to be myself/to be master of myself" (*"maître à moi-même/m'être à moi-même,"* Lacan 1991 [1969–1970], p. 178). In the meantime, this "I," or ego, has lost its real body and will do anything to rejoin it again. The attempt to rejoin it takes place through the Other, through the

Other's signifier with which the ego identifies in order to represent its own body. Precisely in this way, the real body becomes even more irrecoverable. Finally, the ego gets stuck at the signified body, that is to say, the body image that comes from the Other. As a result, not only does the gap remain, it is perpetually reconfirmed.

Third, the formation of the subject. The divided subject appears and disappears under the Other's signifiers in an attempt to answer the Other's lack and thereby mend the separation. Nevertheless, such an answer is formulated in phallic signifiers, while the underlying lack in the Other lies beyond the signifier. Every phallic answer thus becomes precisely a confirmation of the initial problem, turning the process into an endless repetition.

This will be the same when the relation between the subject and the Other becomes a relation between a man and a woman. The original circular but nonreciprocal relation between life and death, between body and ego, between Other and subject, is ultimately repeated between man and woman. The repetition always produces the same effect: an encore on a subsequent level. From a structural perspective, we encounter two heterogeneous elements each time, one of which functions as a pole of attraction for the other that tries to return to it, although this return only reconfirms the original loss. Already in 1948, Lacan wrote that a fundamental gap lies at the heart of the human organism: "This relation to nature is altered by a certain dehiscence at the heart of the organism, a primordial Discord" (Lacan 1977 [1949], p. 4). The human being is always divided between something that it is not or doesn't have, and something that it will never be nor have. As a border or gap structure, this division keeps insisting, enabling one to recognize a homologous structure in the body, the drive, the unconscious, and subject. This impossible relation is not so much the relation between nature and culture, as between the Real and the Symbolic. Between the two lies the unconscious: "The unconscious is surely the veritable intermediary between the somatic and the psychic: perhaps it is the missing link one is so much looking for" (Groddeck 1977, letter of 5 June 1917, my translation).

10
Conclusion: The Subject's Position in Relation to Anxiety, Guilt, and Depression

In the previous chapter we discussed the question of etiology in terms of the bigger picture. Were we to ask the same question at the level of the subject, we would inevitably come up against the problem of guilt, as we already saw in the conclusion to Part 1. By way of concluding Part II, we here take up the question of guilt again, this time in the light of our metapsychology. As we will see, it has everything to do with two central clinical phenomena: anxiety and depression.

The importance of these phenomena in the contemporary clinic scarcely needs stating. At the end of the day, one finds no form of psychopathology without some feelings of depression and/or anxiety. Before the hype of the personality disorders, it seemed as if the DSM diagnostic would almost exclusively be based on these feelings. While anxiety has always been at the center of clinical work, depression seems to have recently increased exponentially to become a "sign of the times" (Roudinesco 1999). This ubiquity requires us to comprehend these two phenomena both from a global perspective and as differentiated within the different pathologies.

In what follows, I will show how anxiety and depression are central to subject-formation and that potential psychopathological effects have to do with the way they are—or are not—processed in relation to the Other. We have seen both of them already at work from the outset of identity formation (in Chapter 6). Following on from this, it will become clear how each is connected with another central clinical phenomenon, namely, guilt. Given its high incidence in the clinic, it is strange that guilt has not received as much attention as the other two states. Its relative absence in contemporary studies stands in stark contrast to the ubiquity of depression.

My thesis will be that anxiety, guilt, and depression present a triptych in every relation between the subject and the Other. As such, they are unavoidable existential elements of identity formation, and hence also of clinical diagnostics.

ANXIETY IN THE SUBJECT–OTHER RELATION

Contemporary research into anxiety is mainly focused on its neurobiological foundation and on psychological learning mechanisms. In both areas, a lot of information has been assembled at fairly specialized levels. The problem is that hardly any attention has been paid to the global aspects. Studies such as *The Essence of Anxiety* (Vestdijk 1968) are an exception; it is only from the angle of anthropological psychiatry (Glas 2001) that we still find some attention being paid to it. The result is well known: one cannot see the forest for the trees. From my point of view, such a study of the fundamental nature of anxiety is essential, in order to give these empirical research results clinical utility.

Globally speaking, we can distinguish two major approaches emerging out of Darwin and Freud (Glas 2001, pp. 28–32). From a Darwinian perspective, anxiety is regarded as an inherited, adaptive biological reaction to an external danger. The subsequent development of this idea took place in biomedical research, whose central hypothesis is that every organism displays a homeostatic internal regulation in which anxiety fulfills a survival role. The anxiety-blocking effect of imipramine (D. Klein 1964, 1980) set the tone for pharmacological research and the accompanying idea of pharmacological treatment. While its therapeutic effects are unmistakable, this line of thought has had a disastrous effect on the clinical psychological study of the phenomenon.

Alongside this we find the Freudian approach, in which anxiety is understood as a reaction to an external and an internal danger, with a focus on the internal (Freud 1978 [1926d]). The child's biological helplessness in relation to its own drive impulses that endanger survival is the foundation of anxiety, and this obliges the human being to turn to a number of coping strategies. Any potential psychopathology has to do with these coping strategies, not with the phenomenon of anxiety per se. This line of reasoning formed the basis for a number of clinical psychological theories, easily recognized for instance in the contemporary cognitive approach of Beck and Clark (Glas 2001, p. 24).

At first sight, these two viewpoints seem opposed and serve to illustrate the difference between the biomedical and psychological approach. Their difference can be summed up in their respective emphases: internal versus external. Nevertheless, this difference disappears the moment that the difference between the internal and the external becomes relative. In our previous chapters, we saw how the organism and the outside world—the subject and the Other—are one whole, and how the division operates in a different fashion than through a simple splitting between internal and external.[1] With this approach, one can begin to understand anxiety in a different light, and one that does justice to both theories. Let us briefly recall this again in order to come to both a clinical and an ontological understanding of anxiety.

The starting point is an experience of what Freud calls unpleasure and pain as a result of an internal imbalance. Its prototypes are hunger and thirst, whose source in the body has the aim of survival—here the connection with Darwin is fairly clear. Because of infantile helplessness, what ensues is an appeal to the Other by means of the cry in an attempt to effect a return to homeostasis. The original unpleasure becomes anxiety the moment that the other's response to the appeal fails. The implication is that, from quite early on, anxiety can take two directions: inward, resulting from the breaking through of the homeostasis, and outward, resulting from the other's failure to restore the balance. From a psychological point of view, anxiety will therefore always be a combination of the somatically experienced unpleasure and separation anxiety.

---

1. We have applied the same line of reasoning to the nature–nurture debate in the previous chapter: there are no two separate elements, they are combined from the outset.

The link between internal and external is patent from the beginning and takes place through language. First, we have a primal, automatic anxiety, in which language/the Other falls short in its answer to the Real of the drive (actualpathology). The subsequent processing in the Symbolic and the Imaginary (psychopathology) give rise to a secondary signal anxiety that remains associatively linked to the original primal form. This processing is endless because of the structural incompatibility between language as representation and the original drive; it is an integral part of subject-formation. This has two consequences: first, anxiety can be hooked onto one of the two processes (alienation-separation) in subject-formation and, second, depending on the specific structure of the subject, will appear in different forms.

On this basis, we can distinguish between several forms of anxiety. The most eye-catching difference is that between panic disorder (or automatic anxiety) and signal or phobic anxiety. This distinction accords with the difference between an actualpathology and a psychopathology, and can be found in each of the three subjective structures. This brings us to the second distinction: depending on the specific structure of the subject, the anxiety—either automatic or signal—will receive a certain coloring. Traditionally, anxiety in psychosis is considered far more monolithic than neurotic anxiety, while anxiety in the perverse subject is scarcely ever discussed. This specific character will be discussed in Part III of this book, where we will encounter the various pathological structures. Following this, we can make another distinction: the anxiety will be different depending on whether it involves a lack or a surplus in the Other's answer to the original unpleasure. Where the Other's answer is lacking, separation anxiety will appear, along with dependency. Where the Other's answer is in excess, we will find anxiety over incorporation/alienation, combined with a striving for autonomy.

The clinical differential diagnostic with regard to anxiety will therefore have to take these three possibilities into account. Each time the following question must be asked: Does the anxiety pertain to a psychotic, a perverse, or a neurotic structure? Is the anxiety automatic, or are we dealing with an already processed signal anxiety? In which way is the anxiety directed? Toward alienation or separation?

ANXIETY AS THE ENGINE OF SUBJECT-FORMATION

My thesis is as follows: anxiety is the engine for three simultaneous processes, namely, subject-formation, symbol development, and the establishment of human reality as such. The implication is that anxiety is a necessary phenomenon in order for the three processes to occur, and that potential pathologies are just that, potential, and not necessary in themselves. Anxiety, on the other hand, is necessary. To illustrate this, let us turn to a classical case study (M. Klein 1930) that can be reread in terms of our metapsychology.

Dick is 4 years old but speaks barely at the level of a 2-year-old. He has, moreover, no desire to speak, as is consistent within the larger framework of his contact disorder. He displays no feelings of pain, doesn't ask for comfort, and as far as he's concerned the therapist is nothing more than a part of the décor. He exhibits plenty of pathological phenomena that can be summed up thus: nothing goes in and nothing comes out, both at the level of words and of food.

Klein notes how the chief symptom is his lack of anxiety, which is associated with a stasis in development. Dick has no form of fantasy play and is barely interested in the surroundings. The only thing that interests him is the opening and closing of doors and, in terms of toys, trains.

It seems clear that the identity-forming dialectic between the subject and the Other is missing. This is confirmed by his case history: Dick is not a wanted child. His grandmother and nanny show him some affection but the mother herself has little interest in him.

Based on her clinical experience, Klein concludes that analysis as such is impossible here—indeed there is no material that could be analyzed. Instead, her therapeutic goal is to put the development back into motion, and she does this by naming the situation for him in the only way he can understand it, that is, in terms of trains. She calls one a papa-train, another a Dick-train, and another the mama-station, and says that the Dick train is locked up in the mama station. The child reacts to this by running away and locking himself in the corridor between two doors and calling for his nanny. With this action he confirms Klein's interpretation—he is locked up—at the same time that he formulates his first demand to an other for help, in this case the nanny. The same scenario is repeated in the second and third sessions when at last the anxiety becomes manifest, together with his first appeal to the therapist and his first interest in toys, accompanied by aggression. Klein does little more than brutally name the process in terms of the relation between the mother and child, linked to introjection and expulsion. The bad parts of the mother are thrown out, destroyed, the good parts are retained.

From the fourth session onward, developments start to move fast. The child touches and names an ever-increasing number of objects, which he tries to destroy and repair, while the vocal exchange and appeals to the other also increase. Klein uses the concept of symbolic equation, indicating by this that the objects the child handles are symbolic equivalents for the primary exchange between the mother and child, based on the dialectics of good (pleasure) and bad (unpleasure).

We can understand this process in terms of our metapsychology. Dick finds himself initially in an undifferentiated position; he has no identity of his own. Klein's interpretation provokes a colossal anxiety, which we must understand as a psychotic existential anxiety: he does not exist, he is simply a part of the Other. His incorporation in the Other is Imaginary, but nonetheless it is total—the child is still "living" in the Other. This anxiety initiates a coping process by which the child separates and identifies himself at the same time. This occurs through the manipulation of ever more objects and their names, across which the initial monolithic anxiety is spread and thereby thinned. This manipulation, moreover, occurs in relation to an Other—the therapist—who not only gives him the words, but also a secure context within which the process becomes possible.

The result is threefold. First, the child's identity starts forming. He begins to learn an increasing number of words for things, and what is striking is that the first series of words are almost completely to do with the body. This implies at the same time an extension of his subjective identity. Indeed, the subject is the result of the self-extending chain of signifiers, through which he can name both "himself" and the "outside world." Secondly, symbol development is put in motion and it is foreseeable that this process of displacement will continue, depending on his growing ability to cope with the anxiety. Thirdly, because of this, his reality is enlarged: he has increasing interest in his surroundings; he can name the things and therefore also master them.

These three processes are three facets of a single whole; subject-formation, symbol development, and the establishment of human reality are all based on dialectical exchanges between the subject and the Other that occur by way of signifiers. The engine is anxiety, that is, the need to make the primal anxiety manageable through language. The process recalls a centrifugal movement, through which increasing numbers of signifiers are layered around an anxiety-provoking kernel. Its schematic representation is then the same as what Freud describes in his "Studies on Hysteria," with the nonverbal trauma as kernel (see Fig. 7–1), which can be inserted dialectically in the relation toward A and (*a*) (see Fig. 8–5).

The case study concerns a pathological situation that Klein calls a case of infantile schizophrenia. In normal circumstances, the confrontation with the initial unpleasure and pain causes the infant to appeal to the Other, resulting automatically in a relation toward this Other. The inadequacy of the Other's answer forces the subject to make its demand again, in an increasing variety of expressive ways. The most well-known manifestations of it are found in the child's endless questions, "Why?" or "How come?" that force new answers from the Other. These expressions—signifiers—will constitute the continuously extending subject as such who thereby also learns how to know and deal with an ever-increasing reality by means of a growing symbolization.[2]

ANXIETY AND GUILT

The question of whether psychopathological determinants are internal or external is part of the larger question of etiology. In clinical practice, this comes down to the hot potato question of guilt, which is preferably quickly passed on to somebody else. Twenty or so years ago,

---

2. This has far-reaching repercussions for "rehabilitation programs" and "community education." The more limited a person's language, the more limited the worldview and identity—as we have seen, the three go together. The acquisition of more signifiers, coming from different others within a positive transferential relation, a requisite for every form of education, is the effective basis for community education. In cases of a restricted and monotonous Other—as in *Pravda* and CNN, not to mention Fox News—the "world" view becomes frighteningly narrow-minded.

it was largely assumed that parents had the central influence on (normal or abnormal) development of their offspring; nowadays this has been dissolved into the influence of "society," the peer group (Harris 1998), and even to the so-called "non-common factors."[3] Recently, more and more voices are heard that exonerate everyone by situating the etiological cause in the body and, particularly, in heredity. As we saw in our previous chapter, this is a naive, dichotomous logic that is assumed above all to the subject's advantage. In that sense, it adheres perfectly to the initial subject-formation, which always lays responsibility elsewhere. This doubtless explains its success.

On this basis, we can say that guilt is a central clinical phenomenon that appears in nearly every form of pathology. It is no coincidence that one of the most frequently heard complaints of children is "It's not my fault!" As we concluded in our first part, it is not enough to scientifically choose sides and either blame or exonerate the patient. Given identity formation's starting point, a certain failure and guilt will be implicit from the start in the relation between the subject and the Other.

Diagnostically and therapeutically, it is of enormous value to interrogate this dialectic so as to find out what the place and function of this sense of guilt are in a particular pathology, and how the treatment can work on them. In the discussion of the specific pathological structures in Part III of this book, it will become clear that the way the neurotic subject handles the lack and the accompanying sense of guilt is completely different from the way perverse and psychotic subjects handle it. Classically, the clinician anticipates a neurotic and therefore shared sense of guilt, hence his or her surprise when confronted with subjective structures that don't conform to this. Doubtless, this expectation has to do with the obligatory sense of guilt within Judeo-Christian culture, as in "*Mea culpa, mea culpa, mea maxima culpa,*" but it actually goes much further than this. Lack is a central element in identity

---

3. Empirical research has recently shown the importance of these non-common factors where siblings adopted into the same family were compared to siblings adopted by different families. Such research demonstrates that the *non*-common factors, that is to say, factors *outside* the specific family, are the most decisive for the differences in identity formation (Plomin and Bergeman 1991).

formation because of the characteristic structure of the Symbolic—this is why the question of guilt is universal.

Regarded from the perspective of our metapsychology, guilt boils down to a way of coping with anxiety. This is because the sense of guilt installs the conviction that anxiety could have been avoided if only someone had said or done the "right" thing. This anxiety is always associated with the Real and the Other's failure with respect to it. In this way, anxiety and, hence, guilt are introduced into the subject–Other dialectic. To the extent that guilt is either ascribed to the Other or taken up by the subject itself, this creates the illusion that the anxiety could have been been mastered, beyond the learned helplessness. An illustration of this can be found in the frequently pseudoscientific discourse of psychosomatics. The confrontation with a somatic experience that cannot be explained by the medical other means, in our terms, that the Other fails to answer. As a result, the patient is forced to take the guilt upon him or herself: she or he must have done something wrong, made a mishandling of emotions, aggression, anger, and so on. Consequently, the patient is guilty for what is inexplicable.[4] Often, the patient's counterreaction is refusal and an even more radical accusation of the (medical) Other who failed to listen, or to listen properly. The "advantage" to such a game of ping-pong is that the

---

4. Sontag (1979) denounced this in a brilliant essay where, among other things, she compares TB to cancer. Before the discovery of the Koch-bacillus, the cause of TB was in the patient—he or she was a romantic loser in love, pining away on Thomas Mann's *Magic Mountain* or as in *La Traviata*. Such accusations disappeared very quickly after the discovery of the bacillus, and TB became a normal disease. Sontag demonstrates how an analogous logic can be found with regard to cancer. She cites a number of typologies in which the cancer patient is described as a malingerer and a complainer, a loser with respect to hate and aggression, incapable of emotional expression or control. Both cases (TB and cancer) demonstrate that when the cause is laid exclusively on the patient, he or she is not only ill but also responsible for his or her disease. Hence Sontag's conclusion: the diagnosis of a disorder as psychosomatic *simply because one cannot find an organic cause* must be avoided at all costs. The contemporary approach to somatization is considerably more nuanced, making a precise distinction between a group where the psychological processing is missing (and, hence, there are literally no *psycho*somatic factors) and a group where it is present. We will return to this later.

confrontation with the naked anxiety, in its encounter with an unnameable Real, is avoided.

Each subjective structure will install a specific form of guilt as a way of handling anxiety in its relation with the Other. One can find a lucid overview of this process in Mooij's wider discussion of the question of guilt (1997, pp. 15–21). In the neurotic subject, the question of guilt is manifestly central. The obsessional tries to avoid guilt by formulating the perfect answer to the Other's norms, thus inevitably inaugurating a downward spiral of guilt. The hysteric takes the guilt upon him- or herself and punishes him/herself for his or her desire, but forces the other to take some of the blame as well. The perverse subject must entirely comply with the Other in order to assure the Other's jouissance and, as a result, guilt is situated unilaterally within this Other. The psychotic subject, with its characteristic lack of the reflective function and inability to take symbolic distance, feels either completely guilty (melancholy), or purely innocent (paranoia) (Soler 1988).

Next, we come upon another quintessentially human phenomenon: shame. At first sight, guilt and shame seem to be opposed. Guilt has to do with one's failure to live up to an interiorized norm. Shame is caused by a loss of face—and, hence, in terms of the mirror stage, the loss of identity—because one has failed with respect to an external norm. Nevertheless, the difference between shame and guilt is not all that clear; the well-known experience of "vicarious shame" provides a good illustration of this. One is ashamed for someone else, based on an identification with the other's failure and the guilt. Again we find the interdependence of the inside and outside, the ego and the Other. The common factor always has to do with a sense of failure. From a clinical point of view, this brings us to a third existential theme alongside anxiety and guilt, namely depression.

DEPRESSION AND THE POSITION OF THE SUBJECT

In Part III of this book we will discuss the differential diagnostics for actualpathologies and psychopathologies, differentiating the three different subject structures. As we saw above, anxiety can be understood from the basis of the specific differential diagnostic. The question now is, Where do we locate depression in this differential diagnostic system?

The fundamental line of reasoning remains the same: just as with anxiety, depression doesn't imply any particular subjective structure. The specific color of the depression will be determined by the specific relation between the subject and the Other in which the depression occurs and, consequently, also by the way the subject positions itself in language. This means that we can use the same differential-diagnostic line of reasoning here as was used for anxiety. Depression may relate to a naked actualpathological form, or an elaborated psychopathological variation. Moreover, depression can occur as easily in neurotic and psychotic structures as in perverse structures, displaying the specific characteristics of that structure each time.

Like anxiety, depression is not a symptom in the psychoanalytic sense of the word in the way that slips of the tongue, dreams, or conversion symptoms are. Both start as an actualpathological phenomenon that, through potential further psychopathological elaborations, can give rise to symptoms. To my mind, depression is the sign of a moment of passage, a transition, that can either be taken or missed, occurring within the larger framework of what is sometimes called the symbolic realization of the subject. This is not to say that certain subjects, independently of their specific structure, are not more prone to depression than other subjects because of their specific history.

It may come as a surprise that I do not consider depression as a separate, independent subjective structure, especially given its very high incidence in the clinic. But the real question is what this prevalence means. Seen from a purely phenomenological perspective and, moreover, in light of the increasing pharmacologization of the clinic, it seems clear that today's omnipresent DSM categorization has caused an enormous increase in the diagnosis. All it takes is for someone to recognize something that seems depressive within a larger pattern of complaints for the diagnosis and medication to be triggered. Afterward, discussion can be restricted to the question of whether it concerns a "minor" or "major" affective disorder, possibly "bipolar," with little concern for the underlying structure. To avoid repeating myself, the reader is referred to my earlier critique of this line of reasoning in Part I of this book (see also Van Hoorde 1992).

The second cause of the success of this diagnosis has more substance and concerns changes in the wider sociocultural discourse. Today's Westerners live in an all-encompassing psy-culture; every psychological and psychiatric theory gains immediate popular recognition, and what was formerly professional lingo is these days part of everyday language. Moreover, we live in a liberal-capitalist society[5] that gives the impression on all sides that happiness and comfort are for sale and, hence, easily attainable simply if you want it. The results are predictable: the "common unhappiness" Freud refers to in the final paragraph of his "Studies on Hysteria," has become unbearable and what was formerly merely part of the human condition has been rechristened today in fashionable psychiatric terminology. One used to be "down"; these days one is "dépri" (it rhymes with déli). Every clinician is familiar with the question, both in clinical practice and at social events: "Am I manic depressive? Things always seem to go well for a few months and then everything starts falling apart." The idea that happiness only exists in comparison with unhappiness seems to have been forgotten. The accompanying expectation is one of immediate relief, by external intervention moreover, which tallies perfectly with today's pharmacological clinic. In terms of discourse theory, this is an appeal to the discourse of the Master at the very moment this discourse is in decline. One expects the therapist as the incarnation of the big Other to make a masterly intervention that will resolve everything in one fell swoop, and without any effort on the side of the patient. In short, one wants Huxley's soma pills from *Brave New World* ("a soma a day keeps your sorrow away").

This has not only caused an increase in the number of depressions, but in addition we can also predict—by interpreting its cause structurally—what the nature of this increase in depression will be. A structural interpretation of contemporary discourse reveals that the symbolic father has disappeared. Consequently, the depression will be of an actualpathological nature (see Part III of this book).

As we saw earlier, the drive arousal is initially mirrored by the mother and symbolically regulated by the signifier of the Name-of-the-Father. This latter is the Freudian Oedipus complex, whose effects can be summarized as follows: the drive is subjected to a conventional

---

5. The connotations of "liberal" in a European context are opposite to those in the United States, that is, signifying right-wing in Europe. This in itself seems to say a lot about the difference between the two continents.

meaning by its introduction into a discourse that is based on the master signifier, and that signifies gender and authority. This is Lacan's symbolic function of the father, and anthropology has shown that while the content of such a function can be quite different throughout different ages and places, the function per se remains the same. In contemporary Western society, however, this is no longer the case (Demoulin 2001b, Verhaeghe 2002a). The symbolic function of the father itself has been undermined, resulting in the impossibility of either a collective signification or an accompanying regulation of the drive. Replacing the earlier discourse of the Master is the discourse of capitalism, a discourse emptied of meaning. For in itself, money merely has exchange value, one cannot "buy" meaning with it. Hence, too, today's more generalized complaints about the loss of meaning, an omnipresent emptiness, and its accompanying anxiety and depression. Because of this loss of meaning, anxiety and depression will mostly be actualpathological.

Based on this structural reading of contemporary discourse, Van Compernolle (2002) has argued that the current increase in depression amounts to an increase in its anxiety-neurotic (see Chapter 11) and hence actualpathological form. Normal depression, that is to say, depression that is concerned with the Other's norm, lies in the psychopathological spectrum and boils down to the conviction that one has been unable to fulfill the ego-ideal, as dictated by the Other (Jonckheere 1998b). In his studies of actualneurosis, Freud already indicates that, should it not receive a psychological elaboration, the somatic pressure of the drive will give rise to an automatic anxiety and depression (Freud 1978 [1892–1899], pp. 178, 183). Such a combination of panic disorder and depression has meanwhile been empirically proven (Clum and Pendrey 1987). Here the drive pressure continues to function at the somatic level without acquiring a signification through the Other. As a consequence, the resulting anxiety and depression are also meaningless. Even more so: it is precisely because of this lack of signification that they remain operative at the level of the body. As a result, actualpathological depression will always be accompanied by somatization. This, too, is largely confirmed by contemporary empirical research, demonstrating again the combination in place between anxiety, depression, and somatization (see Chapter 11).

On the basis of this structural understanding of the disappearance of the symbolic father function, we can now grasp the larger complex of the "new" symptoms of today: automutilation, eating disorders, and aggressive and/or sexual acting out.[6] Phenomena such as these remain caught in the somatic starting point, as opposed to the classic symptoms of psychopathology that fully undergo symbolic and imaginary processing. Demoulin (2001a) talks about *"une clinique de la jouissance égarée,"* a clinic of rambling jouissance.

As a result, actualpathological depression involves a failure in the somatic passage of the drive's psychological elaboration and regulation through the Other. Depression in psychopathological structures has already gone through this transition where the subject at first succeeded in answering the image of the Ego-Ideal presented to it by the Other, but then subsequently failed, resulting in the depression. Let us look at this failure now within the larger context of subject-formation.

DEPRESSION AS AN ESSENTIAL POSSIBILITY FOR EVERY SUBJECT

The most important Freudian text in this respect is "Mourning and Melancholia" (1978 [1917e]), and it is the term "melancholia" that is immediately striking. It is only later that one begins to speak of "neurotic depression"; Freudian melancholy pertains to the field of psychosis. In this paper, the central analogy is between depression and the mourning process, whose common factor is the loss of the object. This is abundantly clear in mourning, and Freud remarks that losing the object in reality (in the external world) has to be followed by its dismantling in the ego (the inside world). Experience makes this clear: when we lose a loved one, it seems as if part of ourselves has also died. The loved object formed, as it were, a part of ourselves; it was inside us and now must be relinquished internally as well. Freud calls this

---

6. We can include addiction in this as well. Addiction can best be understood in the context of actualpathology, as the subject's attempt to directly intervene in its own drive, without a detour through the Other (Loose 2002). Moreover, these phenomena are not really new, they only seem more frequent today; that, at least, is the general impression. From our perspective, they pertain for the most part to actualpathology, and fit seamlessly with today's changes in the symbolic function of the father. For a sociological discussion of these sociocultural changes, see Ehrenberg (1991, 1998).

the work of mourning, a slow and painful process that has a strong resemblance to melancholy. At two points, however, this resemblance ends: in melancholy, the object loss is not always so apparent, while in a normal mourning process the vociferous self-reproaches, so typical of the melancholic patient, are missing.

Before taking a closer look at these differences, let us first concentrate on the common factors, taking identification as the central concept. Indeed, the process that lies at the heart of both depression and mourning is evidently the need to dismantle the inner image and, hence, identification. This is why depression is a key phenomenon in subject-formation: because it can be considered the reverse process, a de-identification.

In the chapter on identity acquisition, identification was described in terms of three logical moments, each having the same motive but using different material: incorporation, identification, alienation. Incorporation continues to reverberate within our language, in expressions in which we say we could "eat someone up" with love, and where the kiss lingers on as an atavistic remainder. In the second logical moment, we get what Freud calls identification, where it is not an object, but the image of an object that is brought inside through the pleasure–unpleasure balance. This mechanism is studied in ethology as well, and it was from there that Lacan got the inspiration for his theory of the mirror stage, among other things.

This stage provides the first grounding identification, enabling us to highlight the crucial aspect of this process—that is, the formative-ontological impact (Lacan 1966 [1946], pp. 188–193). In the Freudian-Lacanian line of thinking, the human organism begins as an empty, albeit purposive, (that is, goal-directed) shell that only acquires psychological content and, hence, identity through successive identifications. The very first identification that takes place in the mirror stage provides the shell, namely, the bodily schema that will hold all later identifications. In other words, our most intimate identity, that which is ourselves and only ourselves, is ultimately nothing but an integrated collection of identifications and hence of "extimate" identities. Lacan will rename this identification *alienation*. The subject identifies with the words and images of the Other and becomes alien, an Other. Consequently, should this alienation disappear, no "true" or "original" identity could come forth, but rather there would be a hole, an emptiness. Kundera's "unbearable lightness of being" is a perfect illustration of this.

Here we come back to depression, which can now be understood from a theoretical basis. Without the perspective of this theoretical aspect, the concept of depression has little value; its metaphoric abilities would refer primarily to the weather forecast or to economic conditions. On the basis of our discussion of subject-formation, however, we can comprehend depression as one side of an opposition, as can also be seen in the concept of manic-depression (bipolar): the emptiness of the depression stands in contrast to the fullness of enthusiasm. Here etymology and classical mythology can be of help. Enthusiasm comes from the ancient Greek *enthousiastikos*, whose etymological meaning is to take the god into oneself; the god fulfills one and makes one ecstatic. One of the Euripidean tragedies tells the story of the Bacchae, the high priestesses of Bacchus who maintained the orgiastic rites that culminated in the devouring of a billy goat representing the god. At that moment, they became "enthusiastic": the god was taken in. The same process can be found in many religions—just think of the Catholic rite of holy communion. There, too, flesh and blood are taken in, albeit in a much more civilized and therefore less satisfying way. Opposed to this, then, is the loss of God, of being forsaken by the god, leaving man devoid of the ecstatic fulfillment that took place a short while ago. It is not too hard to find an exemplary case of this in the final residue that remains for the human being of the fusion process, namely, coitus. The "enthusiasm" of the coital fusion with the other is mirrored by the de-fusion, the postcoital dissolution of the *"omne animal triste."*

This theoretically generated opposition between full and empty accords beautifully with clinical experience. Contemporary popular approaches focus on the affect, and people quickly come to associate depression with certain negative emotions. But this is not the crux of it, quite the opposite in fact: as Lacan tells us, *"le senti-ment"*—feelings—are deceptive.[7] At the heart of depression, as is clinically not hard to see, is a lack of emotion, and a confrontation with emptiness and the

---

7. Translator's Note: Lacan is here playing on *sentiment*, the French word for feelings and emotion, and *mentir*, to lie. *Le senti-ment*, that is, *"le sentiment ment"* can be translated as "emotion lies."

loss of meaning. Hence Kierkegaard's negative name for his melancholy: despair, the loss of hope (see Mallet 1955).

Depression can thus be conceived as the reverse of identity acquisition, the loss of an identificatory anchoring point in the Other. In this way, depression is an essential possibility for every subject, so that the question now turns to a consideration of what specific factors in the relation between the subject and the Other provoked this reversal. The manifestation of depression itself will then wholly be determined by the specific subjective structure (neurosis, psychosis, perversion).

DEPRESSION AND GUILT

The relation between depression and guilt—and thereby anxiety—in every subjective structure is readily apparent to anyone who listens. Besides the comparison with mourning, this represents Freud's second important discovery in "Mourning and Melancholia." Depression always comes with the self-reproach that one has failed to satisfy the Other's desire. The idea that this self-reproach is a covert accusation of the other at the same time was already suggested by Freud, and is still verifiable in clinical practice,[8] albeit on the same condition: that someone does indeed listen.

---

8. This enables Freud to extend his theory considerably. More specifically, his second topology (ego, superego, id) originates in his study of melancholy because it is precisely the division between the ego and the superego that plays such an important role in the depression–enthusiasm dichotomy. The term superego had not yet appeared by the time of "Mourning and Melancholia." There, Freud talks about the "critical instance" in the ego. By differentiating between these two, he is able to describe the internal mirroring of the external loss of the object. In psychotic melancholy, the image of the lost object takes the place of the ego, resulting in the ego being severely condemned by the superego: it is nothing, it can do nothing, it has never been able to do anything and never will be able to. The ego thus sinks into a deep lethargy and is scarcely able to speak. What the clinician hears are the harsh superego condemnations of this ego, so vociferous that these reproaches ultimately testify to a colossal self-conceit. Freud's clinical genius showed that these so-called "self"-reproaches are nothing but hidden accusations *of the other*, where the self has taken the place of the object upon which the superego revenges itself because that object dared to leave the ego. Note that once again the internal and external worlds are interchangeable.

In psychotic depression, these self-reproaches come through loud and clear, in neurotic depression this vociferousness is absent. The neurotic for the most part will try to hide his or her failures, and doesn't show off his or her sense of being worthless. In this context, one often hears people speak of a "hidden" depression, that is to say, a depression that is hidden from the outside world, from the Other. Guilt and shame merge together here. One can hear anything in the depressive, empty neurotic complaints, from fatigue, boredom, the feeling of being worn down, having no desire, to a generalized *tedium vitae*. The totality can be summed up as, "I've no longer any desire" as well as "I'm not desired by anyone," by which one should understand "I can't do anything, I am inadequate."[9] Again, this must be understood in terms of the subject–Other dialectic of identification whose driving idea is "desire is the desire of the Other."

Through the dialectics of desire, the subject acquires an identity of its "own." Should the subject fall out of the Other's desire, it finds itself as a result in emptiness. It loses (part of) itself from the moment it is convinced that the Other no longer desires it, and is directing his or her desire elsewhere. This is provoked when the Other, in the form of a loved one, a boss, an elder, says or does something that gives the subject the idea that she or he no longer satisfies it (Vanheule 2001a,b,c).

How do we now understand this provocation as a loss of identification? During subject-formation, identity was acquired in the relation to the Other. The subject's original appeal to the Other to provide an answer to the inner drive arousal (*a*) resulted in a situation where the subject identified with the Other's response. In Lacanian terms, the subject identifies itself with the desire of the Other. This means that the subject sees itself from the position of the Other and moulds itself according to the ideal form it thinks this Other desires (Lacan 1966 [1958], p. 677; 1994 [1964], p. 256). This can likewise be understood from the perspective of the anxious-depressive counterpart of "desire is the desire of the Other." This counterpart is the "*Veut-il me perdre?*" or "Can he lose me?" Here, "he" stands for the Other, as in "Am I good

---

9. This explains another typical characteristic, namely, that time stands still for the depressive patient. Time's passing has everything to do with a scansion, where the subjective ordering is determined by desiring or being desired. Should the latter disappear, the scansion also disappears and, consequently, time comes to a standstill.

enough for him or her, do I satisfy his or her desire?" (Lacan 1994 [1964], p. 214). Depression begins when, for one reason or another, the subject is convinced that she or he no longer satisfies the Other's desire. As a result, the subject plunges from his or her fantasy into the empty void. The subject falls out of "itself," indicating at the same time the relativity of this "self."

Precisely for this reason, then, depression is an ontological possibility: it forms part of the subject's essence, although this essence has to be understood ironically: identity always comes from the Other, is built for another and can be lost through the Other. "I is another," is thus the proper psychoanalytic ontology.[10]

Now we can elucidate both the foundation and the eliciting factors of so-called psychopathological depression. As we saw above, this foundation is part of every subject-formation, independent of any specific structure. This does not exclude the way certain elements in the course of subject-formation may operate as a predisposition for a later depression. Typical in such a case is an original subject–Other relation where the Other defines the subject-to-be as perpetually inadequate. The subject is by definition inadequate and guilty, no matter what it does, "it" will never be enough. The second predisposing factor doubtless involves certain singular events in life, particularly during early subject-formation, such as the loss of the Other through disease, divorce, or other causes. It is striking how, confronted with such a loss, children always ask themselves whether they were somehow responsible

---

10. Rimbaud, "*Je est un autre.*" A similar idea can be found in Melanie Klein. She begins with the idea that the dependent child initially distinguishes between a good (gratifying) and a bad (persecuting) object, in relation to which the child assumes a split position. This is the paranoid-schizoid position whose mechanisms (introjection–projection) and effect (splitting) can fruitfully be compared to the Lacanian-derived process I have described above. For Klein this first position is relieved and resolved by the depressive position. The child will integrate the originally split good and bad object, resulting in an anxiety about losing this object and guilt caused by its own earlier aggression toward (what was experienced as) the persecuting other. This anxiety and guilt are the main components of the depressive position, whose solution must result in a tenable separation of the mother and child. For Klein, the depressive position thus holds a key function in psychological development, and the way it is resolved is determinative for normality (M. Klein 1986 [1935], 1986 [1946]; Leader 2000).

for it and hence are also to "blame" for it. Indeed, the other's disappearance makes it difficult to ascribe the guilt to the Other. The only "solution" is for the subject to take this guilt upon itself.

These predisposing factors will therefore often evoke a fall back onto a foundation that was constituted during early identity acquisition, and can be summed up thus: anything that damages the subject's certitude that it satisfies the Other's desire provokes depression. This can be anything from professional failure to rejection in love, and ranges over humiliation, failure, and devalorization. Here it must be stressed that this experience resides in the subject itself and is not necessarily the same as what an objective observer might see. The most typical accompanying phenomenon is the craving for recognition, or a fishing for compliments, with a far-reaching dependence on the public and the public scene that reassures a subject that he or she is doing well.

DEPRESSION AS A POSSIBILITY OF PASSAGE

The concept of depression has received relatively little attention in psychoanalysis, usually being studied in the context of a larger framing pathology. In addition, there has been a fair amount of interest in it from another angle that might seem a little strange at first sight. I refer here to the end of the treatment, where the idea of a moment of passage is raised. This idea appears in both Melanie Klein and Lacan, who each conceive of the end of the treatment in terms of depression (Cottet 1985). The end point, or better, the finality of the treatment is conceived as a mourning process, with the emphasis on the work of mourning or depression-work.

This shows that one can make a clear analogy between the work of mourning and analytic work. In mourning, one searches for the really lost object, the object that is lost in reality, which ultimately comes down to an unremitting production of all associative memories. What was originally brought inside is now slowly brought outside, bit by bit. In terms of Freud's libidinal-economic metaphor, all of the cathexes must be relinquished. In analytic work, the analysand searches for the object that he or she is. Through free association, the analysand looks for his or her own identity and his or her own accompanying desire. The paradoxical result is that the analysand rapidly discovers that there is nothing to find beyond an identity that derives from elsewhere and a desire that is dependent upon an other—and regardless of whether that desire is for or in opposition to that other, it is no less dependent upon it all the same. "For in this labor which he undertakes to reconstruct for another, he rediscovers the fundamental alienation that made him construct it like another, and which has always destined it to be taken from him by another" (Lacan 1977 [1953], p. 42). In short, one discovers nothing other than the continuous spiral of alienation in which one's so-called own identity becomes ever less accessible and, indeed, increasingly put into question. This is what Lacan aptly called subjective destitution and it is undeniably of the order of mourning, over both one's own and the Other's identity.[11]

The most important difference between the work of mourning in depression and in psychoanalytic treatment has to do with the idea of passage. One is "cured" of depression, frequently through medication but more especially through a repetition of the same pattern. On the horizon, a newly desired or desiring object appears, a new identification is installed in place of the previous one. Nevertheless, the underlying structure remains the same, the fundamental fantasy is restored. Depression here is a moment of passage from the same to the same again; nothing has been gained. There has merely been a quest for and reinstallation of a figure that incarnates the master figure, guaranteeing "the whole course of existence" once more (Freud 1978 [1912–1913], p. 43). It is this process that Freud recognizes in the case history of Haizmann, where he mentions the "eternal sucklings who cannot tear themselves away from the blissful situation at the mother's breast, and who, all through their lives, persist in a demand to be nourished by someone else" (Freud 1978 [1923d (1922)], p. 104).

Characteristic of this process, which has its own sociocultural allures as well, is that the crown—that is to say, the master and his function—can never be allowed to be exposed, only replaced ("the King is dead, long live the King"). Anyone who dares to point out that the King has no clothes must immediately be punished. Traditionally, only the

---

11. In 1964, at the time of *Seminar XXI* (1973–1974), the goal of the treatment is given in terms of separation. Lacan will later further specify this in terms of "traversing the fantasy" (Lacan 1994 [1964], p. 274), and still later, as "subjective destitution" (*"la déperdition subjective"*).

Fool is permitted this, which immediately assigns an appropriate place to the analyst . . . Should the King's nudity be revealed, a collective despair arises, an historical example of which is the generalized depression among European Communists at the time of Kruschev's exposure of "Papa" Stalin. They had indeed lost their (collective) identity. But this is a great exception: ordinarily the incarnation of the big Other is maintained or silently replaced. There is no actual passage to something new.

The aim of the treatment, on the other hand, is to break through such repetition. In concrete terms, it aims to break through the fundamental fantasy to the extent that it is the habitual relation toward the Other through which the same stumbling blocks and frequently enough the same depression are repeated. What Lacan calls "traversing the fantasy" aims to redefine identity in relation to the Other, halting the repetition, while the working through of the depression implies a passage to something new.[12] If the treatment should fail on this point, it

---

12. In case this sounds a bit esoteric, let us first distinguish it from what it is not. In the relation between the subject, the Other, and the lost object (*a*), any one of these elements can be chosen, albeit wrongly, as a finishing point. Identifying with the position of the subject boils down to being in the position of the Hegelian slave who must either fill in the master's lack or flee from it. This is the neurotic position. Identifying with the Other is an identification with the master figure as guarantee—one has found "the truth." This is the most typical therapeutic end, with a clearly alienating effect. Balint has described this, remarking that such a process usually ends in a kind of manic euphoria (Balint 1950, 1955). It is not hard to recognize in this the enthusiasm described above, where the patient leaves therapy with the therapist in his belly. Identifying with the lost object (*a*) and, hence, with the lack, results in a generalized fatalism. This amounts to remaining stuck in the mourning process as such, thus devaluing everything—see postmodern cynicism. Each of these three identifications, however, remains within the system of alienation and therefore fails to bring about an essential change. This can only be achieved if the transition to separation is made. The best way of understanding this is in terms of choice and sublimation, understood in the Lacanian sense (De Kesel 2002). In Freud, sublimation implies that the drive aims at a new, nonsexual goal, that is to say, the original "real" goal is replaced by something else. Lacan will go further, because for him there is no originally correct sexual aim; the drive always makes a detour around an object that can never be reached and it is the detour itself that is the drive's goal. In his reading, there is no question of replacing an original "something," because that something was never there; every object is a substitute object. Hence the Freudian conclusion of the interchange-

will result in the well-known phenomenon of the "revolving door" patient.

SUMMARY

- Anxiety, guilt, and depression pertain to subject-formation as such and take on specific appearances in accordance with the specific subjective structures.
- The original anxiety is the motive for subject-formation and sets the development of the Symbolic and therefore of human reality in motion.
- The question of guilt involves the processing of the original anxiety by way of the Other, raising the question of who is responsible for the lack.
- Both anxiety and depression begin from an actualpathological position, where the transition from (*a*) to A has not yet been carried out; in such cases, neither possesses signification and their appearance will contain somatic phenomena.
- In anxiety, subsequent processing through the secondary elaboration and subject-formation gives rise to a signifying signal anxiety.
- In depression, the same processing gives rise to a de-identification and implies, in terms of subject-formation, a regression in the dialectics of desire.
- The treatment must aim at a change in the relation between the subject and the Other. Depression may function as a moment of passage to something new.

---

ability of objects. When Lacan discusses sublimation, he describes a process in which the subject "elevates an object to the dignity of the Thing" as the basis for the creative process itself (Lacan1992 [1959–1960], p. 112).

To leave the preceding alienations behind for such a *conscious* sublimation—as the foundation for a continuously changing creative process—doesn't seem so bad as the treatment's final goal, whose additional bonus is that one can then tolerate both difference as such, in contrast to the narcissism of minor differences, and lack, as opposed to the endless neurotic reprocessing of castration anxiety.

III
POSITIONS AND STRUCTURES OF THE SUBJECT

Overview

This third and final part deals with structural diagnostics as such. Based on the theory sketched out in Part II, we can make a distinction between positions and relational structures. Each subject can be situated on a continuum between the actualpathological and psychopathological positions. The former implies a direct, unmediated confrontation with (a) whose chief effect on the subject is automatic anxiety. Progression to the psychopathological position implies a processing at the level of the signifier and the construction of symptoms as defensive attempts to process the Real. Besides the position, we distinguish three different structures between the subject and the Other, each implying a specific way of being-in-language and a particular relation toward others. These are the neurotic, perverse, and psychotic structures. Accompanying my explanation of the various positions as they appear in each specific subjective structure will be an indication of its relevance for how the treatment should be approached.

One might imagine that, organized logically, the discussion of psychosis should come first, starting with its actualpathological variation (schizophrenia) and followed by its psychopathological elaboration (paranoia). The perverse structure should come next, divided once more between its actualpathological and psychopathological positions. Last but not least should come the typical neurotic structure, again with the two possible positions. However, clinical praxis is not logical. I have thus organized this part in a way that I see as more clinically relevant. Nevertheless, the reader should be able to recognize the implicit logic behind it without too much difficulty.

Chapter 11 discusses a problem that formerly was rarely seen in the clinic but is increasingly being referred to us from the medical world. That these patients seldom come to us voluntarily has to do with the overwhelming actualpathological character of the complaint: somatization. However, in cases where the accent is on the chief actualpathological phenomenon, anxiety, there tends to be a more rapid demand for clinical psychological consultation. The following discussion will enable us to understand contemporary panic disorder as a synonym for Freud's anxiety neurosis.

In Chapter 12 we encounter the main protagonist of today's clinic: post-traumatic stress disorder (PTSD). Empirical research emphasizes the intensely relative nature of the pathogenic effect of actual trauma, with the result that the etiology of PTSD must be sought elsewhere. We will see how little use it is as a descriptive category, and that PTSD must be reconsidered in terms of its relation to actual- and psychopathology as well as from the perspective of the three subjective structures. In connection with this, we will discuss the problem of borderline personality and show how it belongs to the actualpathological side of the neurotic structure.

In Chapter 13 we enter into familiar territory. Hysteria and obsessional neurosis have always been classics of the clinic. This is not by coincidence: they pertain to the psychopathological position and present classically interpretable symptoms founded upon the fundamental fantasy. I will pay special attention to the relational aspect through which these symptoms are constructed and must be understood. Particularly for cases of hysteria, this is the only feasible way of obtaining a correct diagnosis.

Lying in wait for us in Chapter 14 is the perverse subject. This largely forensic clinical aspect is anything but straightforward and its diagnosis pertains predominantly to the juridical field, with the emphasis on the "perpetrator." As a result, we must clear away a certain amount of brushwood before we can actually discuss the perverse relation. More than ever, the relational structure through which the perverse subject has been installed will need to be emphasized as the basis for clinical psychodiagnostics and potential treatment.

In the final chapter, I examine the most enigmatic of all structures of the subject, that is, psychosis. I chose to present psychosis last because it confronts us with the limits of our own symbolically determined subjectivity. With it, too, the difference between the actualpathological and the psychopathological position can be applied, and there, too, the psychotically installed relation is determinative for the diagnosis. In its otherness, psychosis above all shows us how each relational structure between the subject and the Other is simultaneously a relation with language.

11
The Actualpathological Position: Panic Disorder and Somatization

Our metapsychological discussion of identity formation has enabled us to distinguish a position of the subject in relation to (*a*) and the Other where the secondary defense and psychological processing have not taken place. The initial problem—which is simultaneously the motive for identity formation—remains focused on the body, that is to say, on the demand arising out of the real body and the impotence of the Other to answer it.

Should such a subject position be empirically verifiable, the consequences would be the following. First, in the psychodiagnostic field, the differential diagnostic becomes relatively simple. For such a subject position, there will be no symptoms a fortiori, that is, no signifying constructions in the Symbolico-Imaginary. The accent will remain on the starting point of the development, namely, on certain somatic phenomena and their accompanying (un-)pleasure and anxiety. Still within the context of diagnosis, this implies that such patients today will initially find themselves in the medical field and only later in a clinical psychological setting. Secondly, at the level of treatment we are confronted with a problem that is structurally different from our customary psychopathology, the latter having already undergone secondary processing. The usual psychotherapeutic treatment will be of little use here, and the potential psychotherapeutic approach to such problems must also be completely reconsidered in the light of the structural diagnostic.

There are two arguments in favor of the existence of such an actual-pathological position. One is classical and conceptual: we must look again at what has long since been a forgotten part of Freudian theory and clinical practice, at what in 1898 he called the "actual neuroses." The other draws on more recent empirical work: we must call upon the flood of contemporary research into somatization, alexithymia, and the panic disorders.

FREUD'S ACTUAL NEUROSIS: A FORGOTTEN CATEGORY

At its outset, clinical practice was utterly unlike that of today. One of the chief differences was its lack of specialization, with the result that doctors could be confronted with more or less any type of patient. Into this often vaguely differentiated group, Freud quickly introduced divisions. On one side is what he called the neuro-psychoses of defense (Freud 1978 [1894a], [1896b] and manuscript B and E).[1] The origin of these disorders must be sought in infantile sexual development; its associated symptoms are signification-rich and their typical characteristic is defense against an inner conflict at the level of sexuality and desire. On the other side are the actual neuroses. Their origin is also sexual, by which we must understand that it is located in the present life of the patient, not in the past. The symptoms are limited to somatic *phenomena* and have no further meaning, the emphasis lying largely on anxiety and the somatic anxiety equivalents (Freud 1978 [1895b], [1896a]).

Throughout the subsequent course of his career, Freud will place his emphasis on elaborating the first group, which will come to form the basis of many of today's psychodiagnostic categories. The second

---

1. Let us not forget that the term "neurosis" originally covered almost the entire field of psychopathology, including what are known today as psychosis and perversion. These latter categories are more recent and appear at least partly thanks to Freud. In order to take account of today's differentiation, we will talk about actual-pathology versus psychopathology.

group remains underdeveloped, despite Freud's continuing to confirm its existence right to the end. The reason for this relative lack of interest is a pragmatic one. This group failed to respond to the psychoanalytic treatment of his time. Indeed, the symptomatic superstructure and accompanying fantasmatic developments are completely absent; there is quite simply nothing to analyze.

Nevertheless, this didn't stop him from providing a thorough description of this group, for whose etiology he offers a number of hypotheses. Within the actual neuroses, he distinguishes between anxiety neurosis and neurasthenia, later adding hypochondria to these (Freud, 1978 [1914c], pp. 82–85).

Freud's emphasis is clearly on anxiety neurosis, whose name and discovery are both Freud's (Freud 1978 [1895b], [1898a]). It is worth recalling his clinical description. He identifies seven characteristics:

1. General irritability. This indicates an increase of excitation and an inability to tolerate it. Sleeplessness is fairly common.
2. Anxious anticipation. There is a quantum of free-floating anxiety that can be secondarily associated with any content whatsoever. For Freud, this is the symptomatic kernel.
3. Anxiety attacks. Such attacks occur suddenly, without any connection with a preceding train of thought. This anxiety can be secondarily associated with fears of dying or of becoming mad. The combination of anxiety with disturbances in certain bodily functions is fairly common, such as "spasms of the heart," respiratory difficulties, sweating, ravenous hunger.
4. A continuum from rudimentary anxiety attacks to somatic anxiety equivalents. The proportional combination of the two varies widely in the clinic, but the central phenomenon remains anxiety. Among the somatic anxiety equivalents, Freud distinguishes heart palpitations, disturbances of respiration, sweating, tremor and shivering, ravenous hunger, diarrhea, locomotoric vertigo, congestion, and paresthesias. Freud calls such somatic anxiety-equivalents "larval anxiety-states" and adds that the anxiety is not always experienced as such by the patient.[2]

---

2. Equivalents, that is to say, not substitutes. With substitutes we would be dealing with signifying symptoms and therefore with psychopathology.

5. Nocturnal fears (pavor nocturnis). An anxiety attack at night, usually in combination with sweating and respiratory difficulties, although not associated with a nightmare.
6. Vertigo. Also usually in combination with anxiety, although not always. The patient's legs feel like they are giving way and it seems impossible to remain standing but without actually falling.
7. Two kinds of phobias. The first group boils down to the reinforcement of previously existing and, according to Freud, probably instinctive aversions in the patients (anxiety about thunderstorms, vermin, darkness), thereby turning them into a phobia. The second group concerns agoraphobia, often beginning with an attack of vertigo and later taking hold of the patient's motor abilities. Freud highlights the difference between both types of phobias and psychopathology: there is no associative link to an underlying repressed train of thought—thus making it impossible to moderate this phobia through analysis or psychotherapy—and the underlying affect is anxiety as such (Freud 1978 [1895b], pp. 92–97).

For Freud, the etiological ground of anxiety neurosis or, more broadly, of the actual neuroses, must lie in the somatic-sexual factor, operating as an endogenic arousal. More specifically, he locates its etiology in the failure to psychically process this excitation and thus abreact it—and hence gives general irritation as its first characteristic. The accumulated tension is immediately transformed into anxiety. Freud will further specify this etiology by referring to the role of sexual abstinence. Its kernel nevertheless remains the absence of psychological elaboration of something that pertains to the body.

The second form of actual neurosis is what was called neurasthenia. Originally described by Beard, this category enjoyed immense success and was extensively developed by Janet, for one. Freud remained critical of this broadening of the term, limiting his description of its core characteristics to three elements.[3] Firstly, the characteristic

---

3. Freud isolated anxiety neurosis from what was then a very broad description of neurasthenia that encompassed practically everything. This is shown in the title of his paper: "On the grounds for detaching a particular syndrome from neurasthenia under the description anxiety neurosis" (Freud 1978 [1895b]).

physical exhaustion that has no physical explanation. Secondly, the accompanying somatic phenomena, normally headaches, dyspepsia, constipation, and spinal paresthesia. Thirdly, the decline of sexual activity. An important difference between this and the previous group is that here anxiety is almost entirely absent. Its etiology is the same as that of anxiety neurosis, that is, the impossibility of psychically processing an internal sexual somatic arousal. In neurasthenia, the cause is not so much anxiety as exhaustion resulting from a conflict between the subject and its drive. As a special etiological factor, Freud mentioned masturbation, something that accorded perfectly with the medical-moral discourse of that time.

This more or less sums up the Freudian theory of actual neurosis (with the exception of hypochondria; see Chapter 15). As I said, it gets little attention in the rest of his oeuvre and, after Freud, this piece of his theory and clinical praxis becomes more or less forgotten. One reason for this has to do with the supposed etiology of the condition: these days, sexual abstinence and masturbation no longer mean the same thing as in the 1900s—although I am still convinced that their psychological impact should not be underestimated even today. However, along with this one tends to forget how these are merely the specific etiological manifestations of an underlying general cause, that is, the fact that the endogenic arousal has not been psychically processed. As far as this arousal is concerned, Freud even accounts for the classic psychiatric *"surmenage,"* or in contemporary terms stress by overwork (Freud 1978 [1898a], [1905d]). The second reason why it has been forgotten doubtless has to do with the fact that, because of the growing medical specialization, such patients tend to arrive in an increasingly exclusive medical setting. We will have to wait for the reconciliation of the medical and clinical psychological discourses before this problem is addressed. However, this brings us to two contemporary topics that have been widely researched: panic disorders and somatization phenomena.

PANIC DISORDER: OLD WINE IN NEW BOTTLES

Panic disorder is a modern success story. Psycinfo cites only 22 studies for the 1970s; this increases to 2.588 in the 1980s, and that number more than doubles over the next decade. As has often happened, the discovery of this condition was purely coincidental, occurring moreover outside the context of any historical awareness. In the 1960s, an American psychiatrist, Donald Klein, conducted research into the pharmacological treatment of schizophrenia. One particular group of schizophrenic patients, characterized by an absence of delusions and hallucinations, and displaying acute anxiety attacks, failed to react to the usual medication of those days. This was in contrast to the other group that did indeed display hallucinations and delusions, along with a chronic anxiety.[4] He then discovered that another drug (imipramine) diminished the acute anxiety and concluded that the anxiety in both groups must be essentially different (D. Klein 1964).

After that, things begin to move fast. This particular form of anxiety is described as the so-called panic attack. This, in turn, will give rise to a number of diagnostic entries in the DSM. We will first discuss the description of the panic attack itself, and then the diagnostic entries in the light of the associated empirical research.

In the *DSM-IV* (American Psychiatric Association 2000, p. 432), panic attack is described as an isolated, acute-anxiety experience in which the patients display at least four of the following symptoms, arriving at a peak in a very short time:

Panic Attack
A discrete period of intense fear or discomfort, in which four (or more) of the following symptoms developed abruptly and reached a peak within 10 minutes:
1) palpitations, pounding heart, or accelerated heart rate
2) sweating
3) trembling or shaking
4) sensations of shortness of breath or smothering
5) feeling of choking
6) chest pain or discomfort
7) nausea or abdominal distress

---

4. Note that this supports the distinction between the actualpathological and a psychopathological position in the psychotic structure. A psychotic structure without symptoms does indeed exist, that is to say, without delusions and hallucinations. Freud's original study of the anxiety neurosis was mainly concerned with the neurotic spectrum. Only later did he add schizophrenia because of the presence of hypochondria (Freud 1978 [1914c]).

8) feeling dizzy, unsteady, lightheaded, or faint
9) derealization (feelings of unreality) or depersonalization (being detached from oneself)
10) fear of losing control or going crazy
11) fear of dying
12) paresthesias (numbness or tingling sensations)
13) chills or hot flushes

Comparing this description with the characteristics of anxiety neurosis described above, we are forced to conclude that they both concern the same thing. Not only does the DSM contain all of the phenomena described by Freud, Freud moreover contains more. The shortcoming of the DSM lies for the most part in its lack of a certain insight not absent in Freud, namely, that the somatic anxiety equivalents can appear in place of anxiety, with the result that the patient is barely aware of his own anxiety. Recent discussion since then has revolved around the paradoxical NFPD, the "non-fearful panic disorder," as yet unmentioned in the DSM. Research has shown that such panic attacks without anxiety may occur in both clinical and nonclinical populations (Kushner and Beitman 1990). The difference between both groups is relatively small, although with the understanding that the nonclinical population suffers less from agoraphobia and expectance anxiety. As such, NFPD remains an unintelligible clinical phenomenon for which even the cognitive approach must rely on the probably unconscious "cognitions" of this group as an explanation (Clark 1986). The explanation today resides in linking NFPD with alexithymia (see below).

The thirteen characteristics can be ordered in line with our theory. The group 1 through 8, 12, and 13 are the somatic anxiety equivalents, where the "chills or hot flushes" signals the connection that Freud already pointed out with menopause. We have previously encountered characteristic Number 9, derealization or depersonalization; both can be understood as a reaction to a failed confrontation with the Real of the body. The failure lies in the absence of the psychic processing, causing these phenomena—derealization and depersonalization—to acquire a dissociative character. Hence, it is not by chance that we will come across the same phenomena later on in our study of the traumatic neuroses. Numbers 10 and 11 are the sole psychological characteristics and can be interpreted as an expression of anxiety over the disappearance of the subject itself, in the wordlessness of the Real.

On the basis of this description, the *DSM-IV-TR* distinguishes between panic disorders with or without agoraphobia. At this point we reencounter the original Freudian description, albeit outside of any conceptual framework. The kernel of the agoraphobia is described as:

> Anxiety about being in places or situations from which escape might be difficult (or embarrassing) or in which help may not be available in the event of having an unexpected or situationaly predisposed Panic Attack or panic-like symptoms. Agoraphobic fears typically involve characteristic clusters of situations that include being outside the home alone; being in a crowd or standing in a line; being on a bridge; and traveling in a bus, train, or automobile. [American Psychiatric Association 2000, p. 433]

This disorder is then described as follows:

Panic disorder with agoraphobia (300.21)

A. Both 1) and 2):
   1) recurrent unexpected Panic Attacks
   2) at least one of the attacks has been followed by 1 month (or more) of one (or more) of the following:
      a. persistent concern about having additional attacks
      b. worry about the implications of the attack or its consequences (e.g., losing control, having a heart attack, 'going crazy')
      c. a significant change in behavior related to the attacks
B. The presence of Agoraphobia
C. The Panic Attacks are not due to the direct physiological effects of a substance (e.g., a drug of abuse, a medication) or a general medical condition (e.g., hyperthyroidism)
D. The Panic Attacks are not better accounted for by another mental disorder, such as Social Phobia (e.g., occurring on exposure to feared social situations), Specific Phobia (e.g., on exposure to a specific phobic situation), Obsessive-Compulsive Disorder (e.g., on exposure to dirt in someone with an obsession about contamination), Posttraumatic Stress Disorder (e.g., in response to stimuli associated with a severe stressor), or Separation Anxiety Disorder (e.g., in response to being away from home or close relatives). [American Psychiatric Association 2000, p. 441]

The need to couple panic attack and agoraphobia with panic disorders comes from the experience that in practice they are frequently found in combination. The majority of studies devoted to this link come to more or less the same conclusion: agoraphobia is a consequence of a preceding panic attack (Clum and Knowles 1991). Such an approach pays most attention to the cognitive factors (catastrophic interpretations and social concerns). For me, however, the most interesting angle is that found in Klein and Gorman (1987), who offer the following typical sequence: the "spontaneous" occurrence of the first panic attack is followed by help-seeking behavior, after which chronic expectance anxiety is installed, succeeded by the final development of avoidance behavior.

The reason I find this the most interesting approach is because it no longer focuses on the phobic "object" that must be avoided—the agora—but rather on the patient's motivation that lies at its base. One can also see this motivation in the DSM's description of the panic attack: "Anxiety about being in places or situations from which escape might be difficult (or embarrassing) *or in which help may not be available.*" To my mind, when understood from our metapsychological perspective, such a panic attack is always a reaction to an internal, unprocessed excitation (a), in response to which the subject makes an almost instant appeal to the Other. Typically, for actualpathology in general, and for anxiety neurosis in particular, the other's intervention will never suffice but the appeal will nevertheless persist. "Agoraphobia" is the expression of this need for the other, and the avoidance of all situations where this other could be absent. In this sense, panic disorder may well be accompanied by claustrophobia, understood as the feeling of being locked up on one's own in a small space. In both cases, agoraphobia and claustrophobia, the anxiety will be tempered by the presence of a significant other, although this presence will never be enough.

Empirical research has meanwhile shown that panic disorders demonstrate a high comorbidity with other anxiety disorders, such as affective disorders and addiction (Rosenbaum 1997).[5] Addiction corresponds

---

5. During a certain period, the relation between hyperventilation attacks and panic disorders was also the topic of intensive research. On the basis of this research, hyperventilation is now considered a side phenomenon that can occur during an anxiety attack, that is, as part of what Freud regarded as respiratory difficulties.

with the phenomenon of auto-medication, and can be minimally understood as the drinking or injecting away of anxiety.[6] Freud already indicated the high correlation between anxiety neurosis (panic disorder) and depression (Freud 1978 [1892–1899], Manuscript B to Fliess). This correlation is indeed pretty high (44 percent in the research by Clum and Pendrey 1987), and again can be understood in light of our conception of subject-formation. Here, depression is the actualpathological position of the subject who was unable to satisfy the Other's desire from the start (see Chapter 10). Typical of this comorbidity is that, in these other disorders, symptoms (in our sense of the word) are also entirely absent: there's no secondary elaboration, making classic psychotherapy all the more problematic.

THE ETIOLOGY OF PANIC DISORDER/ANXIETY NEUROSIS

Comparing recent studies with Freud's classical notions of actual neurosis and of anxiety neurosis in particular reveals certain similarities. This is probably true for classical neurasthenia and contemporary chronic fatigue syndrome as well, although I will not go into that here. The questions now concern etiology: What is the source of the actualpathology? Can contemporary studies provide an answer for this? and What relevance will it have for the treatment?

The etiological question is all the more of a challenge because the anxiety is always described as spontaneous. Given the pharmacological discoveries, it is no surprise that its etiology was initially purely sought in the biological discourse. The fact that imipramine has a favorable effect on panic attacks but not on chronic anxiety led Klein and his colleagues (1987) to hypothesize that there were two different neurobiological systems at work that could be considered the cause of two different anxieties. This theory contains an error of logic; although certain pharmacological items operate selectively on anxiety, that doesn't

---

6. Through research into primates, it was shown that there is a clear relation between addiction (alcoholism) and separation (Higly et al. 1996). As we will see later on, the failure of the primary relation between the subject and the Other is also central to actualpathology.

mean that the cause of anxiety must be sought in the absence of those molecules. Other research concentrated on "challenge tests" that artificially provoked or inhibited anxiety attacks through the administration of certain products (caffeine, among others). This produced a surprising result: the substances worked on a number of different systems in the human body. The hypothesis that panic attacks were caused by one specific bodily system or function consequently had to be rejected (McNally 1994).

A second explanatory model was found in psychology, with the accent on learning and cognitive psychology. Here, the cause of a panic attack was thought to lie in the so-called catastrophic misinterpretation of bodily sensations (Beck 1988; Clark 1986). These bodily sensations can be quite diverse (anger, excitation), and the emphasis is on the patient's mistaken and thereby anxiety-provoking interpretation (heart attack, suffocating, becoming mad), resulting in an increasingly vicious circle. This view received extensive research (Barlow and Craske 1988; Craske and Barlow 1988; Rachman et al. 1988; Wolpe and Rowan 1988), and produced the following result. Catastrophic misinterpretations are developed only *after* the first panic attack and therefore cannot explain this attack. What this model does explain, however, is the spiral that sets in after the first attack and that gives rise to agoraphobia, for example, and other avoidant behaviors.

The conclusion is that neither a simple neurobiological line of reasoning, nor a cognitive learning psychological approach can provide a conclusive answer to the question of etiology. This means that we can return to Freud's hypothesis, albeit with a number of important additions. The starting point of the first anxiety attack lies in the body, and more specifically in an increase in arousal or excitation. It is not at all clear whether this arousal is of a phallic-sexual nature: neurobiological research indicates that this excitation can be associated with a number of different bodily systems. To my mind, this argues for the certainly vague, but nevertheless causal character of (a) as the drive excitation that only after the secondary processing through the oedipal structure acquires a phallic character. The rise in tension itself is not the cause of anxiety per se, but rather the fact that such excitation cannot be adequately psychically elaborated. It is precisely this lack of secondary processing that lies at the basis of the development of anxiety and/or somatic anxiety equivalents.

With this we return to Freud's general hypothesis: *the absence of psychological processing of the endogenous excitement is the cause of the actual neurosis*. Nevertheless, such a hypothesis remains relatively biological-medical. The crucial supplement we can and must add to it is founded on recent research.

The first aspect concerns the experience of analysts in the course of treating patients with panic disorders (Milrod 1995, 1998; Milrod et al. 1997; Shear et al. 1993; Shear and Weiner 1997). Time and again, it became clear that for such patients the stress factors preceding the panic disorder invariably had to do with physical or emotional separation from significant persons or with fantasies concerning this. Faravelli's research (Faravelli and Pallanti (1989); Faravelli et al. 1985) confirms that, compared with a normal control group, such patients were significantly more frequently confronted with the death or a life-threatening disease of a partner or relative or good friend. The crux of the problem lies in these patients' inability to express situations of conflict, or even simply the impossibility of experiencing such situations in a psychological way; we will discuss the pertinent connection with alexithymia shortly.

These studies were confirmed from a different angle by research into biological psychiatry. Recently it has been shown that there is a correlation between separation anxiety and panic disorder (de Ruiter and van IJzendoorn 1992; Free et al. 1993; Miliora and Ulman 1996; Silove et al. 1995). Separation anxiety is defined as an intense anxiety about losing contact with a caretaker or a protective person. Here, it is not so much the actual departure of this person that is anxiety provoking but the loss of the subjective feeling of union with him or her. Hence, even a purely fantasized experience of loss can be as effective as a real loss.

No Answer by the Other

We can therefore conclude that the causal factor of actualpathology, and of anxiety neurosis/panic disorder in particular, *lies in the fact that the subject's internal drive excitation is not—or is insufficiently—answered by the Other.* The transition from (a) to A through which the Other supplies an answer and sets the secondary processing into motion does not occur, with the result that the initial arousal turns into anxiety and even into separation anxiety (see the element of separation in so-called *agora*-phobia). Anxiety neurosis is situated between (*a*) and A, and has no further reach. The ensuing phenomenon we are now in a position to examine—somatization disorder—also lies in between, if somewhat closer to (*a*) and therefore probably closer to neurasthenia.

SOMATIZATION, MUS, AND ALEXITHYMIA

Following the explosion of medical science and the power of its application, it is becoming increasingly clear that a number of apparently organic disorders escape medical discourse. These are indicated as "MUS" —as in medically unexplained symptoms, or somatization phenomena.[7] Epidemiological studies are constantly demonstrating their high frequency in both the normal population (Drossman et al. 1993; Kroenke and Price 1993) and in every medical setting (Escobar et al. 1998; Fink 1992). The numerous studies attempting to understand this phenomenon often make the following distinction. On the one hand is a group of patients possessing a relatively clear link between somatization and an underlying psychological complaint; for them, the question then concerns the nature of this link. On the other hand, we have a group of patients where this relation is not at all clear, and where somatization occurs in itself, apparently without any connection to psychological history (De Gucht 2001; De Gucht and Fischler 2002).

The confusion here (see below) has to do with the disappearance of the category of hysteria in the DSM, thus making it necessary to place one of its core symptoms, conversion, into another category. Ever since Briquet (1859) and Freud (1978 [1894a]), conversion has been understood as the somatic and meaningful expression of a psychological conflict and its accompanying defense (repression) within a certain psychopathology, namely, hysteria; conversion is, thus, a symptom. The DSM's atheoretical approach has thrown out this category, resulting in the need for a new distinction as far as the problem of somatization is concerned.

---

7. Lipowski (1988, p. 1359) classically defines it as "the tendency to experience and communicate somatic distress and symptoms unaccounted for by pathological findings, to attribute them to physical illness, and to seek medical help for them."

The solution was the creation (from the *DSM-III* onward) of the categories of Somatization on the one hand, and Conversion Disorder on the other, whose connection with psychological factors was presupposed. Thus we end up with two different categories, as is confirmed over and over again by research: somatization as such and somatization as the bodily expression of psychological distress. The two categories are sometimes called "functional" somatization and "presenting" somatization (Kirmayer and Robbins 1991), and have been amply confirmed by other research (Escobar 1997; Fava et al. 1995; P. Fink 1996; Portegijs et al. 1996).

The difference between these two groups is then defined as follows: the presenting somatization group is typified by the presence of an affective disorder (anxiety, depression) and the manner in which these patients present their symptoms to the doctor (MUS instead of, or in combination with, psychological symptoms). Here, the dimension of the Other is quite clear. In contrast, patients with functional somatization fail to mention any relation with psychological problems or even explicitly deny a relation between their complaints and a supposedly psychosocial origin. The latter—the real, functional or idiopathic somatization patients—are in the minority (Craig et al. 1993; Kirmayer and Robbins 1991; Kirmayer et al. 1993). The comorbidity between somatization on the one hand, and anxiety and the depressive disorders on the other is fairly high: up to 53 percent for affective disorder (depression), up to 40 percent for anxiety disorder (P. Fink 1995; Rief et al. 1992). Nevertheless, in the *DSM-IV*, the emphasis is on functional somatization and the other group is confusingly spread out over a number of categories.[8]

With respect to the "presenting somatization" group, the question remains whether one can consider somatic symptoms as a *substitute for* psychological problems or as mere *manifestations of* those problems. The first thesis follows the classical conception of conversion hysteria, where somatic phenomena are regarded as meaningful symptoms (see

---

8. The major confusion lies in the way Conversion belongs to the description of the Somatization Disorder (300.81, ad B4), while also receiving its own separate category (300.11 Conversion Disorder). Moreover, in yet a third category, "Pain Disorder," a relation with psychological factors is also presupposed (American Psychiatric Association 2000, p. 503), so that part of the "old" conversion hysteria also assumes its place here (more specifically: paresthesias).

Chapter 13). The second thesis, in all its vagueness, is right but of little value, and testifies largely to the absence of any theoretical support.[9] The contemporary notion is that somatization can be understood as a somatic *equivalent* of anxiety disorder or depression (Bridges and Goldberg 1985; De Gucht 2001). The connection with the classical Freudian position regarding actual neurosis (phenomena rather than symptoms) is easily made but is ignored by contemporary research.

Alexithymia

As I said earlier, the high frequency of the somatization phenomenon has given rise to extensive research. One of the aims was to find an explanation: What is the difference between this group and a normal population, and what is the underlying mechanism? Today's research results come to the same conclusion: at the root of MUS is a personality factor, called alexithymia (De Gucht 2001; De Gucht and Heiser 2003b). Translated literally, this means "to have no words for feelings." The concept comes from psychoanalytic discourse (Sifneos 1973) and was later taken up in the cognitive model as a defect in the "cognitive processing and regulation of emotions" (Bagby and Taylor 1997). The concept itself was initially understood as having four dimensions; after empirical verification, a threefold structure was maintained: (1) a difficulty identifying feelings; (2) a difficulty describing feelings to others; and (3) externally oriented thinking.

Further investigation of the results (De Gucht 2001; De Gucht and Heiser 2003b) delivered the following.[10] All English empirical studies (1985–2000) demonstrate a significant correlation between alexithymia and the number of reported MUS-phenomena, particularly with regard to the first factor. The correlation with the second factor is lower, but

---

9. What has been confirmed up till now is a parallel increase in the number of MUS-symptoms on the one hand, and the extent of psychological distress reported by the patients on the other (Simon et al. 1996; Simon and Gureje 1999). To imagine that there is a relation between them would call for a theory but clearly that would be going too far today.

10. The most validated and internally consistent instrument is the TAS-R (the Toronto Alexithymia Scale) (Bagby et al. 1994).

still significant; the correlation with the third is unclear. All studies comparing patients from the functional somatization group to a healthy control group demonstrate a significantly higher presence of alexithymia in the patient group. Conversely, all except one find a significantly higher presence of somatization phenomena in the alexithymia group as compared to a normal control group (that is to say, without alexithymia). The temporal stability of alexithymia in both clinical and in nonclinical populations has moreover been confirmed; this is in contrast to anxiety, depression, and negative affect, which can change considerably during the follow-up period (Haviland et al. 1988; Marinez-Sanchez et al., 1998; Salmien et al. 1994; Schmidt et al. 1993; Wise et al. [all as quoted in De Gucht 2001]). With regard to this latter affect, it is worth looking at the item analysis of De Gucht's research (2001). Analysis of the applied instrument (the TAS-R) clearly shows how the highest correlation between the MUS and alexithymia is to be found in the first subscale "Difficulty identifying feelings," and then particularly with regard to the following items: "I have physical sensations which even the doctors do not understand" and "I am often puzzled by sensations in my body." This corresponds moreover with earlier research cited in the same paper.

What can we conclude from this? First, we find a confirmation of our thesis—namely, that a subject position characterized by an absence of psychological processing with regard to bodily excitations and/or phenomena does exist, and that such a structure is quite stable. Second, there are evidently two groups that can be distinguished from one another, one in which such somatizations are apparently unrelated to a psychological problem, and another that shows a clear correlation, particularly with regard to anxiety and depression but also with other psychopathological disorders, and which is brought up as such by the patients.

The DSM categorization is therefore insufficient. Despite its isolation of somatization from depression and anxiety disorder, the entry contains a confusing mix. The core description is as follows:

300.81 *Somatization Disorder*
B. Each of the following criteria must have been met, with individual symptoms occurring at any time during the course of disturbance:
   1. *four pain symptoms*: a history of pain related to at least four different sites or functions (e.g., head, abdomen, back, joints, extremities, chest, rectum, during menstruation, during sexual intercourse, or during urination)

2. *two gastrointestinal symptoms*: a history of at least two gastrointestinal symptoms other than pain (e.g., nausea, bloating, vomiting other than during pregnancy, diarrhea, or intolerance of several different foods)
3. *one sexual symptom*: a history of at least one sexual or reproductive symptom other than pain (e.g., sexual indifference, erectile or ejaculatory dysfunction, irregular menses, excessive menstrual bleeding, vomiting throughout pregnancy)
4. *one pseudoneurological symptom*: a history of at least one symptom or deficit suggesting a neurological condition not limited to pain (conversion symptoms such as impaired coordination or balance, paralysis or localized weakness, difficulty swallowing or lump in throat, aphonia, urinary retention, hallucinations, loss of touch or pain sensation, double vision, blindness, deafness, seizures; dissociative symptoms such as amnesia; or loss of consciousness other than fainting. [American Psychiatric Association 2000, p. 490]

Characteristic Number 4 is called "conversion," and the description itself is in fact quite classical (pseudoneurological syndromes). In this way, one opens the door to psychopathology, while in their isolated character characteristic Numbers 1 to 3 pertain to actualpathology. In addition, there is a separate category in the DSM for conversion—thus making the confusion complete. It is striking that the above-mentioned research is far more nuanced in this respect than the DSM.

The explanation found in contemporary research—alexithymia as a stable personality trait—is simply a redefinition of what used to be called actual neurosis. The Freudian definition corresponds perfectly with the previously mentioned item analysis of the TAS-R, and makes the core problem clear: "something" bodily presents itself but is neither nameable nor communicable. In a further development, this "something" clearly correlates with a psychological problem, resulting in a different population from the purely actualpathological or alexithymic. Yet this correlation is not a necessary one. What is unmistakable is how the presence of what is called "negative affect"—beside alexithymia—is the best predictor for MUS (De Gucht 2001; De Gucht and Fischler 2002; P. Fink 1995; Simon et al. 1996). This, too, fits in perfectly with what we have already described in identity formation.

Here we find ourselves back in our metapsychology. Something bodily presents itself in a negative way (unpleasure) and calls for processing. It is by way of the Other that this processing is expected to occur. Should it fail, the only possibility for the subject is to maintain this problematic at the same somatic level; the secondary elaboration is absent. That this frequently gives rise to anxiety and depression is confirmed by empirical research, and was predicted by our metapsychology. Opposed to this are the conversion symptoms, where the somatic problem is also present—albeit in a completely different way: conversion belongs to the psychopathological relation toward the Other (see Chapter 13).

What is initially a little unclear is the failure of the Other. For us, it is indeed not so much the somatic arousal itself that is the cause of the actualpathology or alexithymia, but the Other's failing intervention. The Other must be understood, moreover, as the concrete first and second others (the parents), as well as the cultural discourse. Indeed, a study by Shorter (1994) shows that the Other, in the sense of the sociocultural discourse, has a clear influence on the specific forms of appearance of somatic symptoms. It seems as if patients obtain their somatic phenomena from a culturally determined symptom pool that varies throughout different times and places. The failure of the first and/or second other is not directly indicated in the cited research results, nor in Freud's description of actual neurosis. As with the panic disorders, therefore, we must take a look at some studies that are more expressly focused on the treatment.

Despite the fact that such studies derive from quite different therapeutic approaches, all of the data point in the same direction. The resultant hypothesis can be summed up thus: the Other has failed in its meaning-providing function and, hence, in its protective interventions with respect to the bodily excitation. A number of studies posit somatic and sexual abuse during childhood as the etiology (Drossman et al. 1995; McCauley et al. 1997; Reilly et al. 1999). In the next chapter we will discuss the post-traumatic stress disorders that center around the Other's impact and the dissociative somatization phenomena. Other studies discuss "social learning" as a causal factor, where once again the Other appears as a decisive factor (Barsky 1992; Pennebaker and Watson 1991; Whitehead et al. 1994). In a metastudy (Medline search, 1990–99), Van Houdenhove (2001) concludes that early attachment problems and emotional, physical, and sexual abuse play a clear role in the etiology of somatization, and that these moreover form the foundation of dysfunctional help-seeking behavior.

Within each of the different theoretical frameworks, then, the same element appears: the Other failed in its answer to the subject's question concerning something at the level of the body.

CONCLUSION: ACTUALPATHOLOGY—IMPLICATIONS FOR THE TREATMENT

The empirical studies cited above persuasively confirm the existence of an actualpathological structure in the subject, understood as the impossibility of translating somatic arousal into psychological representations. The correlation with the Other's failure is also confirmed by the frequently mentioned problem of separation. The connection with our metapsychology, particularly with regard to primary identity acquisition, is clear. Clear, too, is the analogy with Fonagy's core argument regarding the development of the subject's first identity through the other's mirroring of the child's somatic arousal, although these authors fail to make the link to actualpathology (Fonagy et al. 2002).

Differential diagnostics in actualpathology must be approached from two aspects. On the one hand, the clinician must distinguish between the neurotic, psychotic, or the perverse structure of the subject. On the other, adequate attention must be paid to the nature of the affect and the accompanying phenomena.

With regard to the subjective structure, it is striking to find that the majority of research has focused almost exclusively on neurotic patients, while the post-Freudian starting point (D. Klein) took off from psychotic patients. The clinician must be aware that the actualpathological position of the subject can occur in *every* subjective structure, and that the typical actualpathological characteristics will be fully colored by that structure. In psychosis, this will often be hypochondria, understood as the subject's anxious preoccupation with "something" in the body that cannot be named. Again, in psychosis, we also encounter paroxysmic anxiety attacks. In perversion, the application is considerably less clear, largely because of the lack of clinical material.

As far as the nature of the affect is concerned, three aspects can be distinguished. The first concerns a special form of anxiety—traumatic, automatic anxiety, or panic. Where this anxiety is predominant, we are facing panic disorder or anxiety neurosis (or, anxiety psychosis—see D. Klein [1964, 1980]—and schizophrenia in particular). The second concerns somatization, whether in combination with the previous form or not. Once more I must underscore how these are not constructed and therefore signifying symptoms, but anxiety equivalents of the accompanying phenomena of anxiety. Their distinction from meaningful conversion symptoms must be taken fully into account. The applicable categories here are functional somatization, neurasthenia, and, in all probability, chronic fatigue syndrome. The third point concerns the possible presence of an affective disorder, chiefly depression. This has to be clearly distinguished from its psychopathological counterpart (see Chapter 10 and Chapters 13 and 15).

These three aspects of the differential diagnostic cannot be easily isolated. The most important argument for a diagnosis of actualpathology has to do with the presence of a specific characteristic relation between the subject and the Other, understood as both language and as concrete others. This relation boils down to the fact that the Other failed in its initial verbalization of (*a*), with the result that the secondary elaboration was not set in motion, or only barely. The above-cited clinical studies describe a problem of separation. Our metapsychology enables us to be more precise: it is in fact a problem of alienation, in the sense that the Other failed to present sufficient signifiers with which the subject could have identified so as to have been able to cope with the bodily arousal. As a result, such patients were unable to have access to separation, being the logical-temporal process that comes *after* the alienation. In such cases, separation lies on the side of the Other: it is the Other that separates from the subject.

Consequently, the clinical diagnostic examination must contain a thorough exploration of the case history. This is all the more imperative because patients themselves seldom make a connection between their actualpathological phenomena on the one hand, and anxiety and depression on the other. This clinical exploration of the primary relation between the subject and the Other is particularly vital because it is precisely this relation that will repeat itself in the transference and become the aim of the treatment. To help such patients, it is this relation that must be changed.

Treatment of the Actualpathology

If we understand actualpathology as an effect of a primary disturbance in the relation between the subject and the Other that results in the impossibility of a secondary elaboration and symptom construction by the patient, it will become clear that the treatment will not just be different from that for psychopathology, but will in fact be the exact opposite. To follow Freud, it is impossible to classically analyze actualpathology precisely because there is no symptom formation. Psychopathologies with accompanying secondary elaborations allow symptoms to be analyzed—to be stripped of their meaning—albeit always with the accent on the relation through which these meanings came into being. In actualpathologies, the primary aim of the treatment is the restoration or even installation of the primary relation between the subject and the Other through the therapeutic relation. It is this that will enable the subject to build up a secondary elaboration and, through the transferential relation, embed the original bodily arousal into signifiers, enabling symptoms to be constructed. To put it concretely, one must begin with an exploration of the original relation between the subject and the Other (with the emphasis on separation anxiety) and on the remaining signifiers, that is, the minimal original inscriptions of the somatic in the Symbolico-Imaginary order.[11] Rather than subject analysis, the therapeutic goal here is *subject amplification*.[12]

---

11. This means that the clinician must look for things like childhood diseases and the parental reaction to them—there are almost always residual signifiers to be found concerning both the original relationship to the Other and its inscription on the body. Beginning with these signifiers, the clinician needs to create the context through which this originally omitted process can nevertheless be carried out inside an expressly guaranteeing therapeutic relation. Where the therapist him or herself produces signifiers and significations from within a University or Master discourse, the risk of inducing guilt on the patient's part is immense (see Note 3 in Chapter 10).

12. It is striking how Fonagy et al. (2002) come to the same conclusion: classical interpretations do not work with these patients. Instead, they propose a therapeutic

Along with subject amplification, the need to make the therapeutic relation the goal of the treatment is shown by empirical outcome studies. Short-term outcome studies demonstrate that cognitive behavioral therapy produces the best results (Barlow 1997; Gould et al. 1995). Outcome studies in long-term treatments that focus solely on the actualpathological phenomena present a considerably less rosy picture: residual symptoms, relapse, alcoholism, and comorbidity with anxiety and affective disorders are the rule (Milrod and Bush 1996; Shear and Weiner 1997; Shear et al. 1993) for 40 to 80 percent of the patients (Rosenbaum 1997). These studies have a larger scope than the former, where improvements are almost exclusively measured in terms of the reduction of the number of somatic phenomena and panic attacks, and not on the basis of the improvement in the overall state of the patient (McNally 1994; Pollack and Otto 1997).[13] It must be admitted that from a scientific perspective this latter is far harder to measure. A recent review of empirical outcome studies of mainly cognitive treatments for panic disorder (Bakker 2001) demonstrates that with longer follow-up periods the risk of relapse is fairly considerable, and that patients run a significantly higher risk of developing depression.

Clearly, to focus on somatic phenomena and/or anxiety is not enough for the treatment. Even more, the failure of such an approach—recently becoming increasingly clear—leads to a repetition of the original problem, hence the higher risk of depression in these patients. Such patients were recently designated "therapy resistant" (Lydiard and Brawman-Mintzer 1997; Rosenbaum 1997). In terms of the dialectics of the therapeutic relation, this amounts to blaming the patient—it is the patient who is the reason for the failure, she or he is "resistant"—leaving the therapist in the position of the Other. This is nothing but a repetition

---

approach in which the original mirroring process is reperformed, founded on the actual reality of the therapeutic interaction.

13. These new studies resulted in a surprising discovery: the majority of patients (up to 80 percent) underwent *additional* treatment during the follow-up period after the first treatment that the outcome studies were attempting to measure. Because most of the studies following the first treatment failed to inquire into the possibility of additional treatment during the follow-up period, their results are dubious (de Beurs et al. 1999).

of the original failed relation between the subject and the Other, where the Other was unable to fulfill its task and left the subject in the lurch. The same process is recognizable in the medical approach as well: realizing that medical science is inapplicable[14]—that is, having inadequate signifiers at his or her disposal, the medical doctor refers the patient to a psychiatrist or clinical psychologist with whom the same process will once again be repeated. This is a painful illustration of what was already described in our metapsychology, where the original, pathogenic relation between the subject and the Other will repeat itself in the subsequent therapeutic relation! As clinicians, we need to be well aware of this so as to make this relation the precise focus of the diagnosis and the therapeutic medium.

Accordingly, merely to focus on the symptoms during the treatment—or more accurately, on the phenomena—will never be enough. There has recently been renewed interest in a broader psychoanalytic treatment of these disorders that combines classical Freudian data with contemporary research results (Bush et al. 1999; Comptom 1998; Hebbrecht 1998; Miliora and Ulman 1996; Milrod et al. 1997). The hardest part in such a therapeutic approach is the analyst's ever-present tendency to interpret somatic phenomena and/or anxiety as meaningful symptoms, while the patient is not yet able to do so. The patient's complaints are thereby turned into metaphors, which is precisely what they are *not*. Inevitably, such a misunderstanding induces guilt in the patient.[15] Rather, the emphasis must be on the creation of a therapeutic context through which the patient—with the help of the Other's interventions—can develop his or her own meanings.

---

14. It is no coincidence that medical doctors experience such patients as "difficult and frustrating." Consequently, their referral is actually a rejection (Hahn et al. 1996; Walker et al. 1997). Nor is it a coincidence that these patients frequently decide to organize self-help groups—that is to say, with the exclusion of the professional Other; sometimes these organizations even take juridical steps to get their members' status as patients officially recognized.

15. In Chapter 10 we referred to Sontag (1979) with regard to the guilt-inducing impact of a certain so-called "psychosomatic" approach. In the words of Sontag herself: "Nothing is more punitive than to give a disease a meaning—that meaning being invariably a moralistic one" (p. 57).

Once more, this testifies to the importance of making a correct diagnosis, one focusing on the original relation between the subject and the Other. The diagnostic distinction between an actualpathology and psychopathology must re-emerge in a clearly differentiated therapeutic approach. This will also be true for the differential diagnostic group to be discussed in Chapter 12: The post-traumatic stress disorders and the borderline spectrum.

12
Between Actualpathology and Psychopathology: Post-Traumatic Stress Disorder and Borderline

POST-TRAUMATIC STRESS DISORDERS

The diagnosis of post-traumatic stress disorder (PTSD) is becoming increasingly common today, suggesting that the clinic has returned to its original starting point (Freud and Breuer 1978 [1895d]). Associated with this is the success of the concept of borderline personality disorder, whose link with a traumatic history is becoming progressively clearer (Herman 1992b). The argument of this chapter will be that both can be understood as situated between the actualpathology and the psychopathology positions, albeit with a very clear stress on actualpathology.

At first—naive—sight, the diagnosis of PTSD doesn't present too many problems. It is one of the few DSM diagnoses that has an etiology. The underlying logic is this: Trauma is an actual, but thankfully relatively uncommon event, and the psychological confusion (that is, disturbance) it causes is not only foreseeable but above all entirely comprehensible. Treatment ought to follow as soon as possible afterward, and the victim will automatically request help.

In practice, things are quite different. A review of virtually all the English language publications of empirical research into PTSD over the period 1990–2001 produces the following surprising results (Lee and Young 2001; Paris 2000; Perkonigg et al. 2000).

Firstly, the experience of trauma (as defined by the *DSM-IV*) is fairly common. More than half the normal Western population sooner or later undergoes such a shattering event. Paris (2000, p. 179) comments dryly: "Throughout history, trauma has been more the norm than the exception in human experience." This is followed by the remarkable conclusion that from this large group only a limited number will effectively develop PTSD. The average figure oscillates between 1 and 9 percent (Paris 2000) and 5 to 12 percent (Lee and Young 2001). Thus we must conclude that trauma in itself is not enough to cause later, longer-lasting disturbances. In most cases, it is immediately after the trauma that an acute stress disorder appears (ASD in the *DSM-IV*, 308.3), lasting a minimum of two days or four weeks maximum. Its subsequent development into a PTSD is rare (Harvey and Bryant 1999).

This brings us to the second conclusion: the occurrence of PTSD is determined not so much by the trauma itself as by other factors. The question then becomes, Which other factors? The obvious answer in our genetically colored times is heredity.[1] Behavioral genetic studies on twins have indeed shown a genetic disposition. Nevertheless, this must be qualified with the following two points: the same behavioral genetic studies demonstrate first of all that the supposedly inherited disposition is nonspecific and can give rise to different pathologies; secondly, environmental factors are responsible for half the variation in nearly every dimension of personality. Moreover, it was also shown that traumatic environmental factors are the cause of long-term neurobiological changes (Paris 2000, pp. 177–178). In other words, we come up once more against the eternally complex imbrication of nature and nurture as determinative of the end result.

A third conclusion further relativizes the importance of actual trauma. Counter to all expectations, there is no relation between trauma and pathology with regard to the nature or burden of what the victim

---

1. As we saw in the first part, an analogy can be made between the genetic answer and the naive trauma model; in both cases the cause is defined as external to the subject, and we find ourselves back in the victim model. As we will see later, this is the worst possible approach to take for PTSD patients because the treatment thus confirms them in their passive position.

literally experienced. This seems to be true even for long-term physical and sexual abuse of children: "Such research has consistently shown that exposure to child abuse increases the risk of developing a wide range of psychological symptoms, but that only a minority of exposed persons are likely to develop clinically significant psychopathology" (Paris 2000, p. 176). What research has proven is a connection between the development of PTSD and certain personality characteristics existing *before* the traumatic event and the repetition of the trauma.[2]

This brings us to the final conclusion of the research from the previous decade. Undergoing traumatic events can cause a number of other psychopathological disorders than PTSD, particularly depression, addiction, and personality disturbances. Comorbidity is less the exception than the rule, and in a large number of cases the other disturbances will appear in isolation, that is to say, without an obvious PTSD present.

Complexity

The diagnosis that seemed so easy at first sight is clearly somewhat more complex, and the question moves from the nature of the trauma to the structure of the subject. Depending on this latter, the reaction will either be limited to an ASD, or a more extensive disorder will develop later. One can even see this shift in emphasis in the evolution of the DSM, the most recent edition of which introduced subjective factors into the diagnostic criteria for PTSD (Lee and Young 2001, p. 151).

To make sense of these subjective factors, we must call on the theoretical foundation set out in Part II of this book. My thesis has already been stated: trauma must be understood in terms of actualpathology. But before going more deeply into this, let us first present a number of arguments in support of this view, which can be found in just about

---

2. Freud, too, discovered that trauma has a particularly traumatic impact when repeated. As I stated at the beginning of this chapter, the contemporary hype around PTSD is a return to the clinic's historical starting point. Hence we can predict the sequel: after an initial focus on the real character of the trauma and the role of the victim ("survivors" in newspeak) it will shift more and more to the personality factors of the patients themselves, making the initially easy diagnosis increasingly hard and raising a number of "new" questions. History will repeat itself, particularly when we ignore it.

every study and research discovery. Firstly, anxiety is the central phenomenon of the clinic. This is why PTSD is classified in the DSM under the heading of anxiety disorders. This anxiety has a very distinct nature: there is no secondary processing, and its manifestation is quite similar to anxiety neurosis and panic attacks.

Secondly, and immediately following on from this, it is impossible for such patients to arrive at a normal, that is to say, associative representation and elaboration of the trauma. This brings us to the problem of memory functioning. It is striking how normal, associative memory fails to function in cases of trauma. In its place appear intrusive phenomena that attack the subject with (fragments of) the raw, nonprocessed trauma. For some authors this is the primary differential diagnostic characteristic ("Intrusive imagery is the hallmark of PTSD"; Lee and Young 2001, p. 151). This is then also the chief common factor between the different descriptions of the *ICD-9* and the *DSM-IV*.

The two previous characteristics already show how psychological processing through a secondary elaboration is not simply absent, but is evidently in itself inherently difficult. My third argument for situating PTSD on the side of actualpathology therefore comes as no surprise: in practically every case we will encounter somatization. Lacking the possibility of being psychologically processed, the Real of the trauma is inscribed onto the body itself. The high frequency of the coincidence of trauma with addiction points to the same thing: patients try to treat their problems by intervening directly with their body.

Finally, I would like to mention something that is less frequently mentioned in diagnostic studies but that comes out all the more during the treatment: the primary effect of chronically traumatic situations on subject-formation. This is particularly clear with regard to the so-called dissociative phenomena that split the psychological functioning in two, but it also contributes to the difficulty of further secondary processing.

Situating PTSD on the side of actualpathology, as I do, has two important diagnostic implications. *Since PTSD belongs to the actualpathological spectrum, it can occur just as easily in neurotic, psychotic, and perverse subject structures.* Contemporary research literature ignores this, and even Freud (1978 [1920g]) spoke exclusively about traumatic *neurosis*. Nearly every study surreptitiously assumes an underlying "normal" structure, with the result that PTSD in psychosis and perversion is hardly ever addressed. The connection between trauma (concentration camp victims) and schizophrenia has been forgotten (Bettelheim 1979). In the study of perversion, the connection between the perpetrator and early infantile sexual abuse is often made, but never, or rarely the reverse: perversion is almost never mentioned in studies of PTSD. The result is that many clinicians take an underlying "normal" neurotic structure for granted.

The differential diagnosis becomes even more tricky in light of the fact that trauma doesn't necessarily lead to an exclusively actualpathological problem. One can find traumatic antecedents in many *psycho*pathological case studies, so one must assume that a number of patients are indeed able to process the secondary elaboration. Again, the question shifts to the structure of the subject itself, as the mediating factor between the actual trauma and the potentially pathological effects.

PTSD as Actualpathology: Structural versus Accidental Trauma

As during the era when the psychotherapeutic clinic began, it has recently seemed as though the cause of all psychological disturbances could be brought back to trauma. In the early days, this became nuanced by the unavoidable discussion of "false memories" and real traumas, a discussion that has returned to us today. My thesis will be an extension and fuller confirmation of this starting point: not only psychological disturbances but *all* development begins with what I have called the *structural* trauma (Verhaeghe 2001b, pp. 49–64). How this structural trauma is—or is not—elaborated through the Other will lay the foundation for potential later disturbances, including PTSD. These disturbances will always involve a repetition, through an *accidental* trauma, of the original structural trauma and its failure to be processed.

As we saw in Part II (Chapter 6), subject-formation begins with an internal experience of unpleasure that is caused by the drive. The impossibility of regulating this is the result of the child's physical helplessness and its accompanying inability to represent the drive. Representation is the necessary condition for the subject to be able to regulate the drive. Such representations, along with the specific actions that release the tension, come from the Other and will set identity acquisition into motion from that moment on.

This means that subject development begins initially with the structural trauma, that is, in the confrontation between the subject-to-be and the nonregulated rise in tension, caused by the wordless Real of the drive. Right from the start, we encounter the principal characteristic of all trauma, namely, the absence of normal, associative representation.[3] In the same movement, the trauma is introduced into the initial relation between the subject and the Other, thus adding an essential element: as a consequence, not only is the drive tension traumatic, but the absence of the Other also comes to carry the same traumatic weight. In that sense, every trauma is at the same time a trauma of separation.

In a secure development, the Other is safely present, offering the guaranteeing signifiers necessary for opening up the ongoing possibilities of representation and elaboration, both for the tension of the drive and the corresponding identity. Both the nature of the original relationship between the subject and the Other and the signifiers that the Other presents will determine the subject's increasing possibilities for representation and elaboration, this being nothing other than subject-formation.[4] Many things can go wrong during this process as well, but because of this elaboration such disorders will belong to the psychopathological spectrum.

---

3. This enables us to give an operational definition of trauma: it is an impact on the subject by a part of the Real that cannot be put into signifiers. Such an operational definition is needed to distinguish between emotionally shattering events and trauma. Lacan talks about a *"trou-matisme"* (1973–1974, lesson of February 19, 1974; Translator's Note: Lacan is making a play here on the French word for gap (*"trou"*) and traumatism (*"traumatisme"*); see Freud's definition: "We apply the term "traumatic" to an experience which within a short period of time presents the mind with an increase of stimulus too powerful to be dealt with or worked off in the normal way, and this must result in permanent disturbance of the manner in which the energy operates" (1978 [1916–1917], SE 16, p. 275). The connection with the drive excitation is clear, and Freud will also describe the confrontation with the drive as a confrontation with a rise in tension that must be psychically processed (Freud 1978 [1905d], SE 7, p. 168). See also his description of the primary repression as the first defense against the drive (see Chapter 7 of this book).

4. We often hear these days about "bottomless children" but it is not exactly clear what "bottom" or baseline they are missing. From our perspective, this baseline concerns that primary relationship in and through which the Other presents the child with the signifiers it needs to enter the world, including the world of its own drives.

Studies based on attachment theory have shown that if the original attachment has been sufficiently secure, the subject will have a firm enough basis to process potential accidental traumas later on. Processing implies that, while an ASD may well appear following an accidental trauma, there will be no further progression on to other pathological disturbances. In fairness, we can assume that such an accidental trauma gives rise to a processing analogous to that of the original trauma, that is, to an appeal for and intervention by the Other, in this case an already interiorized Other; it is precisely this processing that inhibits further progression into PTSD.

In cases where the original processing of the structural trauma and the accompanying separation either failed to take place, or took place insufficiently, one can predict that subsequent accidental traumas will not be processed normally either. Attachment theory calls this type of attachment group "unresolved." Quite so; the original problem of (a) was indeed not "solved" and it is precisely this that will give rise to a further disturbance, built on the already existing subjective structure and the nature of the accidental trauma.

In such cases we will once again encounter the characteristic actualpathological phenomena, recognizable from their lack of processing through the signifier, and with emphasis on primary anxiety and somatization. If our line of reasoning is correct—that PTSD is a regression to the subject's preexisting actualpathological position—this position ought to be visible and detectable prior to the development of PTSD resulting from an accidental trauma. This presence is confirmed by a large-scale epidemiological study ($N = 3021$) of the so-called premorbid personality, demonstrating that more than 60 percent of the patients already had a preexisting disorder, particularly somatization disorders (63.6%), social phobias (62.2%), or simple phobias (71.4%) (Perkonigg et al. 2000). From our perspective, this seems quite telling, as it points in the same direction: there was no or only insufficient original processing of (a) through the Other, hence the somatization and (social) phobia.

Such a regression to actualpathology resulting from an accidental trauma implies a renewed confrontation with the unprocessable, an inner rise in tension that Lacan calls "jouissance." The peculiarity of this term notwithstanding, it can easily be recognized in contemporary terminology as post-traumatic *stress* disorder. The word stress gives a poor indication of what patients internally experience as an unbearable rise in tension and anxiety that they often try to put an end to through automutilation and dypsomania. Freud (1978 [1920g]) came up against this too. It is far from coincidental that his most significant paper here is called "Beyond the Pleasure Principle." What traumatic patients repeat is anything but pleasurable, and yet the repetition continues to function as an attempt at mastery nonetheless. For Freud, this takes place through the "binding" of the energy to word representations; for Lacan, through the signifiers of the Other (see Chapter 9, Note 20).

Certain research data on accidental trauma in children confirm this. Time and again it becomes clear that it is the parents who must provide the child the language through which the trauma can be processed. By this we must understand, so as to be able literally to re-member it,[5] enabling the trauma to be emotionally regulated (Salmon and Bryant 2002, pp. 174–176). The worst possible thing to do is what many parents end up doing, namely, keeping quiet about it so as to forget as quickly as possible (Yehuda et al. 1998).

One study reveals something striking. As had been anticipated, the children of Holocaust survivors run a higher risk of PTSD compared to other children. What is remarkable is how these *children display far more PTSD disturbances than their parents* (Yehuda et al. 1998). Naturally this is very delicate material to interpret. From our perspective, this could indicate that the central mediating factor is not so much the actual traumatic experiences themselves but the Other. The same thing is confirmed by studies on the impact of the social environment, with the Other as a social-cultural discourse. The presence or absence of social support quite clearly influences the appearance of PTSD (Paris 2000, pp. 179–180). This explains, for example, why Vietnam vets suffered many more traumatic disturbances than their World War II cousins. The latter were seen as heroes; the tickertape parades on Fifth Avenue and elsewhere were all-inclusive. The former were jeered after their "tour of duty" and, above all, forced to keep quiet about their experiences.

A further confirmation of our thesis is found in the conclusion that trauma is especially traumatic when it is repeated. By original trauma,

---

5. Translator's Note: The Dutch verb to remember, "*te herinneren*" literally means "to bring back inside," to re-internalize.

these studies refer not only to actual experiences that can be neatly isolated, but more particularly to so-called "life experiences" (see Craig et al. 1993). These are fairly extensive, but can be summed up in terms of underprivileged circumstances, early infantile abuse, and early separation from the parents. What is central, particularly in the last two cases, is either the absence or the dysfunction of the Other. This is quite closely connected with another given of clinical experiences, namely, that one frequently finds an increased separation anxiety in cases of PTSD (Perrin et al. 2000, p. 278; Yule 2001). The traumatic experience drives us back toward the Other.

A clear analogy can be made, moreover, between our line of reasoning and contemporary ideas about the cognitive processing of those life experiences. "Cognitive" is the fashionable word today for "psychological," and has the disadvantage of suggesting that the emotional-affective element is not involved. Even within this cognitive approach, one begins from the idea that the trauma has to be "encoded" ("the attribution of meaning") through the construction of "schemas" or "constructs," which are "cognitive-affective memory structures and beliefs" (Cason et al. 2002). This is based on the understanding of the psyche as an information processing and associative system.[6]

This description is not far from what we developed earlier but it misses the crucial point, namely, that the development of such "constructs, responses, and meanings" occurs *through the Other*, and that it is in the course of this development that the subject's identity, the identity of the Other, and the outside world emerge. This is not merely a difference in diagnostic outlook, it has serious repercussions for the treatment. In the cognitive approach, it seems as though it is enough just to confront the patient with new and, above all, corrective information, "resulting in new learning and more diverse, elaborated associative connections" (Cason et al. 2002, p. 148). It is, in other words, a

---

6. "Emotions are stored in memory networks that contain information about stimuli, responses, and meanings related to emotional events. Retrieval occurs when external or internal cues result in 'spreading activation' along associative linkages to memory structures representing past events" (Bower and Sivers 1998). "Adapting this theory to PTSD, Foa et al. (1989) proposed that following a traumatic event, a fear network that stores information about sources of threat is formed," . . . and so on. (Salmon and Bryant 2002, p. 168).

University discourse, as described in Part I of this book. The fact that this new information can only be taken in from within the framework of a therapeutic, workable relation with the Other, and that this relation acquires all the weight of the preceding primary relation, moreover, making the process therefore far from self-evident, has received far too little attention. At most, we hear about the patient's "resistance" to the new information, which we are told we must understand as the patient's resistance to the therapist as the Other.

All of this proves that there are sufficient arguments for tracing the distinction between a restricted ASD and the larger PTSD back to the preceding, unresolved actualpathological position. Subsequent actual trauma will always have a retroactive effect that depends on this preceding position.[7] Both the diagnosis and the treatment must take this fully in account. Our explanation began with the idea of a temporal split between an original, unprocessed structural trauma, and a later accidental trauma. In clinical practice, however, we encounter yet another situation where the structural and the accidental trauma are intertwined with one another. This occurs in cases of chronic sexual and/or physical abuse of children, and will not only result in a classic, actualpathological position, but will also have serious effects on the subject-formation itself. That is why this group must be treated separately here.

Early Infantile Abuse and Subject-formation: Basic Distrust, Dissociation, Passive–active Reversal

Ordinary development takes place in a situation of what Anglo-American psychoanalysis calls "basic trust": the Other assumes a regulating and caretaking function through which identity development and drive regulation come into being. The confrontation with (a) can be processed through signifiers coming from the Other. In cases of

---

7. This idea of the requirement of a double trauma for PTSD to develop, where the effect of the second trauma builds on the first, can be found in Freud from the outset. Freud will later extend this line of reasoning: adult defense, fantasy, and the function of the father are grounded in a primary form and acquire their respective weight from it (see Verhaeghe 1999b, pp. 33–35 and 149–203).

chronic sexual and physical abuse, however, we encounter exactly the opposite, namely, "basic distrust": the Other as a guarantee is not installed, the drive has not been psychologically elaborated. Not only is the internal drive insufficiently processed, a confrontation with the Other's drive takes place on top of that.

The effects of this on subject-formation are far-reaching. As we saw in Part II, through the normal dialectics of alienation and separation, identity formation initially takes place by way of a dual mirroring with the Other, and later through a triangular distancing of this Other. In this way, a synthesis of different identifications comes into being and the Ego is developed. At the same time, the Other's identity is internally represented, along with the relationship toward this Other. In both identities, the good and bad parts are integrated. From the classical Freudian perspective, this leads to the so-called dynamic unconscious where the pleasurable and the unpleasurable parts operate in an associative network, and where the splitting of the subject is never complete. It is precisely this aspect of integration that fails to be installed in cases of chronic child abuse. In its place, dissociation is installed.

This idea seems a recent one, but in fact it is not. It is just a contemporary translation of Freud's original concept of the unconscious, formulated precisely during his clinical work with traumatized patients. In this early period, he discovered how such patients' psychological functioning entails a radical *Spaltung*, a splitting, where one part is associatively separated from the other. At first it was only in what Freud called severe cases of hysteria that this splitting was recognized, but let us not forget that he was working with traumatic disturbances at the time (Freud and Breuer 1978 [1895d], pp. 12–13). Later, once he began to concentrate on the psychoneuroses, he had to conclude that such a splitting is found in these patients as well, albeit in a much less radical way: the conscious and unconscious run through one another, and the patient is able to make associative connections.

In dissociation this doesn't happen. There, a split between the unpleasurable, "bad" part and the pleasurable "good" part of the Other is installed. This split is mirrored in the subject in such a way that it installs an analogous split between the "bad" (because abused) and "good" (because "normal") parts of identity. Such a dissociative splitting comes into being as a defense during the abuse: the child "switches itself off" and is psychologically "gone"; the child itself is not being abused, only the "bad" part, and by the "bad" part of the other, moreover.[8] After the abuse, a return to the preceding situation that was cut off takes place, allowing the "normal" relation between the subject and the Other to function once more. In some cases, dissociation becomes a system according to which the identity of the different "alters" can be distinguished, that is to say, through subidentities who function completely independently of each other. The relation with dissociative identity disorder is clear.

As a defense, dissociation has a clear advantage. The child needs the Other, the relation cannot be severed.[9] Through the radical splitting, both can continue to function in a seemingly normal relation. The loss is nevertheless immense. The Symbolico-Imaginary processing of the dialectics between (a), subject, and Other through the normal Oedipal structure is impossible. As a result, there can be no symptom formation either. In its place, actualpathological phenomena are formed, together with repetition compulsion.

Such phenomena contain the primary anxiety and somatization, but here the latter in particular appears in a much more severe form. Because of the repeated abuse, the child lives in a constant state of anxiety and alertness ("When will 'it' happen again?") that establishes a chronic hyperactivation in all bodily systems. After a while, this leads to exhaustion, with diffuse effects on the body (heightened blood pressure, digestive disorders, sleeplessness) and, finally, the hyperalertness reverts into the opposite, that is, a general numbness.

---

8. A patient who was anally and genitally abused by her father at a very young age described it thus: "Henrietta recalls initially welcoming his attention (even encouraging it) and gradually, when 'the pain' started, going blank, which helped him to get inside her. She describes imagining herself as one of her dolls. This meant that she blocked any awareness of thoughts and feelings in herself or the other" (Fonagy and Target 2000, p. 866).

9. Traumatized children need the Other even more than normal children, albeit with a characteristic ambiguity because the primary need for a securing Other was not fulfilled. This is why abused children often hide the abuse from the external world—usually they are very much aware of the consequences of discovery, consequences that always come down to separation. This is precisely what is unbearable for them, because they have never lived through normal separation and still need the Other. This explains the frequently paradoxical bond between the child and the abuser, which appears very strange from outside and often leads to accusations of complicity in the child.

The repetition compulsion operates monolithically, intrusively, and incomprehensibly. Fragments of the abuse impose themselves through "intrusive imagery," frequently found in the play of small children in performative ways. These intrusive phenomena are often triggered by minimal cues in the environment, setting the reexperiencing of the trauma in motion, and instigating the flip from one side of the dissociation to the other.

As far as identity development is concerned, there is no integration through triangular distancing, to the contrary even. The world, and therefore others, are seen entirely in black and white, and defined as either good or bad, with very rapid switches between the two. The same goes for the subject's own identity. The general relation toward the Other is similarly characterized by such a splitting—either he or she is entirely trustworthy, or completely untrustworthy. The regulation of the drive either runs through aggressive automutilation, or through projective identification, where the bad part of the subject's identity is usually projected onto the other in an attempt to master it. Here we find a passive–active reversal in an attempt at mastery; rather than taking on the role of victim oneself, it is the Other who must become the victim. Such projective identifications are often accompanied by forceful actings-out, setting a vicious cycle in motion (see Chapter 14). As adults, these patients may display a strange combination of sexual promiscuity and anxiety about intimacy.

The result is a combination of a number of disturbances, almost always in the actualpathological range, with an emphasis on acting out and aggression, often in combination with addiction. These make it difficult to see the traumatic ideology underying the initial reasons for the consultation that almost always occurs at the demand of a third party.

The Nature of the Trauma and the Handling of Guilt

The majority of recent empirical studies are concerned with the characteristics and classifications of PTSD. Because most studies have no foundation in a metapsychology, this means that such classifications tend to be pretty arbitrary—the DSM again being the best example of this. We will shortly examine the DSM category of PTSD in light of the above-described structure, namely, the retreat to an earlier actualpathological position through an accidental trauma. But before we go into this, let us first look at another classificatory criterion: the nature of the accidental trauma.

As mentioned above, factual experience is of less significance than the structure of the subject, but this doesn't mean we can ignore these facts! We must distinguish between an individual and a collective trauma—which itself can be further differentiated on the basis of its acute or chronic nature. Typical collective chronic traumata are war situations, but also the sexual abuse of a number of children in the same family. Temporally isolated accidents or disasters are collective acute traumata. Both may also involve merely a single individual, which is not without its own effects, particularly in the way guilt is experienced. The difference between these different forms must be taken into account in the differential diagnostics.

A typical example of an acute, individual trauma is rape. In most cases, the resulting ASD will not give rise to a PTSD, particularly if there is enough support from the surrounding environment. Such support always boils down to the same thing: the ability to talk and talk and talk again, within a guaranteeing supportive relationship. Hence the complaints of rape victims of former times: the police didn't listen to them, did not take them seriously—luckily this has since changed. The guaranteeing function is even more expected from those in positions of authority. Where such an embedment in the signifier is missing, the chance of later disturbances is increased. This will be even truer in cases of a preceding actualpathological position. Moreover, the two will interact. Because of the actualpathological position, the victim will be unwilling to talk about the recent trauma in any event, with the result that the surrounding environment will remain silent as well, and so on. In such cases the demand for help will not be so evident.

The most frequent form of chronic individual trauma, child abuse, has already been discussed. Its most visible forms are physical and sexual abuse, but that doesn't mean that abuse can't happen without such acts. I am referring to situations where children grow up psychically terrorized, without a single hair of their head being touched, as it were. This latter may indeed be taken literally, and immediately shows the poverty of positive affect in such a psychologically traumatizing upbringing. These patients, moreover, don't have the relative advantage of being able to point to objective factual abuse, while the effects can be at least as severe.

In both cases, what initially seems like a remarkable phenomenon emerges, one that is less apparent in the collective forms of trauma, namely, the victim's sense of guilt, or "survivor's guilt." The public's inability to understand this is immense: How could this be? Not only did the poor victims have it happen to them, they feel guilty now? The well-meaning answer is then to press the role of victim onto the subject, forcing patients to remain silent about this sense of guilt, yet without freeing them from it. Where does this sense of guilt come from? For the answer we must look once more at the way the original structural trauma failed to be processed. In the dual relationship with the Other, there are only two options: either the responsibility is laid on the other, or the subject takes it upon itself. In cases where the Other doesn't respond, all the subject can do is take the guilt upon itself, and this is precisely what happens in these patients. Mostly they will rationalize this sense of guilt, which comes down to a way of coping with anxiety: "If I hadn't done this or that, then 'it' wouldn't have happened." Or—and typically along the lines of the original trauma—during the course of the treatment of sexually abused patients, the other will be blamed, usually the mother who could not or did not want to see "It"; she failed to intervene, to notice, and so on (remarkably enough, the perpetrator tends to be blamed less).

The two final forms are the collective traumas, whether chronic or acute. Acute trauma involves a single disaster situation for a group, while chronic trauma is usually associated with war situations. From a diagnostic point of view, the relative advantage is that the etiology is known—which isn't always the case in the two forms discussed earlier. Their chief difference from the previous, individual forms is that in case of collective trauma the question of guilt is handled differently because of the way the event was shared with others. The processing will almost always happen in the group, which in it itself creates the possibility for the construction of a collective discourse—an Other—that enables the Real to be more smoothly embedded in the signifier. Here, as before, the foundation for a subsequent appearance of PTSD will always have to do with a preceding actualpathological position.

To conclude this introduction, we must mention one more striking fact, namely, that there is often a time lapse between the trauma and the appearance of PTSD, sometimes even a long one during which there have seemingly been no troubles at all. The DSM specification includes "with delayed onset" when the disturbance begins six months or even more after the event (Hermann and Eryavec 1994; Solomon et al. 1991a,b; Solomon and Singer, 1995). The explanation must be sought in the typical characteristic of the actual pathological position: there is no speech, the "elaboration" takes place in silence. Even more, in many cases such patients don't want to know about it and actually know nothing more about it because of the dissociative splitting of the associative networks. There are no symptoms, only phenomena at the level of the body and, should a consultation for these phenomena occur, it usually comes much later precisely because these patients have little inclination to approach the Other; the Other didn't give much of an answer in the past after all . . .

This means that in a large number of cases the diagnosis is made considerably more difficult, not only because of the temporal gap between the accidental trauma and the disturbances, but also because the patients themselves are unable or unwilling to make the connection. Research has shown that many patients come for consultation without connecting their troubles to their sexual or physical abuse as a child (Price et al. 2001, pp. 1096–1097). This, in combination with what is sometimes even the complete absence of a demand for help, requires the diagnostician to be all the more attentive to a number of often vague indications and characteristics. We will now address these from the perspective of their underlying structure, starting with the description in the *DSM-IV*.

Descriptive Characteristics in Light of the Underlying Structure

PTSD is classified under the heading of anxiety disorders, but it will soon become clear that it overflows into a number of other categories as well. The *DSM-IV* description is as follows

309.81 Posttraumatic Stress Disorder
A. The person had been exposed to a traumatic event in which both the following were present:
   (1) The person had experienced, witnessed, or was confronted with an event or events that involved actual or threatened

death or serious injury, or a threat to the physical integrity of self or others.
(2) The person's response involved fear, helplessness, or horror. **Note:** In children, this may be expressed instead by disorganised or agitated behaviour.

B. The traumatic event is persistently re-experienced in one (or more) of the following ways:
(1) Recurrent and intrusive distressing recollections of the event, including images, thoughts, or perceptions. **Note:** In young children, repetitive play may occur in which themes or aspects of the trauma are expressed.
(2) Recurrent distressing dreams of the event. **Note:** In children, there may be frightening dreams without recognisable content.
(3) Acting or feeling as if the traumatic event were recurring (includes a sense of reliving the experience, illusions, hallucinations, and dissociative flashback episodes, including those that occur on awakening or when intoxicated). **Note:** In young children, trauma-specific re-enactment may occur.
(4) Intense psychological distress at exposure to internal or external cues that symbolise or resemble an aspect of the traumatic event.
(5) Physiological reactivity on exposure to internal or external cues that symbolise or resemble an aspect of the traumatic event.

C. Persistent avoidance of stimuli associated with the trauma and numbing of general responsiveness (not present before the trauma), as indicated by three (or more) of the following:
(1) Efforts to avoid thoughts, feelings, or conversations associated with the trauma.
(2) Efforts to avoid activities, places, or people that arouse recollections of the trauma.
(3) Inability to recall an important aspect of the trauma.
(4) Markedly diminished interest or participation in significant activities.
(5) Feeling of detachment or estrangement from others.
(6) Restricted range of affect (e.g., unable to have loving feelings).
(7) Sense of foreshortened future (e.g., does not expect to have a career, marriage, children, or a normal life span).

D. Persistent symptoms of increased arousal (not present before the trauma) as indicated by two (or more) of the following:
(1) Difficulty falling or staying asleep.
(2) Irritability or outbursts of anger.

(3) Difficulty concentrating.
(4) Hypervigilance.
(5) Exaggerated startle response.
E. Duration of the disturbance (symptoms in criteria B, C, and D) is more than one month.
F. The disturbance causes clinically significant distress or impairment in social, occupational, or other important areas of functioning. [American Psychiatric Association 2000, pp. 467–468]

Criterion A concerns the etiology and immediately gives an indication of its complexity. It is not just a question of having experienced the trauma oneself, one may have been witness to or—even more vaguely—been confronted with it. The subject's own reaction, moreover (Ad 2), is decisive. Here we come up against the "indirect" trauma that helps to explain why children of concentration camp victims suffer more from PTSD than their parents. This is the step toward an imagined trauma, which immediately brings us to the discussion about a trauma's real or imagined nature, a discussion that has already reappeared several times in history. Such an indirect effect once more diminishes the importance of the factual nature of the trauma, and shifts the focus onto the subject itself. In its relation with the Other, the subject may take over the Other's trauma through incorporation or identification, which is literally an "imagining," an "in-imaging"[10] Clearly, such an imagined trauma can have effects just as important as the actually experienced trauma.

The emphasis here is on the *threat* of death or injury, not necessarily on the actual injury. In cases of war trauma, Freud suggested that an actual injury may reduce the chance of developing a subsequent PTSD, but as far as I know this hypothesis has not been confirmed. Under this heading fall those forms of usually chronically traumatic situations, where the trauma is said to be merely psychic, and is therefore much more difficult to detect.

At A(2) we find the traumatic, automatic anxiety that is quite close to panic attack. At its heart is the fact that the subject is obliged to take the *passive* position, thus forcing it to collapse back into the original, early infantile position of helplessness where only the Other can provide the specific actions and signifiers that makes coping possible.

---

10. Translator's Note: In Dutch, *"inbeelding"* means literally to make or bring images inside.

Intrusive Reexperiencing

Under Criterion B we find the repetition compulsion, and intrusive reexperiencing that has nothing to do with memory. The typical characteristic of trauma is precisely that it cannot be remembered through signifiers. The inscription took place on the body, in a different memory system than of declarative memory.[11] Consequently, there is also no return of the repressed, nor is there any psychopathological symptom construction and its resultant repetition. Instead, we find a repetition compulsion that the subject is unable to control; it is a reexperiencing followed by a defense against it, often with somatization phenomena as a result. The patient tries to grasp what was never originally psychically inscribed in the declarative memory. The so-called memories are always monolithic, unprocessable, and intrusive, always imposing themselves under the form of the same verbal fragments, flashbacks, bodily sensations.

The same goes for traumatic dreams as well, which for Freud were the sole exception to what he considered the central function of the dream, namely, to maintain sleep through wish fulfillment. Their effect, in fact, is precisely the opposite, because the dreamer is woken up by what Lacan calls a missed encounter with the Real (Lacan 1994 [1964], pp. 53–56, 68–70). The missed aspect lies in the impossibility of turning the traumatic Real into signifiers, and this is why one wakes up precisely at the moment "it" is going to happen. Such traumatic

---

11. Contemporary neuropsychology has shown the existence of at least two different memory systems. The conscious, declarative memory functions through the hippocampus, while the unconscious memory operates through a system based on the amygdala. Both are operative at the same time, independently of each other. Bridges between them are indirect (LeDoux 1998, pp. 239–252). This is a further reason—in addition to the traumatizing effect of imagined trauma—why it is so difficult to make a distinction between a real and an imagined trauma. The implication is that the traumatized patient will never be able to remember the trauma in any normal way. Freud rapidly and intuitively understood this, long before contemporary neurology and any discussion of "repressed" and "false memories." Already in 1896, he asked whether it is correct to say that the vanished memories of the trauma have really disappeared, or rather if it is the case that the therapist is confronted here with a cognitive process *that never took place*, meaning that the treatment has to enable the patient to perform a psychic operation that she or he was unable to carry out at the time of the trauma itself (Freud and Breuer 1978 [1895d], *SE* 2, p. 300).

dreams often engage a vicious cycle. A secondary signal anxiety is developed against sleeping, precisely because of the nightmares, resulting in a reversal of the day and night rhythm that in turn causes further disturbances in somatic and social functioning, with serious somatization effects.

In this way, the idea of "symbolizing the traumatic event" must be interpreted and revised. Here it has nothing to do with symbolization at all, but with an automatic evocation of the trauma through triggers, provoking an uncontrollable reexperiencing. Once symbolization proper becomes possible, the psychic-associative processing of the trauma can take place, together with its (literal) re-covery.

Hypervigilance and Distrust

Criteria C and D present different elements that could be better organized. Psychologically, the inability to recall (C3) is the core problem: the traumatic experience has not been inscribed in an ordinary psychological way and therefore cannot be associatively processed. This characteristic deserves a much more central place in the diagnostic description and belongs, moreover, to Criterion B.

Under C1 and C2 we find secondary avoidance behaviors, and the entire criterion D could be included in here as well. Sleep disorders (D1) always have to do with the continued vigilance and desire to avoid traumatic dreams. D (3 to 5) needs explanation because it seemingly contains a paradox (difficulty concentrating versus hypervigilance). PTSD patients do not pay "normal" attention to the surroundings, thus giving the impression that they are not paying any attention at all. Nevertheless they are hyperconcentrated and hypervigilant, albeit with respect to (the avoidance of) reexperiencing the trauma and the desire to control the Other, or, more broadly, the surrounding environment. When such hypervigilance lasts too long, somatization phenomena occur from exhaustion. Often this leads to abuse of medication (alternating between sleeping pills and pep pills), thus creating further problems (e.g., addiction). Aggressive reactions (D2) also belong in this category, and may additionally turn into their opposite, that is, a total lack of reaction.

Immediately following from this, we can isolate a final group of characteristics (C 4 to 7), namely, the PTSD patient's characteristic relationship with the Other. This too finds insufficient elaboration in the DSM description. The heart of the matter is that trust in the Other is missing because she or he originally failed to respond, or didn't respond sufficiently at the moment of the structural trauma. In its place we find a distancing from or fundamental distrust of the Other. The effect is social isolation as a choice, and this takes a totally different form from the neurotic variety of loneliness and its accompanying complaints.

A final remark concerns the way the link with the preceding structural trauma—more broadly, with the premorbid personality—is not just missing in the DSM categorization, but is even rejected ("not present before the trauma"), while almost all research results have shown this link to be necessary. This absence follows from a certain naiveté: the DSM description begins with the idea that the trauma, as the cause of the disorder, is already known. In clinical practice, this is often not the case. Many referrals take place as a result of the secondary phenomena, without any knowledge of a link to a trauma. The sole finger pointing in this direction is the specification "with delayed onset." If we were to add to this the impossibility of remembering the trauma, combined with a negative relation toward the Other—and therefore toward the clinician—it becomes clear why diagnosis here is not a simple matter.

Differential Diagnostic Difficulties and Implications for the Treatment

First and foremost, we must stress that PTSD in itself does not determine a specific structure of the subject. But this doesn't prevent us from approaching it structurally: PTSD always goes back to the actual-pathological position of the subject, where the psychopathological processing only barely took place. The specific structure of the subject (neurosis, psychosis, perversion) fully determines how it appears. Later we will discuss its most well-known manifestation, namely, the neurotic structure, better known as borderline.

In addition, what must be emphasized is how frequently PTSD is a missed diagnosis (particularly in cases of a psychotic or perverse structure), or one that is made far too late. We have already seen the reasons for this. The effects of a chronic traumatic history can be very diverse, and moreover spread their visible effects over a large number of diagnostic categories. Such effects are often so striking that they claim all of the attention. The typical example here is female alcoholism.

As clinicians, we must be aware that we are being confronted with a complex final product, thus proving once more the need for a very thorough investigation of the case history. Here, the difference between a real or imagined trauma is less important than a continued attentiveness to the relation between the subject and the Other; indeed, it is precisely the structure of this relation that will determine whether or not PTSD is developed, not the nature of the "event."[12]

Its spillage over into other categories is evident anywhere one looks in the literature—between 60 and 90 percent of PTSD patients receive at least a double diagnosis (for a summary, see Lee and Young 2001, pp. 152–153). In fact, any referral beyond the classical psychopathological spectrum can hide a traumatic history. Classic in this respect are the affective and anxiety disorders and somatoform and dissociative disorders, together with sleep disorders, because these directly connect with actualpathological phenomena as effects of the structural trauma. The roomy catchall of what are known as adaptive disorders carries many features that refer simultaneously to PTSD, particularly if we understand these as coping mechanisms for (the effects of) the trauma by way of a passive–active reversal. With this, I am thinking of aggressive acting-out, sexual promiscuity, automutilation and suicidal behavior, and disturbances in impulse control. Addiction is ubiquitous, and even eating disorders are not uncommon.

No wonder that many are calling for a revision of the category. A well-known example is Herman's idea of a "complex post traumatic stress disorder" (Herman 1992a) or even a DESNOS ("Disorders of Ex-

---

12. In cases of a hysterical structure, with its typical susceptibility to suggestion, there is a high risk that the therapist's suggestions concerning traumatic antecedents may be taken on by the patient, resulting indeed in false memory syndrome (cf infra). Once again, the diagnostic attention must be on the relation between the subject and the Other because it is the hysterical tendency to identify with the words of the other that makes such false memories possible. In PTSD and the underlying actualpathological position, this will be absent. A rule of thumb here (with all the obligatory restrictions concerning such rules) could be the following: When the etiology lies in the Real, the phenomena it causes will also occur in the Real; if the etiology lies in the Symbolico-Imaginary, the symptoms will belong to that field.

treme Stress Not Otherwise Specified," [Herman 1992b]). For me, this proves once more how a categorical descriptive diagnosis will inevitably fail and how one must fully attend to the underlying structure of the subject in its relation to the Other.

This latter idea is the most important conclusion for differential diagnostics. An initial diagnostic evaluation will almost always have to do with the actualpathological phenomena in the Real, along with their accompanying defensive avoidant behavior. The step toward diagnostic recognition of the importance of the relation with the Other is made only when one realizes that such phenomena always boil down to a passive–active reversal: what one passively underwent is now actively repeated in an attempt to master it, albeit beyond the realm of the signifier and therefore the Other. This brings us, finally, to the most crucial element of diagnosis. Chances are that when there is an underlying actualpathological structure that has been reactivated by an accidental trauma, the Other—and hence the clinician as well—will be warded off. The perpetual attempt to rejoin the Other notwithstanding, the Other is not to be trusted. It is even more so in cases of a preceding chronic trauma: the Other must be kept under control.

What the clinician normally expects, in other words—the attribution of a position of assistance along with the guaranteeing aspect of the position he or she occupies as the subject "supposed-to-know"—is anything but assured here. In a number of cases, she or he will meet the exact opposite, that is, a repetition of the original basic distrust. A silent, uncooperative patient with a series of vague complaints, often combined with addiction, doesn't lend herself to a very positive attitude in the clinician. If, within a short period of time, this patient should then try to take hold of the reins, a negative countertransference is usually installed, even a rejection on the part of the therapist. The result is a repetition of the original actualpathology and, hence, a confirmation of the problem: the Other takes off, the subject is left alone.

This is all the more debilitating because the central aim of the treatment here is the creation of a therapeutic relation that will enable the patients to take the active position. This latter is not so much oriented toward action but toward an active mastery of the Real through language that simultaneously allows the subject to acquire a new layer of identity. Any approach that maintains or even puts the patient in the role of passive victim merely reconfirms the original structure.

As far as treatment is concerned, it has become clear in the meantime that a classic psychoanalytic approach, directed toward the analysis of symptoms through interpreting the underlying conflict, doesn't work. Indeed, because of the actualpathological position of the subject, there are no symptoms. In their place, the emphasis must be on the installation of an effective therapeutic relation, through which *subject amplification* can occur. This is nothing but the redoing of the original process of subject-formation, through which the subject acquires the signifiers necessary for processing the Real of the body. In this respect, it is not so much a question of presenting the patient with the "correct" signifiers as of creating a relationship in and through which these signifiers can be taken in and assumed from a guaranteeing Other.

Much the same line of reasoning can be found in the development of cognitive behavioral therapy. In place of the earlier systematic desensitization and flooding, now the emphasis is on the "imaginal exposure." As far as I can see, this comes down to an installation of a secondary processing in and through the presence of a security-providing Other, in which it is frequently the therapist who, as the Other, repeatedly puts the traumatic experience into detailed words: "Imaginal exposure involves the trauma survivor *or the therapist* narrating repeatedly the traumatic experience in detail" (Livanou 2001, p. 181; my italics). Everything is then taped so the patient can listen to it again at home. What is insufficiently stressed in this approach is the underlying structural ground and the need to construct an effective relationship as such. It is precisely the failure or the success of this that will determine the therapeutic outcome.

All this is even more true for a clinical category that is (in)famous for the difficulties it presents in the transference. I mean the so-called borderline disorders, whose interrelation with PTSD is seen almost everywhere today. This will be our next topic.

BORDERLINE DISORDERS: THE ACTUALPATHOLOGICAL POSITION IN THE NEUROTIC STRUCTURE

In today's hit parade of personality disorders, borderline personality disorder (BPD) tops the list. What has recently become increasingly clear is that it is connected with PTSD. First, on a purely phenomenological level, it is easy to see an analogy—it suffices just to compare the DSM descriptions of PTSD and BPD (Herman 1992b). Furthermore, in a large number of empirical studies a trauma is discovered at the base of BPD.

At first sight, this might seem to indicate that BPD could be interpreted as if it were a special case of PTSD. To me, this doesn't seem like a fruitful line of reasoning. So-called PTSD, as described above, comes down to the purely phenomenological summary of the effects following an accidental trauma in someone with a prior existing actualpathological structure. The latter, in any case, is the necessary condition for PTSD phenomena to develop. The implication is that PTSD is not in itself determining for any specific subjective structure, but can occur just as easily within a neurotic, a perverse, or a psychotic structure.

Since it is based on observation, the DSM category is unable to take this into account and, hence, doesn't allow one to make a structural diagnosis. The discussion above described in general terms the interaction between an actualpathological position and the retroactive effect of an accidental trauma. "General" here implies that it can be recognized in the three subject structures, with the proviso that each structure will determine a number of specific characteristics. We will shortly examine this in relation to the perverse structure. This, too, can be approached from the actualpathological side of the continuum.

My argument is that what we understand as BPD today amounts to an actualpathological position of the neurotic relation between the subject and the Other. Remember: it involves a neurotic subject who, in its initial confrontation with drive arousal, received neither the Other's signifiers—or not enough of them—nor the Other's guarantee, needed to set the secondary processing in motion and to make the step toward the psychopathological side of things. I am following Jonckheere (1993) here, although his emphasis was on the anxiety neurosis.

With this, I distance myself from the original conception of borderline, which located it between psychosis and neurosis (Kernberg 1975).[13] Instead, I see the classical borderline as situated between the

---

13. Kernberg, whose original concept it was, later extended it to all the *DSM-IV* personality disorders except obsessive-compulsive personality disorder (Kernberg 1996a; see also Vermote and Auwerkerken 1999). From my perspective, actualpathology may indeed be present in every subject structure. In this chapter, we will focus on "classical" borderline, that is, its neurotic form.

actualpathological and the psychopathological position of the neurotic structure, albeit with a very clear shift toward the actualpathological side. It is precisely an unfamiliarity with Freud's original differential diagnostics that lies at the bottom of the classic idea that locates BPD between neurosis and psychosis. The same logic can be applied to the perverse and psychotic structures. There too we can make a diagnosis based on the subject's position in the continuum from actualpathological to psychopathological positions.[14] Anticipating what follows, I can already list a number of well-known clinical characteristics of BPD that prove my point. The chief argument for understanding classical borderline as pertaining to the neurotic structure has to do with the presence of so-called reality-testing. For me, this means that the oedipal triangularization has been carried through and that the dual-Imaginary functioning has been superseded by the Symbolic. Thus it doesn't so much concern reality-testing as a sense of symbolically determined and shared reality. This is not so in the psychotic structure that remains glued, as it were, to the Real (see Chapter 15). The implication is that BPD pertains to the neurotic structure.

The actualpathological character of BPD is illustrated by two well-known clinical facts (Vermote 2000). For the borderline patient, the emphasis is on the present, in the therapeutic interaction as well. From here it follows that the patient expects concrete proof of the therapist's commitment, if not to say his or her "love." The connection with the original relationship between mother and child, where the child required a "specific action" (Freud) from the mother, is clear. The same idea appears in what Vermote (2000, p. 669) calls the third and fourth directions taken in the psychoanalytic conceptualization of BPD, despite the fact that the authors he cites fail to make this connection with Freud's actualpathology.

In the third movement (Winnicott, Balint, Kohut, Bion), the focus is on the failure of the basic experience between the mother and child, be it based on a trauma or on not "good enough mothering." Instead of the necessary "holding environment" (Winnicott), "primary love"

---

14. This is not just a question of changing the wording. By applying Freud's structural distinction between actual- and psychopathology to the three possible relations between the subject and the Other, one can make a much better diagnosis with regard to treatment. Today's vague and generalized interpretation of the BPD category is not very helpful here.

(Balint), "primary empathy" (Kohut), or "containment" (Bion), a "basic fault" (Balint) appears, a "primitive agony" (Winnicott), a "fear of fragmentation" (Kohut) or a "nameless dread" (Bion). The latter expression expresses best what is involved here: the structural trauma of the drive is not (or is insufficiently) represented by a guaranteeing Other; the confrontation with the nameless drive keeps on insisting. Fear of fragmentation can easily be understood as a failure in the mirror stage, making it impossible to install the bodily image as a totality.

The fourth direction (Fonagy, Target, Bateman) is characterized by an emphasis on the Other, more specifically, on his or her failure, and its effects. In the language of contemporary attachment theory, this failure of the Other implies that the subject will not be able to "mentalize," that is to say, to regulate the drive through internal representations and constructions about the subject's identity and the identity of the Other. Instead, projective identifications are installed, along with an immediate abreaction of the drive arousal in the present, whether on the other, or on the subject's body.

It is largely from this last approach that my discussion of BPD will begin because it is closest to my own Freudo-Lacanian approach to subject-formation. It is true that little attention has been paid to BPD from a strictly Lacanian perspective (Jonckheere 1993). I will begin not with the narrow DSM definition but with today's broader understanding of it. The indicative characteristics are: dramatic regression, psychotic-like episodes, intense (counter)transference and acting out.[15] The most recent rundown goes like this (Fonagy et al. 2002, p. 346):

---

15. There are many different descriptions of diagnostic criteria, mostly relying on Kernberg (for a summary, see Verhaeghe 1993). Kernberg's structural analysis possesses the following characteristics: "1. Nonspecific Manifestations of Ego Weakness (a. lack of anxiety tolerance; b. lack of impulse control; c. lack of developed sublimatory channels). 2. Shift Toward Primary-Process Thinking. 3. Specific Defensive Operations at the Level of Borderline Personality Organization (a. splitting; b. primitive idealization; c. early forms of projection and especially projective identification; d. denial; e. omnipotence and devaluation). 4. Pathology of Internalized Object Relationships" (Kernberg 1975, pp. 8–40). His criteria for the differential diagnostics for Borderline Personality Organization are: "1. The presence of identity diffusion (that is, of a lack of integration of the concepts of the self and of significant others, in other words, of self- and object-representations). 2. The predominance of a constellation of primitive defensive operations centering around splitting. 3. The maintenance of reality testing" (Kernberg 1979).

- Disorganized and dysfunctional self-organization and consequent problems in affect regulation and emotional self-control (including feelings of emptiness, lack of a stable sense of self, emotional instability, and impulsivity);
- Dysfunctional and distorting "social-reality-testing" abilities: the dominance of defensive modes of functioning in intimate relationships, and in the analytic transference characterized by splitting and projective identification;
- Vulnerability to trauma, serious difficulties in maintaining intimate attachment relations, proneness to provoke abandonment, and consequent suicidality.

In what follows, I will work through these descriptive characteristics from a structural point of view, focusing on identity formation.

BPD and Subject-formation: Projective Identification, Splitting, Enactment

In normal subject-formation, the mirror stage provides the first layer of identity through which the partial drives are taken up in the total body image and their first regulation is installed. As I showed in Part II (Chapters 6 and 8), this is first of all a dual functioning without any distinction between the subject and the Other. The Oedipal structure introduces a third point and, hence, difference, making symbolic distancing and further representational processing possible. As a result, three things develop at the same time: symbolization, the human reality it determines, and the subject itself.

In cases of BPD, the original mirroring process takes a different course. The child doesn't receive a guaranteeing S_1-signifier from the Other for processing its (a). Instead, the child is confronted with a mirroring that gives it no way of handling its drive. Patrick et al. (1994) and Fonagy et al. (1996 and 2002) discovered a high correlation between the BPD-diagnosis and a preoccupied attachment style, concluding that the traumatic experiences remained unresolved and there is a striking reduction in reflective capability.

The effect of such an attachment style must be understood within the broader theory of attachment; focusing purely on the attachment style itself is not enough (Fonagy et al. 2002, pp. 344, 349 ff; and see Chapter 6). In attachment theory, development is described in this way: the internalizations of the representations of the "internal states" (what I have been calling the primal alienation through which (*a*) is introduced into representations) depends on a sensitive mirroring by the caregiver (the first and second Other). On this basis, a teleological model of the mind is initially developed in the child, being a combination of the representation of the self-experience and the representation of the reactions by the caregiver. This model enables the child to interpret both its own drive and the Other.

The next step in development is that from a teleological to an intentional position. This depends on how much security the child experiences in its exploration of the caregiver's mind, that is to say, it depends on the nature of the attachment. In a secure attachment, a safe exploration of the other becomes possible. In avoidant attachments, the mental state of the other is avoided. In resistant attachments, a focus on one's own "distress" follows, which excludes intersubjective interactions. Finally, in disorganized attachments, there is a hypervigilance toward the other, but without any positive consequence for self-organization—such children are immensely capable of reading the other's mind, but cannot read their own.[16] The final step in normal development takes place through the oedipal triangle and implies a stepping away from the equivalence between internal and external reality to a mentalized internal world, through which subjective experiences are recognized as just a single version of the external world, being a "representation of reality."

Empirical research has repeatedly shown the presence of a preoccupied attachment in combination with the unresolved character of early traumas in adult BPD patients. Consequently, there is no differentiation between external and internal "reality," by which we must understand that there is no differentiation between the subject's identity and the identity of the Other. The first alienation comes down to an identification with emptiness or with a rejecting Other. Therefore, no secure basic

---

16. For utter clarity: children's attachment styles (secure; anxious/avoidant; anxious/resistant; disorganised/disoriented) do not perfectly coincide with those of adults (secure/autonomous; dismissing; preoccupied; unresolved) although there is a clear correlation.

identity is developed, no "authentic, organic self-image built around internalized representations of self-states" (Fonagy and Target 2000, p. 864).[17] This has a number of typical consequences. A chaotic sense of self or even an inner emptiness is installed as far as identity is concerned, a void combined with anxiety. Normal affect regulation and control are absent because self-regulation through the Other's normalizing signifiers has not been established. Next, this gives rise to a craving for identity and a propensity to drink in the meaning-providing signifiers of the Other through physical proximity-seeking, albeit in combination with psychological avoidance as a result of the primary rejection by the Other. No coherence or synthesis gets developed at the level of identity.

Psychological functioning continues to operate in the equivalence mode, the dual-Imaginary, with a reversibility between the subject and the Other. Little Symbolic distance-taking or reflective functioning is possible, and the secondary processing or mentalizing (Lecours and Bouchard 1997) fails to develop. Here, an important differential diagnostic criterion must not be missed: the sense of reality, as determined by the symbolic order, comes into being in a *thinglike* way. What fails to be installed is a sense of *social* reality; at that level the psyche remains stuck in a dualistic mode. Whatever is thought in relation to the other and his or her intentions, is experienced as monolithic, real and actual. "Monolithic" and "real" mean that there can be none of the nuances of distance taking; "actual" means that no associative link to the subject's history can be found. In brief, there is no integration of the equivalence and the pretend modes (Fonagy and Target 2000, p. 855; and see Chapter 6).

In daily life, this may lead to a hyperalertness that attachment theory calls "hypermentalization": the patient has an excessive though selective awareness for detecting psychic states and intentions in the Other, and reacts to them in a black-and-white manner. This is translated into the need for the other's physical presence as well, albeit always in combi-

---

17. "Authentic" is misleading here, because throughout the whole book these authors show how this primary "authentic" self-image does indeed come from the other, that is, through his or her reactions to and interpretations of the child's drive arousal (i.e., the "organic"). This gives rise to an inner representation in which the internal drive arousal and its external interpretation by the Other form a mirror-subject or "identity."

nation with an anxiety about this presence—this is the need for a physically present "mirror" that enables one to know what one is actually feeling by way of the other's gaze. One step further and such a demand for physical presence gives rise to acting-out, whether sexually, aggressively, or—frequently enough—a combination of the two. Throughout this entire functioning, thought and reality concerning the other, the relation and the subject's own identity remain synonymous; moreover, the reversibility between the subject and the Other is maintained. As a result, the clinician encounters the characteristic division of the subject (splitting), the characteristic mechanism of defense (projective identification), and the typical BPD proneness for action (enactment).

The subject will then process its drive by sending out what is experienced as the bad or dangerous part to the outside and unilaterally situating it in the Other. Rather than the integration of alienation (the taking in) and separation (the distance taking), we come up against a projective identification (Ogden 1979). This implies that the unmanageable drive is unilaterally projected onto the Other and treated defensively there. The nature of projective identification is such that the other becomes reduced to it and seems to be left with only two possibilities: she or he can either behave in that way, or pull out entirely.

The intent of such projective identification is defensive in two ways: the drive (a) can be controlled by sending it outside and, by the same token, the other can be controlled as well. The latter can take two forms, presumably mirroring what the borderline patient originally experienced from the mother and/or the father: aggressive punishment or overconcern. This has been demonstrated in young children with a "disoriented/disorganized" attachment, from ages 5 to 7 onward (Main and Cassidy 1988; Solomon et al. 1995).

As a result, the construction of social reality and interpersonal relations runs in tandem with subject-formation, that is, in terms of black-and-white, and the latter will be called "splitting." Its difference from normal subject division boils down to the fact that the separate identificatory layers remain distinct and are unintegrated. The "inner" and the "outer," the subject and the Other remain both separated and reversible. Hence the typical adult interpersonal relations: it is always either everything or nothing, either extremely positive and intimate, or extremely negative and rejecting. There can be no nuancing through the reflective function. Hence the rigidity of interpersonal relations; the dual mode of functioning allows no distance taking; normal reflectivity is absent. Beyond the black-and-white pattern of relations, the borderline subject faces an inner emptiness (i.e., the lack of a primal identification) and its accompanying feeling of disorganization.

The link with dissociation in PTSD is clear. On the basis of two prospective longitudinal studies in adolescents, one can make a correlation between one of the most important PTSD symptoms, that is, dissociative phenomena, and disorganized attachment (Carlson 1998; Ogawa et al. 1997), and, therefore, to borderline pathology. Nevertheless, what is called splitting goes much further than the dissociative reexperiencing of unrepresentable trauma. It is used to deal not merely with the isolated, intrusive reexperiencing of traumatic elements, but with identity per se.

In addition to splitting and projective identification, the persistence of dual functioning—where thoughts and reality regarding social interactions are synonymous—has still another consequence. The equation between thought and reality gives rise to a quasi-immediate putting into action of what is thought, known as "enactment."[18] Classically, this can take two directions: an aggressive and/or sexual attack or seduction, each time in an unveiled manner. The sexual aspect can at first sight give the impression of an easy-going, unfrustrated attitude, but a closer look reveals that a proper intimate relationship is very difficult and is even experienced by this subject as threatening. The borderline patient has great difficulties acknowledging the other in its otherness; she or he cannot internally imagine or remember what the other thinks or desires. Because of projective identification, the other is completely colored by the drive arousal that must be warded off.

Interpersonal relations then become profoundly equivocal: an intense separation anxiety is combined with an accompanying need for physical presence, yet it is almost impossible to enter into intimate psychological relations. The other may not come too close and must, above all, be kept under control. This latter brings us to the often-mentioned traumatic etiology of the borderline pathology.

---

18. It is not difficult to make a comparison with neurotic acting-out. The neurotic subject begins acting out when the representational elaboration (the symptom as a Symbolico-Imaginary construct) no longer functions; in that sense, neurotic acting-out indicates a border. In case of borderline, the same border is much closer, precisely because of the absence of the representational processing of the drive.

Relation to Trauma

Over the past decade, empirical evidence for the relation between borderline pathology and infantile sexual abuse has been steadily appearing (Herman 1992b; Johnson et al. 1999; Paris et al. 1993). In itself this is not an explanation, far from it. As argued above, trauma alone is not sufficient as an etiological ground for a later pathological disturbance. This obliges us to reconsider the idea of trauma once more. My argument is that borderline pathology does indeed go back to trauma, but to an early infantile *traumatic relationship* toward the Other, through which mentalization and reflective functioning fail to arrive at a normal development; sexual abuse is the most well-known variety of such a traumatic relationship, but the latter can take more subtle and less visible forms as well.

Recent research has focused on the relation between reflective functioning and borderline. The clear result was that BPD patients scored very low on reflective functioning, and that in more than 80 percent of the cases there had been sexual abuse during childhood (Fonagy and Target 1996a). In an inverse study, the starting point was a group of patients whose sexual abuse as children was already known. In this group it was possible to isolate a subgroup that met the diagnostic criteria for BPD, and it was precisely this group that had very low reflective functioning (Fonagy et al. 1996). Consequently, the conclusion is that not everyone who experiences sexual abuse develops BPD, and that those who do have low reflective functioning abilities.

Actual trauma in itself, therefore, is not the direct cause of borderline disorder. Its etiology lies in the fact that this trauma occurs in an early child–Other interaction that doesn't permit the development of secondary processing and the fundamental fantasy. This has to do with the failure of the Other's guaranteeing function, the failure of "parental mirroring." The grounds for this failure can either be constitutional and/or traumatic and/or a psychopathology in the parents. With regard to the latter, depression in the mother is a well-known factor (Murray and Cooper 1997). Fonagy and Target (2000) observe that the core etiology has to do with a certain parental inability to imagine themselves in the child; and such a situation can also arise without a clear parental pathology or actual trauma (Fonagy et al. 2002). The psychoanalytic understanding of the effect of trauma is thus confirmed: the impossibility of representing the internal drive arousal and the absence of the representational processing of separation (see Chapter 6).

Should real abuse be present, the first alienation and mirroring occurs with a traumatizing Other. As a first result, the first layer of one's "own" identity is only narrowly related to the drive arousal (a), but is instead related to the Other's drive; thus, there is no representation of nor knowledge about one's own drive. The second consequence is that this identity is threatening for the subject, because it contains persecution and abuse. Hence the ever-present risk of masochistic behavior and the self-provocation of new abuse.

Indeed, where the previously mentioned hypermentalization takes place in a history of sexual abuse, this can have unfortunate consequences. The patient him- or herself actively seeks new abusers so as in this way to regulate its own drive, as well as to build some kind of identity, albeit through identification with the aggressor. The patient looks for "abusers, who, through maltreating her, helped her temporarily to reduce her unbearable sense of diffused identity" (Fonagy and Target 2000, p. 868). In contrast, tender intimacy is dreaded. The trauma is thus repeated and the traumatic relationship toward the Other maintained.

Implications for Differential Diagnostics and Treatment

Let us resume from our initial thesis. The classic borderline patient pertains to the neurotic structure, more specifically to a level of neurotic structure that has only barely left the actualpathological position. In this sense, there is no development of the fundamental fantasy, nor is there any secondary processing through triangular structuration. The defensive processing is limited to actualpathological phenomena and there are no Symbolico-Imaginary symptoms properly speaking. As far as the position toward the Other is concerned, that is, toward language and the other, dual-Imaginary functioning predominates, characterized by reversibility and the inseparability of thought and reality with regard to social relations. Hence the rigid, black-and-white nature of the exchanges. The relation between the subject and the Other remains within the dual-Imaginary (the "splitting") and is mainly experienced through unmediated projective identification and enactment. Processing by way of the symbolic phallus, as the opening between the subject and the first and second Others, doesn't occur.

In place of such processing, we find actualpathological phenomena, with their inevitable focus on the body. Again, this indicates an underlying process, or rather the failure to introduce the drive tension into the representational order. The most well-known examples of this in borderline are automutilation and addiction. Both are direct attempts at coping with the arousal of the organism to control the drive.

Addiction, to both legal and illegal products, is not hard to understand. It is a pseudomedical practice, which Loose aptly calls "administration" (Loose 2002). The addictive product is used as a "floodgate" for controlling the subject's jouissance, resulting in the creation of a new problem, addiction.

Automutilation is also fairly well-known in the borderline pathology (Fonagy et al. 1993; Fonagy and Target 1995). It must be understood within the larger context of the ever-present tendency toward impulsiveness and enactment in view of the reversibility between thought and action. Moreover, the "auto" is also relative, again in light of the reversibility of the subject and the Other. Aggression can go in both directions here. In contrast to anorexia-bulimia, the emphasis is not on the refusal of the relationship with the other (see Chapter 8), but on the relationship between the subject and (*a*). When one can get these patients to talk about their automutilation—something that is far from easy—one usually gets a variation of the following: they experience an ever-growing internal tension that provokes more and more anxiety—anxiety about disappearing, exploding, becoming completely mad. The cutting or burning occurs at the moment the climax becomes almost unbearable, and always has a tension-reducing effect—order returns. The defensive processing through the Other is almost entirely absent here—hence the inherent difficulty for these patients of talking about it; the processing is instead real and unmediated.[19]

From a differential diagnostic perspective, the relationship the borderline patient establishes, both inside and outside the consultation room, is of decisive importance. The proximity of the Other is at once both

---

19. Like anorexia, automutilation has been recuperated by normal hysteria in the shape of piercing and its related forms. The main difference from primary automutilation is that the hysterical form is a very explicit appeal to the Other, it must be

sought—as an answer to (*a*)—and avoided. Both the subject's and the Other's fantasies are experienced as real and therefore dangerous—the dual-functioning mode does not allow any distance taking. Moreover, projective identification imposes the subject's drive onto the other in such a way that the other becomes reduced to it.[20] Because of the actual-pathological position, drive regulation and a coherent identity are missing—hence the instability of every relationship, together with an intense impulsiveness. Out of the lack of sufficient symbolization, the step toward action takes place very rapidly, something that is also demanded from the other. The instability of the relation doesn't prevent there from being a patent rigidity, in the sense that psychic reality and objective reality are regarded as identical. Their contents can rapidly revert to the opposite, hence the instability. This, in turn, gives rise to splitting, both in the subject's identity and in the identity of the other.[21]

Like the characteristic borderline phenomena, the nature of the relation can be understood from the perspective of actualpathology. The maintenance of the sense of reality and of the desire to connect to the Other, moreover, indicate the presence of a neurotic structure. It is in this sense that I regard classical borderline as the actualpathological position of the neurotic structure, alongside anxiety neurosis and actualpathology.

Differential diagnosis with psychosis has become more difficult with the ever-increasing expansion of research into both psychosis and borderline pathology. Once we limit ourselves to the classical borderline definition, however, it becomes less problematic. The psychotic subject has no sense of reality. Particularly during the acute episode,

---

"shown" in a provocative way. Actualpathological automutilation—usually going back to a traumatic history—eliminates the Other; the patient acts on his or her own. The reversal from passive to active positions is quite clear here.

20. "Not being able to feel themselves from within, they are forced to experience the self from without" (Fonagy 2001, p.178).

21. The distinction between the first Other (the mother) and the second Other (the father) is absent from this description of the borderline's characteristic relationship with the Other. Very little attention has been paid to the father in the Anglo-American formulation. The focus is almost entirely on the mother. This is probably an artifact of the theory. On the other hand, to the extent that it belongs to the actualpathological position, the borderline will relate to a nondifferentiated Other. Clearly further research is needed here.

words and things are synonymous, and reflective functioning is absent entirely (see Chapter 15). On the other hand, while the borderline patient has no sense of *social* reality, the objective side of symbolically determined reality presents him or her with few difficulties. The differential diagnosis with psychosis becomes a lot easier, moreover, when one assumes that the actualpathological position can occur in the psychotic structure as well.

As far as perversion is concerned, the differential diagnosis becomes simultaneously both simpler and more problematic. The simplicity has to do with the predominance of the juridical diagnostic system that today stresses the transgressive behavior in perversion. But from a clinical perspective a number of things become a lot more complex. "Splitting" can be found in perversion, too, as well as an emphasis on enactment. The chief difference has to do with the specific mechanism of defense (disavowal) and the relation toward the first and second Others (see Chapter 14).

Therapeutic Consequences

To conclude, let us examine the therapeutic consequences of the relationship with regard to the borderline patient. As this pathology leans toward the actualpathological position, psychoanalytic treatment in a classical sense is difficult, if not impossible. Symptoms, in the classical meaning of the word, are barely present. An analysis of the transference based on the case history of subject-formation is very tricky because of the ahistorical character of the actualpathological position. In this sense, the mere possibility of a transference analysis can already be considered a positive result of the treatment.

Interpretation, in the Freudian sense, has neither effect nor ground—indeed, there is scarcely any secondary processing present, because the development of significations in the Imaginary failed (see Fonagy and Target 2000). Rather, the treatment will have to focus on creating the possibility for developing a secondary elaboration, the $a \rightarrow \mathcal{S}$. The anxiety, as a reaction to the incomprehensibility of the drive, appears in its primary form and the subject literally has not "come to terms" with it. Indeed, no adequate representation was developed for it. Therapy must provide a new beginning through the therapeutic relationship, understood as a largely supportive and name-giving relationship with a security-providing Other. This implies that a significant number of the interventions have to be focused on the here and now so as to enable one to establish a later and an elsewhere, that is to say, an ability to take symbolic distance and to cope.

In a positive working alliance, the secondary elaboration can be stimulated, with the emphasis on a growing amendment of the image of the self and the Other. In a negative working alliance, the therapist must be able to contain the negative image so as to make it clear through the treatment that other options are possible. The effective goal, then, is the enlargement of the secondary elaboration and the accompanying reflective functioning.

This sounds easy. In reality it is anything but. The transferential relationship is very difficult to manage. Because of the actual pathological position, there is barely any coherent sense of identity, and it is precisely this that causes a very strong physical separation anxiety. Without the actual presence of another, the borderline patient does not exist. The inner image of the self is empty, the other is vital as the constant mirror in which patients confirm their existence. The ensuing appeal to the therapist can take on a very demanding, even compelling nature. Another outcome is the high risk of suicide, which is almost always triggered by what the patient has experienced as separation. Furthermore, the aggression can go in two directions: toward the patient him- or herself or toward the other. Freud's original theory that in a number of cases murder can be regarded as a disguised form of suicide, is illustrated by this (Fonagy and Target 2000, pp. 965–869). "Lighter" versions are physical aggression toward the subject's own body (automutilation, addiction) or toward the body of the other.

In the same strain, we encounter the effects of projective identification and enactment. There is a huge difference between this and the normal-neurotic transference where the therapist is always staged in an Imaginary scenario to which he or she can react fairly easily with the requisite abstinence. The borderline patient skips over the imaginarization and thereby comes much closer to the Real, and frequently enough to what functions in Lacanian discourse theory in the position of the truth. Time and again, the borderline patient performs miracles in the provocation of heated (counter)-transferential reactions, getting under the therapist's skin. The next step to "enactment" on the therapist's part is not all that rare.

13
The Psychopathological Position of the Subject: Hysteria and Obsessional Neurosis

PSYCHONEUROSIS AS THE *NORMAL* STRUCTURE OF THE SUBJECT

As we saw, subject-formation emerges out of the relation between the subject's own body and the Other. An originally internal, somatic drive arousal gives rise to a demand for an answer from the Other after which the processing of the Real can begin within the Symbolico-Imaginary. At the same time, both the subject and the Other acquire specific contents and an accompanying relation toward each other, and toward desire and jouissance.

$$a \to A \to S_1$$
$$\downarrow \to \mathcal{S}$$
$$S_2$$

Actualpathology has been characterized as that group of disorders where the subject remains stuck in primary development: the Other doesn't answer, or failed to answer sufficiently. As a result, the initial (un)pleasure and anxiety, together with their somatic anxiety equivalents, persist in an unelaborated form. The resulting disorder centers on somatization and anxiety, accompanied by reactive avoidance behavior.

No processing occurs in the representational order, hence the absence of a fundamental fantasy and symptoms. An important differential diagnostic effect of this is that such patients often initially address themselves to the medical clinical setting, and only later come for psychological consultation. For the characteristics and complaints of this group I have coined the term actualpathological *phenomena*, in order to distinguish them from symptoms, which as Symbolico-Imaginary constructions are secondary processings and can only appear in the psychopathological position.

When subject-formation does develop further, we encounter the psychopathological group, classically known as neurosis, perversion, and psychosis. These also begin from the actualpathological position but, because this position subsequently gets elaborated in the Symbolico-Imaginary, this group looks completely different. We can understand this elaboration as the Oedipal structuring of the relation between the subject and the Other with respect to the original anxiety and jouissance, which then acquires form in the so-called fundamental fantasy and, eventually, in the symptoms based on it. The differential diagnostic effect is that these patients usually come directly to the clinical psychological and/or psychiatric setting.

One cannot overestimate the impact of this oedipal structuring. The Other is split into a first and second Other, making a transition from the dual-Imaginary to the symbolic triangle possible. With this, gender differentiation is immediately introduced, with the result that (a) becomes phallically reworked into $(a)/-\varphi$. Consequently, the initial confrontation shifts to another level, where, rather than being confronted with the original jouissance (i.e., the drive arousal), the subject can now concentrate endlessly on desire. The advantage is that the original traumatic, automatic anxiety is processed into signal anxiety, which Freud classically called castration anxiety. This latter will need to be reconsidered, along with the way we fill in the concept of the "phallus."[1] The effects of this oedipal restructuring will now be discussed in relation to the first psychopathological structure, namely, neurosis.

---

1. See also B. Fink (1997), pp. 112–164.

From the Other to the First and Second Others

The transition from the actualpathological to the psycho(patho)logical position also pertains to normal development[2]—in the latter case, it is simply psychological development, without the pathology. Even more: it is precisely via this transition that the norm, in the sense of shared social rules, is installed. Its appearance can best be understood through Lacan's discourse theory, which is at the same time his formal rereading of the Freudian Oedipus complex. The discourse of the Hysteric gives its starting point:

$$\begin{array}{ccc} \$ & \rightarrow & S_1 \\ \uparrow & & \downarrow \\ a & // & S_2 \end{array}$$

This formula shows how the divided subject seeks an answer to (a) from the Other in the position of the master. His answer is the Master's discourse

$$\begin{array}{ccc} S_1 & \rightarrow & S_2 \\ \uparrow & & \downarrow \\ \$ & // & a \end{array}$$

where the subject is introduced into the endless signifying elaboration of (a)—endless precisely because no signifier can come up with the final answer to jouissance. This is indicated in discourse theory by the disjunction of impotence. The master's answer always rests on shared conventions about the manner in which one's own body and the body of the other is to be handled, and hence the answer is always relative to a certain time and place. Its only constancy, throughout all cultures, is the prohibition against incest and the obligation for exogamy, understood

---

2. This boils down to a reinterpretation of Freud's Oedipus complex. Through the intervention of the symbolic Name-of-the-Father, the child is able to leave the original dual-Imaginary relationship with the mother that centered around jouissance. The net result is separation and the development of a desire beyond the mother. Castration anxiety is a secondary defensive elaboration that acts as a hinge between the original anxiety about completely disappearing into the mother and later "social" anxieties. See Verhaeghe (1999b and 2001b, pp. 9–16).

as the necessity of leaving the original symbiosis and of repeating it later on in a different way with someone else.³

Discourse theory shows how the normal starting point for every subject is the hysterical position toward a master figure—an oedipal father—who is called on to intervene. Hence, for Lacan (1991 [1969–1970]), the hysterical position is at the same time synonymous with the normal position, which must be taken in its literal meaning: the acquisition of a *norm* that must be followed. Discourse theory also shows how, from this installation onward, the subject no longer needs to concentrate on defending against jouissance (the lower level of each discourse) but can safely proceed to the never-ending meanderings of desire in relation to the Other (the upper level). Nevertheless, beneath the dialectics of desire, the confrontation with jouissance remains.

What discourse theory fails to show is how the Other doubles into a first and a second Other during subject-formation. From a classically Freudian point of view, one would expect this to be the mother and father, but Lacan's theory is more complex and takes a certain distance from the patriarchal model of Freud (Lacan 1991 [1969–1970], pp. 99–167). The first Other is that of the body, the second Other is that of law and knowledge. Neither is forced to be localized in a single concrete figure: the concrete mother will make statements about both the body and the law; the same goes for the father. Nor does the first Other by definition have to be biologically female and the second Other male. What is crucial is that there is a transition from a dual relationship between a subject and one Other to a triangular structuration, enabling the subject to shift the dialectics of (a) from the first to a second Other.⁴

---

3. It is not coincidental that the Latin root of "education," *educere*, not only means "to educate," but in the first instance "to lead outside." We can even recognize the etymological origins of the master's role: *dux* means leader, "*educere*" is indeed to *lead* outside.

4. What we gain from such a formal reading of Freud's oedipal theory is immense. It implies that the oedipal structure can be applied to *every* triangular situation, regardless of the biological sex of the participants or of the particular family situation in which this occurs. Conversely, it also means that the mere real presence of three characters does not necessarily imply an oedipal structuring. Generally speaking, the specific manifestation of every triangular situation will have specific effects each time, and this applies for the *norma*l situation of a mother, a father, and a child as well.

As a result of the internal drive arousal, the subject-to-be appeals to the Other. The first Other interprets this appeal as a demand, based on her own stance toward the body, and in this way formulates an answer that contains her own desire. The implication is that from this moment onward, the subject's lack is mixed up in the desire of the first Other, and that the subject—to receive an answer to its own lack—must pass though the desire of this first Other (Lacan 1994 [1956–1957]). A simple example: the child's arousal is interpreted by the first Other as a demand for food and, as a consequence, the child not only has to eat but, based on this interpretation, is invited to interpret its own arousal as caused by a lack of food.[5] With this interpretation, the first Other expresses his or her own desire—which can never be fully verbalized—and to which the child has to submit if it is to receive an answer to its *own* drive. This means that a striking reversal takes place: in order to get an answer to its own lack, the subject has to model itself according to the Other's desire; it must identify with it. From that moment, the difference between the subject's and the Other's desire becomes blurred: "The desire of the subject is the desire of the Other." Furthermore, both the subject and the Other have to *interpret* this desire; the demand can never fully express desire because of the incompatibility between the Real and the signifier.

Every answer will be inadequate, and there will always be a remainder. This in turn gives rise to the displacement of this demand onto the second Other who is assumed to possess the answer—all the more so because the first Other's desire is ordinarily directed toward this second Other, that is to say, beyond the child. The first Other's referral to a third point thus breaks through the dual situation where the child had to be everything for the Other and vice versa. In the oedipal constellation, this second Other is assigned the position of the one who is supposed to know and who must therefore have the answer. From this period onward, the underlying drive tension acquires a

---

5. In reality, this simple example is almost always more complex. The mother can interpret the child's cry as anger, rejection, as proof of her own failure as a mother. Her position toward her identity as a mother, in relation to her own mother and father and her actual partner, is decisive here. It is precisely this aspect—the mother's mirroring of what the child experiences but cannot verbalize—that is at the heart of contemporary attachment theory as well.

more specific character, that is to say, it becomes introduced into the dialectics of desire between two others of different genders.[6] Such a differentiation is based on the phallic signifier, which causes a retroactive "phallicization," that is, a phallic interpretation of the object (*a*).[7] In schematic form:

$$a \to A \to A_1 \to \frac{a}{-\varphi} \to A_2 \to S_1$$
$$\downarrow \to \$$$
$$S_2$$

From Traumatic Jouissance (*a*) and Automatic Anxiety to Phallic Pleasure (*a*)/–φ and Signal Anxiety

The child's original drive tension can be characterized by the specific needs arising out of the interaction between the organism and the outside world, with the emphasis on the oral and the anal. The first Other's reaction introduces these component drives into the dialectic of desire and adds two other component drives from then on: the scopic and the invocative drives.[8] Besides the oral and the anal, the eye and

---

6. Here, too, we must introduce Lacan's important correction of Freud, specifically, the Freudian biological interpretation of gender. For Lacan, gender implies the position chosen by the subject toward the phallic signifier (Lacan 1998 [1972–1973]). A biological woman may take the masculine position and vice versa. This is why it is possible to have a difference in gender within a couple with the same biological sex. It is striking how in contemporary research, despite the generally accepted difference between sex and gender, research populations and matched control groups are still composed solely on the basis of sex, thus introducing a considerable bias. Admittedly, composing them on the basis of gender would be a lot more difficult. But so is reality.

7. By "phallicization" I mean that, from the oedipal period onward, the earlier drive tensions that went back to the component drives are now rewritten in a phallic way, combining the oral with the phallic, for example. This may seem like a new Lacanian concept, but in fact it isn't. See Freud (1978 [1906a], p. 278, and 1978 [1905d], p. 166). What Lacan added is the idea of making "genital" synonymous with "phallic"—but even this is not new since it can also be found in Freud.

8. These drives are "component" in view of an assumed total-genital drive to which they are submitted after genital maturity. For both Freud and Lacan, such a total genital drive is an illusion; adult sexual life remains marked by the pregenital, albeit under a phallic flag.

the ear will acquire their specific pathways based on the Other's desire, which will always color these with particular emphases. This will determine the form of the subject's drive life, by way of his or her identification with the desire of the Other (Lacan 1994 [1964]).

The first Other will never be able to provide a total answer to the subject's demand, just as the subject will never be able to fully coincide with the first Other's desire. The ball is then passed to the second Other in the expectation of its answer. In this way, gender differentiation is introduced: this second Other is supposed to have the answer to desire. In Lacanian terms: this second Other is clothed with the phallic signifier.

The term "phallus" is central here, signalling the difference between Lacan and the biological, Freudian interpretation of gender difference. The phallus is a signifier for gender difference, which is founded upon biology but at the same time supersedes it (Lacan 1977 [1958b]).[9] As a signifier, the phallus is essentially empty, or meaningless, with one exception: it is the signifier that marks the difference between the two genders, in the sense that what one possesses or is, as far as sexuation is concerned, is supposed to be an answer to the other's lack. Clinically, this is found in the perpetually shifting meanings attributed to the other in the expectation that this other has the answer to sexualized desire.

The consequences are far reaching. The original jouissance becomes phallicized, that is to say, the pregenital drives acquire a phallic meaning that will remain in place (Freud 1978 [1906a], p. 278; [1905d], p. 166). In general terms, here we find the oral, anal, scopic, and invocative sexuality. The Freudo-Lacanian addition of "phallic" indicates the

---

9. As a signifier, the phallus can be handled Imaginarily or Symbolically. An Imaginary handling implies a meaning fixation. This is the case for every symptom (in the psychoanalytic sense of the word); as the phallus is essentially empty, this fixed Imaginary meaning is hidden and unknown—hence the characteristic neurotic belief that the symptom has meaning, although of what is not clear. Handled Symbolically, the emphasis is on the lack and the accompanying possibilities for meaning displacements, thus opening a window toward creativity. Hence the aim of psychoanalytic interpretation: not to reveal the hidden meaning (for that would be an endorsement of the Imaginary), but to free the symptomatic signifier from its fixation, thus making the normal game of perpetually shifting signifiers and creativity possible again.

central position of the phallic signifier in the process of sexuation.[10] Oral-phallic sexuality is well known in hysteria; obsessional neurosis is typified by anal-phallic; scopic-phallic is quite common in perversion; while the invocative-phallic colors all of them. In addition, it should be emphasized that these are not exclusive relations: any phallicized partial drive can appear in any psychopathological structure, although in each certain ones will usually be preponderant.

Such a phallic rewriting of the original jouissance implies an attribution of meaning to the Real of (*a*), bringing us immediately into the order of the Imaginary. Insofar as this rewriting is limited to the Imaginary, we encounter a typical psychoneurotic illusion: there is a single Other who possesses the perfect phallic answer that would completely satisfy my desire. All one needs to do is to find the right lover, the correct relation, the perfect (sexual) position, and the Sunday of Life will begin. In reality, however, one confronts a perpetual displacement: it concerns, after all, the phallic *signifier*; the complete filling out of desire is therefore impossible. The assumption of this structural impossibility and its accompanying loss of being is what Lacan calls symbolic castration, which immediately opens up the possibility of choice. This is Lacan's reading of the Freudian concept of sublimation, based on the symbolic order (De Kesel 2002).

The advantage of this rewriting lies in the fact that the subject no longer must directly confront its own drive tension. From this moment on, it is a mediated confrontation between the signifier and the Other. The original, automatic anxiety is processed and dispersed through the displacement of the associative exchanges with the Other at the level of desire. Within the associative network, certain signifiers may acquire the function of referring to the original underlying anxiety and as such become anxiety-loaded themselves. This anxiety—known as "signal anxiety"—is clinically far less intense than the original anxiety, precisely because of its association with signifiers. In this way, an active

---

10. The phallic signifier is the basic signifier for Lacan because it introduces basic difference (masculine/feminine). As such, the phallus grounds the Symbolic order precisely because of the way this order is founded on difference (de Saussure 1976). This can be shown through a simple empirical observation: *anything* in language can have a phallic-sexual meaning, hence the essential equivocalness of all speech.

coping possibility is opened up for the subject, which was precisely what was missing from the direct confrontation with jouissance.

For Freud, this is the evolution of automatic, traumatic anxiety into "castration anxiety," whose female variation is penis envy and anxiety about losing the other's love. His reading must be amended on at least three points. The first concerns the phallic signifier. The second is the sexual specificity of his account, which must be extended to a broader gender identity. And third, the anxiety is not just about a loss, but equally about a surplus.

On the basis of our metapsychology, we can say that here the traumatic anxiety of the confrontation with the Real of (a) becomes displaced into an anxiety about the phallic desire of the Other. We can make out two distinct possibilities: anxiety about being unable to answer the desire of the Other, or of being unable to satisfy it sufficiently, along with its opposite, anxiety about satisfying this desire only too well.

The first (predominantly hysterical) form is the one most closely connected to classical "castration anxiety": the subject feels itself phallically falling short in relation to the other, and must constantly remain on his tippy toes to come up with "it." This "it" is originally situated in the parent–child relationship, later in the gender relation, and is therefore precisely signified in a phallic way. As a signifier, "it" can mean just about *anything*, beyond as well as within the narrowly sexual field. Popular forms of it range from "fear of failure" to "inferiority complexes." The "fear of losing the other's love" is closely connected with these. Alongside it, we find "penis envy," the subject's jealous conviction that a third party does have the correct phallic answer. These three forms are not specific for any one gender and can be found in both men and women.

The second form received much less attention from Freud, a situation that has to do with the preponderance of hysteria in his theory. The anxiety about oversatisfying the phallic desire of the other is typical for obsessional neurosis, but can be recognized in perversion and psychosis as well, resulting in precisely the opposite situation. In this case, the subject needs a barrier between him- or herself and the other in order to avoid being reduced merely to the object of this other. Clinically, this is where we find a strange combination of anxiety about success and narcissistic feelings of superiority. An important form of this combination is the obsessional neurotic inhibition, where the movement toward the other is arrested (Vanheule 2001d).

Such a translation of the original traumatic anxiety into phallic terms causes an endless displacement, both in the objects of anxiety and of satisfaction—the difference between the two frequently being fairly minimal. The initial advantage for the subject is further filled out with a second, namely, in the way guilt is handled. In the primary relationship between the subject and the as yet undifferentiated Other, one of them must take *respons*ibility. In the case of actualneurosis, this falls entirely on the shoulders—more precisely, on the body—of the subject itself. In cases of psychopathology, the responsibility for desire can be passed on from the subject to the first Other and then onto the second Other. As a result, this leads to the quintessentially human ping-pong game of guilt and lack, the endless nature of which produces nothing but misery at first sight. But this is not the whole truth, because one tends to forget that such a displacement in itself is a defensive answer to the underlying problem. As long as the subject can concentrate on the dialectics of desire and guilt, it can maintain some distance from a confrontation with the Real and jouissance. The principal way of keeping this distance is to argue about who is to blame.

In connection with this, we must direct our attention to an important consequence of the transition from the dual to the triangular dialectic. The opening that is created as a result of separation (every signifier coming from the Other has to be interpreted) has the consequence that the subject is able to distance itself from alienation and to reflect: this is why alienation is never total. Clinically, this finds expression in the way the subject, even during acute psychopathological states, is always able to take its distance from this state and can look at it—at him or herself, that is—from the "outside" as it were. In diagnostic terms, this is regarded as insight into the illness, usually combined with a sense of guilt. In practice, this comes down to a consciousness of the effect of alienation, resulting in the subject's own self-accusation that his or her pathology is not real or genuine.[11]

---

11. This is not limited to psychoneurosis, moreover. The same phenomenon can be seen in the psychotic structure, where the psychotic subject may also show a certain insight into the illness. The difference is that in psychosis the part originating in the Other through the alienation is not considered a part of the subject, but is expe-

Division of the Subject, the Fundamental Fantasy, and Symptoms

The Other's division into the first and second Others is not without consequences for subject-formation. The previously discussed alienation-separation process follows the same division. The subject acquires an identity and an accompanying division both at the level of the body (the first Other) and at the level of knowledge and authority (the second Other). How this first Other answered his or her own desire determines both the content of its gender identity and—more broadly—how the subject relates to jouissance. This forms the basis of the Ego-Ideal, and is how the subject must see itself in the mirror. That the reactions of the Other are determining in this respect is fairly well known, starting from small remarks ("You have to comb your hair") to global judgments or convictions ("You look like a whore" or "you're so beautiful"). The same goes for the subject's relation toward the law and authority. From a classical point of view, here we find the formation of the superego. In fact, this can barely be distinguished from the above; Ego-Ideal and superego continuously run through one other, just like the subject's position toward jouissance and the law.

In this way, both gender and generational identities are formed through the flywheel movement of alienation and separation. Both gender and generational identity will be the points where a potential later psychopathology will break through. This is well known in clinical praxis: both the confrontation with sexuality and with generation are privileged points for psychopathological breakdown. To become a "man" or a "woman," to become a "father" or "mother" is not always a self-evident process.

The fact that a breakdown may take place precisely at these points has to do with a typical characteristic of subject-formation, namely, division as a result of conflict. The Other's messages about sexuality and authority are never unidimensional; on the contrary, they will

---

rienced as coming from the outside in an intrusive manner. Classical psychiatry called this "xenopathic." The psychoneurotic subject, on the other hand, regards a number of contents (often the most pathological ones) as strange and senseless, but nevertheless as forming part of its own subjectivity and therefore as coming from the "inside." This can only be understood in light of the intermingling of inside and outside during subject-formation.

always contain inner contradictions. This is even more true when the messages come from two Others. As a result, the subject-to-be has to choose which part of the story (narrative identity) to identify with and which part to reject. The basis of such a choice always confronts the child with the perpetually impossible question: "Who do you love best, Mommy or Daddy?" The result is an internal division that is associatively hooked onto certain signifiers and which, when these signifiers are reactivated, will be evoked. Clinical practice is full of examples of this.

A clinical fragment: an adult woman breaks down when her mother dies. This is not a normal mourning process because anxiety predominates and there are serious repercussions in the way she experiences her female identity. The background history reveals that she grew up in a family where her Don Juan–like father called her first "the princess," then later regarded her as a sexually attractive woman, while simultaneously rejecting his wife, her mother, as a domestic drudge. As an adult, she chooses a househusband for a partner and macho men for lovers. At the moment of her mother's death, she is forced to take responsibility for her younger brother, meaning that she has to take on the motherly position. The self-division leaps massively into the foreground and can no longer be managed through the construction of a symptom, hence the overflow of anxiety and depression.

This division is located at the level of desire, in the relationship between the subject–first Other and subject–second Other. Below it, however, yet another division is at work, namely, the ever-present dualism of the drive (see Chapter 9). The Eros drive tends toward symbiosis and therefore to alienation and identification. The Thanatos drive tends toward disintegration and therefore to separation and expulsion. The two tendencies are always at work at the same time, with the result that every choice the subject makes in this respect will be structurally countered by the other tendency. Consequently, the drive never reaches definitive satisfaction.

The solution for this division lies in the construction of a fundamental fantasy that may or may not be accompanied by symptoms built on top of it. A *fundamental fantasy* is a lasting, representational construction, a particular theory of the mind by which the structural relationship between the subject and the Other is delineated with regard to desire, and through which both the subject's and the Other's identities are determined. Its general formula is: $S \lozenge (a) \lozenge A$. We will shortly examine its specific manifestation in hysteria and obsessional neurosis. In any case, each fundamental fantasy contains a distinction at the level of gender and generational identity that signifies the subject's respective positions toward the body and jouissance (the first Other), and toward knowledge and authority (the second Other). This implies that the fundamental fantasy is an Imaginary construction at those precarious points of the Real for which the Symbolic has no definitive answer. Lacan summarized these points in what appear to be three slogans: "The Woman does not exist," "The Other of the Other does not exist," "The Sexual Relationship does not exist." Their inner logic can be understood as follows. In the Symbolic, there is no final form of gender differentiation; the distinction is made on the basis of just one signifier (the phallus), making female identity precarious. This absence of a final Symbolic form in its turn has to do with the lack of an ultimate authority; indeed, the Symbolic order is based on normative conventions that can always be put into question. As a result, the relation between the different gender identities cannot be conclusively symbolized either. The denial in the three formulas is explicitly connected to the definite article, "The," indicating that the one-and-only (woman, authority, sexual relationship) does not exist.

The fundamental fantasy is constructed in and through the first concrete relationships toward the first and second Others. It forms the basis for all later relationships, where it will be repeated with other others. This is nothing but Freud's theory of the transference as a general phenomenon. With Lacan (1994 [1964]) we must underline here how this repetition always brings with it the possibility for change. This is why both the diagnosis and the treatment must focus on it.

Freud already stated that symptoms are always based on underlying primal fantasies (in his terms, infantile-sexual theories) (Freud 1978 [1905d], p. 226; see also Verhaeghe 1999b, pp. 160–166). Such symptoms are constructions in the signifier, and therefore can be analyzed. Classic examples are slips of the tongue and mistaken actions in general, dreams (with the exception of traumatic dreams), conversion symptoms, phobias inside the psychoneurotic structure, delusions and hallucinations, obsessional thoughts and acts. Symptoms such as these should never be studied, diagnosed, or treated in isolation; they acquire their meaning and function only in the light of the accompanying position of the subject toward the Other, based on the fundamental fantasy (Declercq 2002). The symptom's goal is always the same: it tries to cope with the anxiety by avoiding the underlying division. In this way, symptoms enable the subject to avoid making a choice, which is quite typical of psychopathology.

Incidentally, symptoms don't necessarily have to be present in the structural relationship the subject builds in relation to the Other. Reich (1949), following Freud (1978 [1916d] and [1931a]) already talked about character pathology, which reappears in today's so-called personality disorders. In these, the relationship itself is pathological and it is the division that comes to the fore—meaning that the fundamental fantasy failed to make the internal division manageable.

Alongside these symptomless character pathologies or personality disorders, we must consider another nonsymptomatic variation: depression. As I said above (see Chapter 10), depression indicates that state where the subject has fallen out of the flywheel movement of alienation and separation and defines itself as "nothing" in the relation toward the Other. This is not to say that both its point of onset and its form of appearance will not be determined by the preceding structural relation of a particular subject toward the Other. There will therefore be a differential diagnostic distinction to be made between hysterical, obsessional neurotic, perverse, and psychotic depressions.

THE HYSTERIC'S RELATION TOWARD THE OTHER AND $\frac{a}{-\varphi}$

You won't find hysterical neurosis per se in the DSM categorization. This can be partially explained by the negative halo surrounding it and the feminist reaction to it (Herman 1992b). Yet there is another more important reason for its disappearance. The inconsistency of hysterical phenomena led a number of researchers to the conviction that it did not exist (Verhaeghe 1999b, pp. 77–95). This is one more illustration of the need of a theory to make something visible. By reason of its very structure, hysteria cannot be captured in merely descriptive terms. I will argue that, despite the variety of its characteristics, the hysterical structure as such remains consistent.

Like every psychopathology, hysteria comes down to a certain structural relationship between the first and second Others with regard to desire. Within this relationship, a number of variable characteristics and/or symptoms can find their place, *whose content and form are entirely determined by the specific way the Other appears*. Consequently, these characteristics and/or symptoms will always obtain their function and/or meaning from this relationship. This can generally be characterized by dependence, a tendency toward identification and conflict avoidance, and so on. Such a characterization is insufficient and fails to make a differential diagnostic distinction, for example, between this and the still to be discussed obsessional structure.

Hysteria's external manifestation is determined by the specific way the Other is colored by the subject, which lends hysteria a chameleon-like appearance. A concentration on the color alone has led to this invariant structure being spread over a number of different categories. In the latest version of the DSM, hysteria is found variously under the headings of conversion disorder (300.11), specific phobia (300.29), and the sexual dysfunctions (302.xx). Its relational aspect appears in the larger group of relational disorders and more specifically in the category of factitious disorders. The best description is found in the histrionic personality disorder (301.50) and the dependent personality disorder (301.6), provided that the descriptions are combined.

Nevertheless, collating all this together doesn't produce a description of the hysterical structure; moreover, it could leave us with the illusion that hysteria can be grasped merely through descriptive characteristics. *This is not so*: *any* symptom or characteristic can be exhibited by the hysteric subject depending on the particular Other on duty. A study of the history of psychopathology will show that hysteria's particular form of appearance depends on the reigning discourse of a specific period. During Charcot's time, in the reigning days of epilepsy, the hysterical patient produced hysterical attacks, thus creating certain difficulties for a differential diagnosis with epilepsy. In the heyday of schizophrenia, hysteria presented a psychotic picture, resulting in different differential diagnostic problems. Today (just as in Freud's early days), the idea of PTSD is omnipresent and there, too, hysteria awaits us either in the form of a victim or a witness. Still earlier in history, before the birth of science, it is easy to see how hysteria directed itself to the reigning discourse of the time, that is, the religious one, and produced "symptoms" in line with that discourse, from saints to witches.[12]

The DSM's "factitious" disorder is a far too pallid description of what it's really about. Imitation connotes the idea of a conscious simulation, even trickery. This certainly does happen, particularly in the context of insurance policies. Nevertheless hysteria per se extends a lot further than mere imitation as we will see in the following section.

Hysteria and Subject-formation: Incorporation, Identification, Alienation

Freud repeatedly stressed hysteria's oral component as its characteristic drive fixation (Freud 1978 [1905e]). For Freud, this had to do with constitutional factors, although it is difficult to separate the impact of these from nurturing factors. The connection with the initial process of subject-formation is not hard to see: incorporation, identification, and alienation will be far more in evidence than separation.[13] The tendency toward the latter nevertheless remains surreptitiously present, and will therefore form the basis of the division. However, the alienation aspect continues to have the upper hand, hence the hysterical subject's associated awareness of being a fake, which is also how others frequently experience it—recall the theatrical, histrionic character combined with emotional instability mentioned in practically every study.

---

12. The evolution of almost all of these forms of the appearance of hysteria is captivatingly described by Veith (1965), beginning with incidents described in Egyptian papyrus rolls and ending in the middle of last century. Nevertheless, her conclusion is disappointing, because she assumes that hysteria has "disappeared" today, that is to say, she fails to rediscover the forms she has just described. Despite her comprehensive study, Veith appears incapable of understanding that hysteria's different forms of appearance each time occur on top of an unchanging structural relationship, as can be proven by her own research (see Verhaeghe 1999b).

13. Still in the Freudian line of reasoning, this preponderance of the oral drive component and its accompanying incorporation/identification implies that hysteria is dominated by the Eros drive, with its propensity toward fusion and symbiosis. Hence, too, the fact that hysteria is well known for its suggestibility, especially as regards sexuality and gender, although its relation toward knowledge and gender is also typical.

As in every psychoneurosis, there is a preceding actualpathological position. Freud described the latter as "*Schreckhysteria*," that is, a panic attack in confrontation with a "psychic lack" (see Chapter 7). Its connection with the previously described anxiety neurosis is quite clear. Hysteria starts out from this but proceeds onto a processing of the signifiers, whose classical effects are phobic and/or conversion hysteria. In this way, the original drive component becomes phallicized: instead of (a), we encounter $(a)/-\varphi$, the oral phallus, in psychoanalytic jargon. Put in more general psychological terms, this is an oral and above all dependent sexuality. This can be understood in both the particular and the more general senses of the word oral. Freud (1978 [1905e]) found that a number of Dora's conversion symptoms (nausea, tussis nervosa) went back to her repressed fantasies of fellatio and cunnilingus in the game of love between her father and his mistress, fantasies, moreover, that centered around her father's impotence. In the wider sense of the word, here we encounter the phallus as an empty signifier: the hysterical subject drinks everything in from the Other, particularly the signifiers for desire, knowledge, and authority.

It is this mechanism in the relationship toward authority in particular that makes diagnosis simultaneously so difficult and so easy. In and through such a transferential relationship, the therapist is transformed into a Master and a subject-supposed-to-know, with the result that the hysterical subject identifies with those symptoms she or he believes the Other is expecting. This was empirically demonstrated by Shoenberg (1975): patients who, in the course of the treatment, were obliged to exchange their medical therapist for a psychotherapist also changed their symptoms accordingly (see also Verhaeghe 1999b). Lacan rightly observes how hysterical patients will produce hysterical attacks and memories of traumatic antecedents in vast quantities if that's what the therapist is crazy about.[14]

---

14. "How convincing the process of remembering was with the first hysterics! But what is at issue in this remembering could not be known at the outset—one did not know that the desire of the hysteric was the desire of the father, to be sustained in his status. It was hardly surprising that, for the benefit of him who takes the place of the father, one remembered things right down the dregs" (Lacan 1994 [1964], pp. 49–50). I leave the applicability of "false memory syndrome" to the reader's own resources.

The first component of the subject-formation process is thus repeated time after time in hysteria: identification with the Other's desire. The fact that this forms part of subject-formation means that it extends beyond mere imitation or simulation. To understand it, we must examine its oedipal history, the repetition of which comprises the later hysterical structure.

The Oedipal History of Hysteria

From the outset of its official status as a psychopathology and continuing today, hysteria has always been associated with unpleasure, trauma, and seduction (Charcot, Freud), if also with controversy ("repressed memory theory" versus "false memory movement"). Both these associations and their accompanying controversies can be understood in the light of hysteria's oedipal background.

In psychoneurosis, the subject expects to get an answer to the tension of its drive from the Other, with the result that the subject identifies with the Other's desire. In hysteria, this general process takes on its particular form by the way the Other reacts and/or how the subject interprets this reaction.[15] The message the hysterical subject-to-be hears—or thinks it hears—is in short: "You are inadequate, you do not satisfy my desire." The result is that the identification/alienation process is reinforced, that is, the subject further identifies with the signifiers of the Other's desire in a desperate attempt to satisfy it. Turning to the second Other also fails to provide an answer because this second Other either invalidates himself or is invalidated by the first Other: "Your father isn't good enough either. He doesn't know the right answer." At the same time, this first Other sends the message that surely there must be someone, somewhere, who can provide a satisfying answer. From a psychoanalytic perspective, this means that neither the father's phallus nor identification with it suffice as answers to the desire of the mother. The result is that the hysterical subject must continue to look for an other Other, someone who can give the right answer.

---

15. It is important to stress this aspect of interpretation in the hysterical subject. Hysteria, or even more broadly, psychoneurosis, always includes the impact of the patient him- or herself, and can never be fully accounted for by the Other.

Such a double message is directly translated into hysterical subject-formation, particularly with regard to the position toward sexuality and authority. Let us take these separately.

In later adult relations, the hysterical subject is convinced that it will never be enough for the sexual partner or, more broadly, for others in general, resulting in its never-ending attempts to satisfy them. In masculine hysteria, this leads to the characteristic "Guinness Book of Records"-type hysteria—and, in a more restricted, sexual sense, to Viagra.[16] In female hysteria, we encounter the "Miss World"–hysteria, eventually accompanied by excesses in plastic surgery. In the wider sense, we find a propensity for following the desires of her partner(s) that can be quite extensive. The masculine version tries hard to *have* the phallus, the feminine version to *be* the phallus, each in relation to an Other who is felt to be unsatisfiable. Precisely for this reason, the hysterical subject will go to extremes to identify with the presumed desire of the Other. Relational life is thereby turned into a never-ending search for someone for whom one will be good enough, someone who will love the subject despite his or her defaults. Essentially, this means that every hysterical subject, whether male or female, searches for the mother in the partner, but the mother in an unconditionally loving version. When such a partner is found, the hysterical subject will never believe it: "Anyone who loves me either doesn't mean it, or is an idiot, and therefore not worth the trouble," thus setting the vicious cycle back in motion. At the same time, the hysterical subject will set up a third figure, an external model and rival it looks up to full of both jealousy and admiration, because he or she does have "it" and is therefore supposed to have "The" answer to the desire of the Other.[17] This brings us to the second relation, toward authority and knowledge.

The positions the hysterical subject takes toward the subsequent replacements of the second Other are also entirely determined by the

---

16. The use of Viagra in itself shows the distance between the penis and the phallus. The penis in itself will never be enough to satisfy the Other's desire and in that sense belongs to the series of partial and phallicized objects. The aim of the hysterical subject is to be loved "totally" by the Other—and the problem lies in the impossibility of this totality.

17. For Dora, this is her father's love, Frau K., and the Madonna of Dresden (Freud 1978 [1905e]). The same triple structure can be seen just as easily in male hysteria.

oedipal history. The hysterical subject goes looking for a master figure who knows "it" and from whom she or he can appropriate this "it." This is familiar from the Lacanian discourse theory, more specifically, from the relation between the Hysterical and the Master discourses (Lacan 1991 [1969–1970]). Such a search is nevertheless always encumbered by the ever-present doubt whether the current master-in-charge is not going to fail too, and of course, sooner or later this will occur. At that point, the relationship is ended and the search for another master figure begins anew ("The king is dead, long live the king!").[18] While the master is accepted as a master, the hysterical subject will fully adopt his signifiers and thus change color. Those signifiers will always touch the delicate points: "the" psychosexual identity, "the" authority, and "the" sexual relationship. Hence the hysterical subject's affinity for everything that tends toward gurus and sects, as these formulate their oracles precisely on these points.

Such adoption goes far beyond mere imitation; at that point it forms part of the subject-formation itself. Hence Freud's remark (1978 [1921c]) that the ego can be analyzed as a multilayered structure, each of whose layers contains an identification with a previous object, be it in matters of love or in matters of authority, or a combination of both. Applied to the psychopathological manifestation, this implies that when hysterical subjects direct themselves as a group to a certain authority (whether religious, medical, psychological, or psychoanalytic), they will model their symptoms according to what they think that particular authority wants.[19] Consequently, the master-in-charge finds the confirmation of his own theory in what is in front of him—indeed, he gets back what he himself sent out. Any potential later divergence from this, once the hysterical subject has been disappointed and leaves this par-

---

18. There is also another possible hysterical solution: identification with the master himself, that is to say, not just limited to his desire. This always results in caricatures, aptly described by Descartes (1968, p. 85) in his "Discourse on Method": "They are like the ivy which does not seek to climb higher than the trees which support it, and which even often comes down again after reaching the top."

19. This can literally be seen when a group of hysterical subjects focus on the same master figure. As a group, they share the same identification/alienation (Freud 1978 [1921c]), causing them to resemble each other in clothing, bodily adornments, and—especially—language, each time boiling down to a shared attitude toward sexuality and authority.

ticular master, is usually rationalized on ideological grounds, thus enabling the master to remain in his conviction of being the One and Only.

The relation between the hysterical structure and unpleasure, potentially trauma, is built into the Oedipal starting point as a result, together with the ensuing debate about its "genuineness." Not being good enough for the first Other is unpleasurable, even traumatic, and sets up a continuing propensity for identification with the Other. The relation with seduction that is classically assumed is not yet clear, nor the link with gender. This will be my next point.

Relation to Gender, Seduction, and Trauma

Hysteria was classically considered a female complaint, one that presupposed an essential relation between women and hysteria.[20] To my mind, this is merely an historical artifact, rooted in age-old patriarchal dominance. One of the primary effects of this dominance is that it obliged women to take the *passive* position toward the Other's desire, and it is precisely this that lies at the base of the hysterical structure. Today, at least in the Western world, patriarchy has lost much of its power, resulting in a reversal: since *eman*cipation, many men have been forced to position themselves passively in their relation to the Other, making the hysterical structure a reality for them, too.[21]

Consequently, the connection between gender and hysteria is only indirect; the true relation lies between the hysterical structure and the need to take a passive stance toward the Other. It is this passive position—in earlier jargon, the "dropsical" position—that is central, and it can be assumed by both men and women. Still, classically speaking, one would expect the hysterical man to search for the woman/mother

---

20. Moreover, this kind of reasoning assumes an analogy between biological sex and gender. In Seminar XX, Lacan elaborated a structurally-based gender difference, based on the relationship between the subject, (*a*) and the phallus (Lacan 1998 [1972–1973]). Based on this, one must conclude that hysteria is situated on the masculine side of the formulas of sexuation.

21. In general, one can say that it is the passive stance toward the Other, particularly as far as sexuality is concerned, that is the most frightening and the cause of much defensive behavior (Verhaeghe 2000b).

who will finally love him unconditionally, and the hysterical woman to search for the man/father who possesses and can provide The Answer. From my perspective, both scenarios can easily be interchanged, meaning that it is better to speak in terms of the hysterical *subject*, without associating this subject specifically with any one gender.

Futhermore, "passive" must be understood properly: a hysterical subject may very well act in extremely active ways to realize the passive position. The activity is directed toward the process of identification with the desire of the Other. At this point, we encounter another classical characteristic and problem: seduction.

Hysterical patients are often generally accused of overerotizing and seducing their environment, and their therapists in particular. Conversely, the hysterical patient frequently accuses the other of seduction, making the differential diagnosis of PTSD problematic. This ambiguity becomes understandable in light of the subject's identification with the Other's desire sketched out above. The hysterical subject identifies with the Other's phallic desire, which frequently creates the impression in the other party that she or he has been offered a sexual invitation. Should this other accept this "offer," she or he will frequently encounter rejection. Indeed, the hysterical subject is convinced that she or he is unable to answer the desire of the other and if there is one thing the hysterical subject wants to avoid, it is to confront failure in this. To lay oneself open, both literally and figuratively, is too great a risk. This is why the hysteric will withdraw, usually at the very last moment, resulting in the other's requisite frustration that ends with the classic indictment ("prick tease!"). When seduction is followed through with action, the hysterical subject will almost always experience this as unpleasurable, even traumatic. Hence the mutual accusations: Who seduced whom? The hysterical subject who, through identification with the other's desire, emitted certain signals? Or the other, who responded to these signals? This is the classic ping-pong game of guilt and responsibility.

In addition, this orientation toward the Other's desire explains another distinguishing feature of hysteria. The hysterical subject is very much conflict-avoidant—the Other must be pleased—and it is precisely for this reason that the hysterical subject will cause a considerable number of conflicts. In trying to satisfy all the desires of all the important others so as to be loved, one soon finds oneself in the most unimaginable difficulties and conflicts. Thus we come across another classic charge: the hysterical subject is manipulative, a fake, a hypocrite, swinging in the wind depending on which master is on duty. This is nothing but a consequence of the symptom's ultimate goal in the fundamental fantasy: "Don't choose. Reconcile."

Hysterical Fundamental Fantasy and Symptom Formation

It is well known that fantasies and daydreaming lie at the heart of neurosis. But by the term "fundamental fantasy" I am referring to the underlying structure that has no specific content in itself. The general formula of the fundamental fantasy above, understood as the structural relationship between the subject and the phallicized desire of the Other, acquires a more specific form in the hysterical fantasy that illustrates the predominance of identification/alienation (Lacan 1991 [1960–1961], pp. 288–291). To put it schematically:

$$\frac{a}{-\varphi} \diamond A$$

Identifying with its perception of the Other's phallic desire, the hysterical subject assumes the position of $(a)/-\varphi$ in an attempt to complete the Other, to fill in its lack; hence the notation A and not divided $\bar{A}$. Through filling in the Other's lack and desire, the hysterical subject aims to cope with the anxiety of its own underlying drive tension (a). In its relation towards the first Other, this comes down to an identification with the Other's sexual identity and position toward phallic pleasure. In its relation to the second Other, it is a question of identifying with the Other's knowledge and authority concerning knowledge of jouissance. At the same time, the conviction holds that one will never be up to it, which then appears in the underlying fear of being rejected by the Other, the "Can he lose me?" (Lacan 1994 [1964], p. 214).

This basic structure determines its typical manifestation through two seemingly contradictory characteristics. On one side, we find the famous hysterical self-sacrifice, on the other, its "revendication."[22]

---

22. Revendication (Latin: *rei vindicatio*, the reclamation of a thing; *vindicare*: to claim rightfully): the legal act of reclaiming something to which one feels entitled. (Lacan 1966 [1959], p. 716).

Sacrificing oneself for the Other('s desire) is a direct result of the fundamental fantasy. The formula itself already shows how the subject barely establishes an existence of its own; everything happens as a result of the other.[23] On the basis of its oedipal history, the hysterical subject heads in search of a sick, possibly injured, maltreated other (see the father figure) so as to restore him. Lacan talks about the hysterical preference for "former fathers," "fathers off-duty," "fathers who are has-beens" (Lacan 1991 [1969–1970], p. 108 ff.). In conjunction with this, a second characteristic enters in: the revendication. Once the other has been restored and installed as a master, he is expected to produce, to provide The Answer; the hysterical subject not only expects this, but mandates it. The moment the master ultimately fails, we come across another typically hysterical complaint: despite all of the subject's efforts, the Other wasn't able to fulfill his duty; he must therefore be removed from his pedestal.

This structure and its accompanying phenomena are to be found in every hysterical patient, in daydreams and in symptoms, as—more broadly—in the choice of partner and profession. The exemplary case of this is the first modern case study, Anna O. (Bertha Pappenheim), who was also the very first patient to be treated by psychotherapy (Freud and Breuer 1978 [1895d]). She called her daydreaming her "private theatre" and even wrote a number of stories that were subsequently published. The theme is very telling: the main character is a man who is living in the deepest misery because his wife has left him. The story ends happily when his apparently lost daughter returns and informs him that his wife (her mother) has died. She gives him back his lust for life and everyone lives happily ever after.[24] Bertha Pappenheim also gave her fundamental fantasy realization in her life: regarded as the first social worker, she devoted her entire life to the

---

23. The connection between the hysterical structure and the larger social sector is well known and not without consequences for the way this sector functions.

24. For a more extensive discussion, see Verhaeghe (1999b) and Freeman (1977). The same themes are also found in her plays. Moreover, these plays—dating from a later period in her life—represent the second act of the hysterical drama, that is, her disappointment when she realizes that the second Other (the father-master) is not up to the task either, with the result that she dismisses him and turns back to the first Other, her mother.

underprivileged, particularly those who had been abused by the Other (unmarried mothers, prostitutes, those in slavery).

By way of its fundamental fantasy, the hysterical subject more or less manages to solve its inner self-division. The same thing can be said of the hysterical symptoms that are always formed on top of the fundamental fantasy and whose explicit aim is to avoid conflict. This can be best understood by examining the typical defense mechanism of hysteria, repression. Freud's original description places too much emphasis on what disappears, and not enough on what appears in its place. As described above (see Chapter 7), the process of repression always implies a double movement: something is pushed away (because of unpleasure), and something with which the subject identifies is put in its place. Repression and the return of the repressed are the one and the same process. Its operational mechanism is condensation (Freud) or metaphor (Lacan), thus bringing together two opposed elements in one, the latter becoming the expression of two internally opposing meanings.

The hysterical relation toward the Other determines at the same time how the hysterical subject will position itself in language, and this is determined precisely by repression and its affiliated trope, metaphor. The hysterical subject has a "normal" way of being in language: everything is linked up associatively; certain signifiers are forgotten because they are too heavily freighted, while others take on a certain weight and meaning from elsewhere. The hysterical subject's entire speech, moreover, foregrounds the lack, and its accompanying doubt about whether "it" can be said.

This condensation of opposing contents is a typical characteristic of hysterical symptom construction, and explains at the same time why every hysterical symptom contains its own failure.[25] Not only does the patient try to answer the opposing desires of various others (the subject's self-conflict within its narrative identity) by way of the symptom and condensation, the underlying drive dualism is at work here as well, namely, the tendency toward separation, the tendency to flee from

---

25. In the blossoming period of hysterical attacks, the most exemplary case of this involved a patient who—during an attack—tried with one hand to undress herself, while preventing herself from doing so with the other (Freud 1978 [1908a], p.166).

the Other's desire, as compared to alienation, the tendency to fulfill the desire of the Other.

The result is predictable: the hysterical symptom is typically unstable and only barely hides the underlying anxiety. From a therapeutic point of view, the symptom provides an associative starting point through which the subject's division in relation to the Other's desire can be recovered. In concrete terms, this minimally hidden conflict is found in every slip of the tongue, hysterical phobia, conversion symptom, and the like. Furthermore, it is impossible to collate an exhaustive list of hysterical symptoms precisely because of the nature of the hysterical structure: any symptom whatsoever is conceivable.

This said, I would nevertheless like to address a symptom that can be considered "typically hysterical," provided that it is not confused with somatization: conversion symptoms. With these, the underlying conflict first acquires representation and is then defensively inscribed on the body, thus creating a medically incomprehensible functional disturbance. In the previous chapter, we discussed its difference from actualpathological somatization, in which the representation of the conflict is missing. In contrast, conversion symptoms are always functionally constructed through the Other, hence their current name: *presenting* somatization. The classic examples go from astasia-abasia (being unable to stand up or to step forward), paresthesias and anesthesias (having either excessive, wrong, or too few perceptual sensations), hysterical nausea, and globus hystericus.

The impression is that such conversion symptoms are less prevalent today than formerly. To the extent that this is true, the explanation probably lies in the fact that contemporary hysterical patients are less inclined to address themselves to the medical master in favor of the psychological-psychiatric master, with an accompanying change in symptoms (Shoenberg 1975, Wajeman 1982). Another explanation is that today's MDs and even psychiatrists and clinical psychologists are less familiar with this symptom, seeing as how it doesn't fit into their scientific discourse, with the result that conversion becomes drowned in the muddy bath of "medically unexplainable symptoms."

At any rate, it is my conviction that there is a fundamental relationship between hysteria and conversion, independent of the inevitably temporally bound manifestation of the master. Indeed, the primal lack the hysterical subject seeks an answer for in the Other always has to do with the body and, as a result, the body assumes a central position in the hysterical relation toward the Other. It will be the imaginar-ized, sexualized body in particular upon which the subject's identification with the Other's desire will be inscribed.[26] Its prevalence does not lessen the fact that, for the time being, conversion remains an incomprehensible process: How can mere thoughts, conflicting and unconscious ones moreover, have such an impact on the body? Regrettably, contemporary science's response is fairly typical: if we don't understand it, it doesn't exist.

Conversion symptoms, and even symptoms in general, are not always to be found in hysteria. It can limit itself simply to the relation, as can be seen in the combination of histrionic and dependent personality disorders. Finally, I would like to draw attention to yet another fairly typical hysterical phenomenon, particularly in light of the essential failure of the fundamental fantasy and its accompanying symptoms: hysterical depression. The combination of the subject's inner conviction of being unable to answer the Other's desire and its perpetual tendency to identify with this desire results in the hysterical subject's constant need to push itself to the limit to satisfy the unsatisfiable, that is, the desire of the Other. Classical psychiatry talks about "hidden depression." The typical hysterical question—"Am I okay?"—has been immortalized by Peter van Straaten's cartoons; sooner or later, the answer will eventually be "no." At that moment, the hysterical subject will fall out of its fundamental fantasy and be confronted with the lack: "I am nothing, I don't mean anything, nobody wants me, I don't want anything." Spitz (1946) talked about *Anlehungsdepression* in this respect, whose rather unfortunate English translation, "anaclitic depression" loses the unmistakable meaning of the original German "to lean on" (*Anlehnung*), depression caused by a

---

26. This is also evident in Veith's historical study of hysteria (1965), indicating that bodily symptoms are one of the few constants throughout different periods and places. Freud provides a precious clinical observation that overcomes the Other's merely imaginary determination of conversion symptoms. Based on his clinical data, he talks about *Somatisches Entgegenkommen* (somatic compliance) (Freud 1978 [1905e], pp. 40–41). With this term, he expresses how something Real of the body plays a role in the imaginary conversion symptoms, literally meeting them halfway. In my reading, this has to do with the specificity of (*a*)'s impact on any particular subject.

failure in this process of leaning on someone else. Spitz associated this form with (the sense of) being abandoned by the mother. This is why hysterical depression melts away like snow the moment a new love object comes on the scene, albeit without any change in the underlying structure.

Implications for Differential Diagnosis and Treatment

Any diagnosis that is based on external, descriptive behavioral characteristics is doomed to fail: absolutely any symptom is possible in the hysterical relation toward the Other. The object of the diagnosis here—even more than elsewhere—will be the structural relationship.[27] Classical psychodiagnostic instruments are inadequate for this. It is the diagnostic interview, spread over several sessions, that indubitably is the best tool, particularly because this relation will typically repeat itself in the clinical situation. The clinician is placed in the position of the Master, the subject-supposed-to-know, which enables one to inquire into the subject's case history. During these interviews, all forms of suggestion must be avoided at all costs because otherwise the interviews will become a self-fulfilling prophecy.

We can anticipate a number of differential diagnostic problems. Firstly, with regard to the other possible subject positions, specifically the psychotic and the perverse ones. Since hysteria is capable of exhibiting any symptom whatsoever, even psychotic forms of appearance are not excluded. The most thorough investigation of this is found in Maleval (1981, 1984; see also Cremniter and Maleval 1989). In this case too, the differential diagnosis must be based on the subject's relation toward the clinician. In cases of psychotic structures, this will be completely different (see Chapter 15). The same goes for the differential diagnosis of perversion; in answering the desire of a potentially perverse Other, the hysterical subject may exhibit plenty of paraphiliac behavior, but here, too, the difference in the structural relation will be definitive (see Chapter 14).

---

27. From a structural perspective, this can be understood as the relation between the hysterical discourse and the discourse of the master. For a discussion, see Verhaeghe (1999b).

The rest of the differential diagnostic difficulties are mainly caused by the descriptive nature of the DSM. Two of its categories are worthy of separate discussion: PTSD and Dissociative Identity Disorder.

Historically, the relation between hysteria and traumatic neurosis was the source of major difficulties right from the beginning. We discussed this already in terms of the effect of a structural trauma: every subject begins with unpleasurable experiences that are experienced as traumatic (for lack of being able to represent them), the answer to which is sought in the Other. Moreover, on the basis of the typical hysterical structure, there is a strong chance that the hysterical subject will later provoke sexual behavior in the other, resulting in an accidental trauma. As is the case in a number of chronic PTSD cases, it is often far from clear who it was that provoked the sexual behavior, the patient or the other. The difference between hysterical and post-traumatic sexual acting-out must be sought in a different field. In cases of hysteria, the sexual acting-out is only narrowly aimed at sexual-genital interaction; the subject wants unconditional love, not sex. In cases of post-traumatic sexual acting-out, the aim is always an accounting, a setting straight of the balances: the traumatized subject wants to gain power over the other and presents the other with the unpaid bill. In both cases, in the hysterical and the post-traumatic, it is not a question of pleasure for the subject that each will experience completely differently. The hysterical subject will try to keep up appearances by focusing on the other's pleasure, and complaining about it afterward. The post-traumatic subject holds itself aloof and operates in an instrumental way, seemingly devoid of feelings.

As a result, the conjunction of a hysterical basic structure and a later accidental trauma is far from uncommon. In such a clinical situation, it is important to attend to its double etiology. Furthermore, there is indeed such a thing as "false memory syndrome," whether combined with a dissociative disorder or not, that can emerge under the influence of a faulty therapeutic suggestion. How it occurs can be described as follows.

A clinician convinced of the omnipresence of the sexual-traumatic etiology will be eager to discover it in his patients. Hysterical subjects will receive this as suggestion and, because of their identification with the signifiers of the Other's desire, will enter into it—all the more so because it tallies perfectly with the structural trauma. As a result, they will produce vague suspicions about an allegedly infantile sexual abuse, which the therapist will interpret as confirmation of his or her expectation, and so on. In a very short time, a "false memory" of something that is experienced as real will be established. This is all the more difficult to distinguish from memory of actual traumatic situations because of the latter's typical characteristic: there are never any normal associative memories about the trauma. This leaves us with a catch-22 situation: anyone who remembers a trauma did not experience it, and vice versa.

Such an unrecognized dialectic between the patient and the clinician may go even further. Based on his expectations and knowledge of PTSD, the well-meaning clinician may make some suggestions about dissociation. The hysterical subject-formation is such that there are a number of identificatory layers in the subject, each going back to an older, already abandoned relation toward a particular other. In the diagnostic and/or therapeutic dialectic, such layers may not only be reactivated, but concretized as well. In this way, the reciprocal conviction is installed that there are "alters" at work. The hysterical subject's ever-present awareness of alienation ("This is not really me") is thus confirmed and reinforced by the clinician's expectation of dissociation. The former "multiple personality disorder" (now Dissociative Identity Disorder) is caused at least partly by such "therapeutic" interactions. To the extent that they appear in PTSD, dissociative phenomena will only rarely acquire such a total form, and are limited in most cases to fragmentary reexperiences of them in the context of a "bad" (because abused) and "good" part of the personality.

What the hysterical structure implies for the treatment can be summarized briefly: treatment is only too successful. Independent of the specific therapeutic approach, the hysterical subject will drink in everything from the therapist, based on the initially almost always positive transferential relationship.[28] As a result, there is relatively rapid suc-

---

28. The most convincing historical example of this is "Justine," Janet's patient, who hallucinated situations where she asked Janet for help, gave herself answers in his place, and then corrected these answers from earlier suggestions of Janet's. The master must be kept in charge, the hysteric will make sure of that (Ellenberger 1970, p. 369; see also Verhaeghe 1999b).

cess at the symptomatic level.[29] Nevertheless, this is *not* a therapeutic result, on the contrary! It is a confirmation and a reinforcement of the problem, namely the subject's typical relation toward the Other. When treatment continues over a longer period, the workable therapeutic relation will either turn into its opposite, or be maintained at enormous cost. In the first case, the master-therapist is replaced once she or he is seen to have failed, and a new master—whether alternative or established—will be found. In the second case, the master-therapist must sustain his or her position as master, meaning that she or he must continue to provide unconditional responses. The treatment thus becomes endless and installs a dependence on the therapist, usually accompanied with a pseudo-ideological group formation. At this level the difference between therapeutic approaches, ideology and sect formation is woefully small.

Consequently, proper treatment of hysteria must be directed toward a change in the relationship and the underlying fundamental fantasy. The most important instrument for this is the transference. The price is thus too high for many therapists: one must relinquish the pedestal upon which one has been installed.

THE OBSESSIONAL RELATION TOWARD THE OTHER AND $\frac{a}{-\varphi}$

Freud identified and isolated obsessional neurosis as a separate clinical entity from a larger group of disorders (including anxiety neurosis, neurasthenia, and cognitive degeneration among others) (Freud 1978 [1896a]). Nevertheless, it is striking how he continued to stress the

---

29. This has enormous implications for contemporary outcome research into the effectiveness of the treatment. Many of these studies measure the therapeutic results on the basis of the concrete reduction of the concrete symptoms, preferably through short-term protocollary treatments. In view of the high prevalence of the hysterical structure, many research subjects will indeed be hysterical and "improve" quite quickly. In the long term, these results will disappear. This is being confirmed by long-term outcome research. It must be admitted that it is much more difficult to measure structural changes in a subject than merely to measure symptom reduction. In this field, there is still plenty of work to be done.

hysterical foundation of every obsessional neurosis. It reappears in the DSM in two forms: as obsessive-compulsive disorder (300.3) within a larger group of anxiety disorders, and as obsessive-compulsive personality disorder (301.81). As we will see, there is a clear connection with the so-called narcissistic personality disorder (301.81) as well.

Like hysteria, obsessional neurosis must be understood as a repetition of the original relation toward the first and second Others with respect to desire. This original relation can give rise to several different characteristics and symptoms, but it has a lot less diversity than hysteria. In general terms, we can describe a tendency toward autonomy and distance, accompanied by feelings of ambivalence and doubt. As always, such a description is insufficient for a differential diagnosis, which must be based on insight into the formal structure.

Obsessional Neurosis and Subject-Formation: Expulsion/Separation

While emphasis in hysteria was on the oral partial drive, in obsessional neurosis Freud sees a preponderance of the anal component (Freud 1978 [1913i]). Here, too, he refers to constitutional and educational factors; the latter having particularly to do with the child's toilet training. The relation between obsessional neurosis and the three basic characteristics of the anal character (Freud 1978 [1908b]) is easy to see: orderliness, parsimoniousness, and obstinacy. These traits reappear in the DSM description of the obsessive-compulsive personality disorder. Moreover, these characteristics can just as easily shift into their opposite without any change in the underlying structure. In such cases, the obsessional neurotic gives up, capitulates to the other, and disappears into filth. "Parsimonious" in particular must be clarified: the obsessional is frequently very generous—except of him- or herself (see below, oblativity and the obsessional's fundamental fantasy).

The anal predominance refers to the second process of subject-formation, namely, the expulsion/separation that are the landmarks of obsessional neurosis. The emphasis on the second process indicates that the first, alienation/identification, was more than adequately present.

This is why obsessional neurosis can be regarded as an evolution of hysteria and why it has an underlying hysterical structure.[30] This must always be understood relatively: the emphasis on separation doesn't lessen the fact that the process of alienation/identification is also present, furnishing the basis for conflict and subject division. From a wider perspective, one can say that the Thanatos drive[31] predominates in obsessional neurosis, albeit—as always—with fusional Eros at work in the background, causing conflict and division.

As an oedipal psychoneurosis, obsessional neurosis implies a phallic interpretation of the original anal drive component (a). From a psychoanalytic perspective, here we encounter anal-phallicism and its associated sexuality. In the restricted meaning of the word, this can be found in the typically anal symptoms (Freud 1978 [1909d]). In general psychology, this anal aspect has received less attention, particularly as compared to that for the oral component, presumably because of the former's unpleasant smell. For Freud, the anal belongs to the most repressed part of human sexuality. This becomes especially clear once we compare its relative absence in the scientific publications to its omnipresence in human sexuality. It is in the widest sense of the term that the anal *phallus* appears in the anal character as described by Freud.

This stress on the anal-phallic must be understood primarily in terms of its accompanying process: the expulsion of separation. In contrast to the hysteric, who absorbs everything from the Other, the obsessional will refuse, even expel everything that comes from the Other: rather than fusion, the aim here is separation. To understand this and to be able to chart the obsessional neurotic structure, we must once again examine the oedipal history.

---

30. Freud even considers obsessional neurosis a "dialect" of hysteria at one point (Freud 1978 [1909d], pp. 156–157).

31. The death drive is one of the most difficult Freudian concepts, partly because Freud didn't fully elaborate it himself. The idea of "death" must be nuanced. The Thanatos drive, with its tendency toward separation and diffusion, chooses in favor of the individual's continuing existence as a separate entity, independent of the Other, and in that sense the "death"-drive operates in favor of the life of the individual. See Verhaeghe (2001a).

Oedipal History of Obsessional Neurosis

While hysteria is associated with a surplus of unpleasure and trauma, the opposite is true for obsessional neurosis: the supposition is that there was an excess of pleasure that in itself was experienced as traumatic (Freud 1978 [1896a], p. 155). This classic conception has meanwhile been forgotten in today's emphasis on phenomenological descriptions that have little concern for its etiology. I would like to go into it regardless, because of its importance for the treatment.

In the transition from the confrontation of its own drive arousal with that of the desire of the first Other and identification with it, the obsessional-subject-to-be interprets the message of the first Other in the following way: "If I just work hard enough to meet her demands, the Other will be satisfied (and will leave me alone)." At the same time, the subject receives the message that the second Other hasn't met those standards. This Other's authority is ridiculed while it is simultaneously indicated that somewhere beyond him is a strict system of rules that can take care of desire in a neat and orderly fashion.

Consequently, at the level of alienation/separation, obsessional subject-formation reaches a satisfactory point, hence the experience of "pleasure"—he or she must and does do well. The hysterical fear of failure, "I will never be good enough for the Other," comes up against its obsessional counterpart: "I must and will always succeed, either for or counter to this Other." The difficulties have to do with the fact that answering the Other's desire always carries the risk of being reduced to this desire and nothing else. In this way, the surplus of pleasure receives a traumatic character, and the emphasis shifts toward the need for separation. Seeing as how the second Other is experienced as unsatisfactory, separation will not be easy and will need continual reconfirmation by way of the obsessional system in the obsessive's typical relation with others. This system is initially taken over from the first Other, but soon becomes elaborated into the obsessional's own system of rules, independent of that Other.

Here the anxiety is of a totally different nature than that of hysterical anxiety. In the latter, the anxiety is about not satisfying the desire of the other, of failing; in obsessional neurosis, the anxiety is about disappearing because of oversatisfying of the other's desire. It must be underscored how the obsessional neurotic affect is considerably less visible to the outside world than its hysterical variety. As a rule, the outside world tends to be irritated by the pedantic obsessional and is barely aware of the underlying anxiety.

Such a double message is translated directly into subject-formation as far as attitudes toward gender and authority are concerned. In later adult relations, the obsessional subject is convinced that he or she is or has "it" for the other. This is why others usually experience obsessionals as haughty and arrogant—the connection with the narcissistic personality disorder is easy to see. Despite this conviction, the subject scarcely dares to act because of the constant threat of being reduced to the other's desire. In the field of sexuality, the obsessional maintains his or her distance, regarding things coolly from the sidelines. In more general relations, the obsessional is characteristically aloof, reinforcing the impression of narcissism.

In my discussion of hysteria, I observed how the hysteric generally installs a third figure between the subject and a possible partner. This third party functions as the hysteric's role model and rival. In obsessional neurosis, one can often similarly detect the existence of a third party, albeit in a completely different way. The obsessional is convinced that she or he is capable of satisfying the desire of the Other. She or he suffers little from (typically hysterical) jealousy, and will compete with him- or herself rather than with the other who is held in lower regard. At the same time, the fear of being reduced to the Other's desire insists, and it is here that a third party can be brought in. Such a figure—often a friend of the subject's partner, who is typically installed and maintained in position by the obsessional subject him or herself—thus functions not as an Ego-Ideal, but as a lightning rod and buffer. In concrete terms, this means that the obsessional performs miracles in creating "ménage-à-trois" where the removal of the third party must be avoided at all costs.

The same equivocalness and ambivalence can be found in the relation toward authority and knowledge. These are never absent in obsessionals. Despite their conviction of their superiority with regard to knowledge and authority, the need for a third point to act as a wedge between the ego and the first Other remains. This commonly appears in the work space, where the obsessional—oddly enough—competes with someone she or he regards as his or her inferior. Rivalry such as this is very draining, because the obsessional must constantly ensure that this other won't lose—for in that case, the third party's protective function would also disappear. In cases of pathology, the obsessional patient will not so much fall back on a third figure as on his or her own obsessional system, composed of thoughts and acts intended to keep the outside world at a distance and under control.

The combination of these original relationships toward the first and second Others in terms of gender and knowledge not only reappears in later transferential relationships, but also often determines the onset of the pathology as such. For the outside world, typically disregarding the underlying structure and used to seeing this individual as a narcissist, this onset is utterly incomprehensible. Finally, the yearned-for promotion is achieved, and now everything falls apart . . . At long last, the partner's lover has gone, the marriage can normalize, but nothing seems to work out anymore . . .

Relation to Gender, Seduction, and Trauma

The proverbial hysterical *woman* finds her mirror image in the obsessional *man*. Here we must make the same amendment as previously: the coupling of the neuroses with a specific gender is only indirect and has to do with historical artifacts. The proper relation is that between obsessional neurosis and the active position toward the Other in the context of separation. Patriarchal society almost exclusively assigns the active position to men, hence the gender associations of the time. By now, in the West, this has almost disappeared; hence associations with specific genders are no longer applicable.

The obsessional subject's specific positioning in relation to the Other's desire is not without its effects for gender relations. Being convinced that one can satisfy the other's desire, while meeting the concurrent need to maintain one's distance, results in a characteristic stance called "oblativity."[32] The obsessional subject gives the other everything so as to keep its own self out of the firing line. The aim is to mortify

---

32. Oblativity (Latin: *offere*; participium perfectum: *oblatus*): the act of committing oneself to a (religious) order by giving all one's goods and promising to follow certain regulations, but without giving up completely the layman's status. See Lacan (1977 [1958a], p. 253).

the other's desire, to "kill" it in order to maintain one's own safety. Such an attitude can initially come across as very seductive, particularly if the other possesses a hysterical structure and is—precisely because of this structure—looking for someone who seems to have special access to knowledge and truth and is prepared to share them. Hysterical revendication finds its perfect mirror image here in the oblative obsessional. This inevitably gives rise to a classic spiral: nothing an obsessional gives will ever be enough, and the hysterical subject soon interprets this refusal to give of "oneself" as rejection, convinced as it is of its own intrinsic failure.

A typical illustration of this interaction is found here in Flanders, obsessed as we are with housing. The obsessional builds his hysterical partner a house, or at least wants to give it the final touch. It must be done, however, with the utmost perfection, with the result that for years every spare moment is spent with this "finishing." Meanwhile, the fact that the couple, and eventually the children, are camping in the shed is simply an unfortunate but temporary detail. The man gives "everything" to his partner while maintaining a safe distance—he's on site all the time after all. His wife shouldn't complain—is he not sacrificing himself? But for the time being she must stay on her own in the shed . . .

Thus the initial trauma is repeated on both sides. What the hysterical subject experiences as personal rejection, in spite of all the obsessional's presents and solutions, confirms the primary (oedipal) rejection. What the obsessional experiences as success is always a surplus, causing anxiety and guilt. Here the feeling of guilt itself is a way of coping with anxiety, in the sense that translating anxiety into guilt creates the illusion of control ("If only I hadn't done that, 'it' wouldn't have happened"). The obsessional's rigidity is connected with this.

The obsessional's control of the other occurs through a set of cardinal rules aimed at making the guilt and anxiety manageable—this is the obsessional hypermorality, and its associated inflexibility are well known. The conflicts that this produces are of a completely different nature from those of hysteria, whose causes are always found in the hysterical tendency to identify with the conflicting desires of different others. Because of its tendency toward separation, the obsessional subject takes the opposite tack and creates a different kind of conflict. Such a rigid attitude nevertheless hides an underlying ambivalence and doubt that we will shortly return to in our discussion of symptom formation.

The Obsessional Fundamental Fantasy and Symptom Formation

Like hysteria, obsessional neurosis has its own specific manifestation of the fundamental fantasy as the lasting result of the original relation with the Other that will reappear in all subsequent relations. The formula is as follows (Lacan 1991 [1960–1961], p. 295 ff):

$$\cancel{A} \quad \Diamond \quad \varphi\,(a', a'', a''', \ldots)$$

Here the divided Other heads the formula as the recipient of the obsessional subject's perpetually new phallicized objects that are intended to keep the subject itself outside the game. From a psychoanalytic perspective, the obsessional buries the Other under a pile of anal objects that will never be enough—hence the constant shifting of objects—but that are intended to maintain the Other's lack; hence the notation $\cancel{A}$. The Other will never be made whole because this would imply the disappearance of the subject itself, which must be avoided at all costs.

The proverbial obsessional aloofness toward the Other stands in direct opposition to hysterical fusion, and the fundamental fantasy illustrates how separation predominates in obsessional neurosis, albeit somewhat equivocally. In the fields of both sexuality and knowledge and authority, the obsessional gives "it" to the Other while keeping itself out of the game. This is why, like hysteria, obsessional neurosis has a self-sacrificing quality, although its nature is completely different. The hysterical subject sacrifices him or herself; the obsessional sacrifices an object.

This is easily seen in Freud's classic case study (1978 [1909d]) of obsessional neurosis. Such a sacrifice can be quite all-embracing; the obsessional may care for the other until death. The amortization of the other's desire can be taken literally here. The conscious appearance of the typically hysterical fantasy of dying and of seeing others' reactions to it takes the opposite form in the obsessional's version. She or he will dream about the *other's* death, following which one's "own" life will finally be able to begin. Such fantasies (the partner has a deadly accident, the father gets cancer, etc.) reinforce the already preexisting feelings of guilt, and must be worked over in a reactive way, that is to say, one must give even more. This, in turn, opens the floodgates to the other side of the conflict and results in further defensive measures to ensure that the other doesn't come too close.

The aim of the fundamental fantasy is to manage the underlying conflict and its accompanying anxiety. Both hysteria and obsessional neurosis present a normal version as well. Its normality depends on the degree of its success or failure with regard to anxiety and conflict management. In more concrete terms, it depends on whether or not the obsessional is able to make a choice. To the extent that the obsessional subject tries to maintain both sides at once—completely satisfying the other's desire while remaining outside the game—the result will be the pathological obsessional spiral.

The obsessional conflict can be described in the same formal terms as that of the hysteric. On the one hand, we find the division based on the narrative identity. On the other hand, we encounter the dualism of the drive. The difference from hysteria has to do with the different emphases of the terms—separation and Thanatos for the obsessional, alienation and Eros for the hysteric—and the different defense mechanisms that lie at the basis of symptom formation.

The obsessional defense mechanism is of a completely different nature, and determines the characteristic obsessional ambivalence and its accompanying doubt. In contrast to hysterical repression, here we find obsessional "isolation" (Freud 1978 [1926d], p. 120).[33] The really

---

33. As a defense mechanism, "isolation" receives little attention from Freud, whose main focus is on hysterical repression. The most important and almost exclusive reference is as follows:

> The second of these techniques which we are setting out to describe for the first time, that of isolation, is peculiar to obsessional neurosis. It, too, takes place in the motor sphere. When something unpleasant has happened to the subject or when he himself has done something which has a significance for his neurosis, he interpolates an interval during which nothing further must happen—during which he must perceive nothing and do nothing. This behaviour, which seems strange at first sight, is soon seen to have a relation to repression. We know that in hysteria it is possible to cause a traumatic experience to be overtaken by amnesia. In obsessional neurosis this can often not be achieved: the experience is not forgotten, but, instead, it is deprived of its affect, and its associative connections are suppressed or interrupted so that it remains as though isolated and is not reproduced in the ordinary processes of thought. The effect of this isolation is the same as the effect of repression with amnesia. This technique, then, is reproduced in the isolations of obsessional neurosis; and it is at the same time given motor reinforcement for magical purposes. [Freud 1978 (1926d), p. 120]

After Freud, this mechanism was largely forgotten, "isolated." Nevertheless, it has clear value for understanding obsessional neurosis.

important signifiers are dissociated from one another and thus function autonomously, without any underlying connection. Moreover, to the extent that the signifier represents one side of the conflict, it will be replaced each time by another that expresses the other side. The chief difference can be illustrated by comparing it to hysterical symptom formation: because of the (return of the) repressed, in hysterical symptom formation the two sides of the conflict are always fused into a single metaphorical whole. In obsessional neurosis, one relieves the other, seemingly without any relation between the two.

This defense mechanism can be understood through the predominance of the separation process. The principal elements are not permitted to touch each other; a requisite distance between them must constantly be maintained. In the restricted meaning of the word, this can sometimes be quite literally heard in the obsessional's speech, which can often sound fairly staccato: every syllable, every word has to be individually pronounced, with a scansion and pause in between. More broadly, this mechanism can be seen in the fear of being touched and of contamination, which are themselves nothing but exaggerations of the obsessional's need for interpersonal distance.

Symptom formation always acts on signifying material inside what we've been calling the secondary processing. The linguistic process connected with this is metonymy, the constant displacement of one isolated signifier into another. However, the term displacement is too feeble here; it is not so much displacement as a reactive replacement of one element by its opposite. This means that the obsessional subject will be positioned differently in language than the hysteric. To the extent that we are dealing with pathology and the absence of a clear choice, the result will be a never-ending series. The obsessional patient will endlessly keep harping on, the pros and cons following in quick succession and reciprocally neutralizing one another.[34]

---

34. This has certain sociocultural consequences. Hysteria, centered on metaphor, creates new meanings. Obsessional neurosis, with its focus on metonymy, fails to do so. Hence the clear relation between hysteria and art on the one hand, and obsessional neurosis and religion, on the other. The hysterical subject is able to innovate; the obsessional subject has to attach itself to an immovable certainty (Freud 1978 [1907b]). Hence, too, the connection between obsessional neurosis and those professions that demand precision, certainty, and clarity.

Such alternation, in which it is impossible to make a choice, is fairly typical of obsessional symptom formation, hence its name: the obsessional spiral. The two sides of the conflict continuously alternate and spiral ever farther apart from the original starting point. It ultimately ends in what seem to be ludicrous details, together with the ever-present doubt. The latter has to do with the obsessional's uncertainty over whether one element has really succeeded in cancelling out the other, this uncertainty standing in striking contrast to the otherwise rigid obsessional character.

The symptom spiral begins with obsessional brooding, self-reproach, and the accompanying guilt feelings. The *self*-reproaches are themselves already an expression of the tendency toward separation: the other cannot reproach the obsessional for anything; the subject will take care of this itself. These reproaches and guilt feelings have to do with the surplus of pleasure following the assumption of the phallic position in relation to the first Other and its resultant anxiety. The brooding is an effect of the continuous alternation of the pros and cons in the thought process. This soon gives rise to obsessional thoughts, always experienced by the patient as intrusive and parasitic. Remember that these are experienced as coming from the Other (which, in view of the process of subject-formation, is seen as quite right), and so must be transformed into one's "own" thoughts. The initial material contains a verbalization of the core conflict: hence, the manifestation of the Other's desire must be countered in an aggressive manner by distancing oneself from this Other. Such aggression is always recognizable at the onset of an obsessional neurosis, if sometimes in the form of over-scrupulousness about not hurting that Other.

In classical psychiatry, such thoughts are divided into ideative, phobic, and impulsive types, although in clinical practice one usually finds them in combination. Ideative thoughts concern those insisting thoughts from which the patient cannot free him- or herself. Their content is often of an aggressive/impulsive nature—the mother who is afraid of letting her baby fall, of accidentally hitting it, and becomes overanxious and overprotective—leading to phobic thoughts: all knives and scissors must be removed. Thoughts such as these present themselves in a spiralling series of pluses and minuses, moving the contents further and further away from the original conflict. Freud talks about "reaction formations" in this respect, where the ambivalent alternations of love (identification) and hate (separation) relieve one another in antagonistic fashion.

At a certain moment, these thoughts are no longer enough and lead to obsessional repetitive acts and rituals aimed at putting an end to the inner doubt but resulting in precisely the opposite. These in turn lead to further elaborations, with an unremitting verification process that attempts to determine whether the defense was adequte. The result is neatly captured by Freud's term, "*Ungeschehenmachen*" (undoing) (Freud 1978 [1909d], pp. 235–236, 243; [1926d], pp. 119–120), or retroactive annulment. Act + (x) expresses aggression, must be undone, and is annulled by act − (x). Its connection with the original content can easily be detected at first: compulsive washing (to remove the other's dirt), compulsive checking to make sure every door is locked (to keep the other outside). As these acts continue to develop in a spiraling fashion, they end up in meaningless rituals that ultimately come to fill the entire psychic space. In its terminal phase, obsessional neurosis results in complete immobility and isolation.

Let me repeat that each symptom must be understood and interpreted in the light of the fundamental fantasy and its isolation mechanism. Separation and the active position have the upper hand, but are each time countered by identification and the desire for the passive position.

Like hysteria, obsessional neurosis also presents two nonsymptomatic variations. Freud already described the obsessive-compulsive character (1978 [1908b]; [1916d]); this reappeared later as obsessive-compulsive personality disorder in the DSM, providing that the latter is combined with certain characteristics of the narcissistic personality disorder. Here, too, the mark of pathology lies in the absence of a clear choice. The second, nonsymptomatic form concerns obsessive-compulsive depression, later called "narcissistic depression." This begins when the obsessional subject is confronted with the failure of its own ideal image, forcing it to realize that it will never be able to reach its own high standards. A similar depressive picture may begin once success has been achieved and a certain ideal realized. In this case, the depression will be primarily characterized by anxiety because of the risk of disappearing beneath the Other's desire.[35] In today's terms, this will be called

---

35. A typical example in academic circles: the postdoctoral depression. In candidates with hysterical structures, this appears out of anxiety that the doctorate wasn't

inhibition, emphasizing the subject's inability to move in the direction of the Other.

Differential Diagnostic and Therapeutic Implications

Diagnosis of the obsessional neurotic structure is easier than it is for the hysterical structure because of the latter's ability to ultimately display any and every form of symptom. This doesn't mean that one should neglect the structure itself, that is to say, the formal relationship toward the first and second Others in question of desire. Otherwise it will be impossible to distinguish between hysterical self-doubt and obsessional doubt, and between hysterical sacrifice and the obsessional way of giving to and caring for the other. From the point of view of differential diagnostics, two special additional difficulties must not be neglected: the difference between obsessional neurosis and the psychotic and perverse structures.

Obsessional sexuality is indeed obsessive, immediately evoking the idea of sexual obsession. Combine this with its not-infrequent ritualization and a predilection for anality, and the final picture suggests something that looks a bit like the perverse structure: a more or less fixed scenario that is repeated over and over again, focused moreover on a single component drive. The differential diagnostic difference lies mainly in the conclusion that the obsessional subject—as opposed to the perverse—does recognize a law and authority outside him or herself, whose consequence is a limitation of jouissance and a continuation of desire. The pervert doesn't recognize this law and goes for jouissance almost entirely at the expense of desire (see Chapter 14). There is also a second aspect where the differential diagnostic with the perverse structure often causes problems, namely, masochism. The active, separating position clearly has the upper hand, but every obsessional subject relishes daydreaming about the opposite attitude (the passive submission to "La Belle Dame Sans Merci," be it in the form of schoolmistress or nurse, or to a macho figure, preferably clad in black leather, complete with motorbike). The guilt-ridden

---

good enough. In those with obsessional structures, it comes out of the anxiety that one has finally satisfied the Other's desire and there is nothing left to do.

confessions of such fantasies might suggest masochistic perversion but the same cautionary remarks concerning desire and jouissance also apply here.

The differential diagnosis with psychosis is a classic psychiatric problem, particularly if one is dealing with a well-developed obsessional neurosis. As psychotics do, ultimately every obsessional develops his or her own version of "the system" full of rituals and magic actions designed to keep the anxiety and conflict under control. In his case study of the Rat Man, Freud talks about "deliria" in obsessional neurosis: "I think such structures as these deserve to be given the name *'deliria'*" (Freud 1978 [1909d], p. 222). Moreover, the patient frequently claims that it seems as if the thoughts are coming from the outside: the acts seem to be externally imposed and must be defended against with counter-thoughts and actions. This has resonances with the xenopathic and intrusive elements in psychosis. As described earlier, the main difference has to do with the fact that, despite their intrusiveness, the obsessional subject remains fully aware that these senseless thoughts and acts come from within. This is mentioned in characteristic A(4) of the DSM category 300.3: "The person recognizes that the obsessional thoughts, impulses, or images are a product of his or her own mind (not imposed from without as in thought insertion)." The most fundamental differential diagnostic indication must nevertheless be sought in the difference between the monolithic psychotic transference (see Chapter 15) and the ambivalent obsessional relation toward the clinician.

As far as treatment is concerned, one can foresee that here, too, the characteristic formal structure will be repeated in the course of the therapy. This is clearest when the patient becomes distant, rejecting anything that comes from the Other. In a number of other cases, this is less obvious. The obsessional patient is often a perfect patient, scrupulously fulfilling the therapist's demands and in this way destroying the therapeutic provision. Free association, for example, is carried out in such a perfect manner that it becomes useless, the same goes for cognitive restructuring tasks and homework. This means that the treatment techniques themselves become obsessionalized while the pathological structure as such remains unchanged. The transferential relation becomes one where the therapist is cut out of everything and the patient takes over his or her job, albeit in a typically obsessional way.[36]

This means that every form of treatment must first be directed toward this relation itself. When this does not happen, there are only two possibilities. Either the cure is prematurely terminated—the therapist was no match for the obsessional who knows a lot more and is much more thorough. Or the therapy becomes part of the obsessional spiral and is interminable. In such cases, it is the therapist's death the obsessional patient is waiting for, the death of the therapist as Other, after which the patient will finally be able to begin living a life of his or her own . . .

---

36. Of course, this is not restricted to therapy but occurs in the outside world as well. An obsessional patient once told me that throughout her studies she dutifully went to all her courses but wouldn't take any notes. Returning home, she would do the whole course over again in her own "autonomous" way. Another obsessional patient with the same tendencies—being unable to take anything in from the other—called this his "mental anorexia."

14
Perverse Structure versus Perverse Traits

PRELIMINARY DIFFERENTIAL DIAGNOSTIC TROUBLES

Perversion is unquestionably one of the most difficult of the clinical categories as far as both research and treatment are concerned.[1] A recent survey of the relevant literature (Gijs 2002) concludes that contemporary etiological theories (mainly from bio-psycho-social and feminist perspectives) have little meaning for clinical praxis. Before anything useful can be said about perversion, we must first clear up a lot of misconceptions—particularly if it is the perverse *structure* that is at issue. As I see it, there are three main problems. One, the ubiquitous, and in most cases explicit moral judgment attending perversion. Two, the omnipresence of the masculine gaze, meaning in most cases a phallic gaze that hinders most studies of perversion. Three, the problem of the differential diagnosis of the quintessentially human polymorphously perverse sexuality on the one hand, and perversion as a subjective structure alongside psychotic and neurotic structures on the other.

---

1. Also see B. Fink (1997), pp. 65–202.

Let us begin with the moral judgment or, better, condemnation. While there is such a thing as a "good neurotic" (Zetzel 1968), and probably even a "good psychotic," the idea of a "good pervert" is a contradiction in terms. The sympathy one has for the victim implies a moral rejection of the perpetrator. The result is not only that it becomes impossible to see anything differently, but also to *treat* both "perpetrators" and "victims," in the proper sense of the word "treatment." Clinical praxis isn't that black-and-white.

In this field, clinical diagnostics runs the risk of becoming confused with juridical diagnostics. Recent history is quite instructive here. Whichever definition of perversion is used, it will always contain the idea of transgressing a norm. The question is, which norm? The answer is of great importance because it will determine both the definition of what perversion constitutes and its treatment. Before Freud, in what were then the barely existing human sciences, the religious-ideological discourse was dominant, exerting a very clear influence on pedagogy and morality. People whom we would consider perverts today were labeled libertines and sinners, that is to say, transgressors of the divine norm. The only "treatment" in this discourse was punishment and repentance. By Freud's time, the medical-psychiatric discourse had taken over, and the previous sinners were rechristened—more correctly, diagnosed—as patients. The remedy became a medical one, although it wasn't clear exactly what this comprised.

This change in discourse also introduced a change in norms. The religious discourse depended on religious norms that, being relative and changing over time, have always been a matter of debate. A medical norm, on the contrary, is "natural" and therefore absolute—there can be no question of interpretation or evolution—fever begins at 37°C or 98.6°F. The work by Masters and Johnson (1966) illustrates this absolute character: the norm is heterosexual coitus between two consenting adults, with mutual orgasm as a bonus. Anything that diverges from this is "dysfunctional," with the result that perversion disappears into the sea of sexual dysfunctions.

The sociocultural shift that followed in the '60s erased this absoluteness. The medical-psychiatric discourse was replaced by a sociological-psychological one. Kinsey's studies (1948, 1953) of the average American's sexual behavior convincingly showed the general inapplicability of the medical norm to the general population.[2] Today, in the aftermath of this discourse, we live with an extreme relativity of the idea of normal sexuality that emphasizes the culturally determined differences of its various manifestations. The vagueness of this postmodern condition is aptly rendered by Money (1988). He speaks of "normophilia": "a condition of being erotosexually in conformity with the standard as dictated by customary, religious, or legal authority" (p. 214). Next to this, he coins the term "paraphilia," for persons who don't fit the prescribed norm. Note the use of *para* (alongside) rather than *patho* (ill).

Initially, this development might seem like a good thing. Indeed, it seems as if we have finally distanced ourselves from our pernicious religious education and the compulsory, absolute medical norm. A free society at last! The evolution of the various editions of the DSM characteristics is a sign of this: certain categories that used to be defined as sexual aberrations have been omitted in recent editions because they have become accepted as "normal."

It's an illusion. Even more so, this "progress" is nothing but a return to pre-Freudian times. Indeed, the pervert—excuse me, the paraphiliac—is someone who transgresses the norm, be it customary, religious, or legal. We are back at the beginning again, with sinners and criminals. The consequences of such a definition are easy to predict and can already be felt. In clinical practice, in an increasingly permissive society, perversion/paraphilia will be measured according to the private norms of the (potentially short-lived) couple. "The" norm then becomes the famous "informed mutual consent": anything is permitted, on condition that the partners agree—penal law interferes little in private matters. As a result, the chief forms of perversion these days, practically the only ones left, are pedophilia and incest, followed by "sexual harassment" in quick succession.[3] This is because in such cases

---

2. The fact that Masters and Johnson still needed to formulate medical norms for that time (their first book dates from 1960; Kinsey's publications go back to 1948 and 1953) proves that history is never linear. The effect of the Kinsey reports came about only retroactively, during the sexual revolution.

3. This is why, in contemporary research, attention has almost exclusively been paid to a number of empirically based diagnostic classification systems of sexual violence against children and adults. A critical evaluation of these systems (Koeck et al.

informed mutual consent is missing.[4] The effect of this on clinical praxis and theory is enormous. Recent studies focus exclusively on sexual violence, with predominantly male perpetrators. What falls outside this scope receives little attention.

History shows something else as well. Accompanying our moral judgment and disgust is an extreme fascination—we can't seem to get enough of it. The aversion covers a barely concealed attraction: How do they do "it"? The perverse character is a preeminent pole of attention for both men and women driven by their own divided desires in sexuality, and this applies equally for researchers as well. It is of the utmost importance, then, to acknowledge this equivocal attitude before one begins the study and treatment of perversion. Neglect this and our fascination with perversion will lead to a poor theory. To the extent that one even arrives at treatment, it will end in characteristic failure, with the pervert assigning the therapist a certain position in his or her perverse scenario (passive object and/or passive onlooker). The need to avoid this means we must now examine the polymorphic "perversity" of normal subjects. On this basis, we will understand how every neurotic subject dreams of being a pervert, that is, he or she dreams of the unlimited gratification the pervert is imagined to enjoy.

The Juridical View

The second difficulty for differential diagnostics follows directly from the previous one. Precisely because of our increasing tolerance, deviant sexual behavior has once more become a fully juridical ques-

---

2002) concluded that while such classifications have not been very useful for the clinic, conceptualizations that do have clinical relevance are so far lacking empirical evidence.

4. Hence the debate over the "age of consent": at what age can children give their consent? This has led to the ridiculous situation where, depending on the (European) country, pedophilia is linked with different age categories, often depending on the child's sex, moreover, and with different ages for homosexual contact as well.

The connection between the clinical and the juridical system has another consequence as well. In a recent postgraduate seminar (October 2001), E. Welldon, who worked for three decades in the Portman Clinic (Tavistock) explained the statistical (rather than clinical) absence of necrophilia and bestialism in this way: the "victims" never complain.

tion. From the juridical point of view, diagnosis will by definition focus on behavior, and more specifically on that aspect of behavior that transgresses the legal norm. This is evident from the use of pseudodiagnostic categories that always emphasize the transgressiveness of this behavior, its element of "harassment." Next, with this diagnosis in hand, treatment is begun with a largely a priori goal in mind: the transgressive behavior must stop and any "relapse" be prevented at all costs.

The DSM categories for sexual deviance and paraphiliac behavior make this quite clear. The sexual norm, moreover, is more or less exclusively male, with an emphasis on erection, coitus, and orgasm. Deviance or paraphilia is that which deviates from these goals or makes them impossible to reach. An often-heard complaint today is that perversion is exclusively male. This is indeed so, given that it is regarded solely through the phallic, male gaze, leaving little room for women and therefore for female perversion. More specifically, this gaze makes it impossible to see the position of the mother/woman in the perverse structure. A radically different conception of female sexuality should make it possible to conceive of a radically different theory of female perversion, which does exist. Here, the gaze must be directed away from the restricted phallic area to the entire body and to the child as an original product of that body.[5]

Beyond the Jurisdictional

The third differential diagnostic difficulty brings us for the first time into the clinical field proper, that is to say, beyond the jurisdictional. Let me put forward two main theses that I have derived from Freud and Lacan. First, each one of us exhibits abnormal sexual behavior. Second, every psychopathological structure (whether it be neurosis,

---

5. Female perversion is different because woman's relation toward the phallic signifier is different. According to Lacan's formula of sexuation (Lacan 1998 [1972–1973]), woman relates both to the phallic signifier and to the not-all. Translated into clinical terms, this means that man invests solely in the phallic and the phallic imaginarization of the pregenital, that is to say, in component objects. Woman invests not only in the phallic but also in her entire body and in her child, as a product of that body.

psychosis, or perversion) implies a disturbance at the level of sexuality, in the narrow sense of the word, and of gender identity understood in the widest sense. As a result, we are immediately confronted with the principal diagnostic difficulty: How does one differentiate between paraphiliac traits, which are of an actualpathological or psychopathological nature and determined by the psychotic or neurotic structure in which they emerge, and the perverse structure as such, that is, a well-defined typical relationship between subject and Other?

PARAPHILIAC TRAITS: THE POLYMORPHOUS PERVERSITY OF EVERY SUBJECT

The two theses are easy to demonstrate, but they run counter to the moral image of our sociocultural norm. The Kinsey studies already confirmed the first thesis—that everyone possesses paraphiliac traits—empirically proving that almost nobody fits the norm, that is, heterosexual coitus in the missionary position with orgasm for both participants. The explanation is found in Freud's study of infantile sexuality, as elaborated in the still magisterial "Three Essays on the Theory of Sexuality" (1978 [1905d]), and developed further in a number of later texts.

In brief, Freud discovers what every nanny had long known, namely, that sexuality begins from childhood onward, if in a very unique manner. There is no such thing as a genital drive that irresistibly thrusts man toward woman and vice versa right from the start. The life of the drive develops through the partial drives that are only later gathered under the coordinating flag of so-called genital sexuality. It is not a question of human instincts, but of drives. These are both partial and autoerotic. Partial means that they fall back on certain bodily areas: oral, anal, or genital, rather than on the body in its entirety. Autoerotic means that these drives focus firstly on parts of the *subject's* body, not on that of the other. On the grounds of these readily observable data, Freud concludes that our sexuality is grounded in a polymorphously perverse predisposition. Even more so, this polymorphously perverse predisposition is the basis of the original and universal predisposition of the human sexual drive as such (Freud 1978 [1905d], pp. 171–172,

231). Almost any adult perverse trait can be seen in the child, putting perversion[6] in a completely different light.[7] Consequently, according to Freudian theory, the distinction between perverse traits and the perverse structure is not easy to make.

Lacan's Structure

The second thesis can best be argued on the basis of Lacan's elaboration of Freud. Firstly, Lacan widens Freud's focus on the individual drive life by understanding it within the primary relationship between the subject and the Other. As elaborated in Part 2 of this book, the subject-to-be addresses itself to the first Other for an answer to its own drive tension. The resulting dialectics lead to the subject's identification with the desire of the Other, a desire that will be successively focused on certain aspects of the drive tension (oral, anal, etc). The oedipal structuring process causes a phallic reinterpretation of these partial objects and introduces the impossibility of ever receiving a final answer—desire is constitutively unsatisfiable. As a result, Lacan elevates a Freudian idea into a general thesis: "There is no sexual relation," to be understood as: there is no ultimate form of the sexual relation between The Man and The Woman, only different forms that are determined each

---

6. This gives us the first Freudian conceptualization of perversion, understood as a developmental inhibition, that is to say, a fixation on a specific component drive that makes the normal goal (adult genital relation) impossible (Freud 1978 [1905d], p. 162, Note 3; note that Freud's footnote was added in 1920). This conception of perversion will be reworked through the formulation of the perverse mechanism of defense, that is, disavowal.

7. This is why the question of perversion has to be reformulated. Not, Why did someone become perverse? But, Why didn't we all remain perverse? Freud's answer is well known: the Oedipus complex is the developmental phase that takes care of normalization. The combination of somatic immaturity of the genitals and anxiety about the father causes the child to keep its distance from its pregenital desire for the mother and to identify with the normative image presented by the father. Later, with the somatic maturity of puberty, the child will address itself to other Others. At that point, the early pregenital drives will be submitted to the genital drive as such and reduced to what precedes coitus.

time by the original dialectic, which is, moreover, framed by a larger, determining discourse.[8]

It is precisely this last that is important for the acquisition of gender identity. The displacement of the first Other's answer onto the second Other introduces gender differentiation and forms the basis for gender identity. This is part of the larger subject-formation and is therefore submitted to the same mechanisms. As a result, identity will never be complete and will always depend on the Other, understood as both the first and second Others, along with the larger, sociocultural discourse. For centuries, this discourse has presented a binary division: man versus woman. This dichotomy has recently been abandoned and replaced by a wider one where homosexuality and bisexuality have found a place.[9] With gender theory's constructivism (Butler 1993), it has been largely accepted that sexual identity depends on the sociocultural discourse, and thus is far from homogenous. The idea of a uniform category for "homosexuality" is considered as absurd today as the idea of a uniform heterosexuality. The result is that gender identity has become problematic for every subject, which is all the more true once we begin talking about psychopathology.

Deviations Concerning the Goal

The conclusion is not so difficult to reach: if everyone exhibits paraphiliac behavior and if gender identity per se has become prob-

---

8. The structure remains the same: the phallic-imaginary universe is never able to present a final answer to the original jouissance. Hence the title of Lacan's most important seminar in this respect: "*Encore*" (again). The more a subject tries to come up with an answer, the more pregenital-phallic elements will dominate the scene. As a result, the "paraphiliac" traits become even more apparent in concrete sexual behavior: "Can one say, for example, that, if Man [*L'homme*] wants Woman [La *femme*], he cannot reach her without finding himself run aground on the field of perversion?" (Lacan 1990 [1974], pp. 37–38). Here, "perversion" must be explicitly understood as a perverse ("paraphiliac") trait.

9. This binary reasoning dies hard. As I see it, we must approach it from a different angle, emphasizing inclusion rather than exclusion (see Verhaeghe 2001b, pp. 99–133). Rather than the classic dichotomy of male and female, we should examine the ongoing and always problematic intertwining of active and passive (see Verhaeghe 2002c).

lematic, the differential diagnostics for perversion must be based on other criteria. Freud (1978 [1905d]) undertook such an attempt with his classic distinction between sexual deviations with regard to the object, and those with regard to the goal. The first category was found to be of little use because the object is the most exchangeable element of the drive. The emphasis must therefore be placed on the second criterion, the deviations concerning the goal. It is precisely this criterion that can be introduced into a differential diagnostics on the basis of the relationship between the subject and the Other with the question: What is the aim of the perverse relationship? To answer this, we will minimally need some empirical data. Therefore, we must consult the clinic with the most significance in perversion: the forensic clinic.

DATA FROM THE FORENSIC CLINIC

It is by no means coincidental that the perverse subject is rarely found in the normal consultation room, contributing to the difficulty of the theoretical formulation of perversion. The most important descriptions come from compulsory treatment, that is to say, the forensic clinic. This introduces an important bias: here we are always dealing with "perpetrators." This must be taken into account, because it clearly concerns a selective group. What do these descriptions teach us, particularly with the criterion "deviations with respect to the goal"? Three characteristics emerge: (1) the enactment in reality of a rigid pregenital scenario (2) that compulsively imposes itself on the pervert subject, and (3) establishes a relationship of power.

The first characteristic is fairly classical: it is not enough just to have perverse fantasies, they must also be carried out in a hands-on manner (with the exception of voyeurism and exhibitionism). Nevertheless, this requires further clarification. Ever since the sexual revolution, neurotic subjects have also performed their fantasies, with the result that this criterion becomes considerably more blurred. Moreover, the perverse character must not be sought in the specific content of the sexual scenario, because any paraphiliac scenario can be enacted in a normal-neurotic context. The specifically perverse aspect lies in its rigidity, combined with its unfree character. Any deviation causes anxiety and tension. From a psychoanalytic perspective, we are dealing here with the repetition compulsion rather than repetition as such. Indeed, the presence of repetition in neurotic sexuality always introduces something new (Lacan 1994 [1964], pp. 42–53) into the proceeding dialectic of desire. Repetition compulsion, in contrast, as Freud discovered in his study of traumatic neuroses, is indeed compulsive and always fails in its repeated attempt to symbolize the traumatic Real.

The second characteristic stands in stark contrast to the neurotic ideal: the perverse subject is not the liberated erotic connoisseur of the neurotic's wet dream, quite the opposite. Empirical research (Ward and Keenan 1999) into the basic unconscious convictions and cognitive schemes of pedophiles found five convictions, including the sense that the tension cannot be controlled, with this occurring within the larger context of an uncontrollable world. The pervert is fundamentally unfree, compulsively driven to repeat the same thing. It is, moreover, frequently enough experienced as bizarre. Its completion will bring relief but sometimes also shame, disgust, guilt, and depression.[10]

The implication is that the perverse subject is preeminently divided, with no awareness of what it is that drives it. This has the clinical consequence that in its day-to-day life the perverse subject often presents a banal normality. In neurotics, the division is less extreme, demonstrating combinations of normal and abnormal behavior.

The third characteristic is the most interesting for a number of reasons. Clinical descriptions show how the perverse subject always directs its scenario toward the other in an explicit relationship of power, by which we must understand, the subject's power. The exhibitionist, for example, only succeeds if the other is shocked, the masochist will explicitly instruct the other what to do, and so on. The above-mentioned empirical research (Ward and Keenan 1999) reveals the pedophile's second basic unconscious conviction: the idea that the world is divided into superior and inferior creatures, the latter being forced to submit themselves to the former. Immediately following from this is the conviction of the need to control the other and the world in general.

---

10. Note that even the perverts don't know what drives them; here, the subject's division is total. In the forensic context, this causes difficulties, because the forensic clinician wants to know what is driving the behavior and expects to get confessions. The "perpetrator" cannot give them for the simple reason that he barely knows his own motives.

The last point already shows how the power relationship is not restricted to perverse acts—the pervert is also frequently the priest of a challenging new "ethic of pleasure" that needs to have an audience to control. Here, power is not necessarily synonymous with brute violence; it has to do with the relational aspect, the need to have the situation under control. It is important to stress this, because it means that not every pervert inevitably comes into contact with the police. This manifestation of perversion tends toward the psychopathological side of the spectrum, and will often go unrecognized. The "facts" are simply not there.

From a differential-diagnostic perspective, this description can give us important indications but in itself it is not enough. After all, "specialized" pregenital scenarios are not so rare in neurosis (less so in psychosis). If this continues for a while it may well give the impression of rigidity, even in a neurotic structure. Nor is an obsessive and even intrusive character at all exceptional in obsessional neurosis, and it can be seen in schizophrenic patients as well. Finally, the power aspect is found in every sexual relationship because of the dialectic between passive (identification/alienation) and active (separation) positions. The clinical description thus needs further specification in light of the perverse oedipal history so as to lay out its specific relational structure.

OEDIPAL HISTORY OF THE PERVERSE STRUCTURE: DISAVOWAL

It's now an open secret that yesterday's victims of sexual abuse run the risk of becoming today's perpetrators. The link between the victim and the abuser is thus considerably more complex than the simple black-and-white picture discussed earlier. Nevertheless, the connection between PTSD and the perverse structure doesn't mean that every victim of sexual abuse becomes a perpetrator, let alone perverse. In conformity with our reading of PTSD (see Chapter 11), we can understand the link between perversion and trauma by studying the underlying actualpathological position. A subject's specific structure will depend on the specific relational structure between it and the Other. If this is of a neurotic nature, the result will be borderline. Another possibility is perversion, or a psychotic structure.

Hence the question is, What sort of original relation between the subject and the Other is necessary for perversion to occur, and where does trauma fit into this process? The forensic descriptions all point toward an abusive Other, traditionally anticipated to be the father or his replacement—fitting well with our phallic-patriarchal expectations. The idea that a mother might abuse her child is incompatible with our conventional myths of motherly love. At least two women were necessary to explode this myth (Badinter 1980; Welldon 1988, 1995, 1996). Empirical research has meanwhile shown that sexual delinquents are significantly less securely attached than other delinquents and, moreover, that this insecurity has to do in particular with attachment to the mother rather than the father (Smallbone and Dadds 1998; Ward et al. 1995).

Let us first return to normal development. The child's inevitable starting point is the passive position, that is to say, it is reduced to being the passive object of the mother's desire, and acquires the basis of its own identity through a mirroring alienation. Once this basic identity is sufficiently stable, the next step will see the child attempting to take the active position. In between is a transitional phase where the child still clings to the secure relationship through the use of the transitional object (classically the pacifier). In this way, the anxiety about losing the mother can be managed. In a normal oedipal situation, the father's function is to create a situation where the child's further development can take place, if only by the fact that the mother's desire is channeled toward him.

In the psychogenesis of perversion this doesn't happen. The mother reduces the child to her passive object, to the thing that makes her whole.[11] Because of this mirroring, the child remains under her con-

---

11. Let me stress that even in cases of clear parental pathology, its effect on the children can never be predicted. As Freud already told us, we can only look back over time and see how something was developed; we can never predict with certainty. The reason for this is quite simple: the child plays a decisive role as well, making choices that determine further choices. In *Seminar IV*, Lacan (1994 [1956–1957]) observes with good reason that on the basis of his mother's interventions, Little Hans could as easily have become perverse as neurotic. The choice in favor of a neurotic solution (Freud's *Neurosenwahl*) lies with the child. It must be said that the concept of choice in this context is somewhat problematic as it evokes the idea of a conscious choice in full awareness of all alternatives. This is not what it is about at all.

trol, a part of herself.¹² The child thus gains no representational entry into its own drive, let alone to any subsequent elaborations of its own desire. In structural terms, it is reduced to the phallicized object (*a*) through which the mother fills in her own lack, the process of separation never taking place.¹³ As a third figure, the father is reduced to a powerless observer defined as insignificant by the mother. This banalizing of the Other of the authority will return later on when the pervert takes the law into its own hands with regard to jouissance.¹⁴

In this manner, the child finds itself in a paradoxical position: on the one hand, it is the imaginary phallus of the mother—a win for the child. On the other hand, the price the child pays for this is high: there is no separation, and any further development into its own identity will be blocked. In response, the child will perform a characteristic reversal in the attempt to safeguard its gain. The child will try to exchange its passive position for the active, taking the reins in its own hands with the aim of maintaining the privileged position.¹⁵

---

12. "This creates in the perverse person the deep belief that she is not a whole being, but her mother's part-object, just as she experienced her mother when she was a very young infant" (Welldon 1988, p. 9).

13. Lacan expresses it as follows: "The whole problem of the perversions consists in conceiving how the child, in his relation to the mother, a relation constituted in analysis not by his vital dependence on her, but by his dependence on her love, that is to say, by the desire for her desire, identifies himself with the imaginary object of this desire in so far as the mother herself symbolizes it in the phallus" (Lacan 1977 [1959], pp. 197–198). See also S. André (1993).

14. This forms the basis for what are today called "cognitive distortions" (Bumby 1996), which are assumed to comprise part of the etiology and, moreover, to sustain the continuation of the perverse behavior (Stermac and Segal 1989). In the cognitive behavioral approach, it has recently been accepted that these distortions contain basic *unconscious* convictions (Van Beek and Mulder 2002). From our perspective, such "cognitions" are taken over during subject-formation through the mother's perverse mirroring. The most important subsequent "distortion" in perversion is that the other enjoys the scenario, with the pervert as the instrument of this enjoyment—this is the kernel of the perverse subject-formation.

15. In clinical terms, this is most evident in masochism. The masochist presents him or herself as an object of enjoyment for the other, albeit in such a way that she or he has created the whole scenario and directs it—this is the instrumental aspect that clearly shows the passive–active reversal, on condition that "active" is interpreted as "leading." The pervert may appear passive, but is not.

Empirical Studies

The question is to what extent our reading of perversion is confirmed by empirical studies. As I indicated above, research in this field is both limited and biased. A rare exception is a recent study on pedosexuality by Bogaerts et al. (2002). These authors adhere to recent conceptual trends regarding sexual delinquency, focusing on the etiological importance of interpersonal factors (Jamieson and Marshall 2000; Marshall 2001; Smallbone and Dadds 1998; Ward et al. 1995). With the use of validated research instruments, they studied four variables in a population of pedosexuals based on the structural equation model: parental sensitivity,[16] trust, adult romantic attachment, and personality disorders. Their results confirm their opening hypothesis and show, among other things, a clear correlation between parental sensitivity and interpersonal factors on the one hand, and between pedosexuality and interpersonal factors on the other. Despite the selective population (pedosexuals) and wider range of inquiry, we can regard these results as at least a partial confirmation of our position.[17] The fact that recent research is increasingly beginning to emphasize interpersonal factors and the original parental attachment suggests that a more decisive answer may be forthcoming in the future.

Disavowal

Like the other pathological structures already discussed, perverse subject-formation has its own distinctive defense mechanism. We already saw how defense is directed each time toward an underlying anxiety, beginning with the subject's own drive tension and subsequently elaborated through the dialectic with first and second Others. With this, I have reinterpreted Freud's castration anxiety in terms of

---

16. The researchers divide parental sensitivity into warmth (versus coldness) and autonomy (versus overprotection). The relation between this and the guaranteeing function of alienation with no possibility for separation is clear.

17. The same goes for an analogous and now classic study (Malamuth et al. 1991, 1995; see also Gijs 2002). Through a path–analytic model, 78 percent of delinquency, sexual promiscuity, and aggression toward women was found to be explicable on the basis of a combination of parental violence and abuse as a child.

an anxiety either about being unable to satisfy the Other's phallic desire, or of being too satisfying for it. In perversion, we are dealing with a particular manifestation of the second situation: the subject is defined as the perfect answer to the phallic desire of the first Other. In Freudian terms, this implies *the lack of castration*, that is to say, the mother's castration (Freud), and the Other's castration (Lacan). At the same time, the phallic lack beyond the mother–child dyad is indeed recognized, particularly in the form of the powerless and insignificant second Other.

This equivocalness is grounded in the perverse defense mechanism: disavowal (Freud 1978 [1927e]). Through disavowal, the pervert adopts a double stance. He denies the phallic lack (for himself and for the mother), while at the same time recognizing its existence (for the rest of the world in general and for the father in particular). The result is a clear-cut split: the pervert lives in a divided world where lack and the regulating law are both recognized and denied at the same time.

Despite this defense mechanism, the underlying anxiety persists, since in this particular situation it involves anxiety about being reduced to the passive object of the Other. Hence the pervert's typical reversal of positions: the perverse subject compels others to assume the passive position of the object, while taking the active position for itself (see Note 15). In this way, the underlying anxiety can be mastered. In practice, this means that not only will the pervert turn itself into the instrument of the Other's enjoyment, but will also submit this other to its own system of rules *à propos* enjoyment.

Perverse anxiety is often understood as an oedipal anxiety, that is, an anxiety about the castrating father. This is wrong; the anxiety is about the maternal superego.[18] It was the first Other who was in control, and the perverse scenario is explicitly aimed at reversing this situation. This is the main reason why behavioral treatments based on the "paternal" superego usually fail: they are beside the point, in that they fail to address the maternal superego of the pervert. The anxiety lies at a much deeper level, closer to the psychotic anxiety about being

---

18. Again, the idea of mother and father must be amended. From a structural perspective, it is more correct to talk about the first Other (instead of the mother) and the second Other (instead of the father). I know at least one female perverse patient whose father took on the role of the first Other and who then defined and discarded the mother as the second Other.

devoured by the Other. The reaction against the imposition of the paternal law will frequently be aggression (see the discussion of "*aggression érotisée*" below).

Disavowal is not restricted to the sexual relationship. It determines the pervert's entire relation to the Others of sexual difference and of authority. In the pervert's own world there is no lack and its own laws are imposed on the Other. In the conventional world, the law will apparently be followed, that is to say, the pervert acts on the assumption that *others will follow the conventional rules,* and he or she will make full use of this knowledge.[19]

Passive–active Reversal

This original relation will repeat itself with the successors to the first and second Others in adult life with regard to the passive–active reversal. The perverse subject will assume an instrumental position toward the subsequent "first" Other, in order to ensure that Other's enjoyment. This is the paradox from a neurotic point of view: the pervert is firmly convinced that it works itself to death for the Other's enjoyment.[20] Hence the persistent ideas that the victims "asked for it," that they "do enjoy it, you know," and so on, ideas that were certainly true for the original first Other. This conclusion may similarly be found—in a reduced version—in the so-called "cognitive distortions," testifying time after time to the conviction that the victim was "cooperative," or even that it was the victim who took the initiative (Hall 1995; Kennedy and Grubin 1992; Ward et al. 1997).

---

19. The association with the old "psychopathy" is quite clear: this pejorative term referred to a group of patients who took the law into their own hands. The uselessness of this category has largely to do with its express connection with the juridical perspective. Nevertheless, as a term, it has at least one advantage over the contemporary ideas of paraphilia or perversion: unlike these, it doesn't accentuate sexually transgressive behavior, but focuses instead on the particular relationship of the subject to the law, of which sexual deviance is only one of a number of effects.

20. "Perversion adds a recuperation of the φ that would scarcely appear original if it didn't interest the Other as such in a very particular way. It is only my formulation of fantasy that enables one to see here how the subject makes itself the instrument of the Other's *jouissance*" (Lacan 1977 [1960], p. 320).

In its adult manifestation, the original relation has one important new merit, the passive–active reversal. Despite his instrumental position in ensuring the Other's total enjoyment, the pervert will only feel he has succeeded if he provokes anxiety in this Other (Feher-Gurewich 2002). This is the pervert's proof that he has escaped being totally reduced to the Other's desire, and proof of the turnaround in the relation. It is the Other who has been reduced to the object of enjoyment, and the anxiety is proof of this.

The stance is even more equivocal, if that is possible, in the pervert's relation to the replacements of the second Other, the Other of law and authority. The Other's law is not only challenged and unmasked as an insipid convention, appropriate only for the little people. In all the relations in which the perverse subject truly participates, the law is completely swept aside. In its place the pervert will substitute his or her own law, that is, a pseudoethos preached with abundant conviction and to which the Other is obliged to submit. Read any book of Sade's and you will see this characteristic, which is never absent from the perverse structure. Pages of meticulous descriptions of perverse scenarios alternate with chapters that outline the Sadean ethos of jouissance in an attempt to convince the other of the rightness of its justice in comparison to the wishy-washy nature of conventional law.

This relation to the law—challenge, ridicule, and replacement—results in the pervert's focus on the gaze of the second Other, intended to make it clear to the Other that he is powerless. This means that there is indeed a triangular structure in the perverse structure, albeit in the equivocal way we saw above. The neurotic, on the other hand, will always experience the gaze of such a third figure as censure, and precisely for this reason will try to avoid it as much as possible.

RELATION TO GENDER, SEDUCTION, AND TRAUMA

In earlier as in more recent studies, the emphasis has been on the connection between perversion and masculinity—as if perverse women didn't exist. To the extent that a woman exhibits paraphiliac behavior, the assumption is that it arises in hysterical response to her perverse partner. The fact that this is probably often true is no reason to conclude that the perverse structure is exclusively masculine.

So far we have identified the woman-mother as the departure point of the perverse structure. This originates from a psychoanalytically inspired forensic clinic and immediately suggests that the perverse position is not exclusively masculine (Welldon 1988, 1996). From a psychoanalytic perspective, one can even say that perversion is ungendered, seeing as how lack—and therefore, sexual difference—is disavowed as such. The pervert, consequently, is hommosexual. I deliberately write it, ho*mm*osexual, so as to clearly distinguish it from homosexuality.[21] The pervert denies sexual difference by presenting itself as the answer to the phallic lack of the other, thus disavowing both lack and gender difference. Perversion is not about a male–female relationship, but about a mother–child relation.

Nevertheless, disavowal is not psychotic foreclosure (see Chapter 15), and depending on the subject's gender there will indeed be a difference between its manifestations. The oedipal psychogenesis described above indicates that perversion must be studied across three generations. This is yet one more reason for conducting a thorough investigation into the case history. In this psychogenesis, the gender distinction becomes more visible. The perverse man and woman share the same aim: to maintain the privileged position in relation to the other through actively controlling it. Nevertheless, the object is different. In most cases, the masculine pervert will present himself as the other's phallic object of enjoyment. The feminine pervert, on the other hand, starts from the maternal position, that is to say, the position that transforms the other into an object that will fill in her own lack and complete her. Female perversion will thus be preeminently directed toward her child or to her own body—the difference is often quite hard to see because she regards her child as part of her own body. The connection with "Münchausen syndrome by proxy" is quite patent (Lievrouw 2001). It is no accident that Freud's major paper on perversion, "A child is being beaten," deals with female patients (Freud 1978 [1919e]).

---

21. In the United States, the question about the relation between perversion and homosexuality has become a hot topic. Personally, I find little interest in this discussion. Homosexuality is a descriptive characteristic that says nothing about a person's subjective structure, appearing just as easily in neurosis and psychosis as perversion.

Psychogenesis of Perversion

The backdrop for perversion is a presumed traumatic history. In today's empirical naiveté, this must be actual abuse: visible, clear-cut, "hands on." Consequently, little attention is paid to psychological abuse, because of its reduced "visibility." Nevertheless, to my mind, this is precisely the most important form of abuse in the psychogenesis of perversion, even more relevant than any "actual" abuse. Indeed, as recent research has shown us, the latter takes effect only to the extent that it takes place within a certain relation between the subject and the first Other (see Chapter 12), and such a relation may be traumatic in itself, without any perceptible actual abuse.

The original relation has serious repercussions for subject-formation and these extend beyond the purely sexual field. The three main descriptive features of PTSD—dissociation, repetition compulsion, and basic distrust—can be understood in accordance with the specific way the perverse subject acquires its identity in relation to the Other.

In cases of incest and sexual abuse, we confront an abnormal development because the oedipal law has not been respected—the prohibition of incest and the obligation for exogamy are not installed. The sexual abuse is initially not understood by the child, and is traumatic in the properly psychoanalytic meaning of the word.[22] The effects are described in studies of PTSD as dissociation, repetition compulsion with passive–active reversal, and fundamental distrust. The victim's aim will always be the same: to acquire control over the other, rather than being controlled. Let us look at these effects through the perverse structure.

Dissociation here is nothing but the radical splitting of the subject, often into bad (because abused or abusing), and good (because asexual) parts. This is the patient's final attempt to gain control over the situation. The analogy with Freudian disavowal is striking: there, too, two separate worlds are created, functioning independently of each other.

---

22. Hence the "confusion of the tongues" Ferenczi described between the child and the abusing adult (Ferenczi 1955). See, too, Freud's original description of trauma as something that the victim comprehends only later on, making it impossible to process in a psychic-representational way. From a psychoanalytic perspective, the specifically traumatic element has to do precisely with the impossibility of normally verbalizing the experience (see Verhaeghe 2001b).

As a result, the perverse subject has no consciousness of what drives it, unlike the neurotic whose subject division means that inner and outer worlds are intermingled.

The subject experiences its perverse behavior—the enactment of the scenario—as split off from the rest of the personality. It functions as a repetition compulsion that repeats the abuse in an active way. Note how the former victim has now become a perpetrator, doing to someone else what was previously done to him or her. What is most striking is the obsessive need for control: the other must be kept under control at all costs; anything else is unbearable. Sexuality thus becomes an instrument, even a weapon. The aim is to escape from the passive position of the past.

The third consequence is the most significant from a differential diagnostic and therapeutic point of view: the pervert's basic distrust of the Other, and therefore of every other. To have been abused by someone who was supposed to be protective means that later on the victim will distrust everyone. At the level of sexuality, this has two consequences: on the one hand, it becomes impossible to have a genuinely intimate relationship (because the necessary trust is missing); on the other, sexuality is used as an instrument. This latter means that the fine line between victim and perpetrator is often transgressed, thus repeating the vicious circle. In fact, the term basic distrust doesn't go far enough in expressing what we are dealing with in the perverse structure. It is not simply a question of basic distrust but of the active imposition of the pervert's own rule system *à propos* enjoyment onto the Other, whether it be the first or second Other.

Strange as this may seem, the latter characteristic gives the pervert a seductive character. As preachers of morals and underminers of the existing system of rules, perverts are frequently irresistible for the (above all hysterical) other confronted with dissatisfaction in his or her own sexual life.

PERVERSE PHENOMENA AND SYMPTOMS OF THE PERVERSE RELATION

In accordance with our theory of subject-formation, every subject is assumed to begin from an actualpathological position and to continue normally into the psycho(patho)logical elaboration. In the perverse structure, it is clear that the emphasis will lie on the actualpathological position, given perversion's etiological link with a traumatic history. In this sense, one would expect perversion to display more actualpathological phenomena than psychopathological symptoms. This expectation is confirmed by the forensic clinic, where sexual deviations always appear in the form of aggressive behavior ("perpetrators"), that is, the enactment of a rigid scenario. The principal element of the underlying anxiety points in the same direction.

But it is questionable whether the perverse structure can be restricted to this actualpathological position. It seems to me that this is the artifact of an exclusively forensic clinic. A wider, psychoanalytic study will show how the perverse subject is also capable of undergoing further psychopathological development, including the construction of a fundamental fantasy. Precisely because of such development there will be fewer confrontations with the law. In such cases, we are no longer talking so much about "perpetrators" as "writers," since writing is the most well-known symptom of perversion and the vehicle through which the perverse ethics, rooted in the fundamental fantasy, are declaimed. Authors such as de Sade, Sacher-Masoch, Gide, and Genet, but also Nabokov (Feher-Gurewich 2002) belong to this perverse psychopathological range.[23]

The Fundamental Fantasy

The formula for the fundamental fantasy of perversion seems relatively simple at first sight. It radically reverses the normal formula, giving us:

$$a \lozenge \mathbb{A}$$

This means that the perverse subject fully identifies with the object of enjoyment that the Other is lacking. The formula becomes less simple once we realize that it is jouissance as such that the pervert aims at,

---

23. Anyone who thinks there are only male perverse writers should read Vanessa Duriès' *Le lien* (Paris: Spengler éditeur, 1993) that gives a perfect illustration of the perverse structure.

rather than hysteria's ever-shifting dialectic of desire. This is its chief difference from the neurotic position, which always aims to avoid the Other's enjoyment—nothing could be more dreadful for the neurotic than being reduced to the jouissance of the Other, but this is precisely what the pervert has in mind.

Lacan did not elaborate the perverse fundamental fantasy in much detail, although the idea described above can be found from the beginning in his theory of fantasy (Lacan 1983 [1958–1959a,b,c]). In this sense, he develops Freud's original idea—that neurosis is the negative of perversion (1978 [1905d], pp. 165, 231)—by indicating the reversal of the positions in the fantasy à propos desire and enjoyment. A further elaboration is found in "Kant with Sade" (Lacan 1966 [1963]), where he describes the perverse subject's positioning as object (a) in terms of a "will to jouissance" ("*volonté de jouissance*") through which the perverse subject saves itself from the Other's alienation. The effect of such a "will" on the Other (ascribed here to the position of subject) is that this Other becomes reduced to a "raw subject of pleasure" ("*sujet brut du plaisir*").

From a Lacanian perspective, the writing that establishes the perverse ethic is the prototypical example of a perverse psychopathological symptom. For Freud, it was the fetish as it appeared in a metonymic structure. In Freud's view, the object elevated to the status of the fetish refers to the maternal phallus. But the ubiquity of fetishistic attributes in normal, that is, neurotic sexuality, means that this standard example is of little help for differential diagnosis.

Given the defense mechanism of disavowal, one can predict how every perverse symptom construction will possess a yes-and-no structure. Clinical experience testifies to this: in perverse speech, yes and no are always exchangeable, hence the notorious untrustworthiness of the perverse subject. This takes us to a characteristic that belongs to each of the subjective structures: the structural relation toward the Symbolic, and toward language. Human language rests on conventions agreed upon by members of the community who accept and believe in it (de Saussure 1976). The pervert refuses to do this, putting himself beyond it and becoming the champion of imposture and make-believe, assisted in this by the inherent qualities of language itself. If a fetish can represent the mother's phallus, anything can represent anything. This is how the perverse subject positions itself in language: the speech act itself is perverted, and the conventions according to which signification and communication operate are constantly undermined.

We must therefore continue to ask whether what we are seeing are actualpathological phenomena or fantasy-based psychopathological symptoms. Actualpathological phenomena are most prominent in the clinic, where the forensic descriptions talk about the "irresistible urge" that sets the chain of events in motion (Welldon 1988, 1994). In such a context, the perverse acts cannot be considered symptoms but rather reactive phenomena aimed at coping with trauma and managing the underlying anxiety. But where the emphasis is on the elaboration of an individual system of rules designed for the other's limitless enjoyment, the subjective structure is to be located more on the psychopathological side. There, the symptom takes the form of the perverse subject's new "morality," whether this appears in writing or not.

Perverse Structure

Regardless of whether it takes the form of phenomena or of symptoms, scenario or fantasy, the structural relation can be traced out. What is a perverse structure, that is to say, a structure of the subject that is different from the neurotic and the psychotic one?

The mechanism of defense is Freudian disavowal, but the accent is to be laid above all on the identification (per Lacan) with the first Other's imaginary phallus and the accompanying splitting. On the one hand, this implies that the pervert wishes to become the instrument of the Other's enjoyment—by which we must understand the Other's total enjoyment, enjoyment without lack. On the other hand, it means that the pervert not only refuses the Other's oedipal law (prohibition of incest; obligation for exogamy), but also challenges, transgresses, and replaces this law. From the pervert's point of view, such law applies only to the lowly masses; it is not for the pervert who holds itself above it.

Consequently, the perverse structure can be specified as follows: it is that relation between the subject, the Other, and lack in which the pervert turns itself into the first Other's (classically the mother) object of enjoyment in an attempt to control that relation. Turning oneself into the object of enjoyment of the Other takes place in relation to a second Other (classically the father) who is in this way confirmed in his position of powerless observer. The underlying mechanism is disavowal of the phallic lack, with the result that the perverse subject experiences a complete *Spaltung* (splitting).

For me, this reasoning proves the superiority of a structural approach as compared to a purely descriptive one. From a structural perspective, perversion is not synonymous with violent transgressive sexual behavior. As a structure, perversion has to do with a certain relation toward law and lack, and any potential transgressive behavior is nothing but an effect of that.

IMPLICATIONS FOR DIFFERENTIAL DIAGNOSIS AND TREATMENT

The diagnosis of perversion ought never to be based on sexually transgressive behavior. Rather, the clinician should focus on the typically perverse structural relationship and the perverse subject's splitting. It is precisely these aspects that will be of the utmost importance in any possible treatment.

The exclusive focus on transgressive behavior felicitously means that there is plenty of room left for a wider diagnostic enquiry, with particular attention paid to etiology. An exemplary recent model of this has been proposed by De Doncker et al. (2002). They suggest three phases, each time focusing on a specific area. At the macro level (life history and general psychopathology), the patient's case history is examined, along with his or her general and intellectual functioning, the social environment, and the DSM categorization. At the micro level (domains specific to sexuality), the emphasis is on the patient's psychosexual development in combination with external causes; personality traits (self-esteem, sexual preferences, cognitive distortions, etc.) are also charted. Finally, as far as criminal offenses are concerned, the accent is on the perverse scenario and the victims' statements. These authors indicate, moreover, those diagnostic techniques and instruments that have been found to be the most useful. Such a wide-ranging approach is undoubtedly valuable, albeit on one condition: that the patient wants to cooperate. What these authors overlook is that the diagnostic situation is entirely colored by the patient's relation to the clinician. It is precisely this aspect that must now be foregrounded.

It is absolutely crucial that perversion is understood in terms of a structurally determined relationship. As always, we must make a distinction between the subject's relation toward a first Other (gender) and a second Other (authority). The difference between a perverse and a neurotic subject can be evident from the first interviews, assuming that these interviews have not been distorted by what is socially desirable (on either side of the desk). Unlike the neurotic subject, the perverse subject never presents itself as a possible object of the therapist's desire. He presents himself as a possible object of enjoyment. This results in a completely different attribution of places. The perverse subject doesn't put the therapist into the position of the all-knowing Other, the "subject-supposed-to-know." To the contrary, the knowledge lies on the pervert's side. The other is approached as the other-supposed-to-enjoy (i.e., the first Other). Of course, another position may be ascribed to the other as well: the passive, powerless onlooker (i.e., the second Other). In contrast to the neurotic subject who always feels guilty under the other's gaze, the perverse subject absolutely needs to have that third gaze. Translated into oedipal terms, the perverse subject functions as the Imaginary phallus of the mother under the gaze of the father whose symbolic authority is erased. Not only must the third figure be convinced of his own powerlessness, in most cases he must be taught a lesson as well, a lesson, that is, in enjoyment rather than in the paltry pleasure of the neurotic.[24] Sade's books are perfect illustrations of this, with the reader in the passive position of observer. It is by no means exceptional for the therapy to take the same direction. This is all the more likely to happen because the pervert is fully aware of the conventional rules of the game: the therapist is bound by professional ethics, meaning that she or he cannot simply bring what was said during therapy out into the open.

The clear-cut distinction between perverse and neurotic structures doesn't mean that a number of differential diagnostic problems do not remain. First of all, with obsessional neurosis, the obsessional subject

---

24. In that sense, the pervert is anything but "functioning on a lower cognitive level." The earlier "deficit" model (the retarded farmer's son with limited social capabilities who fucks his sheep for lack of anything better) has now been replaced by the "expert" model (Ward 1999). Yes, the pervert is indeed an expert compared to the neurotic as far as enjoyment is concerned.

can also be defined as the answer to the phallic desire of the first Other, with a resultant anxiety about being reduced to a mere object of that Other. Combined with a pregenital, frequently anal scenario that is executed, moreover, in compulsively rigid ways, this may lead to significant differential diagnostic difficulties. Its chief difference from perversion lies in the subject's attitude toward the second Other of the law: for the obsessional, the law is thoroughly present *outside*, albeit not usually incarnated in a third figure but in a highly abstract system of rules; moreover, this law has to be scrupulously obeyed. This external law is disavowed by the perverse subject, who replaces it with his own system.

A second differential diagnostic difficulty concerns the hysterical position. In the hysterical relation, the hysterical subject will typically challenge the master and reveal his failure. This failure will always have to do with the master's system of rules regarding sexual identity and sexual relations, and in so doing the hysterical subject may demonstrate significant paraphiliac behavior. What distinguishes this from the perverse challenging of the master lies in the way the hysterical subject always challenges the master *in view of another master* that the hysteric construes as the better one. It is identification with the desire of this alternative and hysterically recognized master that is the cause of potentially paraphiliac behavior in the hysteric. Incidentally, it is not by chance that this alternative master is in fact, you guessed it, a perverse subject into whose shoes the hysteric has put herself by virtue of his seductive strategies.

If we take the relation toward the second Other into account, the differential diagnosis with the neurotic position is not so hard to make. In cases of neurosis, the desire of the mother goes beyond the child, but also beyond the father: somewhere in the outside world there is either someone (hysteria) or a system of rules (obsessional neurosis) that can satisfy her desire. Hence the typical neurotic stance toward sexuality: "Am I doing well?" In cases of psychosis, the mother's entire attention is on her child, which is this case is reduced to object (a) in its pure form, that is to say, it is nonphallicized. The father and the outside world fail to come into the picture, and the psychic processes take place at a much more primitive level (see Chapter 15). From this perspective, the perverse structure can be psychogenetically understood as being situated between psychosis and neurosis.

Redoubling of Reality

Besides the relation towards the first and second Others, the perverse subject's characteristic split must also be taken into account for the differential diagnosis. In the neurotic position, inside and outside are dynamically intertwined, enabling one to send feelings of guilt back out. Because of the disavowal of perversion, the split is much more radical—the term "dissociation" gives a pretty good idea of what we are talking about. Here the unconscious and the conscious do not dynamically course through one another as they do in the neurotic mechanisms of defense.

The clinical effect of this radical split in perversion is the redoubling both of the subject, the Other, and—even more broadly—of reality itself. On the one hand, the perverse subject is hyperconventional and follows the rules of the outside world. On the other hand, it creates a private world that has its own set of rules. Between the two, there is hardly any connection—thus the recurrent public surprise when a pervert is unmasked.[25] An important consequence is that the pervert barely knows what it is that drives it—and for the subject, too, there is scarcely any connection between the two worlds. Consequently, the integration of these two separate entities will be the most significant and difficult goal of the treatment.

Aggression

Because of the forensic dominance of the perverse clinic, it seems clear that in most cases we will be confronted with the actualpathological position of perversion, that is, with the "perpetrators." In this context, we must point to the presence of a fairly common clinical phenomenon,

---

25. This aspect of unmasking has to do with the previously mentioned split and its effects: on the one hand, a hyperconventional life, on the other, a hidden "other" life. There is an additional reason for this. Because of the perverse structure, the pervert is often driven to professions that center around law, education, and regulating, so as to be able to impose its own "law." The unmasking of the umpteenth educator, judge, or ethicist elicits the public's obligatory indignation ("How could someone like that . . ." etc.). But on the grounds of the structural reasoning described above, it is precisely such a link between perversion and law that can be foreseen.

namely, aggression, understood as a *"passage à l'acte"*—the Lacanian concept of a passage into action—the moment the relationship threatens to fail. With this, I am not referring to aggression in the perverse scenario per se. The aggressive *passage à l'acte* I am referring to is frequently not diagnostically recognized as belonging to the perverse structure. Based on his forensic experience, Mooij (1999) has argued that such a passage is far from rare and always takes place inside a typical constellation. He distinguishes between two situations. The first concerns a situation where the child is reduced to the mother's phallic object and where the child addresses itself to the father in an attempt to escape this reduction. In such cases, chances are that the perverse mother will try to kill the child. The second situation concerns the confrontation between an adult perverse subject and someone who assumes the position of the symbolic father, imposing and continuing to impose the law, thus creating a potential exit for the pervert's victim. In both cases, a violent *passage à l'acte* is not at all uncommon.[26]

Depression

Finally, I would like to draw attention to something that is scarcely ever addressed because of the sociocultural rejection of the pervert, and that is depression. Rather than an aggressive reaction following the breaking-through of the perverse dyad, the perverse subject can also suffer a depressive reaction. The breakdown of the situation where the pervert held all the cards and was "everything" for the Other can also

---

26. "This constellation is fairly typical in cases of partner murder, where the partner [of the perverse subject] solicits help from a third party, thus installing triangulation. As a result, the partner falls victim to an "eroticized aggression" (*"aggression érotisée"*). The same thing occurs in a specific form of child murder, where the child—at around two or three—becomes more autonomous and leans more toward the father, for example, resulting in its murder by the mother. In both cases, we are dealing with a constellation where one (partner, child) is forced to be everything for the other (man, woman or mother) but who is threatening to leave this position through the intervention of someone representing the symbolic function of the father. The subjective position of the perpetrator thus corresponds, one can assume, with the perverse structure as described by Lacan" (Mooij 1999, p. 4, my translation).

result in the exact opposite: being reduced to nothing. Such a perverse depression has seldom been described in the literature (Welldon 1988, p. 96; 1994) and will be closer to psychotic melancholia than to neurotic depression. The reason is the either/or character of the perverse subject structure, based as it is on a radical split.

Treatment

In light of the structural relation, it is clear that treatment will be difficult in any form. A recent review of outcome studies (Emmelkamp et al. 2002) gives little reason to celebrate. All the studies come from a cognitive behavioral perspective, and most have serious methodological flaws. The research population, in accordance with the contemporary redefinition of perversion, was made up of sexually aggressive delinquents, with the main accent on child abusers and rapists. The pitiful conclusion of the best research from a methodological perspective (Marques 1999)—the only one with long-term follow-up incidentally—is that there is scarcely any difference between the treated and the nontreated groups. Other studies talk about "limited results." In addition, a review studying the risk of recidivism concludes that contemporary instruments deliver no better results than a coin toss, and that such diagnostic instruments remain in an experimental phase (Van Nieuwenhuizen and Philipse 2002).

Such negative conclusions have at least partly to do with the forensic setting and the type of research population that (to my mind) probably only forms part of a much larger group. A second reason may have to do with the centrality of the juridical goal in such treatments—avoidance of recidivism—at the cost of other aims more closely linked to the subject structure. Nevertheless, seeing that there is no empirical evidence for these considerations, I must remain cautious with these remarks.

If nothing else, at least a number of predictions can be made on the basis of the perverse structure. First of all, in the majority of cases, treatment per se will not be easy to come by. Because of his disavowal, the perverse subject will by and large present us with a socially acceptable story that denies all guilt—the pervert is an expert in using the social conventions for his own benefit.

Moreover, there will almost never be any genuine demand for help, again because of the specific relation of the perverse structure. The neurotic subject positions the other as the subject-supposed-to-know with regard to lack. This in itself explains why the neurotic subject always has a demand: the neurotic wants something from the Other that the subject lacks. The perverse subject begins from the opposite position: there is no lack; on the contrary, the pervert has something to offer. For the pervert, the other is either obliged to enjoy—with the pervert acting as instrument—or to passively observe.

This structural relation will be repeated in the treatment. The situation where the pervert presents itself as the instrument for the total enjoyment of the other is rare but not impossible. But the most typical transferential relationship is one in which the therapist is reduced to the position of passive onlooker. With a neurotic therapist, this will be all the more enforced because of the neurotic's fascination with anyone who presents themselves as holding the secret to total enjoyment. Such a couple forms a perfect match: the neurotic is fascinated by the lack of *à propos* enjoyment, and the pervert is confirmed in his position of the first Other's imaginary phallus. Therapy itself becomes perverted.

The good news is that such a situation can be used as a diagnostic instrument. Confronted with another neurotic, the normal-neurotic therapist reacts with empathy: Imaginary castration is recognized in the mirror. Confronted with a psychotic patient, the same therapist reacts with an uncanny feeling, the Freudian *Unheimlichkeit*—the *"heim"* (home) of sameness is not reflected and the mirror shatters. Confronted with a pervert, the therapist is fascinated, full of anxiety and horror at the promise of total enjoyment. As a result, the typical one-to-one encounter of the analytic setting is not without danger for the treatment of perversion. Free association and free-floating attention can give rise to a reversal where it is the therapist who is "treated" by the patient. No wonder that analysts who regularly work with perverse patients prefer group treatment so as to prevent such a dual enmeshing of the transference (Welldon 1998).

To the extent that one manages to actually start treatment, one must fully take into account the fact that the perverse behavior or scenario itself is a solution for the underlying problematic structure. Focusing exclusively on relapse prevention means one removes the perverse subject's attempt at solution without addressing the underlying problem. To the extent that relapses do stop, this must occur as a result of the treatment, not as the primary goal. This is why one must focus on establishing an effective therapeutic working alliance through which the original pathological mother–child structure can be reworked.

Recent thoughts on the treatment are heading increasingly in this direction and emphasize interpersonal psychotherapy (Bogaerts et al. 2002), even from a cognitive-analytic approach (Kear-Colwell and Sawle 2001). The "cognitive distortions"—understood as the subject's identity as it sees itself in relation to that Other—can only be changed if the signifying relationship toward that Other is changed.

Concretely, this means that the analytic working-through of the perverse patient's history undoes his or her original identity in relation to the primordial first Other. At this point, treatment is no longer classically psychoanalytic, that is to say, the classical process in which interpretation and analysis of symptoms through free association occurs. Instead, one must open up the possibility for a process analogous to subject-formation. In normal development, the subject acquires identity through the double processes of alienation and separation in relation to the Other. Normally, this process is set in motion by the desire of the first Other, the "good enough mother," but in perversion she makes this impossible. The desire of the analyst must take over this function in the treatment so as to make it possible for the subject to choose its own identity in relation to someone who does not reduce it to a passive object of enjoyment. In this way, an opening is created through which the originally failed alienation and, particularly, separation can be redone. This is the immense challenge of treating the perverse structure.

15
The Psychotic Structure of the Subject

INTRODUCTION: PATHOLOGY AS A LINGUISTIC DISORDER

Neurosis mirrors, perversion fascinates and terrifies, psychosis confronts us with an uncanny riddle. While in the old days people used to listen to the psychotic patient, nowadays the whole focus is on pharmacological and neurobiological solutions and we risk losing the rich clinical knowledge of former times.

In the previous chapters, we understood the various pathologies in terms of a certain structural relation of the subject with the Other. By this, the Other was understood both as language and as first and second Others; however, we have not yet focused directly on this coincidence of Other and language. This means that an important aspect of the subjective structure has received too little emphasis: each pathology, understood as a certain characteristic relation toward the Other, simultaneously implies that each subjective structure possesses a certain way of being-in-language. This is unquestionably the clearest in psychosis, which is why I have reserved discussion of it for this chapter.

Becoming a subject always means becoming a linguistic subject. In neurosis, this is so self-evident that we pass right over it, being as we are, in the very midst of it. The Other furnishes the subject with language that enables it to process its jouissance (*a*) in a specific way: the Other's answer becomes reinterpreted through the phallic signifier and displaced onto an other, thereby shifting the accent onto desire and as far away as possible from the originally all-too-Real jouissance. The result is our uniquely human capacity for language acquisition. In sharing a conventional language, we thereby share the illusion that the Real can be completely mastered. In addition, we are conscious of its illusory aspects: each of us "believes" in language and in the rules and norms that are passed through language, but everyone also has intimate doubts. Is The Sexual Relationship (as our sociocultural discourse presents it) the right one? What is the best way to assume my gender identity? Are the law and the authorities really right? Our conventions enable us to live our lives, but at the end of the day they are nothing but a collectively shared illusion. We continue to invent words for desire, but there will never be a definitive answer to it. The underlying lack is shifted back and forth between the subject and others with collective responsibility and guilt. The subject's normality can be measured by the extent to which it was able to make some of this collective discourse its own and, on that basis, to make choices.

In perversion, we confront a different relational structure from neurosis, and, accordingly, a different way of being in language. Because of his or her disavowal, the perverse subject does indeed recognize lack and the regulating law—but for others, not for itself. One half makes us suspect we are dealing with an equal, even a hyper-equal who is more *au fait* with the conventions than we are. The other half confronts us with the perversion of these conventions that are useful only for being replaced by the lack-disavowing perverse law. The pervert's speech testifies to this equivocalness: yes and no are interchangeable, any word can mean what the perverse subject wants it to mean, and the only law that matters is that which imposes jouissance on the other.

Psychotic subject-formation is radically different. Every attempt to understand it from the standard neurotic model will hit a brick wall—but since there is no other entry, we must at least be fully conscious of this otherness. This doesn't mean that we won't approach the diagnosis from the same direction, namely, the structural relation of the psychotic subject toward the Other. Here, more than ever, the focus must be on the Other as language. As a result, diagnosis of psychosis must focus on two interrelated structural characteristics: firstly, the psychotic way of being-in-language; secondly, the relation toward others resulting from that linguistic position. Anticipating what has yet to be elaborated, I can already state that the psychotic subject doesn't have the luxury of a conventional language and hence of a conventional, shared solution for the Real. This is why the psychotic must create a private solution, namely, delusion. That this delusion is the psychotic's solution—perhaps even the only possible one—has not been adequately recognized in today's approaches.

With psychosis, as with the others, the DSM categorization is purely descriptive. While in the early days of psychiatry the focus was initially on paranoia, this has shifted in the DSM to schizophrenia and "other psychotic disturbances" (295.xx), of which paranoia is a subtype. The diagnosis is based on the presence of delusions, hallucinations, incoherent speech, serious chaotic or catatonic behavior, and negative symptoms, each in a variety of combinations. Thus a distinction can be made between the following subtypes: the paranoid type (295.30), the disorganized type (295.10), the catatonic type (295.20), the undifferentiated type (295.90), and the residual type (295.60).[1] We will presently examine these subtypes from a dynamic perspective.

Here, the need for a theory of the mind is more patent than ever.[2] In most contemporary theories of psychosis, not only are the internal

---

1. Accompanying these are a number of more-restricted forms: schizophreniform disorder (limited in time) and brief psychotic disorder (limited in time and with limited symptoms); schizoaffective disorder, that is, schizophrenia combined with a mood disorder; delusional disorder (no schizophrenic disorder and nonbizarre delusions); shared psychotic disorder; psychotic disorder due to a general medical condition or substance abuse; psychotic disorder not otherwise specified.

2. Unless understood from within a conceptual framework, "hard" data have little meaning. Researchers in the field of neuropsychology have meanwhile come to the same conclusion. Frith's (1992) attempt to construct a "theory of the mind" for schizophrenia, based on data from neuropsychological research, is an example of this. His unilateral emphasis on so-called "meta-cognitive" functions is nevertheless the source of an important handicap. The ongoing emphasis on this in both neuropsychology and cognitive psychology is all the more deplorable since it has been shown, from precisely a neuropsychological perspective, that patients who are "intact" at the cognitive-neuropsychological level but whose neuronal-emotional faculties are disturbed, are unable to make even banal decisions (Damasio 1995, p. 81). Pioneering new neuropsychological research is increasingly taking its leave from the purely cognitive field (Panksepp 1998) and is even making overtures toward contemporary psychoanalysis (Kaplan-Solms and Solms 2000).

dynamics entirely absent, but also scarcely any attention is paid to the characteristic psychotic relation toward the Other. This is less so for psychotic personality disorders (paranoid, schizoid, and schizotypal), which—through reordering—can give us a picture of psychosis before it becomes full blown (see the discussion below).

Because psychosis is without question the most severe of the disorders, diagnosis seems to present fewer difficulties, particularly in cases of obvious delusion. This is far less true of the onset of the psychotic process. Freud's warning of a hundred years ago, that nothing more resembles the onset of a psychosis than neurosis (Freud 1978 [1911c]; see also Lacan 1993 [1955–1956], p. 191), still holds. And even a full-blown psychosis can sometimes present a number of important diagnostic difficulties. There are thus more than enough reasons for thoroughly going into the underlying dynamics so as to be able to understand and recognize psychotic manifestations. As always, this will have significance for the treatment as well.

THE ETIOLOGICAL AND OEDIPAL (?) PREHISTORY OF AN UNDIALECTIZABLE DUALITY

The debate over the pre-Oedipal or Oedipal nature of psychosis is testimony to the fact that we are asking the wrong question. The oedipal structure is typically neurotic and retroactively determines the significance of the preoedipal period. Seeing as how the neurotic oedipal structure as such is absent in psychosis, the question of whether there is a preoedipal determination is beside the point. To my mind, psychosis should be seen in terms of a problematic of duality,[3] as is clear from both its history and its actual clinical manifestations, namely, the impossibility of entering into a dialectical exchange.[4]

---

3. Also see B. Fink (1997), pp. 79–111.

4. Freud called psychosis a "narcissistic neurosis," indicating in this way his attentiveness to its "dual" character. Today's wider use of the concept of narcissism has made the Freudian term confusing. Dual-type problematics are found in neurosis and perversion as well, albeit with one important difference: in the latter two, there is always a potential for triangulation. In psychosis this is not so, with the result that the possibility for a dialectical exchange—something we always strongly anticipate—is simply not there.

The question now concerns the nature of this prehistory. A few decades ago, the etiology of psychosis was thought to lie in the original family; today, empirical research has shown that its cause is to be found in a combination of hereditary and environmental factors. A recent classic in this respect is the longitudinal "Finnish Adoptive Family Study of Schizophrenia" (Tienari et al. 1994), which tracked all adopted children of schizophrenic mothers in Finland and compared them with their normal "matched controls." It showed that the risk of schizophrenia was significantly higher in the first group (with schizophrenic mothers) as compared to the control group, confirming the importance of the genetic factor. However, it appeared that this higher risk was *only* true for those high-risk children who were raised in dysfunctional families. This confirms the environmental factor. In a subsequent overview, Vonk et al. (1998) reach the same conclusion: the genetic risks of schizophrenia are realized only in and through the presence of negative environmental factors. Nevertheless, in professional circles all the talk these days is of "susceptibility" or "vulnerability genes."

Today's debate can best be understood as a retake of what I described in Part I as the opposition between "monists" (represented here by an exclusive emphasis on organic etiology) and "functionalists" (where psychosis is conceived as a functional disturbance, based on an as-yet undecipherable interaction between nature and nurture). The latter view has the upper hand today. The most important overview of recent neuroscientific research (Heinrichs 2001) concludes that there is no structural measure for abnormalities in psychotic patients' brains, and that it is above all the functional disturbances that provide the most convincing diagnostic evidence for schizophrenia. Ultimately, this leads to the conclusion that genetic research into schizophrenia has produced few or no relevant results of use for the treatment, and that the emphasis should be laid on these functional disturbances (Delespaul 2001).

From a clinical perspective, the emphasis must be on the negative "triggering" environmental factors.[5] A review article summarizes these

---

5. "Triggering" is the wrong word, as it gives the idea of something lying in wait, ready to pounce at the slightest provocation. As I argued in Chapter 9, it is always a question of the combination of both nature and nurture, each having a *mutual* influence.

as follows: a dysfunctional upbringing climate, the absence of the father during childhood, cannabis, prenatal complications, stressful life events, unknown environmental factors associated with urbanization, and belonging to specific ethnic groups (Van Os and Marcelis 1998).

From a psychoanalytic perspective, the principal question has to do with the nature of the dysfunctional family environment in combination with the absence of the father. Research by Huttunen and Niskanen (1973), quoted in Van Os and Marcelis [1998]) has shown that the loss of the father in early childhood does not necessarily increase the risk of schizophrenia. The same authors refer to a study by Walker et al. (1981) that demonstrates how it is only in combination with genetic vulnerability that the risk increases. Besides, there are plenty of schizophrenics whose father was present throughout their childhood and on into adulthood. My own hypothesis, a Lacanian one, is that it is more a question of the lack of a certain *function*, regardless of whether it is the father that assumes it.

In comparison with the normal neurotic, psychotic subject-formation can be understood primarily in negative terms. Lacan (1977 [1959]) describes its underlying process as the foreclosure of the Name-of-the-Father.[6] By this concept, he signals a radical absence: the Other's lack is not signified in phallic terms, the phallus as a signifier is missing.

---

6. Lacan first put forward the Name-of-the-Father as the typical psychotic defense mechanism in 1959. This concept subsequently was to undergo considerable evolution, along with his theory of psychosis. His original formulation remains fairly close to his first reading of the Freudian Oedipus complex. Lacan will later subject this to a severe critique, obliging him also to revise his theory of psychosis. This is particularly so with regard to his changing ideas about the function of the father. In his final, so-called "Borromean" clinic, founded on topology, he understands psychosis in terms of an incorrect knotting of the Real, the Symbolic, and the Imaginary, with the accent on jouissance. One of the chief differences between this and his first formulation is that the original concept of foreclosure implied a clear-cut structural differentiation: either one is psychotic, neurotic, or perverse; later, this becomes far less the case. His earlier views regarding the onset of psychosis (through a confrontation with the "*un-père*"—the "un/one father") also undergo a significant change. A detailed consideration of the evolution of Lacan's theory of psychosis can be found in Maleval (2000). For me, the term "foreclosure" refers to a *negative* process, that is to say, something in the course of subject-formation is *not* signified, namely the phallic lack in the Other. The cause of this negative process is not clear.

The original drive tension (a) that, normally speaking, is phallically elaborated and displaced onto the second Other is here maintained in its original form. This means that the normal basis for coping with the lack and managing desire is missing.

As a result, the psychotic is confronted with a *surplus* of jouissance that has no remedy. This explains why the psychotic, particularly during the episode's onset, is confronted with an enigma, often described as such by the patient. The typical effect of such a confrontation is a paroxysmic anxiety. It is not by chance that bodily phenomena take central stage during the onset of psychosis, often in the form of hypochondria. The difference with somatization phenomena, as described above, lies in its monolithic and intrusive character. These phenomena overwhelm the psychotic subject, whose hypochondria is an expression of the impossibility of symbolizing what is experienced in the Real. This is the actualpathological position of psychosis. The subsequent evolution of the psychotic process will be one long-drawn-out attempt to defensively process this Real of bodily tension through a psychotic attempt at its symbolization and thus displacement onto the Other. In this way, psychosis shifts into psychopathology. Compared with the neurotic secondary elaboration, this is a horrendous task: the psychotic must construct its symbolic screen entirely on its own, concluding in the systematized delusion.

At the level of identity, there is no division, neither in subject nor in the Other. This absence is the result of the foreclosure: no S_1 is recognized in relation to S_2, there is no phallically signified lack that would enable normal associative displacement to take place (see the discussion of hysteria, Chapter 13). Lacan coins this the *holophrase* (see below): two foundational signifiers are tangled up together; there is no function pointing toward a third position outside. The Other remains a single, monolithic, intact whole, just like the subject. In terms of discourse theory, this implies that there is no installation of the Master discourse, with the result that none of the other discourses function either. Consequently, the psychotic remains outside the discourses, that is to say, outside the social bonds as determined by the four discourses. The psychotic does nevertheless find itself inside language, albeit a psychotic language, without the normal social bonds founded on lack and desire (Lacan 1975, p. 47).

Total Alienation

The absence of the phallic elaboration of (a), along with the division of both the Other and the subject, makes normal subject-formation (alienation and separation) impossible. In normal formation, inside (subject) and outside (Other) typically loop through one another around a shared lack $(a/-\varphi)$. In psychosis, however, an undivided subject has to relate to an undivided Other during its confrontation with the Real of the jouissance. The psychotic process undergoes a development that sees this confrontation processed in different ways, resulting in a different differential diagnostic picture each time. The common factor is the absence of the interweaving of the subject with the Other, hence the dualistic nature of every psychotic relation with an other. The psychotic either positions itself in opposition to a malevolent, almighty Other who is out to get it (by which we must understand, who is trying to make the psychotic subject the object of its enjoyment). Or the psychotic itself is the almighty intact Other. Both positions are expressions of total alienation. Where the emphasis is on separation, the psychotic subject is reduced to nothingness. Such a subject is empty, has nothing, doesn't exist—is a member of the living dead. This is psychotic melancholia, where the psychotic subject develops an infinite delusion of guilt. So-called "manic-depressive" psychosis can be understood as a vacillation between this and the megalomaniac position.[7]

Fundamental Fantasy

Along with its formal-structural aspects, the contents of psychotic subject-formation can also be described. These contents are identical

---

7. For the layman, the idea of manic-depression (nowadays, bipolar disorder) evokes an image of neatly separated and successive periods of either extreme depression or extreme mania. In clinical practice, such an alternation is far from self-evident, as illustrated by the difficulties of describing such an alternation in the DSM. Clinical experience proves that there is no uniform picture. In my view, it is both diagnostically and therapeutically more relevant to examine the dynamics of the psychotic process through which the (megalo-) maniac and depressive periods can be understood. This is why manic-depressive psychosis is allotted no individual position here, unlike its treatment in many other studies, both inside and outside psychoanalysis.

to those in neurosis: the father ("The Other of the Other does not exist"), gender identity ("The Woman does not exist"), and the relation between the genders ("The Sexual Relationship does not exist"). This is no coincidence, having to do with the structurally determined failure of the relation between the Imaginary and the Symbolic on these three precarious points. The normal neurotic constructs a solution by way of the Imaginary, that is, through the fundamental fantasy according to which she or he assumes a gender identity and a sexual relationship in accordance with conventional authority. This occurs in the context of the collective appearances of gender, gender relations, and authority, based on a collectively shared discourse. The psychotic subject does not share this conventional symbolic order and must create its own solution. The psychotic's position is guaranteed through the delusion of genealogy, coined by Freud the "family romance": the psychotic is the son or daughter of God, of Lindbergh, of Napoleon . . .[8] The riddle of gender is answered by assuming the feminine position (what Lacan calls the "*pousse-à-la-femme*," the "plunge" toward woman).[9] The sexual relation also takes shape in the systematized delusion, typified by its asexual (i.e., nonphallic) character: insemination takes place through the word, rays, waves, and so on.

Solutions such as these are themselves testimony to a further evolution of the psychotic process that sees the systematized delusion increasingly getting the upper hand. The delusion is the psychotic equivalent of the fundamental fantasy. It has the same themes, but the

---

8. Freud originally introduced the concept of the "family romance" solely as an indication for the genealogical delusion in paranoia (Freud 1978 [1892–1899], letter of January 24, 1897, letter of May 25, 1897, letter of June 20, 1898, and Manuscript M). Later on, he recognized the same process in the neurotic, who similarly dreams of a different family background (Freud 1978 [1909c]). In the first case, we are dealing with a psychotic delusion, in the second with a neurotic fantasy. Again, this testifies to the fact that the difference between neurosis and psychosis must be sought not at the level of its contents but in the structural relation toward the Other.

9. This causes additional differential diagnostic problems in the decision about whether to surgically intervene in cases of male transsexuals. To make myself quite clear: not every transsexual has a psychotic structure. Conversely, it must be admitted that a number of male transsexuals develop a psychosis following their surgical transformation into a woman, highlighting the vital need for thorough screening beforehand.

relational structure toward the Other is radically different. It is striking, moreover, how the onset of psychosis often occurs after a confrontation in reality with one of those three elements. A psychotic breakthrough at the moment of becoming a father or a mother is far from uncommon; the same goes for the first orgasmic experience, while, for Lacan, the confrontation with the authority of *"un-père"* is the classic moment of onset (Lacan 1977 [1959]).

There is one constant between the dualism of the psychotic position and the content of its delusions: the structural relation to language. This is indubitably the most significant differential diagnostic characteristic of psychosis.

PSYCHOSIS AS A SPECIFIC WAY OF BEING-IN-LANGUAGE

As differential-diagnostic indications for psychosis, language disturbances have a long history. Classical psychiatry carries many rich and nuanced descriptions of these disorders, which are being approached in contemporary psychiatry through empirical-positivism.[10] Attempts to grasp the psychotic use of language through a limited number of speech disorders each time are countered by the observation that the same characteristics can also be found in normal subjects (Chaika 1974; Fromkin 1975; Schwartz 1982). Contemporary theories assume there must be a cognitive deficit at the heart of psychotic speech, disrupting linguistic performance.[11]

In response to this, let me offer two remarks. Firstly, the highly gifted psychotic patient is not in the least bit rare, exhibiting intact

---

10. Already in 1920 Kraepelin emphasized linguistic disturbances as a differential diagnostic criterion for psychosis. In the wider field of psychiatry, these have been described as: stereotypy, neologism, paralogism, illogism, alogism, agrammatism, glossomania, schizophasia, alliteration, assonance, logolatry, logorrhea, verbal fetishism, perseveration, discordance, and so on.

11. In a fascinating study, Vanheule (1999) compared the Lacanian conception of psychotic speech disturbances to recent neuropsychological research into psychosis and language. The fact that there is a clear difference (focusing on the particular clinical instance of a patient as opposed to scientific generalization) does not exclude an interaction.

cognitive functioning each time as long as the delusional content is not touched upon.[12] Secondly, these studies concentrate on the difference between psychotic and nonpsychotic speech independently of the clinical situation, that is to say, independently of the structural relation toward the other, often using written material upon which computer programs are then set loose. By then, of course, it has indeed become impossible to tell neurotic and psychotic speech apart.[13] In the clinical situation, however, centered as it is around speech and listening, such a distinction can be made, precisely because the clinician, intuitively or not, takes the relational aspect into account.

---

12. The expectation of a cognitive defect is one more illustration of a double prejudice: that the madman is *completely* mad, and mad, moreover, precisely because she or he has a cognitive defect (something *must* be defective), and therefore must be a lesser person than ourselves. Based on his year-long study, Maleval concludes: "one knows how convincing psychotics can sometimes be, both to those who are close to them and to even larger groups. There is nothing to suggest that the onset of a delusion is accompanied by a diminution of the cognitive faculties" (Maleval 2000, p. 173, my translation). High or low cognitive functioning has nothing to do with psychopathology. This very idea is testimony rather to the function of segregation: we, that is, we normals, want nothing to do with them, those abnormals, whom we regard as cognitively "weaker," that is to say, weak-minded, retarded. There are both highly intelligent and stupid psychotics, perverts, and neurotics. A high intelligence usually just makes it easier for the subject to hide its structural differences from others, that is to say, makes it easier to follow the social conventions. There is doubtless a high inverse correlation between the psychiatric residential population and intelligence, meaning that research based on this population will be flawed in this respect. Classical examples of brilliant psychotics are: von Mayer (1842, first principle of thermodynamics), Cantor (founder of the set theory), Comte (founder of positivism), Bolyai (founder of the first, non-euclidian geometry), Nash (Nobel prize in economics, 1994). They all transgressed the limits of normal knowledge and thus found themselves in a symbolic void (Maleval 2000, p. 288). Moreover, psychotic structure and cognitive functioning are unquestionably interrelated, albeit not in the sense of "defective." The psychotic subject is not hindered by phallic lack. Thus the signifiers are not contaminated by eroticism (i.e., by phallicism), and it is precisely this kind of contamination that hinders normal neurotic cognitive functioning.

13. No diagnosis can be based purely on written material. Nevertheless, there is a special relation between writing and psychosis. Writing will always represent a psychotic's attempt to get a hold on the jouissance. One of the most famous illustrations of this is Wolfson (1984), a psychotic patient who tried to cope with his psychosis through experiments on his mother tongue, literally through a form of continuous "translation."

This means that we must once more base our diagnosis on the structural relation toward the Other, understood always as both language and as others. This emphasis on the relation has an additional advantage: a considerable number of psychotic patients seem to produce fairly normal speech; the typically psychotic linguistic disturbances are fairly discrete. But in these, too, the structural relation toward the Other and others will be revealed as psychotic, and because of this, seemingly normal speech will be revealed as possessing a psychotic function.

Psychosis is a certain structural relation toward language and others, and these are scarcely possible to tell apart. As enumerated by classical psychiatry, linguistic disturbances can be grouped, following Freud and Lacan, into two opposing types: on the one hand, those where the fullness of signification has the lead, and on the other those that emphasize the empty formulas (Lacan 1977 [1959], pp. 179–187). Moreover, each of these oppositions will ascribe a specific position to the other.

Such division of linguistic disturbances is of considerable more interest than a purely descriptive classification. As an illustration of this, neologisms, often regarded as the hallmark of psychosis, are not always so evident in clinical praxis because of the way that normal words can be used in a "neologistic" way.[14] Moreover, while the psychotic neologism can be brimful of (new) meaning—as one expects—it can also be the opposite, that is, completely hollowed out, reduced to the repetition of an empty refrain.[15]

This oversaturation of meaning corresponds with Freud's approach: in treating "word presentations" as if they were "thing presentations," words acquire literal and thus overly replete meanings for the psychotic; they become "glued" to the thing (Freud 1978 [1915e], p. 198). Such is

---

14. Again, this multiplicity gets diluted in the more refined classical descriptions: active, passive, lexical, semantic, glossolalic (etc.) neologisms. And again, this doesn't work. We need a broader understanding of psychotic language, based on its function for the psychotic subject, one that will go beyond mere descriptive classification and that is founded in a metapsychology of the psychic functioning of the psychotic subject.

15. "Neologism," moreover, suggests the idea of an isolated expression—which is in fact often so. Nevertheless, the identical function with the same identical extremes (oversignifying or nonsignifying) can be found to a much wider extent in the entire speech, the so-called "glossolalia." This boils down to a speech that appears to have all the characteristics of normal language, but is at the same time entirely incomprehensible and is unlike any existing language (Samarin 1972).

the effect of an *Augenverdreher*, for example (an imposter, literally, someone who turns one's eyes) on a psychotic patient who is convinced her eyes are being physically turned. Psychotic patients themselves feel such expressions to be unique,[16] carrying an uncontestable certainty and self-sufficiency. Such expressions, in other words, are non-dialectizable; the normal displacement through the chain of signifiers is impossible. To the contrary, it is more the reverse: all other signifiers are delusionally reorganized around a specific overreplete expression. As a result, the psychotic has no "sense of reality," by which we must understand that psychotics cannot share our reality because they have no access to the ever-shifting determinations of our symbolic reality. This is the fundamental differential diagnostic difference between psychosis and classical borderline (Fonagy and Target 2000, pp. 854–855).

Lacan coins this unique, non-dialectizable character "holophrasis" (1994 [1964], p. 237); it is solely through the relation between the psychotic patient and the other that it can be diagnosed. Here a written text will be of no use. Holophrasis implies that two or more signifiers are monolithically tied together, having no normal-neurotic space between them. The absence of this inter-space means that associative displacement becomes impossible, as do the fluctuations of meaning. The result is that the holophrase signifies only itself, with an utmost certainty (Stevens 1987).[17] As we will see, holophrases are always

---

16. This gives rise to expressions like "logolatry" or "verbal fetishism" in classical psychiatry. The fact that the psychotic patients themselves experience them as unique and unusual gives the illusion that they are aware of being ill. But this is indeed an illusion. As I showed in Part I, the normal neurotic "insight" into illness is always an "insight" into one's own guilt, that is to say, the recognition that the subject itself plays a part in the problem. This does not happen in psychosis.

17. The first studies of holophrasis focused on isolated examples. It quickly became clear that holophrastic speech is a wider phenomenon and must be understood as a characteristic of psychotic speech as such, and that it is therefore also typical of how the psychotic interprets the speech of others. In his extensive study of the holophrase, Stevens describes a patient who became threatened by the advertisement "The BBL is thinking of you" (Translator's Note: BBL was a European bank) following an attack by the terrorist group CCC on a BBL office. Purely by coincidence, the patient was then working for a firm with the initials CCC when he heard the news and saw the ad on the street. For the patient, it was a forgone conclusion: the BBL was after him. What he read and heard combined into a single, monolithic conviction and there was no way of dissuading him (Stevens 1987).

indications of the paranoid evolution toward a fully Meaningful delusional system—the capital "M" indicates its subjective significance for the patient. The capitals of religion are never far off here either.[18] This linguistic disturbance can also appear in the way the psychotic subject listens to and interprets the language of others. The over-repletion of meaning is then visible in the psychotic's well-known delusional interpretations: the psychotic awards a fully self-centered meaning to the other's words that corresponds perfectly with the developing delusion.[19] Classic psychiatry calls this sensitive delusion (Kretschmer: *sensitive Beziehungswahn*).

Its opposite is seen in the obverse process where unsignifying, purely phonological linguistic productions are found. Here, the word presentations become disconnected from things, and are thus turned into meaningless, frequently repetitive refrains, sometimes in syntagmatically correct forms, sometimes reduced to syllables, "word salads." Classical psychiatry speaks of "schizophasia." The tenacity with which the patient holds onto the repetition of these meaningless expressions makes it clear that it is precisely this repetition that is important. From a Lacanian point of view, these expressions are the final ramparts against the patient's total disappearance into the Real, a desperate attempt to maintain the linguistic network as automaton, divorced from any meaning (Maleval 2000, pp. 188–189). Here, the subject is barely able to be seen anymore as contrasted with the other psychotic linguistic disturbance where the subject is "Absolutely" present in its Absolute Meaning.

Clinical practice has shown how these two linguistic disturbances are themselves two ends of the continuum along which psychotic development takes place. Note how we are once more dealing with a logi-

---

18. It is not uncommon for the psychotic's linguistic disturbances to formally appear in handwriting: capitals, calligraphy, special signs are very well known.

19. Here is an example of a classical division of forms of delusional interpretation (Guiraud 1921, quoted by Maleval 2000, pp. 209–210): (1) verbal allusions (the patient interprets others' sentences as equivocal and hostile); (2) kabbalistic interpretations (numbers are processed in order to prove something); (3) homonymic interpretations, fairly similar to (4); (4) word games ("Thule" = tue-les, kill them; cacao = caca + eau, shit and water). I provide this classification not as a diagnostic specification but to show the reader how such forms may just as easily occur in neurotic subjects (particularly in obsessional neurosis). Once more, a symptom's psychotic or neurotic nature entirely depends on the structural relation toward the Other.

cal rather than chronological time. Such an evolution may evolve over a longer stretch of time, but it can also occur within a very short period; in both cases, moreover, retroactivity will come into play. These dynamics are important, both at the differential-diagnostic and the therapeutic level, which is why we must go into them more thoroughly.

FROM ACTUALPATHOLOGICAL SCHIZOPHRENIA TO PSYCHOPATHOLOGICAL PARAPHRENIA, WITH PARANOIA AS THE HALFWAY POINT

We find the same development in the psychotic structure that we have already seen in the neurotic and the perverse structures: from actualpathology, where the subject is unable to process the original jouissance through the Symbolico-Imaginary, to psychopathology, where the subject develops a fundamental fantasy or delusion. There is no concept of dynamics in the DSM, although traces of this can be seen even in this purely descriptive approach.

Here, as in the other subjective structures, it is important to underscore how we are dealing with a continuum whose beginning and end points in particular can be clearly distinguished from both a clinical and a conceptual perspective. The idea of a continuum implies, however, that most patients have exited the departure point but haven't always reached the end. As we will see, this starting point is clinically quite palpable. This is much less the case for the end point, not only because of its relative rarity, but also because it implies—as a terminal point—a kind of stabilization, meaning that patients manage to maintain themselves outside the clinic. The idea of a continuum also implies that patients can move in both directions: one can "regress" to a previous level; again, we are dealing with a logical time sequence.

The idea of psychotic evolution has been extensively described in classical psychiatry, that is, before the dominance of pharmacology. Billiet (1989) and Maleval (2000, pp. 309–326) have recently taken this up again from a psychoanalytic angle. Neither makes the connection with the continuum of actual- to a psychopathology, but this is not hard to apply. Maleval replaces the psychiatric threefold classification—initial perplexity, intermediary elaboration, final megalomaniac solution—with a Lacanian-inspired fourfold evolution. Nevertheless, whether it is divided into three or four phases is only incidental: the emphasis must be on its dynamic nature. The underlying idea is that the psychotic subject is confronted with an un-phallically processed jouissance as a result of the mechanism of foreclosure. The psychotic elaboration is thus a different attempt at solution than that of the neurotic or the perverse, different precisely because the phallic solution is and remains impossible.

The impossibility of arriving at a normal representational processing of the original drive tension results in the psychotic's completely different experience of the body compared to neurosis. Next to the linguistic disturbances, this is the most important diagnostic indication—except that "next to" is not really the right expression since the disturbances of language and bodily awareness are interwoven. In his introduction to his qualitative empirical study, Soenen (2002) refers to classical psychiatric studies that pay careful attention to schizophrenic disturbances having to do with questions of bodily awareness.[20] Kraepelin, Bleuler, Schneider, Rümke, and Ey also attend closely to this topic. Soenen (2002, p. 148) notes how this focus disappears after 1980, partly because the emphasis from then on is increasingly on the neurobiological approach, and partly because clinical psychology then began to address eating disorders and their associated disturbances in bodily awareness. Of course, this doesn't mean that such bodily disturbances disappeared in schizophrenia. It is just that the discourse changed and, thus, so did the center of attention.

The outbreak or onset of psychosis implies a confrontation between the subject and this jouissance. It is no coincidence that psychosis usually begins during adolescence.[21] An empirical study (Emck et al. 2001)

---

20. The emphasis is on co-anesthesia, uncanny sexual sensations, hypochondria, bodily hallucinations and delusions, somatic depersonalization, and loss of somatic borders. The classic psychoanalytic study of this is by Tausk (1919).

21. Classical psychiatry calls this hebephrenia. Incidentally, it is not just psychosis that sees the period of puberty and adolescence as typical for the outbreak of pathology. Practically every psychopathology emerges during this period; the only difference is that a psychotic breakthrough is much more spectacular. Moreover, a (neurotic) "puberty crisis" is simply par for the course, and therefore gets less attention.

This argument can be further developed. It is not by chance that pathology often begins during periods of confrontation between the mind and the body, forcing the subject to find a new equilibrium: midlife, peno- and menopause, post-surgery, and so on. This is only further confirmation of our metapsychology, in which the shows that schizophrenia in 12- to 18-year olds has a clear predevelopment (school problems, distrust, introversion, sleeping disorders), along with symptoms that can barely be distinguished from adult symptoms. In adolescence, the human being is both somatically and socioculturally confronted with adult sexuality, in the narrow genital sense of the word. The psychotic subject has no means of responding to it. Soenen's research (2002, p. 593 ff) shows how such a confrontation with the libido can be systematically recovered (falling in love, sexual arousal, conflict with the father, etc.).

The Moment of Onset

The first logical moment[22] is the moment of onset, namely, the actualpathological confrontation with (a) in the psychotic structure. There are no symptoms in the psychoanalytic sense, only phenomena related to the bodily experiences. The subject's initial reaction is perplexity (compare this with panic disorder), often coupled with hypochondria. Qualitative research into schizophrenic adolescents has shown that in a number of cases such hypochondriac disturbances existed long before the psychotic breakthrough, anchored mostly in bizarre bodily sensations (de Bois 1989, p. 101, quoted in Soenen 2002, p. 154). Freud already accounted for such hypochondria as actualpathological and psychotic (Freud 1978 [1914c], pp. 82–85): something at the level of the body makes a demand, but the psychotic subject has no way of answering it except through anxious preoccupation.

The hypochondria points to the source of this anxiety: a painfully experienced drive arousal combined with an impossibility of representing what is experienced (André 1986, pp. 127–128). The patient senses

---

organism's demand on the psyche is regarded as the causal factor. Causality nevertheless has to be understood in a Lacanian sense here, that is to say, as the opposite of determination (Lacan 1994 [1964]). The latter will have to do with the subjective structure as such.

22. This first "logical" moment doesn't imply that every psychosis breaks through at this point. In clinical practice, one can encounter onsets even during the paranoid phase. Because of this, the patient will always be able to retroactively point to a preceding actualpathological period, the processing of which is represented precisely by the paranoid delusion. Schreber is a classic example (Freud 1978 [1911c]).

an aggressive, autodestructive force at work in its body that causes it to fragment (e.g., knives slicing through the body, feeling like one is about to explode, of being laced up and deformed by "nerves," etc; Soenen 2002, p. 591 ff). The subject's perplexity is an expression of the impossibility of answering the drive's jouissance. Soenen's research also confirms this impossibility. The body is crisscrossed by uncanny experiences that cannot be verbalized or symbolized in any way. Schizophrenic patients are confronted with "a yawning emptiness wherein life and all meaning is annihilated and swallowed up" (Soenen 2002, pp. 596, 169; my translation).[23]

The dualism of the psychotic structure means that, even in this first period, it is possible to switch over to the other side, that is, for the subject to experience a short-lived fusion with (*a*). Well known in former times, this was rediscovered by Soenen: in the naked confrontation with jouissance, the psychotic subject may experience an extreme sense of satiety and ecstasy, combined with the disappearance of every feeling of uncertainty or lack. One literally feels such experiences "in one's bones" (Soenen 2002, p. 594).

Both classical and contemporary psychiatry will regard this first logical moment as falling partly under the initial phenomena and partly within the second logical moment.

Second Phase

The second phase sees the initial perplexity and hypochondria evolve into classical schizophrenia. In DSM terms, this is schizophrenia of the disorganized type (295.10). The anxiety is monolithic although it doesn't always appear as such, that is, in a neurotic and therefore easily recognizable form. Its typical form will be catatonia: the patient is paralyzed by fear. Clinically, this second period is the acute psychotic phase, where the body is experienced as fragmented, and its different parts no longer refer to one other or add up to a whole

---

23. The analogy between this and what Freud described at the foundation of *Schreckhysteria* is striking: "its primary symptom is the *manifestation of fright* accompanied by a *gap* in the psyche (1978 [1892–1899], p. 228; "A Christmas Fairy Tale," Draft K, d.d. January 1, 1896; my italics; see also Chapter 7 of this book).

(Soenen 2002, p. 587 ff).[24] There is no unifying S_1, hence the fragmentation. The same effect can be found in the verbal productions. Here the patient frequently refers to an enjoyment that is forced upon him or her. Hallucinations and the first forms of delusions (hypochondriac hallucinations and/or delusions of influence on the body) are also fragmented but do not yet have any stabilizing effects. The auditory hallucinations are full of reproaches, typically focusing on enjoyment ("Fag!" "Whore!"). It is only afterward that the patient will be able to talk about what was experienced during this period.[25] The auditory hallucinations—one of the most alienating of the experiences—can be understood on the basis of the dualistic character of psychosis. All neurotic subjects hear voices in their heads as well, voices that forbid or oblige them to do things. But the neurotic subject is fully aware that this is its own voice, albeit framed by neurotic division and conflict with regard to desire. For the psychotic subject, on the other hand, such a voice is real, coming from an external Other, and therefore feels intrusive and threatening.

Third Phase

The third phase represents a clear departure from the actualpathological position and contains a psychopathological attempt to process the jouissance through an increasingly systematic delusional system. In classical psychiatric terms, this is paranoia; in the DSM it is called

---

24. Soenen (2002) found the following phenomena in his patients: peculiar sensations, forces, or rays, a "crippling" excess of energy in the body, the feeling of being torn to shreds, a hyperconsciousness of all bodily sensations, extensive hypochondriac anxiety, bizarre representations of bodily disintegration, (fragmented) persecutory delusions of one's body being taken over, physical hallucinations and disorganized psychomotorics, disintegrated representations of one's insides, fragmentation anxiety, and vertical splitting of physical awareness (left–right) (p. 587). Note that these phenomena are almost never found in patients with a systematized delusion. The latter clearly has a stabilizing effect (p. 589).

25. The famous *Memoirs of My Nervous Illness* (2000 [1903]), Schreber's own report of his psychosis, is exemplary. Looking back from the end phase of his psychopathological psychosis, he gives a detailed report of its psychotic evolution. The book was written with his social rehabilitation in mind, fully convinced as he was of his psychosis being right. As a document, this is obligatory reading for anyone who wishes to understand psychosis.

schizophrenia of the paranoid type (295.30) and delusional disorder (297.1). In practice, the elaboration amounts to a hunt for the Other as the cause of the jouissance the patient was attacked with (and therefore the guilty one). The psychotic feels persecuted by a controlling Other who is using the subject for its personal enjoyment. The way the patient describes this control can be bizarre and thus clearly pathological (poisoned food, waves, rays, . . .) but it can also seem quite normal (conflicts in the family, on the work floor, with neighbors). The anxiety is no longer primarily directed toward the subject's own body but becomes processed into a secondary form directed against fears of the Other's interventions on the life and body of the patient.

This processing aspect is once more confirmed by the research cited above. As a result of its elaboration through a delusional system, the body is no longer overrun by diffuse, uncanny, and lacerating sensations, and the body's boundaries become more consolidated. The destructive experiences of the drive tension disappear to the background, being projected out of the body and ascribed to a malevolent Other; it thus becomes possible to articulate the affect. The delusion also makes it possible to demarcate the bodily image from the outside world. Such stabilizing effects are missing from the fragmentary delusions that belong to the previous phase (Soenen 2002, pp. 589–599).

This third phase centers on oppositional resistance, with the patient frequently taking juridical steps. In the words of Lasègue: "They voluntarily present themselves as advocates of their delusions" (quoted in Maleval 2000, p. 325). Just about every study confirms how paranoid patients initially often succeed in convincing their immediate environment that someone is doing them an injustice—the systematic power of the paranoid patient's conviction should not be underestimated—with the result that the pathology per se often goes unrecognized at the time.[26] Aggressive acting-out is also not uncommon, and not without danger for those close to the patient (Maleval 1991).

---

26. Whenever a neurotic files a complaint, his inner conviction of his own part in it means that he makes the case in a less convincing way. The neurotic's doubt and feelings of guilt will cause the juridical other to doubt as well. When a paranoid psychotic lodges a complaint, she is thoroughly convinced of the other's guilt and of her own innocence. The result is that her complaint is far more convincing than the neurotic's and is frequently believed, particularly when it belongs to the usual range of human vexations.

Along with the defense directed toward the Other, the patient will also seek protection in the Other, who then is attributed with an idealized, sometimes even deified, fatherly function. These two positions can be spread across two different others, but—as any therapist with psychotic patients knows—they can also fluctuate on the same figure. In this advanced stage, the originally fragmented schizophrenic delusions become increasingly systematized, reaching their final form in the delusional system of the paranoid patient. With this, the subject construes a positive explanation for what the Other has done to it. People thus speak of the psychotic's "loss of reality" and "lack of a sense of illness"; this is because for the psychotic these explanations are literally "out of one's mind," all the while that their Truth remains unshakable for the patient. Throughout its delusion, the subject will assume the active position and become the organizer of a new world for which it constructs a new and supportable identity. The initial perplexity, followed by defense, slides toward reconciliation.

Fourth Phase

The fourth and final phase, the "paranoia vera" (true paranoia) or "systematized paraphrenia" of classical psychiatry, depicts a patient who has finally come to rest. In DSM terms, this is schizophrenia of the residual type (295.60). By means of his or her delusional system, the psychotic has literally "come to terms" with the jouissance that the Other (who has meanwhile been identified) has caused. Moreover, throughout these delusions, the subject has gained access to an essential Knowledge, whose veracity is incontestable. The fact that we call this "megalomania" speaks as much about our own doubts as about the psychotic's certainty.

With this final phase, the psychotic has developed a coping strategy whose "encapsulated" delusions (again, a term from classical psychiatry) protect it and even enable it to lead an apparently normal, if usually isolated life. The psychotic has "cured" himself. Consequently, this final form is encountered much less frequently in clinical practice.

IMPLICATIONS FOR DIFFERENTIAL DIAGNOSTICS

Diagnosis of a full-blown psychosis is usually not so difficult except in the case of paranoiacs who, because of their absolute certainty, can often be very convincing. The diagnosis must always be based on the linguistic disturbances and the subject's relation to the Other. The decisive criterion will be the subject's inability to enter into any dialectical exchange, both at the level of language and in the structural relation. The aim of the diagnostic process will not only be the diagnosis of the psychotic structure, but also to assess the extent of the psychotic evolution. The latter will largely determine the treatment, including any pharmacology.

The straightforwardness of the diagnosis doesn't mean that there are no differential-diagnostic difficulties needing further attention. The prodrome or pre-onset psychosis is one of the most important of these. In addition, we must attend to hysterical delusions. The third difficulty has to do with psychotic depression or melancholia.

Prodrome or Pre-onset

Like the symptom-free neuroses we have already seen, there are symptom-free psychoses as well, usually described as "pre-onset." Structurally speaking, this is not so strange: just as there are successful neuroses, there is such a thing as a successful psychosis. The "successful" aspect of it has to do with the subject's ability to handle the internal conflict and its accompanying anxiety. The surprising element in the idea of a "successful" psychosis is in the fundamental difference between the psychotic and normal structures, making it difficult to conceive of a "normal" psychotic subject who can hold its own in normal social interactions. As far as I know, there are no actual studies about its incidence, but clinicians with a lot of experience with psychotic patients often note its high recurrence.

The basis upon which the psychotic subject is able to maintain itself in normal social exchanges is typically summarized by two concepts: "*suppletion*" and as-if identification. The concept of suppletion comes from Lacan's final theory of psychosis, developed through his study of James Joyce (Lacan 1976 [1975–1976a,b]). The essential idea is that the psychotic is able to avoid a psychotic outbreak by putting something in place of the foreclosure (Billiet 1992b, p. 77). Subsequent work on this concept has convinced me that it boils down to the construction of a successful psychotic symptom. In this sense, there is hardly any difference between this and a successful neurotic symptom—in neurosis, too, symptoms act as solutions to the underlying conflict—except for the fact that symptom construction progresses in a structurally different way. The concept of suppletion can be used to explain why creativity and art are commonly found in cases of psychosis and often work to stabilize it.

The as-if identification causes considerably more differential-diagnostic problems. Originally described by Deutsch ([1934]; see also Billiet [1986]) and taken up again by Lacan (1993 [1955–1956]), it denotes a special kind of identification through which the psychotic manages to behave in a hypernormative way in social reality. The extreme difficulty this presents for making a diagnosis is not hard to see. The term "as-if" gives a fairly clear idea of what it is about: the psychotic subject has chosen a model with whom it identifies in an unmediated and total way. Lacan takes his example from Katan (Lacan 1993 [1955–1956], pp. 191–193) with the case of an adolescent who copies his friend in "everything": he falls in love with the same girl, masturbates and stops masturbating exactly like his friend, assumes the same prohibitions and punishments his friend is subjected to by his father, and so on. One of the psychotic patients I met talked about "humaning" as a verb to indicate how she tried to behave in social situations in the same way that she saw other people behaving. She did it pretty well too.

The special character of such an identification has to do with the psychotic structure. Normal neurotic identification is triangular and mediated, thus permitting a certain distance-taking to take place. In psychosis there is only a dual structure, an all-or-nothing. Either alienation/identification is total or it is entirely absent. When such an identification takes place with an ideal role model, a seemingly normal picture results. The pathology lies in the nature of the identification, and it is on this that the diagnosis has to be based.

The concept of the "as-if," however, conjures up the wrong image: the psychotic does not know it is behaving as-if; it *is* the picture. The consciousness of the as-if aspect belongs to the neurotic realm, because the neurotic is always aware of not being "real," of never fully being able to play its part and, precisely because of this, is terrified of being unmasked. In psychosis, it is all about a falling together with, a self-coinciding. Such identification is not uncommon in the treatment, when psychotic patients—often in the context of so-called "resocialization"—fully identify with the therapeutic discourse, even describing themselves to everyone as "schizophrenic"—they are literally the flesh-and-blood image of what they ingested from the Other. Nevertheless, I remain unsure about whether this can be regarded as therapeutic suppletion.

Personality Disorders and Pre-onset Psychoses

The diagnostic recognition of a suppletion and/or dual identification is far from simple. Here, too, we must put the emphasis on the structural relation, toward both language and the Other. In this respect, the DSM descriptions of psychotic personality disorders (Cluster A) can be useful, because in them one can recognize this relational structure. With the help of a little reordering, one can even recognize in these three personality disorders the dynamics we have already sketched out, this time in a pre-onset form. The reordering I see as necessary would put the schizoid personality disorder first, because it is the closest to the actualpathological position, independent of the Other. Next comes the paranoid, where the subject already names the Other as guilty and defends itself against it. The schizotypical personality disorder can be considered as the third phase because of its delusional elements. Let us examine them in this order.

The schizoid personality disorder (301.20) is the easiest to understand: both (a) and the Other are kept at a distance in every possible way; all of the characteristics stress the negative: no desire for close relations or intimate friends, a propensity for solitary activities, no interest in sexual experiences with a partner, pleasure in few, if any, activities, cold and detached affect, indifference (American Psychiatric Association 2000). With such a relational modality, one can foresee that such patients only rarely come into contact with the clinic.

In the paranoid personality disorder (301.0), the central relation is toward a malevolently styled Other. The core description of the *DSM*

(American Psychiatric Association 2000) requires the presence of four of the following seven characteristics for its diagnosis:

1. Suspects without sufficient basis, that others are exploiting, harming, or deceiving him or her
2. Is preoccupied with unjustified doubts about the loyalty or trustworthiness of friends or associates
3. Is reluctant to confide in others because of unwarranted fear that the information will be used maliciously against him or her
4. Reads hidden demeaning or threatening meanings into benign remarks or events
5. Persistently bears grudges, i.e., is unforgiving of insults, injuries, or slights
6. Perceives attacks on his or her character or reputation that are not apparent to others and is quick to react angrily or to counterattack
7. Has recurrent suspicions, without justification, regarding fidelity of spouse or sexual partner. [APA 2000, p. 694]

We can see in this description of the typical paranoid relation a number of classical items from psychiatry. First of all, the delusion of reference (going back to Kretschmer's sensitive delusion): everything from the other is interpreted as an attack that needs to be defended against. Secondly, the obstinate certainty that excludes any part the subject itself might have played. Thirdly, the social isolation, as an effect of the previous characteristics. With respect to this isolation, the description under heading (3) needs to be slightly corrected: such patients selectively take others into their total confidence in an attempt to create allies against the malevolent other. The ambivalence of this psychotic transference (either a malevolent other, or an ally) is missing from the DSM description. The result is that the patient frequently institutes legal proceedings against others and gets tangled up in endless juridical disputes.

The schizotypical personality disorder (301.22) can be considered—if interpreted in a certain way—as a further stage in the psychotic dynamic. Along with the ideas of reference (characteristic 1), suspicion and paranoid ideation (characteristic 5), the following characteristics are also found: 2. peculiar convictions, and magical thinking that influences behavior and is inconsistent with subcultural norms; 3. unusual perceptual experiences including bodily illusions; 4. bizarre thought and speech; 6. inappropriate or constricted affect; 7. behavior or appearance that is odd, eccentric, or peculiar; 8. a lack of close friends or confidants other than first-degree relatives; and 9. excessive social anxiety that does not diminish with familiarity and tends to be associated with paranoid fears rather than negative judgments about the self (American Psychiatric Association, 2000).

From my perspective, this disorder should be considered more in terms of a combination of disorders. On the one hand, it describes the schizoid structure (see characteristics 3, 7, 8, and 9) at the moment of onset, but it also possesses a number of characteristics that refer to an evolution from paranoia to paraphrenia, dominated by the construction of a systematized delusion (see characteristics 1, 2, 4, and 5). On the basis of the dynamics of psychosis described above, I am persuaded that one can identify a "paraphrenic personality disorder" as the end phase of a successful psychotic defense. Paraphrenics, like those suffering from schizoid personality disorder, and because of their relational structure, will rarely be found in clinical practice.

Hysterical Delusions

In addition to the differential-diagnostic difficulties with pre-onset psychosis, it is also extremely difficult to differentiate it from so-called hysterical delusions and—to a lesser extent—from obsessional neurosis. Concerning the latter, a review of the literature shows that obsessional symptoms frequently appear in schizophrenic patients (De Beuk and De Haan 2000). Such symptoms nevertheless occur within a completely different relational structure that is usually not too difficult to recognize (see Chapter 13). This shows again that a purely descriptive diagnosis is not enough.

It is less easy to make a differential-diagnostic distinction between hysterical delusions and the psychotic structure. Clinically, hysterical delusion refers to a situation where the (usually female) patient develops a delusion for a short period (from several hours to a couple of weeks). Following this period is a complete return to the previous state, regarded as hysterical. Maleval has studied this extensively and his conclusion is a little disheartening: during the delusional period itself there is no clear differential-diagnostic criterion to enable one to make a decisive distinction between the hysterical and the psychotic structures. There are just a number of rules of thumb (chiefly the predominance of auditory rather than visual hallucinations in psychosis), but no structural indications (Maleval and Cremniter 1986). It is only afterward, once the delusional period is over, that can one can come to a clear diagnosis.

This has at least two consequences. First and foremost, it compels one to exercise diagnostic prudence, and especially pharmacological prudence. A too hasty bombardment with antipsychotic neuroleptic drugs can lead the pharmacological effects to blur the clinical picture to such an extent that a differential diagnosis ultimately becomes impossible. Secondly, the occurrence of these kinds of delusions seriously puts the exclusivity of the subject structures (either psychotic, perverse, or neurotic) into question. As I mentioned earlier, Lacan's final theory of psychosis puts far less emphasis on such an exclusivity. Anglo-American psychiatry has always allowed for a possible continuity between psychosis and neurosis, along with the idea of a psychotic decompensation. Such brief psychotic disorders are described under heading 298.8 in the *DSM-IV*, where it is also indicated how there is a full return to premorbid level of functioning (American Psychiatric Association 2000, p. 332).

Psychotic Depression

A final differential-diagnostic difficulty in psychosis concerns "psychotic depression" or melancholy (Freud 1978 [1917e]). As we saw in Part II of this book, the depressive position is integral to the ontological possibilities of every subject. Its particular appearance will be determined by the subject's specific structure. In psychosis, we are dealing with an all-or-nothing structure. Thus psychotic depression will have an all-encompassing character. The subject takes the entire guilt of the world onto its shoulders, and this is the sole reason for its existence. The all-encompassing guilt and its accompanying need for punishment invariably display a delusional character. Outside of it, the subject disappears, is reduced to nothing in its relation to the Other. From the moment the guilty delusion develops, its difference from neurotic depression is easily seen. But as long as the delusion remains undeveloped, the psychotic depressive state compares fairly well to a deep neurotic depression.

TREATMENT IN RELATION TO THE DIAGNOSIS

Freud was convinced that psychotic patients could not develop transferential relationships, making psychoanalytic treatment impossible as far as he was concerned. Since then, Freud's position has been reversed and it has largely been accepted that psychotic transference is characteristically intense, massive, fusional, and ambivalent. Such transference has a number of general characteristics that will acquire specific forms depending on where the subject lies in the continuum of psychotic dynamics described above.

Despite the differences found in the different stages, there are two constants. Given the impossibility of dialectizing and the absolute certainty of the psychotic subject, interpretation is impossible. The transference is simultaneously monolithic and ambivalent; the therapist is either a persecutor or an ally. Lacan (1966, p. 72) coins the term "mortifying erotomania" (*"une érotomanie mortifiante"*) for the psychotic transference. With this term, he gives a structural interpretation of what Anglo-American analysts already described as the "terror of closeness" in the psychotic patient. The psychotic ascribes to the therapist a "will to jouissance" that the subject, feeling itself to be the object (*a*) of this jouissance, resists.[27] Any therapeutic handling of the transference must focus on the positive version so as to enable the patient to elaborate his or her attempts at mastery; negative transference should be avoided as much as possible because it makes treatment untenable.[28] Moreover,

---

27. Naturally, this strongly recalls the perverse structure (see Chapter 14). The most important difference is that the object (*a*) in psychosis has not been phallically elaborated. Perversion, on the other hand, centers on the phallic interpretation of (*a*).

28. Important analysts in the treatment of psychosis are Bion, Federn, Little, Fromm-Reichmann, Green, Sullivan, Searles, Kernberg, Segal. Recent Lacanian approaches to it can be found in Laurent, Silvestre, Czermak, Billiet, Soler, Zenoni, and Maleval among others.

negative transference is not without its own dangers as aggressive actings-out do occur.

As far as treatment is concerned, it is of vital importance to realize that the psychotic evolution is in itself a stabilization attempt, in the sense of a subjective acceptance and elaboration of what was originally experienced as intrusive.[29] The conclusion of this stabilization process may then be madness but it is still often livable for both the patient and his or her environment. It is questionable whether an extensive pharmacological treatment is a better option, particularly in view of the irreversible extrapiramidal side-effects. Sacks (1995), for example, is convinced that it isn't, arguing that "Certainly the tranquillizers, if given in massive doses, may, like surgery, induce 'tranquillity,' may still the hallucinations and delusions of the psychotic, but the stillness they induce may be like the stillness of death—and, by a cruel paradox, deprive patients of the natural resolution that may sometimes occur with psychoses and instead immure them in a lifelong, drug-caused illness" (p. 60, footnote 10). However, it must be said that pharmacological treatment is usually necessary during the acute phase. Sacks's comment is aimed at the unnuanced and long-term prescription of pharmacological "cocktails."

In an acute phase, the subject is constantly defending itself against something that has been intrusively forced in on it from the Real, and that always involves jouissance: the subject is affected by rays or waves coursing through the body, often the genitals (Rümke 1971, p. 374). The constant defense against it—through writing, speech, yelling, playing loud music to blot out the inner voices, continuous masturbation—is not only exhausting but is accompanied by an often paroxysmic anxiety as well. It is at this point that pharmacological intervention is necessary, presumably intervening directly in what are for us the unrepresentable bodily experiences of the psychotic subject. Nevertheless, even here the influence of the Other should not be underestimated.

---

29. The best description is found in Billiet (1992b, pp. 94–95, my translation): "Curing in neurosis is the bridging of the gap between the conscious and the unconscious through the lifting of repression; it is the self-recognition of what lies inside. Reconciliation in psychosis is the bridging of the gap between the inner and outer; it is the acceptance of an exterior determination. It is no longer a question of assuming an unconscious truth, but of assuming a compelling task."

In view of the actual pathological nature of this period, the focus must once more be on the creation of an effective working relationship that will enable the subject to come to an elaboration on its own. A recent review by De Haan and Bakker (2000) gives empirical proof that long-term individual psychotherapy has clear positive results (measured in terms of the decrease in the number of psychotic and affective episodes in patients living with their families). Moreover, it was shown that the emphasis must be on the construction of a positive and long-term contact. This suggests to me that, for schizophrenia, the central goal of the treatment must be the installation of an effective working alliance.

Reconciliation

Subsequent psychotic development goes from an initial hypochondriac anxiety to a systematized, paranoid delusion in which the Other is identified as the culprit. In this way, the original psychotic anxiety is processed into a secondary version through its link to a threatening Other. Starting points for therapy may be found in this processing, although this carries the risk that the therapist then becomes part of the delusional system. The step from being a "witness" to being the "secretary" of the psychotic delusion can frequently lead to the therapist's being perceived as a persecutor. But a balanced handling of the positive transference that aims to enable the psychotic subject to reconcile itself with what it regards and will continue to regard as unilaterally coming from the outside world can be very productive. The perpetually relative success of rehabilitation programs must be seen in this context. It is striking the way psychopharmalogical treatments become less and less effective depending on the extent of the psychotic development.

In the final phase, paraphrenia, things have once again calmed down, although the psychotic structure is maintained. Here, rehabilitation and guided living services can be quite useful, provided that the appeal to the Other comes from the paraphrenic subject itself.

CONCLUSION: DIAGNOSIS AND TREATMENT

DIAGNOSIS

In Part I of this book we saw how a descriptive categorical diagnosis founded on the Master discourse carries a structural failure, both at the level of the diagnostic process itself and in the figure of the master. A regression to the University discourse occurs in response to this, being a discourse that is particularly protective and supportive of the agent. But here it is the patient who comes off badly. It is thus not so much the specific content of the theories themselves as the formal structure of the discourse that is determining.

On these grounds, I have argued that the central issue is the relation between the diagnostician and the subject, and that this extends far beyond any specific individual relationship. In Part II, we saw how identity formation is an effect of structural relations. The point of departure for subject-formation is an a priori, evolutionarily determined purposiveness in combination with the primordial tension of the drive. It is precisely because of this purposiveness that the drive is introduced into the relation with the Other. This shows how the subject and the Other are not two separate entities but rather the opposite. Subject-formation is a process through which both the subject's identity and the identity of the Other—or even more broadly, reality itself—come into being; a theory of the mind is always a theory of the world as well.

The content of identity is of less significance than the specific structural relation that is developed at the same time. This can be approached from two angles. The first concerns the degree to which subject-formation offers a representational mode for processing what arises in the body. The second has to do with the specific structure that is installed between the subject and the Other, the latter understood as both language and others. On this basis, we were able to put forward a differential diagnostics founded on the structural relation between the subject, (a), and the Other.

In Part III, this structural diagnostics was further elaborated along two main axes: on the one hand, along the continuum from actualpathology to psychopathology, and on the other, across the three different relational structures between the subject and the Other: neurosis, psychosis, and perversion. The underlying cause is identical: the (un)pleasurable confrontation with (a) and its accompanying anxiety. The subsequent determination of the automaton comes into being through the subject's specific relation towards the Other. Each of the three relational structures can be placed on the continuum from actualpathology to psychopathology. Across the three structures themselves no transition is possible.

Such a continuum is clearest in the study of psychosis. The onset is situated at the actualpathological position, the next step is schizophrenia of the disorganized type, followed by paranoia and eventually paraphrenia (schizophrenia of the residual type). The same evolution can be seen in the neurotic structure, although this received less attention in the text. The starting point is anxiety neurosis or panic disorder and somatization followed by anxiety hysteria and borderline. The next step leads to phobic and conversion hysteria, and the final point is obsessional neurosis. The dynamics of this continuum from actualpathology to psychopathology is least evident in the perverse structure, whose sole discernable evolution is the one from "perpetrator" to "writer."

One must once again underscore how such an evolution—or dynamic—is never linear and must be understood in terms of a *logical* time frame. Each subsequent period contains the previous ones, and a pathological outbreak can occur at any point in the continuum. Progression toward a later moment may occur, but is not automatic. The same goes for regression.

Treatment

Historically, psychotherapy began with the aim of consciousness-raising and insight; later, the emphasis shifted toward behavioral changes, only to turn more recently again toward insight and cognitive restructuring. For me, the aim of the treatment is neither simply to acquire insight nor to effect behavioral changes—these belong rather to its effects. Where the focus is solely on insight and knowledge, it will result in a caricatural subject who "knows" perfectly well why it is doing certain things, but without this knowledge effecting the slightest change in daily life. Where the focus is solely on behavior, one inevitably will end up with normative adaptation (see Van Haute 2002).

Normative adaptation carries the risk that both the diagnosis and the therapy will be reduced to the juridical field. In opposition to this, I have instituted an ethical imperative, centered on the subject's own demand. To make this ethical choice is a far from straightforward process. Firstly, and above all, there may be no such demand. But even when it is present, the demand itself can constitute a part of the pathology. Its presence must be considered as the basis for the establishment of a therapeutic working alliance, and in this sense it is an important point of departure. But it is no more than that.

Hence, the therapeutic aim is neither knowledge nor behavior. Even symptoms are just starting points, if very useful ones. In accordance with what we have developed here, the aim of the treatment is the same as the diagnostic goal: the structural relation between the subject and the Other. At this level, the differential diagnostic presented here can provide us with a first operational distinction. Insofar as this relation pertains to the actualpathological position, the entire focus of the treatment must be on installing a guaranteeing relation through which the subject can bring its problems into psychic elaboration. In today's practice, the importance of the therapeutic frame is often mentioned. To the extent that this relation belongs to the psychopathological side, the focus must be on the repetition of the previously constructed relation and toward the potential symptoms that are founded upon this construction.

THE THERAPEUTIC RELATION

From a medical perspective, the chief therapeutic aim is to cure. In psychiatric and clinical psychological practice, this must be approached from a different angle. The irreversibility of the three subjective structures consequently means that curing a psychosis, for example, by transforming it into a neurosis, is impossible. The treatment must be conceived *within* the existing structure of the subject.

This is easiest to formulate for the actualpathological position. The aim is to open up the possibility for the subject to relinquish this position and to make a transition to the psychopathological position. The entire and even exclusive means for this is the therapeutic relation. Here, interpretation is unworkable and, moreover, can induce guilt. The offer of a possible signifying processing must indeed be an offer, not an imposition. Former ideas of strengthening the ego have been reduced today to the idea of "supportive therapy." The vagueness of this formulation makes it of little value—What is there to be supported? Instead, our metapsychology enables us to suggest the idea of *subject amplification*. Through the guaranteeing therapeutic relation, the possibility must be opened for the subject to assume an increasing number of signifiers from the Other, accordingly extending its identity, possibilities for symbolization, and reality. Therapy must thus start out from the residual signifiers that go back to the original relationship between the subject and the Other, with the aim of bringing these into a dialectic.

Discourse theory is an excellent guideline for this. It may seem surprising to some but it is the analytic discourse that is indubitably the most useful in cases of actualpathology, beginning as it does with the (a) as agent and opening up the possibility for the divided subject to install an S_1 itself. If this succeeds, a secondary elaboration may be set in motion. The specific structure of the subject will continue to play a role in this elaboration. In such a view, the evolution from schizophrenia of the disorganized type to paranoia is considered progress, as strange as this may seem. In any event, it is experienced in this way by the patient because he or she is better able to handle the primary anxiety. But it is also clear that treatment shouldn't stop at this point.

In cases where the subject comes for consultation from a psychopathological position, the aim of the treatment will be completely different. The guaranteeing relation has already been installed, together with the secondary elaboration. With this, we have to take into account that this secondary elaboration and even the symptoms themselves are already a subject's attempt at recovery (usually literally, re-covery), in the sense of an elaboration of the underlying conflict and way of coping with the anxiety. In light of the synchronicity of subject-formation, symbolization, and reality, this elaboration process amounts to the subject's interpretation of the Real and the Other.

Every form of treatment attempts to change the psychopathological part in this interpretation through another interpretation, these days called cognitive restructuring. On the basis of the foregoing, I can make two comments.

The first is operational: every interpretation gains its efficacy from the subject's previously installed structural relation toward the therapist. Consequently, therapy must also focus on that relation, since otherwise nothing can be changed. Hence the diagnostic need to account for this in advance.

My second comment is both operational and ethical. Assuming that the relation between the subject and the Other is elaborated in such a way that interpretation does take effect, the question then becomes, Which direction do we take? To the extent that the therapist's interpretations are corrective and, after that, stabilizing, clearing away the pathological complexion of the patient, the result will inevitably be a certain banalization of the subject. The subject is reduced to the collectively shared discourse by way of an identification/alienation with the signifiers of the Other. In a number of cases, this doubtless alleviates the subjective suffering. But the price of this is being caught in the flytrap.

As opposed to this, one can consider a different interpretive goal, one where it is not so much a question of going further but of taking quite a few steps back. Around the time of *Seminar XI*, Lacan surprised his audience (1994 [1964]) with the comment that the goal of analytic interpretation was ultimately to empty meaning, to attain a point of meaninglessness or non-sense. Every symptom is framed by a fundamental fantasy, and is therefore inevitably an interpretation that comes from the Other. Correcting this interpretation by another better interpretation, coming from yet another Other, changes nothing in the system itself. To the extent that the therapeutic treatment aims to enable the subject to make choices of its own, this is surely not the most direct way of going about it. Its minimal precondition is that one distances oneself from the imposed choices found in the interpretations of both the patient and the therapist. Hence the need to empty them that Lacan indicates. That something like a choice can come into being, always in a relatively independent relationship with the Other, would seem to me the ultimate aim of every treatment.

This brings me to something I have saved for the end. It's a cliché but, as it happens, clichés have an annoying habit of generally being true. An aim such as I have described presupposes respect for the patient as a subject. At this point, our discipline—psychoanalysis—comes once more into conflict with today's demand for a collectivizing and objectifying scientificity. To ignore this would be foolhardy, to pursue it uncritically a disaster.

> *Clov:* "What is there to keep us here?"
> *Hamm:* "The dialogue."
> Samuel Beckett, *Endgame*

References

Abell, F., Happe, F., and Frith, U. (2000). Do triangles play tricks? Attribution of mental states to animated shapes in normal and abnormal development. *Cognitive Development* 15:1–16.

Adams, D. (1992). *The Hitchhiker's Guide to the Galaxy: A Trilogy in Four Parts*. London: Pan Books.

Ainsworth, M., et al. (1978). *Patterns of Attachment: A Psychological Study of the Strange Situation*. Hillsdale, NJ: Lawrence Erlbaum.

American Pychiatric Association. (1983). *DSM-III, Manuel diagnostique et statistique des troubles mentaux*. Paris: Masson.

——— (1987). Diagnostic and Statistical Manual of Mental Disorders, 3rd ed., revised. Washington, DC: American Pychiatric Association.

——— (2000). *Diagnostic and Statistical Manual of Mental Disorders*, fourth edition, Text Revision. Washington, DC: American Psychiatric Association.

André, S. (1986). *Que veut une femme?* Paris: Navarin.

——— (1993). *L'imposture perverse*. Paris: Seuil.

Assoun, P.-L. (1997a). *Corps et Symptôme*. Tome 1: *Clinique du Corps*. Paris: Anthropos.

——— (1997b). *Corps et Symptôme*. Tome 2: *Corps et Symptôme*. Paris: Anthropos.

Badinter, E. (1980). *L'amour en plus: Histoire de l'amour maternel (XVIIe–XXe siècle)*. Paris: Flammarion.

Bagby, R. M., and Taylor, G. J. (1997). Affect dysregulation and alexithymia. In *Disorders of Affect Regulation: Alexithymia in Medical and Psychiatric Illness*, ed. G. J. Taylor, R. M. Bagby, and J. D. A. Parker, pp. 26–45. Cambridge, UK: Cambridge University Press.

Bagby, R. M., Taylor, G. J., and Parker, G. J. (1994). The twenty-item Toronto Alexithymia Scale-II. Convergent, discriminant and concurrent validity. *Journal of Psychosomatic Research* 38:33–40.

Bakker, A. (2001). Recente ontwikkelingen in de behandeling van paniekstoornis en agorafobie. *Tijdschrift voor Psychiatrie* 43:385–394.

Balint, M. (1950). On the termination of analysis. *International Journal of Psychoanalysis* 31:196–199.

——— (1955). The final goal of psycho-analytic treatment. In *The Outline of Psychoanalysis*, ed. C. Thompson, et al., pp. 423–435. New York: Random House.

Barlow, D. H. (1997). Cognitive-behavioral therapy for panic disorder: current status. *Journal of Clinical Psychiatry* 58 (supp. 2):32–36.

Barlow, D. H., and Craske, M. G. (1988). The phenomenology of panic. In *Panic: Psychological Perspectives*, ed. S. Rachman and J. D. Maser, pp. 11–35. Hillsdale, NJ: Lawrence Erlbaum.

Barsky, A. J. (1992). Amplification, somatization, and the somatoform disorders. *Psychosomatics* 33:28–34.

Bateman, A., and Fonagy, P. (2000). Effectiveness of psychotherapeutic treatment of personality disorder. *British Journal of Psychiatry* 177:138–143.

Beauchesne, H. (1986). *Histoire de la psychopathologie*. Paris: P.U.F.

Beck, A. T. (1988). Cognitive approaches to panic disorder. In *Panic: Psychological Perspectives*, ed. S. Rachman and J. D. Maser, pp. 91–109. Hillsdale, NJ: Lawrence Erlbaum.

Beel, V. (2000). *Dag vreemde man: Over partners met autisme*. Berchem: EPO.

Beenen, F. and Stoker, J. (1998). Nederlandse vertaling van de Reflective Functioning Scale, interne publicatie van het Nederlands Psychoanalytisch Instituut.

Benedict, R. (1988). *The Chrysanthemum and the Sword*. New York: Mariner Books.

Bennis, H. (2001). *Tegengestelde krachten in taal*. Rede bij de aanvaarding van het ambt van bijzonder hoogleraar in de taalvariatie binnen het Nederlands aan de Faculteit der Geesteswetenschappen van de Universiteit van Amsterdam. Amsterdam: Vossiuspers, UvA, September 13.

Bercherie, P. (1980). *Les fondements de la clinique: Histoire et structure du savoir psychiatrique*. Paris: Seuil-Navarin.

——— (1981). Pidgin ou Pêle-Mêle, à propos du *DSM-3*. *L'Ane* 3:40–41.

Berden, G.F.M.G. (1986). 'Diagnostische' criteria, essentieel maar controversieel: overwegingen vanuit een kinderpsychiatrische praktijk. *Tijdschrift voor Psychiatrie* 28(7):443–458.

Bergin, A. E. (1980). *The search for a psychotherapy of value.* Rede uitgesproken ter gelegenheid van het vijftigjarig bestaan van de Nederlandse Vereniging voor Psychotherapie, unpublished. Quoted and discussed in J. H. Dijkhuis and J.H.M. Mooren, (1988), zie aldaar en in H. de Haan (1980), zie aldaar.

Bettelheim, B. (1979). *Surviving and Other Essays.* London: Thames and Hudson.

——— (1983). *Freud and Man's Soul.* London: Hogarth.

Beyaert, F.H.L. (1987). Redactioneel. *Tijdschrift voor psychiatrie* 29(6):327–328.

Billiet, L. (1986). 'Als of' en identificatie. Een theorie voor een aantal problemen uit de kliniek van de psychose. *Psychoanalytische Perspektieven* 8:101–115.

——— (1988). Freud en Lacan over de psychose. *Rondzendbrief uit het Freudiaanse Veld* 30:3–10.

——— (1989). Narcisme versus homoseksualiteit. *Rondzendbrief uit het Freudiaanse Veld* 36:3–30.

——— (1992a). De behandeling van psychotische patiënten vanuit de psychoanalyse. *Psychoanalytische Perspektieven* 16:59–66.

——— (1992b). Over suppletie in de psychose. *Psychoanalytische Perspektieven* 16:75–102.

——— (1996). *Het gebroken oor: Lacan voor de kliniek van de psychose.* Ghent: Idesça.

Bion, W. R. (1962a). *Learning from Experience.* London: Heinemann.

——— (1962b). A theory of thinking. *International Journal of Psychoanalysis* 43:306–310.

Blois, M. S. (1980). Clinical judgement and computers. *New English Journal of Medecine* 303:192–195.

Bogaerts, S., Goethals, J., and Vervaeke, G. (2002). Interpersoonlijke factoren bij de verklaring van pedoseksueel gedrag op grond van structurele equatiemodellen. *Tijdschrift voor Seksuologie* 26:26–36.

Bohman, M. (1996). Predisposition to criminality: Swedish adoption studies in retrospect. In *Genetics of Criminal and Antisocial Behavior,* ed. M. Rutter. Chichester, UK: J. Wiley.

Boon, L., and De Vries, G. (1989). *Wetenschapstheorie, de empirische wending.* Groningen: Wolters-Noordhoff.

Bordewijk, F. (1946). *Karakter: Roman van zoon en vader.* Rotterdam: Nijgh en Van Ditmar.

Bouhuys, A. L., and Van Den Hoofdakker, R. H. (1986). Humane ethologie en psychopathologie. In *Ontwikkelingen in de klinische psychologie,* ed. B. G. Deelman et al., pp. 81–98. Deventer: Van Loghum Slaterus.

Bower, G., and Sivers, H. (1998). Cognitive impact of traumatic events. *Development and Psychopathology* 10:625–653.

Bowlby, J. (1969). *Attachment and Loss. Vol. I: Attachment.* New York: Basic Books.
——— (1973). *Attachment and Loss. Vol. II: Separation.* New York: Basic Books.
Braeckman, J. (1997). *De natuurlijke orde tussen noodzaak en toeval, welwillendheid en vijandschap, ontwerp en evolutie: de Darwinistische transitie.* Gent: s.n.
Bram, F. (1965). The gift of Anna O. *British Journal of Medical Psychology* 38:53–58.
Bridges, K. W., and Goldberg, D. P. (1985). Somatic presentation of *DSM-III* psychiatric disorders in primary care. *Journal of Psychosomatic Research* 29:563–569.
Briquet, P. (1859). *Traité clinique et thérapeutique de l'hystérie.* Paris: Bailliére & fils.
Bucci, W. (1997). *Psychoanalysis and Cognitive Science: A multiple code theory.* New York: Guilford.
Bumby, K. (1996). Assessing the cognitive distortions of child molesters and rapists: development and validation of the MOLEST and RAPE scales. *Sexual Abuse: A Journal of Research and Treatment* 8:37–54.
Bush, F. N., Milrod, B. L., and Singer, M. B. (1999). Theory and technique in psychodynamic treatment of panic disorder. *Journal of Psychotherapy Practice and Research* 8:234–242.
Butler, J. (1993). *Bodies that Matter: On the Discursive Limits of "Sex."* New York: Routledge.
Cambien, J. (1981). De (on)wetenschappelijkheid van de psychoanalyse. *Tijdschrift voor Psychiatrie* 23(4):203–215.
——— (1987). De (on)-wetenschappelijkheid van de psychotherapie. *Tijdschrift voor Psychiatrie* 29(8):528–539.
Carlson, E. A. (1998). A prospective longitudinal study of attachment disorganization/disorientation. *Child Development* 69:1107–1128.
Cason, D., Resick, P., and Weaver, T. (2002). Schematic integration of traumatic events. *Clinical Psychology Review* 22:131–153.
Chaika, E. (1974). A linguist looks at schizophrenic language. *Brain and Language* 1:257–276.
Changeux, J. (1983). *L'Homme neuronal.* Paris: Fayard.
Clark, D. M. (1986). A cognitive approach to panic. *Behaviour Research Therapy* 24:461–470.
——— (1988). A cognitive model of panic attacks. In *Panic: Psychological Perspectives,* ed. S. Rachman and J. D. Maser, pp. 27–54. Hillsdale, NJ: Lawrence Erlbaum.
Clum, G. A., and Knowles, S. L. (1991). Why do some people with panic disorders become avoidant? A review. *Clinical Psychology Review* 11:295–313.

Clum, G. A., and Pendrey, D. (1987). Depression symptomatology as a nonrequisite for successful treatment of panic with anti-depressant medications. *Journal of Anxiety Disorders* 1:337–344.

Coles, E. M. (1996). A comment on *DSM-IV*'s diagnostic taxa. *Psychological Reports* 78:688–690.

Comptom, A. (1998). An investigation of anxious thoughts in patients with *DSM-IV* agoraphobia/panic disorder: rationale and design. *Journal of the American Psychoanalytic Association* 46:691–721.

Cooper, D. (1967). *Psychiatrie en anti-psychiatrie*. Meppel: Boom.

Cosmides, L., and Tooby, J. (2001). *What Is Evolutionary Psychology? Explaining the New Science of the Mind*. New Haven, CT: Yale University Press.

Cottet, S. (1985). La belle inertie (note sur la dépression). *Ornicar?* 32:68–87.

Craig, T.K.J., Boardman, A. P., Mills, K., Daly-Jones, O., and Drake, H. (1993). The South London somatisation study I: Longitudinal course and the influence of early life experiences. *British Journal of Psychiatry* 163:579–588.

Craske, M. G., and Barlow, D. H. (1988). A review of the relationship between panic and avoidance. *Clinical Psychology Review* 8:667–685.

Cremniter, D., and Maleval, J.-Cl. (1989). Contribution au diagnostic de psychose. *Ornicar?* 48:69–89.

Csibra, G., and Gergely, G. (1998). The teleological origins of mentalistic axtion explanations: a developmental hypothesis. *Developmental Science* 2:255–259.

Czermak, M. (1986). *Passions de l'objet: Études psychanalytiques des psychoses*. Paris: J. Clims.

Damasio, A. R. (1995). *Descartes' Error*. New York: Avon.

——— (2000). *The Feeling of What Happens*. New York: Heinemann.

Dawkins, R. (1976). *The Selfish Gene*. Oxford,UK: Oxford University Press.

De Beuk, N., and De Haan, L. (2000). Dwangsymptomen bij schizofrenie: aanwijzingen voor een aparte groep. *Tijdschrift voor Psychiatrie* 42:347–351.

de Beurs, E., van Balkom, A.J.L.M., Van Dyck, R., and Lange, A. (1999). Long-term outcome of pharmacological treatment for panic disorder with agoraphobia: a two-year naturalistic follow-up. *Acta Psychiatrica Scandinavica* 99:59–67.

Declercq, F. (1995). De psychotische dimensie in de opvoeding. *Psychoanalytische Perspektieven* 28:27–40.

——— (1998). La sexualité est toujours traumatique en tant que telle: références freudiennes. In *Aux sources de la psychanalyse*, G. Van de Vijoer and F. Geerardyn, pp. 192–203. Paris: L'Harmatan.

——— (2000a). *Het reële bij Lacan: over de pulsie en de finaliteit van de analytische kuur*. Gent: Idesça.

——— (2000b). *L'inquiétante étrangeté du corps*. Colloque de Psychanalyse et Recherches Universitaires, March.

——— (2002). The other side of the symptom. *The Letter* 24:38–47.
De Doncker, D., Schotte, C., and Koeck, S. (2002). De klinisch psychologische diagnostiek van plegers van seksueel misbruik: een diagnostische strategie en instrumentarium. *Tijdschrift voor Seksuologie* 26:46–58.
Deelman, B. G. (1986). Ontwikkelingen in de klinische neuropsychologie. Lessen uit de frenologie? In *Ontwikkelingen in de klinische psychologie*, ed. B. G. Deelman et al., pp. 134–157. Deventer: Van Loghum Slaterus.
De Gucht V. (2001). *Neuroticism, Alexithymia, Negative Affect, and Positive Affect as Predictors of Medically Unexplained Symptoms in Primary Care* (doctoraatsscriptie). Leiden: s.n.
De Gucht, V. (2003). Stability of neuroticism and alexithymia in somatization. *Comprehensive Psychiatry* 44(6):466–471.
De Gucht, V., and Fischler, B. (2002). Somatization: a critical review of conceptual and methodological issues. *Psychosomatics: Journal of Consultation Liaison Psychiatry* 43:1–9.
De Gucht, V., and Heiser, W. (2003). Alexithymia and somatisation: A quantitative review of the literature. *Journal of Psychosomatic Research* 54(5):425–434.
de Haan, H. (1980). Een bedorven verjaardagspartij. Vijftig jaar Nederlandse Vereniging voor Psychotherapie. *De Psycholoog* 15:516–517.
De Haan, L., and Bakker, J. (2000). Effectiviteit van individuele psychotherapie bij schizofrenie. Een overzicht van recent onderzoek. *Tijdschrift voor Psychiatrie* 42:751–758.
de Jong, A., and van de Brink, W. (1986). Ontwikkelingen in de psychiatrische classificatie: voorstel voor een prototypische kernclassificatie. *Tijdschrift voor Psychiatrie* 28(7):426–442.
de Jong, S. (2001). Reactie op 'Het Groene Huis.' *Tijdschrift voor Psychiatrie* 43:3.
De Kesel, M. (2002). *Eros en Ethiek*. Leuven: Acco.
De Kroon, J. (1999). *Omzien naar de psyche. Een kritisch-historische benadering van de psychiatrie*. Amsterdam: Boom.
Delespaul, P. (2001). Boekbespreking 'In search of madness: schizophrenia and neurosciences' (R. W. Heinrichs). *Tijdschrift Klinische Psychologie* 4:236–237.
Demoulin, C. (2001a). De la pratique Lacanienne: éthique, technique et clinique face au malaise du désir aujourd'hui. *Psychoanalytische Perspektieven* 45:9–17.
——— (2001b). Enjeux de la théorie lacanienne. *Psychoanalytische Perspektieven* 46:7–18.
Den Boer, J. A. (1987). Psychoanalyse tussen interpretatie en empirie. *Tijdschrift voor Psychiatrie* 29(7):404–416.

De Ridder, D.T.D. (1987). Diagnose als vonnis, de taak van de psychiater in het strafrecht 1890–1910. *Tijdschrift voor Psychiatrie* 29(6):329–342.
de Ruiter, C., and van Ijzendoorn, M. H. (1992). Agoraphobia and anxious-ambivalent attachment: an integrative review. *Journal of Anxiety Disorders* 6:179–183.
de Saussure, F. (1976). *Cours de linguistique générale*. Édition critique, préparée par Tullio de Mauro. Paris: Payot.
Descartes, R. (1968). *Discourse on Method and the Meditations*. London: Penguin.
De Swaan (1984). *De mens is de mens een zorg*. Amsterdam: Meulenhoff.
Deutsch, H. (1934). Ueber einen Typus der Pseudoaffektivität 'Als ob.' *Internationale Zeitschrift für Psychoanalyse* 10. In het Nederlands vertaald door L. Billiet (1986): Over een type van pseudoaffektiviteit 'als of.' *Psychoanalytische Perspektieven* 8:87–100.
de Vries, G. H. (1994). *De Ontwikkeling van Wetenschap: Een inleiding in de wetenschapsfilosofie, derde geheel herziene en uitgebreide druk*. Groningen: Wolters Noordhoff.
De Witte, A., and Van Houdenhove, B. (2001). Posttraumatische stress-stoornis en chronische pijn. *Tijdschrift voor Psychiatrie* 43:651–654.
Di Gennaro, G. (1987). Het afwijzen van de drugcultuur. *Koerier* 167:10–14.
Dijkhuis, J. H., and Mooren, J.H.M. (1988). *Psychotherapie en levensbeschouwing*. Baarn: Ambo.
Drossman, D. A., Talley, N. J., Leserman, J., Olden, K. W., and Barreiro, M. A. (1995). Sexual and physical abuse and gastrointestinal illness. Review and recommendations. *Archives of Internal Medicine* 123:782–794.
Drossman, D. A., Zhiming, L. I., Andruzzi, E., et al. (1993). U.S. householder survey of functional gastrointestinal disorders. Prevalence, sociodemography and health impact. *Digestive Diseases and Sciences* 38:1569–1580.
Drost, M. (2001). Reactie op 'Het Groene Huis.' *Tijdschrift voor Psychiatrie* 43:432–424.
Dunn, J. (1996). Children's relationships: bridging the divide between cognitive and social development. *Journal of Child Psychology and Psychiatry* 37:507–518.
Duyckaerts, F. (1988). De la justice du monde! *Quarto* 33/34:11–14.
Edelman, G. (1990). *Remembered Present*. New York: Basic Books.
Ehrenberg, A. (1991). *Le culte de la performance*. Paris: Calmann-Levy.
——— (1998). *La fatigue d'être soi*. Paris: Odile Jacob.
Ellenberger, H. F. (1970). *The Discovery of the Unconscious: The History and Evolution of Dynamic Psychiatry*. New York: Basic Books.
Elstein, A. S., Shulman, L. S., and Sprafka, S. A. (1978). *Medical Problem Solving:*

An Analysis of Clinical Reasoning. Cambridge, MA: Harvard University Press.

Emck, C., Schothorst, P., and van Engeland, H. (2001). Psychosen bij jeugdigen. *Tijdschrift voor Psychiatrie* 43(11):757–765.

Emmelkamp, P., Emmelkamp, J., de Ruiter, C and de Vogel, V. (2002). Effectiviteit van psychotherapeutische behandeling bij plegers van seksueel geweld. *Tijdschrift voor Seksuologie* 26:97–104.

Escobar, J. I. (1997). Developing practical indexes of somatization for use in primary care. *Journal of Psychosomatic Research* 42:323–328.

Escobar, J. I., Waitzkin, H., and Silver, R. C., et al. (1998). Abridged somatization: a study in primary care. *Psychosomatic Medicine* 60:466–472.

Ey, H., Bernard, P., and Brisset, C. (1974). *Manuel de psychiatrie.* 4ième édition, revue et complétée. Paris: Masson.

Faravelli, C., and Pallanti, S. (1989). Recent life events and panic disorder. *American Journal of Psychiatry* 146:622–626.

Faravelli, C., Webb, T., Ambonetti, A., et al. (1985). Prevalence of traumatic early life events in 31 agoraphobic patients with panic attacks. *American Journal of Psychiatry* 142:1493–1494.

Fava, G. A., Freyberger H. J., Bech P., et al. (1995). Diagnostic criteria for use in psychosomatic research. *Psychotherapy and Psychosomatics* 63:1–8.

Fechner, G. (1873). *Einige Ideen zur Schöpfungs- und Entwicklungsgeschichte der Organismen.* Leipzig: Breitkopf und Härtel.

Federn, P. (1952). *Ego Psychology and the Psychoses.* New York: Basic Books.

Feher-Gurewich, J. (2002). The philanthropy of perversion. In *Lacan in America,* ed. J.-M. Rabaté, pp. 361–377. New York: Other Press.

Ferenczi, S. (1955). Confusion of the tongues between adult and child. In *Final Contributions to the Problems and Methods of Psychoanalysis,* ed. M. Balint, pp. 155–167. London: Hogarth.

Feynman, R. (1999). *The Pleasure of Finding Things Out: The Best Short Works of Richard Feynman,* ed. J. Robbins. Cambridge, MA: Helix.

Fink, B. (1995). *The Lacanian Subject: Between Language and Jouissance.* Princeton, NJ: Princeton University Press.

——— (1997). *A Clinical Introduction to Lacanian Psychoanalysis: Theory and Technique.* Cambridge, MA: Harvard University Press.

Fink, P. (1992). The use of hospitalisations by persistent somatizing patients. *Psychological Medicine* 22:173–180.

——— (1995). Psychiatric illness in patients with persistent somatisation. *British Journal of Psychiatry* 166:93–99.

——— (1996). Somatization—Beyond symptom count. *Journal of Psychosomatic Research* 40:7–10.

Fischer, A., and van Vliet, K. (1986). Geslachtsverschillen, idealen en ideologieën. In *Psychologische Praktijken, een twintigste-eeuwse geschiedenis,* ed. J. Van Ginneken and J. Jansz, pp. 116–155. 's-Gravenhage: VUGA.

Fonagy, P. (2001). *Attachment Theory and Psychoanalysis.* New York: Other Press.

Fonagy, P., Gergely, G., Jurist, E., and Target, M. (2002). *Affect Regulation, Mentalization, and the Development of the Self.* New York: Other Press.

Fonagy, P., Leigh, T., Steele, M., et al. (1996). The relation of attachment status, psychiatric classification, and response to psychotherapy. *Journal of Consulting and Clinical Psychology* 64:22–31.

Fonagy, P., Moran, G. S., Edgcumbe, R., et al. (1993). The roles of mental representations and mental process in therapeutic action. *Psychoanalytic Study of the Child,* 49:9–48. New Haven, CT: Yale University Press.

Fonagy, P., Moran, G. S., & Target, M. (1993). Aggression and the psychological self. *International Journal of Psychoanalysis* 74:471–485.

Fonagy, P., Steele, M., Steele, H., et al. (1991). The capacity for understanding mental states: the reflective self in parent and child and its significance for security of attachment. *Infant Mental Health Journal* 13:200–217.

Fonagy, P., and Target, M. (1995). Understanding the violent patient: the use of the body and the role of the father. *International Journal of Psychoanalysis* 77:217–233.

——— (1996a). Playing with Reality: I. Theory of the mind and the normal development of psychic reality. *International Journal of Psychoanalysis* 77:217–233.

——— (1996b). Predictors of outcome in child psychoanalysis. A retrospective study of 763 cases at the Anna Freud Centre. *Journal of the American Psychoanalytic Association* 44:27–77.

——— (1997). Attachment and reflective function: their role in self-organization. *Development and psychopathology* 9:679–700.

——— (2000). Playing with reality: III. The persistence of dual psychic reality in borderline patients. *International Journal of Psychoanalysis* 81:853–873.

Fonagy, P., Target, M., and Gergely, G. (1999). *A new transgenerational theory of self-development.* Paper presented at the IPTAR Conference on the Evolution and Dissolution of the self, New York, March.

Foucault, M. (1972). *Histoire de la folie à l'âge classique.* Paris: Gallimard.

——— (1975). *L'ordre du discours: leçon inaugurale au Collège de France prononcée le 2 décembre 1970.* Paris: Gallimard.

——— (1977). *Surveiller et punir: naissance de la prison.* Paris: Gallimard.

——— (1997). *The Birth of the Clinic: An Archaeology of Medical Perception,* trans. A. Sheridan. London: Routledge.

Foudraine, J. (1973). *Wie is van hout . . . Een gang door de psychiatrie.* Bilthoven: Ambo.

Free, N. K., Winget, C. N., and Whitman, R. M. (1993). Separation anxiety in panic disorder. *American Journal of Psychiatry* 150:595–599.

Freeman, L. (1977). *L'histoire d'Anna O.*, trans.W. and B. Ashe. Paris: P.U.F.

Freud, A. (1979). *The Ego and the Mechanisms of Defence.* New York: International Universities Press.

Freud, S. (1978 [1892–99]). Extracts from the Fliess Papers. *The Standard Edition of the Complete Psychological Works of Sigmund Freud* (1:175–282). London: Hogarth.

——— (1978 [1893c]). Some points for a comparative study of organic and hysterical motor paralyses. *Standard Edition* 1:155–172. London: Hogarth.

——— (1978 [1894a]). The neuro-psychoses of defence. *Standard Edition* 3:41–61. London: Hogarth.

——— (1978 [1895b]). On the grounds for detaching a particular syndrome from neurasthenia under the description 'Anxiety Neurosis.' *Standard Edition* 3:87–115. London: Hogarth.

——— (1978 [1896a]). Heredity and the aetiology of the neuroses. *Standard Edition* 3:141–156. London: Hogarth.

——— (1978 [1896b]). Further remarks on the neuro-psychoses of defence. *Standard Edition* 3:157–185. London: Hogarth.

——— (1978 [1898a]). Sexuality in the aetiology of the neuroses. *Standard Edition* 3:261–285. London: Hogarth.

——— (1978 [1899a]). Screen memories. *Standard Edition* 3:299–322. London: Hogarth.

——— (1978 [1900a]). *The Interpretation of Dreams. Standard Edition* 4–5. London: Hogarth.

——— (1978 [1901b]). The psychopathology of everyday life. *Standard Edition* 4:1–279. London: Hogarth.

——— (1978 [1905c]). Jokes and their relation to the unconscious. *Standard Edition* 8:1–258. London: Hogarth.

——— (1978 [1905d]). Three essays on the theory of sexuality. *Standard Edition* 7:123–245. London: Hogarth.

——— (1978 [1905e]). Fragment of an analysis of a case of hysteria. *Standard Edition* 7:1–122. London: Hogarth.

——— (1978 [1906a]). My views on the part played by sexuality in the aetiology of neuroses. *Standard Edition* 7:269–279. London: Hogarth.

——— (1978 [1907b]). Obsessive actions and religious practices. *Standard Edition* 9:116–128. London: Hogarth.

——— (1978 [1907c]). The sexual enlightenment of children. *Standard Edition* 9:129–139. London: Hogarth.

——— (1978 [1908a]). Hysterical phantasies and their relation to bisexuality. *Standard Edition* 9:157–166. London: Hogarth.

——— (1978 [1908b]). Character and anal erotism. *Standard Edition* 9:167–175. London: Hogarth.
——— (1978 [1908c]). On the sexual theories of children. *Standard Edition* 9:205–226. London: Hogarth.
——— (1978 [1909b]). Analysis of a phobia in a five-year-old boy. *Standard Edition* 10:1–149. London: Hogarth.
——— (1978 [1909c]). Family romances. *Standard Edition* 9:235–244. London: Hogarth.
——— (1978 [1909d]). Notes upon a case of obsessional neurosis. *Standard Edition* 10:151–318. London: Hogarth.
——— (1978 [1910i]). The psycho-analytic view of psychogenic disturbance of vision. *Standard Edition* 11:211–218. London: Hogarth.
——— (1978 [1911b]). Formulations on the two principles of mental functioning. *Standard Edition* 12:215–226. London: Hogarth.
——— (1978 [1911c]). Psycho-analytic notes on an autobiographical account of a case of paranoia (dementia paranoides). *Standard Edition* 12:3–82. London: Hogarth.
——— (1978 [1912–1913]). Totem and taboo. *Standard Edition* 13:1–162. London: Hogarth.
——— (1978 [1913c]). On beginning the treatment (further recommendations on the technique of psycho-analysis, I). *Standard Edition* 12:121–144. London: Hogarth.
——— (1978 [1913i]). The disposition to obsessional neurosis. *Standard Edition* 12:313–325. London: Hogarth.
——— (1978 [1914c]). On narcissism: an introduction. *Standard Edition* 14:67–102. London: Hogarth.
——— (1978 [1915a]). Observations on transference-love (further recommendations on the technique of psycho-analysis, III). *Standard Edition* 12:157–171. London: Hogarth.
——— (1978 [1915c]). Instincts and their vicissitudes. *Standard Edition* 14:109–140. London: Hogarth.
——— (1978 [1915d]). Repression. *Standard Edition* 14:141–158. London: Hogarth.
——— (1978 [1915e]). The unconscious. *Standard Edition* 14:159–215. London: Hogarth.
——— (1978 [1915f]). A case of paranoia running counter to the psycho-analytic theory of the disease. *Standard Edition* 14:261–272. London: Hogarth.
——— (1978 [1916d]). Some character-types met with in psycho-analytic work. *Standard Edition* 14:311–333. London: Hogarth.
——— (1978 [1916–1917]). Introductory lectures on psycho-analysis, Part III:

General theory of the neuroses. *Standard Edition* 16:243–463. London: Hogarth.

——— (1978 [1917a]). A difficulty in the path of psycho-analysis. *Standard Edition* 17:135–144. London: Hogarth.

——— (1978 [1917e]). Mourning and melancholia. *Standard Edition* 16:237–260. London: Hogarth.

——— (1978 [1918b]). From the history of an infantile neurosis. *Standard Edition* 17:1–123. London: Hogarth.

——— (1978 [1919a]). Lines of advance in psycho-analytic therapy. *Standard Edition* 17:157–168. London: Hogarth.

——— (1978 [1919e]). A child is being beaten. *Standard Edition* 17:175–204. London: Hogarth.

——— (1978 [1920g]). Beyond the pleasure principle. *Standard Edition* 18:7–64. London: Hogarth.

——— (1978 [1921c]). Group psychology and the analysis of the ego. *Standard Edition* 18:65–143. London: Hogarth.

——— (1978 [1923b]). The ego and the id. *Standard Edition* 19:1–66. London: Hogarth.

——— (1978 [1923d (1922)]). A seventeenth-century demonological neurosis. *Standard Edition* 19:67–105. London: Hogarth.

——— (1978 [1924d]). The dissolution of the Oedipus complex. *Standard Edition* 19:173–182. London: Hogarth.

——— (1978 [1925h]). Negation. *Standard Edition* 19:233–239. London: Hogarth.

——— (1978 [1926d]). Inhibitions, symptoms, and anxiety. *Standard Edition* 20:75–175. London: Hogarth.

——— (1978 [1927e]). Fetishism. *Standard Edition* 21:149–158. London: Hogarth.

——— (1978 [1930]). Civilization and its discontents. *Standard Edition* 21:57–145. London: Hogarth.

——— (1978 [1931a]). Libidinal types. *Standard Edition* 21:215–220. London: Hogarth.

——— (1978 [1931b]). Female sexuality. *Standard Edition* 21:221–243. London: Hogarth.

——— (1978 [1937c]). Analysis terminable and interminable. *Standard Edition* 23:209–253. London: Hogarth.

——— (1978 [1939a (1937–1939)]). Moses and monotheism. *Standard Edition* 23:1–137. London: Hogarth.

——— (1978 [1940a]). An outline of psycho-analysis. *Standard Edition* 23:141–207. London: Hogarth.

——— (1978 [1940e]). Splitting of the ego in the process of defence. *Standard Edition* 23:271–278. London: Hogarth.

——— (1978 [1941f]). Findings, ideas, problems. *Standard Edition* 23:299–300. London: Hogarth.
——— (1978 [1950a (1895)]). A project for a scientific psychology. *Standard Edition* 1:281–397. London: Hogarth.
Freud, S., and Breuer, J. (1978 [1893a]). On the psychical mechanism of hysterical phenomena: preliminary communication. *Standard Edition* 2:3–17. London: Hogarth.
——— (1978 [1895d]). Studies on hysteria. *Standard Edition* 2. London: Hogarth.
Frith, C. D. (1992). *The Cognitive Neuropsychology of Schizophrenia*. Hillsdale, NJ: Lawrence Erlbaum.
Fromkin, V. A. (1975). A linguist looks at "A linguist looks at schizophrenic language." *Brain and Language* 2:498–503.
Fromm-Reichmann, F. (1959). *Psychoanalysis and Psychotherapy*. Chicago: University of Chicago Press.
Gallagher, C., and Darby, M. (1994). The historical development and clinical implications of Jacques Lacan's "optical schema." *The Letter* 2:101–138.
Gauron, E. F., and Dickinson, J. K. (1970). The influence of seeing the patient first on diagnostic decision making in psychiatry. *American Journal of Psychiatry* 126:199–205.
George, C., Kaplan, N., and Main, M. (1996). *The Adult Attachment Interview Protocol*. 3rd edition. Berkeley: University of California Press.
Gergely, G., and Watson, J. (1996). The social biofeedbackmodel of parental affect-mirroring. *International Journal of Psychoanalysis* 77:1181–1212.
Giel, R., Wiersma, D., and De Jong, A. (1987). Sociale klasse en psychische stoornissen: een Hollands drama? *Tijdschrift voor Psychiatrie* 29(3):129–146.
Gijs, L. (2002). Etiologische theorieën over seksueel agressief gedrag: een inleidend overzicht. *Tijdschrift voor Seksuologie* 26:9–25.
Glas, G. (2001). *Angst*. Amsterdam: Boom.
Gould, R. A., Otto, M. W., and Po, M. H. (1995). A meta-analysis of treatment outcome for panic disorder. *Clinical Psychology Review* 15:819–844.
Gould, S. J. (1984). *The Mismeasure of Man*. Harmondsworth,UK: Penguin Books.
Green, A. (1972). *On Private Madness*. London: Hogarth. Reprinted by Rebus Press, London (1996).
Groddeck, G. (1977). *Ça et moi: lettres à Freud, Ferenczi et quelques autres*, trans. from German by Roger Lewinter. Paris: Gallimard.
Hahn, S. R., Kroenke, K., Spitzer, R. L., et al. (1996). The difficult patient: prevalence, psychopathology, and functional impairment. *Journal of General Internal Medicine* 11:1–8.

Hall, G. (1995). Sexual offender recidivism revisited: a meta-analysis of recent treatment studies. *Journal of Consulting and Clinical Psychology* 63:802–809.
Harris, J. R. (1998). *The Nurture Assumption*. New York: Free Press.
Hartmann, H. (1939). Psychoanalysis and the concept of health. *International Journal of Psychoanalysis* 10:308–321.
Harvey, A., and Bryant, A. (1999). A two-year prospective evaluation of the relationship between acute stress disorder and posttraumatic stress disorder. *Journal of Consulting and Clinical Psychology* 67:985–988.
Hebbrecht, M. (1998). Psychodynamische psychotherapie en paniekstoornis. *Tijdschrift voor psychiatrie* 40:319–322.
Heinrichs, R. (2001). *In Search of Madness: Schizophrenia and Neurosciences*. New York: Oxford University Press.
Hellinga, G. (1992). De classificatie van persoonlijkheidsstoornissen: problemen in de praktijk. *Tijdschrift voor Psychiatrie* 34(6):400–411.
Herman, J. L. (1992a). Complex PTSD: a syndrome in survivors of prolonged and repeated trauma. *Journal of Traumatic Stress* 5:377–391.
——— (1992b). *Trauma and Recovery*. New York: Basic Books.
Hermann, N., and Eryavec, G. (1994). Delayed onset post-traumatic stress disorder in World War II veterans. *Canadian Journal of Psychiatry* 39(7):439–441.
Hermans, W. F. (1976). *Nooit meer slapen*. Amsterdam: Bezige Bij.
Higly, J., Suomi, S., and Linnoila, M. (1996). A nonhuman primate model of type II excessive alcohol consumption. (1) Low cerebrospinal fluid 5-hydroxyindoleaccetic acid concentrations and dinminished social competence correlate with excessive alcohol consumption. *Alcoholism—Clinical and Experimental Reseach* 20:629–642.
Hodiamont, P. (2000). De meester-gezelrelatie in perspectief. *Tijdschrift voor Psychiatrie* 42:219–223.
Huttunen, M., and Niskanen, N. (1973). Prenatal loss of father and psychiatric disorders. *Archives of General Psychiatry* 35:429–431.
Israel, L. (1984). *Hysterie, sekse en de geneesheer*. Leuven/Amersfoort: Acco.
Jacobson, E. (1964). *The Self and the Object World*. New York: International Universities Press.
Jamieson, S., and Marshall, W. (2000). Attachment styles and violence in child molesters. *The Journal of Sexual Aggression* 5:88–98.
Jansz, J. (1986). Intelligentie, individuele verschillen gemeten. In *Psychologische Praktijken, een twintigste-eeuwse geschiedenis*, ed. J. Van Ginneken and J. Jansz, pp. 52–87. 's-Gravenhage: VUGA.
Johnson, J., Cohen, P., Brown, J., Smailes, E., et al. (1999). Childhood maltreatment increases risk for personality disorders during early adulthood. *Archives of General Psychiatry* 56:600–605.
Jonckheere, L. (1993). Borderline. *Psychoanalytische Perspektieven* 18:81–98.

——— (1998a). Latent Freudian thoughts towards a theory of neurotic depression. Part one: The anxiety-neurotic depression. *The Letter* 13:1–25.

——— (1998b). Latent Freudian thoughts towards a theory of neurotic depression. Part two: A purely hysterical depression. *The Letter* 13:26–38.

Jones, E. (1931). The concept of the normal mind. *International Journal of Psychoanalysis* 20:1–8.

Jongedijk, R. (2001). Psychiatrische diagnostiek en het DSM-systeem. Een kritisch overzicht. *Tijdschrift voor Psychiatrie* 43:309–319.

Kalus, O., Bernstein, D., and Siever, L. (1993). Schizoid personality disorder: a review of current status and implications for *DSM-IV*. *Journal of Personality Disorders* 7(1):43–52.

Kaplan-Solms, K., and Solms, M. (2000). *Clinical Studies in Neuro-Psychoanalysis: Introduction to a Depth Neuropsychology*. London: Karnac.

Kear-Colwell, J., and Sawle, G. (2001). Coping strategies and attachment in pedophiles: Implications for treatment. *International Journal of Offender Therapy and Comparative Criminology* 45:171–182.

Kennedy, H., and Grubin, D. (1992). Patterns of denial in sex offenders. *Psychological Medicine* 22:191–196.

Kernberg, O. (1975). *Borderline Conditions and Pathological Narcissism*. New York: Jason Aronson.

——— (1979). Psychoanalytic psychotherapy with borderline adolescents. *Adolescent Psychiatry* 7:294–321.

——— (1984). *Severe Personality Disorders*. New Haven, CT: Yale University Press.

——— (1996a). A psychoanalytic theory of personality disorders. In *Major Theories of Personality Disorders*, ed. J. Clarkin and M. Lenzenweger, pp. 103–137. New York: Guilford.

——— (1996b). Thirty methods to destroy the creativity of psychoanalytic candidates. *International Journal of Psychoanalysis* 77:1031–1041.

Kernberg, P. F. (1984). *Reflections in the Mirror: Mother–Child Interactions, Self-Awareness, and Self-Recognition*. New York: Basic Books.

Kinsey, A., Pomeroy, W., and Martin, C. (1948). *Sexual Behavior in the Human Male*. Philadelphia: W. B. Saunders.

Kinsey, A., Pomeroy, W., Martin, C., and Gebhard, P. (1953). *Sexual Behavior in the Human Female*. Philadelphia: W. B. Saunders.

Kirmayer, L. J., and Robbins, J. M. (1991). Three forms of somatization in primary care: prevalence, co-occurrence, and sociodemographic characteristics. *The Journal of Nervous and Mental Disease* 179:647–655.

Kirmayer, L. J., Robbins, J. M., Dworkind, M., and Yaffe, M. (1993). Somatization and the recognition of depression and anxiety in primary care. *American Journal of Psychiatry* 150:734–741.

Klein, D. F. (1964). Delineation of two-drug responsive anxiety syndromes. *Psychopharmacologiea* 5:397–408.

——— (1980). Anxiety reconceptualized. *Comprehensive Psychiatry* 21:411–427.

Klein, D. F., and Gorman, T. M. (1987). A model of panic and agoraphobic development. *Acta Psychiatrica Scandinavica* 76:87–95.

Klein, M. (1930). The importance of symbol-formation in the development of the ego. *International Journal of Psychoanalysis* 11:24–39.

——— (1986 [1935]). A contribution to the psychogenesis of manic-depressive states. In *The Selected Melanie Klein*, ed. J. Mitchell, pp. 445–495. Harmondsworth, UK: Penguin.

——— (1986 [1946]). Notes on some schizoid mechanisms. In *The Selected Melanie Klein*, ed. J. Mitchell, pp. 175–200. Harmondsworth, UK: Penguin.

Klompenhouwer, J. (2001). Het Groene Huis. *Tijdschrift voor Psychiatrie* 43(1):3–6.

Koeck, S., van Beek, D., and De Doncker, D. (2002). Classificatie van pedoseksuelen en verkrachters. *Tijdschrift voor Seksuologie* 26:37–45.

Kohut, H. (1971). *The Analysis of the Self*. New York: International Universities Press.

——— (1977). *The Restoration of the Self*. New York: International Universities Press.

Konner, M. (1982). *The Tangled Wing. Biological Constraints on the Human Spirit*. Harmondsworth, UK: Penguin.

Kortmann, F. (2000). Beschouwingen over paternalisme en autonomie in de psychiatrie. *Tijdschrift voor Psychiatrie* 5:319–326.

Koster van Groos, G.A.S. (1989). De werkelijkheid achter de feitelijkheid. *Tijdschrift voor Psychiatrie* 31(6):351–353.

Kraepelin, E. (1920). *Psychiatrie. Ein Lehrbuch für Studierende und Ärtzte*. 8te Auflage, Band I. Leipzig: Engelman.

Kroenke, K., and Price, R. K. (1993). Symptoms in the community. Prevalence, classification, and psychiatric comorbidity. *Archives of Internal Medicine* 153:2474–2480.

Kübler-Ross, E. (1969). *On Death and Dying*. New York: Macmillan.

Kuhn, T. (1970). *The Structure of Scientific Revolutions*. Chicago: University of Chicago Press.

Kuiper, P. C. (1988). *Ver heen: verslag van een depressie*. 's-Gravenhage: SDU.

Kushner, M. G., and Beitman, B. D. (1990). Panic attacks without fear: an overview. *Behavior Research and Therapy* 28:469–479.

Lacan, J. (1962–63). *Le Séminaire, Livre X: L'angoisse* (unpublished seminar).

——— (1966). *Écrits*, texte établi par J.-A. Miller. Paris: Seuil.

——— (1966 [1946]). Propos sur la causalité psychique. In *Écrits*, pp. 151–193. Paris: Seuil.

——— (1966 [1950]). Introduction théorique aux fonctions de la psychanalyse en criminologie. In *Écrits*, pp. 125–149. Paris: Seuil.

——— (1966 [1955]). Variantes de la cure-type. In *Écrits*, pp. 323–362. Paris: Seuil.

——— (1966 [1958]). Remarque sur le rapport de Daniel Lagache: "Psychanalyse et structure de la personnalité." In *Écrits*, pp. 647–685. Paris: Seuil.

——— (1966 [1959]). Sur la théorie du symbolisme d'Ernest Jones. In *Écrits*, pp. 697–717. Paris: Seuil.

——— (1966 [1961]). La direction de la cure et les principes de son pouvoir. In *Écrits*, pp. 585–645. Paris: Seuil.

——— (1966 [1963]). Kant avec Sade. In *Écrits*, pp. 765–790. Paris: Seuil.

——— (1966 [1964]). Position de l'inconscient. In *Écrits* pp. 829–854. Paris: Seuil.

——— (1966 [1966]). La science et la vérité. In *Écrits*, pp. 855–877. Paris: Seuil.

——— (1968 [1967]). Proposition du 9 octobre 1967 sur le psychanalyste de l'École. *Scilicet* 1.

——— (1973 [1964]). *Le Séminaire, Livre XI: Les quatre concepts fondamentaux de la psychanalyse*, texte établi par J.-A. Miller. Paris: Seuil.

——— (1973–1974). *Le Séminaire, Livre XXI: Les non-dupes errent*. Onuitgegeven manuscript.

——— (1975). *L'Étourdit*. *Scilicet* 4. Paris: Seuil.

——— (1975 [1953–1954]). *Le Séminaire, Livre I: Les écrits techniques de Freud*, texte établi par J.-A. Miller. Paris: Seuil.

——— (1975 [1972–1973]). *Le Séminaire, Livre XX: Encore*, texte établi par J.-A. Miller. Paris: Seuil.

——— (1976 [1975–1976a]). *Le Séminaire, Livre XXIII: Le Sinthome*, texte établi par J.-A. Miller. *Ornicar?* 6:3–20.

——— (1976 [1975–1976b]). *Le Séminaire, Livre XXIII: Le Sinthome*, texte établi par J.-A. Miller. *Ornicar?* 7:3–18.

——— (1977). *Écrits, A selection*, trans. A Sheridan. London: W. W. Norton & Company, Inc.

——— (1977 [1949]). The mirror stage as formative of the function of the I. In *Écrits, A Selection*, pp. 1–7. New York: Norton.

——— (1977 [1953]). The function and field of speech and language in psychoanalysis. In *Écrits, A selection*, pp. 30–113. New York: Norton.

——— (1977 [1958a]). The direction of the treatment and the principles of its power. In *Écrits, A selection*, pp. 226–280. New York: Norton.

——— (1977 [1958b]). The signification of the phallus. In *Écrits, A selection*, pp. 281–291. New York: Norton.

——— (1977 [1959]). On a question preliminary to any possible treatment of psychosis. In *Écrits, A selection*, pp. 179–225. New York: Norton.

——— (1977 [1960]). The subversion of the subject and the dialectic of desire in the Freudian unconscious. In *Écrits, A selection*, pp. 298–325. New York: Norton.

——— (1977 [1969]). Premier impromptu de Vincennes: le discours de l'Universitaire 3/12/1969 (Première de quatre conférences devant avoir lieu dans le cadre du Séminaire 1969–70 réunies sous le titre "Analyticon"). *Magazine Littéraire* 121:21–24.

——— (1981 [1955–1956]). *Le Séminaire, Livre III: Les psychoses*, texte établi par J.-A. Miller. Paris: Seuil.

——— (1983 [1958–1959a]). L'objet Ophélie, texte établi par J.-A. Miller. *Ornicar?* 25–26:7–19.

——— (1983 [1958–1959b]). Le désir et le deuil. *Ornicar?* 25–26:20–31.

——— (1983 [1958–1959c]). Phallophanie, texte établi par J.-A. Miller. *Ornicar?* 25–26:32–44.

——— (1986 [1959–1960]). *Le Séminaire, Livre VII: L'éthique de la psychanalyse*, texte établi par J.-A. Miller. Paris: Seuil.

——— (1990 [1974]). *Television: a Challenge to the Psychoanalytic Establishment*, ed. D. Hollier. New York: Norton.

——— (1991 [1953–1954]). *The Seminar of Jacques Lacan, Book I: Freud's Papers on Technique*, trans. S. Tomaselli. New York: Norton.

——— (1991 [1960–1961]). *Le Séminaire, Livre VIII: Le transfert*, texte établi par J.-A. Miller. Paris: Seuil.

——— (1991 [1969–1970]). *Le Séminaire, Livre XVII: L'Envers de la psychanalyse*, texte établi par J.-A. Miller. Paris: Seuil.

——— (1992 [1959–1960]). *The Seminar of Jacques Lacan, Book VII: The Ethics of Psychoanalysis* (tr. with notes by D. Porter). London: Routledge.

——— (1994 [1956–1957]). *Le Séminaire, Livre IV: La relation d'objet*, texte établi par J.-A.Miller. Paris: Seuil.

——— (1994 [1964]). *The Four Fundamental Concepts of psychoanalysis*, ed. J.-A. Miller, trans. A. Sheridan. London: Penguin.

——— (1997 [1955–1956]). *The Seminar of Jacques Lacan: Book III: The Psychoses*, trans. R. Grigg. New York: Norton.

——— (1998 [1957–1958]). *Le Séminaire, Livre V: Les formations de l'inconscient*, texte établi par J.-A.Miller. Paris: Seuil.

——— (1998 [1972–1973]). *On Feminine Sexuality: The Limits of Love and Knowledge*, trans. B. Fink. New York: Norton.

——— (2001). *Autres Écrits*. Paris: Seuil.

Laing, R. D. (1960). *The Divided Self*. Harmondsworth, UK: Penguin.

Lange, A., and Van der Valk, F. (1983). Labelingsprocessen en het oordeel van psychotherapeuten, een experimenteel onderzoek. *Nederlands Tijdschrift Psychologie* 38:286–300.

Langer, E. J., and Abelson, R. P. (1974). A patient by any other name. *Journal of Consulting Clinical Psychology* 42:4–9.

Laplanche, J. (1980). *Problématiques I: L'Angoisse; Problématiques II: Castration Symbolisations*. Paris: P.U.F.

Laurent, E. (1983). Le transfert délirant. *Actes de l'ecole de la cause freudienne* 4:32–33.

——— (1987). Discipline de l'entretien avec le sujet psychotique. *Quarto* 28–29:18–20.

Leader, D. (2000). The depressive position for Klein and Lacan. In *Freud's Footnotes*, D. Leader, pp. 189–236. London: Faber and Faber.

Lecours, S., and Bouchard, M.-A. (1997). Dimensions of mentalisation: outlining levels of psychic transformation. *International Journal of Psychoanalysis* 78:855–875.

Lee, D., and Young, K. (2001). Post-traumatic stress disorder: diagnostic issues and epidemiology in adult survivors of traumatic events. *International Review of Psychiatry* 13:150–158.

Le Doux, J. (1998). *The Emotional Brain*. London: Phoenix.

Leslie, A., and Thaiss, L. (1992). Domain specificity in conceptual development: neuropsychological evidence from autism. *Cognition* 43(3):225–251.

Lévi-Strauss, C. (1976). *La pensée sauvage*. Paris: Plon.

Lievrouw, A. (2001). Münchausen syndroom (by proxy): classificatie versus klinische diagnostiek. *Tijdschrift Klinische Psychologie* 4:218–230.

Lipowski, Z. (1988). Somatization: the concept and its clinical application. *American Journal of Psychiatry* 145:1358–1368.

Little, M. (1991). *Des états-limites*. Paris: Des femmes.

Livanou, M. (2001). Psychological treatments for post-traumatic stress disorder: an overview. *International Review of Psychiatry* 13:181–188.

Livesley, W., Schroeder, M., Jackson, D., and Jang, K. (1994). Categorical distinctions in the study of personality disorder: implications for classification. *Journal of Abnormal Psychology* 103:1, 6–17.

Loose, R. (2002). *The Subject of Addiction. Psychoanalysis and the Administration of Enjoyment*. London: Karnac.

Lorenz, K. (1966). *Evolution and Modification of Behavior*. Londen: Methuen.

——— (1975). *De weerzijde van de spiegel. Over de evolutie van de menselijke kennis*. Amsterdam: Ploegsma.

——— (1984). *Onze laatste kans. Blauwdruk voor een menselijke toekomst*. Amsterdam: Elsevier.

Luborsky, L., and Crits-Christoph, P. (1998). *Understanding Transference*. Washington, DC: American Psychological Association.

Lydiard, R. B., and Brawman-Mintzer, O. (1997). Panic disorder across the life span: a differential diagnostic aproach to treatment resistance. *Bulletin of the Menninger Clinic* 61(supp. A):66–94.

Mahler, M. (1968). *On Human Symbiosis and the Vicissitudes of Individuation, Infantile Psychosis.* New York: International Universities Press.

Mahler, M., and McDevitt, J. B. (1982). Thoughts on the emergence of the sense of self, with particular emphasis on the body self. *Journal of the American Psycho-Analytic Association* 30:827–848.

Mahler, M., Pine, F., and Bergman, A. (1975). *The Psychological Birth of the Human Infant.* New York: Basic Books.

Main, M., and Cassidy, J. (1988). Categories of response to reunion with the parent at age 6: Predictable from infant attachment classifications and stable over a 1-month period. *Developmental Psychology* 24:415–426.

Main, M., and Goldwyn, S. (1995). Interview based adult attachment classification: related to infant–mother and infant–father attachment. *Developmental Psychology* 19:237–39.

Malamuth, N., Linz, D., Haevely, C., et al. (1995). Using the confluence model of sexual aggression to predict men's conflict with women: A 10 year follow-up study. *Journal of Personality and Social Psychology* 69:353–369.

Malamuth, N., Sockloskie, R., Koss, M., and Tanaka, J. (1991). The characteristics of aggressors against women: testing a model using a national sample of college students. *Journal of Consulting and Clinical Psychology* 52:670–681.

Maleval, J.-Cl. (1981). *Folies hystériques et psychoses dissociatives.* Paris: Payot.

——— (1984). Les psychothérapies des hystéries crépusculaires (II). *Ornicar?* 31:98–128.

——— (1991). Logique du meurtre immotivé. In *Psychose naissante—psychose unique,* H. Grivois, pp. 43–65. Paris: Masson.

——— (2000). *La forclusion du nom-du-père. Le concept et sa clinique.* Paris: Seuil.

Maleval, J.-Cl., and Cremniter, D. (1986). Délire psychotique ou delirium névrotique. Essai de différentiation structurelle. *Bulletin de Psychologie* 376:21–36.

Mallet, J. (1955). La dépression névrotique. *Evolution Psychiatrique* 3:483–501.

Marques, J. (1999). How to answer the question "Does sex offender treatment work?" *Journal of Interpersonal Violence* 14:437–451.

Marshall, W. (2001). Attachment problems in the etiology and treatment of sexual offenders. In *Sexual Appetite, Desire and Motivation: Energetics of the Sexual System,* ed. W. Everaerd, E. Laan & S. Both, pp. 135–143. Amsterdam: Koninklijke Nederlandse Academie van Wetenschappen.

Masson, J. (1995). *The Complete Letters of Sigmund Freud to Wilhelm Fliess (1887–1904),* tr. and ed. J. Masson. Cambridge, MA/London: Belknap Press of Harvard University.

Masters, W., and Johnson, V. (1966). *Human Sexual Response*. Boston: Little, Brown.

Matthaei, I. (2001). Reactie op 'Het Groene Huis.' *Tijdschrift voor Psychiatrie*, 43(3):200–202.

McCauley, J., Kern, D. E., Kolodner, K., et al. (1997). Clinical characteristics of women with a history of childhood abuse. *Journal of the American Medical Association* 277:1362–1368.

McGuire, W., ed. (1994). *The Freud/Jung Letters: The Correspondence Between Sigmund Freud and C. G. Jung*, trans. R. Manheim et al. London: Routledge and the Hogarth Press.

McNally, R. J. (1994). *Panic Disorder: A Critical Analysis*. New York: Guilford.

Miliora, M. T., and Ulman, R. B. (1996). Panic disorder: a bioself-psychological perspective. *Journal of the American Academy of Psychoanalysis* 24:217–257.

Miller, J.-A. (1982). Symptôme-fantasme. *Actes de l'Écoles de la Cause Freudienne* 3:12–19.

——— (1984). Transfert et interprétation. *Actes de l'Écoles de la Cause Freudienne* 6:33–37.

Millon, T. (1993). Negativistic (passive-aggressive) personality disorder. *Journal of Personality Disorders* 7(1):78–85.

Millon, T., and Davis, R. (1996). *Disorders of Personality: DSM-IV and Beyond*, 2nd ed. New York: Wiley.

Milrod, B. (1995). The continuing usefulness of psychoanalysis in the treatment of panic disorder. *Journal of the American Psychoanalytical Association* 43:151–162.

——— (1998). Unconscious pregnancy fantasies as underlying dynamism in panic disorder. *Journal of the American Psychoanalytic Association* 46:673–690.

Milrod, B., and Busch, F. (1996). The long-term outcome of treatments for panic disorder: a review of literature. *Journal of Nervous and Mental Disease* 184:723–730.

Milrod, B., Busch, F., Cooper, A., and Shapiro, T. (1997). *Manual of Panic-Focused Psychodynamic Psychotherapy*. Washington, DC: American Psychiatric Press.

Minderaa, R. B., Van Gemertt, T.L.M., and Van De Wetering, B.J.M. (1988). Onverwachte presentatiewijzen van het syndroom van Gilles de la Tourette. *Tijdschrift voor Psychiatrie* 30:437–445.

Mitchell, J. (1986). *The Selected Melanie Klein*. Harmondsworth, UK: Penquin.

Money, J. (1988). *Gay, Straight, and In Between: The Sexuology of Erotic Orientation*. New York: Oxford University Press.

Monod, J. (1970). *Le hasard et la nécessité, essai sur la philosophie naturelle de la biologie moderne*. Paris: Seuil.

Mooij, A. (1975). *Taal en verlangen*. Meppel: Boom.
——— (1988). *De psychische realiteit. Over psychiatrie als wetenschap.* Meppel-Amsterdam: Boom.
——— (1997). *Schuld in strafrecht en psychiatrie*. Deventer: Gouda Quint.
——— (1999). *Het optreden als een 'un père.'* Ongepubliceerd manuscript.
Moyaert, P. (1994). *Ethiek en sublimatie. Over de 'ethiek van de psychoanalyse' van Jacques Lacan*. Nijmegen: SUN.
Murray, L., and Cooper, P. (1997). The role of infant and maternal factors in postpartum depression, mother–infant interactions and infant outcome. In *Postpartum Depression and Child Development*, ed. L. Murray and P. Copper, pp. 111–135. New York: Guilford Press.
Nicolai, N. (2001a). Hechting en psychopathologie: een literatuuroverzicht. *Tijdschrift voor Psychiatrie* 43:333–342.
——— (2001b). Hechting en psychopathologie: de reflectieve functie. *Tijdschrift voor Psychiatrie* 43:705–714.
Nijs, P. (1987). Redactioneel. *Tijdschrift voor psychiatrie* 29(9):547–549.
Nobus, D., ed. (1998). *Key Concepts of Lacanian Psychoanalysis*. London: Rebus.
Noordenbos, G., Oldenhave, A., Terpstra, N., and Muschter, J. (2000). Kenmerken en behandelingsgeschiedenis van patiënten met chronische eetstoornissen. *Tijdschrift voor Psychiatrie* 42:145–155.
Norretranders, T. (2001). *Het bewustzijn als bedrieger*. Amsterdam: Arbeiderspers.
Ogawa, J. R., Sroufe, L. A., Weinfeld, N. S., et al. (1997). Development and the fragmented self: longitudinal study of dissociative symptomatology in a nonclinical sample. *Development and Psychopathology* 9:855–879.
Ogden, T. (1979). On projective identification. *International Journal of Psychoanalysis* 60:357–373.
Orbach, S. (2001). *Hunger Strike: Starving Amidst Plenty*. New York: Other Press.
Palombo, S. (1999). *The Emergent Ego: Complexity and Coevolution in the Psychoanalytic Process*. New York: International Universities Press.
Panksepp J. (1998). *Affective Neuroscience: The Foundations of Human and Animal Emotions*. New York: Oxford University Press.
Paris, J. (2000). Predispositions, personality traits, and posttraumatic stress disorder. *Harvard Review of Psychiatry* 8(4):175–183.
Paris, J., Zweig-Frank, H., and Guzder, H. (1993). The role of psychological risk factors in recovery from borderline personality disorder. *Comprehensive Psychiatry* 34:410–413.
Patrick, M., Hobson, P. D., Castle, C., et al. (1994). Personality disorder and the mental representation of early social experience. *Development and Psychopathology* 6:375–388.
Pennebaker, J. W., and Watson, D. (1991). The psychology of somatic symp-

toms. In *Current Concepts of Somatization*, ed., L. J. Kirmayer and J. M. Robbins, pp. 21–35. Washington, DC: American Psychiatric Press.

Perkonigg, A., Kessler, R. C., Stortz, S., and Wittchen, H. U. (2000). Traumatic events and post-traumatic stress disorder in the community: prevalence, risk factors and comorbidity. *Acta Psychiatrica Scandinavica* 101: 46–59.

Perrin, S., Smith, P., and Yule, W. (2000). Practitioner review: the assessment and treatment of post-traumatic stress disorder in children and adolescents. *Journal of Child Psychology and Psychiatry and Allied Disciplines* 41:277–289.

Phillips, D. L. (1963). Rejection: a possible consequence of seeking help for mental disorders. *American Sociological Review* 28:963–972.

Pichot, P. (1968). Histoire des idées sur l'hystérie. *Confrontations Psychiatriques* 1:9–28.

Plomin, R., and Bergeman, C. (1991). The nature of nurture: genetic influences on "environmental" measures. *Behavior and Brain Sciences* 14:373–386.

Pollack, M. H., and Otto, M. W. (1997). Long-term course and outcome of panic disorder. *Journal of Clinical Psychiatry* 58(supp. 2):57–64.

Pols, J. (1984). *Mythe en macht, over de kritische psychiatrie van Thomas S. Szasz*. Nijmegen: Sun.

Ponjaert, I., and Vertommen, H., eds. (1985). *Therapiegerichte diagnostiek*. Leuven: Acco.

Portegijs, P. J., van der Horst, F. G., Proot, I. M., et al. (1996). Somatization in frequent attenders of general practice. *Social Psychiatry and Psychiatric Epidemiology* 31:29–37.

Povinelli, D., Landry, A., Theall, L., et al. (1999). Development of young children's understanding that the recent past is causally bound to the present. *Developmental Psychology* 35:1426–1439.

Povinelli, D., and Simon, B. (1998). Young children's understanding of briefly versus extremely delayed images of the self: emergence of the autobiographical stance. *Developmental Psychology* 34:188–194.

Price, J., Hilsenroth, M., Petretic-Jackson, P., and Bonge, D. (2001). A review of individual psychotherapy outcomes for adult survivors of childhood sexual abuse. *Clinical Psychology Review* 21(7):1095–1121.

Rachman, S., Lopatka, C., and Levitt, K. (1988). Experimental analyses of panic. II. Panic patients. *Behavior Research and Therapy* 12:33–40.

Radin, S. (1962). Mental health problems in school children. *Journal of School and Health* 32:392.

Reich, W. (1949). *Character Analysis*, 3rd ed. New York: Orgone Institute Press.

Reilly, J., Baker, G. A., Rhodes, J., and Salmon, P. (1999). The association of sexual and physical abuse with somatization: characteristics of patients

presenting with irritable bowel syndrome and non-epileptic attack disorder. *Psychological Medicine* 29:399–406.
Repacholi, B., and Gopnik, A. (1997). Early reasoning about desires: evidence from 14- and 18- month-olds. *Developmental Psychology* 33:12–21.
Rief, W., Schäfer, S., Hiller, W., and Fichter, M. (1992). Lifetime diagnoses in patients with somatoform disorders: Which came first? *European Archives of Psychiatry and Clinical Neuroscience* 241:236–240.
Rogers, L. (2001). *Sexing the Brain*. New York: Columbia University Press.
Romains, J. (1923). *Knock, ou le triomphe de la médecine*. Oudenaarde: Sanderus
Rooymans, H.G.M. (1986). Over oordelen en vooroordelen in de diagnostiek. In *Ontwikkelingen in de klinische psychologie*, ed. B. G. Deelman, et al., pp. 15–26. Deventer: Van Loghum Slaterus.
Rosen, J. (1953). *Direct Analysis*. New York: Grune & Stratton.
Rosenbaum, J. F. (1997). Treatment-resistant panic disorder. *Journal of Clinical Psychiatry* 58(supp. 2):61–64.
Rosenhan, D. L. (1973). On being sane in insane places. *Science* 179:250–258.
——— (1975). The contextual nature of psychiatric diagnosis. *Journal of Abnormal Psychology* 84:462–474.
Roudinesco, E. (1986). *La bataille de cent ans. Histoire de la psychanalyse en France 1 (1885–1939)*. Paris: Seuil.
——— (1999). *Pourquoi la psychanalyse?* Paris: Fayard.
Rümke, H. C. (1971). *Psychiatrie, II. De Psychosen* (bewerkt door S. J. Nijdam). Amsterdam-Haarlem: Scheltema en Holkema.
Sacks, O. (1986). *De man die zijn vrouw voor een hoed hield*, vert. P. M. Moll-Huber. Amsterdam: Meulenhoff.
——— (1995). *An Anthropologist on Mars: Seven Paradoxal Tales*. London: Picador.
Salmon, K., and Bryant, R. (2002). Posttraumatic stress disorder in children. The influence of developmental factors. *Clinical Psychology Review* 22:163–188.
Samarin, W. S. (1972). *Tongues of Men and Angels*. New York: Collier Macmillan.
Sandifer, M. S., Hordern, A., and Green, L. M. (1970). The psychiatric interview: the impact of the first three minutes. *American Journal of Psychiatry* 126(7):968–973.
Schokker, J., and Schokker, T. (2000). *Extimiteit. Jacques Lacans terugkeer naar Freud*. Amsterdam: Boom.
Schopp, L., & Trull, T. (1993). Validity of the *DSM–III–R* personality disorder clusters. *Journal of Psychopathology and Behavioral Assessment* 15(3):219–237.
Schotte, C., and De Doncker, D. (2000). De *ADP–IV*: een vragenlijst voor een therapeutisch georienteerde diagnostiek van persoonlijkheidsstoornissen. *Psychopraxis* 2:267–273.

Schreber, D. P. (2000 [1903]). *Memoirs of My Illness*. New York: New York: Memoir Books.
——— (1986). *Schreber inédit*. (Textes présentés par D. Devreese, H. Israels, et J. Quackelbeen.) Paris: Seuil.
Schwartz, S. (1982). Is there a schizophrenic language? *Behavioral and Brain Sciences* 5:579–626.
Searles, H. (1977). *L'effort pour rendre l'autre fou*. Paris, Gallimard.
Segal, H. (1987). *Délire et créativité*. Paris: Des femmes.
Shaw, D. S., et al. (1996). Early risk factors and pathways in the development of early disruptive behavior problems. *Development and Psychopathology* 8:679–699.
Shear, M. K., Cooper, A. M., and Klerman, G. L. (1993). A psychodynamic model of panic disorder. *American Journal of Psychiatry* 150:859–866.
Shear, M. K., and Weiner, K. (1997). Psychotherapy for panic disorder. *Journal of Clinical Psychiatry* 58(supp. 2):38–45.
Shoenberg, P. (1975). The symptom as stigma or communication in hysteria. *International Journal of Psychoanalytic Psychotherapy* 4:507–516.
Shorter, E. (1994). *From Mind into Body: The Cultural Origins of Psychosomatic Symptoms*. New York: Free Press.
Sifneos, P. E. (1973). The prevalence of 'alexithymic' characteristics in psychosomatic patients. *Psychotherapy and Psychosomatics* 22:255–262.
Silove, D., Harris, M., Morgan, A., et al. (1995). Is early separation anxiety a specific precursor of panic disorder agoraphobia? A community study. *Psychological Medicine* 25:405–411.
Silvestre, M. (1981). Vocations de la psychiatrie des années 80. *L'Ane* 3:27; overgenomen in M. Silvestre, *Demain la psychanalyse*, pp. 241–243. Paris: Seuil-Navarin, 1987.
——— (1987). *Demain la psychanalyse*. Paris: Seuil-Navarin.
Simon, G., Gater, R., Kisely, S. R., and Piccinelli, M. (1996). Somatic symptoms of distress: an international primary care study. *Psychosomatic Medicine* 58:481–488.
Simon, G., and Gureje, O. (1999). Stability of somatization disorder and somatization symptoms among primary care patients. *Archives of General Psychiatry* 56:90–95.
Slater, E. (1961). Hysteria 311. *The Journal of Mental Science* 448:359–381.
——— (1965). Diagnosis of "Hysteria." *British Medical Journal* 1:1395–1399.
Smallbone, S., and Dadds, M. (1998). Childhood attachment and adult attachment in incarcerated adult male sex offenders. *Journal of Interpersonal Violence* 13:555–573.
——— (2001). Further evidence for a relationship between attachment in-

security and coercive sexual behavior in nonoffenders. *Journal of Interpersonal Violence* 16:22–35.

Soenen, S. (2002). *Schizofrenie en lichaamsbeleving. Theoretische verheldering en gevalsstudie bij jongvolwassenen vanuit psychodynamisch perspectief.* Doctoraat KUL, promotor Prof. J. Corveleyn, Leuven, pp. 1–704.

Soler, C. (1986). Le choix de la névrose. *Quarto* 24:47–58.

——— (1988). Innocence paranoïaque et indignité mélancolique. *Quarto 33/ 34*:23–28.

——— (1993). L'expérience énigmatique du psychotique, de Schreber à Joyce. *La Cause freudienne. Revue de psychanalyse* 23:50–59.

Solomon, J., George, C., and Dejong, A. (1995). Children classified as controlling at age six: Evidence of disorganised representational strategies and aggression at home and at school. *Development and Psychopathology* 7:447–463.

Solomon, Z., Mikulincer, M., Waysman, M., and Marlowe, D. (1991a). Delayed and immediate onset posstraumatic stress disorder. I. Differential clinical characteristics. *Social Psychiatry and Psychiatric Epidemiology* 26:1–17.

Solomon, Z., Mikulincer, M., and Waysman, M. (1991b). Delayed and immediate onset posstraumatic stress disorder. II. The role of battle experiences and personal resources. *Social Psychiatry and Psychiatric Epidemiology* 26:8–13.

Solomon, Z., and Singer, Y. (1995). Clinical characteristics of delayed and immediate-onset combat-induced post-traumatic stress disorder. *Military Medicine* 160:425–430.

Sontag, S. (1979). *Illness as Metaphor.* Harmondsworth, UK: Penguin.

Southwick, S. M., Morgan, C. A., Nicolaou, A. L., and Charney, D. S. (1997). Consistency of memory for combat-related traumatic events in veterans of Operation Desert Storm. *American Journal of Psychiatry* 154:173–177.

Spitz, R. (1946). Anaclitic depression. *Psychoanalytic Study of the Child* 2:313–42. New York: International Universities Press.

Stengers, E. (1989). Boîtes noires scientifiques, boîtes noires professionnelles. In *La psychanalyse, une science?* VIIes Rencontres psychanalytiques d'Aix-en-Provence, pp. 159–199. Paris: Les Belles Lettres.

Sterba, E. (1990 [1933]). Een abnormaal kind. Uit zijn ziektegeschiedenis en behandeling, vert. D. Vanderwegen. *Rondzendbrief uit het Freudiaanse Veld* 41:5–41.

Stermac, L., and Segal, S. (1989). Adult sexual contact with children: an examination of cognitive factors. *Behavior Therapy* 20:573–584.

Stern, D. (1985). *The Interpersonal World of the Infant.* New York: Basic Books.

Steunpunt Algemeen Welzijnswerk Gent (s.d.). *Leerprojecten voor daders van seksueel geweld. Een kennismaking.* [Brochure]

Stevens, A. (1987). L'holophrase, entre psychose et psychosomatique? *Ornicar?* 42:45–79.

Sullivan, H. S. (1974). *Schizophrenia as a Human Process.* New York: Norton.

Sulloway, F. J. (1979). *Freud, Biologist of the Mind: Beyond the Psychoanalytic Legend.* London: Burnett Books.

Suomi, S. (1997). Early determinants of behaviour: Evidence from primate studies. *British Medical Bulletin* 53:170–184.

——— (2000). A biobehavioral perspective on developmental psychopathology: excessive aggression and serotonergic dysfunction in monkeys. In *Handbook of Developmental Psychopathology*, A. Sameroffr, M. Lewis, and S. Miller, eds., pp. 237–256. New York: Plenum.

Szasz, T. (1972). *De waan van de waanzin, de psychiatrie als voortzetting van de inquisitie.* Bilthoven: Ambo.

——— (1983). *La schizophrénie, le symbole sacré de la psychiatrie*, vert. M. Manin. Paris: Payot. (See also Szasz, T. (1976). *Schizophrenia.* New York: Basic Books.)

Target, M., and Fonagy, P. (1996). Playing with reality: II. The development of psychic reality from a theoretical perspective. *International Journal of Psychoanalysis* 77:459–476.

Tausk, V. (1919). Ueber die Entstehung des "Beeinflussungsapparates" in der Schizofrenie. *Internationale Zeitschrift für Arztliche Psychoanalyse* 5:1–33.

Temerlin, M. K. (1968). Suggestion effects in psychiatric diagnosis. *Journal of Nervous and Mental Disease* 147:349–353.

Tienari, P., Wynne, L., Moring, J., et al. (1994). The Finnish Adoptive Family Study of Schizophrenia. Implications for family research. *British Journal of Psychiatry* 164(supp. 23):20–26.

Tomasello, M. (1999). *The Cultural Origins of Human Cognition.* Cambridge, MA: Harvard University Press.

Torrey, E., Bowler, A., Taylor, E., and Gottesman, I. (1994). *Schizophrenia and Manic-Depressive Disorders: The Biological Roots of Mental Illness as Revealed by the Landmark Study of Identical Twins.* New York: Basic Books.

Treffers, P. (1988). Reizend Circus. *Tijdschrift voor Psychiatrie* 30(9):565–567.

Vallas, P. (1986). Horizons de la psychosomatique. In *Le phénomène psychosomatique et la psychanalyse (Analytica* nr. 48, pp. 89–99). Paris: Navarin.

van Beek, D., and Mulder, J. (2002). De rol van cognitieve vervormingen in het plegen van pedoseksuele delicten en hun plaats in de behandeling. *Tijdschrift voor Seksuologie* 26:79–86.

Van Compernolle, E. (2002). *Depression, sign of the times? On the Real in clinical work.* Paper presented at the 8th Annual Conference, Understanding Subjectivity in Culture: Psychoanalysis/Ethnography/Cultural Studies,

George Washington University, Washington, DC: April 12–14. *The Letter* 25-26:212–229.

van den Brink, W. (1990). Persoonlijkheidsstoornissen; conceptualisering, operationalisering en onderzoeksthema's. *Tijdschrift voor Psychiatrie* 32(2):105–125.

Vandereycken, W. (1988). Weg met de statistiek?! *Tijdschrift voor Psychiatrie* 30(2):79–81.

Vandermeersch, P. (1978). *Het gekke verlangen*. Antwerpen: De Nederlandsche Boekhandel.

Van Haute, P. (2002). *Against Adaptation: Lacan's Subversion of the Subject*. New York: Other Press.

Vanheule, S. (1999). Taalgebruik in de psychose: een vraag naar kruisbestuiving tussen Lacan en enig experimenteel onderzoek. *Tijdschrift voor Psychoanalyse* 5:89–102.

——— (2001a). Burnout en psychoanalyse: van een procesvisie naar een conflictmodel. *Tijdschrift voor Psychotherapie* 27:278–295.

——— (2001b). Burnout and psychoanalysis: a Freudo-Lacanian point of view. *Journal for the Psychoanalysis of Culture and Society* 6:265–271.

——— (2001c). Psychoanalytic considerations on a case of burnout. *Anamorphosis* 4:73–87.

——— (2001d). Inhibition: "I am because I don't act." *The Letter* 23:109–126.

Van Hoorde, H. (1986a). Psychiatrische diagnostiek en *DSM-III*. *Rondzendbrief uit het Freudiaanse Veld* 5:3–13.

——— (1986b). 'Statistiatrie,' nosologie en structuur: een vraag? *Tijdschrift voor Psychiatrie* 28:6–14.

——— (1987). Redactioneel. *Tijdschrift voor Psychiatrie* 29:251–252.

——— (1991). Psychoanalyse en recht: de toerekening van een verantwoordelijkheid. *Rondzendbrief uit het Freudiaanse Veld* 9:3–11.

——— (1992). *Psychiatrie en Psychoanalyse: Scheiding van Tafel en Bank?* Ghent: Idesça.

——— (1993). De articulatie van kanker, psychosomatiek en psychoanalyse in de praktijk. *Rondzendbrief uit het freudiaanse veld* 53:35–52.

Van Houdenhove, B. (2001). State of the art-artikel: somatoforme stoornissen. *Tijdschrift voor Psychiatrie* 2:83–93.

Van Ijzendoorn, M. H. (1992). Intergenerational transmission of parenting. A review of studies. *Developmental Review* 12:76–99.

——— (1995). Adult attachment representations, parental responsiveness, and infant attachment: a meta-analysis on the predictive validity of the Adult Attachment Interview. *Psychological Bulletin* 117:387–403.

Van Ijzendoorn, M. H., and Bakermans-Kranenburg, M. J. (1996). Attachment representations in mothers, fathers, adolescents and clinical groups: a metaanalytic search for normative data. *Journal of Consulting and Clinical Psychology* 64:8–21.

Van Lieshout, P., Brook, G., and Van Dijk, P. (1987). Consistentie van psychiatrische diagnosen, Mededelingen uit het Patiëntenregister Intramurale Geestelijke Gezondheidszorg (20). *Tijdschrift voor Psychiatrie* 29:232–244.

Van Neygen, A. (1991). Strafrecht en psychoanalyse. *Rondzendbrief uit het Freudiaanse Veld* 9:35–56.

Van Nieuwenhuizen C., and Philipse, M. (2002). Risicotaxatie bij zedendelinquenten: een globaal literatuuroverzicht. *Tijdschrift voor Seksuologie* 26:70–78.

Van Os, J., and Marcelis, M. (1998). Opkomst van de psychiatrische ecogenetica: psychose. *Tijdschrift voor Psychiatrie* 40:95–107.

Van Os, J., Driessen, G., Gunther, N., and Delespaul, P. (2000). Neighbourhood variation in incidence of schizophrenia. Evidence for person-environment interaction. *British Journal of Psychiatry* 176:243–248.

Van Praag, H. (1994). Zorgen over depressie. Lezing gehouden op symposium, *Het Symptoom*, Psychiatrisch Centrum Sint-Jozef, Sleidinge 11 juni.

―――― (2000). Verrijkt biologisch depressieonderzoek de diagnostiek van depressies? *Tijdschrift voor Psychiatrie* 41:11–18.

Veith, I. (1965). *Hysteria: The History of a Disease*. Chicago: University of Chicago Press.

Verhaeghe, P. (1989). Determinisme en causaliteit in de psychoanalyse: tuchè en automaton. *Rondzendbrief uit het Freudiaanse Veld* 7:15–30.

―――― (1993). Borderline, een gewichtige zaak. *Psychoanalytische Perspektieven* 18:99–115.

―――― (1997). Trauma en hysterie bij Freud en Lacan. *Tijdschrift voor Psychoanalyse* 3:86–99.

―――― (1998). Causation and destitution of a pre-ontological non-entity: on the Lacanian subject. In *Key Concepts of Lacanian Psychoanalysis*, ed. D. Nobus, pp. 164–189. London: Rebus; New York: Other Press.

―――― (1999a). *Love in a Time of Loneliness*. London: Rebus.

―――― (1999b). *Does The Woman Exist? From Freud's Hysteric to Lacan's Feminine*. London: Rebus, revised edition [original dutch version: Verhaeghe, P. (1987). *Tussen hysterie en vrouw. Een weg door honderd jaar psychoanalyse*. Leuven/Amersfoort: Acco.

―――― (2000b). Activité versus passivité: l'au-delà du principe de genre. *Che vuoi?* 13:111–122.

―――― (2001a). Freuds drifttheorie. Van partiële pulsie naar eros/thanatos. *Tijdschrift voor Filosofie* 63:465–492.

―――― (2001b). *Beyond Gender: From Subject to Drive*. New York: Other Press.

——— (2002a). Vers un nouvel Oedipe: pères en fuite. *Revue française de psychanalyse* 1:145–158.
——— (2002b). Causality in science and psychoanalysis. In *Lacan and Science*, J. Glynos and Y. Stavrakakis, pp. 119–145. London: Karnac.
——— (2002c). Phallacies of binary reasoning: drive beyond gender. Conference on Sexuality and Gender, Stockholm, September (see also Verhaeghe, P. (forthcoming). In *Sex and Gender*, I. Matthis, ed.
——— (2003). Causality in science and psychoanalysis. In *Lacan and Science*, ed. J. Glynos and Y. Stavrakakis, pp. 119–145. London: Karnac.
Vermote, R. (2000). Psychoanalytische en psychiatrische diagnostiek bij persoonlijkheidsstoornissen. *Tijdschrift voor Psychiatrie* 42:667–674.
Vermote, R., and Auwerkerken, F. (1999). Een structureel diagnostische benadering van de *DSM-IV* as II persoonlijkheidsstoornissen. *Diagnostiek-Wijzer* 4:171–184.
Vertommen, H. (1996). Klinische psychodiagnostiek: een specifieke competentie van de klinisch psycholoog. In *De psyche als zorg: klinische psychologie in Vlaanderen*, ed. J. Vereycken, B. Cools, and M. Van Gael, pp. 27–46. Kapellen: Uitgeverij Pelckmans.
Vestdijk, S. (1968). *Het wezen van de angst*. Amsterdam: De Bezige Bij.
Vonk, R., van de Wetering, B., and Niermeijer, M. (1998). De erfelijkheid van psychiatrische aandoeningen. Recente ontwikkelingen deel II: bevindingen bij schizofrenie, stemmingstoornissen en de ziekte van Alzheimer. *Tijdschrift voor Psychiatrie* 40:82–91.
Wajeman, G. (1982). *Le Maître et l'Hystérique*. Paris: Seuil-Navarin.
Walgrave, L. (1979). *Afwijkend gedrag bij jongeren*. Welzijnsgids, Deel I. Antwerpen: Van Loghum Slaterus.
Walker, E., Hoppes, E., Emory, E., et al. (1981). Environmental factors related to schizophrenia in psychophysiologically liable high-risk males. *Journal of Abnormal Psychology* 90:313–320.
Walker, E. A., Katon, W. J., Keegan, D., et al. (1997). Predictors of physician frustration in the care of patients with rheumatological complaints. *General Hospital Psychiatry* 19:315–323.
Ward, T. (1999). Competency and deficit models in the understanding and treatment of sexual offenders. *Journal of Sex Research* 36:298–305.
Ward, T., Hudson, S., Marshall, W., and Siegert, R. (1995). Attachment style and intimacy deficits in sex offenders: a theoretical framework. *Sexual Abuse: A Journal of Research and Treatment* 7:317–355.
Ward, T., Hudson, S., Johnston, L., and Marshall, W. (1997). Cognitive distortions in sex offenders: an integrative review. *Clinical Psychology Review* 17:479–507.

Ward, T., and Keenan, T. (1999). Child molestors' implicit theories. *Journal of Interpersonal Violence* 14:141–157.

Welldon, E. (1988). *Mother, Madonna, Whore: The Idealization and Denigration of Motherhood.* New York: Guilford.

——— (1994). Forensic pychotherapy. In *The Handbook of Psychotherapy*, ed. P. Clarkson and M. Pokorny, pp. 470–493. London: Routledge.

——— (1995). Female perversion and hysteria. *British Journal of Psychotherapy*, 3:406–414.

——— (1996). Contrasts in male and female perversions. In *Forensic Psychotherapy*, ed. C. Cordess and M. Cox, pp. 273–289. London: Jessica Kingsley Publishers.

——— (1998). Group therapy for victims and perpetrators of incest. *Advances in Psychiatric Treatment* 4:82–88.

Whitehead, W. E., Crowell, M. D., Heller, B. R., et al. (1994). Modeling and reinforcement of the sick role during childhood predicts adult illness behavior. *Psychosomatic Medicine* 56:541–550.

Wilson, E. O. (1975). *Sociobiology*. Cambridge, MA: Harvard University Press, Belknap Press.

Wing, J. K. (1978). *Reasoning about Madness*. New York: Oxford University Press.

Winnicott, D. W. (1967). The location of cultural experience. *In Playing and Reality*, pp. 112–121. London: Tavistock Publications, 1971.

Wolfson, L. (1984). *Ma mère, musicienne, est morte* . . . Paris: Navarin.

Wolpe, J., and Rowan, V. V. (1988). Panic disorder: a product of classical conditioning. *Behavior Research and Therapy* 26:441–450.

World Health Organization (1973). *Report of the International Pilot Study of Schizophrenia. Vol. I: Results of the Initial Evaluation Phase.* Geneva: WHO.

World Health Organization (1992). *ICD-10: The ICD-10 classification of mental and behavioural disorders: clinical descriptions and diagnostic guidelines.* Geneva: WHO.

Wyshak, G. (1994). The relation between change in reports of traumatic events and symptoms of psychiatric distress. *General Hospital Psychiatry* 16:290–297.

Yehuda, R., Schmeidler, J., Giller E. Jr., et al. (1998). Relationship between posttraumatic stress disorder characteristics of Holocaust survivors and their adult offspring. *American Journal of Psychiatry* 155:841–843.

Yule, W. (2001). Post-traumatic stress disorder in children and adolescents. *International Review of Psychiatry* 13:194–2000.

Zarifian, E. (1988). *Les jardiniers de la folie*. Paris: O. Jacob.

Zenoni, A. (1997). La construction dans la clinique des psychoses. *Quarto* 63:62–66.

Zenoni (1991). *Le corps de l'être parlant. De l'évolutionnisme à la psychanalyse.* Brussel: De boeck-Wesmael.

Zetzel, E. (1968). The so-called good hysteric. *International Journal of Psychoanalysis* 49:256–260.

Zwemstra, J. (2001). Reactie op 'Het Groene Huis.' *Tijdschrift voor Psychiatrie* 43:202–204.

Index

Abell, F., 166n16
Abelson, R. P., 21
Abnormality
   analytic paradigm, 108–112
   categorical diagnostics, 20–22
   categorization, 10
   clinical psychodiagnostics, 6–8
Abraham, K., 12n9, 22–23, 114, 123
Actual neurosis, category of, 290–293
Actualpathological schizophrenia, to psychopathological paraphrenia, psychotic structure, 443–449
Actualpathology, 289–312. *See also* Borderline personality disorder; Panic disorder; Post-traumatic stress disorder
   actual neurosis (Freud), 290–293
   borderline personality disorder, 336–350
   panic disorder, 293–301
   post-traumatic stress disorder, 313–336, 317–322
   psychopathology versus, 202–205
   somatization phenomenon, 301–307
   subject-formation, 351–352
   treatment, 307–312
Adams, D., 61n29
Addiction, panic disorder, 297–298
Adler, A., 102
Agent, Other and, categorical diagnostics, 33–35
Age of consent, 400n4
Aggression, perversion, 423–424
Agoraphobia, panic disorder with, 296–297
Ainsworth, M., 156
Alexithymia, 303–307
Alienation
   depression, 273–274
   hysteria, 366–368
   linear to circular model, 213–220
   psychosis, 436
   psychotherapy, 9–10
   separation anxiety, identity, 158–159

Index

Analytic paradigm, 108–125
   deterioration, 121–125
   flight into health, 108–112
   scientism to ethics, 112–121
Anatomist, functionalists and, medical-biological paradigm, 80–82
Anato-pathological paradigm, medical-biological paradigm, 82–85
André, S., 409n13, 445
Anna O. case (Freud and Breuer), 11, 187–188, 374–375
Anorexia, linear to circular model, 231–232
Anxiety. *See also* Panic disorder
   defenses, 185–186
   guilt and, 265–268
   pathogenesis, 191–192
   pathological forms, defenses, 202–206
   subject-formation and, 263–265
   in subject-other relation, 260–262
   traumatic jouissance to phallic pleasure, 356–360
Aristophanes, 252
Aristotle, 38, 46
Assoun, P.-L., 218
Attention deficit hyperactivity disorder, 22
Auwerkerken, F., 337n13

Badinter, E., 408
Bagby, R. M., 303
Bakermans-Kranenburg, M. J., 209n3
Bakker, A., 102, 310
Bakker, J., 458
Balint, M., 280n12, 338–339
Barlow, D. H., 299, 310
Barsky, A. J., 306
Basic trust, post-traumatic stress disorder, 322–325
Bateman, A., 339
Bayle, 82–83, 84
Beard, 292
Beauchesne, H., 79n6
Beck, A. T., 261, 299

Beckett, S., 464
Beitman, B. D., 295
Benedict, R., 128n1
Bercherie, P., 40, 79n6
Berden, G. F. M. G., 45n10
Bergeman, C., 266n3
Bergin, A. E., 105n26
Bettelheim, B., 9n3, 73n1, 317
Beyaert, F. H. L., 11
Billiet, L., 443, 451, 456n28, 457n29
Binet, A., 15n10
Binswanger, L., 73
Bion, W., 160, 162n12, 338, 339, 456n28
Blame, depression and guilt, 277–278
Bleuler, E., 23n2, 67, 444
Blois, M. S., 24
Bogaerts, S., 410, 427
Bohman, M., 86n10
Borderline personality disorder, 336–350
   categorical diagnosis, 337–340
   differential diagnosis and treatment, 346–350
   DSM, 43–44
   post-traumatic stress disorder and, 336–337, 344
   subject-formation, 340–344
   trauma, 345–346
Borges, J. L., 42n6
Bouchard, M.-A., 342
Bouhuys, A. L., 86
Bower, G., 321n6
Bowlby, J., 160
Braeckman, J., 237n3
Bram, F., 11
Brawman-Mintzer, O., 310
Breuer, J., 11, 96n17, 100, 125n40, 178, 187–188, 193n17, 313, 323, 331n11, 374
Bridges, K. W., 303
Briquet, P., 301
Bryant, A., 314
Bryant, R., 320, 321n6
Bucci, W., 228–229n28, 245

Bulimia, linear to circular model, 231–232
Bumby, K., 409n14
Burnout, referral and flight, clinical psychodiagnostics, object to relationship, 65–68
Burton, R., 73
Busch, F., 310
Bush, F. N., 311

Cambien, J., 69n39
Carlson, E. A., 344
Carroll, L., 61n31
Cason, D., 321
Cassidy, J., 343
Cassirer, E., 95n16
Castration anxiety
   Other to first and second Others, 353n2
   phallus as signifier, identity, 171
Categorical diagnostics, 19–36. *See also* Clinical psychodiagnostics; *Diagnostic and Statistical Manual of Mental Disorders*
   abnormality, 20–22
   borderline personality disorder, 337–340
   clinical psychodiagnostics, 143–147
   Diagnostic and Statistical Manual of Mental Disorders, 24–31
      personality research, 27–29
      personality types, 29–30
      pros and cons of, 30–31
      success of, 26–27
      treatment modalities, 29
   form and content in, 31–35
   hysteria, 365–366
   hysterical delusions, 455
   medically unexplained symptoms (MUS), 301–307 (*See also* Somatization phenomenon)
   obsessional neurosis, 381–382, 392
   panic disorder, 293–298
   perversion, 399, 401, 420

post-traumatic stress disorder, 313–317, 328–333
power relationship, 35–36
psychosis, 431, 446–450
psychotic personality disorders, 452–454
subject and, 459–461
suggestibility effect, 22–24
treatment, 19–20
Categorization, clinical psychodiagnostics, 40–46
Chaika, E., 438
Changeux, J., 78
Charcot, J.-M., 50n14, 67, 72, 85, 90, 365, 368
Childhood sexual abuse
   borderline personality disorder, 345–346
   hysteria, 380
   perversion, 317, 415–416
   post-traumatic stress disorder, 315, 317, 322–327
   somatization disorder, 306–307
Chomsky, N., 242
Circular model. *See* Linear to circular model
Clark, D. M., 261, 295, 299
Clinical paradigms, 71–125. *See also* Categorical diagnostics; Metapsychology
   analytic, 108–125
      deterioration, 121–125
      flight into health, 108–112
      scientism to ethics, 112–121
   characteristics of, 76–78
   exemplary cases, 72–76
   guilt, 127–128
   medical-biological, 78–91
      anatomist and functionalists, 80–82
      anato-pathological paradigm, 82–85
      dualism, 78–80
      uniform syndrome, 85–86
      University discourse, 86–91

500 Index

Clinical paradigms (*continued*)
  moral treatment, 92–107
    exoneration and infantilization, 97–100
    Guislan, 94
    Pinel, 92–94
    Primal Father, 103–107
    Protagoras, 95–97
    rejection of subject, 101–103
  overview, 71–72
Clinical psychodiagnostics, 3–18. *See also* Categorical diagnostics; Clinical paradigms; Metapsychology
  categorical diagnostics, 143–147
  epistemology, 46–58
    DSM approach, 51–53
    Lacan's discourse theory, 56–58
    naive approach, 46–50
    science as symbolic system, 53–56
  goals of, 129–133, 142–143
  medical model, 3–4
  normality
    abnormality and, 6–8
    as developmental process, 11–13
    as ideal, 8–11
  object of, 38–46
  object to relationship, 58–70
    as cover-up, 60–65
    ethics and social bond, 68–70
    nominalist diagnostics, 58–60
    referral, flight, and burnout, 65–68
  pitfalls of, 133–136
  post-traumatic stress disorder, 333–336
  prognosis, 13–15
  referral and treatment, 15–17
  symptoms to syndrome, 4–6
Clum, G. A., 271, 297, 298
Coles, E. M., 44n8
Comorbidity
  panic disorder, 297–298
  post-traumatic stress disorder, 315
Comptom, A., 311
Condillac, 46, 79
Conflict, pathology, 208

Content, form and, categorical diagnostics, 31–35
Conversion disorder, 302
Conversion symptoms, hysteria, 377
Cooper, D., 20
Cooper, P., 345
Cosmides, L., 48n12, 240n5, 241, 242, 245
Cottet, S., 278
Craig, T. K. J., 302, 321
Craske, M. G., 299
Cremniter, D., 378, 455
Crits-Christoph, P., 228–229n28
Csibra, G., 166
Culture, guilt, 128
Czermak, M., 456n28

Dadds, M., 408, 410
Damasio, A. R., 177, 431n2
Dante, 125n40
Darwin, C., 39–40, 48, 85, 236, 260, 261
Darwin, E., 236
Davis, R., 29n8
Dawkins, R., 245
Death drive, obsessional neurosis, 383
De Beuk, N., 454
de Beurs, E., 310n13
de Bois, 445
Declercq, F., 165, 193, 200, 364
De Doncker, D., 134, 420
Deelman, B. G., 22
Defenses, 181–206
  analytic paradigm, 113–114
  clinical illustration, 186–188
  identity, 177–178
  obsessional neurosis, 390
  pathogenesis, 188–197
  pathological forms, 202–206
  primary/secondary, 181–186
  symptom as hinge, 197–202
De Gucht, V., 301, 303, 304, 305
de Haan, H., 105n26
De Haan, L., 454, 458

De Jong, A., 42n6, 76n3
De Kesel, M., 53n20, 280n12, 358
De Kroon, J., 79n6
De La Mettrie, 78
Delespaul, P., 433
Delusions
  hysterical, 454–455
  psychosis, 447–449
Democritus, 78
Demoulin, C., 271, 272
Den Boer, J. A., 48n12
Depression
  as essential possibility of subject, 272–275
  guilt and, 275–278
  perversion, 424–425
  position of subject and, 268–272
  as possibility of passage, 278–281
  psychotic, 455–456
Depressive reaction, separation anxiety, identity, 157
De Ridder, D. T. D., 11
de Ruiter, C., 300
De Saussure, F., 5n1, 49–50, 51, 211, 358n10, 418
Descartes, R., 38–39, 47, 78, 370n18
de Swaan, 197n23
Deutsch, H., 451
Developmental perspective
  Freudianism, 154
  Oedipal structure, 166–173
  Other, 137–140
De Witte, A., 154
Diagnostic and Statistical Manual of Mental Disorders, 24–31, 90, 259. *See also* Categorical diagnostics
  clinical psychodiagnostics, 42–45, 143
  epistemology, 51–53
  hysteria, 364, 365, 366
  hysterical delusions, 455
  medically unexplained symptoms (MUS), 301–307
  metapsychology, 134
  nominalist diagnostics, 59, 60n28

obsessional neurosis, 381–382, 392
panic disorder, 294–297
personality research, 27–29
personality types, 29–30
perversion, 399, 401, 420
post-traumatic stress disorder, 313–317, 328–333
pros and cons of, 30–31
psychosis, 431, 446–450
psychotic personality disorders, 452–454
somatization disorder, 304–305
success of, 26–27
treatment modalities, 29
Diagnostics. *See* Categorical diagnostics; Clinical paradigms; Clinical psychodiagnostics; Differential diagnosis; Metapsychology
Dickinson, J. K., 24
Differential diagnosis
  borderline personality disorder, 346–350
  hysteria, 378–381
  linear to circular model, 229–232
  obsessional neurosis, 393–395
  perversion, 397–402, 420–425
  post-traumatic stress disorder, 333–336
  psychotic structure, 450–456
Di Gennaro, G., 75
Dingemans, 26
Disavowal, perversion, 410–412
Discourse theory, 56–58
  categorical diagnostics, 33–35
  Other to first and second Others, 353–354
Displacement, science as symbolic system, 54
Distrust, post-traumatic stress disorder, 332–333
Division of subject, psychoneurosis, 361–364
Dolto, F., 138–139n8
Dora case (Freud), 367, 369n17
Doxa. *See* Clinical paradigms

Dreams
  memory, 184n3
  post-traumatic stress disorder, 331–332
Drive theory
  evolution, 237, 246–253
  Other to first and second Others, 355
Drossman, D. A., 301, 306
Dualism, medical-biological paradigm, 78–80
Duriès, V., 417n23
Duyckaerts, F., 128

Edelman, G., 177
Edwards, P., 95n16
Ego psychology, analytic paradigm, 123
Ehrenberg, A., 272n6
Einstein, A., 47, 48n12
Eitingon, 23
Ellenberger, H. F., 73, 79n6, 202
Elstein, A. S., 24
Emck, C., 444
Emmelkamp, P., 425
Emotion, memory, 321
Enactment, borderline personality disorder, 340–344
Epistemology, 46–58
  discourse theory (Lacan), 56–58
  DSM approach, 51–53
  naive approach, 46–50
  science as symbolic system, 53–56
Eryavec, G., 328
Escobar, J. I., 301, 302
Esquirol, 80, 81, 93
Ethics
  scientism, analytic paradigm, 112–121
  social bond and, clinical psychodiagnostics, 68–70
Evolution, 235–257
  circular, nonreciprocal structure, 253–257
  drive theory, 246–253
  metapsychology compared, 244–246
  organogenesis versus psychogenesis, 240–244
  purposiveness, 236–240

Exemplary cases, clinical paradigms, 72–76
Exoneration, infantilization and, moral treatment paradigm, 97–100
Ey, H., 84, 122, 243n8, 444

Fantasy
  fundamental
    hysteria, 373–378
    obsessional neurosis, 388–393
    perversion, 417–419
    psychoneurosis, 361–364
    psychosis, 436–438
  subject and Other, linear to circular model, 225–229
Faravelli, C., 300
Father, Primal, moral treatment paradigm, 103–107
Fava, G. A., 302
Federn, P., 456n28
Feher Gurewich, J., 413, 417
Ferenczi, S., 138n8, 415n22
Feynman, R., 174n26
Finality, drive theory, evolution, 250–253
Fink, B., 210n5, 352n1, 397n1, 432n3
Fink, P., 301, 302, 305
Fischer, A., 91
Fischler, B., 301, 305
Fixation, symptom, 200–201
Fliess, 114, 298
Flight, referral and burnout, clinical psychodiagnostics, object to relationship, 65–68
Flight into health, analytic paradigm, 108–112
Flournoy, 72
Foa, 321n6
Fonagy, P., 86, 91n14, 158, 161, 162n12, 163–164n13, 166, 167, 168, 209n3, 212n8, 213–214n9, 218n13, 228–229n28, 230, 243, 245, 307, 309n12, 324n8, 339, 341, 342, 345, 346, 347, 348n20, 349, 350, 441
Forensic clinics, perversion, 405–407

Forgetting, remembering and, 198
Form, content and, categorical diagnostics, 31–35
Foucault, M., 32, 46, 69, 79n6, 90, 102, 130
Foudraine, J., 100n22, 223n20
Fournier, 83
Free, N. K., 300
Freeman, L., 11, 374n24
Freud, A., 123
Freud, S., 8, 11, 12, 30n9, 34, 52, 54, 55–56, 64–65n32, 67n36, 70, 73, 85, 93, 94, 96n17, 100, 101, 102, 104n24, 105n26, 106, 107n27, 108–125, 138n8, 151, 153–161, 163n13, 168n19, 169, 171, 173, 174n27, 175, 177, 178, 183, 184, 188–193, 196–200, 202–203, 207, 211, 214n10, 216–217, 218n11, 220n17, 221, 223, 226, 236, 237, 239, 246–254, 260–261, 265, 270, 271, 272, 275, 278–279, 290–293, 295, 298, 299–300, 301, 306, 309, 313, 315n2, 316, 318n3, 320, 322n7, 323, 331, 338, 352, 354, 356n6–8, 357–359, 363–364, 365, 366–367, 368, 369n17, 370, 374–375, 377n26, 381–384, 388–390, 392, 394, 398, 401–403, 405, 411, 414, 418, 432, 437, 440–441, 445, 446n23, 455, 456
Frith, C. D., 431n2
Fromkin, V. A., 438
Fromm-Reichmann, F., 456n28
Functionalists, anatomist and, medical-biological paradigm, 80–82
Fundamental fantasy
  hysteria, 373–378
  obsessional neurosis, 388–393
  perversion, 417–419
  psychoneurosis, 361–364
  psychosis, 436–438

Gall, 22, 80–81
Gauron, E. F., 24

Gender
  hysteria, 371–373
  hysterical delusions, 454–455
  obsessional neurosis, 386–387
  perversion, 401, 413–416
Georget, 81–82
Gergely, G., 151, 166, 166n16
Giel, R., 76n3
Gijs, L., 397, 410n17
Glas, G., 260, 261
Goldberg, D. P., 303
Goldwyn, S., 228–229n28
Gopnik, A., 167n17
Gorman, T. M., 297
Gould, S. J., 28n6, 310
Green, A., 456n28
Griesinger, 40
Groddeck, G., 257
Grubin, D., 412
Guilt
  anxiety and, 265–268
  clinical paradigms, 127–128
  depression and, 275–278
  post-traumatic stress disorder, 325–328
Guiraud, 442n19
Guislain, 94, 208
Gureje, O., 303n9

Hahn, S. R., 311n14
Hall, G., 412
Hallucination, psychosis, 447
Harris, J. R., 266
Hartmann, H., 9n3, 103
Harvey, A., 314
Haviland, 304
Hebbrecht, M., 311
Hegel, G. W. F., 46, 101
Heinrichs, R., 433
Heiser, W., 303
Hellinga, G., 28, 29
Heraclitus, 38
Herman, J. L., 313, 334–335, 337, 345, 364
Hermann, N., 328

Higley, J., 298n6
Hite, S., 110
Holophrasis, 441–442
Homosexuality, categories, 404. *See also* Perversion
Huxley, A., 11, 270
Hypervigilance, post-traumatic stress disorder, 332–333
Hysteria, 364–381
　analytic paradigm, 111
　differential diagnosis and treatment, 378–381
　fundamental fantasy and symptoms formation, 373–378
　gender, seduction, and trauma, 371–373
　Oedipal history, 368–371
　structure, 364–366
　subject-formation, 366–368
Hysterical delusions, psychosis, 454–455

Ideal, enforcement of, moral treatment paradigm, 99–100
Identification, hysteria, 366–368
Identity, 153–179. *See also* Subject-formation
　categorical diagnostics, 459–461
　language, 173–178
　Oedipal structure, 166–173
　　Other, 168–170
　　phallus as signifier, 170–172
　Other, 151–152
　separation anxiety, 153–166
　　depressive reaction, 157
　　lack and alienation, 158–159
　　mirroring, 159–166
　subject-formation, 208, 210–213
Incorporation, hysteria, 366–368
Infancy, mirroring, identity, 159–166
Infantilization, exoneration and, moral treatment paradigm, 97–100
International Classification of Diseases (ICD), 25–26, 316
Israel, L., 108

Jacobson, E., 162n12
Jamieson, S., 410
Janet, P.-M.-F., 67, 72, 124, 220n17, 292
Jansz, J., 15n10
Jaspers, K., 88n11
Johnson, J., 345
Johnson, V., 110, 398–399
Jonckheere, L., 271, 337, 339
Jones, E., 9n3
Jongedijk, R., 30
Jouissance
　of the body, 193
　psychosis, 435
　stress, 319–320
　traumatic, to phallic pleasure, psychoneurosis, 356–360
Jouissance concept, analytic paradigm, 113, 115
Joyce, J., 98n19, 450
Jung, C. G., 30n9, 73, 144–145
Juridical-social diagnostics
　goals of, 130–132
　perversion, 400–401

Kalus, O., 28n7
Kant, I., 39–40, 48, 55n23, 95
Kaplan-Solms, K., 177, 431n2
Kear-Colwell, J., 427
Keenan, T., 406
Kennedy, H., 412
Kernberg, O., 67, 162n12, 337, 456n28
Kierkegaard, S., 275
Kinsey, A., 398–399
Kirmayer, L. J., 302
Klein, D. F., 260, 294, 297, 298, 307, 308
Klein, M., 123, 146, 263–264, 277n10, 278
Knowledge
　truth versus, clinical psychodiagnostics, 60–65
　University discourse, medical-biological paradigm, 87
Knowles, S. L., 297
Kohut, H., 162n12, 338, 339
Konner, M., 15n10, 34–35n12

Koster van Groos, G. A. S., 7
Kraepelin, E., 30n9, 82, 84, 85, 87, 88n11, 438n10, 444
Kretschmer, 442
Kroenke, K., 301
Kübler-Ross, E., 12–13n9
Kuhn, T., 35–36, 71
Kundera, M., 274
Kushner, M. G., 295

Labeling, clinical psychodiagnostics, 40–46
Laborit, 102
Lacan, J., 5, 9, 20, 32, 33n11, 34, 38–39n2, 44–45n9, 51n16, 51n17, 53n20, 55–56, 56–58, 60, 62, 64, 66n34, 68n37, 87, 88n11, 100n23, 102, 106, 107, 109, 111, 114, 115, 116n33, 120, 122, 125n40, 136, 137, 138–139n8, 139n9, 140, 146, 151–152, 158, 159, 162, 163–164, 168–170, 171–172, 174, 181, 185, 186n7, 193, 195n20, 197–199, 201, 208–214, 216–227, 243n8, 246, 254–257, 273–274, 276–281, 318n3, 319, 320, 331, 353, 354, 356n6–8, 357–358, 363, 367, 370, 371n20, 373–375, 386n32, 388, 401, 403–404, 406, 408n11, 409n13, 411, 412n20, 418, 424, 432, 434–435, 437–438, 440–441, 450–451, 455, 456, 463–464
Lack, separation anxiety, identity, 158–159
Laing, R. D., 20
Lange, A., 21
Langer, E. J., 21
Language
 clinical psychodiagnostics, 48–49, 54–55
 defenses, 181–182
 discourse theory, 56–58
 identity, 173–178
 perversion, 418–419
 psychosis, 429–432, 438–443

University discourse, medical-biological paradigm, 86–91
Laplace, P.-S. de, 22
Laplanche, J., 207–208n1
Laurent, E., 456n28
Leader, D., 277n10
Lecours, S., 342
LeDoux, J., 331n11
Lee, D., 314, 315, 316, 334
Lerner, M. J., 128
Lesègue, 448
Leslie, A., 166n16
Leuret, 79–80
Lévi-Strauss, C., 48
Lievrouw, A., 414
Linear to circular model, 207–210, 207–233
 alienation, 213–220
 differential diagnosis, 229–232
 evolution, 253–257
 fantasy, 225–229
 separation, 220–225
 subject-formation, 210–213
Linguistics, clinical psychodiagnostics, 49–50
Lipowski, Z., 301n7
Little, M., 456n28
Little Hans case (Freud), 120
Livanou, M., 336
Livesley, W., 29n8
Loose, R., 272n6, 347
Lorenz, K., 20, 68n38, 241
Luborsky, L., 228–229n28
Lydiard, R. B., 310

Magritte, R.-F.-G., 55n22
Mahler, M., 139, 162n12
Mahoney, 83–84
Main, M., 228–229n28, 343
Make-believe, analytic paradigm, 111–112
Malamuth, N., 410n17
Maleval, J.-Cl., 23n2, 73, 214, 378, 434n6, 439n12, 442, 443, 448, 455, 456n28

Mallet, J., 275
Malraux, A., 96n17, 256
Mann, T., 267n4
Marcelis, M., 434
Marinez-Sanchez, 304
Marques, J., 425
Marshall, W., 410
Marx, K., 46
Masson, J., 114n32
Masters, W., 110, 398–399
McCauley, J., 306
Mcdevitt, J. B., 162n12
McGuire, W., 30n9
McNally, R. J., 299, 310
Medical-biological paradigm, 78–91
   anatomist and functionalists, 80–82
   anato-pathological paradigm, 82–85
   dualism, 78–80
   uniform syndrome, 85–86
   University discourse, 86–91
Medically unexplained symptoms (MUS), 301–307
Medical model
   clinical psychodiagnostics, 3–4, 6, 19, 38
   evolution, 237–238
Medline search, 306
Memory
   dreams, 184n3
   trauma, 321, 331
Menaker, D., 121n36
Mendel, G. J., 236n2
Metapsychology, 127–147
   categorical diagnostics, 143–147
   clinical psychodiagnostic goals, 129–133
   clinical psychodiagnostic pitfalls, 133–136
   evolution compared, 244–246
   guilt, 127–129
   treatment, 135–143
Miliora, M. T., 300, 311
Miller, J.-A., 226
Millon, T., 28n7, 29n8

Milrod, B., 300, 310, 311
Minderaa, R. B., 22
Mirroring
   alienation, 215, 219
   separation anxiety, identity, 159–166
Moguchi, 83
Moll, 76n4
Moment of onset, psychotic structure, 445–446
Money, J., 10n7, 399
Monod, J., 9n3, 95
Mooij, A., 52n18, 69, 268, 424
Mooren, 105n26
Moral treatment paradigm, 92–107
   exoneration and infantilization, 97–100
   Guislan, 94
   Pinel, 92–94
   Primal Father, 103–107
   Protagoras of Abdera, 95–97
   rejection of subject, 101–103
Morel, 76n3
Murray, L., 345

Name-of-the-Father
   identity, 166–173
   psychosis, 434–435
Nature/nurture debate, evolution, organogenesis versus psychogenesis, 240–244
Neologism, 440n15
Neurosis
   actual neurosis, 290–293
   choice of, analytic paradigm, 112–121, 221–222
   guilt, 127–128
   trauma, 195
Newton, I., 78
Nietzsche, F., 101
Nijs, P., 85
Nominalist diagnostics, clinical psychodiagnostics, object to relationship, 58–60
Noordenbos, G., 232n29

Normality. *See also* Psychoneurosis
  abnormality and, clinical psychodiagnostics, 6–8
  analytic paradigm, 108–112
  as developmental process, clinical psychodiagnostics, 11–13
  as ideal, clinical psychodiagnostics, 8–11
  perversion, 398–399
  psychoneurosis, 351–364
Normophilia, 10
Norretransders, T., 104n25

Object to relationship, nominalist diagnostics, clinical psychodiagnostics, 58–60
Observation, clinical psychodiagnostics, 40–46
Obsessional neurosis, 381–395
  categorical diagnostics, 381–382
  differential diagnosis and treatment, 393–395
  fundamental fantasy and symptom formation, 388–393
  gender, seduction, and trauma, 386–387
  Oedipal history, 384–386
  subject-formation, 382–383
Occam's razor, 49
Oedipal structure
  analytic paradigm, 116, 120
  discourse theory, 57
  hysteria, 368–371
  identity, 166–173
    Other, 168–170
    phallus as signifier, 170–172
  obsessional neurosis, 384–386
  Other to first and second Others, 353
  perversion, 407–413
  psychotic structure, 432–438
  subject-formation, 352
Ogawa, J. R., 344
Ogden, T., 343
Opinion. *See* Clinical paradigms

Organogenesis, psychogenesis versus, evolution, 240–244
Orwell, G., 11, 97n18
Other
  acutalpathology, 307–312
  agent and, categorical diagnostics, 33–35
  alienation, 213–220
  anxiety in subject-other relation, 260–262
  clinical psychodiagnostics, 12
  defenses, 181–182
  depression and guilt, 275–278
  to first and second Others, psychoneurosis, 353–356
  hysteria, 365, 368, 375–377
  identity, 151–152
  metapsychology, 137–140
  mirroring, identity, 159–166
  obsessional neurosis, 384–386, 391
  Oedipal structure, identity, 168–170, 171
  panic disorder, 300–301
  pathogenesis, 188–197
  perversion, 403–404, 407–413
  post-traumatic stress disorder, 317–325
  psychosis, 434–438, 448
  subject and, 140–142
    fantasy, linear to circular model, 225–229
  subject-formation, 210–213
  therapeutic relation, 462–464
  unconscious and, 136–137
Otto, M. W., 310

Pallanti, S., 300
Palombo, S., 236n2
Panic disorder, 293–301. *See also* Anxiety
  diagnostic categories, 293–298
  etiology, 298–301
  pathogenesis, 191–192
Panksepp, J., 244n10, 431n2

Pappenheim, Bertha. *See* Anna O. case (Freud and Breuer)
Paranoia, psychotic structure, 443–449
Paris, J., 314, 320, 345
Passive-active reversal, perversion, 412–413
Patient Register of Intramural Mental Health Care, 25
Pavlov, I. P., 73
Pendrey, D., 271, 298
Pennebaker, J. W., 306
Perkonigg, A., 314, 319
Perrin, S., 321
Personality disorders, psychotic, 452–454
Personality research, DSM, 27–29
Personality types, DSM, 29–30
Perversion, 397–427. *See also* Sexuality
  childhood sexual abuse, 317
  differential diagnosis, 397–402, 420–425
  forensic clinics, 405–407
  gender, seduction, and trauma, 413–416
  guilt, 127–128
  Oedipal history, 407–413
  paraphiliac traits, 402–405
  symptoms, 416–420
  treatment, 425–427
Phallic pleasure, from traumatic jouissance, psychoneurosis, 356–360
Phallus, as signifier, identity, 170–172
Pharmacology
  depression, 270
  hysterical delusions, 455
  psychosis, 457
Phenomenon, symptom, 203
Philipse, M., 425
Phillips, D. L., 20, 21, 24
Phobia, pathogenesis, 191–192
Picasso, P., 175n28
Pichot, P., 67n36
Pinel, P., 40, 67, 80, 81, 92–93, 95, 137n7

Plato, 38, 46, 78, 252
Plomin, R., 266n3
Plutarch, 74n2
Poe, E. A., 44
Pollack, M. H., 310
Portegijs, P. J., 302
Post-traumatic stress disorder, 154, 313–336
  actualpathology, 317–322
  basic trust, 322–325
  borderline personality disorder and, 336–337, 344
  categorical diagnostics, 313–317, 328–333
  differential diagnosis and treatment, 333–336, 379–380
  nature of trauma, 325–328
  perversion, 407
Power relationship
  categorical diagnostics, 35–36
  perversion, 406–407
Price, J., 328
Price, R. K., 301
Primal Father, moral treatment paradigm, 103–107
Primary defenses, secondary defenses and, 181–186
Primary repression, pathogenesis, 189–190
Procrustes, 74n2
Prognosis, clinical psychodiagnostics, 13–15
Projective identification, borderline personality disorder, 340–344
Protagoras of Abdera, 95–97
Proton pseudos, 193
Psychogenesis, organogenesis versus, evolution, 240–244
Psychoneurosis, 351–364
  division of subject, fundamental fantasy, and symptoms, 361–364
  Other to first and second Others, 353–356
  subject-formation, 351–352

traumatic jouissance to phallic
    pleasure, 356–360
Psychopathological paraphrenia,
    actualpathological schizophrenia
    from, psychotic structure, 443–
    449
Psychopathological position, 364–395.
    See also Hysteria; Obsessional
    neurosis
    hysteria, 364–381
    obsessional neurosis, 381–395
Psychotherapy, alienation, 9–10
Psychotic depression, 455–456
Psychotic structure, 429–458
    actualpathological schizophrenia to
        psychopathological paraphrenia,
        443–449
    differential diagnosis, 450–456
    etiology and Oedipal prehistory,
        432–438
    guilt, 127–128
    language, 429–432, 438–443
    treatment, 456–458
    University discourse, 122–124
Purposiveness, human behavior,
    evolution, 236–240

"Q"-factor, drive theory, 246

Rachman, S., 299
Radin, S., 112
Rank, O., 156
Rape, post-traumatic stress disorder,
    326
Real
    analytic paradigm, 113, 116–118
    defenses, 185
    discourse theory, 57–58
    linguistics, clinical
        psychodiagnostics, 49–50, 55
    nominalist diagnostics, clinical
        psychodiagnostics, 59–60
    pathogenesis, 196
    transference, analytic paradigm, 114–
        118

Referral
    flight and burnout, clinical
        psychodiagnostics, 65–68
    treatment and, clinical
        psychodiagnostics, 15–17
Reilly, J., 306
Rejection of subject, moral treatment
    paradigm, 101–103
Relationship, object to, nominalist
    diagnostics, clinical
    psychodiagnostics, 58–60
Remembering, forgetting and, 198
Repacholi, B., 167n17
Repetition compulsion
    analytic paradigm, 117n34
    post-traumatic stress disorder, 325,
        331
Repression
    analytic paradigm, 110
    defenses, 182–185
    pathogenesis, 189–190
    symptom, 199
Rief, W., 302
Rimbaud, A., 277n10
Robbins, J. M., 302
Rogers, L., 177
Romains, J., 23n3
Rooymans, H. G. M., 24, 52n18
Rosenbaum, J. F., 297, 310
Rosenhan, D. L., 23
Roudinesco, E., 124, 259
Rowan, V. V., 299
Rümke, H. C., 84, 444, 457
Rush, B., 10n6

Sacks, O., 22, 457
Salmien, 304
Salmon, K., 320, 321n6
Samarin, W. S., 440n15
Sandifer, M. S., 24
Sawle, G., 427
Schaudinn, 83
Schizophrenia. See Psychotic structure
Schmidt, 304
Schneider, 444

Schopenhauer, A., 101
Schopp, L., 28
Schotte, C., 134
Schreber, D. P., 52, 74
Schwartz, S., 438
Science
  medical-biological paradigm, 78–91
  as symbolic system, epistemology, 53–56
Scientism, ethics, analytic paradigm, 112–121
Searles, H., 456n28
Secondary defenses, primary defenses and, 181–186
Secondary elaboration, categorical diagnostics, 23
Seduction
  hysteria, 371–373
  obsessional neurosis, 386–387
  perversion, 413–416
Segal, H., 456n28
Separation, linear to circular model, 220–225
Separation anxiety
  identity, 153–166
    depressive reaction, 157
    lack and alienation, 158–159
    mirroring, 159–166
  panic disorder, 300
  symptom, 203
Sexual abuse
  borderline personality disorder, 345–346
  hysteria, 380
  perversion, 317, 415–416
  post-traumatic stress disorder, 315, 317, 322–327
  somatization disorder, 306–307
Sexuality. *See also* Perversion
  analytic paradigm, 110, 116
  evolution, 237–239
  Freud, 153
  hysteria, 368–371
  psychoneurosis, 361–364

Sexual offenders, violent, metapsychology, 135–136
Shakespeare, W., 47, 75
Shame, guilt and, 268
Shear, M. K., 300, 310
Shoenberg, P., 367, 376
Shorter, E., 306
Sifneos, P. E., 303
Signifier(s)
  analytic paradigm, 118
  clinical psychodiagnostics, 5, 62
  defenses, 183–184
  linguistics, clinical psychodiagnostics, 49–50
  moral treatment paradigm, 97
  pathogenesis, 195
  phallus as, 357–358
  science as symbolic system, 53–56
  University discourse, medical-biological paradigm, 87–89
Silove, D., 300
Silvers, H., 321n6
Silvestre, M., 7, 456n28
Simon, G., 303n9, 305
Singer, Y., 328
Skinner, B. F., 242
Slater, E., 103
Smallbone, S., 408, 410
Social bond, ethics and, clinical psychodiagnostics, 68–70
Socrates, 71
Soenen, S., 445, 446, 447, 448
Soler, C., 60n28, 268, 456n28
Solms, M., 177, 431n2
Solomon, J., 343
Solomon, Z., 328
Somatization disorder, 304–305
Somatization phenomenon, 301–307
Sontag, S., 267n4, 311n15
Sophocles, 127
Southwick, S. M., 205
Spinoza, 125n40
Spitz, R., 377–378

Splitting
  analytic paradigm, 111
  borderline personality disorder, 340–344
Spurzheim, 22
Stengers, E., 53
Sterba, E., 55n21
Stern, D., 139
Stevens, A., 441
Stress, jouissance, 319–320
Subject, 259–281
  analytic paradigm, 124–125
  anxiety
    guilt and, 265–268
    subject-formation and, 263–265
    in subject-other relation, 260–262
  categorical diagnostics, 459–461
  depression and guilt, 275–278
  depression and position of, 268–272
  depression as essential possibility, 272–275
  depression as possibility of passage, 278–281
  division of, psychoneurosis, 361–364
  Other and, 140–142
  Other and, fantasy, linear to circular model, 225–229
  rejection of, moral treatment paradigm, 101–103
Subject-formation. *See also* Identity
  anxiety and, 263–265
  borderline personality disorder, 340–344
  hysteria, 366–368
  identity, 208, 211–213
  linear to circular model, 210–213
  obsessional neurosis, 382–383
  psychoneurosis, 351–352
Suggestibility effect, categorical diagnostics, 22–24
Suggestion, clinical paradigms, 77
Sullivan, H. S., 456n28
Sulloway, F. J., 76n4, 118
Suomi, S., 86n10

Survivor guilt, post-traumatic stress disorder, 327
Sydenham, 46, 90
Symbol, linguistics, clinical psychodiagnostics, 49–50
Symbolic, defenses, 184
Symptoms
  clinical psychodiagnostics, 4–6
  as hinge, defenses, 197–202
  hysteria, 373–378
  medical model, 3–4
  obsessional neurosis, 388–393
  perversion, 416–420
  psychoneurosis, 361–364
Syndrome
  clinical psychodiagnostics, 4–6
  medical model, 3–4
Systemic theory, clinical psychodiagnostics, 5
Szasz, T., 10, 20, 67n36, 88, 101, 102–103

Target, M., 168n18, 213–214n9, 228–229n28, 324n8, 339, 342, 345, 346, 347, 349, 350, 441
Tausk, V., 444n20
Taylor, G. J., 303
Temerlin, M. K., 21, 22, 24
Testing, clinical psychodiagnostics, 14–15
Thaiss, L., 166n16
Therapeutic effects, metapsychology, 134–135
Therapeutic relation, treatment, 462–464
Thomä & Kächele, 48n12
Tienari, P., 86n10, 433
Tomasello, M., 166
Tooby, J., 48n12, 240n5, 241, 242, 245
Tourette's syndrome, 22
Training, Other, 137n7
Transference
  analytic paradigm, 120–121
  real, analytic paradigm, 114–118

Trauma. *See also* Post-traumatic stress disorder
  analytic paradigm, 116n33
  borderline personality disorder, 337, 345–346
  hysteria, 371–373
  incidence of, 314
  memory, 321, 331
  nature of, post-traumatic stress disorder, 325–328
  neurosis, 195
  obsessional neurosis, 386–387
  perversion, 413–416
Traumatic jouissance, to phallic pleasure, psychoneurosis, 356–360
Treatment
  acutalpathology, 307–312
  borderline personality disorder, 346–350
  categorical diagnostics, 19–20
  clinical psychodiagnostics, 9–10, 15–17
  Diagnostic and Statistical Manual of Mental Disorders, 29
  goals of, 461
  hysteria, 378–381
  metapsychology, 135–143
  obsessional neurosis, 393–395
  perversion, 425–427
  post-traumatic stress disorder, 333–336
  psychosis, 456–458
  therapeutic relation, 462–464
Trull, T., 28
Truth, knowledge versus, clinical psychodiagnostics, 60–65

Ulman, R. B., 300, 311
Unconscious
  clinical psychodiagnostics, 5
  defenses, 196–197
  Other and, 136–137
Uniform syndrome, medical-biological paradigm, 85–86

University discourse
  medical-biological paradigm, 86–91
  post-traumatic stress disorder, 321–322
  psychosis, 122–124

Value judgments, metapsychology, 134
Van Compernolle, E., 271
van de Brink, W., 42n6
Van Den Hoofdakker, R. H., 86
Vandereycken, W., 42, 88n11
Vandermeersch, P., 61, 93
Van der Valk, F., 21
Van Groos, K., 60n28
Van Haute, P., 139n9
Vanheule, S., 9n4, 360, 438n11
Van Hoorde, H., 41, 133–134, 269
Van Houdenhove, B., 154, 306
Van Ijzendoorn, M. H., 209n3, 300
Van Lieshout, P., 16, 25
Van Nieuwenhuizen, C., 425
Van Os, J., 434
Van Praag, H., 28n6, 88n11
van Straaten, Peter, 377
van Vliet, K., 91
Veith, I., 202, 366n12, 377n26
Verhaeghe, P., 20n1, 33n11, 38–39n2, 51n16, 57, 104n24, 110n30, 156, 171, 210, 226n23, 249n15, 251, 271, 317, 322n7, 339n15, 353, 363, 364, 366n12, 367, 371n21, 374n24, 378n27, 380n28, 383n31, 404n9, 415n22
Vermote, R., 337n13, 338
Vertommen, H., 134
Vestdijk, S., 260
Violent sexual offenders, metapsychology, 135–136
Virchow, 83
Voltaire, 71
Vonk, R., 433
"Von Sackel" treatment, 110

Wajeman, G., 376
Walgrave, L., 75–76
Walker, E. A., 311n14, 434

Ward, T., 406, 408, 410, 412, 421n24
Watson, D., 306
Watson, J., 151, 166n16
Weiner, K., 310
Welldon, E., 400n4, 408, 409n12, 414, 419, 425, 426
Whitehead, W. E., 306
Wiersma, D., 76n3
William of Occam, 49
Wilson, E. O., 236n2
Winnicott, D. W., 162n12, 338, 339
Wise, 304

Wolfson, L., 439n13
Wolpe, J., 299
Wyshak, G., 205

Yehuda, R., 320
Young, K., 314, 315, 316, 334
Yule, W., 321

Zarifian, E., 41n5
Zenoni, A., 236n2, 456n28
Zetzel, E., 398
Zimmerman, 90